PENGUIN REFERENCE

Penguin Pocket Famous People

David Crystal was born in 1941 and spent the early years of his life in Holyhead, North Wales. He went to St Mary's College, Liverpool, and University College, London, where he read English and obtained his Ph.D. in 1966. He was a lecturer in linguistics at the universities of Bangor and Reading, becoming Professor of Linguistics at the University of Wales, Bangor. He is editor of *The Penguin Encyclopedia* and related publications, the former editor of the Cambridge family of general encyclopedias, compiler of several dictionaries, and author of publications on the theory and practice of reference works. He currently directs a company which manages a large reference database and which is developing systems for improving document classification and internet search. A past president of the Society of Indexers, in 2001 his book *Words on Words* (co-authored with Hilary Crystal) was awarded the Wheatley Medal for an outstanding index. In 1995 he was awarded the OBE for services to the English language.

PENGUIN POCKET FAMOUS PEOPLE

Edited by David Crystal

PENGUIN BOOKS

PENGUIN BOOKS

Published by the Penguin Group
Penguin Books Ltd, 80 Strand, London WC2R 0RL, England
Penguin Group (USA) Inc., 375 Hudson Street, New York, New York 10014, USA
Penguin Group (Canada), 90 Eglinton Avenue East, Suite 700, Toronto, Ontario, Canada M4P 2Y3
(a division of Pearson Penguin Canada Inc.)
Penguin Ireland, 25 St Stephen's Green, Dublin 2, Ireland (a division of Penguin Books Ltd)
Penguin Group (Australia), 250 Camberwell Road, Camberwell, Victoria 3124, Australia
(a division of Pearson Australia Group Pty Ltd)
Penguin Books India Pvt Ltd, 11 Community Centre, Panchsheel Park, New Delhi – 110 017, India
Penguin Group (NZ), cnr Airborne and Rosedale Roads, Albany, Auckland 1310, New Zealand
(a division of Pearson New Zealand Ltd)
Penguin Books (South Africa) (Pty) Ltd, 24 Sturdee Avenue, Rosebank, Johannesburg 2196, South Africa

Penguin Books Ltd, Registered Offices: 80 Strand, London WC2R 0RL, England

www.penguin.com

First published 2006
1

The moral right of the author has been asserted

Set in ITC Stone Sans and ITC Stone Serif
Typeset by Data Standards Ltd, Frome, Somerset
Printed in England by Clays Ltd, St Ives plc

ISBN-13: 978-0-141-02717-3
ISBN-10: 0-141-02717-7

Contents

Acknowledgements   vii
Preface   ix
Penguin Pocket Famous People   1

Acknowledgements

Crystal Reference

GENERAL EDITOR
David Crystal

DEVELOPMENT EDITOR
Ann Rowlands

EDITORIAL MANAGER
Hilary Crystal

DATABASE MANAGEMENT
Tony McNicholl

TECHNOLOGY DEVELOPMENT
Philip Johnstone
Dan Wade

CRYSTAL REFERENCE
ADMINISTRATION
Ian Saunders
Rob Phillips

Penguin Books

COMMISSIONING EDITOR
Georgina Laycock

EDITORIAL MANAGERS
Jodie Greenwood
Ellie Smith

PRODUCTION
Kristen Harrison

TEXT DESIGN
Richard Marston

TYPESETTING
Data Standards Ltd

Preface

Famous people. It sounds like such an easy concept, but it is full of complications. Fame, to begin with, is not the same as being 'well-known' or 'popular'. Real fame transcends time and nation. It lasts after you are dead, and while you are alive it takes you beyond national popularity into an international world. A television weather-forecaster, for example, will certainly be well-known within his or her country, but will have no recognition abroad.

However, such a stringent criterion would make for a very small book. Only a few of the many monarchs, politicians, generals, artists, novelists, philosophers, film stars, scientists, and other leading personalities would qualify. Nor would it make for a very interesting book, for the people we are most interested in tend to be our contemporaries – the celebrities of today, not of fifty years ago.

So this book is an amalgam of old and new. It is aimed at a British readership, so a great deal of space is devoted to – for example – UK political, cricket, and media personalities. Bearing in mind that living memories still include World War 2, I have included several leaders from that period.

The 'pocket book' concept also suggests a very general interest range, and I have therefore included rather more people from such fields as sport, fashion, films, stage, and television, and not so many from more specialized domains, such as philosophy and the sciences. It contains far more Oscars than Nobels.

There is another bias. Bearing in mind the rather obvious point that anyone who buys this book is likely to have an interest in reading, I have included proportionately more writers than other artists. The book also contains a good selection of characters from the Bible, given the frequent reference made to them both in religion and in literature.

Lastly, there are also people who are famous without us realizing it, in that their name has become a part of the language or part of our daily lives. Into this category fall such people as Ferdinand Porsche, Heath Robinson, and Frank Woolworth. They are here too, for their achievements add greatly to the browsability of a book of this kind.

David Crystal

Aaron (15th–13th-c BC) Biblical patriarch, the elder brother of Moses. He and his sons were ordained as priests after the construction of the Ark of the Covenant, and he was confirmed as hereditary high priest by the miracle of his rod blossoming into an almond tree (hence various plants nicknamed 'Aaron's Rod').

Aaron, Hank, popular name of **Henry Louis Aaron,** nickname **Hammerin' Hank** (1934–) Baseball player, born in Mobile, AL. A right-handed batting outfielder, he set almost every batting record in his 23-season career with Milwaukee Braves, Atlanta Braves, and Milwaukee Brewers. He received the Presidential Medal of Freedom in 2002.

Abba Swedish pop singing group, formed in 1973 by **Björn Ulvaeus** (1945–), married to **Agnetha Fältskog** (1950–), and **Benny Andersson** (1945–), married to **Anni-Frid Lyngstad** (1945–). They came to international attention by winning the 1974 Eurovision Song Contest with 'Waterloo', which was followed by hits throughout the 1970s and 1980s. Ulvaeus and Andersson wrote the musical *Mamma Mia!* (1999).

Abbado, Claudio (1933–) Musical conductor, born in Milan, Italy. He was conductor and director of La Scala, Milan (1968–86), and principal conductor of the London Symphony Orchestra (1979–87) and of the Berlin Philharmonic Orchestra (1989–2001).

Abbott, Bud *see* Abbott and Costello

Abbott and Costello Comedy film partners: **Bud Abbott**, originally **William A Abbott** (1896–1974), born in Asbury Park, NJ, and **Lou Costello**, originally **Louis Francis Cristillo** (1908–59), born in Paterson, NJ. They teamed up as a comedy double act, Costello playing the clown and Abbott his straight man, and made many successful comedy films, beginning with *Buck Privates* (1941).

à Becket, Thomas *see* Becket, St Thomas

Abel Biblical character, the brother of Cain and second son of Adam and Eve. He is described as a shepherd, whose offering God accepts; but he was then murdered by Cain.

Aberdeen, George Hamilton Gordon, 4th Earl of (1784–1860) British prime minister (1852–5), born in Edinburgh. He was foreign secretary (1828–30, 1841–6), then resigned over the repeal of the Corn Laws. In 1852 he became prime minister of a popular coalition government, but vacillating policy during the Crimean War led to his resignation.

Abraham, Abram, or **Ibrahiz** (after 2000 BC) Biblical character revered as the ancestor of Israel and of several other nations. According to *Genesis* he migrated with his family to the 'Promised Land' of Canaan, and lived to be 175 years old. At 100 years of age he is said to have had a son, Isaac, by his previously barren wife, Sarah (*Gen* 21). In Judaism, Isaac was seen as the fulfilment of the divine promises, although Abraham was ordered by God to sacrifice his heir at Moriah as a test of faith (*Gen* 22). He is traditionally regarded as the father of Judaism, Christianity, and Islam.

Abram *see* Abraham

Abramovich, Roman Arkadyevich (1966–) Multi-billionaire businessman and entrepreneur, born in Saratov, Russia. He rapidly made a name for himself within the oil industry and joined the board of the Sibneft company, eventually completing a merger which made it the fourth biggest oil company in the world. Since 1999 he has been a member of the lower house of the Russian parliament representing Chukotka in Siberia. He has become a familiar face in England since his acquisition of Chelsea Football Club in 2003.

Abse, Dannie (1923–) Writer and physician, born in Cardiff. His literary output includes several volumes of poetry, the novel *Ash on a Young Man's Sleeve* (1954), and the autobiographical *A Strong Dose of Myself* (1983).

Abu-Bakr or **Abu-Bekr** (c.573–634) Muslim caliph, born in Mecca, the father of Mohammed's wife, Aïshah. He became the prophet's most trusted follower, succeeded him as the first caliph (632), and began the compilation of the Qur'an. During his short reign he put down a revolt and initiated conquests.

Achebe, Chinua, originally **Albert Chinualumogo** (1930–) Novelist, born in Ogidi, Nigeria. Four novels written between 1958 (*Things Fall Apart*) and 1966 (*A Man of the People*) describe the tensions of pre- and post-colonial Nigerian society. After a period in politics and education, he wrote *Anthills of the Savannah* (1987). Heralded as a fresh voice in African literature, he has also written short stories, poetry, essays, and children's books.

Acheson, Dean (Gooderham) (1893–1971) US secretary of state (1949–53) born in Middletown, CT. In the Truman administration he formulated the Truman Doctrine (1947), helped to establish the Marshall Plan (1947), and promoted the formation of NATO (1949).

Ackroyd, Peter (1949–) Writer, born in London. He is known chiefly for his biographical studies of Pound, T S Eliot, and Dickens, and for his fiction, including *The Last Testament of Oscar Wilde* (1983), *Hawksmoor* (1985), and *First Light* (1989).

Acosta, Carlos (1973–) Ballet dancer and choreographer, born near Havana, Cuba. He studied with the Turin Ballet in Italy (1990), and went on to win the top prize at the prestigious Prix de Lausanne. He gained international prominence with the Houston Ballet and in 1998 joined the Royal Ballet, where he became guest principal (from 2000).

Adair, Red, popular name of **Paul Neal Adair** (1915–2004) Fire-fighting specialist, born in Houston, TX.

Called in as a troubleshooter to deal with major oil fires, he attended the disaster on the Piper Alpha oil rig in the North Sea (1988), and the fires in Kuwait at the end of the Gulf War (1991).

Adam, Adolphe (Charles) (1803–56) Composer, born in Paris. The son of the pianist **Louis Adam** (1758–1848), he is chiefly remembered for the ballet *Giselle* (1841).

Adam, Robert (1728–92) Architect, born in Kirkcaldy, Fife. He established a practice in London in 1758, where he and his brother **James Adam** (1730–94) transformed the prevailing Palladian fashion in architecture by a series of romantically elegant variations on diverse classical originals, as in Home House, Portland Square, London. They also designed furniture and fittings.

Adam and Eve Biblical characters described in the Book of Genesis as the first man and woman created by God. Traditions describe their life in the garden of Eden, their disobedience and banishment, and the birth of their sons Cain, Abel, and Seth. Their fall into sin is portrayed as a temptation by the serpent.

Adams, Douglas (Noel) (1952–2001) Writer, born in Cambridge, Cambridgeshire. He is known for his humorous science-fiction novels, especially the series beginning with *The Hitch-hiker's Guide to the Galaxy* (1979, originally a radio series, 1978, 1980, later televised; filmed 2005).

Adams, Gerry, popular name of **Gerald Adams** (1948–) Northern Ireland politician, born in Belfast. In 1978 he became vice-president of Sinn Féin

and later its president. He was elected to the UK parliament in 1983–92, but declined to take up his seat at Westminster. He achieved national prominence as the chief contact with the IRA during the events relating to the IRA ceasefire (1994–6), and regained his seat in the 1997, 2001, and 2005 general elections.

Adams, John (1735–1826) US statesman and second president (1797–1801), born in Braintree (now Quincy), MA. Of strongly colonial sympathies, he led the protest against the Stamp Act (1765), and was 'the colossus of the debate' on the Declaration of Independence. He became the first US vice-president under Washington (1789); they were re-elected in 1792, and in 1796 Adams was chosen president by the Federalists.

Adams, John Quincy (1767–1848) US statesman and sixth president (1825–9), born in Quincy, MA, the son of John and Abigail Adams. As secretary of state under Monroe, he negotiated with Spain the treaty for the acquisition of Florida (1819), and was alleged to be the real author of the Monroe Doctrine (1823).

Adams, Richard (George) (1920–) Novelist, born in Newbury, Berkshire. He came to prominence with his first novel, *Watership Down* (1972). Later novels include *Shardik* (1974), *The Bureaucrats* (1985), and *Tales from Watership Down* (1996).

Adams, Tony (1966–) Footballer, born in Romford, Essex. He joined Arsenal Football Club as a centre back in 1983, became team captain, and was the Professional Footballers' Association Young Player of the Year in 1987. He captained England in 1994, 1995, and during the 1996 European Cup, and won 66 caps. From 2003–4 he was manager of Wycombe Wanderers.

Adamson, Joy (Friedericke Victoria), *née* Gessner (1910–80) Naturalist and writer, born in Austria. Living in Kenya with her third husband, British game warden **George Adamson** (1906–89), she is known for her series of books about the lioness Elsa, such as *Born Free* (1960) and *Elsa and Her Cubs* (1965). She was murdered in her home by tribesmen.

Addams, Charles Samuel (1912–88) Cartoonist, born in Westfield, NJ. A contributor to *The New Yorker* from 1935, he is known for the ghoulish group which was immortalized on television in the 1960s as *The Addams Family*.

Adderley, Cannonball, popular name of **Julian Edwin Adderley** (1928–75) Jazz saxophonist and composer, born in Tampa, FL. In 1956 he formed a successful combo with his brother **Nat** (1932–2000). His many recordings include the album *Kind of Blue* (1958–9) with the Miles Davis sextet and John Coltrane, and his film work included *Play Misty for Me* (1971).

Addington, Henry *see* Sidmouth, 1st Viscount

Addison, Joseph (1672–1719) Essayist and politician, born in Milston, Wiltshire. He became an MP in 1708, while building a literary career with regular contributions to the *Tatler*, started by Richard Steele (1709), and the *Spectator* which they co-founded in 1711. In 1717 he was made secretary of state, but resigned through failing health.

Addison, Thomas (c.1793–1860) Physician, born in Longbenton, Northumberland. His chief research was on the disease of the suprarenal capsules now known as **Addison's disease**, and into pernicious anaemia, **Addisonian anaemia**.

Adenauer, Konrad (1876–1967) German statesman, born in Cologne, Germany. He was president of the Prussian State Council (1920–33), and became the first chancellor of the Federal Republic of Germany (1949–63). His policy was to rebuild West Germany and establish closer post-war links with other European nations, with the ultimate aim of reunifying Germany.

Adie, Kate, popular name of **Kathryn Adie** (1945–) News reporter and correspondent, born in Sunderland, Tyne and Wear. As a reporter for BBC TV News (1979–81), correspondent (1982), and chief correspondent (1989–2003), she became a familiar figure presenting reports from the heart of war-torn countries around the world. Since 2003 she has freelanced for the BBC and presents a weekly radio programme, *From Our Own Correspondent*.

Adler, Alfred (1870–1937) Psychiatrist, born in Vienna. His *Study of Organ Inferiority and its Psychical Compensation* (trans, 1907) aroused great controversy, and led to one of the early schisms in psychoanalysis. His main contributions include the concept of the inferiority complex and his special treatment of neurosis as the exploitation of shock.

Adrian IV, also **Hadrian**, originally **Nicholas Breakspear** (c.1100–59)

The only Englishman to become pope (1154–9), born in Abbots Langley, Hertfordshire. He is said to have issued a controversial bull granting Ireland to Henry II.

Aeschylus (c.525–c.456 BC) Playwright, known as 'the founder of Greek tragedy', born in Eleusis, near Athens. Of some 60 plays ascribed to him, only seven are extant, including the trilogy of the *Oresteia* (458): *Agamemnon*, *Choephori*, and *Eumenides*.

Aesop (?6th-c BC) Legendary Greek fabulist, supposedly of Phrygia. The fables, anecdotes which use animals to make a moral point, were popularized by the Roman poet Phaedrus in the 1st-c AD, and rewritten by La Fontaine in 1668.

Affleck, Ben(jamin Geza) (1972–) Film actor, born in Berkeley, CA. He became known following his appearance in *Good Will Hunting* (1997), for which he shared an Oscar for best original screenplay with co-star Matt Damon. Later films include *Shakespeare in Love* (1998), *Forces of Nature* (1999), *Pearl Harbor* (2001), and *Man About Town* (2005).

Aga Khan I, originally **Hasan Ali Shah** (1800–81) Imam of the Nizari Ismailite sect of the Shiite Muslims. He claimed to be descended from Ali, the son-in-law of the Prophet Mohammed. Appointed governor of the Iranian province of Kerman, he was granted the title of Aga Khan in 1818 by the Shah of Iran. In 1838 he rose in revolt against Mohammed Shah but was defeated and fled to India. He helped the British in the first Anglo-Afghan War (1839–42) and in the conquest of Sindh (1842–3).

Agassi, Andre (Kirk) (1970–) Tennis player, born in Las Vegas, NV. His singles titles include Wimbledon (1992), the US Open (1994, 1999), the Australian Open (1995, 2000, 2001, 2003), and the French Open (1999). He is also known for his work in relation to youth community projects, notably the Andre Agassi Foundation (1994). He married Steffi Graf in 2001.

Agatha, St (?–251) Christian martyr from Catania, Sicily, who is said to have rejected the love of the Prefect Quintilianus, and suffered a cruel martyrdom in 251. She is the patron saint of Catania and of bell-founders, and is invoked against fire and lightning.

Agnew, Spiro T(heodore) (1918–96) US Republican vice-president (1969–73), born in Baltimore, MD. Nixon's running-mate in the 1968 election, he resigned in 1973, after an investigation into alleged tax violations.

Agostini, Giacomo (1942–) Motorcyclist, born in Lovere, Italy. He won a record 15 world titles between 1966 and 1975, including the 500 cc title a record eight times (1966–72, 1975). He also won 10 Isle of Man TT Races (1966–75).

Agutter, Jenny, popular name of **Jennifer (Ann) Agutter** (1952–) Actress, born in Taunton, Somerset. She became known following her role in *The Railway Children* (1970), and among later films are *The Snow Goose* (1971) and *Equus* (1977, BAFTA). Television work includes a new adaptation of *The Railway Children*

(2000) and *The Alan Clark Diaries* (2004).

Ahab (9th-c BC) King of Israel (c.873–c.852 BC), the son of Omri. His reign was marked by battles against Syria, and a religious crisis when his wife Jezebel introduced worship of the Phoenician god, Baal, thus arousing the hostility of the prophet Elijah.

Ahern, Bertie (1951–) Irish politician and prime minister (1997–), born in Dublin. From 1982 he held various ministerial posts, became leader of the opposition and president of Fianna Fáil (1994), and then prime minister (1997), re-elected in 2002. He was a key participant in the Northern Ireland peace process following the signing of the Good Friday Agreement.

Aidan, St, known as the **Apostle of Northumbria** (?–651) A monk from the Celtic monastery on the island of Iona, born in Ireland. In 635 he founded the Northumbrian Church in England, becoming its first bishop and establishing the monastery at Lindisfarne.

Aiken, Joan (Delano) (1924–2004) Writer, the daughter of Conrad Aiken, born in Sussex. Her many books for children include *The Kingdom and the Cave* (1960) and *The Witches of Clatteringshaws* (2005, posthumously). Among her adult novels are *Mansfield Revisited* (1985) and *Cold Shoulder Road* (1995).

Ailey, Alvin (1931–89) Dancer and choreographer, born in Rogers, TX. In 1958 he formed the Alvin Ailey American Dance Theater, a multiracial modern dance ensemble.

Aïshah or **Ayeshah** (c.613–78) The favourite of the nine wives of the prophet Mohammed, and daughter of Abu-Bakr. On Mohammed's death, she resisted Ali, the prophet's son-in-law, and secured the caliphate for her father. She opposed Ali again in 656, but was defeated and exiled.

Akabusi, Kriss (Kezie Uche-Chukwu Duru) (1958–) Athlete, born in London. He won gold medals in the 4 x 100 m relay at the 1986 European Championships and Commonwealth Games, the 400 m hurdles at the 1990 European Championships and Commonwealth Games, the 4 x 400 m relay at the 1991 World Championships, and the 4 x 400 m relay in the 1993 European Cup. He also won Olympic silver in the 4 x 100 m relay in 1984.

Akbar the Great, in full **Jalal ud-Din Muhammad Akbar** (1542–1605) Mughal Emperor of India, born in Umarkot, Sind, India. He assumed power in 1560 and within a few years had gained control of the whole of India N of the Vindhya Mts. He promoted economic reforms, encouraged science and the arts, and pursued a tolerant religious policy.

Akhmatova, Anna, pseudonym of **Anna Andreeyevna Gorenko** (1889–1966) Poet, born in Odessa, Ukraine. In 1910 she married Nicholas Gumilev, and with him started the Neoclassicist Acmeist movement. Her work was banned between 1922 and 1940, and again in 1946, but she was 'rehabilitated' in the 1950s, and is now recognized as the greatest woman poet in Russian literature.

Akihito (1933–) Emperor of Japan (1989–), the eldest son of Emperor

Hirohito, born in Tokyo. In 1959 he became the first crown prince to marry a commoner, **Michiko Shoda** (1934–). They have three children.

Alanbrooke (of Brookeborough), Alan Francis Brooke, 1st Viscount (1883–1963) British field marshal, born in Bagnères-de-Bigorre, France. In World War 2 he commanded the 2nd corps of the British Expeditionary Force (1939–40), covering the evacuation from Dunkirk. He became Chief of the Imperial General Staff (1941–6), and was principal strategic adviser to Churchill.

Alban, St (3rd-c) Roman soldier, venerated as the first British Christian martyr. When living in Verulamium (now St Albans), he was scourged and beheaded for protecting a Christian priest who had converted him.

Albee, Edward (Franklin) (1928–) Playwright, born near Washington, DC. His major works include *The Zoo Story* (1958), *The American Dream* (1960), and *Who's Afraid of Virginia Woolf?* (1962; filmed 1966). *A Delicate Balance* (1966), *Seascape* (1975), and *Three Tall Women* (1991) won Pulitzer Prizes.

Albert, Prince, in full **Francis Albert Augustus Charles Emmanuel, Prince of Saxe-Coburg-Gotha** (1819–61) Prince Consort of Queen Victoria, born at Schloss Rosenau, near Coburg, Germany. In 1840 he married his cousin, an infatuated Queen Victoria, and became her chief adviser, first as Consort (1842), then as Prince Consort (1857). His death from typhoid occasioned a long period of seclusion by his widow, and the Albert Memorial was erected to his memory in 1871.

Albertus Magnus, St, Graf von (Count of) **Bollstädt**, known as **Doctor Universalis** ('Universal Doctor') (c.1200–80) Philosopher, bishop, and doctor of the Church, born in Lauingen, Germany. A Dominican, he helped to bring together theology and Aristotelianism, and had several famous pupils, notably Thomas Aquinas. He was canonized in 1931.

Albright, Madeleine K(orbel) (1937–) US secretary of state (1997–2000), born in Prague. Formerly permanent US representative to the UN, in the second Clinton administration she became the first woman to head the State Department.

Alcock, Sir John William (1892–1919) Aviator, born in Manchester, Greater Manchester. On 14 June 1919, with Arthur Whitten Brown, he became the first to fly the Atlantic. The nonstop trip, from Newfoundland to Ireland, was made in a Vickers-Vimy biplane, and took 16 h 27 min.

Alcott, Louisa May (1832–88) Writer, born in Germantown, PA. She achieved success with the children's classic, *Little Women* (1868), followed by *Good Wives* (1869), *An Old-Fashioned Girl* (1870), *Little Men* (1871), and *Jo's Boys* (1886).

Alda, Alan (1936–) Actor, director, and writer, born in New York City. He is best known for the award-winning television series *M*A*S*H* (1972–83). His acerbic sense of humour is evident in such films as *Canadian Bacon* (1995), and later films include *The Aviator* (2004).

Alderton, John (1940–) Actor, born in Gainsborough, Lincolnshire. He became popularly known on television with series such as *Please Sir*, *My Wife Next Door*, and *Forever Green*. Among his films are *Please Sir* (1971), *It Shouldn't Happen to a Vet* (1976), and *Calendar Girls* (2003).

Aldiss, Brian (Wilson) (1925–) Writer, born in East Dereham, Norfolk. Best known as a writer of science fiction, his novels include *Hothouse* (1962) and *Dracula Unbound* (1991). Other works include histories of science fiction, and edited collections of short stories, such as *Cultural Breaks*, published to mark his 80th birthday.

Aldrin, Buzz, popular name of **Edwin Eugene Aldrin** (1930–) Astronaut, born in Montclair, NJ. During the Gemini 12 Mission in 1966, he set a world record by walking in space for 5 h 37 min. He was the second man to set foot on the Moon in the Apollo 11 mission in 1969.

Alexander (of Tunis), Sir Harold (Rupert Leofric George) Alexander, 1st Earl (1891–1969) British soldier, born in London. He served in Burma (1942), became commander-in-chief Middle East (1942–3) achieving a historic victory in his North African campaign, and was supreme allied commander in the Mediterranean.

Alexander the Great (356–323 BC) King of Macedonia (336–323 BC), born at Pella, the son of Philip II. After crushing all opposition at home, he conquered Achaemenid Persia, defeating Darius III, taking Babylon, Persepolis, and other major cities, and founding the city of Alexandria. In India his exhausted army mutinied, and he died during the return journey.

Alexandra, Princess, the Hon Lady Ogilvy (1936–) Daughter of George, Duke of Kent, and Princess Marina of Greece. In 1963 she married Sir **Angus James Bruce Ogilvy** (1928–2004). They have a son, **James Robert Bruce** (1964–), and a daughter, **Marina Victoria Alexandra** (1966–).

Al Fayed, Mohamed (1933–) Businessman, born in Egypt. He became owner of the Ritz Hotel in Paris in 1979, and of Harrods in London in 1985. One of his children, **Dodi** (1955–97), received worldwide publicity when the press discovered his relationship with Princess Diana. He was killed along with Diana in a car accident in Paris while trying to escape the attentions of paparazzi.

Alfred, known as **Alfred the Great** (849–99) King of Wessex (from 871), born in Wantage, Oxfordshire, the fifth son of King Ethelwulf. He inflicted on the Danes their first major reverse, at Edington (878), reorganized his forces into a standing army, built a navy, and established fortifications. He revived religion and learning, and provided his successors with the means to reconquer the Danelaw. The famous story of his being scolded by a peasant woman for letting her cakes burn is first recorded in the 11th-c.

Ali (?–661) Fourth caliph (656–61), the cousin of Mohammed, whose daughter, Fatima, he married. He encountered much opposition during his reign and was assassinated in the mosque at Kufa. He is held by Shiah Muslims to be the only true successor to the prophet.

Ali, Muhammad, originally **Cassius (Marcellus) Clay, Jr** (1942–) Boxer, born in Louisville, KY. He won the world heavyweight title in 1964, defeating Sonny Liston. At that time he joined the Black Muslims and adopted the name Muhammad Ali. In 1971 he was beaten by Joe Frazier, but beat him in 1974. In 1978 he was defeated by Leon Spinks, but regained the title later that year – the first man to win the world heavyweight title three times. His flamboyant style made him a legend. The film, *When We Were Kings* (Oscar), recounting the 1974 Ali v. Foreman fight, appeared in 1996.

Allcock, Tony, popular name of **Anthony Allcock** (1955–) British bowls player, born in Leicestershire. His titles include world outdoor champion (1980, 1984, 1988), world outdoor singles champion (1992, 1996), world indoor singles champion (1986–7, 1997, 2002), and world indoor pairs champion with David Bryant (1986–7, 1989–92). The holder of a record 15 world bowls titles, he retired in 2003.

Allen, Sir George Oswald Browning, known as **Gubby Allen** (1902–89) Cricketer, born in Sydney, New South Wales, Australia. He played for England in 25 Tests, and is the only player to have taken all 10 wickets in an innings at Lord's (1929).

Allen, Woody, originally **Allen Stewart Konigsberg** (1935–) Film actor and director, born in New York City. His major films, exploring the themes of mortality, sexual inadequacy, show-business nostalgia, psychoanalysis, and urban living, include *Annie Hall* (1977), *Hannah and Her Sisters* (1986, Oscar), *Bullets Over Broadway* (1994, Oscar), and *Match Point* (2005).

Allingham, Margery (Louise) (1904–66) Detective-story writer, born in London. The creator of the fictional detective Albert Campion, her novels include *Flowers for the Judge* (1936) and *The China Governess* (1963).

Aloysius, St *see* Gonzaga, Luigi, St

Alston, Richard (1948–) Choreographer and director, born in Stoughton, West Sussex. In 1972 he co-founded Strider, the forerunner of the contemporary dance company Second Stride (1982). He later became artistic director of the Rambert Dance Company (1986–92), and the Richard Alston Dance Company (from 1994).

Altichiero (c.1330–c.1395) Painter and possible founder of the Veronese School, born near Verona, Italy. He worked in Verona, then moved to Padua, where his frescoes are in the Basilica of San Antonio (painted 1372–9) and the Oratory of San Giorgio (1377–84).

Alzheimer, Alois (1864–1915) Psychiatrist and neuropathologist, born in Marktbreit, Germany. He is remembered for his full clinical and pathological description (1906) of pre-senile dementia (*Alzheimer's disease*).

Ambler, Eric (1909–98) Writer, born in London. He specialized in the writing of spy thrillers, such as *Epitaph for* *a Spy* (1938), *Dirty Story* (1967), and *The Intercom Conspiracy* (1970).

Ambrose, St (c.339–97) Roman clergyman, born in Trier, Germany. He is remembered for his preaching, literary works, and hymns. He also made improvements in the liturgy, notably the *Ambrosian ritual* and *Ambrosian chant*.

Amies, Sir (Edwin) Hardy (1909–2003) Couturier, and dressmaker by appointment to Queen Elizabeth II. Known for his tailored suits for women, he founded his own fashion house in 1946, and started designing for men in 1959, receiving the British Fashion Council Hall of Fame Award in 1989.

Amin (Dada), Idi (c.1925–2003) Ugandan soldier and dictator, born in Koboko. He staged a coup deposing Obote, and established a military dictatorship (1971–9). Throughout his rule there were many reports of atrocities, making his regime internationally infamous. Deposed by exiled Ugandans with the help of the Tanzanian army in 1979, he fled abroad, and eventually settled in Saudi Arabia.

Amis, Sir Kingsley (William) (1922–95) Novelist and poet, born in London. He achieved success with his first novel, *Lucky Jim* (1954). Later books include *Jake's Thing* (1978), *The Old Devils* (1986, Booker), and *The Russian Girl* (1992).

Amis, Martin (Louis) (1949–) Novelist and journalist, the son of Kingsley Amis, born in Oxford, Oxfordshire. His works include the novels *The Rachel Papers* (1973) and *Time's Arrow* (1991), and the collected short stories

Einstein's Monsters (1986) and *'Heavy Water' and Other Stories* (1999).

Amos (835–765 BC) Old Testament prophet, the earliest prophet in the Bible to have a book named after him. He denounced the iniquities of the N kingdom of Israel.

Ampère, André Marie (1775–1836) Mathematician and physicist, born in Lyon, France. He laid the foundations of the science of electrodynamics. His name was given to the basic SI unit of electric current.

Amundsen, Roald (Engelbregt Gravning) (1872–1928) Explorer, born in Borge, Norway. His Antarctic expedition of 1910 reached the Pole in December 1911, one month ahead of Scott. In 1926 he flew the airship *Norge* across the North Pole, but was lost on a later expedition.

Andersen, Hans Christian (1805–75) Writer, born in Odense, Denmark. His works include collections of poems (1831–2), travel books, novels, and plays, but he is mainly remembered for his fairy-tales for children, such as *The Tin Soldier*, *The Tinderbox*, and *The Ugly Duckling*.

Anderson, Clive (Stuart) (1953–) Television presenter and barrister, born in London. He joined BBC Radio 4 as chairman of the popular *Whose Line Is It Anyway?* (1988). The programme later transferred to Channel 4 television, where he was also given his own chat-show *Clive Anderson Talks Back* (1989–96). Later shows include *What If...?* (2003).

Anderson, Elizabeth Garrett, *née* **Garrett** (1836–1917) Physician, the first English woman doctor, born in London. She faced difficulty qualifying as a doctor because of opposition to the admission of women, finally receiving an MD degree from the University of Paris in 1870.

Anderson, Gerry (1929–) British creator of puppet-character programmes for television. Among his best-known adventure series are *Fireball XL-5* (1961), *Thunderbirds* (1964–6), *Captain Scarlett and the Mysterons* (1967), and *Terrahawks* (1983–4).

Anderson, Gillian (1968–) Actress, born in Chicago, IL. She became known for her role as Dana Scully in the television series *The X-Files* (1993–2002), and starred in the film *The X-Files: Fight the Future* (1998). In 2005 she appeared as Lady Dedlock in BBC television's serialization of Charles Dickens' *Bleak House*.

Anderson, Lindsay (Gordon) (1923–94) British stage and film director, born in Bangalore, India. He began with short documentary films, such as *Thursday's Children* (1955, Oscar), and became a leading proponent of the Free Cinema critical movement, his feature films including *This Sporting Life* (1963) and *O Lucky Man!* (1973).

Andersson, Benny *see* Abba

Andress, Ursula (1936–) Film actress, born in Bern. She made her international debut in *Dr No* (1963), her later films including *What's New, Pussycat?* (1965), *Casino Royale* (1967), and *The Clash of the Titans* (1981).

Andrew (Albert Christian Edward), Duke of York (1960–) British prince, the second son of Queen Elizabeth II. In 1986 he married **Sarah (Margaret) Ferguson** (1959–), and was made Duke of York. They have two children, **Princess Beatrice Elizabeth Mary** (1988–) and **Princess Eugenie Victoria Helena** (1990–). The couple separated in 1992, and divorced in 1996.

Andrew, St (d.c.60) One of the 12 apostles, the brother of Simon Peter. He preached the Gospel in Asia Minor and Scythia, and was crucified in Achaia. He is the patron saint of Scotland and of Russia.

Andrews, Eamon (1922–87) Broadcaster, born in Dublin. He began as a sports commentator in Ireland in 1939, and became well known as the host of several BBC television series, such as *What's My Line?* (1951–63, 1984–7) and *This is Your Life* (1955–87).

Andrews, Dame Julie, originally **Julia Elizabeth Wells** (1935–) Singer and actresss, born in Walton-on-Thames, Surrey. Her film debut was in the musical *Mary Poppins* (1964, Oscar), later films including *The Sound of Music* (1965), *A Fine Romance* (1992), and *The Princess Diaries* (2001).

Angeles, Victoria de los, originally **Victoria Gómez Cima** (1923–2005) Lyric soprano, born in Barcelona, Spain. She achieved international recognition as both a concert and an operatic singer, and was noted for her 19th-c Italian roles and for her performances of Spanish songs.

Angelico, Fra, originally **Guido di Pietro**, monastic name **Giovanni da Fiesole** (c.1400–55) Early Renaissance painter, born in Vicchio, Italy. He entered the Dominican monastery at Fiesole in 1407. His most important frescoes are those in the Convent of S Marco (now a museum) in Florence, and in the Vatican chapel of Nicholas V in Rome.

Angelou, Maya, pseudonym of **Marguerite Ann Johnson** (1928–) Writer, singer, and dancer, born in St Louis, MO. In the 1960s she was involved in African-American civil rights, then spent several years in Ghana as editor of *African Review*. She received success with her autobiographical *I Know Why the Caged Bird Sings* (1970). The *Complete Collected Poems of Maya Angelou* appeared in 1995.

Ångström, Anders (Jonas) (1814–74) Physicist, born in Lögdö, Sweden. He studied heat, magnetism, and spectroscopy, and the unit for measuring wavelengths of light is named after him.

Aniston, Jennifer (Joanne) (1969–) Actress, born in Los Angeles, CA. She became known through her role as Rachel Green in the acclaimed television series *Friends* (1994–2004). Film roles include *She's the One* (1996), *Bruce Almighty* (2003), and *Rumor Has It* (2005). She was married to actor Brad Pitt (2000–5).

Annan, Kofi (Atta) (1938–) UN secretary-general (from 1997), born in Kumasi, Ghana. After joining the UN secretariat, he was under-secretary-general for peacekeeping operations (from 1993), and in 1997 became the first secretary-general from sub-Saharan Africa. Jointly with the UN, he was awarded the 2001 Nobel Peace Prize.

Annas (1st-c) Israel's high priest, appointed in AD 6 and deposed by the Romans in 15, but still described later by this title in the New Testament. He apparently questioned Jesus after his arrest (*John* 18) and Peter after his detention (*Acts* 4).

Anne (1665–1714) Queen of Great Britain and Ireland (1702–14), born in London, the second daughter of James II. In 1683 she married **Prince George of Denmark** (1653–1708), bearing him 17 children, but only **William, Duke of Gloucester** (1689–1700) survived infancy. During much of her life she was greatly influenced by her close friend and confidante, Sarah Churchill, the future Duchess of Marlborough. In 1701 Anne signed the Act of Settlement designating the Hanoverian descendants of James I as her successors.

Anne, St (fl.1st-c BC–1st-c AD) Wife of **St Joachim**, and mother of the Virgin Mary, first mentioned in the *Protevangelium* of James, in the 2nd-c. She is the patron saint of carpenters.

Anne (Elizabeth Alice Louise), Princess (1950–) British Princess Royal, the only daughter of Queen Elizabeth II and Prince Philip, born in London. She married **Mark Anthony Peter Phillips** (1948–), in 1973 (divorced, 1992). Their children are: **Peter Mark Andrew** (1977–) and **Zara Anne Elizabeth** (1981–). She married **Timothy Laurence** (1952–) in 1992.

Anne Boleyn *see* Boleyn, Anne

Anne of Cleves (1515–57) German princess, the fourth queen of Henry VIII (Jan 1540). Of plain appearance, she was chosen for purely political reasons after the death of Jane Seymour. The marriage was annulled by parliament six months later, and she remained in England until her death.

Annigoni, Pietro (1910–88) Painter, born in Milan, Italy. He employed the technical methods of the old masters, his most usual medium being tempera. His work included portraits of Queen Elizabeth II and President Kennedy.

Anouilh, Jean (Marie Lucien Pierre) (1910–87) Playwright, born in Bordeaux, France. He was influenced by the Neoclassical fashion inspired by Giraudoux, his many plays including *Antigone* (1944), *Becket* (1959), and *The Trousers* (trans, 1978).

Anselm, St (1033–1109) Theologian and philosopher, born in Aosta, Italy. Appointed Archbishop of Canterbury (1093), he was often in conflict with William II and Henry I. The main figure in early scholastic philosophy, he devised the ontological proof for the existence of God. He may have been canonized as early as 1163.

Anthony, St *see* Antony, St; Antony of Padua, St

Antonioni, Michelangelo (1912–) Film director, born in Ferrara, Italy. He made several documentaries (1945–50) before turning to feature films, and gained an international reputation with *L'avventura* (1959). Later films include *La notte* (1961), *Blow-up* (1966), and *Beyond the Clouds* (1995).

Antonius, Marcus or **Mark Antony** (c.83–30 BC) Roman statesman and soldier. After Caesar's assassination, his speeches caused the flight of the conspirators from Rome, and left him with almost absolute power. He formed a triumvirate with Octavian and Lepidus to share the Roman world, defeating Brutus and Cassius at Philippi (42 BC). He then met and was captivated by Queen Cleopatra, whom he followed to Egypt (41 BC). In 40 BC a new division of the Roman world gave Antony the East, and he married Augustus's sister Octavia. His renewed liaison with Cleopatra provided Octavian with reasons to arouse the Roman people against him. Defeat at Actium (31 BC) followed, and Antony and Cleopatra both committed suicide.

Antony or **Anthony, St**, known as **Antony the Great**, also called **Antony of Egypt** (c.251–356) Religious hermit, the father of Christian monasticism, born in Coma, Upper Egypt. He spent 20 years in the desert, where he withstood a famous series of temptations, and in 305 founded a monastery near Memphis – one of the earliest attempts to instruct people in the monastic way of life.

Antony or **Anthony of Padua, St** (1195–1231) Monk, born in Lisbon. In 1220 he entered the Franciscan order, and became known for his preaching. Canonized in 1232, he is the patron saint of Portugal, lost property, and the lower animals.

Appleton, Sir Edward (Victor) (1892–1965) Physicist, born in Bradford, West Yorkshire. He discovered the existence of a layer of electrically charged particles in the upper atmosphere (the *Appleton layer*), which plays an essential part in long-distance radio communication. He received the Nobel Prize for Physics in 1947.

Aquinas, St Thomas, known as **Doctor Angelicus** ('angelic doctor') (1225–74) Scholastic philosopher and theologian, born near Aquino, Italy. He entered the Dominican order, and became widely known as a teacher. He was the first among 13th-c metaphysicians to stress the importance of sense perception and the experimental foundation of human knowledge. His best-known works are two encyclopedic syntheses: the *Summa contra Gentiles* (1259–64) and the incomplete *Summa theologiae* (1266–73), which includes the famous 'five ways' or proofs of the existence of God. He was canonized in 1323.

Aquino, Cory, popular name of **(Maria) Corazon Aquino**, *née* **Cojuangco** (1933–) Philippines president (1986–92), born in Tarlac province. In 1956 she married **Benigno Aquino** (1932–83), the chief political opponent to Ferdinand Marcos. The couple lived in exile in the USA until 1983, when Benigno returned to the Philippines and was assassinated. She took up her husband's cause, leading a non-violent 'people's power' movement which brought the overthrow of Marcos.

Arafat, Yasser, originally **Mohammed Abd al-Ra'u Arafat** (1929–2004) Palestinian president (1996–2004), born in Jerusalem. In 1959 he co-founded the Fatah resistance group, which in 1969 took control of the Palestine Liberation Organization (PLO). After the 1988 declaration of Palestinian statehood he was elected president of the PLO, negotiating international recognition of Palestine in 1993. He shared the Nobel Peace Prize in 1994.

Arc, Joan of *see* Joan of Arc, St

Archer (of Weston-Super-Mare), Jeffrey (Howard) Archer, Baron (1940–) Writer and former politician, born in Weston-super-Mare, Somerset. He became a Conservative MP (1969–74), but resigned following bankruptcy. He began writing fiction, and his many best-selling novels include *First Among Equals* (1984) and *The Fourth Estate* (1996). He served a prison sentence (2001–3) for perjury, and published *A Prison Diary* (2002).

Archimedes (c.287–212 BC) Greek scientist, born in Syracuse. He studied the theory of mechanics and hydrostatics, proving that a body plunged in a fluid becomes lighter by an amount equal to the weight of the fluid it displaces (*Archimedes' principle*) – a discovery which in popular tradition is remembered by his uttering *eureka* ('I have found it'). He was the first to evaluate areas and volumes of solids systematically, and gave a good approximation to π.

Arden, Elizabeth, originally **Florence Nightingale Graham** (1878–1966) Beautician and businesswoman, born in Woodbridge, Ontario, Canada. She opened a beauty salon in New York City in 1910, producing cosmetics on a large scale, and developed a worldwide chain of salons.

Arden, John (1930–) Playwright, born in Barnsley, South Yorkshire. His works, which include *Serjeant*

Musgrave's Dance (1959) and *The Workhouse Donkey* (1963), often experiment with dramatic form and theatrical technique.

Aristophanes (c.448–c.388 BC) Greek playwright. He is said to have written 54 plays, but only 11 are extant. His works fall into three periods. to the first (up to c.425 BC), belong *The Acharnians*, *The Knights*, *The Clouds*, *The Wasps*, and *Peace*; to the second (up to 406 BC), *The Birds*, *Lysistrata*, *Thesmophoriazusae*, and *Frogs*; to the third (up to c.388 BC), *The Ecclesiazusae* and *The Plutus*.

Aristotle (384–322 BC) Greek philosopher, scientist, and physician, born in Stagira, Macedonia. Associated with Plato's Academy for 20 years, in 335 BC he opened his own school (the Lyceum). He wrote the first systematic treatises on logic; made major contributions to the study of natural change, psychology, and biology; and wrote some of the most influential philosophical works in the history of thought, notably his *Metaphysics*, *Nicomachean Ethics*, *Politics*, *Rhetoric*, and *Poetics*.

Arius (Gr *Areios*) (c.250–336) Founder of Arianism, born in Libya. He claimed (c.319) that, in the doctrine of the Trinity, the Son was not co-equal or co-eternal with the Father, but only the first and highest of all finite beings, created out of nothing by an act of God's free will. He won some support, but was excommunicated in 321.

Arjan Dev, known as **Guru Arjan Dev** (1581–1606) Sikh leader, the compiler of the Adi Granth in 1604, born in Goindwal, Punjab, India. The expanded text used today is revered by all Sikhs. He began the construction of the Harimandir, or Golden Temple, at Amritsar. The Mughal emperor, Jahangir, began to oppress the Sikhs and ordered Guru Arjan to eliminate all sections of the Adi Granth that offended Hindus or Muslims. He refused and was tortured to death.

Arkwright, Sir Richard (1732–92) Inventor of mechanical cotton-spinning, born in Preston, Lancashire. In 1768 he set up his celebrated spinning-frame in Preston, but popular opinion believed that his inventions threatened jobs, and in 1779 his mill was destroyed by a mob.

Arlott, (Leslie Thomas) John (1914–91) Writer, journalist, and broadcaster, born in Basingstoke, Hampshire. He became a popular cricket commentator for BBC radio and television. His many books on cricket included *How to Watch Cricket* (1949, 1983) and *Arlott on Cricket* (1984).

Armani, Giorgio (1934–) Fashion designer, born in Piacenza, Italy. He became a designer for **Nino Cerruti** (1930–) in 1961, before setting up his own company in 1975, designing first for men, then also for women. In 2003 he became the first fashion designer to exhibit at London's Royal Academy.

Armstrong, Lance (1971–) Racing cyclist, born in Plano, TX. He made a remarkable comeback from cancer to become a record-breaking seven times winner of the Tour de France (1999–2005). He established the Lance Armstrong Foundation in

1996, a charity to aid the fight against cancer. He retired in 2005.

Armstrong, Louis (Daniel), nicknames **Satchmo** and **Pops** (1901–71) Jazz trumpeter and singer, born in New Orleans, LA. After joining King Oliver's band (1922), his melodic inventiveness established the central role of the improvising soloist in jazz, especially in a series of recordings known as the 'Hot Fives' and 'Hot Sevens' (1925–8). Film appearances include *Pennies from Heaven* (1936) and *High Society* (1956).

Armstrong, Neil (Alden) (1930–) Astronaut, born in Wapakoneta, OH. As commander of the Apollo 11 Moon-landing mission, he became the first man to set foot on the Moon, on 20 July 1969.

Armstrong-Jones, Antony *see* Snowdon, 1st Earl of

Arnold, Sir Malcolm (Henry) (1921–) Composer, born in Northampton, Northamptonshire. His works include nine symphonies, 18 concertos, ballets, operas, and film music, notably *Bridge over the River Kwai* (1957, Oscar).

Arnold, Matthew (1822–88) Poet and critic, born in Laleham, Surrey, the eldest son of Dr Arnold of Rugby. An inspector of schools (1851–86) and professor of poetry at Oxford (1857–67), he also wrote several works of criticism, such as *Culture and Anarchy* (1869), and books on religious themes.

Arthur (?6th-c) A semi-legendary king of the Britons. He is said to have fought the pagan invaders (5th–6th-c AD) in a series of battles, starting with a victory at 'Mount Baden' (?516) and

ending with defeat and death at 'Camlan' (537), after which he was buried at Glastonbury. His story became interwoven with legends of the Round Table of Camelot and the Holy Grail.

Arthur, Chester A(lan) (1830–86) US lawyer and 21st president (1881–5), born in Fairfield, VT. A Republican Party leader, he was made US vice-president under Garfield in 1881, and president after Garfield's assassination.

Ashcroft, Dame Peggy, originally **Edith Margaret Emily Ashcroft** (1907–91) Actress, born in Croydon, Greater London. Her notable stage roles included Juliet (1935), Cleopatra (1935), and Hedda Gabler (1954). Among her films were *The Thirty-nine Steps* (1935) and *A Passage to India* (1984, Oscar).

Ashdown, Paddy, popular name of **Lord Jeremy John Durham Ashdown of Norton-sub-Hamdon** (1941–) British politician, born in New Delhi, India. Elected to parliament in 1983, he served as leader of the Social and Liberal Democratic Party (1988–99). In 2002 he became the international community's representative in Bosnia and Herzegovina with responsibility for implementing the Dayton peace accord.

Asher, Jane (1946–) Actress and cake designer, born in London. Her films include *Alfie* (1966), *Henry VIII and His Six Wives* (1970), and *Closing Numbers* (1994). Among her many books on baking are *Jane Asher's Complete Book of Cake Decorating Ideas*

(1993). She is married to the cartoonist Gerald Scarfe.

Ashkenazy, Vladimir (1937–) Pianist and conductor, born in Nizhni Novgorod (formerly Gorky), Russia. After earning an international reputation as a concert pianist, he turned increasingly to conducting, directing the Royal Philharmonic Orchestra (1987–95), the Radio Symphony Orchestra, Berlin (1989–99), the Czech Philharmonic Orchestra (1998–2003), and the Tokyo NHK Symphony Orchestra (2004–).

Ashley, Laura, *née* **Mountney** (1925–85) Fashion designer, born in Merthyr Tydfil, S Wales. In 1949 she started a business designing and producing furnishing materials, later developing this into an international chain of boutiques selling clothes, furnishing fabrics, and wallpapers.

Ashton, Sir Frederick (William Mallandaine) (1904–88) British dancer and choreographer, born in Guayaquil, Ecuador. He became co-director of Sadler's Wells (later The Royal Ballet) (1952–63), then director (1963–70).

Asimov, Isaac (1920–92) Novelist, critic, and popular scientist, born in Petrovichi, Russia. His family emigrated to the USA in 1923. Best known for his science-fiction writing, his works include the short-story collection *I, Robot* (1950), and the novels known as *The Foundation Trilogy* (1953).

Askey, Arthur, nickname **Big-hearted Arthur** (1900–82) Comedian, born in Liverpool, Merseyside. He achieved national recognition on radio with *Band Wagon* (from 1938).

He used his smallness of stature (1.6 m/5 ft 2 in) to comic advantage, and his twangy pronunciation of 'I thank you!' became a catchphrase.

Aspel, Michael (Terence) (1933–) Broadcaster and writer, born in London. He worked as a television newsreader (1960–8), later becoming known as host of *Aspel and Company* (1984–93), and as presenter of *This is Your Life* (1988–2003) and *The Antiques Roadshow* (from 2000).

Asquith, Herbert Henry Asquith, 1st Earl of Oxford (1852–1928) British prime minister (1908–16), born in Morley, West Yorkshire. A Liberal MP, he rose to be home secretary (1892–5), Chancellor of the Exchequer (1905–8), and prime minister. His office was notable for the Parliament Act (1911), suffragette troubles, the declaration of war (1914), and the Sinn Féin rebellion (1916).

Astaire, Fred, originally **Frederick Austerlitz** (1899–1987) Actor and dancer, born in Omaha, NE. With partner Ginger Rogers, he revolutionized the film musical with his original tap-dance routines in such films as *Top Hat* (1935). Later turning to straight acting, he received an Oscar nomination for *The Towering Inferno* (1974).

Astor, John Jacob (1763–1848) Businessman, founder of the Astor family, born in Waldorf, Germany. In 1784 he went to the USA, where he founded the America Fur Co, and rose to become one of the country's most powerful financiers.

Atatürk, originally **Mustafa Kemal** (1881–1938) Turkish army officer, politician, and president of Turkey (1923–38), born in Thessaloniki, Greece. After a nationalist rebellion, he became virtual dictator, and launched a social and political revolution introducing Western fashions, the emancipation of women, educational reform, and the replacement of Arabic script with the Latin alphabet. In 1935 he assumed the surname Atatürk ('Father of the Turks').

Athanasius, St (c.296–373) Christian theologian and prelate, born in Alexandria. He led the opposition to the doctrines of the heretic Arius, and his teaching was supported after his death at the Council of Constantinople (381). The *Athanasian Creed* was little heard of until the 7th-c.

Athelstan or **Æthelstan** (c.895–939) Anglo-Saxon king, the son of Edward the Elder, whom he succeeded as King of Wessex and Mercia in 924. He successfully invaded Northumbria, thus establishing himself as effectively the first King of all England in 927.

Atherton, Mike, popular name of **Michael Andrew Atherton** (1968–) Cricketer, born in Manchester, Greater Manchester. He joined Lancashire in 1987, made his debut for England in 1989 against Australia, and captained England in a record 51 Tests (1993–8). His best-remembered innings was an 11-hour, match-saving 188 against South Africa in Johannesburg in 1996. He retired from first-class cricket in 2001.

Atkins, Robert Coleman (1930–2003) Cardiologist and businessman, born in Columbus, OH. He developed a dietary system based on the theory that people can lose weight by following a high-protein, high-fat, and very low carbohydrate diet, published in *Dr. Atkins' Diet Revolution* (1972). The approach gained a huge following during the early 2000s but had faded in popularity by 2006.

Atkinson, Rowan (Sebastian) (1955–) Comic actor and writer, born in Newcastle upon Tyne, Tyne and Wear. His television roles include *Blackadder* (1983–9), *Mr Bean* (1990–4), and *The Thin Blue Line* (1995–6), and among his films are *Four Weddings and a Funeral* (1994), *Bean: the Ultimate Disaster Movie* (1997), and *Johnny English* (2003).

Atlas, Charles, originally **Angelo Siciliano** (1893–1972) Body-builder, born in Acri, Italy. He settled in the USA, and became popularly known as 'America's Most Perfectly Developed Man'.

Attenborough, Sir David (Frederick) (1926–) Naturalist and broadcaster, born in London, the brother of Richard Attenborough. He joined the BBC in 1952, and became director of programmes (1969–72). He is known for his many documentary series on wildlife in its natural habitat, such as *Life on Earth* (1979), *The Living Planet* (1984), *The Life of Birds* (1998), and *Planet Earth* (2006).

Attenborough, Sir Richard (Samuel), Baron (1923–) Film actor, producer, and director, born in Cambridge, Cambridgeshire, the brother of David Attenborough. He became well known following his role in *Brighton Rock* (1947). Major successes as a director include *Oh, What a Lovely War!* (1969), *Gandhi* (1982, 8 Oscars), *Cry Freedom* (1987), *Chaplin* (1992), and *Shadowlands* (1993).

Attila, known as **the Scourge of God** (c.406–53) King of the Huns (434–53). His dominion extended from the Rhine to the frontiers of China. He defeated Emperor Theodosius II (ruled 408–50), and in 451 invaded Gaul, but was routed by Aëtius and Theodoric I on the Catalaunian Plains.

Attlee, Clem, popular name of **Clement Richard Attlee, 1st Earl Attlee** (1883–1967) British Labour prime minister (1945–51), born in London. He served as dominions secretary (1942–3) and deputy prime minister (1942–5) in Churchill's War Cabinet. As prime minister, he carried through a vigorous programme of nationalization, and introduced the National Health Service.

Attwell, Mabel Lucie (1879–1964) Artist and writer, born in London. She was noted for her 'cherubic' child studies, with which she illustrated her own and other stories for children.

Atwood, Margaret (Eleanor) (1939–) Writer and critic, born in Ottawa, Ontario, Canada. Best known as a novelist, her works include *Lady Oracle* (1976), *The Handmaid's Tale* (1985; filmed 1990), *The Blind Assassin* (2000, Booker), and *Oryx and Crake* (2003).

Auden, W(ystan) H(ugh) (1907–73) Writer, born in York, North Yorkshire. His first volume of verse placed him in the forefront of a group of poets of left-wing sympathies. In 1939 he emigrated to New York, becoming a US citizen. His conversion to Anglicanism became evident in a more reflective style of writing, seen in *Homage to Clio* (1960) and *City Without Walls* (1969).

Audubon, John James, originally **Jean-Jacques Fougère** (1785–1851) Ornithologist and bird artist, born in Les Cayes, Haiti. He went to the USA in 1804, where he built up a vast collection of bird illustrations, as shown in *The Birds of America* (1827–38). The National Audubon Society was founded in his honour in 1866.

Augustine, St, also known as **Augustine of Canterbury** (?–604) Clergyman, the first Archbishop of Canterbury, born probably in Rome. He was prior of a Benedictine monastery at Rome, when in 596 Pope Gregory I sent him with 40 other monks to convert the Anglo-Saxons to Christianity. He was made Bishop of the English in 597.

Augustine, St, originally **Aurelius Augustinus**, also known as **Augustine of Hippo** (354–430) The greatest of the Latin Fathers, born in Tagaste, Numidia (modern Algeria). He became a Christian (387), then a priest (391), and was appointed Bishop of Hippo (396). A formidable antagonist to the heretical schools in the Donatist and Pelagian controversies, he wrote a famous autobiography, *Confessions* (397) and a vindication of the Christian Church, *De Civitate Dei* (413–26).

Augustus (Gaius Julius Caesar Octavianus) (63 BC–AD 14) Founder of the Roman Empire, the great nephew of Julius Caesar. On Caesar's assassination (44 BC), he raised an army and defeated Antony. When Antony returned from Gaul in force later that year with Lepidus, Octavian made a deal with his former enemies, joining them in a triumvirate, and taking Africa, Sardinia, and Sicily as his province. A later redivision of power gave him the entire western half of the Roman world, and Antony the eastern. In 31 BC, the Battle of Actium made Octavian victorious as sole ruler.

Aung San Suu Kyi, Daw (1945–) Political leader, born in Yangon, Myanmar (formerly Rangoon, Burma), the daughter of the assassinated General Aung San, the father of Burmese independence. When the military took power, she co-founded the National League for Democracy, and was arrested (1989–95). A further period of house arrest followed (2000–3), and in 2003 she was detained at Insein Prison near Rangoon and later placed under house arrest. She was awarded the Nobel Peace Prize in 1991.

Austen, Jane (1775–1817) Novelist, born in Steventon, Hampshire. Of her six great novels, the first four were published anonymously during her lifetime: *Sense and Sensibility* (1811), *Pride and Prejudice* (1813), *Mansfield Park* (1814), *Emma* (1816); *Persuasion* and *Northanger Abbey* (both 1818).

Auster, Paul (1947–) Novelist, born in Newark, NJ. His use of detective-story techniques to explore modern urban identity is evident in *The New York Trilogy* (1985–6). Later books include *The Music of Chance* (1990), *Oracle Night* (2003), and *The Brooklyn Follies* (2005).

Austin (of Longbridge), Herbert Austin, Baron (1866–1941) Car manufacturer, born in Little Missenden, Buckinghamshire. In 1895 he produced his first car, the Wolseley, and in 1905 opened his own works near Birmingham, producing an enormous output which included the popular 'Baby' Austin 7 (1921).

Avon, 1st Earl of *see* Eden, Sir Anthony

Ayckbourn, Sir Alan (1939–) Playwright, born in London. The first of many West End successes was *Relatively Speaking* (1967), and he was quickly established as a master of farce. Among his best-known plays are *Absurd Person Singular* (1973), *The Norman Conquests* (1974), and *Joking Apart* (1979). Later plays include *Invisible Friends* (1991), and *My Sister Sadie* (2003).

Ayer, Sir A(lfred) J(ules) (1910–89) Philosopher, born in London. His book *Language, Truth and Logic* (1936) was hailed as a lucid exposition of logical positivism. Later works include *The Problem of Knowledge* (1956) and *The Central Questions of Philosophy* (1972).

Ayeshah *see* Aïshah

Aykroyd, Dan (1952–) Actor, born in Ottawa. A stand-up comedian, he joined the anarchic show *Saturday Night Live* (1975–9). He starred in *The Blues Brothers* (1980), and earned a Best Supporting Actor Oscar nomination for his role in *Driving Miss Daisy* (1989). Later films include *Bright Young Things* (2003).

Babbage, Charles (1791–1871) Mathematician and pioneer computer scientist, born in Walworth, London. He worked on the theory of logarithms, and built a calculating machine, the forerunner of the computer. His assistant was Byron's daughter, Augusta Ada, Lady Lovelace.

Babington, Antony (1561–86) Conspirator, born in Dethick, Derbyshire. In 1586 he was induced to lead a conspiracy to murder Queen Elizabeth I and release Queen Mary of Scotland (the Babington Plot). The plan was discovered, and he was executed.

Bacall, Lauren, originally **Betty Joan Perske** (1924–) Actress, born in New York City. Her first leading role was in *To Have and Have Not* (1944), opposite Humphrey Bogart, whom she later married. Other films include *The Big Sleep* (1946), *Key Largo* (1948), *The Shootist* (1976, BAFTA), and *Birth* (2004).

Bach, C(arl) P(hilipp) E(manuel), known as **the Berlin Bach** or **the Hamburg Bach** (1714–88) Composer, born in Weimar, Germany, the second surviving son of Johann Sebastian Bach. He published *The True Art of Clavier Playing* (1753), the first methodical treatment of the subject, introduced the sonata form, and composed numerous concertos, keyboard sonatas, church music, and chamber music.

Bach, J(ohann) C(hristian), known as **the London Bach** or **the English Bach** (1735–82) Composer, born in Leipzig, Germany, the youngest son of Johann Sebastian Bach. His works include two Masses, a Requiem, a 'Te Deum', and operas. In 1762 he was appointed composer to the London Italian opera, and became musician to Queen Charlotte.

Bach, Johann Sebastian (1685–1750) Composer, one of the world's greatest musicians, born in Eisenach, Germany. In 1711 he became chapel master to Prince Leopold of Anhalt-Cöthen, where he wrote mainly instrumental music, including the 'Brandenburg' Concertos (1721) and *The Well-tempered Clavier* (1722). In 1723 he was appointed cantor of the Thomasschule in Leipzig, where his works included c 300 church cantatas, the *St Matthew Passion* (1727), and the *Mass in B Minor*. The most outstanding member of the celebrated Bach family, his main achievement was his development of polyphony.

Bach, W(ilhelm) F(riedemann), known as **the Halle Bach** (1710–84) Composer, born in Weimar, Germany, the eldest and most gifted son of J S Bach. The greatest organ player of his time, he held posts at Dresden (1733) and Halle (1747).

Bacharach, Burt (1929–) Composer, born in Kansas City, MO. He teamed up with Hal David to write such hits as 'Magic Moments' (1957) and 'Raindrops Keep Fallin' on My Head' (1969, Oscar Best Song). In the 1970s he began working with lyricist and future wife (1982–90) Carol Bayer Sager. His album *At This Time* appeared in 2005.

Bacon, Francis, Viscount St Albans (1561–1626) Philosopher and statesman, born in London, the younger son of Sir Nicholas Bacon. He became attorney general (1613), privy counsellor (1616), Lord Keeper (1617), and Lord Chancellor (1618). His philosophy is best studied in *The Advancement of Learning* (1605) and *Novum Organum* (1620), where his stress on inductive methods influenced later scientific investigation.

Bacon, Francis (1909–92) Artist, born in Dublin. In England from 1928, he treated religious subjects in a highly individual surrealist manner, and is best known for his 'Three Studies for Figures at the base of a Crucifixion' (1945).

Bacon, Kevin (1958–) Actor and musician, born in Philadelphia, PA. His films include *National Lampoon's Animal House* (1981), *The River Wild* (1993, Golden Globe Best Actor nomination), *Apollo 13* (1995), *Mystic River* (2003), and *Where the Truth Lies* (2005). Along with brother Michael, he performs with The Bacon Brothers folk-rock group.

Baden-Powell, Robert Stephenson Smyth Baden-Powell, Baron (1857–1941) British general, born in London. He won fame during the Boer War as the defender of Mafeking (1899–1900). In 1908 he founded the Boy Scout movement, and in 1910, with his sister **Agnes** (1858–1945), the Girl Guides.

Bader, Sir Douglas (Robert Stuart) (1910–82) Wartime aviator, born in London. He lost both legs in a flying accident in 1931, but overcame his disability and returned to the RAF in 1939, commanding the first Canadian Fighter Squadron. Captured in 1941, his example of fortitude and heroism became legendary.

Baez, Joan (1941–) Folk singer, born in New York City. During the revival of traditional folk music in the 1960s, she became popular with young audiences for her songs and political views in support of civil rights, peace, and other causes.

Baffin, William (c.1584–1622) Navigator, probably born in London. He was pilot in several expeditions in search of the Northwest Passage (1612–16), during which they explored Baffin Bay (1615) and found Lancaster, Smith, and Jones Sounds (1616).

Bailey, David (Royston) (1938–) Photographer, born in London. Initially a fashion photographer, he became known for his portraits expressing the spirit of the 1960s, and for outstanding nude studies. In 1999 a major retrospective of his work, 'Birth of the Cool', opened in London.

Bainbridge, Dame Beryl (Margaret) (1934–) British writer, born in Liverpool, Merseyside. She became known for her terse, black comedies, such as

The Dressmaker (1973; filmed 1979) and *Filthy Lucre* (1986). Later novels include *Master Georgie* (1998) and *According to Queeney* (2001), and she has also published plays, stories, and collections of her journalistic essays.

Baird, John Logie (1888–1946) Television pioneer, born in Helensburgh, Argyll and Bute. In 1926 he gave the first demonstration of a television image. His 30-line mechanically scanned system was experimentally broadcast by the BBC in 1929; and during 1936, transmissions of his improved 240-line system alternated with the rival Marconi-EMI 405-line electronic system, which was adopted in 1937.

Baker, Dame Janet (Abbott) (1933–) Mezzo-soprano, born in Hatfield, South Yorkshire. She has had an extensive operatic career, especially in early Italian opera and the works of Benjamin Britten, and is also a noted interpreter of Mahler and Elgar.

Baker, Richard (Douglas James) (1925–) Broadcaster and author, born in London. He joined the BBC as an announcer in 1950, and became known as a television newsreader (1954–82), and as a commentator on major state occasions.

Bakewell, Joan (Dawson) (1933–) Broadcaster and writer, born in Stockport, Greater Manchester. She became known for her BBC television series, such as *Late Night Line Up* (1965–72) and *Heart of the Matter* (1988–2000). Among her later books is *Belief* (2005).

Balanchine, George, originally **Georgi Melitonovich Balanchi-**vadze** (1904–83) Ballet dancer and choreographer, born in St Petersburg, Russia. After a period in the Russian Ballet in Paris, he opened the School of American Ballet in New York City (1934), and became director of the New York City Ballet (1948).

Baldwin, Mark (Phillip) (1954–) Choreographer and dancer, born in Fiji. Raised in New Zealand, he became a dancer with the New Zealand Ballet and Australian Dance Theatre before joining the Rambert Dance Company in London (1982–92), also as choreographer (1992–4). He became resident choreographer with Sadler's Wells (1994–5) and with the Scottish Ballet (1996), and was appointed artistic director of the Rambert Dance Company in 2002.

Baldwin (of Bewdley), Stanley Baldwin, 1st Earl (1867–1947) British Conservative prime minister (1923–4, 1924–9, 1935–7), born in Bewdley, Hereford and Worcester. He was President of the Board of Trade (1921–2) and Chancellor of the Exchequer (1922–3). He resigned as premier after criticism of his apparent failure to recognize the threat from Nazi Germany.

Balenciaga, Cristóbal (1895–1972) Fashion designer, born in Guetaria, Spain. He left Spain for Paris as a result of the Spanish Civil War, where he produced clothes noted for their dramatic simplicity and elegance.

Balfour, Arthur James Balfour, 1st Earl (1848–1930) British Conservative prime minister (1902–5), born in Whittingehame, Lothian. He was chief secretary for Ireland (1887), and as foreign secretary (1916–19) was responsible for the *Balfour Declaration* (1917) on Palestine.

Ball, Michael (Ashley) (1962–) Actor and singer, born in the West Midlands. He made his West End debut in *Les Miserables* in 1985. Other major productions include *Phantom of the Opera* (1987), *Aspects of Love* (1989), and *The Woman in White* (2005).

Ballard, J(ames) G(raham) (1930–) Writer, born in Shanghai, China. Among his works are the science-fiction novel *The Drowned World* (1962), the autobiographical novel *Empire of the Sun* (1984; filmed 1987), and its sequel *The Kindness of Women* (1991). Later works include *Millennium People* (2003).

Ballesteros, Sevvy, popular name of **Severiano Ballesteros** (1957–) Golfer, born in Pedrena, Spain. His successes include the British Open (1979, 1984, 1988), the US Masters (1980, 1983), and the World Matchplay (1981–2, 1984–5, 1991).

Balmain, Pierre (Alexandre Claudius) (1914–82) Fashion designer, born in St Jean-de-Maurienne, France. He opened his own house in 1945. Famous for elegant simplicity, his designs included evening dresses, tailored suits, sportswear, and stoles.

Balzac, Honoré de, originally **Honoré Balssa** (1799–1850) Novelist, born in Tours, France. His chief work was *The Human Comedy* (trans, 1827–47), a complete picture of modern civilization, which includes such masterpieces as (trans titles) *Father Goriot*, *Lost Illusions*, and *The Peasants*.

Banderas, Antonio, in full **José**

Antonio Domínguez Banderas (1960–) Actor, born in Málaga, Spain. He worked with Spanish director Pedro Almodóvar in such films as *Matador* (1985) and *La ley del deseo* (1986). Moving to Hollywood, his films include *Philadelphia* (1993), *Evita* (1996), and *The Legend of Zorro* (2005). He married actress Melanie Griffith in 1996.

Banks, Lynne (Reid) (1929–) Writer, born in London. Her best-known novel is *The L-Shaped Room* (1960; filmed 1962), and she has also written plays and biographical novels. Her many books for children include *The Indian in the Cupboard* (1980; filmed 1995) and *Alice By Accident* (2000).

Bannister, Sir Roger (Gilbert) (1929–) Athlete and neurologist, born in Harrow, Greater London. He was the first man to run the mile in under 4 minutes (3 min 59·4 s), at Oxford (6 May 1954).

Barabbas (1st-c) Political rebel and murderer (*Mark* 15, *Luke* 23). He was arrested but apparently released by popular acclaim in preference to Pilate's offer to release Jesus of Nazareth.

Barber, Samuel (1910–81) Composer, born in West Chester, PA. His early music includes the popular *Adagio for Strings*. Later works lay more emphasis on chromaticism and dissonance, and include the ballet *Medea* (1946) and the opera *Vanessa* (1958, Pulitzer).

Barbera *see* Hanna-Barbera

Barclay, Robert (1843–1913) British banker, who oversaw the merger of 20 banks to form Barclay & Co Ltd in

1896. In 1917 the name was changed to Barclay's Bank Ltd.

Bardeen, John (1908–91) Physicist, the first person to receive two Nobel Prizes for Physics, born in Madison, WI. In 1947 he helped to develop the point contact transistor, for which he shared the Nobel Prize in 1956. His second prize (1972) was shared for his work on the first satisfactory theory of superconductivity.

Bardot, Brigitte, originally **Camille Javal** (1934–) Film actress, born in Paris. The film *And God Created Woman* (trans, 1956), directed by husband Roger Vadim, established her international reputation as a sex kitten. Later films include *The Truth* (trans, 1960) and *If Don Juan Were a Woman* (trans, 1973).

Barker, Pat(ricia Margaret) (1943–) Novelist, born in Thornby-on-Tees, Cleveland. She is especially known for an acclaimed trilogy about World War 1: *Regeneration* (1991), *The Eye in the Door* (1993, Guardian Fiction Award), and *The Ghost Road* (1995, Booker). Later novels include *Double Vision* (2003).

Barker, Ronnie, popular name of **Ronald William George Barker** (1929–2005) Comic actor, born in Bedford, Bedfordshire. His many radio and television appearances include *Porridge* (1974–7; filmed 1979), *Open All Hours* (1976, 1981–5) and, in partnership with Ronnie Corbett, *The Two Ronnies* (1971–87).

Barnabas (1st-c) Christian missionary, originally a Levite from Cyprus called Joseph. He was a companion and supporter of Paul during Paul's early ministry to the Gentiles. The so-called *Letter of Barnabas* is a spurious 2nd-c work.

Barnard, Christiaan (Neethling) (1922–2001) Surgeon, born in Beaufort West, South Africa. At Groote Schuur Hospital he performed the first successful human heart transplant (1967), though the patient, Louis Washkansky, died of double pneumonia 18 days later. Later transplants proved to be increasingly successful.

Barnardo, Thomas John (1845–1905) Physician and philanthropist, born in Dublin. In London in 1867 he founded the East End Mission for destitute children in Stepney, and a number of homes in Greater London, which came to be known as the *Dr Barnardo's Homes*.

Barnes, John (Charles Bryan) (1963–) Footballer, born in Kingston, Jamaica. A winger, he played for Watford (1981), Liverpool (1988), Newcastle (1997), and Charlton (1998), then joined Kenny Dalglish at Celtic as team coach (1999–2000). During his career he won 79 caps for England, making him England's highest capped black football player. Since retirement he has worked in the media.

Barrie, Sir J(ames) M(atthew) (1860–1937) Novelist and playwright, born in Kirriemuir, Angus. Chiefly remembered for *Peter Pan* (1904), other notable plays include *The Admirable Crichton* (1902) and *Dear Brutus* (1917).

Bart, Lionel (1930–99) Composer and lyricist, born in London. His successful musicals include *Lock Up Your*

Daughters (1959), *Oliver* (1960), *Blitz!* (1962), and *Maggie May* (1964).

Bartók, Béla (1881–1945) Composer, born in Nagyszentmiklós, Hungary. His compositions were greatly influenced by Hungarian and Balkan folk music. In 1939 he settled in the USA, where his many works include the opera *Duke Bluebeard's Castle* and the ballet *The Wooden Prince*.

Bartoli, Cecilia (1966–) Mezzo-soprano, born in Rome. She gave her debut performance in Zurich in 1988. Winner of four Grammy Awards, her albums include *The Vivaldi Album* (1999), *The Salieri Album* (2003), and *Opera Proibita* (2005).

Baruch (7th–6th-c BC) Biblical character, described as the companion and secretary of the prophet Jeremiah (*Jer* 36). His name became attached to several Jewish works of much later date.

Basie, Count, popular name of **William Allen Basie** (1904–84) Jazz pianist, and bandleader, born in Red Bank, NJ. He joined the Benny Moten band in 1929, forming his own band in 1935 which became the Count Basie Orchestra. Nearly 50 years as a bandleader, his most popular compositions include 'One O'Clock Jump' and 'Jumpin' at the Woodside'.

Basil, St, known as **Basil the Great** (c.329–79) One of the greatest of the Greek fathers, born in Caesarea, Cappadocia, the brother of Gregory of Nyssa. A fierce opponent of Arianism, he improved monastic standards and wrote many seminal works.

Basinger, Kim (1953–) Film actress, born in Athens, GA. A former top model, her films include *The Real McCoy* (1993), *L.A. Confidential* (1997, Oscar), *8 Mile* (2002), and *Cellular* (2004). Her second marriage (1993–2001) was to actor Alec Baldwin.

Bassey, Dame Shirley (Veronica) (1937–) Singer, born in Tiger Bay, Cardiff. She began performing at local clubs, soon turned professional, and went on to international success. Her best-known songs include 'As Long as He Needs Me' (1960), 'What Now My Love' (1962), 'Goldfinger' (1964), and 'Diamonds are Forever' (1971).

Bates, Sir Alan, originally **Arthur Bates** (1934–2003) Actor, born in Allestree, Derbyshire. His films included *The Entertainer* (1960), *A Kind of Loving* (1962), and *Women in Love* (1969), and the television productions of *An Englishman Abroad* (1982, BAFTA) and *Love in a Cold Climate* (2001).

Bates, H(erbert) E(rnest) (1905–74) Writer, born in Rushden, Northamptonshire. A noted exponent of the short story, his best-known works are *Fair Stood the Wind for France* (1944), *The Jacaranda Tree* (1949), and *The Darling Buds of May* (1958), which became a popular UK television series.

Bates, (Michael) Jeremy (1962–) Tennis player, born in Solihull, West Midlands. After winning national tennis titles at junior level, he turned professional in 1980. A member of the Davis Cup team (1984–95), his titles include the Wimbledon mixed doubles (1987), Australian Open mixed doubles (1991), and the Korean Open singles (1994). A former British number 1, he retired in 1996 and since then has been the Lawn Tennis Association's head of performance. In January 2004 he became Davis Cup captain.

Batten, Jean (1909–82) Pioneer aviator, born in Rotorua, New Zealand. In 1934, in a Gypsy Moth, she broke Amy Johnson's record for the solo flight from England to Australia, and became the first woman to complete the return journey.

Baudelaire, Charles (Pierre) (1821–67) Symbolist poet, born in Paris. His masterpiece is a collection of poems, *Les Fleurs du mal* (1857), for which he was prosecuted for impropriety in 1864. Later works include *Les Paradis artificiels* (1860) and *Petits Poèmes en prose* (1869).

Baudot, Jean-Maurice-Emile (1845–1903) Electrical engineer, born in Magneux, France. In 1874 he patented the Baudot code, used in telegraph systems, and in 1894 a system which allowed several messages to be sent along the same wire simultaneously (*multiplexing*).

Baum, Vicki, originally **Vicki Hedvig** (1888–1960) Novelist, born in Vienna. Her works include *Grand Hotel* (1930), *Headless Angel* (1948), *The Mustard Seed* (1953), and several short stories and plays. She emigrated to the USA in 1931.

Bausch, Pina, popular name of **Philippine Bausch** (1940–) Choreographer and dancer, born in Solingen, Germany. In 1973 she became ballet director of the Wuppertal Dance Theatre, and later founded her own company, where her expressionist productions were highly influential.

Beach Boys, The US singing/instrumental group, formed in California in 1961, consisting originally of brothers **Brian Wilson** (1942–), **Carl Wilson** (1946–98), and **Dennis Wilson** (1944–83), with cousin **Mike Love** (1941–) and **Al(an) Jardine** (1942–), later also **Bruce Johnstone** (1944–) and others. Their hit songs included 'I Get Around', 'California Girls', and 'Good Vibrations'. In 2004 Brian Wilson completed his album *Smile* begun in the 1960s.

Beaconsfield, Earl of *see* Disraeli, Benjamin

Beatles, The (1960–70) British pop group, formed in Liverpool in 1960, originally **John Lennon** (1940–80), **Paul McCartney** (1942–), **George Harrison** (1943–2001), and **Pete Best** (1941–), replaced in 1962 by **Ringo Starr** (1940– , real name **Richard Starkey**). Success came after appearances at the Cavern Club in Liverpool and 'Love Me Do' became the first of a string of international hit singles and albums. Their films included *A Hard Day's Night* (1964) and *Help!* (1965). The group dissolved in 1970.

Beaton, Sir Cecil (Walter Hardy) (1904–80) Photographer and designer, born in London. Known as a photographer of high-society celebrities, including royalty, he later designed scenery and costumes for stage and film productions including *My Fair Lady* and *Gigi*.

Beatrix, in full **Beatrix Wilhelmina Armgard** (1938–) Queen of The Netherlands (1980–), born in Soestdijk, The Netherlands, the eldest daughter of Queen Juliana and Prince Bernhard Leopold. In 1966 she married West German diplomat **Claus-Georg Wilhelm Otto Friedrich Gerd von Amsberg** (1926–2002). They have three sons.

Beatty, Warren, originally **Henry Warren Beaty** (1937–) Actor and film-maker, born in Richmond, VA, the younger brother of actress Shirley MacLaine. Film appearances include *Splendor in the Grass* (1961), *Bonnie and Clyde* (1967), *Reds* (1981, Oscar for Best Director), *Bulworth* (1998), and *Town and Country* (2001).

Beauvoir, Simone de *see* de Beauvoir, Simone

Beaverbrook (of Beaverbrook and of Cherkley), (William) Max(well) Aitken, Baron (1879–1964) Newspaper magnate and British politician, born in Maple, Ontario. In 1916 he took over the *Daily Express*, founded the *Sunday Express* (1921), and bought the *Evening Standard* (1929). During World War 2, he was made minister of supply (1941–2) and Lord Privy Seal (1943–5).

Bechstein, Karl (1826–1900) Piano manufacturer, born in Gotha, Germany. He founded his famous factory in Berlin in 1856.

Beckenbauer, Franz, nickname **the Kaiser** (1945–) Footballer, born in Munich, Germany. He led West Germany to success in the European Nations Cup (1972) and the World Cup (1974). Voted European Footballer of the Year in 1972, he retired in 1983, and became manager of Germany (1986). He is currently president of FC Bayern Munich and

in 1998 was appointed vice-president of the German Football Association.

Becker, Boris (1967–) Tennis player, born in Leiman, Germany. The youngest winner of the men's singles at Wimbledon (17 years 227 days) in 1985, he retained the title in 1986 and 1989, and in 1992 won the Association of Tennis Professionals World Title.

Becket, St Thomas, also called **Thomas (à) Becket** (1118–70) Saint and martyr, born in London. In 1155 he became Chancellor, the first Englishman since the Conquest to hold high office. When created Archbishop of Canterbury (1162), he resigned the chancellorship, and came into conflict with Henry II's aims to keep the clergy in subordination to the state. Henry's rashly voiced wish to be rid of 'this turbulent priest' led to Becket's murder in Canterbury Cathedral (29 Dec 1170) by four of the king's knights. He was canonized in 1173.

Beckett, Margaret (Mary) (1943–) British stateswoman, born in Ashton-under-Lyne, Greater Manchester. Elected an MP in 1974, she became deputy leader of the Labour Party (1992–4). She was president of the Board of Trade and secretary of state for trade and industry (1997), Leader of the House of Commons (1998–2001), secretary of state for environment, food and rural affairs (2001–6), and foreign secretary (2006–).

Beckett, Samuel (Barclay) (1906–89) Writer and playwright, born in Dublin. He settled in France in 1937. Writing first in English, he later wrote in French, notably the novels *Molloy* (1951) and *Malone Dies* (trans, 1951) and the plays *Waiting for Godot* (trans, 1954) and *End Game* (trans, 1956). He was awarded the 1969 Nobel Prize for Literature.

Beckham, David (Robert Joseph) (1975–) Footballer, born in London. A midfield player, he joined Manchester United in 1993, and the England team in 1996, captain from 2002. By the start of 2006 he had won 86 caps. His many honours with United include the treble of FA Cup, Premier League Championship, and European Cup in the 1998–9 season, before signing for Real Madrid in 2003. He married Victoria Adams ('Posh Spice') in 1999.

Becquerel, (Antoine) Henri (1852–1908) Physicist, born in Paris. He discovered the *Becquerel rays* emitted from the uranium salts in pitchblende (1896), which led to the isolation of radium, and shared the Nobel Prize for Physics with the Curies in 1903.

Bede or **Baeda, St**, known as **the Venerable Bede** (c.673–735) Anglo-Saxon scholar, theologian, and historian, born near Monkwearmouth, Durham. His greatest work was the Latin *Ecclesiastical History of the English People* (trans, 731), the single most valuable source for early English history. He was canonized in 1899.

Beecham, Sir Thomas (1879–1961) Conductor and impresario, born in St Helens, Merseyside. Principal conductor (1932) at Covent Garden, and founder of the Royal Philharmonic Orchestra (1946), he was noted for his candid views on musical matters, his

'Lollipop' encores, and his after-concert speeches.

Beecher Stowe, Harriet *see* Stowe, Harriet (Elizabeth) Beecher

Beethoven, Ludwig van (1770–1827) Composer, born in Bonn, Germany. His music is usually divided into three periods. The first (1792–1802) includes the first two symphonies, the first six quartets, and the 'Pathétique' and 'Moonlight' sonatas. The second (1803–12) begins with the 'Eroica' symphony (1803), and includes his next five symphonies, the 'Kreutzer' sonata (1803), the Violin Concerto, and the 'Archduke' trio (1811). The third begins in 1813, and includes the Mass, the 'Choral' symphony (1823), and the last five quartets. His career was marred by deafness, which began in 1801 and was total by the early 1820s.

Beeton, Isabella Mary, *née* **Mayson**, known as **Mrs Beeton** (1836–65) Cookery writer, born in London. Her *Book of Household Management* (1859–60), covering cookery and other branches of domestic science, made her name a household word.

Bell, Alexander Graham (1847–1922) Educationist and inventor, born in Edinburgh, the son of Alexander Melville Bell. He invented the articulating telephone, sending the first intelligible message to his laboratory assistant in 1875, and formed the Bell Telephone Company in 1877.

Bell, Martin (1938–) Television journalist and politician, born in Cambridge, Cambridgeshire. He joined the BBC in 1962, becoming one of their best-known foreign correspondents. He fought an 'anti-sleaze' campaign in the 1997 general election and was returned as Independent MP for Tatton, but was unsuccessful in the 2001 general election.

Bellamy, David (James) (1933–) British botanist, writer, and broadcaster. He is widely known for his televison programmes on the natural environment, such as *Bellamy's Britain* (1975), *Bellamy's Border Raids: The Peak District* (1994), and *A Welsh Herbal* (1998–9). He established the Conservation Foundation in 1988.

Bellini A family of 15th-c Venetian painters. **Jacopo Bellini** (c.1400–70) studied under Gentile da Fabriano, painting a wide range of subjects. His son **Gentile Bellini** (c.1429–1507) painted many portraits. His other son, **Giovanni Bellini** (c.1430–1516), was the greatest Venetian painter of his time. His innovations of light and colour became the hallmark of Venetian art, continued by his pupils Giorgione and Titian.

Belloc, (Joseph) Hilaire (Pierre René) (1870–1953) Writer, born in Saint-Cloud, near Paris. A British Liberal MP (1906–10), he left politics and continued as a writer, producing travel books, historical studies, religious works, and nonsensical verse for children, such as *Cautionary Tales* (1907). He was a leading Roman Catholic of his day.

Bellow, Saul, originally **Solomon Bellows** (1915–2005) Writer, born in Lachine, Quebec, Canada. His novels include *The Dangling Man* (1944), *Henderson the Rain-King* (1959), *Herzog* (1964), and *Humboldt's Gift* (1975,

Pulitzer). He was awarded the Nobel Prize for Literature in 1976.

Belshazzar, Gr **Balt(h)asar** (?–539 BC) Ruler of Babylon (550–539 BC). In the Book of Daniel, mysterious writing appears on the wall of his palace, which Daniel interprets as predicting the fall of the empire. He died during the capture of Babylon.

Benaud, Richie, popular name of **Richard Benaud** (1930–) Cricketer, broadcaster, and international sports consultant, born in Penrith, New South Wales, Australia. An all-rounder, he played in 63 Test matches for Australia (captain in 28), scored 2201 Test runs, and took 248 wickets. He became a well-known cricket commentator.

Benedict of Nursia, St (c.480–c.547) The founder of Western monasticism, born in Nursia, Italy. At Subiaco he founded 12 small monastic communities, and his *Regula monachorum* (c.515) became the common rule of all Western monasticism (*the Benedictine rule*). He was declared the patron saint of all Europe by Pope Paul VI in 1964.

Benedict XVI, originally **Joseph Ratzinger** (1927–) Pope (2005–), born in Marktl am Inn, Bavaria, Germany. He was ordained in 1951, became advisor to Cardinal Frings of Cologne during Vatican Council II, and gained a reputation as a reformist. Made Archbishop of Munich in 1977, he was created a cardinal the same year. He became a close friend and confidant of Pope John Paul II, and served as head of the congregation of the Doctrine of the Faith in the Vatican for over 20 years.

Benesh, Rudolph (1916–75) Dance notator, born in London. A painter, he married **Joan Rothwell** (1920–), born in Liverpool, a former member of the Sadler's Wells Ballet. Their dance notation system, Choreology (1955), is now used to document all important Royal Ballet productions. They opened their own institute in 1962.

Ben-Gurion, David, originally **David Gruen** (1886–1973) Israeli statesman and prime minister (1948–53, 1955–63), born in Plonsk, Poland. In 1930 he became leader of the Mapai (Labour) Party, in 1948 the first ruling party in the state of Israel. After his retirement, he came to symbolize the Israeli state.

Benigni, Roberto (1952–) Film director and actor, born in Arezzo, Tuscany, Italy. He appeared in the films *I Love You Berlinguer* (trans, 1976), *The Son of the Pink Panther* (1993), *Asterix and Obelix Take on Caesar* (trans, 1999), and *Coffee and Cigarettes* (2003). *Life is Beautiful* (trans, 1997) he wrote, directed, and starred in, gained Oscars for Best Actor and Best Foreign Language Film.

Benn, Anthony (Neil) Wedgwood, known as **Tony Benn** (1925–) British statesman, born in London, the son of Viscount Stansgate. He became a Labour MP (1950–60), but was debarred from the House of Commons on succeeding to his father's title. He renounced his title, was re-elected (1963), and went on to hold several ministerial posts.

Bennett, Alan (1934–) Playwright, actor, and director, born in Leeds,

West Yorkshire. His many plays include *Kafka's Dick* (1986), *Single Spies* (1988), and *The History Boys* (2004). He has also written much for television, including a series of monologues, *Talking Heads* (1987), and the autobiographical *The Lady in The Van* (1999).

Bennett, (Enoch) Arnold (1867–1931) Novelist, born near Hanley, Staffordshire. Among his many novels are *Anna of the Five Towns* (1902), *The Old Wives' Tale* (1908), and the *Clayhanger* series, all of which reflect life in the Potteries. His *Journals* were published posthumously.

Bennett, Brian *see* Shadows, The

Bennett, Sir Richard Rodney (1936–) Composer, born in Broadstairs, Kent. Well known for his music for films, such as *Murder on the Orient Express* (1973), he has also composed operas, orchestral works, chamber music, experimental works, and jazz pieces.

Benny, Jack, originally **Benjamin Kubelsky** (1894–1974) Comedian, born in Waukegan, IL. A child prodigy violinist, he went on to Broadway success, later earning his own radio series and television show, *The Jack Benny Show* (1950–65).

Bentinck, William Henry Cavendish, 3rd Duke of Portland (1738–1809) British prime minister (1783, 1807–9), born in Bulstrode, Buckinghamshire. He was also home secretary under Pitt, with charge of Irish affairs (1794–1801).

Bergerac, Savinien Cyrano de *see* Cyrano de Bergerac, Savinien

Bergman, (Ernst) Ingmar (1918–) Film director and writer, born in Uppsala, Sweden. His films became something of a cult for art-cinema audiences, such as (trans titles) *The Seventh Seal* (1956), *Wild Strawberries* (1957), *Through a Glass Darkly* (1961, Oscar), and *Autumn Sonata* (1978). Later films include *Fanny and Alexander* (1982, Oscar) and *Saraband* (2005).

Bergman, Ingrid (1915–82) Film actress, born in Stockholm. Her early film successes included *Casablanca* (1942) and *Gaslight* (1944, Oscar), and she later won Oscars for *Anastasia* (1956) and *Murder on the Orient Express* (1974).

Berkeley, Busby, originally **William Berkeley Enos** (1895–1976) Choreographer and director, born in Los Angeles, CA. He became one of the cinema's most innovative choreographers, noted for his mobile camerawork and kaleidoscopic routines involving spectacular multitudes of chorus girls, in such films as *Forty Second Street* (1933).

Berlin, Irving, originally **Israel Baline** (1888–1989) Composer who helped to launch 20th-c American popular music, born in Temun, Russia. Taken to the USA as a child, his 'Alexander's Ragtime Band' became an international hit in 1911. The 1940s saw him at the peak of his career, with the hit musicals *Annie Get Your Gun* (1946) and *Call Me Madam* (1950).

Berlioz, (Louis-)Hector (1803–69) Composer, born in Côte-Saint-André, France. His works include the *Symphonie Fantastique* (1830), the symphonies *Harold en Italie* (1834) and *Roméo et Juliette* (1839), the cantata *La Damnation de Faust* (1846),

and the operas *Les Troyens* (1856–8) and *Béatrice et Bénédict* (1860–2).

Berlitz, Charles (Frambach) (1914–) Languages educationist, born in New York City. He is the grandson of **Maximilian Delphinus Berlitz** (1852–1921), who founded the Berlitz School in 1878 as a German emigré to the USA.

Bernadette of Lourdes, St, originally **Marie Bernarde Soubirous** (1844–79) Visionary, born in Lourdes, France, the daughter of a miller. She claimed in 1858 to have received 18 apparitions of the Blessed Virgin at the Massabielle Rock, which has since become a notable place of pilgrimage. She became a nun with the Sisters of Charity at Nevers, and was canonized in 1933.

Bernard of Clairvaux, St, known as **the Mellifluous Doctor** (1090–1153) Theologian and reformer, born in Fontaines, France. The first abbot of the newly founded monastery of Clairvaux (1115), he founded over 70 monasteries. He was canonized in 1174. The monks of his reformed branch of the Cistercians are often called *Bernardines*.

Bernard of Menthon, St, known as **the Apostle of the Alps** (923–1008) Clergyman, born in Savoy, Italy. As archdeacon of Aosta he founded the hospices in the two Alpine passes that bear his name. *St Bernard dogs* are also named after him. He was canonized in 1115.

Berners-Lee, Sir Tim (1955–) Network designer, the inventor of the World Wide Web, born in London. In 1984 he took up a physics fellowship at CERN, Geneva, and in 1989 proposed a global hypertext project which was implemented on the Internet in 1991. He is director of the World Wide Web Consortium.

Bernhardt, Sarah, originally **Henriette Rosine Bernard** (1844–1923) Actress, born in Paris. Her most famous roles included the title role in *Phèdre* (1877) and as Marguerite in *La Dame aux camélias* (1884). A legendary figure, she founded the Théâtre Sarah Bernhardt in 1899.

Bernstein, Leonard (1918–90) Conductor, pianist, and composer, born in Lawrence, MA. His compositions include three symphonies, a Mass, a ballet, and many choral works and songs, but he became most widely known for his two musicals, *On the Town* (1944) and *West Side Story* (1957).

Berry, Chuck, popular name of **Charles Edward Anderson Berry** (1926–) Rock singer and songwriter, born in St Louis, MO. His successes include 'Rock And Roll Music' (1957), 'Johnny B Goode' (1958), and 'My Ding A Ling' (1972).

Berry, Halle (1966–) Actress, born in Cleveland, OH. Her films include *The Flintstones* (1994), *Die Another Day* (2002), and *Catwoman* (2004). In 2002 she made Hollywood history as the first black woman to win an Academy Award for Best Actress for her role in *Monster's Ball*.

Bessemer, Sir Henry (1813–98) Inventor and engineer, born in Charlton, Hertfordshire. He originated over 100 inventions, but is best known for the *Bessemer process* (1856), whereby molten pig-iron can be turned directly into steel by blowing air through it in a tilting converter.

Best, George (1946–2005) Footballer, born in Belfast. A highly gifted player, he was the leading scorer for Manchester United (1967–8), European and English Footballer of the Year in 1968, and played for Northern Ireland 37 times. His tempestuous lifestyle hastened his retirement. He underwent a successful liver transplant operation in 2002 but was frequently beset by health problems.

Betjeman, Sir John (1906–84) Writer and broadcaster, born in London. He became especially known for his light verse, as seen in his *Collected Poems* (1958) and verse autobiography, *Summoned by Bells* (1960). He became poet laureate in 1972.

Bettany, Paul (1971–) Actor, born in London. Born into a show business family, his feature film roles include *A Beautiful Mind* (2001), *Master and Commander* (2003), and *Firewall* (2005). He married actress Jennifer Connelly in 2002.

Bevan, Aneurin, known as **Nye Bevan** (1897–1960) British statesman, born in Tredegar, Blaenau Gwent, S Wales. As Labour minister of health (1945–51), he introduced the National Health Service (1948). 'Bevanism' was a left-wing movement to make the Labour Party more socialist and less 'reformist'.

Biggs, Ronald (1929–) Member of the gang who perpetrated the Great Train Robbery in 1963. One of the first to be arrested for the robbery, he escaped from Wandsworth Prison in 1965, eventually settling in Brazil, where he continued to attract press publicity. Attempts at extradition failed, but he finally returned to Britain voluntarily in 2001 and was imprisoned.

Biko, Stephen (Bantu), known as **Steve Biko** (1946–77) South African black activist, born in King William's Town. The founder of the Black Consciousness Movement, in 1973 he was served with a banning order severely restricting his movements, and died in police custody, allegedly as a result of beatings. He was the subject of the film *Cry Freedom* (1987).

Bilk, Acker, popular name of **Bernard Stanley Bilk** (1929–) Jazz musician, composer, and band leader, born in Pensford, Somerset. He joined Ken Colyer's Band as clarinettist, and formed the Bristol Paramount Jazz Band in 1951. His best-known hit single was 'Stranger on the Shore' (1961, first number 1 simultaneously in UK and USA).

Billy the Kid *see* Bonney, William H

Binchy, Maeve (1940–) Writer, born in Dublin. Best known as a romantic novelist, her books include *Light a Penny Candle* (1982), *The Glass Lake* (1994), and *Nights of Rain and Stars* (2004).

bin Laden, also **Usama bin Laden** *see* Osama bin Laden

Binoche, Juliette (1964–) Film actress, born in Paris. She received international success with the film version of Milan Kundera's novel, *The Unbearable Lightness of Being* (1988). Later films include *The English Patient* (1996, Oscar for Best Supporting Actress), *Chocolat* (2000), and *Hidden* (2005).

Bird, Dickie, popular name of **Harold**

Dennis Bird (1933–) Cricket umpire, born in Barnsley, South Yorkshire. He played county cricket for Yorkshire (1956–9) and Leicestershire (1960–4) before establishing himself as a popular and respected umpire. He retired as a Test umpire in 1996. His autobiography in 1998 was the best-selling hardback book in British publishing.

Birdseye, Clarence (1886–1956) Businessman and inventor, born in New York City. He is best known for developing a process for freezing food in small packages suitable for retailing, and became president of Birdseye Frosted Foods (1930–4).

Birt (of Liverpool), John Birt, Baron (1944–) Broadcasting executive, born in Liverpool, Merseyside. He joined Granada Television (1968), moving to London Weekend Television (1971) as producer of *The Frost Programme*. In 1987 he was appointed deputy director of the BBC, becoming director-general (1993–2000).

Birtwistle, Sir Harrison (1934–) Composer, born in Accrington, Lancashire. Among his later works are the operas *Punch and Judy* (1966–7), *The Masque of Orpheus* (1973–84), and *Slow Frieze* (1996). In 1993 he became composer in residence to the London Philharmonic Orchestra at the South Bank Centre.

Bismarck, Otto Eduard Leopold, Fürst von (Prince of) (1815–98) The first chancellor of the German Empire (1871–90), born in Schönhausen, Germany. Appointed prime minister in 1862, he was made a count in 1866, and created a prince and chancellor of the new German

Empire. After the Peace of Frankfurt (1871), his policies aimed at consolidating the young Empire. In 1879, to counteract Russia and France, he formed the Austro-German Treaty of Alliance. Called the 'Iron Chancellor', he resigned the chancellorship in 1890, disapproving of Emperor William II's policy.

Bizet, Georges, originally **Alexandre César Léopold Bizet** (1838–75) Composer, born in Paris. His incidental music to Daudet's play *L'arlésienne* (1872) was remarkably popular, and survives in the form of two orchestral suites. His masterpiece was the opera *Carmen* (1875).

Black (of Crossharbour), Conrad Moffat Black, Baron (1944–) London-based financier, born in Montreal, Quebec, Canada. He achieved control of the Argus Corporation in Canada, becoming chairman in 1979 and chief executive in 1985. He bought many newspapers in Canada and the USA, and London's *Daily Telegraph* (1985–2003).

Black Prince *see* Edward the Black Prince

Blaine, David (1973–) Illusionist, born in Brooklyn, NY. Modelling himself on Harry Houdini, he began to perform seemingly impossible feats of endurance. In 2003, he apparently endured starvation in solitary confinement for 44 days in a perspex box suspended by a crane over the R Thames, the stunt gaining worldwide media coverage.

Blair, Tony, popular name of **Anthony Charles Lynton Blair** (1953–) British politician and prime minister (1997–), born in Edinburgh.

Labour MP for Sedgefield from 1983, he became shadow secretary of state for energy (1988), employment (1989), and home affairs (1992), and was elected leader of the Labour Party in 1994, leading it to power in 1997 and 2001. In 2001 he made history as the only Labour leader to have won three successive general elections. His wife, **Cherie Blair** (1954–), is a barrister.

Blake, Quentin (Saxby) (1932–) Children's writer and illustrator, born in London. He produced cartoons for *Punch* and provided illustrations for the works of Roald Dahl, among others. His own books include *The Quentin Blake Book of Nonsense Verse* (1996). He was the first ever Children's Laureate (1999–2001).

Blake, William (1757–1827) Poet, painter, engraver, and mystic, born in London. His first book of poems, the *Poetical Sketches* (1783), was followed by *Songs of Innocence* (1789) and *Songs of Experience* (1794), which express his belief in the freedom of the imagination. These ideas found their fullest expression in his prophetic poems, especially *Jerusalem* (1804–20). His finest artistic work is to be found in the 21 *Illustrations to the Book of Job* (1826).

Blanc, Mel (1908–89) Entertainer, born in Los Angeles, CA. For over fifty years he provided the voices for some of the most famous cartoon characters including Bugs Bunny, Daffy Duck, Sylvester, Tweety Pie, Woody Woodpecker, and the stammering Porky Pig. He was also the voice of Barney Rubble in the television cartoon series *The Flintstones* (1960–6).

Blanchett, Cate (1969–) Actress, born in Melbourne, Victoria, Australia. She made her film debut in *Paradise Road* (1997), and further successes include *Elizabeth* (1998, Golden Globe, BAFTA, Oscar nomination), *The Lord of the Rings* trilogy (2001–3), and *The Aviator* (2004, Oscar and BAFTA Best Supporting Actress).

Blatter, (Joseph) Sepp (1936–) Sports administrator, born in Visp, Switzerland. He has served the Fédération Internationale de Football Association (FIFA) in a variety of posts, and in 1998 was elected FIFA president (re-elected in 2002). He has been a member of the International Olympic Committee since 1999.

Blériot, Louis (1872–1936) Airman, born in Cambrai, France. He made the first flight across the English Channel from Baraques to Dover, on 25 July 1909, in a small 24-hp monoplane.

Blethyn, Brenda (1946–) Actress, born in Ramsgate, Kent. Her television work includes the series *Outside Edge* (1994–6) and *Belonging* (2004). She received international acclaim for her role in *Secrets and Lies* (1996, Best Actress, Cannes), and among later films is *Pride and Prejudice* (2005).

Bligh, William (c.1754–c.1817) Naval officer, born in Plymouth, Devon. In 1787 he was sent as commander of HMS *Bounty* to Tahiti. On the return voyage, the men mutinied under his harsh treatment, and in April 1789, he and 18 others were cast adrift in an open boat without charts. In June

they arrived in Timor, having sailed 3618 miles.

Bliss, Sir Arthur (Edward Drummond) (1891–1975) Composer, born in London. In 1953 he became Master of the Queen's Musick. His works include the ballet *Checkmate* (1937), the opera *The Olympians* (1949), chamber music, and works for piano and violin.

Blix, Hans (1928–) Diplomat, born in Uppsala, Sweden. He became widely known following his appointment in 2000 as head of the UN Monitoring, Verification and Inspection Commission, leading the investigation into the whereabouts of Iraq's weapons of mass destruction. In 2003 he was appointed head of a Sweden-sponsored international commission on such weapons.

Blondel or **Blondel de Nesle** (12th-c) French minstrel. According to legend he accompanied Richard I to Palestine on the Crusades, and located him when imprisoned in the Austrian castle of Dürrenstein (1193) by means of the song they had jointly composed.

Blondin, Charles, originally **Jean François Gravelet** (1824–97) Acrobat and tightrope-walker, born in Hesdin, France. In 1859 he crossed Niagara Falls on a tightrope, and later repeated the feat with variations (eg blindfolded, on stilts).

Bloom, Claire (1931–) Actress, born in London. A noted Shakespearean actress, she is also known for her film roles, such as *Limelight* (1952) and *Look Back in Anger* (1959). Her television work includes *Brideshead*

Revisited (1981), *Shadowlands* (1985, BAFTA), and *Imogen's Face* (1998).

Bloom, Orlando (1977–) Actor, born in Canterbury, Kent. He became well known following his film role as the warrior elf Legolas Greenleaf in *The Lord of the Rings* trilogy (2001–3). Other films include *Black Hawk Down* (2001) and *Kingdom of Heaven* (2005).

Bloom, Ursula, pseudonym of **Mrs Gower Robinson** (1892–1984) Writer, born in Chelmsford, Essex. Her novels are mainly historical romances, such as *Pavilion* (1951) and *The First Elizabeth* (1953). Most of her plays were written for radio.

Blücher, Gebhard Leberecht von, Fürst von (Prince of) **Wahlstadt**, nickname **Marshal Forward** (1742–1819) Prussian field marshal, born in Rostock, Germany. In 1813 he took chief command in Silesia, defeated Napoleon at Leipzig, and entered Paris in 1814. In 1815 he saved Wellington from defeat at Waterloo by his timely appearance on the field.

Blue, Lionel (1930–) British rabbi and broadcaster. He is well known for his humorous and off-beat comments on life, both on radio and in such books as *A Taste of Heaven* (1977) and *Blue Horizons* (1989). His autobiography *Hitchhiking to Heaven* appeared in 2004.

Blunkett, David (1947–) British statesman, born in Sheffield, South Yorkshire. He became an MP in 1987, was chairman of the Labour Party (1993–4), and became secretary of state for education and employment (1997) and home secretary (2001). He resigned in 2004 following accusations that he fast-tracked a visa for personal reasons. He was recalled to the cabinet in 2005 but resigned later that year.

Blunt, Anthony (Frederick) (1907–83) Art historian and Soviet spy, born in Bournemouth, Dorset. At Cambridge he supplied Burgess with names of likely recruits to the Communist cause and, during his war service in British Intelligence, passed on information to the Russian government. In 1964, after the defection of Philby, he confessed in return for immunity, and his role was made public only in 1979.

Blyth, Chay, popular name of **Charles Blyth** (1940–) Yachtsman, born in Hawick, Scotland, the first to sail single-handed 'the hard way' round the world. He rowed the Atlantic from W to E with John Ridgeway (1966), before making his epic voyage westward around the globe (1970–1).

Blyton, Enid (Mary) (1897–1968) Children's writer, born in London. In the late 1930s she began writing her many children's stories featuring such characters as Noddy, the Famous Five, and the Secret Seven. She published over 600 books, but in the 1980s her work was criticized in some quarters for racism, sexism, and snobbishness.

Boadicea *see* Boudicca

Bocelli, Andrea (1958–) Tenor, born in Lajatico, Tuscany, Italy. Blind from childhood, he shot to fame with his recording of the duet 'Miserere' (1992) with Pavarotti. International success followed with the single 'Time To Say Goodbye' (1996), recorded with Sarah Brightman, and his albums include *Romanza* (1997) and *Aria: The Opera Album* (2005).

Boeing, William (Edward)
(1881–1956) Aircraft manufacturer, born in Detroit, MI. He formed the Pacific Aero Products Co in 1916 to build seaplanes. Renamed the Boeing Airplane Co in 1917, it became the largest manufacturer of military and civilian aircraft in the world.

Bogarde, Sir Dirk, originally **Derek Niven van den Bogaerde** (1921–99) Actor and writer, born in London. His first film roles were mostly in light comedy, such as *Doctor in the House* (1954), but more challenging parts followed in such films as *The Servant* (1963) and *Death in Venice* (1971).

Bogart, Humphrey (DeForest)
(1899–1957) Film actor, born in New York City. Many of his performances have become classics, notably in *The Maltese Falcon* (1941) and *Casablanca* (1942). Later films include *The Big Sleep* (1946), *The African Queen* (1951, Oscar), and *The Caine Mutiny* (1954).

Bohr, Niels (Henrik David)
(1885–1962) Physicist, born in Copenhagen. He greatly extended the theory of atomic structure when he explained the spectrum of hydrogen by means of an atomic model and the quantum theory (1913). He founded the Institute of Theoretical Physics at Copenhagen, and was awarded the Nobel Prize for Physics in 1922.

Boleyn, Anne, also spelled **Bullen** (c.1507–36) English queen, the second wife of Henry VIII (1533–6). She secretly married Henry, and was declared his legal wife; but his pas-

sion for her rapidly cooled. It was not revived by the birth (1533) of a princess (later Elizabeth I), still less by that of a stillborn son (1536). She was charged with treason and beheaded.

Bolingbroke *see* Henry IV(of England)

Bolívar, Simón, known as **the Liberator** (1783–1830) The national hero of Venezuela, Colombia, Ecuador, Peru, and Bolivia, born in Caracas. He played the most prominent part in the wars of independence, and in 1819 proclaimed the vast Republic of Colombia, becoming its president.

Bonaparte *see* Napoleon I; Napoleon III

Bonaventure or **Bonaventura, St**, known as **Doctor Seraphicus** ('Seraphic Doctor'), originally **Giovanni di Fidanza** (c.1221–74) Theologian, born near Orvieto, Italy. He became a Franciscan (1243), general of his order (1257), and Cardinal Bishop of Albano (1273). He was canonized in 1482.

Bondi, Sir Hermann (1919–2005) Mathematical physicist and astronomer, born in Vienna. He became director-general of the European Space Research Organisation (1967–71), and was one of the originators of the steady-state theory of the universe.

Bonham-Carter, Helena (1966–) Actress, born in London. Her gift for playing quintessential English heroines brought her early fame; she made her cinematic debut as Lady Jane Grey in *Lady Jane* (1985). Later film credits include *Hamlet* (1990), *Twelfth Night* (1996), and *Charlie and the Chocolate Factory* (2005).

Bonhoeffer, Dietrich (1906–45) Lutheran pastor and theologian, and opponent of Nazism, born in Wrocław, Poland (formerly Breslau, Prussia). Deeply involved in the German resistance movement, he was arrested (1943), imprisoned, and hanged.

Boniface, St, originally **Wynfrith**, known as **the Apostle of Germany** (c.680–c.754) Anglo-Saxon Benedictine missionary, born in Wessex, England. He set out in 718 to preach the Gospel to German tribes, and became Primate of Germany in 732. He was killed at Dokkum by heathens.

Bonington, Sir Chris(tian John Storey) (1934–) Mountaineer, born in London. He was a member of the first British team that conquered the N face of the Eiger (1962), and later climbed Annapurna South Face (1970) and Everest (1972, 1975 SW face).

Bonney, William H, known as **Billy the Kid**, originally (?) **Henry McCarty** (1859–81) Bandit and gunfighter, born in New York City. A killer from the age of 12, he achieved legendary notoriety for his robberies in the SW. He was finally tracked down and shot by Sheriff Pat Garrett.

Bonnie and Clyde Notorious robbery partners: **Clyde Barrow** (1909–34), born in Telico, TX, and **Bonnie Parker** (1911–34), born in Rowena, TX. The pair met in 1932. With their gang, they committed a number of robberies and murders. They were shot dead at a police road-block in Louisiana.

Bonnie Prince Charlie see Stuart, Prince Charles Edward

Boole, George (1815–64) Mathematician and logician, born in Lincoln, Lincolnshire. He is best known for his *Mathematical Analysis of Logic* (1847) and *Laws of Thought* (1854), employing mathematical symbolism to express logical processes (*Boolean algebra*).

Boone, Daniel (c.1734–1820) Legendary pioneer, born in Berks Co, PA. He made a trail through the Cumberland Gap (1767) and became one of the first to explore Kentucky (1769–73). Twice captured by Indians, he repeatedly repelled Indian attacks on his stockade fort, now Boonesborough.

Boot, Sir Jesse, Baron Trent (1850–1931) Drug manufacturer, born in Nottingham, Nottinghamshire. In 1877 he opened his first chemist's shop in Nottingham, and by 1900 had built up the largest pharmaceutical retail trade in the world.

Booth, John Wilkes (1839–65) Assassin, born near Bel Air, MD, the brother of Edwin Thomas Booth. He became an actor and was popular in the South. In 1865 he joined a conspiracy to avenge the defeat of the Confederates, and shot President Lincoln at Ford's Theatre, Washington, DC. He fled to Virginia, but was tracked down and shot.

Booth, William (1829–1912) Founder and 'general' of the Salvation Army, born in Nottingham, Nottinghamshire. In 1865 he founded the Army (so named in 1878) on military lines with mission work in London's East End. His wife, **Catherine Booth** (1829–90), was fully associated with him, and his first son **Bramwell Booth** (1856–1929) and daughters

Kate Booth (1859–1955) and **Evangeline Booth** (1865–1950) succeeded him in the work.

Border, Allan (Robert) (1955–) Cricketer, born in Sydney, New South Wales, Australia. A prolific batsman, on his retirement in 1994 he held the record for highest run-scorer in the history of Test cricket with a record 11 174 runs. West Indian Brian Lara broke his record in 2005.

Borg, Björn (Rune) (1956–) Tennis player, born in Södertälje, Sweden. He became Wimbledon singles champion five times (1976–80), a modern-day record, losing to McEnroe in the 1981 final. He also won the French singles title six times, and was the World Championship Tennis singles champion in 1976.

Borge, Victor, originally **Børge Rosenbaum** (1909–2000) Entertainer and pianist, born in Denmark. From 1940 he worked in the USA for radio, television, and theatre, best known for his comedy sketches combining music and narrative.

Borges, Jorge Luis (1899–1986) Writer, born in Buenos Aires. From 1918 he lived in Spain, where he joined the avant-garde Ultraist literary group, returning to Argentina in 1921. From 1941 he wrote mainly short stories, including *Fictions* (trans, 1945) and *The Aleph* (trans, 1949).

Bormann, Martin (1900–?45) Nazi politician, born in Halberstadt, Germany. One of Hitler's closest advisers, he became *Reichsminister* (1941) after Hess's flight to Scotland, and was with Hitler to the last, though his own fate is uncertain.

Borodin, Alexander Porfiryevich (1833–87) Composer and scientist, born in St Petersburg, Russia. His compositions include the unfinished opera, *Prince Igor*, three symphonies, and the symphonic sketch *In the Steppes of Central Asia*.

Boswell, James (1740–95) Man of letters, born in Edinburgh. He met Dr Johnson in 1763, and took him on a journey to the Hebrides. The success of *Journal of a Tour to the Hebrides* (1785) led him to plan his masterpiece, the *Life of Samuel Johnson* (1791).

Botham, Ian (Terence) (1955–) Cricketer, born in Heswall, Merseyside. An all-rounder, he played for England in 102 Test matches, scored 5200 runs, took 383 wickets, and held 120 catches. He retired from first-class cricket in 1993.

Botticelli, Sandro, originally **Alessandro Filipepi** (1445–1510) Painter, born in Florence, Italy. He produced mostly religious works, but is best known for his mythological subjects, notably 'Spring' (c.1477) and the 'Birth of Venus' (c.1485), both in the Uffizi.

Boudicca, also known as **Boadicea** (1st-c) British Celtic warrior-queen, wife of Prasutagus, king of the Iceni, a tribe inhabiting what is now Norfolk and Suffolk. Her army destroyed Camulodunum, Londinium, and Verulamium. Defeated in battle by Suetonius Paulinus, she took poison.

Boulez, Pierre (1925–) Conductor and composer, born in Montbrison, France. He was conductor of the BBC Symphony Orchestra (1971–5) and of the New York Philharmonic (1971–7), after which he took up a post at the Pompidou Centre in Paris (1977–91).

Boult, Sir Adrian (Cedric) (1889–1983) Conductor, born in Chester, Cheshire. He became musical director of the BBC, conductor of the newly formed BBC Symphony Orchestra, and conductor-in-chief of the London Philharmonic Orchestra until 1957.

Bourne, Matthew (1960–) Choreographer and dancer, born in London. He gained a reputation for his unconventional interpretations of classical ballets, such as *Swan Lake* (1995, Olivier Award, Tony), using bare-chested male dancers. Later works include *Mary Poppins* (2004, Olivier Award) and *Edward Scissorhands* (2005).

Bowdler, Thomas (1754–1825) Doctor and man of letters, born in Ashley, Somerset. He is immortalized as the editor of *The Family Shakespeare* (10 vols, 1818), in which 'those words and expressions are omitted which cannot with propriety be read aloud in a family'. *Bowdlerizing* has since become a synonym for prudish expurgation.

Bowie, David, originally **David Robert Jones** (1947–) Rock singer, born in London. His albums include *The Rise and Fall of Ziggy Stardust and the Spiders from Mars* (1972) and *Heroes* (1977). He has also acted in films, including *The Man Who Fell to Earth* (1976) and *Basquiat* (1996).

Boycott, Geoffrey (1940–) Cricketer and broadcaster, born in Fitzwilliam, West Yorkshire. In 1981 he overtook Sobers' world record of 8032 Test runs, and in 108 Tests for England scored 8114 runs. Captain of Yorkshire (1971–8), he retired from first-class cricket in 1986.

Boyd, Michael (1955–) Stage director, born in Belfast. He became an associate director of the Royal Shakespeare Company (RSC) in 1996, and won an Olivier Award for best director for the *Henry VI* trilogy (2000). In 2003 he succeeded Adrian Noble as artistic director of the RSC.

Boyer, Charles (1899–1978) Actor, born in Figeac, France. A star of the French stage and cinema, he settled in Hollywood in 1934, and was known as the screen's 'greatest lover' from such romantic roles as *Mayerling* (1936) and *Algiers* (1938).

Boy George, popular name of **George O'Dowd** (1961–) Pop singer and songwriter, born in Eltham, Kent. In 1981 he formed his own band, Culture Club, and their hits included a number 1 single, 'Karma Chameleon' (1983). A flamboyant cross-dresser and admitted drug user, controversy dogged his career. During the 1990s he forged a new career as a DJ on the club scene.

Boylan, Clare (1948–2006) Writer, born in Dublin. Her first novel, *Holy Pictures*, appeared in 1983, as did a book of short stories, *A Nail in the Head* (1983). Later fiction included *Black Baby* (1998), *Beloved Stranger* (2000), and *Emma Brown* (2003).

Boyle, Danny, popular name of **Daniel Boyle** (1956–) Director, born in Bury, Greater Manchester. He made his name with *Mr Wroe's Virgins*, a television period drama. His directorial film debut was with *Shallow Grave* (1994, BAFTA for Best British Film), and he consolidated this success with *Trainspotting* (1996). Later films include *A Life Less Ordinary* (1997) and *The Beach* (2000).

Boyle, Robert (1627–91) Chemist and natural philosopher, born at Lismore Castle, Co Waterford, Ireland. He carried out experiments on air, vacuum, combustion, and respiration, and in 1662 arrived at *Boyle's law*, which states that the pressure and volume of gas are inversely proportional.

Brabham, Jack, popular name of **Sir John Arthur Brabham** (1926–) Motor-racing driver, born in Sydney, New South Wales, Australia. He became Australia's first world champion in 1959, repeating his success in 1960 and 1966.

Bradbury, Sir Malcolm (Stanley) (1932–2000) Writer and critic, born in Sheffield, South Yorkshire. His novels included *Eating People is Wrong* (1959), *Stepping Westward* (1965), *The History Man* (1975, also a television series), *The Atlas of Literature* (1996), and *To the Hermitage* (2000).

Bradbury, Ray(mond Douglas) (1920–) Writer of science fiction, born in Waukegan, IL. Primarily a short-story writer, his best-known stories are *The Day It Rained Forever*, *R Is for Rocket*, and those collected as *The Martian Chronicles* (1950; filmed 1966). His novels include *Fahrenheit 451* (1953), *Quicker than the Eye* (1996), and *Let's All Kill Constance* (2002).

Bradford, Barbara Taylor (1933–) Journalist and novelist, born in Leeds. She worked for several newspapers and magazines, both in the UK and USA, before gaining success with her first novel, *A Woman of Substance* (1980). Later books include *Where You Belong* (2000) and *Just Rewards* (2005).

Bradman, Sir Don(ald George) (1908–2001) Cricketer, born in Cootamundra, New South Wales, Australia. He played for Australia (1928–48), and was captain from 1936. His batting records include the highest score (452 not out) which he held until 1994, and an average in Test matches of 99·94 runs per innings.

Brady, Ian (1938–) Convicted murderer, born in Glasgow. He and his lover **Myra Hindley** (1942–2002) were described as the 'Moors Murderers' because they buried most of their victims on Saddleworth Moor in the Pennines.

Bragg, Billy, popular name of **Steven William Bragg** (1957–) Rock singer, musician, and songwriter, born in Barking, Essex. He began performing in the 1970s with the punk group Riff Raff. Starting a solo career, he became known as the leading figure of the anti-folk movement of the 1980s. His albums include *Must I Paint You a Picture? The Essential Billy Bragg* (2003).

Bragg (of Wigton), Melvyn Bragg, Baron (1939–) Writer and broadcaster, born in Wigton, Cumbria. His novels include *A Time to Dance* (1990) and *Crossing the Lines* (2003). He has presented ITV's *The South Bank Show* since 1978. For BBC Radio 4 his work includes *Start the Week* (1988–98) and *In Our Time*.

Brahe, Tycho (1546–1601) Astronomer,

born in Knudstrup, Sweden. In 1573 he discovered serious errors in the astronomical tables, and rectified this by observing the stars and planets with unprecedented positional accuracy.

Brahms, Johannes (1833–97) Composer, born in Hamburg, Germany. He earned his living as a pianist until 1853, when he was able to concentrate on composition. Major works include four symphonies, two piano concertos, a violin concerto, chamber and piano music, and many songs. His greatest choral work is the *German Requiem* (first performed complete in 1869).

Braille, Louis (1809–52) Educationist, born in Coupvray, France. Blind from the age of three, in 1829 he devised a system of raised-point writing which the blind could both read and write.

Branagh, Kenneth (Charles) (1960–) Actor and director, born in Belfast. He joined the Royal Shakespeare Company (1984) and in 1998 co-founded the Shakespeare Film Company. He starred in several films, such as *Henry V* (1989), *Much Ado About Nothing* (1993), *Hamlet* (1997), and *Love's Labour's Lost* (2000), all of which he directed. He was married to actress Emma Thompson (1989–96).

Brando, Marlon (1924–2004) Film and stage actor, born in Omaha, NE. His many films include *Mutiny on the Bounty* (1962) and *Last Tango in Paris* (1972). An Oscar winner for *On the Waterfront* (1954) and *The Godfather* (1972), he refused the latter honour in protest at the film industry's treatment of American Indians.

Branson, Sir Richard (Charles Nicholas) (1950–) Businessman, born in Sharnley Green, Surrey. He opened his first shop in London in 1971, under the name Virgin, and went on to found a series of highly successful business enterprises, including the Voyager Group (1980), Virgin Atlantic (1984), Virgin Radio (1993), Virgin Direct (1995), V2 Music (1996) and Virgin Trains (1996). His sporting achievements include the record-breaking Atlantic crossing in *Virgin Atlantic Challenger II* in 1986, and the first crossing by hot-air balloon of the Atlantic (1987) and Pacific (1991).

Braque, Georges (1882–1963) Painter, born in Argenteuil, France. He was one of the founders of classical Cubism, and worked with Picasso (1908–14). His paintings, mainly of still-life, include 'The Port of La Ciotat' (1907) and 'The Black Birds' (1957).

Braun, Eva (1910–45) Mistress of Adolf Hitler, born in Munich, Germany. She is said to have married him before they committed suicide together in the air-raid shelter of the Chancellery during the fall of Berlin.

Braun, Wernher von (1912–77) Rocket pioneer, born in Wyrzysk, Poland (formerly Wirsitz, Germany). In 1936 he directed a rocket research station at Peenemünde, but refused to cooperate over the V-2 project. He became a US citizen, and in 1958 was responsible for launching the first US artificial Earth satellite, Explorer 1.

Brautigan, Richard (Gary) (1933–84) Writer, born in Tacoma, WA. He became a cult figure as one of the San

Francisco poets and an embodiment of the 1960s counterculture, writing surrealistically random novels and poems about alienation. His books include the novel, *Trout Fishing in America* (1967), and the collected poems, *The Pill Versus the Springhill Mine Disaster* (1968).

Brazil, Angela (1868–1947) Writer of girls' school stories, born in Preston, Lancashire. She produced over 50 school novels, from *The Fortunes of Philippa* (1906) to *The School of the Loch* (1946).

Breakspear, Nicholas *see* Adrian IV

Brecht, (Eugene) Bertolt (Friedrich) (1898–1956) Playwright and theatre director, born in Augsburg, Germany. Popularity came with *The Threepenny Opera* (trans, 1928). After leaving Nazi Germany, his major plays include (trans titles) *Mother Courage and her Children* (1938) and *The Caucasian Chalk Circle* (1945). In East Berlin from 1948, his work with the Berliner Ensemble established him as a major influence on 20th-c theatre.

Bremner, Rory (Keith Ogilvy) (1961–) Satirical impressionist, writer, and performer, born in Edinburgh. He began performing in tours and one-man shows in 1985. He made several series for BBC television (1986–92) and *Rory Bremner – Who Else?* for Channel 4 (from 1992), as well as a number of videos. Awards include the Top Male Comedy Performer BAFTA (1994, 1995, 1996).

Breughel *see* Brueghel

Brezhnev, Leonid Ilich (1906–82) Russian statesman, general secretary of the Soviet Communist Party (1964–82), and president of the Supreme Soviet (1977–82), born in Kamenskoye, Ukraine. He was the first to hold simultaneously the position of general secretary and president.

Briers, Richard (David) (1934–) Actor, born in Croydon, Surrey. He has played many major theatre roles, but is probably better known for such television series as *The Good Life*, *Ever Decreasing Circles*, and the later *Monarch of the Glen* (2000–2).

Bristow, Eric, nickname **the Crafty Cockney** (1957–) Darts player, born in London. He was world professional champion a record five times (1980–1, 1984–6), and also won the World Masters (1977, 1979, 1981, 1983–4) and the World Cup individual (1983, 1985).

Britten (of Aldeburgh), (Edward) Benjamin Britten, Baron (1913–76) Composer, born in Lowestoft, Suffolk. His works were largely vocal and choral, major works including the operas *Peter Grimes* (1945), *Billy Budd* (1951), and *Gloriana* (1953).

Broderick, Matthew (1962–) Actor, born in New York City. He made his film debut in *War Games* (1983), and earned Tony awards for his Broadway appearances in *Brighton Beach Memoirs* (1982–3) and *How to Succeed in Business Without Really Trying* (1995). Later films include *Election* (1999) and *Strangers with Candy* (2005).

Bron, Eleanor (1938–) Actress and writer, born in Stanmore, Greater London. From the early 1960s she made regular stage appearances, and on television became known in *Not So Much a Programme, More a Way of*

Life (1964). Her films include *Alfie* (1966), *Black Beauty* (1994), and *Wimbledon* (2004).

Brontë, Anne, pseudonym **Acton Bell** (1820–49) Poet and novelist, born in Thornton, West Yorkshire. She wrote two novels: *Agnes Grey* (1848) and *The Tenant of Wildfell Hall* (1848).

Brontë, Charlotte, pseudonym **Currer Bell** (1816–55) Novelist and poet, born in Thornton, West Yorkshire. Her first novel, *The Professor*, was not published until after her death (1857). Her masterpiece, *Jane Eyre*, appeared in 1847, and this was followed by *Shirley* (1849), and *Villette* (1853). *Emma* remained unfinished at her death.

Brontë, Emily (Jane), pseudonym **Ellis Bell** (1818–48) Novelist and poet, born in Thornton, West Yorkshire. Her single novel, *Wuthering Heights* (1847), remains one of the major works of English prose fiction.

Brook, Peter (Stephen Paul) (1925–) Theatre and film director, born in London. In 1962 he joined the Royal Shakespeare Company in Stratford, his productions including *King Lear* (1962) and *A Midsummer Night's Dream* (1970). Among his films are *Lord of the Flies* (1962) and an adaptation of *The Mahabharata* (1989), and *The Tempest* (1990).

Brooks, Mel, originally **Melvin Kaminsky** (1926–) Film actor and director, born in New York City. He is known for his zany comedies satirizing established movie styles, among them *Blazing Saddles* (1974) and *Dracula: Dead and Loving It* (1995). He adapted his 1967 film, *The Producers*, into a musical comedy for

the New York stage (2001), taking the show to London in 2004. He married actress **Anne Bancroft** (1931–2005) in 1964.

Broome, David (1940–) Show jumper, born in Cardiff. He won the World Championship on *Beethoven* (1970), was three times European champion, on *Sunsalve* (1961) and *Mister Softee* (1967, 1969), and was the individual bronze medallist at the 1960 and 1968 Olympics.

Brosnan, Pierce (1953–) Actor, born in Navan, Co Meath, Ireland. He became known when he took on the role of James Bond in *Goldeneye* (1995), followed by *Tomorrow Never Dies* (1997), *The World is Not Enough* (1999), and *Die Another Day* (2002). Other films include *The Matador* (2005).

Brown, Sir Arthur Whitten (1886–1948) Aviator, born in Glasgow. As navigator with Alcock he made the first non-stop crossing of the Atlantic in a Vickers-Vimy biplane on 14 June 1919.

Brown, Capability *see* Brown, Lancelot

Brown, Dan (1964–) Novelist, born in Exeter, NH. He gained success with his first novel, *Digital Fortress* (1998), a political thriller. Later novels include *Angels and Demons* (2000), *Deception Point* (2001), and the controversial best seller, *The Da Vinci Code* (2003).

Brown, George (Alfred) *see* George-Brown, Baron

Brown, (James) Gordon (1951–) Labour politician, born in Glasgow. He became Opposition chief secretary to the Treasury (1987–9),

Opposition trade and industry secretary (1989–92), and shadow Chancellor (1992–97), and Chancellor of the Exchequer (1997–2001, 2001–) in the Labour government.

Brown, John (1800–59) Militant abolitionist, born in Torrington, CT. In 1859 he led a raid on the US Armory at Harper's Ferry in Virginia, trying to launch a slave insurrection, but the raid failed, and he was hanged. The song 'John Brown's Body' commemorates the raid.

Brown, Lancelot, known as **Capability Brown** (1715–83) Landscape gardener, born in Kirkharle, Northumberland. He established a purely English style of garden design, using simple artifices to produce natural effects, such as those at Blenheim and Kew.

Browning, Elizabeth Barrett, *née* **Barrett** (1806–61) Poet, born in Durham, Co Durham. She seriously injured her spine (c.1821), and was long an invalid. In 1845 she met Robert Browning, with whom she eloped in 1846. Her best-known work is *Sonnets from the Portuguese* (1850).

Browning, Robert (1812–89) Poet, born in London. *Bells and Pomegranates* (1841–6) included several of his best-known lyrics, such as 'How they Brought the Good News from Ghent to Aix'. In 1846 he married Elizabeth Barrett, and they settled in Florence, where their son **Robert Barrett Browning** (1849–1912), the sculptor, was born. After his wife's death (1861) he wrote his masterpiece, *The Ring and the Book* (1869).

Brubeck, Dave, popular name of **David Warren Brubeck** (1920–)

Pianist, composer, and bandleader, born in Concord, CA. He formed the Dave Brubeck Quartet in 1951, and went on to make many popular recordings, such as *Time Out* (1958), featuring 'Take Five' and 'Blue Rondo à la Turk'.

Bruce, Robert (1274–1329) King of Scots (1306–29) as Robert I, and hero of the Scottish War of Independence. As Earl of Carrick, he joined the Scottish revolt under Wallace, and in 1306 was crowned king at Scone. He defeated the English at the Battle of Bannockburn (1314), and sporadic war with England continued until the Treaty of Northampton (1328), which recognized the independence of Scotland.

Bruckheimer, Jerry (c.1944–) Film producer, born in Detroit, MI. In 1983 he teamed up with Don Simpson (1943–96) to head a company that produced such successful films as *Beverly Hills Cop* (1984) and *Dangerous Minds* (1995). His later productions include *Pearl Harbor* (2001), *Pirates of the Caribbean* (2003), and *King Arthur* (2004).

Bruckner, Anton (1824–96) Composer and organist, born in Ansfelden, Austria. His fame chiefly rests on his nine symphonies (the last unfinished), but he also wrote four Masses, several smaller sacred pieces, and many choral works.

Brueghel, Pieter, also spelled **Bruegel** or **Breughel**, known as **the Elder** (c.1520–69) Flemish painter, probably born in the village of Brueghel, near Breda. He settled in Brussels, where he painted his genre pictures of peasant life, such as the 'Peasant

Dance' (c.1568). His eldest son, **Pieter Brueghel the Younger** (c.1564–1637), is known as 'Hell' Brueghel, because of his paintings of devils, hags, and robbers. His younger son, **Jan Brueghel** (1568–1625), known as 'Velvet' Brueghel, painted still-life, landscapes, and religious subjects.

Bruijn, Inge de (1973–) Swimmer, born in Barendrecht, Netherlands. In 2000 she set world records in the 50 m and 100 m freestyle and the 50 m and 100 m butterfly. At the 2000 Sydney Olympics, she won gold medals in the 50 m and the 100 m freestyle and the 100 m butterfly, and set new world records in each of these events.

Brummell, George Bryan, known as **Beau Brummell** (1778–1840) Dandy, born in London. A leader of early 19th-c fashion, he became a close friend and protégé of the prince regent (the future George IV), but after a quarrel, gambling debts forced him to flee to France (1816).

Bruna, Dick (1927–) Dutch artist and writer, creator of a highly successful series of picture books for young children. Favourite characters include Miffy the rabbit and the small dog Snuffy.

Brundtland, Gro Harlem, *née* **Harlem** (1939–) First woman prime minister of Norway (1981, 1986–9, 1990–6), born in Bærum, Norway. She was appointed environment minister (1974–9) and became leader of the Labour Party group. In 1987 she chaired the World Commission on Environment and Development which produced the report *Our Common Future*. She served as director-general of the World Health Organization (1998–2003).

Brunel, Isambard Kingdom (1806–59) Engineer, born in Portsmouth, Hampshire, the son of Marc Brunel. He designed the *Great Western* (1837), the first steamship built to cross the Atlantic, the *Great Britain* (1843), the first ocean screw-steamer, and the *Great Eastern* (1853–8), then the largest vessel ever built.

Brunel, Sir Marc Isambard (1769–1849) Engineer and inventor, born in Hacqueville, France. He solved many of the problems of underwater tunnelling, and his main achievement was the 460 m/503 yd Thames Tunnel from Rotherhithe to Wapping (1825–43).

Bruno of Cologne, St (c.1030–1101) Clergyman, born in Cologne, Germany. In 1084 he withdrew to the mountains of Chartreuse, near Grenoble, where he founded the austere Carthusian order on the site of the present Grande Chartreuse.

Brutus, Marcus Junius (c.85–42 BC) Roman politician. When the civil war broke out, he submitted to Caesar, and was appointed Governor of Cisalpine Gaul. Cassius persuaded him to join the conspiracy against Caesar (44 BC), but he killed himself after the defeat at Philippi.

Bryson, Bill (1951–) Writer, born in Des Moines, IA. His travel books include *Notes From A Small Island* (1995) and *Notes From a Big Country* (1998). Later books include *A Short History of Nearly Everything* (2003, Aventis Prize). He lived in England during 1977–95, returning again in 2003.

Buchanan, James (1791–1868) Fifteenth president of the USA (1857–61), born near Mercersburg, PA. A Democrat, he became secretary of state in 1845, and as president was strongly pro-slavery.

Buddha ('the enlightened one') (c.563–c.483 BC) The title of Prince **Gautama Siddhartha**, the founder of Buddhism, born the son of the rajah of the Sakya tribe ruling in Kapilavastu, Nepal. When about 30 years old he left the luxuries of the court, his wife, and all earthly ambitions for the life of an ascetic; after six years of austerity and mortification he saw in the contemplative life the perfect way to self-enlightenment. The goal is *Nirvana*, the absorption of the self into the infinite. For the next 40 years he taught, gaining many disciples, and died at the age of about 80 in Kusinagara, Oudh. His teaching is summarized in the *Four Noble Truths*.

Buerk, Michael (Duncan) (1946–) Television journalist and presenter, born in Solihull, West Midlands. He joined the BBC in 1970, becoming a special correspondent (1981–2) and Africa correspondent (1983–7). He has presented Radio 4's *The Moral Maze* (from 1990), and for television the new format *Ten O'Clock News* (2000–2).

Buffalo Bill *see* Cody, William F

Bull, Deborah (Clare) (1963–) Ballerina, born in Derby, Derbyshire. In 1981 she joined the Royal Ballet (principal dancer from 1992), and retired in 2001. She was then appointed artistic director of the Linbury Studio Theatre and Clore Studio Upstairs at the Royal Opera House.

Bull, John (c.1562–1628) Musician, born in Somerset. A Catholic, he fled abroad in 1613 to escape persecution, and became organist of Antwerp Cathedral. He was one of the founders of contrapuntal keyboard music, and has been credited with composing the air 'God Save the King'.

Bunsen, Robert Wilhelm (1811–99) Chemist and physicist, born in Göttingen, Germany. He shared with Kirchhoff the discovery of spectrum analysis (1859), and among the inventions from his laboratory are the *Bunsen burner* and the grease-spot actinometer.

Buñuel, Luis (1900–83) Film director, born in Calanda, Spain. His first films were a sensation with their Surrealistic, macabre approach: *An Andalusian Dog* (trans, 1928) and *The Golden Age* (trans, 1930). Later films include *Viridiana* (1961), *The Discreet Charm of the Bourgeoisie* (1972), and *That Obscure Object of Desire* (1977).

Bunyan, John (1628–88) Writer, born in Elstow, Bedfordshire. In 1653 he joined a Christian fellowship, and in 1660 was arrested and spent 12 years in Bedford county gaol, where he wrote *Grace Abounding* (1666). Briefly released, he was reimprisoned for six months, and there wrote the first part of his allegorical work *The Pilgrim's Progress* (1678). The second part was published in 1684.

Buonaparte *see* Napoleon I

Burford, Eleanor *see* Hibbert, Eleanor

Burgess, Anthony, pseudonym of **John Anthony Burgess Wilson** (1917–93) Writer and critic, born in

Manchester, Greater Manchester. His novels include *A Clockwork Orange* (1962), *Malayan Trilogy* (1965), and *Earthly Powers* (1980). Other works include critical studies, film scripts, and musical compositions.

Burghley or **Burghleigh, Lord** *see* Cecil, William

Burke, Edmund (1729–97) British statesman and political philosopher, born in Dublin. He became secretary for Ireland, and entered parliament in 1765. His *Reflections on the French Revolution* (1790) was influential throughout Europe.

Burke, William (1792–1829) Murderer, born in Orrery, Ireland. With his partner, **William Hare** (c.1790–c.1860), born in Londonderry, he carried out a series of infamous murders in Edinburgh in the 1820s, with the aim of supplying dissection subjects to an anatomist. Hare turned king's evidence, and died a beggar in London; Burke was hanged.

Burnet, Alastair, popular name of **Sir James William Alexander Burnet** (1928–) British journalist and television news presenter. He was editor of *The Economist* (1965–74) and *The Daily Express* (1974–6), and became a nationally known personality when he joined ITN as a news presenter (1976–91), later becoming associate editor for *News at Ten* (1982–91).

Burnett, Frances (Eliza) Hodgson, *née* **Hodgson** (1849–1924) Writer, born in Manchester, Greater Manchester. In 1865 her family emigrated to Tennessee. She wrote several plays and over 40 novels, notably *Little Lord Fauntleroy* (1886) and *The Secret Garden* (1911).

Burnett, Ivy Compton *see* Compton-Burnett, Dame Ivy

Burns, George, originally **Nathan Birnbaum** (1896–1996) Comedian and actor, born in New York City. He made his debut at the age of 13, and in 1923 teamed up with **Gracie Allen** (1905–64). They became a husband-and-wife comedy duo popular for over three decades in vaudeville, radio, films, and television. Well known for his omnipresent cigar, dry wit, and comic timing, he received an Oscar for his role in *The Sunshine Boys* (1975).

Burns, Robert (1759–96) Scotland's national poet, born in Alloway, South Ayrshire. The Kilmarnock edition of his poems (1786) brought him great acclaim, followed by the famous epistolary flirtations with 'Clarinda' (Agnes Maclchose). Among his best-known poems are 'The Jolly Beggars' (1785) and 'Tam o' Shanter' (1790). In 1788 he married **Jean Armour** (1767–1834).

Burroughs, Edgar Rice (1875–1950) Writer, born in Chicago, IL. He made his name with the 'Tarzan' stories, beginning with *Tarzan of the Apes* (1914).

Burton, Richard, originally **Richard Walter Jenkins** (1925–84) Stage and film actor, born in Pontrhydyfen, S Wales. His early films include *The Robe* (1953), for which he received one of his six Oscar nominations. His romance with Elizabeth Taylor during the making of *Cleopatra* (1962) and their eventual marriage (1964–74, 1975–6) projected them both into the 'superstar' category. Among his later films were *Becket*

(1964), *Equus* (1977), and *1984*
(released after his death).

Burton, Sir Richard (Francis)
(1821–90) Explorer, born in Torquay,
Devon. In 1856 he set out with Speke
on the journey which led to the discovery of L Tanganyika (1858). **Lady
Burton**, *née* **Isabel Arundell**
(1831–96), burned her husband's
journals after his death.

Busby, Sir Matt(hew) (1909–94)
Footballer and football manager,
born in Bellshill, North Lanarkshire.
After playing with Manchester City
and Liverpool, he became manager
of Manchester United in 1945.
Severely injured when his team
was involved in an air crash at
Munich (1958), he rebuilt the side to
achieve European Cup success in
1968.

Bush, George (Herbert Walker)
(1924–) US statesman and 41st
president (1989–93), born in Milton,
MA. In 1980 he campaigned for the
Republican nomination, but lost to
Reagan, later becoming his vice-
president. In 1988 he won the nom-
ination, and defeated Michael
Dukakis in the election. He lost to Bill
Clinton in 1992.

Bush, George W(alker), also known
as **George Bush Jr** (1946–) US
statesman and 43rd president
(2001–), born in New Haven, CT, son
of former president George Bush. In
2000 he was declared president following five weeks of complex legal
argument over the voting procedure,
and in 2004 won a second term. His
period of office has seen the terrorist
attack on the World Trade Center in
New York City (11 Sep 2001) and the

controversial involvement of US-led
coalition forces in the Iraq War
(2003).

Bush, Laura Welch (1946–) US First
Lady (2001–), born in Midland, TX.
In her role as First Lady, she promotes
the importance of libraries and
reading for children, and is a member
of many education advisory boards.
She also supports the Texas Health
Department, the American Cancer
Society, and other health organiza-
tions.

Bussell, Darcey (Andrea) (1969–)
Ballerina, born in London. She
joined the Royal Ballet as soloist in
1988, and went on to become the
company's youngest principal dancer. In 2005 she announced her
retirement as principal dancer, but
remains as guest dancer.

Butlin, Billy, popular name of **Sir
William (Edmund) Butlin**
(1899–1980) Holiday camp promoter,
born in South Africa. In Britain, he
opened his first camp at Skegness in
1936, followed by others at Clacton
and Filey, and several more camps
and hotels after World War 2.

Byatt, Dame A(ntonia) S(usan), *née*
Drabble (1936–) Writer and critic,
the sister of Margaret Drabble. Her
novels include *The Virgin in the Garden* (1978), *Still Life* (1985), *Possession*
(1990, Booker), and *A Whistling
Woman* (2002).

Bygraves, Max (Walter) (1922–)
Entertainer, born in Rotherhithe,
Greater London. A professional
entertainer since 1946, his catchphrase, 'I wanna tell you a story', is
also the title of his autobiography
(1976).

Byron (of Rochdale), George (Gordon) Byron, 6th Baron, known as **Lord Byron** (1788–1824) Poet, born in London. The popular *Childe Harold's Pilgrimage* (1812) gave to Europe the concept of the 'Byronic hero'; later works include *Don Juan* (1819–24). He actively helped the Italian revolutionaries, and in 1823 joined the Greek insurgents who had risen against the Turks, but died of a fever at Missolonghi.

Cabot, John, Ital **Giovanni Caboto** (1425–c.1500) Navigator, born possibly in Genoa, who discovered the mainland of North America. He settled in Bristol c.1490, and set sail in 1497 with two ships, accompanied by his three sons, sighting Cape Breton I and Nova Scotia.

Cabot, Sebastian (1474–1557) Explorer and navigator, born in Venice or Bristol, the son of John Cabot. He accompanied his father to the American coast, then served Ferdinand V of Spain as a cartographer (1512). He later explored the coast of South America (1526).

Cabral or **Cabrera, Pedro Alvarez** (c.1467–c.1520) Explorer, born in Belmonte, Portugal. In 1500 he sailed from Lisbon for the East Indies, but was carried to Brazil, which he claimed on behalf of Portugal. He then made for India, but was forced to land at Mozambique, and provided the first description of that country.

Cadbury, George (1839–1922) Businessman, born in Birmingham, West Midlands, the son of John Cadbury.

In partnership with his brother **Richard Cadbury** (1835–99), he expanded his father's cocoa and chocolate business, and established for the workers the model village of Bournville (1879).

Caesar, in full **Gaius Julius Caesar** (c.101–44 BC) Roman politician, a member of the Julii, an aristocratic Roman family. His military genius, as displayed in the Gallic Wars (58–51 BC), enabled Rome to extend her empire to the Atlantic seaboard, but his ruthless ambition led to the breakdown of the Republican system of government at home. In 60 BC he joined with Pompey and Crassus (the First Triumvirate) to protect his interests in the state, and in 49 BC, to avoid being humbled by his enemies at Rome, led his army across the R Rubicon into Italy, plunging the state into civil war. Victory over the Pompeian forces (48–45 BC) left him in sole control, and he took the title 'Dictator for Life' in 44 BC. He was murdered by Republican-minded Romans under the leadership of Brutus and Cassius.

Cage, Nicolas, originally **Nicholas Coppola** (1964–) Film actor, born in Long Beach, CA. He became well known after his appearance in *The Cotton Club* (1984) and won critical acclaim for *Leaving Las Vegas* (1995, Oscar). Later films include *Con Air* (1997), *Adaptation* (2002), and *Lord of War* (2005).

Cagney, James (1899–1986) Film actor, born in New York City. His film performance as the gangster in *The Public Enemy* (1931) brought him stardom. Later films include *Angels* *with Dirty Faces* (1938) and *Yankee Doodle Dandy* (1942, Oscar).

Caiaphas (1st-c) Son-in-law of Annas, eventually appointed by the Romans to be his successor as high priest of Israel (c.18–36). In the New Testament he interrogated Jesus after his arrest (*Matt* 26) and Peter after his detention in Jerusalem (*Acts* 4).

Cain Biblical character, the eldest son of Adam and Eve. He is portrayed (*Gen* 4) as a farmer whose offering to God was rejected, in contrast to that of his herdsman brother, Abel. This led to his murder of Abel, and Cain's punishment of being banished to a nomadic life.

Caine, Sir Michael, properly **Sir Maurice Micklewhite** (1933–) Film actor, born in London. His many films include *Zulu* (1963), *The Ipcress File* (1965), *Educating Rita* (1983), *Hannah and Her Sisters* (1986, Oscar), *The Cider House Rules* (1999, Oscar for Best Supporting Actor), *The Quiet American* (2002, Oscar nomination), and *Batman Begins* (2005).

Calamity Jane, popular name of **Martha Jane Burke** or **Burk**, *née* **Cannary** (?1852–1903) Legendary frontier figure, born in Princeton, MO. She became an expert markswoman and rider, and (dressed as a man) was companion to **'Wild Bill' Hickok** (1837–76). She is said to have threatened 'calamity' for any man who tried to court her, but in 1891 she married Clinton Burk(e) in El Paso, TX.

Caligula, nickname of **Gaius Julius Caesar Germanicus** (12–41) Roman emperor (37–41), the youngest son of Germanicus and Agrippina, born in Antium. Brought up in an army camp, he was nicknamed Caligula from his little soldier's boots (*caligae*). Extravagant, autocratic, vicious, and mentally unstable, he wreaked havoc with the finances of the state, and terrorized those around him, until he was assassinated.

Callaghan (of Cardiff), (Leonard) James Callaghan, Baron, known as **Jim Callaghan** (1912–2005) British statesman and prime minister (1976–9), born in Portsmouth, Hampshire. He was Chancellor of the Exchequer (1964–7), home secretary (1967–70), and foreign secretary (1974–6), and became prime minister on Harold Wilson's resignation.

Callas, Maria (Meneghini), originally **Maria Anna Sofia Cecilia Kalogeropoulos** (1923–77) Operatic soprano, born in New York City of Greek parents. She sang with great authority in all the most exacting soprano roles, excelling in the intricate *bel canto* style of pre-Verdian Italian opera.

Calvin, John (1509–64) Protestant reformer, born in Noyon, France. At Basel he issued his influential *Institutes of the Christian Religion* (trans, 1536), and at Geneva was persuaded by Farel to help with the reformation. The reformers proclaimed a Protestant Confession of Faith, but the Libertines party rose against this and Calvin and Farel were expelled (1538). In 1541 he was recalled, and by 1555 his authority was confirmed into an absolute supremacy. He left a double legacy to Protestantism by systematizing its doctrine and organizing its ecclesiastical discipline.

Calzaghe, Joe, popular name of

Joseph Calzaghe (1972–) Boxer, born in London. The son of an Italian father and Welsh mother, he settled with his family in Newbridge, South Wales. He won three consecutive British ABA titles (1991–3) in welter, light-middle, and middleweight divisions, then turned professional, and in 1997 defeated Chris Eubank for the WBO super-middleweight crown. In 2006 he became the undisputed world super-middleweight champion after defeating Jeff Lacy.

Cameron, David (William Donald) (1966–) British statesman, born in Oxfordshire. Elected MP for Witney in Oxfordshire (2001), he became deputy chairman of the Conservative Party (2003) and shadow education secretary (2004). In December 2005 he was voted party leader, taking over from Michael Howard.

Cameron, James (1954–) Film director, screenwriter, and producer, born in Kapuskasing, Ontario, Canada. His credits as writer/director include *The Terminator* and its sequel (1984, 1991), *Aliens* (1986), and *Titanic* (1997, 11 Oscars, including Best Film and Best Director). He directed and produced *Aliens of the Deep* in 2005.

Campbell, Donald (Malcolm) (1921–67) Speed-record contestant, born in Horley, Surrey, the son of Sir Malcolm Campbell. In 1964 he set a water-speed record of 276·33 mph on L Dumbleyung, and a land-speed record of 403·1 mph at L Eyre salt flats, both in Australia. He was killed when his *Bluebird* turbo-jet hydroplane crashed on Coniston Water in England.

Campbell, Sir Malcolm (1885–1948) Speed-record contestant, born in Chislehurst, Kent. He held land and water speed records from 1927 onwards, and in 1935 achieved 301·1292 mph at Bonneville Salt Flats, UT. In 1939 he achieved his fastest speed on water with 141·74 mph.

Campbell, Sir Menzies, known as **Ming Campbell** (1941–) British politician, born in Glasgow. He studied law, and was elected MP for North East Fife in 1987. For the Liberal Democrat Party he has served as shadow foreign secretary (1997–2003), deputy party leader (2003–6), and shadow secretary of state for foreign and Commonwealth affairs (2003–). In 2006 he succeeded Charles Kennedy as party leader.

Campbell-Bannerman, Sir Henry (1836–1908) British statesman and prime minister (1905–8), born in Glasgow. He was chief secretary for Ireland (1884), war secretary (1886, 1892–5), and Liberal leader (1899). His popularity united the Liberal Party.

Campion, Jane (1954–) Film director, born in Waikanae, New Zealand. Her film *Peel* (1984) won the 1986 Cannes Palme d'Or for best short film. Among later films are *Sweetie* (1989), *An Angel at My Table* (1990), *The Piano* (1993), and *In the Cut* (2003).

Camus, Albert (1913–60) French existentialist writer, born in Mondovi, Algeria. He earned an international reputation with his nihilistic novel, *The Outsider* (trans, 1942). Later novels include (trans titles) *The Plague* (1947) and *The Fall* (1956), and he also wrote plays and several political works. He received the Nobel Prize for Literature in 1957.

Canaletto, originally **Giovanni Antonio Canal** (1697–1768) Painter, born in Venice, Italy. He painted a renowned series of views in Venice, and in England (1746–56) his views of London and elsewhere proved extremely popular.

Canning, George (1770–1827) British statesman, born in London. Nominated Governor-General of India (1822), he was set to leave when Castlereagh's suicide saw him installed as foreign secretary. He was the first to recognize the free states of Spanish America, contended earnestly for Catholic Emancipation, and prepared the way for a repeal of the Corn Laws. In 1827 he formed an administration with the aid of the Whigs, but died the same year.

Cano, Juan Sebastian del (?–1526) The first man to circumnavigate the globe, born in Guetaria, Spain. In 1519 he sailed with Magellan in command of the *Concepción*, and after Magellan's death navigated the *Victoria* home to Spain.

Cantona, Eric (1966–) Footballer, born in Paris. He made his professional debut for Auxerre in 1983, became a French international, then moved to the UK (Leeds United, 1991; Manchester United, 1993). An aggressive and tempestuous player, his career has been interrupted by a series of suspensions. He announced his retirement in 1997, and began a career in films.

Canute or **Cnut**, sometimes known as **the Great** (c.995–1035) King of England (from 1016), Denmark (from 1019), and Norway (from 1028), the younger son of Sweyn Forkbeard. He defeated Edmund Ironside at Assandun (1016), secured Mercia and Northumbria, and became king of all England after Edmund's death. The story of his failure to make the tide recede was invented by a 12th-c historian.

Capone, Al(phonse) (1899–1947) Gangster, born in Brooklyn, NY. He achieved worldwide notoriety as a racketeer during the prohibition era in Chicago. In 1931 he was sentenced to 11 years' imprisonment for tax evasion, but was released on health grounds in 1939.

Capriati, Jennifer (Marie) (1976–) Tennis player, born in New York City. She turned professional in 1990 and went on to win a gold medal at the Barcelona Olympics in 1992. After an extended break from tennis, she made a successful comeback winning the French Open and Australian Open singles titles in 2001, and retaining the Australian title in 2002. At the start of 2005 she was ranked world number 10, but a shoulder injury has since kept her out of the game.

Caravaggio, originally **Michelangelo Merisi** (1573–1610) Baroque painter, born in Caravaggio, Italy, whence his nickname. His works include altarpieces and religious paintings, notably several of St Matthew (1599–1603) and 'Christ at Emmaus' (c.1602–3).

Cardin, Pierre (1922–) French fashion designer, born in Venice, Italy. He went to Paris in 1944, where he worked on costume design, notably for Cocteau's film *Beauty and the Beast* (1947). He opened his own house in 1953, producing fashion for both women and men.

Carey, George (Leonard) (1935–) Anglican clergyman, born in London. He became Bishop of Bath and Wells in 1987 and Archbishop of Canterbury (1991–2002).

Carling, Will, popular name of **William David Charles Carling** (1965–) Player of rugby union football, born in Bradford-on-Avon, Wiltshire. He made his England debut in 1988, was made captain (1988–96), and played a major role in the Grand Slam victories of 1991, 1992, and 1995. His 73 international appearances are a record for an English centre.

Carluccio, Antonio (Mario Gaetano) (1937–) Restaurateur, born in Vietri Sul Mare, Italy. He joined the Neal Street Restaurant in London as restaurateur (1981), became proprietor (1989), and joint proprietor (with his wife) of Carluccio's food retailers (1992). His television series include *Antonio Carluccio's Italian Feasts* (1996) with accompanying book.

Carlyle, Robert (1961–) Actor, born in Glasgow. He became known for his role in the television series *Hamish Macbeth* (1995–7), and his film credits include *Trainspotting* (1996), *The Full Monty* (1996), *Angela's Ashes* (1999), and *The Mighty Celt* (2005).

Carlyle, Thomas (1795–1881) Man of letters, born in Ecclefechan, Dumfries and Galloway. His best-known works are *Sartor Resartus* (1833–4), and studies on the French Revolution (3 vols, 1837) and on Frederick the Great (1858–65).

Carr, Philippa *see* Hibbert, Eleanor

Carrey, Jim, popular name of **James**

Eugene Carrey (1962–) Actor and entertainer, born in Newmarket, Ontario. He moved to Los Angeles in 1981, where he worked in nightclubs as a stand-up comedian and impressionist. His films include *Earth Girls Are Easy* (1989), *The Mask* (1994), *The Truman Show* (1998), and *Fun with Dick and Jane* (2005).

Carroll, Lewis, pseudonym of **Charles Lutwidge Dodgson** (1832–98) Writer, born in Daresbury, Cheshire. His nursery tale *Alice's Adventures in Wonderland* (1865), and its sequel *Through the Looking-Glass* (1872), quickly became classics. He also wrote much humorous verse, such as 'The Hunting of the Snark' (1876).

Carrott, Jasper, originally **Bob Davies** (1945–) Comedy entertainer, born in Acocks Green, Birmingham. In 1978 he starred in his own television show *An Audience with Jasper Carrott*. Later series include *Carrott Confidential* (1987–9), *Canned Carrott* (1990–1), and *The Detectives* (1989, 1992–4).

Carson, Johnny, popular name of **John William Carson** (1925–2005) Television personality and businessman, born in Corning, IA. He starred in *The Johnny Carson Show* (1955–6), after which he hosted the hugely popular *The Tonight Show* (1962–92).

Carson, Kit, popular name of **Christopher Carson** (1809–68) Frontiersman, born in Madison Co, KY. He acted as guide in John Frémont's explorations (1842), was Indian agent in New Mexico (1853), and fought for the Union in the Civil War. Several places are named after him.

Carte, Richard D'Oyly *see* D'Oyly Carte, Richard

Carter, Howard (1874–1939) Archaeologist, born in Swaffham, Norfolk. Under the patronage of George Herbert, Earl of Carnarvon, his discoveries included the tombs of Hatshepsut (1907) and Tutankhamen (1922).

Carter, Jimmy, popular name of **James (Earl) Carter** (1924–) US statesman and 39th president (1977–81), born in Plains, GA. In 1976 he won the Democratic presidential nomination, and defeated Gerald Ford. He arranged the peace treaty between Egypt and Israel (1979), and was much concerned with human rights at home and abroad. His administration ended in difficulties over the taking of US hostages in Iran and the Soviet invasion of Afghanistan, and he was defeated by Reagan in 1980. He has since been much involved in international diplomacy. He was awarded the Nobel Peace Prize in 2002.

Cartier-Bresson, Henri (1908–2004) Photographer, born in Paris. He worked only in black-and-white, concerned exclusively with illustrating contemporary life. In the mid-1970s he gave up photography, and returned to his earlier interests of painting and drawing.

Cartland, Dame (Mary) Barbara (Hamilton) (1901–2000) Popular romantic novelist, born in Edgbaston, West Midlands. Following her first novel, *Jigsaw* in 1923, she wrote over 700 books, mostly romantic novels but also biographies, books on food, health, and beauty, and several volumes of autobiography.

Cartwright, Edmund (1743–1823) Inventor of the power loom (1785–90), born in Marnham, Nottinghamshire. Attempts to use the loom met with fierce opposition, and it was not until the 19th-c that it came into practical use.

Caruso, Enrico (1873–1921) Operatic tenor, born in Naples, Italy. He made his debut in Naples in 1894. The extraordinary power of his voice, combined with his acting ability, won him worldwide recognition.

Casanova (de Seingalt), Giacomo Girolamo (1725–98) Adventurer, born in Venice, Italy. Alchemist, cabalist, and spy, he visited Europe, mixed with the best society, and had always to 'vanish' after a brief period of felicity. His main work is his autobiography, in which he emerges as one of the world's great lovers.

Cash, Johnny (1932–2003) Country music singer, songwriter, and guitarist, born in Kingsland, AR. He signed for Sun Records in 1955, and early songs included 'Cry, Cry, Cry', 'I Walk The Line', and 'Folsom Prison Blues' (1956). He married **June Carter** (1929–2003) in 1968. A biopic of his life, *Walk the Line*, appeared in 2005.

Cassidy, Butch, originally **Robert LeRoy Parker** (1866–?1909) Outlaw, born in Beaver, UT. He joined the infamous Wild Bunch and was partner with the Sundance Kid. They roamed America, robbing banks, trains, and mine stations, until they were trapped and killed.

Cassius, in full **Gaius Cassius Longinus** (?–42 BC) Roman soldier and politician. Despite gaining political advancement through Caesar, he played a leading part in the conspiracy to murder him (44 BC). He raised an army in Syria and marched against the Triumvirate, but was defeated at Philippi (42 BC) and committed suicide.

Castle, Roy (1932–94) Entertainer, born in Scholes, West Yorkshire. He starred in cabaret, theatre, film, and television, becoming known for such programmes as BBC television's *Record Breakers*. Following his death from lung cancer, the Roy Castle Cause for Hope Foundation, a research centre into the disease, was launched in Liverpool in 1994.

Castlereagh, Robert Stewart, Viscount (1769–1822) British statesman, born in Dublin. His major achievements date from 1812 when, as foreign secretary, he was at the heart of the coalition against Napoleon (1813–14). He represented England at Chaumont and Vienna (1814–15), Paris (1815), and Aix-la-Chapelle (1818), advocating 'Congress diplomacy' to avoid further warfare.

Castro (Ruz), Fidel (1927–) Cuban revolutionary, prime minister (1959–), and president (1976–), born near Birán, Cuba. In 1958 he mounted a successful attack against Batista, and as premier proclaimed a Marxist–Leninist programme. His overthrow of US economic dominance was balanced by his dependence on Russian aid.

Catesby, Robert (1573–1605) Chief conspirator in the Gunpowder Plot, born in Lapworth, Warwickshire. A Catholic, he had suffered much as a recusant, and was shot dead while resisting arrest after the failure of the plot (1605).

Catherine II, known as **Catherine the Great**, originally **Princess Sophie Friederike Auguste von Anhalt-Zerbst** (1729–96) Empress of Russia (1762–96), born in Szczecin (Stettin), Poland. In 1745 she was married to the heir to the Russian throne (later **Peter III**, r.1761–2), and succeeded him after a palace coup. She carried out an energetic foreign policy, extended the Russian Empire S to the Black Sea after the Russo-Turkish Wars (1774, 1792), and brought about the three partitions of Poland (1772, 1793, 1795). Despite pretensions to enlightened ideas, her domestic policies achieved little for most Russians, and in 1774 she had to suppress a popular rebellion led by Pugachev. Her private life was dominated by a long series of lovers, notably Potemkin.

Catherine of Aragón (1485–1536) Queen of England, the first wife of Henry VIII (1509–33), born in Alcalá de Henares, Spain, the fourth daughter of Ferdinand and Isabella of Spain. She was first married in 1501 to **Arthur** (1486–1502), the son of Henry VII. Soon widowed, in 1509 she married her brother-in-law Henry, and bore him five children, but only the Princess Mary survived. Henry divorced her in 1533, and she retired to a religious life.

Causley, Charles (Stanley) (1917–2003) Poet, born in Launceston, Cornwall. He became known as a poet of the sea, and also as a children's poet. His *Collected Poems 1951–1997* were published in 1997.

Cavell, Edith (1865–1915) Nurse, born in Swardeston, Norfolk. Matron of the Berkendael Medical Institute, Brussels, she tended friend and foe alike in 1914–15, but was executed by the Germans for helping fugitives to escape capture.

Caxton, William (c.1422–c.1491) The first English printer, born possibly in Tenterden, Kent. In Cologne he probably learned the art of printing (1471–2), and printed the first book in English, *The Recuyell of the Historyes of Troye* (1475). He set up his wooden press at Westminster, producing the first books printed in England.

Cecil, Robert (Arthur Talbot Gascoyne), 3rd Marquess of Salisbury (1830–1903) British statesman and prime minister (1885–6, 1886–92, 1895–1902), born in Hatfield, Hertfordshire. He was Conservative prime minister on three occasions, much of the time serving as his own foreign secretary.

Cecil, Robert (Arthur James Gascoyne), 5th Marquess of Salisbury (1893–1972) British statesman, born in Hatfield, Hertfordshire. In the Churchill government of 1951 he became secretary of state for Commonwealth relations and Lord President of the Council, but resigned in 1957.

Cecil, William, 1st Baron Burghley or **Burghleigh** (1520–98) English statesman, born in Bourne, Lincolnshire. In 1558 Elizabeth appointed him chief secretary of state, and for the next 40 years he was the chief architect of Elizabethan greatness, influencing her pro-Protestant foreign policy, securing the execution of Mary, Queen of Scots, and preparing for the Spanish Armada. In 1572 he became Lord High Treasurer, an office he held until his death.

Cecilia, St (2nd-c or 3rd-c) Christian martyr, and patron saint of music. According to tradition, she was compelled to marry despite a vow of celibacy, but her husband respected her vow, and she converted him to Christianity. They were both put to death.

Celsius, Anders (1701–44) Astronomer, born in Uppsala, Sweden. He devised the centigrade scale (*Celsius scale*) of temperature in 1742.

Cervantes (Saavedra), Miguel de (1547–1616) Writer of *Don Quixote*, born in Alcalá de Henares, Spain. Tradition maintains that he wrote *Don Quixote* (1605) in prison at Argamasilla in La Mancha. He produced the second part in 1615, after writing many plays and short novels.

Cézanne, Paul (1839–1906) Post-Impressionist painter, born in Aix-en-Provence, France. He abandoned his early sombre Expressionism for the study of nature, using his characteristic glowing colours. After 1886 he constructed pictures from a rhythmic series of coloured planes, thus becoming the forerunner of Cubism. Among his best-known paintings are 'L'estaque' (c.1888) and 'The Card Players' (1890–2).

Chabrol, Claude (1930–) Film critic and director, born in Paris. Identified with the French *Nouvelle Vague*, his most widely known films are dramas of abnormality in the provincial bourgeoisie, notably (trans titles) *The*

Butcher (1970), *Red Wedding* (1973), and *Inspector Lavardin* (1986).

Chagall, Marc (1887–1985) Artist, born in Vitebsk, Belarus. During World War 2 he moved to the USA. He illustrated several books, but is best known for his Surrealist paintings of animals, objects, and people from his life, dreams, and Russian folklore.

Chalmers, Judith (1937–) Television presenter, born in Manchester. In 1972 she joined Thames Television and from 1973 presented the long-running holiday programme *Wish You Were Here...?*. She has been commentator for many royal and state occasions.

Chamberlain, (Arthur) Neville (1869–1940) British Conservative prime minister (1937–40), born in Birmingham, West Midlands, the son of Joseph Chamberlain. He became Chancellor of the Exchequer (1923–4, 1931–7) and minister for health (1923, 1924–9, 1931). As prime minister, he advocated 'appeasement' of Italy and Germany, returning from Munich with his claim to have found 'peace for our time' (1938).

Chamberlain, Wilt(on) Norman, nickname **Wilt the Stilt** (1936–99) Basketball player, born in Philadelphia, PA. Height 1·85 m/7 ft 1 in, he played for the Philadelphia 76ers, and was seven times the National Basketball Association leading scorer (1960–6). During his career (1960–73) he scored 31 419 points.

Chandler, Raymond (Thornton) (1888–1959) Writer, born in Chicago, IL. His 'private-eye' novels include *The Big Sleep* (1939) and *Farewell, My Lovely* (1940), several of which were filmed. He is the creator of the detective anti-hero, Philip Marlowe.

Chanel, Coco, popular name of **Gabrielle Chanel** (?1883–1971) Fashion designer, born in Saumur, France. She revolutionized women's fashions during the 1920s, her designs including the 'chemise' dress and the collarless cardigan jacket.

Chaplin, Charlie, popular name of **Sir Charles Spencer Chaplin** (1889–1977) Film actor and director, born in London. He went to Hollywood in 1914, and in his early silent comedies he adopted the bowler hat, out-turned feet, moustache, and walking-cane which became his hallmark, as in *The Kid* and *The Gold Rush*. His first sound film was *The Great Dictator* (1940). In *Limelight* (1952) he acted, produced, directed, and composed the music.

Chardin, Pierre Teilhard de *see* Teilhard de Chardin, Pierre

Charlemagne or **Charles the Great** (742–814) King of the Franks (sole ruler, 771–814), and emperor of the West (800–14), the eldest son of Pepin the Short. He defeated the Saxons (772–804) and the Lombards (773–4), and took control of most of Christian W Europe. He later consolidated his vast empire, promoting Christianity, education, agriculture, the arts, manufacture, and commerce, and the period has become known as the *Carolingian Renaissance*.

Charles I (of England) (1600–49) King of Britain and Ireland (1625–49), born in Dunfermline, Fife, the second son of James I. He married the French princess, Henrietta Maria, thus disturbing the nation, for she was permitted the free exercise of the Catholic religion. He warred with France (1627–9), and in 1630 made peace with Spain, but his continuing need for money led to unpopular economic policies, and his attempt to anglicize the Scottish Church brought active resistance (1639). In 1642 he entered into the Civil War, was annihilated at Naseby (14 Jun 1645), and surrendered at Newark (1646). After a second Civil War (1646–8), he came to trial at Westminster, where his dignified refusal to plead was interpreted as a confession of guilt. He was beheaded at Whitehall.

Charles II (of England) (1630–85) King of Britain and Ireland (1660–85), born in London, the son of Charles I. On his father's execution (1649), he assumed the title of king, and was crowned at Scone (1651). Leading poorly organized forces into England, he was defeated at Worcester (1651), and lived in exile until an impoverished England summoned him back as king (1660). In 1662 he entered into a childless marriage with the Portuguese princess, Catherine of Braganza. His war with Holland (1665–7) was unpopular, and led to the dismissal of Lord Clarendon (1667), who was replaced by a group of ministers (the Cabal).

Charles (Philip Arthur George), Prince of Wales (1948–) Eldest son of Queen Elizabeth II and Prince Philip, Duke of Edinburgh, and heir apparent to the throne, born at Buckingham Palace, London. He was given the title of Prince of Wales in 1958, and invested at Caernarfon (1969). He served in the RAF and Royal Navy (1971–6), and in 1981 married Lady Diana Frances Spencer. They had two sons: **Prince William Arthur Philip Louis** (1982–) and **Prince Henry Charles Albert David** (1984–). The couple separated in 1992, and were divorced in 1996. He married divorcée Camilla Parker Bowles in 2005 in a civil ceremony at Windsor Guildhall.

Charles, (William) John, nickname **the Gentle Giant** (1931–2004) Footballer, born in Swansea, S Wales. He joined Leeds United Football Club in 1949 and gained his first cap for Wales the next year. In 1957 he made history as the first British player to sign for a foreign club when he transferred to Italy's Juventus for a then British record £65 000. He gained a total of 38 caps and was never booked or sent off.

Charles, Ray, originally **Ray Charles Robinson** (1930–2004) Singer and pianist, born in Albany, GA. Blind from childhood, he became influenced by jazz and blues, and developed an original blend of music identified as 'soul'. He gave over 10 000 concerts during his career and in 2005 was honoured with eight posthumous Grammy Awards.

Charles Edward Stuart see Stuart, Prince Charles Edward

Charlton, Bobby, popular name of **Sir Robert Charlton** (1937–) Footballer, born in Ashington, Northumberland, the brother of Jack Charlton. He played for Manchester United throughout his career (1954–73). He won 105 caps for England, scoring a record 49 goals.

Charlton, Jack(ie), popular name of **John Charlton** (1935–) Footballer, born in Ashington, Northumberland, the brother of Bobby Charlton. He played for Leeds United (1965–75), and was capped for England late in his career. He became manager of the Ireland team (1986–96), taking them to the last stages of the World Cup in 1990 and 1994.

Charteris, Leslie, originally **Leslie Charles Bowyer Yin** (1907–93) Crime-story writer, born in Singapore. He became a US citizen in 1941, and is especially known as the creator of Simon Templar, 'the Saint'.

Chatham, 1st Earl of *see* Pitt, William, 1st Earl of Chatham

Chaucer, Geoffrey (c.1343–1400) Poet, probably born in London. Travelling extensively abroad in the king's service, he also held royal posts at home, including that of Comptroller of the Petty Customs (1382). His early writings, such as *Troilus and Criseyde*, were greatly influenced by Italian authors, notably Boccaccio. His later period includes his most famous work, the unfinished *Canterbury Tales*. Chaucer was the first great poet of the English nation; and in the Middle Ages he stands supreme.

Che Guevara *see* Guevara, Che

Chekhov, Anton (Pavlovitch) (1860–1904) Playwright and master of the short story, born in Taganrog, Russia. His early full-length plays were failures, but when *The Seagull* (trans, 1896) was revived in 1898 it was a great success. He then wrote his masterpieces: (trans titles) *Uncle Vanya* (1900), *The Three Sisters* (1901), and *The Cherry Orchard* (1904).

Cheney, Dick, popular name of Richard B(ruce) Cheney (1941–) US Republican politician, born in Lincoln, NE. Secretary of defence under President George Bush (1989–93), he formed the coalition to execute Operation Desert Storm. In 2000 he was George W Bush's running-mate, and he became vice-president in 2001.

Cher, in full **Cherilyn La Piere Sarkisian** (1946–) Singer and actress, born in El Centro, CA. She originally sang with her husband as Sonny and Cher, best known for the rock anthem 'I Got You Babe' (1965), but later found success as a solo singer. Her films include *Moonstruck* (1987, Oscar) and *Tea With Mussolini* (1999).

Cheshire (of Woodhall), (Geoffrey) Leonard Cheshire, Baron (1917–92) British bomber pilot and philanthropist. He was an official British observer of the atomic bomb over Nagasaki in 1945. The experience determined him to establish co-operative communities for ex-servicemen, from which grew the Cheshire Homes for the Disabled.

Chesterton, G(ilbert) K(eith) (1874–1936) Critic and writer, born in London. He wrote articles, poetry, and critical studies, gaining popularity with the amiable detective-priest introduced in *The Innocence of Father Brown* (1911). He became a Catholic in 1922, and thereafter wrote mainly on religious topics.

Chevalier, Maurice (1888–1972) Film and vaudeville actor, born in Paris. He became known for his individual, straw-hatted, *bon-viveur* personality and his distinctive French accent, in such films as *The Innocents of Paris* (1929) and *Gigi* (1958).

Chiang Kai-shek *see* Jiang Jieshi

Chichester, Sir Francis (Charles) (1901–72) Pioneer air navigator, adventurer, and yachtsman, born in Barnstaple, Devon. In 1953 he took up ocean sailing, winning the first solo transatlantic yacht race (1960) in *Gipsy Moth III*, sailing from Plymouth to New York in 40 days. He also made a solo circumnavigation of the world (1966–7) in *Gipsy Moth IV*.

Chippendale, Thomas (1718–79) Furniture-maker and designer, baptized at Otley, West Yorkshire. He set up a workshop in London in 1754, and became famous for his Neoclassical furniture. *The Gentleman and Cabinet-maker's Director* (1754) was the first comprehensive trade catalogue of its kind.

Chirac, Jacques (René) (1932–) French prime minister (1974–6, 1986–8) and president (1995–). Appointed prime minister by Giscard d'Estaing, he resigned over differences with him, and broke away to lead the Gaullist Party. He was unsuccessful in the 1981 and 1988 presidential elections, but won in 1995.

Chopin, Frédéric (François) (1810–49) Composer and pianist, born in Zelazowa Wola, Poland. His works for the piano include 50 mazurkas, 27 études, 25 préludes, 19 nocturnes, 13 waltzes, 12 polonaises, four ballades, three impromptus, three sonatas, two piano concertos, and a funeral march. He lived with the novelist George Sand between 1838 and 1847.

Chou En-lai *see* Zhou Enlai

Christian, Fletcher (18th-c) Seaman and ringleader of the mutiny on the *Bounty* (1789), born in Cockermouth, Cumbria. After the mutiny, he settled on Pitcairn I, where his descendants were found in 1808.

Christie, Dame Agatha (Mary Clarissa), *née* Miller (1890–1976) Writer, born in Torquay, Devon. She wrote more than 70 detective novels featuring the Belgian detective, Hercule Poirot, or the enquiring village lady, Miss Marple. Several of her stories have become popular films, such as *Murder on the Orient Express* (1974) and *Death on the Nile* (1978).

Christie, John Reginald Halliday (1898–1953) Murderer, born in Yorkshire. He was hanged at London for the murder of his wife, and confessed to killing six other women, including the wife of Timothy John Evans (hanged for the murder in 1950). Evans was granted a free pardon in 1966.

Christie, Julie (1940–) British actress, born in Chukua, Assam. Her many films include *Billy Liar* (1963), *Darling* (1965, Oscar), *The Go-Between* (1971), *Fools of Fortune* (1990), and *Troy* (2004).

Christopher, St (3rd-c) Syrian Christian martyr, traditionally a man of gigantic stature who carried the Christ-child across a river. He is said to have suffered martyrdom under Emperor Decius (reigned 249–251), and is the patron saint of wayfarers and motorists.

Church, Charlotte (1986–) Soprano,

born in Cardiff. At age 11 she performed 'Pie Jesu' on a television talent show, and was immediately signed to a recording contract. With her debut album, *Voice of an Angel* (1998), she became the youngest ever artist to make number 1 in the UK classical charts. In 2005 she released her first pop album, *Tissues and Issues*.

Churchill, Sir Winston (Leonard Spencer) (1874–1965) British prime minister (1940–5, 1951–5), born in Blenheim Palace, Oxfordshire. Initially a Conservative MP (1900), he joined the Liberals in 1904, and was colonial under-secretary (1905), President of the Board of Trade (1908), home secretary (1910), and First Lord of the Admiralty (1911). After World War 1 he was secretary of state for war and air (1919–21), and Chancellor of the Exchequer (1924–9). In 1929 he returned to the Conservative fold, and on Chamberlain's defeat (May 1940) formed a coalition government, leading Britain through World War 2 with great oratory and steely resolution. Defeated in the July 1945 election, he was prime minister again in 1951, and after 1955 remained a venerated backbencher. He was awarded the Nobel Prize for Literature in 1953. His widow, **Clementine Ogilvy Hozier** (1885–1977), whom he had married in 1908, was made a life peer in 1965 for her indefatigable charitable work (**Baroness Spencer-Churchill of Chartwell**).

Cicero, Marcus Tullius, also known in English as **Tully** (106–43 BC) Roman orator, statesman, and philosopher, born in Arpinum, Latium. He foiled Catiline's revolutionary plot, and was exiled when Clodius became tribune in 58 BC. Recalled by the people, he lost the esteem of both Caesar's and Pompey's factions by vacillating between the two. Living in retirement (46–44 BC), he wrote his chief works on rhetoric and philosophy. In 43 BC he delivered his famous speeches against Antony, the so-called 'Philippics', and was murdered by Antony's soldiers.

Cid, El, popular name of **Rodrigo** or **Ruy Díaz de Vivar** (c.1040–99) Spanish hero, born in Burgos, Spain. He became known as the *Cid* (from the Moorish *Sidi*, 'lord'). His great achievement was the capture of Valencia in 1094.

Clapton, Eric (1945–) Rock guitarist and singer, born in Ripley, Surrey. In the 1960s he was in British rhythm-and-blues bands The Yardbirds and John Mayall's Bluesbreakers, then in Cream and Blind Faith. 'Layla' (1970) is considered a rock classic by many, as are 'I Shot the Sheriff', 'Lay Down Sally', and 'Wonderful Tonight'.

Clare of Assisi, St (1194–1253) Abbess, born of a noble family in Assisi, Italy. In 1215 she founded with St Francis the order of Franciscan nuns known as the Poor Clares. She was canonized in 1255, and in 1958 was designated patron saint of television.

Clare, Anthony (Ward) (1942–) British psychiatrist and broadcaster. He became widely known through his BBC television series, *In the Psychiatrist's Chair* (from 1982). Among his books are *Depression and How to*

Survive It (1993, with Spike Milligan) and *On Men* (2000).

Clark, Alan (Kenneth McKenzie) (1928–99) British politician, military historian, and diarist. Elected a Conservative MP in 1974, he held posts at employment (1983–6), trade (1986–9), and defence (1989–92). He left parliament before the 1992 general election but returned in 1997. Three volumes of his diaries have been published (1994, 2000, 2002).

Clarke, Sir Arthur C(harles) (1917–) Writer of science fiction, born in Minehead, Somerset. A prolific writer, he is especially known for *2001: a Space Odyssey* (1968), which became a highly successful film, and the sequels, *2010: Space Odyssey II* (1982; filmed 1984), *2062: Odyssey III* (1988), and *3001: the Final Odyssey* (1997).

Clarke, Kenneth (Harry) (1940–) British Conservative statesman, born in Nottingham, Nottinghamshire. He became secretary of state for health (1988), home secretary (1992), and Chancellor of the Exchequer (1993–7). In 2005 he launched his third unsuccessful bid for the party leadership.

Clarkson, Jeremy (Charles Robert) (1960–) Journalist and television presenter, born in Doncaster. He joined the BBC as presenter on *Top Gear* (1989–1998, 2002–), and is a regular columnist for leading newspapers and for *Top Gear* magazine, which he founded in 1993. His publications include the best-selling *The World According to Clarkson* (2005).

Claude Lorrain, originally **Claude Gellée** (1600–82) Landscape painter, born in Lorraine, France. He painted about 400 landscapes, including several with biblical or Classical themes, such as 'The Sermon on the Mount' (1656, New York City). He also produced many drawings and etchings.

Claudius, in full **Tiberius Claudius Caesar Augustus Germanicus** (10 BC–AD 54) Roman emperor (41–54), the grandson of the Empress Livia. Kept in the background because of his physical disabilities, he devoted himself to historical studies, and thus survived the in-fighting of the imperial house. Through his public works and reforms, he made a lasting contribution to the government of Rome and the empire, and through the annexation of Britain, Mauretania, and Thrace, a significant extension of its size. He died poisoned, probably by his fourth wife Agrippina.

Clay, Cassius *see* Ali, Muhammad

Cleese, John (Marwood) (1939–) Comic actor and writer, born in Weston-super-Mare, Somerset. He joined *Monty Python's Flying Circus* (1969–74), wrote and starred in the television series *Fawlty Towers* (1975, 1979), and has appeared in several films, such as *A Fish Called Wanda* (1988) and *Around the World in 80 Days* (2004).

Clement I, St, known as **Clemens Romanus** or **Clement of Rome** (late 1st-c) One of the apostolic Fathers of the Church, reckoned variously as the second or third successor of St Peter at Rome, possibly 88–97 or 92–101. The first of two epistles attributed to him is generally accepted as his.

Cleopatra VII (69–30 BC) Queen of Egypt (51–48 BC, 47–30 BC), the daughter of Ptolemy Auletes. Caesar, to whom she bore a son Caesarion, supported her claim to the throne (47 BC), while Antony, by whom she had three children, restored to her much of the old Ptolemaic empire. Defeated with Antony at Actium (31 BC), she used an asp to commit suicide.

Clerk Maxwell, James *see* Maxwell, James

Cleveland, (Stephen) Grover (1837–1908) US statesman and the 22nd and 24th president (1885–9, 1893–7), born in Caldwell, NJ. In 1895 he caused worldwide excitement by applying the Monroe Doctrine to Britain's dispute with Venezuela.

Clijsters, Kim (1983–) Tennis player, born in Bilzen, Belgium. By the end of 2003 she had won 19 titles, including the Australian and French Opens (2000), and she won her first Grand Slam title, the US Open, in 2005. At the start of 2006 she was ranked world number 2.

Clinton, Bill, popular name of **William Jefferson Clinton**, born **William Jefferson Blythe** (1946–) US Democratic statesman and 42nd president (1993–2000), born in Hope, AR. He entered Arkansas politics as state attorney general, becoming governor (1979–81, 1983–92). He defeated George Bush for the presidency in 1992, and Bob Dole in 1996. The US Congress voted to impeach him in 1998 on charges of perjury and obstruction over his alleged sexual relationship with Monica Lewinsky, a White House intern. A Senate trial took place in 1999 and he was acquitted.

Clinton, Hillary (Rodham) (1947–) Lawyer and US first lady (1993–2000), born in Park Ridge, IL. She married fellow law graduate Bill Clinton in 1975. She performed an active political role following his election as president, heading a task force on national health reform in 1993. In 2000 she won a senate seat representing New York State.

Clive (of Plassey), Robert Clive, Baron (1725–74) Soldier, and administrator in India, born in Styche, Shropshire. In 1755 he was called to avenge the so-called Black Hole of Calcutta, and at Plassey (1757) defeated a large Indian–French force. For three years he was sole ruler of Bengal in all but name.

Clooney, George (1961–) Actor and director, born in Lexington, KY. He became well known for his role as Dr Doug Ross in the TV series *ER* (1994–9). His film credits include *Batman and Robin* (1997), *O Brother, Where Art Thou?* (2000, Best Comedy Actor Golden Globe), and *Syriana* (2005, Best Supporting Actor Oscar and Golden Globe).

Clooney, Rosemary (1928–2002) Singer, born in Maysville, KY. In 1950 she recorded a dialect song, 'Come On-a My House' and became a pop star, following it with a string of hits including 'Hey There' (1951) and 'This Ole House' (1952). She co-starred in the film *White Christmas* (1954) and hosted TV's *The Rosemary Clooney Show* (1956–7).

Clough, Brian (1935–2004) Footballer and manager, born in Middlesbrough. As manager, he took Derby County and Nottingham Forest to League championship wins and the latter to two European Cup successes (1979, 1980). His son, Nigel (1966–), is also a footballer, who became manager of Burton Albion in 1998.

Cnut *see* Canute

Coates, Eric (1886–1957) Composer, born in Hucknall, Nottinghamshire. Among his best-known compositions are the *London Suite* (1933), *The Three Elizabeths* (1944), and a number of popular waltzes and marches.

Cobbett, William (1763–1835) Journalist and reformer, born in Farnham, Surrey. In 1802 he started his *Weekly Political Register*, which moved from its original Toryism to an uncompromising Radicalism. His works include a *History of the Protestant Reformation* (1824–7) and *Rural Rides* (1830).

Cochise (?1812–74) Chiricahua Apache chief, born in present-day Arizona or New Mexico. The main war chief of the Apaches, he surrendered in 1872, after winning assurances from the US government that he and his band could remain in the Chiricahua Mts.

Cockerell, Sir Christopher (Sydney) (1910–99) Engineer, born in Cambridge, Cambridgeshire. Working on hydrodynamics, in the early 1950s he invented the amphibious hovercraft.

Cocteau, Jean (1889–1963) Poet, playwright, and film director, born in Maisons-Lafitte, France. His best-known works include (trans titles) the novel *Children of the Game* (1929), the play *Orpheus* (1926), and the film *Beauty and the Beast* (1945).

Cody, William F(rederick), known as **Buffalo Bill** (1846–1917) Showman, born in Scott Co, IA. He received his nickname after killing nearly 5000 buffalo in eight months for a contract to supply workers on the Kansas Pacific Railway with meat. From 1883 he toured with his Wild West Show.

Coe (of Ranmore), Sebastian (Newbold) Coe, Lord (1956–) Athlete, born in London. He broke eight world records, including the mile three times, and at the 1980 Olympics won the gold medal in the 1500 m and the silver in the 800 m, repeating the achievement in 1984. He served as a Conservative MP (1992–7). In 2004 he was appointed the new leader of London's successful campaign to host the 2012 Olympics.

Coetzee, J(ohn) M(axwell) (1940–) Writer and critic, born in Cape Town. His novels include *Dusklands* (1974), *In the Heart of the Country* (1977), *Life and Times of Michael K* (1983, Booker), *Disgrace* (1999, Booker), and *Slow Man* (2005). He received the 2003 Nobel Prize for Literature.

Coggan (of Canterbury and of Sissinghurst), (Frederick) Donald Coggan, Baron (1909–2000) Clergyman, born in London. He was Archbishop of York (1961–74), and Archbishop of Canterbury (1974–80), subsequently becoming a life peer.

Colbert, Claudette, originally **Lily Claudette Chauchoin** (1903–96) Film actress, born in Paris. She became a star with *It Happened One Night* (1934, Oscar), followed by several romantic comedy successes, such as *The Palm Beach Story* (1942). Her stage career continued into the 1980s.

Cole, George (1925–) Actor, born in London. His many films include the *St Trinian's* series, but he is probably best known in the UK as Arthur Daly from the 1980s television series, *Minder*.

Cole, Nat King, originally **Nathaniel Adams Cole**, family name formerly **Coles** (1919–65) Entertainer, born in Montgomery, AL. During the 1930s he became popular as a jazz pianist and singer, his many hit records including 'Route 66', 'Walking My Baby Back Home', and 'Unforgettable'. His daughter, **Natalie Cole** (1950–), is also an entertainer.

Coleman, Ornette (1930–) Alto saxophonist, multi-instrumentalist, and composer, born in Fort Worth, TX. Following early recordings with Don Cherry (1936–95), he persevered through a discouraging climate for avant-garde jazz, becoming accepted in the 1960s as a major innovator.

Coleridge, Samuel Taylor (1772–1834) Poet, born in Ottery St Mary, Devon. His friendship with William and Dorothy Wordsworth resulted in a new poetry reacting against neoclassic artificiality: *Lyrical Ballads* (1798) opens with his 'Rime of the Ancient Mariner'. In 1800 he moved to the Lake District, but his career prospects were blighted by his moral collapse, partly due to opium. In 1816 he published 'Christabel' and 'Kubla Khan', both written in his earlier period of inspiration, and went on to write critical and other essays.

Collins, Joan (Henrietta) (1933–) Actress, born in London. After a film debut in *Lady Godiva Rides Again* (1951), her sultry appeal and headline-catching private life made her an international celebrity, best known for her role in the television soap opera *Dynasty* (1981–9). Her sister is the best-selling novelist **Jackie Collins** (1942–).

Collins, Michael (1930–) US astronaut, born in Rome. He was one of the members of the Gemini 10 project, and remained in the command module during the successful Apollo 11 Moon-landing expedition.

Collins, Pauline (1940–) Actress, born in Exmouth, Devon. She starred in the popular television series *Upstairs, Downstairs* (1971–3), and later series include *Forever Green* (1989–91), with actor husband John Alderton, and *Bleak House* (2005). Her film credits include *Shirley Valentine* (1989, Best Actress Oscar nomination).

Collins, (William) Wilkie (1824–89) Novelist, born in London. A master of the mystery story, his best-known works are *The Woman in White* (1860) and *The Moonstone* (1868).

Colt, Samuel (1814–62) Inventor, born in Hartford, CT. In 1835 he took out his first patent for a revolver, which was adopted by the US army, thus founding the fortunes of his company, Colt's Patent Fire-Arms.

Coltrane, John (William) (1926–67) Jazz saxophonist and composer, born in Hamlet, NC. He emerged in the 1950s working with Dizzy Gillespie, Bud Powell, and Miles Davis, then led his own small groups, becoming a controversial and influential avant-garde figure.

Columba, St, also **Columcille** or **Colm** (521–97) Missionary and abbot, born in Gartan, Co Donegal, Ireland. He founded monasteries at Derry (546), Durrow (553), and Iona (c.563), from where he and his followers brought Christianity to Scotland.

Columbus, Christopher, Ital **Cristoforo Colombo**, Span **Cristóbal Colón** (1451–1506) European discoverer of the New World, born in Genoa, Italy. His plans to reach India by sailing W were supported by Ferdinand and Isabella of Spain. He set sail from Saltes (1492) in the *Santa Maria*, reaching the Bahamas, Cuba, and Hispaniola (Haiti). His second voyage (1493–6) led to the discovery of several Caribbean islands, and on his third voyage (1498–1500) he discovered the South American mainland. His last voyage (1502–4) was along the S side of the Gulf of Mexico.

Comaneci, Nadia (1961–) Gymnast, born in Onesti, Moldova. Representing Romania, she was the star of the 1976 Olympic Games when, aged 14, she won gold medals in the beam, vault, and floor disciplines. In 1989 she defected to the USA, and began a career as a model.

Como, Perry, nickname **Mr C** (1912–2001) Popular singer, born in Canonsburg, PA. He sang with the Ted Weems band for six years and recorded many hit records in the 1940s and 1950s. He released the hit song 'It's Impossible' in 1970.

Compton, Denis (Charles Scott) (1918–97) Cricketer, born in London.

He played cricket for England 78 times, scoring 5807 runs, and during his career (1936–57) made 38 942 runs and took 622 wickets.

Compton-Burnett, Dame Ivy (1884–1969) Novelist, born in Pinner, Greater London. Her novels, set in upper-class Victorian or Edwardian society, include *Pastors and Masters* (1925) and *Mother and Son* (1955, James Tait Black).

Conan Doyle *see* Doyle, Arthur Conan

Confucius, Latin name of **Kongfuzi** or **K'ung Fu-tse** (Chin 'Venerated Master Kong') (551–479 BC) Chinese philosopher, born in the state of Lu (modern Shantung). Largely self-educated, in 531 BC he began his career as a teacher. His ideas for social reform made him the idol of the people; but his enemies caused him to leave Lu, and he travelled widely, followed by many disciples. The *Confucian Analects* compiled soon after his death, are a collection of his sayings and doings. His teachings later inspired a cult of veneration, and Confucianism became the state religion of China.

Connelly, Jennifer (Lynn) (1970–) Actress, born in Catskill Mountains, NY. Her first film role was in *Once Upon a Time in America* (1984), and later films include *Mulholland Falls* (1996), *A Beautiful Mind* (2001, Best Actress Golden Globe, BAFTA, Oscar nomination), and *Dark Water* (2005). She married actor Paul Bettany in 2002.

Connery, Sir Sean, originally **Thomas Connery** (1930–) Film actor, born in Edinburgh. In 1963 he was cast in *Dr No* as Ian Fleming's secret agent

James Bond, a part he played on seven occasions. Later films include *The Untouchables* (1987, Oscar) and *Indiana Jones and the Last Crusade* (1989).

Connolly, Billy (1942–) Comedian and actor, born in Glasgow. He became well known during the 1980s for his one-man theatre comedy acts and television appearances. His film credits include *Mrs Brown* (1997) and *The Man Who Sued God* (2003). In 2004 he presented *World Tour of New Zealand* for BBC television.

Conrad, Joseph, originally **Józef Teodor Konrad Nalecz Korzeniowski** (1857–1924) Novelist, born in Berdichev, Ukraine. His books include *The Nigger of the Narcissus* (1897), *Lord Jim* (1900), *Nostromo* (1904), *The Secret Agent* (1907), and *Under Western Eyes* (1911). His fiction has been a favourite subject for film and television adaptation.

Conran, Jasper (1959–) Fashion designer, born in London, the son of Sir Terence Conran. He produced his first collection of easy-to-wear, quality clothes in London in 1978.

Constable, John (1776–1837) Landscape painter, born in East Bergholt, Suffolk. Among his best-known works are 'Haywain' (1821) and 'The White Horse' (1819). He is today considered, along with Turner, as the leading painter of the English countryside.

Constantine I, known as **the Great**, originally **Flavius Valerius Constantinus** (c.274–337) Roman emperor, born in Naissus, Moesia. He became emperor of the West after his defeat of Maxentius (312), and

emperor of the East after his victory over Licinius (324). Believing that his victory in 312 was the work of the Christian God, he became the first emperor to promote Christianity, whence his title 'Great'.

Conti, Tom, popular name of **Thomas A Conti** (1942–) Actor and director, born in Paisley, Scotland. He made his acting debut in 1960 and has since performed and directed regularly in London theatres. Among his films are *Merry Christmas, Mr Lawrence* (1982) and *Shirley Valentine* (1989).

Cook, James (1728–79) Navigator, born in Marton, North Yorkshire. In the *Endeavour*, he carried a Royal Society expedition to Tahiti, circumnavigated New Zealand, and charted parts of Australia. In his second voyage he sailed round Antarctica (1772–5), and discovered several Pacific island groups. His third voyage (1776–9) aimed to find a passage round the N coast of America from the Pacific; but he was forced to turn back, and was killed by natives on Hawaii.

Cook, Peter (Edward) (1937–95) Comedian and actor, born in Torquay, Devon. He became known as one of the performers in *Beyond the Fringe* (1959–64), and for his collaboration with Dudley Moore in the television series *Not Only... But Also* (1965–71).

Cook, Robin, popular name of **Robert Finlayson Cook** (1946–2005) British statesman, born in Bellshill, Lanarkshire. He became an MP in 1974, held various posts in the shadow cabinet, and was chairman of the Labour

Party (1996–8). He became foreign secretary in the Labour government (1997) and Leader of the Commons (2001), but resigned in 2003 over his opposition to the Iraq War.

Cook, Sue, popular name of **Susan Lorraine Cook** (1949–) British broadcaster. She joined Capital Radio as a producer and presenter (1974–6), then moved to the BBC. She became well known for her television work, including *Breakfast Time*, *Holiday*, and *Crimewatch UK*. In 2005 she began presenting *Making History* for BBC Radio 4.

Cook, Thomas (1808–92) Railway excursion and tourist pioneer, born in Melbourne, Derbyshire. He organized his first railway excursion in 1841, from Leicester to Loughborough, and his travel agency is now a worldwide organization.

Cooke, (Alfred) Alistair (1908–2004) Journalist and broadcaster, born in Manchester, Greater Manchester. He settled in the USA in 1937, where he became a commentator on current affairs. At his death, his 'Letter from America', (1946–2004), was the longest-running solo BBC radio feature programme.

Cookson, Dame Catherine (Ann) (1906–98) Novelist, born in East Jarrow, Tyne and Wear. She published her first book, *Kate Hannigan*, in 1950. Most of her novels are set in the NE of England, several belonging to a series about a single character or family, such as *Tilly Trotter* (1981).

Coolidge, (John) Calvin (1872–1933) US statesman and 30th president (1923–29), born in Plymouth, VT. A strong supporter of US business interests, he was triumphantly re-elected by the Republicans in 1924, but refused renomination in 1928 after the stock-market crash which began the depression.

Cooper, Gary (Frank), popular name of **Frank James Cooper** (1901–61) Film actor, born in Helena, MT. He was the archetypal hero of many Westerns, notably in *High Noon* (1952, Oscar), and starred in the Hemingway epics *A Farewell to Arms* (1932) and *For Whom the Bell Tolls* (1943).

Cooper, Sir Henry (1934–) Boxer, born in Bellingham, Kent, the only man to win the Lonsdale Belt outright on three occasions. He won his first British heavyweight title in 1959. His only world title fight was in 1966, losing to Muhammad Ali. After losing to Joe Bugner in 1971, he announced his retirement.

Cooper, James Fenimore (1789–1851) Novelist, born in Burlington, NJ. He is best known for his frontier adventure stories such as *The Last of the Mohicans* (1826; filmed 1936, 1992) and *The Pathfinder* (1840).

Cooper, Jilly, *née* **Sallitt** (1937–) Writer and journalist, born in London. A Sunday columnist for many years, her books include general interest works, such as *Angels Rush In* (1990). Among her novels are *Polo* (1991) and *Wicked!* (2006).

Cope, Wendy (Mary) (1945–) Poet, writer, and journalist, born in Kent. Her first collection of poems, *Making Cocoa for Kingsley Amis*, was published in 1986. She won the Cholmondeley Award for poetry in 1987 and the Michael Braude Award for

Light Verse in 1995. She has also written many books for children.

Copernicus, Nicolas, Polish **Mikolaj Kopernik** (1473–1543) The founder of modern astronomy, born in Toruń, Poland. His treatise *On the Revolutions of the Celestial Spheres* (trans, completed 1530) had a hostile reception when it was published (1543), as it challenged the ancient teaching of the Earth as the centre of the universe.

Copland, Aaron (1900–90) Composer, born in New York City. Among his compositions are those tapping a deep vein of US tradition and folk music, as in the ballets *Billy the Kid* (1938) and *Appalachian Spring* (1944). He also composed film scores, two operas, and three symphonies.

Coppola, Francis Ford (1939–) Film director and screenwriter, born in Detroit, MI. Among his outstanding productions are *The Godfather* (1972; *Part II*, 1974; *Part III*, 1990) and his controversial study of the Vietnam War, *Apocalypse Now* (1979).

Corbett, Ronnie, popular name of **Ronald Balfour Corbett** (1930–) Comedian, born in Edinburgh. His diminutive stature and comic monologues gained him national popularity, known especially for the television series *Sorry!* (1981–8) and *The Two Ronnies* (1971–87), with Ronnie Barker.

Corbusier, Le *see* Le Corbusier

Corneille, Pierre (1606–84) Playwright, born in Rouen, France. A master of the alexandrine verse form, his major tragedies include *Le Cid* (1636), *Horace* (1639), and *Polyeucte* (1640). *The Liar* (trans, 1642) entitles

him to be called the father of French comedy as well as of French tragedy.

Cornwall, Duchess of, formerly **Camilla (Rosemary) Parker Bowles,** née **Shand** (1947–) Consort of Charles, Prince of Wales, the eldest son of Elizabeth II of the United Kingdom. She first met Prince Charles in 1970. In 1973 she married cavalry officer Andrew Parker Bowles (divorced 1995); they have two children. Following Charles's divorce from Princess Diana (1996), Camilla became Charles's constant companion. The couple were married in 2005 at a civil ceremony in Windsor Guildhall.

Cornwallis, Charles Cornwallis, 1st Marquess (1738–1805) British general and statesman, born in London. In the American War of Independence, he defeated Gates at Camden (1780), but was forced to surrender at Yorktown (1781). As Governor-General of India (1786), he defeated Tippoo Sahib, and introduced the series of reforms known as the *Cornwallis Code.*

Cornwell, Patricia (Daniels) (1957–) Novelist, born in Miami, FL. In the 1990s she became one of the world's best-selling women novelists, known especially for the character of medical examiner Dr Kay Scarpetta introduced in her first novel *Postmortem* (1990). Later books include *Blow Fly* (2003) and *Predator* (2005).

Correggio, originally **Antonio Allegri** (c.1494–1534) Renaissance painter, born in Correggio, Italy. In 1518 he began his great series of mythological frescoes for the convent of San Paolo at Parma. His many pictures on religious themes include 'The Adoration of the Shepherds', known as 'The Night' (c.1530).

Cortés, Hernán, also spelled **Cortéz** (1485–1547) The conqueror of Mexico, born in Medellín, Spain. In 1519 he commanded an expedition against Mexico, founded Vera Cruz, then marched on the Aztec capital, capturing the king, Montezuma. After the Mexicans rose, he was forced to flee, but a siege of the capital led to its fall in 1521.

Cosby, Bill, popular name of **William Henry Cosby** (1937–) Comedian, born in Philadelphia, PA. His television successes include the series *I Spy* (1965–8), for which he won three Emmy Awards, and his own *The Cosby Show* (1984–92, 1996) which consistently topped the ratings. His films include *California Suite* (1978) and *Leonard: Part VI* (1987).

Cosmas and **Damian, Saints** (3rd-c) Arabian twin brothers, said to have been physicians at Aegaea, Cilicia. They were cast into the sea as Christians, rescued by an angel, but then beheaded by Diocletian. They are the patron saints of physicians.

Costello, Elvis, originally **Declan Patrick MacManus** (1955–) Singer and songwriter, born in London. His debut album, *My Aim Is True*, established his reputation. For his second album, *This Year's Model* (1978), he was joined by The Attractions, a three-piece group who worked with him on most of his albums over the next eight years. His work on the soundtrack for *Cold Mountain* (2003) earned him an Oscar nomination.

Costello, Lou *see* Abbott and Costello

Costner, Kevin (1955–) Film actor and director, born in Compton, CA. He established his acting career with *Bull Durham* (1988) and *Field of Dreams* (1989), then directed and starred in *Dances With Wolves* (1990, 7 Oscars). Later films include *JFK* (1991), *Waterworld* (1995), and *The Upside of Anger* (2005).

Cotten, Joseph (1905–94) Film actor, born in Los Angeles, CA. A member of Orson Welles Mercury Theater radio ensemble from 1937, his films include *Citizen Kane* (1941), *The Magnificent Ambersons* (1942), and *The Third Man* (1949).

Coulomb, Charles (Augustin de) (1736–1806) Physicist, born in Angoulême, France. He invented the torsion balance for measuring the force of magnetic and electrical attraction. The *coulomb*, the unit of quantity in measuring current electricity, is named after him.

Courrèges, André (1923–) Fashion designer, born in Pau, France. He opened his own house in Paris in 1961. Famous for stark, futuristic, 'Space Age' designs, he produces ready-to-wear as well as couture clothes.

Courtenay, Tom, popular name of **Sir Thomas Daniel Courtenay** (1937–) Actor, born in Hull. He won acclaim for his stage performance as Norman in the Ayckbourn comedy trilogy, *The Norman Conquests* (1974). His films include *The Loneliness of the Long-Distance Runner* (1962), *Billy Liar* (1963), *Doctor Zhivago* (1965), and *The Dresser* (1983). Television work includes *A Rather English Marriage* (1998, BAFTA).

Cousins, Robin (1957–) Ice skater, born in Bristol. In 1980 he became only the second British male to win an Olympic figure-skating gold medal, and he was world freeskating champion for three successive years (1978–80). He turned professional in 1980, and has been artistic director of the Ice Castle International Training Center in California since 1989. He retired from professional ice skating in 2000.

Cousteau, Jacques (Yves) (1910–97) Naval officer and underwater explorer, born in Saint-André, France. He invented the aqualung diving apparatus (1943) and a process of underwater television. He wrote widely on his subject, and his films included *The Golden Fish* (1960, Oscar).

Coward, Sir Noel (Pierce) (1899–1973) Actor, playwright, and composer, born in London. His many successful plays include *The Vortex* (1924), *Hay Fever* (1925), *Private Lives* (1930), and *Blithe Spirit* (1941), all showing a strong satirical humour. He wrote the music and lyrics for most of his works, and was an accomplished singer.

Cowdrey (of Tonbridge), Lord (Michael) Colin (1932–2000) Cricketer, born in Putumala, India. He captained Kent, played in 114 Tests for England (23 as captain), and scored 7624 runs, including 22 centuries. He became chairman of the International Cricket Council (1989–93). His son, **Chris Cowdrey** (1957–), has also captained England.

Cowell, Simon (1959–) Record producer and manager, born in Brighton, East Sussex. In 2001 he was a judge on the first series of UK's Pop Idol show, and again for American Idol (2002–). With his production company, Syco, he created, and was a judge on, British TV talent show, *The X Factor* (2004–). Known for his acerbic humour, he published *I Don't Mean to be Rude, But...* in 2004.

Cowper, William (1731–1800) Poet, born in Berkhamsted, Hertfordshire. He collaborated with the clergyman John Newton to write the *Olney Hymns* (1779). His ballad of John Gilpin (1783) was highly successful, as was his long poem about rural ease, *The Task* (1785).

Cox (Arquette), Courteney (1964–) Actress, born in Birmingham, AL. She became well known through her role as Monica Geller in the acclaimed television series *Friends* (1994–2004). Her feature film roles include *Scream* and its sequel (1996, 1998). She married actor David Arquette in 1999.

Cradock, Fanny, *née* **Phyllis Primrose-Pechey** (1909–94) British writer and television cook. From 1955 she became known for the television programmes presented with her husband, Johnny. She wrote cookery books, children's books, novels, and press columns which were notorious for their social pretension and outspoken opinions.

Cram, Steve, popular name of **Stephen Cram** (1960–) Athlete, born in Gateshead, Tyne and Wear. He won the World Championship gold medal at 1500 m in 1983, and the Commonwealth Games gold medals at 1500 m (1982, 1986) and 800 m (1986). In 1985 he set three world records in 20 days at 1500 m, 1 mi, and 2000 m.

Cranmer, Thomas (1489–1556) Archbishop of Canterbury (from 1523), born in Aslockton, Nottinghamshire. He annulled Henry VIII's marriages to Catherine of Aragon and to Anne Boleyn (1536), divorced him from Anne of Cleves (1540), and was largely responsible for the Book of Common Prayer (1549, 1552). On Henry's death, he agreed to the plan to divert the succession from Mary I to Lady Jane Grey (1553), for which he was arraigned for treason and burned alive.

Crawford, Joan, originally **Lucille Fay Le Sueur** (1904–77) Film actress, born in San Antonio, TX. Her films include *Mildred Pierce* (1945, Oscar) and *Whatever Happened to Baby Jane?* (1962), in which she co-starred with her long-standing rival, Bette Davis.

Crawford, Michael (1942–) Actor and singer, born in Salisbury, Wiltshire. The 1970s television series, *Some Mothers Do 'Ave 'Em*, made him a household name in Britain. He went on to star in such musicals as *Barnum* (1981), *The Phantom of the Opera* (1986, Tony), and *The Woman in White* (2004). His films include *Hello Dolly* (1968) and *Condorman* (1980).

Crazy Horse, Sioux name **Tashunka Witco** (c.1842–77) Oglala Sioux chief, born near the Black Hills, SD. He fought in all the major Sioux actions to protect the Black Hills against white intrusion, defeating Custer's forces at Little Bighorn in 1876. He is regarded as a symbol of Sioux resistance and as their greatest leader.

Crick, Francis (Harry Compton)
(1916–2004) Biophysicist, born in Northampton, Northamptonshire. In 1953, he and J D Watson constructed a molecular model of the genetic material DNA, and in 1958 he proposed that DNA determines the sequence of amino acids in a polypeptide through a triplet code. He shared the Nobel Prize for Physiology or Medicine in 1962.

Crippen, Hawley Harvey, known as **Dr Crippen** (1862–1910) Physician and murderer, born in Michigan, USA. After poisoning his second wife, he and his mistress attempted to escape to Canada on board the SS *Montrose*, but they were arrested, and he was hanged in London.

Crockett, Davy, popular name of **David Crockett** (1786–1836) Backwoodsman, born in Green Co, TN. He distinguished himself against the Creek Indians in Jackson's campaign of 1814, and died fighting for Texas at the Battle of the Alamo.

Crompton, Samuel (1753–1827) Inventor of the spinning-mule, born in Firwood, Greater Manchester. In 1779 he devised a machine which produced yarn of astonishing fineness, and although he was forced to sell his idea to a Bolton manufacturer, he was later awarded a national grant.

Cromwell, Oliver (1599–1658) English soldier and statesman, born in Huntingdon, Cambridgeshire. A convinced Puritan, he sat in both the Short and the Long Parliaments (1640), and when war broke out (1642) he formed his unconquerable Ironsides, combining rigid discipline with strict morality, securing victory at Marston Moor (1644) and Naseby (1645). He brought Charles I to trial, and was one of the signatories of his death warrant (1649). Having established the Commonwealth, he suppressed the Levellers, Ireland (1649–50), and the Scots (1650–1), and established a Protectorate (1653). He was succeeded by his son, Richard, who was forced into French exile in 1659.

Cromwell, Richard (1626–1712) English statesman, the third son of Oliver Cromwell. In 1658 he succeeded his father as Lord Protector, but fell out with parliament, which he dissolved in 1659. He recalled the Rump Parliament but was forced to abdicate in 1659.

Cronenberg, David (1943–) Film director and screenplay writer, born in Toronto, Ontario, Canada. A prolific and acclaimed exponent of the horror film genre, his works include *The Dead Zone* (1983) and *The Fly* (1986), which gave him cult status. Among later films are *Crash* (1996) and *A History of Violence* (2005).

Cronin, A(rchibald) J(oseph) (1896–1981) Novelist, born in Cardross, Argyll and Bute. His books include *The Citadel* (1937) and *The Keys of the Kingdom* (1942). The television series *Dr Finlay's Casebook* was based on his stories.

Crosby, Bing, popular name of **Harry Lillis Crosby** (1904–77) Singer and film star, born in Tacoma, WA. His distinctive style of crooning made his recordings of 'White Christmas' and 'Silent Night' the hits of the century. He starred in many films, notably the *Road* films with Bob Hope and **Dorothy Lamour** (1914–96), *Going My Way* (1944, Oscar), *White Christmas* (1954), and *High Society* (1956).

Crowe, Russell (1964–) Actor, born in Wellington, New Zealand. His films include *The Insider* (1999, Oscar nomination), *Gladiator* (2000, Best Actor Oscar), *A Beautiful Mind* (2001, Best Actor Golden Globe, BAFTA), *Master and Commander* (2003), and *Cinderella Man* (2005).

Cruft, Charles (1852–1939) British showman who organized the first dog show in London in 1886. The annual shows have since become world-famous, and have helped to improve standards of dog-breeding.

Cruise, Tom (1962–) Film actor, born in Syracuse, NY. His films include *Top Gun* (1985) and *Rain Man* (1988), and he won Oscar nominations for *Born on the Fourth of July* (1989) and *Jerry Maguire* (1996). Among later films are *The Last Samurai* (2003) and *War of the Worlds* (2005). He was married (1990–2001) to actress Nicole Kidman.

Cruyff, Johann (1947–) Footballer, born in Amsterdam. A player for Ajax, in 1974 he captained Holland in the World Cup final (beaten by West Germany). He joined Barcelona as manager in 1988, guiding the Spanish champions to the European Cup in 1992.

Cruz, Penélope (1974–) Actress, born in Madrid. Her work for the Spanish cinema includes *Belle Epoque* (1993) and *All About My Mother* (1999), both of which won Best Foreign Film Oscars. Among her Hollywood film credits are *Captain Corelli's Mandolin* (2001) and *Sahara* (2005).

Crystal, Billy (1947–) Film actor, born in Long Beach, NY. Well known for his role in the American comedy series, *Soap*, his feature films include *Throw Momma From the Train* (1987), *When Harry Met Sally* (1989), *Forget Paris* (1995), which he also directed, and *Analyze This* (1999, sequel 2002).

Cummings, E(dward) E(stlin) (1894–1962) Writer and painter, born in Cambridge, MA. His several successful collections of poetry, starting with *Tulips and Chimneys* (1923), are striking for their unorthodox typography and linguistic style. *Complete Poems* appeared in 1968.

Cunard, Sir Samuel (1787–1865) Shipowner, born in Halifax, Nova Scotia, Canada. He emigrated to Britain in 1838, and in 1839 helped to found the British and North American Royal Mail Steam Packet Co, later known as the Cunard Line.

Cunningham, Jack, popular name of **John Cunningham** (1939–) British statesman, born in Felling, Durham. A Labour MP from 1970, he served as minister for energy (1976–9) in the Callaghan government, and under Blair was minister for agriculture (1997–8) and chancellor of the Duchy of Lancaster (1998–9).

Cunningham, Merce (1919–) Dancer, choreographer, teacher, and director, born in Centralia, WA. He danced with the Martha Graham Company (1939–45), starting his own company in 1952.

Cunobelinus *see* Cymbeline

Curie, Marie, *née* **Manya Sklodowska** (1867–1934) Physicist, born in War-saw, who worked in Paris with her French husband **Pierre Curie** (1859–1906) on magnetism and radioactivity. Together they discovered and isolated polonium and radium in 1898, and shared the 1903 Nobel Prize for Physics with Becquerel for the discovery of radioactivity. In 1910 she published her treatise on radioactivity, and was awarded the Nobel Prize for Chemistry in 1911.

Curtis, Tony, originally **Bernard Schwarz** (1925–) Actor, born in New York City. He proved he could play comedy roles as in *Some Like It Hot* (1959) while also displaying his dramatic ability in *The Boston Strangler* (1968). Other films include *Spartacus* (1960) and *The Mirror Crack'd* (1980). He was formerly married to actress Janet Leigh. Their daughters, **Kelly Curtis** (1956–) and **Jamie Lee Curtis** (1958–), are both actresses.

Cushing, Peter (1913–94) Actor, born in Kenley, Greater London. He was chiefly known for his long association with the Gothic horror films produced by Hammer Studios, such as *The Curse of Frankenstein* (1956) and *Dracula* (1958), as well as films in which he played Sherlock Holmes.

Custer, George Armstrong (1839–76) US soldier, born in New Rumley, OH. He led his 7th US Cavalry to a massive defeat by a combined Sioux–Cheyenne force at the Little Bighorn, MT (25 Jun 1876), with no survivors from his immediate command ('Custer's Last Stand').

Cuthbert, St (c.635–87) Missionary, born in Ireland or Northumbria. He became Bishop of Hexham (684) and of Lindisfarne, but soon returned to his hermit cell on the island of Farne.

Cymbeline, also known as **Cunobelinus** (?–c.43) Pro-Roman king of the Catuvellauni, who from his capital at Camulodunum (Colchester) ruled most of SE Britain. Shakespeare's character was based on Holinshed's half-historical Cunobelinus.

Cyprian, St, originally **Thascius Caecilius Cyprianus** (c.200–58) One of the great Fathers of the Church, probably born in Carthage. As Bishop of Carthage (248), his zealous efforts to restore strict discipline forced him to flee, eventually suffering martyrdom under Valerian.

Cyrano de Bergerac, Savinien (1619–55) Satirist and playwright, born in Paris. In his youth he fought more than a thousand duels, mostly on account of his extremely large nose. His life was the subject of the play by Edmond Rostand (1897).

Cyril, St (c.827–69) Christian missionary and saint, born in Thessaloniki, Greece, who with his brother **St Methodius** (c.825–85), also born in Thessaloniki, became missionaries to the Slavs. They went to Moravia, where they prepared a Slavonic translation of the Scriptures and the chief liturgical books, and introduced a new, Greek-based alphabet (the *Cyrillic alphabet*).

Dafoe, Willem (1955–) Film actor, born in Appleton, WI. He made his film debut in *Heaven's Gate* (1980), and went on to the Oscar-nominated role of Sergeant Elias in *Platoon* (1986) and the controversial title role in *The Last Temptation of Christ* (1988). Later films include *The English Patient* (1996) and *Manderlay* (2005).

Dahl, Roald (1916–90) Writer, born in Llandaff, Cardiff, of Norwegian parents. A specialist in short stories of unexpected horror and macabre surprise, his children's books also display a taste for the grotesque, such as *James and the Giant Peach* (1961), *Charlie and the Chocolate Factory* (1964), and *The BFG* (1982).

Daimler, Gottlieb (Wilhelm) (1834–1900) Engineer, born in Schorndorf, Germany. In 1885 he patented a high-speed internal combustion engine, and in 1889 designed one of the earliest roadworthy motor cars. He founded the Daimler Automobile Co in 1890.

Dalai Lama (Mongolian, 'ocean-like guru') (1935–) Spiritual and temporal head of Tibet, currently **Tenzin Gyatso** (1935–), born in Taktser, China, into a peasant family. He was designated the 14th Dalai Lama in 1937. Following Chinese suppression, he was forced into exile in India, where he established a democratically-based alternative government. He was awarded the Nobel Peace Prize in 1989.

Daldry, Stephen (1960–) Film and theatre director, born in Dorset. In London he became artistic director of the English Stage Company (1992–9) and associate director of the Royal Court (1999). He received Best Director Oscar nominations for the films *Billy Elliot* (2000) and *The Hours* (2002), and directed the West End stage musical version of *Billy Elliot* (2005).

Dalglish, Kenny, popular name of **Kenneth Mathieson Dalglish** (1951–) Footballer and manager, born in Glasgow. He joined Glasgow Celtic in 1967, transferring to Liverpool in 1977, and won 102 caps for Scotland. He later became manager of Liverpool, while still a player. He joined Newcastle United as manager (1997–8), returning to Celtic as director of football in 1999.

Dali, Salvador (Felipe Jacinto), Span Dalí (1904–89) Artist, born in Figueras, Spain. A principal figure of the Surrealist movement, his study of abnormal psychology and dream symbolism led him to represent 'paranoiac' objects in landscapes remembered from his boyhood. One of his best-known paintings is 'The Persistence of Memory' (known as 'The Limp Watches', 1931).

Dalton, John (1766–1844) Chemist,

born in Eaglesfield, Cumbria. He first described colour blindness (*Daltonism*) in 1794. His chief physical research was into mixed gases, the force of steam, the elasticity of vapours, and the expansion of gases by heat, his law of partial pressures being also known as *Dalton's law*. In chemistry, his work on atomic theory (c.1810) gave a new basis for all quantitative chemistry.

Damocles (4th-c BC) Legendary courtier of the elder **Dionysius, tyrant of Syracuse** (405–367 BC). Damocles was shown the precarious nature of fortune in a singular manner: while seated at a richly spread table, he looked up to see a keen-edged sword suspended over his head by a single horse-hair.

Damon, Matt (1970–) Film actor, born in Cambridge, MA. He starred in *The Rainmaker* (1997), and *Good Will Hunting* (1997), for which he shared an Oscar for Best Original Screenplay with co-star Ben Affleck. Later films include *Saving Private Ryan* (1998), *The Talented Mr Ripley* (1999) and *The Bourne Identity* (2002, sequel 2004).

Damon and Pythias, also found as **Phintias** (4th-c BC) Two Pythagoreans of Syracuse, remembered as the models of faithful friendship. Condemned to death by the elder **Dionysius, tyrant of Syracuse** (405–367 BC), Pythias begged to be allowed home to arrange his affairs, and Damon pledged his own life for his friend's. Pythias returned just in time to save Damon from death. Struck by so noble an example, the tyrant pardoned Pythias.

Dampier, William (1652–1715) Navigator and buccaneer, born in East Coker, Somerset. In 1683 he crossed the Pacific, visiting the Philippines, China, and Australia. He later led voyages to the South Seas, exploring the NW coast of Australia, and naming the *Dampier Archipelago* and *Strait*.

Danes, Claire (Catherine) (1979–) Actress, born in New York City. She became known through her role in the US television series *My So-Called Life* (1994–5), and went on to star as Juliet in *William Shakespeare's Romeo and Juliet* (1996). Later films include *Igby Goes Down* (2002) and *Stage Beauty* (2004).

Dankworth, Sir John (Philip William), known as **Johnny Dankworth** (1927–) Jazz musician, composer, and arranger, born in London. An accomplished saxophonist, and bandleader since 1953, he has also composed works for combined jazz and symphonic ensembles, and film scores. He has recorded many albums with his wife, singer **Cleo Laine** (1927–), and in 1993 formed the Dankworth Generation Band, with son Alec.

Dannay, Frederic, originally **Daniel Nathan** (1905–82) Novelist, born in New York City. First cousin to **Manfred B Lee** (originally **Manford Lepofsky** (1905–71)), also born in New York City. They wrote many popular books, using 'Ellery Queen' both as their pseudonym and as the name of their detective. They also used the pseudonym **Barnaby Ross** as the author of their other detective, Drury Lane.

Dante (Alighieri) (1265–1321) Poet, born in Florence, Italy. In 1274, a meeting with **Beatrice** (c.1265–90), possibly the daughter of Florentine aristocrat Folco Portinari, influenced the rest of his life. The *Vita nuova*, which tells of his boyish passion for Beatrice, is probably his earliest work. By far the most celebrated is the *Divina commedia* (Divine Comedy), a vision of hell, purgatory, and heaven which gives an encyclopedic view of the highest culture and knowledge of his age.

Danton, Georges (Jacques) (1759–94) French revolutionary politician, born in Arcis-sur-Aube, France. He formed the Cordelier's Club (1790), voted for the death of the king (1793), and was a member of the Committee of Public Safety. He tried to abate the severity of his own Revolutionary Tribunal, but lost the leadership to Robespierre, and was guillotined.

Darling, Grace (1815–42) Heroine, born in Bamburgh, Northumberland. She lived with her father, **William** (1795–1860), the lighthouse keeper on one of the Farne Islands. In 1838, she braved raging seas in an open rowing boat to rescue the survivors of the stranded *Forfarshire*.

Darwin, Charles (Robert) (1809–82) Naturalist, born in Shrewsbury, Shropshire, the grandson of Erasmus Darwin. He studied medicine at Edinburgh (1825), then biology at Cambridge (1828). In 1831–6 he was the naturalist on HMS *Beagle*, surveying South American waters. From 1842 he devoted himself to his epoch-making work, *On the Origin of Species by Means of Natural Selection* (1859).

He wrote many other works on plants and animals, but is remembered primarily as the leader in the field of evolutionary biology.

Davenport, Lindsay (1976–) Tennis player, born in Palos Verde, CA. In 1996 she won the Olympic gold medal, in 1997 four titles, and in 1998 three, including the US Open. Later achievements include the Wimbledon singles title (1999) and the Australian Open (2000). She began 2005 and 2006 as the world number 1.

David (?–c.962 BC) Second king of Israel. According to Jewish tradition he is the author of several of the Psalms, and according to some Christian traditions the ancestor of Jesus. A warrior under King Saul, his successes against the Philistines (including the killing of Goliath) caused the king's jealousy, and he was forced to become an outlaw. After Saul's death, he became king of all Israel, making Jerusalem the centre of his kingdom, and building his palace on its highest hill, Zion (the 'city of David'). He was succeeded by Solomon, his son by Bathsheba.

David or **Dewi, St** (?–601) Patron saint of Wales, born near St Bride's Bay, Pembrokeshire. He was Bishop of Moni Judeorum, or Menevia (afterwards St David's), and founded many churches in S Wales.

David, Hal (1921–) Lyricist, born in Brooklyn, NY. He teamed up with composer Burt Bacharach in 1957 and among their many successful songs are '24 Hours From Tulsa' (1964), 'Walk On By' (1964), and 'What's New, Pussycat?' (1965). He received an Academy Award for 'Raindrops Keep Falling On My Head' (1969).

Davies, Sir Peter Maxwell (1934–) Composer, born in Manchester, Greater Manchester. He founded and co-directed the Pierrot Players (1967–70) and was founder/artistic director of The Fires of London (1971–87). A prolific composer, his works include *Taverner* (1972) and three other operas, symphonies, concertos, songs, and chamber music. He was made composer laureate in 1994 and Master of the Queen's Musick in 2004.

Davies, Siobhan, originally **Susan Davies** (1950–) Dancer and choreographer, born in London. She started her own modern dance company in 1981, joined with Ian Spink to found Second Stride, and in 1988 launched the Siobhan Davies Company.

da Vinci, Leonardo *see* Leonardo da Vinci

Davis, Sir Andrew (Frank) (1944–) Conductor, born at Ashridge House, Hertfordshire. He became musical director of the Toronto Symphony Orchestra (1975–88), then music director of the Glyndebourne Festival Opera, and (from 1989) chief conductor of the BBC Symphony Orchestra. In 2000 he was appointed director of the Chicago Lyric Opera.

Davis, Bette, popular name of **Ruth Elizabeth Davis** (1908–89) Film actress, born in Lowell, MA. Her leading roles included *Of Human Bondage* (1934), *Dangerous* (1935, Oscar), *Jezebel* (1938, Oscar), and *Whatever Happened to Baby Jane?* (1962).

Davis, Carl (1936–) Composer and conductor, born in New York City. Among his works for ballet are *Liaison Amoureuses* (1988) and *Alice in Wonderland* (1995). His music for television includes *The World at War* (1972, Emmy) and *Pride and Prejudice* (1995), and for film *The French Lieutenant's Woman* (1981, BAFTA).

Davis, Sir Colin (Rex) (1927–) Conductor, born in Weybridge, Surrey. He was chief conductor of the BBC Symphony Orchestra (1967–71), and musical director at Covent Garden (1971–86) where his production of *The Ring* gained him international standing as a Wagner conductor. He became principal conductor of the London Symphony Orchestra in 1995.

Davis, Geena (1957–) Film actress, born in Wareham, MA. She won a Best Supporting Actress Oscar for *The Accidental Tourist* (1988), and critical acclaim for her role as Thelma in *Thelma and Louise* (1991). Later films include *The Long Kiss Goodnight* (1996) and *Stuart Little* (1999, sequels 2002, 2005).

Davis, Jefferson (Finis) (1808–89) US statesman, president of the Confederate States during the Civil War (1861–5), born in Christian Co, KY. In the US Senate he led the extreme States' Rights Party, supported slavery, and was chosen president of the Confederacy. At the close of the Civil War he was imprisoned for two years, and included in the amnesty of 1868.

Davis, Miles (Dewey) (1926–91) Trumpeter, composer, and bandleader, born in Alton, IL. He became the most admired instrumentalist of the post-war era, from 1948 leading a nonet that introduced the style known as 'cool jazz', as in 'Round About Midnight' (1955) and 'Milestones' (1958).

Davis, Sammy, Jr (1925–90) Singer, actor, and dancer, born in New York City. He starred on Broadway in *Mr Wonderful* (1956) and in *Golden Boy* (1964), and his films include *Porgy and Bess* (1959), *Robin and the Seven Hoods* (1964), and *Taps* (1980).

Davis, Steve (1957–) Snooker player, born in London. He dominated snooker in the 1980s, winning the world championship six times: 1981, 1983–4, and 1987–9. In 1997 he made a comeback winning the Benson & Hedges Masters title.

Davy, Sir Humphry (1778–1829) Chemist, born in Penzance, Cornwall. He found that chemical compounds could be decomposed into their elements using electricity, and in this way discovered potassium, sodium, barium, strontium, calcium, and magnesium. In 1815 he invented the miner's safety lamp.

Dawkins, (Clinton) Richard (1941–) British zoologist, born in Nairobi, Kenya. His work on animal behaviour and genetics emphasizes that apparently selfish behaviour is designed to ensure survival of the gene, apparently above that of the carrier. Known for his successful scientific popularizations, as well as for his aggressive atheism, his works include *The Selfish Gene* (1976) and *The Ancestor's Tale* (2004).

Day, Doris, originally **Doris Kappelhoff** (1924–) Singer and film actress, born in Cincinnati, OH. Her sunny personality made her a star of many musicals, her films including *Calamity Jane* (1953), *The Pajama Game* (1957), and the comedy *Pillow Talk* (1959), which earned her an Oscar nomination.

Day, Sir Robin (1923–2000) Journalist and broadcaster, born in London. He presented BBC television's *Panorama* (1967–72) and *Question Time* (1979–89), brought an acerbic freshness to interviewing techniques, and proved a formidable inquisitor of political figures.

Dayan, Moshe (1915–81) Israeli general and statesman, born in Deganya, Palestine. He won international acclaim as defence minister in 1967 when his heavily outnumbered forces triumphed over Egypt, Jordan, and Syria in the Six Day War. As foreign minister, he helped to secure the historic peace treaty with Egypt (1977).

Day-Lewis, C(ecil) (1904–72) Poet, born in Ballintubber, Co Kildare, Ireland. During the 1930s he was known as a leading left-wing writer. His *Collected Poems* appeared in 1954, and he became poet laureate in 1968. He also wrote detective stories under the pseudonym of **Nicholas Blake**.

Day-Lewis, Daniel (1957–) Film actor, born in London. His films include *My Beautiful Launderette* (1985), *Room With A View* (1985), the much-acclaimed portrayal of handicapped Irish writer Christy Brown in *My Left Foot* (1989, Oscar), and *Gangs of New York* (2002, BAFTA, Oscar nomination).

Dean, Christopher *see* Torvill and Dean

Dean, Dixie, popular name of **Wil-**

liam Ralph Dean (1907–80) Footballer, born in Birkenhead, Merseyside. He joined Everton in 1925, and scored 349 goals in 399 games. He still holds the scoring record of 60 League goals in one season.

Dean, James (Byron) (1931–55) Film actor, born in Marion, IN. He gained overnight success in the film *East of Eden* (1955), and made only two more films, *Rebel Without a Cause* (1955) and *Giant* (1956), before his early death in a car crash turned him into a cult figure.

Deayton, (Gordon) Angus (1956–) Writer and broadcaster, born in Caterham, Surrey. He became well known for his role in BBC television's *One Foot in the Grave* (from 1989), and went on to host *Have I Got News for You* (1990–2002). He later presented the series *Help Your Self* (2006).

de Beauvoir, Simone (1908–86) Existentialist writer, born in Paris. Closely associated with Sartre, her works provide existentialism with an essentially feminine sensibility, notably in *The Second Sex* (trans, 1949) and her masterpiece *Les Mandarins* (1954, Prix Goncourt).

de Bono, Edward (Francis Charles Publius) (1933–) Psychologist and writer, born in Malta. He is involved with various organizations to promote the skills of thinking which break out of the limitations of the traditional (*lateral thinking*). His books include *The Use of Lateral Thinking* (1967) and *I Am Right, You Are Wrong* (1990).

Debussy, (Achille-) Claude (1862–1918) Composer, born in St Germain-en-Laye, France. His early

successes, notably *Prelude to the Afternoon of a Faun* (trans, 1894) and the piano pieces, *Images* and *Préludes*, led to his work being described as 'musical Impressionism', seen also in such orchestral music as *The Sea* (trans, 1905).

Dee, Jack (1962–) British comedian and actor. He became known for his deadpan humour, and since 1990 has toured extensively with his one-man show. Television credits include five series of his own show for Channel 4 and two series of *Jack Dee's Happy Hour* (BBC 2000–1).

Defoe, Daniel (1660–1731) Writer, born in London. Known for his political pamphleteering, he achieved lasting fame with *Robinson Crusoe* (1719–20). His other major works include *A Journal of the Plague Year*, *Moll Flanders* (both 1722), and *Roxana* (1724).

Degas, (Hilaire Germain) Edgar (1834–1917) Artist, born in Paris. He associated with the Impressionists and took part in most of their exhibitions from 1874 to 1886. Among his best-known works are 'Dancer Lacing her Shoe' (c.1878, Paris) and 'Jockeys in the Rain' (1879).

de Gaulle, Charles (André Joseph Marie) (1890–1970) French general and first president of the Fifth Republic (1958–69), born in Lille, France. With the fall of France, he fled to England to raise the standard of the 'Free French', and led a liberation force into Paris in 1944. As president he practised a high-handed yet successful foreign policy, repeatedly surviving political crises by the use of the referendum. He developed an independent French nuclear deterrent, granted independence to former colonies, signed a historic reconciliation treaty with West Germany, and blocked Britain's entry into the European Economic Community.

de Havilland, Sir Geoffrey (1882–1965) Aircraft designer, born in Haslemere, Surrey. He built his first plane in 1908 and became director of the firm bearing his name, producing such aircraft as the Tiger Moth, Mosquito, and Vampire jet.

De Havilland, Olivia (Mary) (1916–) Actress, born in Tokyo. Brought up in the USA, she joined Warner Brothers (1935–42). She received Best Supporting Actress nominations for her roles in *Gone With the Wind* (1939) and *Hold Back The Dawn* (1941), and won Oscars for *To Each His Own* (1946) and *The Heiress* (1949).

Deighton, Len, popular name of **Leonard Cyril Deighton** (1929–) Thriller writer, born in London. A leading author of spy novels, notable titles are *The Ipcress File* (1962), *Funeral in Berlin* (1964), and the trilogy *Berlin Game* (1984), *Mexico Set* (1985), and *London Match* (1986).

de Klerk, F(rederick) W(illem) (1936–) South African president (1989–94), born in Johannesburg, South Africa. He set about the dismantling of apartheid, releasing Nelson Mandela (1990), and signing a new constitutional agreement with him (1993), for which both men were awarded the Nobel Peace Prize. From 1994–6 he served as vice-president in the Mandela administration.

de la Mare, Walter (John) (1873–1956) Writer, born in Charlton, Kent. Among his best-known works are the prose romance *Henry Brocken* (1904), the poetic collection *The Listeners* (1912), and his fantastic novel *Memoirs of a Midget* (1921).

de la Renta, Oscar (1932–) Fashion designer, born in Santo Domingo, Dominican Republic. In 1965 he started his own company, producing opulent, ornately trimmed clothes, particularly evening dresses, and also day wear and accessories.

Delibes, (Clément Philibert) Léo (1836–91) Composer, born in St Germain du Val, France. He wrote light operas, of which *Lakmé* had the greatest success, but he is chiefly remembered for the ballet *Coppélia* (1870).

DeLillo, Don (1936–) Writer, born in New York City. His novels, recognized as leading examples of American postmodernism, include *Americana* (1971), *White Noise* (1984), and *Cosmopolis* (2003). A play, *Love-Lies-Bleeding*, premiered in 2006.

Delius, Frederick (1862–1934) Composer, born in Bradford, West Yorkshire, of German–Scandinavian descent. After 1890 he lived almost entirely in France. He wrote six operas, including *A Village Romeo and Juliet* (1901), and a variety of choral and orchestral works, notably *On Hearing the First Cuckoo in Spring* (1912). In 1924 he became paralyzed and blind, but with the assistance of **Eric Fenby** (1906–97), his amanuensis from 1928, he continued to compose.

Delors, Jacques (1925–) French and European statesman, born in Paris.

He joined the Socialist Party in 1973, served as minister of economy and finance under Mitterrand (1981–4), and was elected President of the European Commission (1985–95).

de los Angeles, Victoria *see* Angeles, Victoria de los

De Mille, Cecil B(lount) (1881–1959) Film producer and director, born in Ashfield, MA. He gained a reputation for box-office spectacles with such films as *The Ten Commandments* (1923, remade 1957), *The Plainsman* (1937), and *The Greatest Show on Earth* (1952).

Demme, Jonathan (1944–) Film director, born in Long Island, NY. He made his cinema directorial debut with *Caged Heat* in 1974. He went on to win a Best Director Oscar for the psychological thriller *Silence of the Lambs* (1991), and later films include *Philadelphia* (1993), *Beloved* (1998), and *The Agronomist* (2004).

Demosthenes (c.383–322 BC) The greatest of the Greek orators. He gained prominence in 351 BC with the first of a series of speeches (the 'First Philippic') advocating resistance to Philip of Macedon. Swayed by his oratory, the Athenians did eventually go to war (340 BC), only to be defeated at Chaeronea (338 BC). Put on trial, he vindicated himself in his oratorical masterpiece, *On the Crown*, but was forced to commit suicide after the failure of the Athenian revolt against Macedon.

Dempsey, Jack, popular name of **William Harrison Dempsey**, nickname **the Manassa Mauler** (1895–1983) World heavyweight champion boxer, born in Manassa, CO. In 1919 he defeated Jess Willard to win the world heavyweight title, which he lost to Gene Tunney in 1926.

Dench, Dame Judi, popular name of **Dame Judith Olivia Dench** (1934–) Actress, born in York, North Yorkshire. A member of the Old Vic Company (1957–61), she became a distinguished classical actress. Her television credits include *A Fine Romance* (1981–4), with husband **Michael Williams** (1935–2001), and her many films include the role of M in the James Bond films *Tomorrow Never Dies* (1997) and *The World is Not Enough* (1999). Among later films are *Iris* (2002, BAFTA Best Actress) and *Mrs Henderson Presents* (2005, Oscar nomination).

Deneuve, Cathérine, originally **Cathérine Dorléac** (1943–) Actress, born in Paris. She became well known through the musical *The Umbrellas of Cherbourg* (trans, 1964), later films including *Repulsion* (1965), *Belle de Jour* (1967), and *The Last Metro* (trans, 1980).

De Niro, Robert (1943–) Actor and director, born in New York City. His films include *The Godfather, Part II* (1974, Oscar), *Taxi Driver* (1976), *The Deerhunter* (1978), *Raging Bull* (1980, Oscar), *Analyze This* (1999, sequel 2002), and *Meet the Fockers* (2004).

Denning (of Whitchurch), Alfred Thompson Denning, Baron (1899–1999) British judge, born in Whitchurch, Hampshire. As Master of the Rolls (1962–82) he was responsible for many often controversial decisions. Among his books are *The Road to Justice* (1955) and *What Next in the Law* (1982).

De Palma, Brian (1940–) Film director, born in Newark, NJ. He made his feature-length debut with *The Wedding Party* (1966), and had commercial success with *Carrie* (1976) and *The Untouchables* (1987). Later films include *Bonfire of the Vanities* (1990), *Mission Impossible* (1996), and *Femme Fatale* (2002).

Dépardieu, Gérard (1948–) Actor, born in Châteauroux, France. His films include *Danton* (1982), *Jean de Florette* (1986), *Cyrano de Bergerac* (1990), *Green Card* (1990), and *San Antonio* (2004). He also directed himself in *Le Tartuffe* (1984).

Depp, Johnny, popular name of **John Christopher Depp II** (1963–) Actor, born in Owensboro, KY. He made his feature film debut in *A Nightmare on Elm Street* (1984) and later films include *Edward Scissorhands* (1990) and *Donnie Brasco* (1997). He received Best Actor Oscar nominations for *Pirates of the Caribbean* (2003) and *Finding Neverland* (2004).

Derby, Edward Geoffrey Smith Stanley, 14th Earl of (1799–1869) British prime minister (1852, 1858–9, 1866–8), born at Knowsley Hall, Lancashire. He entered parliament as a Whig in 1828, and became chief-secretary for Ireland (1830), and colonial secretary (1833), then joined the Conservatives and became party leader (1846–68). His third administration passed the Reform Bill (1867).

Derrida, Jacques (1930–2004) French philosopher-linguist, born in Algeria. His critique of the referentiality of language and the objectivity of structures founded the school of criticism called *deconstruction*. His works include (trans titles) *Of Grammatology* (1967) and *Dissemination* (1972).

Descartes, René, Lat **Renatius Cartesius** (1596–1650) Rationalist philosopher and mathematician, born in La Haye, France. His task was to refound human knowledge on a basis secure from scepticism, expounded in the *Meditations on First Philosophy* (trans, 1641) – a work which introduced his famous principle that one cannot doubt one's own existence as a thinking being, *cogito ergo sum* ('I think, therefore I am'). He virtually founded co-ordinate or analytic geometry, and made major contributions to optics.

de Sica, Vittorio (1901–74) Actor and film director, born in Sora, Italy. A romantic star of Italian stage and screen in the 1930s, he became a director in 1940, achieving international success in the neo-Realist style with (trans titles) *Shoeshine* (1946) and *Bicycle Thieves* (1948).

Dettori, Frankie, popular name of **Lanfranco Dettori** (1970–) British jockey, born in Milan, Italy. His major wins include The Oaks (1994, 1995, 2002), St Leger (1995, 1996), Two Thousand Guineas (1996, 1999), and One Thousand Guineas (1998). He was champion jockey for two successive seasons (1994, 1995), and again in 2004.

de Valera, Eamon (1882–1975) Irish prime minister (1932–48, 1951–4, 1957–9) and president (1959–73), born in New York City. A commandant in the 1916 rising, he became leader of

Sinn Féin (1917–26), was elected president of Dáil Eireann, and in 1926 became leader of Fianna Fáil.

Dewar, Donald (Campbell) (1937–2000) British statesman, born in Glasgow. He became a Labour MP in 1966, becoming Labour chief whip (1995–7). He was secretary of state for Scotland (1997–9), and became Scotland's inaugural first minister in the new Scottish Parliament (1999–2000).

Dewey, John (1859–1952) Philosopher and educator, born in Burlington, VT. A leading exponent of pragmatism, he developed a philosophy of education which stressed development of the person, understanding of the environment, and learning through experience.

Diaghilev, Sergei Pavlovich (1872–1929) Ballet impresario, born in Novgorod, Russia. His company was founded in 1909, and triumphantly toured Europe. Many of the great dancers, composers, and painters of his period contributed to the success of his Ballets Russes, and he also encouraged several major choreographers.

Diamond, Neil (Leslie) (1941–) Singer and songwriter, born in New York City. He wrote the hit 'I'm A Believer' (1966) for the Monkees, and had his first number 1 hit with 'Cracklin' Rosie' (1970). Later albums include *Tennessee Moon* (1996) and *12 Songs* (2005).

Diana, Princess of Wales, formerly **Lady Diana (Frances) Spencer** (1961–97) Former wife of Charles, Prince of Wales, born at Sandringham, Norfolk, the youngest daughter of the 8th Earl Spencer. She married the Prince of Wales in 1981 (separated 1992; divorced 1996). They had two sons, **Prince William (Arthur Philip Louis)** (1982–) and **Prince Henry (Charles Albert David)** (1984–). Seriously interested in social concerns, she became a popular public figure in her own right. She continued to travel and work with a range of good causes, both in Britain and abroad, while receiving unprecedented worldwide media attention, with newspapers competing to report on her family situation and on her (real or imaginary) personal relationships; and it was while trying to escape the pursuit of paparazzi in Paris that she died in a car accident in August 1997. A British inquest into her death was opened in 2004 and was ongoing in 2006.

Diaz or **Dias, Bartolomeu** (c.1450–1500) Navigator and explorer, probably born in Portugal. In 1487 he sailed round the Cape of Good Hope, and discovered Algoa Bay. He also travelled with Vasco da Gama (1497) and with Cabral (1500), but was lost in a storm.

Diaz, Cameron (1972–) Film actress, born in San Diego, CA. In 1994 she auditioned for a small part in *The Mask* and was offered the lead. Later films include *There's Something About Mary* (1998), *Gangs of New York* (2002), and *In Her Shoes* (2005).

Dibdin, Michael (John) (1947–) Novelist, born in Chichester, West Sussex. In 1988 he won the Crime Writers' Award, the Gold Dagger, for *Ratking*. Later books include *Dirty*

Tricks (1991), *Cosi Fan Tutti* (1996), and *Back to Bologna* (2005).

DiCaprio, Leonardo (1974–) Film actor, born in Los Angeles. He became known after his Oscar-nominated role for Best Supporting Actor in *What's Eating Gilbert Grape?* (1993). Later films include *Titanic* (1997), *Gangs of New York* (2002), and *The Aviator* (2004, Golden Globe Best Actor).

Dickens, Charles (John Huffam) (1812–70) Novelist, born in Landport, Hampshire. He joined a London newspaper as a journalist, and in 1836 published his *Sketches by Boz* and *Pickwick Papers*. He wrote several successful novels, often campaigning against the social evils of his time, notably *Oliver Twist* (1837–9), *Nicholas Nickleby* (1838–9), and *The Old Curiosity Shop* (1840–1). Later books include *David Copperfield* (1849–50), *Bleak House* (1852–3), *A Tale of Two Cities* (1859), *Great Expectations* (1860–1), and the unfinished *The Mystery of Edwin Drood* (1870).

Dickinson, Emily (Elizabeth) (1830–86) Poet, born in Amherst, MA. At the age of 23 she withdrew from all social contacts, and lived a secluded life, writing in secret over 1000 poems. Hardly any of her work was published before her death.

Diderot, Denis (1713–84) Writer and philosopher, born in Langres, France. He was chief editor of the *Encyclopédie* (1745–72), a major work of the age of the Enlightenment. A prolific and versatile writer, he published novels, plays, satires, essays, and letters.

Didrikson, Babe, nickname of **Mil-dred Ella Zaharias**, *née* **Didrikson** (1914–56) Golfer and athlete, born in Port Arthur, TX. A great all-round athlete, she won two gold medals at the 1932 Olympics. Excelling also in swimming, tennis, and rifle-shooting, she turned to golf, winning the US Women's Open three times (1948, 1950, 1954).

Diesel, Rudolf (Christian Carl) (1858–1913) Engineer, born in Paris. He patented a design in 1892 and, subsidized by the Krupp company, constructed a 'rational heat motor', demonstrating the first compression-ignition engine in 1897.

Dietrich, Marlene, originally **Maria Magdalene von Losch** (1904–92) Film actress, born in Berlin. She became famous in a German film *The Blue Angel* (trans, 1930), and developed a glamorous and sensual film personality in such Hollywood films as *Morocco* (1930) and *Blond Venus* (1932).

Dillane, Stephen, professional name of **Stephen Dillon** (1958–) Actor, born in London. He has worked for many of Britain's leading theatre companies, including the Royal Shakespeare Company. In 1999 he won the Evening Standard Theatre Award for best actor in *The Real Thing*. His feature films include *The Hours* (2002) and *King Arthur* (2004).

Dillinger, John (Herbert) (1903–34) Gangster, born in Indianapolis, IN. He specialized in armed bank robberies, terrorizing Indiana and neighbouring states (1933–4). After escaping from jail, he was shot dead by FBI agents.

Dillon, Matt (1964–) Film actor, born

in Larchmont, NY. His first major film role was in Francis Ford Coppola's *The Outsiders* (1983), later films including *Beautiful Girls* (1996), *City of Ghosts* (2002), and *Loverboy* (2005).

DiMaggio, Joe, popular name of **Joseph (Paul) DiMaggio**, nicknames **Joltin' Joe** and **the Yankee Clipper** (1914–99) Baseball player, born in Martinez, CA. He spent his entire career with the New York Yankees (1936–51), holding the record for hitting safely in 56 consecutive games (1941). His second wife was Marilyn Monroe.

Dimbleby, David (1938–) Broadcaster, born in London, the son of Richard Dimbleby. Since the 1970s he has become a leading presenter and interviewer on BBC television current-affairs programmes, such as *Panorama* and *Election and Results*, and is also chairman of the BBC's *Question Time* (from 1994).

Dimbleby, Jonathan (1944–) Broadcaster, writer, and journalist, born in London, the son of Richard Dimbleby. Well known as a presenter of many television current-affairs documentaries, his controversial 'official' biography of the Prince of Wales appeared in 1994.

Dimbleby, Richard (Frederick) (1913–65) Broadcaster, born in Richmond on Thames, Greater London. He became the BBC's first foreign correspondent and its first war correspondent. In the post-war era he established himself as a magisterial TV anchorman on *Panorama*, and a commentator on major events.

Dionne, Cécile, Yvonne, Annette, Emilie, and **Marie** (1934–) Quintu-

plets, born near Callander, Ontario, Canada. They were the first documented set of quintuplets to survive, and became international child celebrities. Emilie died in 1954, Marie in 1970, and Yvonne in 2001.

Dior, Christian (1905–57) Fashion designer, born in Granville, France. He founded his own Paris house in 1945, and achieved worldwide fame with his long-skirted 'New Look' (1947). Later designs included the 'H' line and the 'A' line.

Dirac, Paul A(drien) M(aurice) (1902–84) Physicist, born in Bristol. His main research was in the field of quantum mechanics, in which he applied relativity theory, developed the theory of the spinning electron, and proposed the existence of 'antimatter'. He shared the Nobel Prize for Physics in 1933.

Disney, Walt(er Elias) (1901–66) Artist and film producer, born in Chicago, IL. He set up a small studio producing animated cartoons, his most famous character being Mickey Mouse (1928). His first full-length coloured cartoon film was *Snow White and the Seven Dwarfs* (1937), followed by *Pinocchio* (1940), *Dumbo* (1941), and *Fantasia* (1940). He also produced nature films, such as *The Living Desert* (1953), and films for young people including *Treasure Island* (1950) and *Mary Poppins* (1964). He opened the first Disneyland amusement park in California in 1955.

Disraeli, Benjamin, 1st Earl of Beaconsfield (1804–81) British prime minister (1868, 1874–80), born in London. As a writer, he is best known for his two political novels, *Coningsby* (1844) and *Sybil* (1846). Chancellor of the Exchequer in Derby's minority governments (1852, 1858–9, 1866–8), he piloted the 1867 Reform Bill through the Commons. During his administration, Britain became half-owner of the Suez Canal (1875), and Queen Victoria became Empress of India (1876).

Docherty, Tommy, popular name of **Thomas Henderson Docherty** (1928–) Footballer and manager, born in Glasgow. He played 25 times for Scotland, and managed 10 clubs including Aston Villa and Manchester United. He also briefly managed the Scotland side (1971–2).

Dodd, Ken(neth) (1929–) Stand-up comedian, singer, and actor, born in Liverpool, Merseyside. His hit songs include 'Tears' and 'Happiness'. He was still performing into the early 2000s.

Dodgson, Charles Lutwidge *see* Carroll, Lewis

Doenitz or **Dönitz, Karl** (1891–1980) German naval commander, born in Grünau, Germany. He planned the U-boat fleet, and in 1943 became commander-in-chief of the German navy. He was responsible for the final surrender to the Allies, and in 1946 was sentenced to 10 years' imprisonment for war crimes.

Dohnányi, Ernst von, Hung **Ernő** (1877–1960) Composer and pianist, born in Pozsony, Hungary (now Bratislava, Slovak Republic). He is best known for his piano compositions, notably *Variations on a Nursery Song* (1913) for piano and orchestra.

D'Oliveira, Basil (Lewis) (1934–) Cricketer, born in Cape Town, South Africa. In England from 1960, he played for England 44 times, and scored five Test centuries. Chosen for the 1968–9 England tour of South Africa, the refusal of the government to admit him (as a Cape Coloured) led to the exclusion of South Africa from international cricket.

Domingo, Plácido (1941–) Tenor, born in Madrid. He first sang in New York City in 1966, and at Covent Garden in 1971. His vocal technique and acting ability have made him one of the world's leading lyric-dramatic tenors, notably in works by Puccini and Verdi.

Dominic, St (c.1170–1221) Founder of the Order of Friars Preachers, born in Calaruega, Old Castile. He devoted himself to missionary work, notably among the Albigenses of S France, and he was canonized in 1234.

Domino, Fats, originally **Antoine Domino** (1928–) Singer, pianist, and composer, born in New Orleans, LA. His cheerful boogie-woogie piano style helped popularize rock-and-roll in the 1950s. His songs include 'Blueberry Hill', 'Ain't That A Shame', and 'I'm Walkin''.

Donatello, originally **Donato di Betto Bardi** (c.1386–1466) Sculptor, born in Florence, Italy. He may be regarded as the founder of modern sculpture, as the first producer since classical times of statues complete in themselves. Among his works are the marble statues of saints Mark and George for the exterior of Or San Michele, Florence.

Donegan, Lonnie, originally **Anthony James Donegan**

(1931–2002) Singer and guitarist, born in Glasgow. During the 1950s he had success both in Britain and the USA with such songs as 'Rock Island Line' (which launched a skiffle craze), 'Gamblin' Man', and 'Cumberland Gap'.

Dönitz, Karl *see* Doenitz, Karl

Donizetti, (Domenico) Gaetano (Maria) (1797–1848) Composer, born in Bergamo, Italy. The work which carried his fame beyond Italy was *Anna Bolena* (1830), and he had several other successes, notably *Lucia di Lammermoor* (1835).

Donleavy, J(ames) P(atrick) (1926–) Writer, born in New York City. His first novel, *The Ginger Man* (1955) was hailed as a comic masterpiece, and later works include *A Singular Man* (1963), *The Onion Eaters* (1971), and *That Darcy, That Dancer, That Gentleman* (1990). He has been an Irish citizen since 1967.

Donne, John (?1572–1631) Poet, born in London. Originally a Catholic, he joined the established Church, and became Dean of St Paul's. His creative years fall into three periods. The first (1590–1601) was a time of passion and cynicism, as seen in his *Elegies* and *Songs and Sonnets*; the second is represented by his *Anniversaries* and funeral poems; and his third includes sonnets and hymns.

Doohan, Mick, popular name of **Michael Doohan** (1965–) Motorcyclist, born in Brisbane, Queensland, Australia. He won 54 Grand Prix before retiring from riding after a serious accident in 1999. He won five successive 500 cc world championships (1994–8), and set a new record for the number of wins in a season (12) in 1997.

Dors, Diana, originally **Diana Fluck** (1931–84) Actress, born in Swindon, Wiltshire. Promoted as a sex symbol, she was cast in various low-budget comedies, achieving more dramatic roles in *Yield to the Night* (1956), *Three Months Gone* (1970), and *The Amazing Mr. Blunden* (1972).

Dorsey, Jimmy *see* Dorsey, Tommy

Dorsey, Tommy, popular name of **Thomas Dorsey** (1905–56) Trombonist and bandleader, born in Shenandoah, PA. His big bands were sometimes co-led by his brother **Jimmy Dorsey** (1904–57, alto saxophone, clarinet). The Dorsey Brothers Orchestra existed from 1932 to 1935, reforming again in 1953 until Tommy's death.

Dostoevsky or **Dostoyevsky, Fyodor (Mikhailovich)** (1821–81) Novelist, born in Moscow. Joining revolutionary circles in St Petersburg, he was sent to hard labour in Siberia. In 1859 he returned to St Petersburg, where his major works include (trans titles) *Crime and Punishment* (1866), *The Idiot* (1868–9), and *The Brothers Karamazov* (1879–80).

Douglas, Kirk, originally **Issur Danielovitch Demsky** (1916–) Film actor, born in Amsterdam, NY. His films include *Champion* (1949), *The Bad and the Beautiful* (1952), *Lust for Life* (1956), and *Spartacus* (1960), and from the 1970s he also worked as a director.

Douglas, Michael (Kirk) (1944–) US film actor and producer, born in New Brunswick, NJ, the son of Kirk Douglas. His acting roles include

Wall Street (1987, Oscar), *Fatal Attraction* (1987), *Traffic* (2000), in which he co-starred with wife Catherine Zeta-Jones (married 2000), and *The In-Laws* (2003).

Douglas-Home, Sir Alec *see* Home of the Hirsel, Baron

Dowell, Sir Anthony (1943–) Dancer and director, born in London. He joined the Royal Ballet company in 1961, becoming one of the premier male ballet dancers of the period, and was later appointed artistic director there (1986–2001).

Downes, Terry (1936–) Boxer, born in London. He was British middleweight champion (1958–62), and held the world championship (1961–2).

Doyle, Sir Arthur Conan (1859–1930) Writer, born in Edinburgh. His first book, *A Study in Scarlet* (1887), introduced the character of Sherlock Holmes, and the whole apparatus of detection mythology associated with Baker Street, Holmes's fictitious home. He also wrote historical romances, such as *The White Company* (1890).

Doyle, Roddy (1958–) Novelist, born in Dublin. His first success came with *The Commitments* (1987), the first book of the internationally acclaimed Barrytown trilogy. Later novels include *Paddy Clarke Ha Ha Ha* (1993, Booker), *A Star Called Henry* (1999), and *Oh, Play That Thing* (2004).

D'Oyly Carte, Richard (1844–1901) Theatrical impresario, born in London. He became a concert agent, and from 1875 produced the first operettas

by 'Gilbert and Sullivan'. In 1881 he built the Savoy Theatre in London.

Drabble, Margaret (1939–) Novelist and critic, born in Sheffield, South Yorkshire. Her novels include *The Ice Age* (1977), *The Gates of Ivory* (1991), *The Peppered Moth* (2001), and *The Red Queen* (2004), and she edited the *Oxford Companion to English Literature* (1985). She married biographer Michael Holroyd in 1982.

Drake, Sir Francis (c.1540–96) Elizabethan seaman, born near Tavistock, Devon. In 1577 he set out for the Pacific through the Straits of Magellan in the *Golden Hind*, returning to England via the Cape of Good Hope in 1580. In 1585 he visited the Spanish Indies, bringing home tobacco, potatoes, and the dispirited Virginian colonists. In the week-long battle against the Spanish Armada (1588), his seamanship and courage brought him further distinction.

Dreyfus, Alfred (1859–1935) French Jewish army officer, born in Mulhouse, France. Falsely charged with delivering defence secrets to the Germans (1894), he was transported to Devil's I, French Guiana. After vigorous efforts to prove him innocent, he was re-tried (1899), found guilty, but pardoned, and in 1906 the verdict was reversed.

Dreyfuss, Richard (1947–) US film actor, born in New York City. Major films include *Jaws* (1975), *Close Encounters of the Third Kind* (1977), *The Goodbye Girl* (1977, Oscar), and *The American President* (1995).

Dryden, John (1631–1700) Poet, born in Aldwinkle, Northamptonshire. He became poet laureate (1668–88) and in 1678 produced his best play, *All for Love*. Called to defend the king's party, he wrote a series of satires, notably *Absalom and Achitophel* (1681). Other works include the didactic poem *Religio laici* (1682) and *The Hind and the Panther* (1687), marking his conversion to Catholicism.

Dubček, Alexander (1921–92) Czechoslovakian statesman, born in Uhrovek, Slovak Republic. As first secretary in the Communist Party (1968), his liberalization policy led to the occupation of Czechoslovakia by Warsaw Pact forces (1968), and in 1969 he was replaced. In 1989, following a popular uprising, he was elected chairman of the Czechoslovak Federal Assembly.

Duchovny, David (1960–) Actor, born in New York City. He became known through the role of Fox Mulder in the cult television series *The X-Files* (1993–2002), for which he received a Golden Globe Best Actor award in 1997. His feature films include *The X-Files: Fight the Future* (1998) and *Full Frontal* (2003).

Dumas, Alexandre, known as **Dumas père** ('father') (1802–70) Writer, born in Villers-Cotterêts, France. He began writing plays, then turned to travelogues and historical novels. Among his best-known works are (trans titles) *The Count of Monte Cristo* (1844–55), *The Three Musketeers* (1845), and *The Black Tulip* (1850).

du Maurier, Dame Daphne (1907–89) Novelist, born in London, the granddaughter of George du Maurier. She wrote several successful period romances and adventure stories,

including *Jamaica Inn* (1936), *Rebecca* (1938), and *The Flight of the Falcon* (1965).

Dunaway, Faye (1941–) Film actress, born in Bascom, FL. Her first starring role was in *Bonnie and Clyde* (1967). Later films include *Chinatown* (1974, Oscar nomination), *Network* (1976, Oscar), *The Thomas Crown Affair* (1999), and *Jennifer's Shadow* (2004).

Duncan, Isadora, originally **Angela Duncan** (1877–1927) Dancer and choreographer, born in San Francisco, CA. She travelled in Europe, performing her own choreography, and founding schools in several cities. A pioneer of modern dance, she was also known for her unconventional views on women's liberation.

Duncan Smith, Iain (1954–) British Conservative politician, born in Edinburgh. He was elected MP in 1992, rising to be shadow secretary of state for social security (1997–99) and defence (1999–2001). In 2001 he became party leader, but was replaced by Michael Howard after losing a vote of confidence by Conservative MPs.

Dunlop, Joey, popular name of **(William) Joseph Dunlop** (1952–2000) Motor-cyclist, born in Ballymoney, Northern Ireland. He won the Isle of Man Senior Tourist Trophy (TT) in 1985 and 1987–8. In 1988 he won the Formula One TT for the sixth successive season, and was Formula One world champion 1982–6.

Dunlop, John Boyd (1840–1921) Inventor, born in Dreghorn, North Ayrshire. In 1888 he obtained patents on a pneumatic tyre (invented 1845), at first used for bicycles.

Dunmore, Helen (1952–) Novelist and poet, born in Leeds, West Yorkshire. In 1996 she won the inaugural Orange Prize for women fiction writers for her novel *A Spell of Winter*, and later novels include *With Your Crooked Heart* (2000) and *House of Orphans* (2006).

Dunstan, St (c.909–88) Abbot, born near Glastonbury, Somerset. He became abbot of Glastonbury in 945, making the abbey a centre of religious teaching. In 960 he was appointed Archbishop of Canterbury.

Dunwoody, Richard (Thomas), nickname **the Prince** (1964–) Jockey, born in Belfast. He was champion jockey in 1993–5, won the Grand National twice (1986, 1994), and rode at least 100 winners in Britain every season from 1989–90. In 1999, he rode home his 1679th winner, setting a National Hunt record.

du Pré, Jacqueline (1945–87) Cellist, born in Oxford, Oxfordshire. She quickly established an international reputation, and in 1967 married the pianist Daniel Barenboim, with whom she gave many recitals. Her career as a player ended in 1973, when she developed multiple sclerosis.

Durante, Jimmy, popular name of **James Francis Durante**, nickname **Schnoz** or **Schnozzle Durante** (1893–1980) Comedian, born in New York City. Known for his large nose (hence his nickname), he was a popular and versatile entertainer on Broadway and radio.

Dürer, Albrecht (1471–1528) Painter and engraver, born in Nuremberg,

Germany. In 1497 he set up his own studio, producing many paintings, then in 1498 published his first great series of designs on wood, the illustrations of the Apocalypse.

Durrell, Gerald (Malcolm) (1925–95) British zoologist, writer, and broadcaster, born in Jamshedpur, India, the brother of Lawrence Durrell. His popular animal stories and reminiscences include *My Family and Other Animals* (1956) and *A Zoo in My Luggage* (1960). He was founder chairman of Wildlife Preservation Trust International in 1972.

Durrell, Lawrence (George) (1912–90) British novelist and poet, born in Darjeeling, India. He is best known for the 'Alexandria Quartet' (1957–60): *Justine*, *Balthazar*, *Mountolive*, and *Clea*. Later novels include *Monsieur* (1974), *Livia* (1978), *Constance* (1982), *Sebastian* (1983), and *Quinx* (1985).

Duvall, Robert (1931–) Actor, born in San Diego, CA. He earned Oscar nominations for *The Godfather* (1972), *Apocalypse Now* (1979), and *The Great Santini* (1980), before winning the award for *Tender Mercies* (1983).

Dvořák, Antonín (Leopold) (1841–1904) Composer, born near Prague. His work, known for its colourful Slavonic motifs, includes nine symphonies, much chamber and piano music, and the acclaimed *Stabat mater* (1880).

Dyke, Greg(ory) (1947–) Broadcasting executive, born in London. He was director of programmes at TVS (1984–7) and LWT (1987–91), becoming managing director and group chief executive of LWT in 1990. In

2000 he took over as director-general at the BBC, but resigned in 2004 after the Hutton Report severely criticized the BBC.

Dyke, Dick Van *see* Van Dyke, Dick

Dylan, Bob, pseudonym of **Robert Zimmerman** (1941–) Folk singer and songwriter, born in Duluth, MN. He rose to fame in the 1960s, his lyrics focusing on pacifism, the nuclear bomb, and racial and social injustice, as in 'Blowin' in the Wind' and 'The Times They are a-Changin''. He remains one of the seminal influences on popular songwriting.

Ee

Earhart, Amelia (Mary) (1897–1937) Aviator, born in Atchison, KS. She was the first woman to fly the Atlantic, as a passenger, and followed this by a solo flight in 1932. In 1937 she set out to fly round the world, but her plane was lost over the Pacific.

Earp, Wyatt (Berry Stapp) (1848–1929) Gambler, gunfighter, and lawman, born in Monmouth, IL. During his stay in Tombstone, AZ, he befriended Doc Holliday, who joined with the Earp brothers against the Clanton gang in the famous gunfight at the OK Corral (1881).

Eastman, George (1854–1932) Inventor and philanthropist, born in Waterville, NY. He produced a successful roll-film (1884), the 'Kodak' box camera (1888), and the transparent celluloid film which made possible the moving-picture industry (1889).

Eastwood, Clint (1930–) Film actor and director, born in San Francisco, CA. He began acting in television Westerns, and rose to international stardom with the 'spaghetti' Western *A Fistful of Dollars* (1964). Later films,

several of which he also directed, include *Dirty Harry* (1971), *Unforgiven* (1992, two Oscars), *Mystic River* (2003), and *Million Dollar Baby* (2004, two Oscars, Golden Globe).

Eco, Umberto (1932–) Novelist and critic, born in Alessandria, Italy. His intellectual mediaeval detective story, *The Name of the Rose* (trans, 1981; filmed 1986), achieved instant fame. Later novels are *Foucault's Pendulum* (trans, 1988) and *L'isola del giorno prima* (1995, The Island of the Day Before).

Eddington, Sir Arthur S(tanley) (1882–1944) Astronomer, born in Kendal, Cumbria. In 1919 his observations of star positions during a total solar eclipse gave the first direct confirmation of Einstein's general theory of relativity. He became a renowned popularizer of science, notably in *The Nature of the Physical World* (1928).

Eddy, Mary Baker, married name **Glover** (1821–1910) Founder of the Christian Science Church, born in Bow, NH. In 1866 she received severe injuries after a fall, but read about the palsied man in Matthew's Gospel, and claimed to have risen from her bed similarly healed. She set out her beliefs in *Science and Health with Key to the Scriptures* (1875), and organized the Church of Christ, Scientist, at Boston (1879).

Eden, Sir (Robert) Anthony, 1st Earl of Avon (1897–1977) British prime minister (1955–7), born at Windlestone Hall, Durham. He became foreign secretary (1935), resigning in 1938 over differences with Chamberlain. Foreign secretary again

(1940–5, 1951–5), he succeeded Churchill as prime minister. In 1956 his controversial order to occupy the Suez Canal Zone led to his resignation.

Edgar or **Eadgar** (943–75) King of Mercia and Northumbria (957) and (from 959) King of all England, the younger son of Edmund I. In c.973 he introduced a uniform currency based on new silver pennies.

Edgar the Ætheling ('Prince') (c.1050–1125) Anglo-Saxon prince, the son of Edward the Ætheling. Though chosen as king after the battle of Hastings, he submitted to William the Conquerer (1066), then rebelled and fled to Scotland (1068). He was reconciled with William in 1074, but later fought against Henry I.

Edinburgh, Prince Philip, Duke of (1921–) The husband of Queen Elizabeth II of the United Kingdom, born in Corfu, Greece, the son of Prince Andrew of Greece and Princess Alice of Battenberg. He became a naturalized British subject in 1947, when he married the Princess Elizabeth. He is a keen sportsman, yachtsman, qualified airman, and conservationist, and in 1956 began the Duke of Edinburgh Award scheme to foster leisure activities for young people.

Edison, Thomas (Alva) (1847–1931) Inventor and physicist, born in Milan, OH. He held patents for over 1000 inventions, including the printing telegraph (1871), the phonograph (1877), the carbon-filament light bulb (1879), and motion picture equipment. He discovered thermionic emission (1883), which became the basis for the electronic valve.

Edmund I (921–46) King of the English (939–46), the half-brother of Athelstan. He re-established control over the S Danelaw (942) and Northumbria (944) and, until his murder by an exile, ruled a reunited England.

Edmund II, known as **Edmund Ironside** (c.980–1016) King of the English for a few months in 1016, the son of Ethelred the Unready. He defeated Canute, but was routed at Ashingdon, and agreed to a partition of the country. He died soon after, leaving Canute as sole ruler.

Edmund, St, originally **Edmund Rich** (1170–1240) Clergyman, born in Abingdon, Oxfordshire. As Archbishop of Canterbury (1234) he became the spokesman of the national party against Henry III, defending Church rights. He was canonized in 1247.

Edward I (1239–1307) King of England (1272–1307), born in London, the elder son of Henry III and Eleanor of Provence. He married Eleanor of Castile (1254) and later Margaret of France. In the Baron's War (1264–7), he defeated Simon de Montfort at Evesham (1265), then won renown as a crusader to the Holy Land in the Eighth Crusade (1270–2). In two campaigns (1276–7, 1282–3) he annexed N and W Wales, building magnificent castles. His claims to the overlordship of Scotland began the Scottish Wars of Independence, and he died while fighting Robert Bruce.

Edward II (1284–1327) King of England from 1307, born in Caernarfon, Wales, the fourth son of Edward I and

Eleanor of Castile. In 1308 he married Isabella, the daughter of Philip IV of France. He was decisively defeated at Bannockburn (1314). In conflict with the barons, who sought to rid the country of royal favourites, he was deposed by Isabella and her lover, Roger Mortimer, Earl of March, and imprisoned. He abdicated in favour of his eldest son (1327), and was murdered in Berkeley Castle.

Edward III, known as **Edward of Windsor** (1312–77) King of England from 1327, born in Windsor, S England, the elder son of Edward II and Isabella of France. He married Philippa of Hainault in 1328. By banishing Queen Isabella from court, and executing her lover, **Roger Mortimer, Earl of March** (c.1287–1330), he began to restore the monarchy's authority. He defeated the Scots at Halidon Hill (1333) and in 1337 revived his hereditary claim to the French crown, thus beginning the Hundred Years' War. He destroyed the French navy at the Sluys (1340), and won a major victory at Crécy (1346).

Edward IV (1442–83) King of England (1461–70, 1471–83), born in Rouen, France, the eldest son of Richard, Duke of York. Recognized as king on Henry VI's deposition, and with the support of his cousin, Richard Neville, Earl of Warwick, he decisively defeated the Lancastrians at Towton. He secretly married Elizabeth Woodville in 1464. Warwick forced him into exile (1470), but he returned to England (1471), killed Warwick at Barnet, and destroyed the remaining Lancastrian forces at Tewkesbury.

Edward V (1470–83) King of England (Apr–Jun 1483), born in London, the son of Edward IV and Elizabeth Woodville. He and his younger brother, **Richard, Duke of York** (?1473–83), were imprisoned in the Tower by their uncle Richard, Duke of Gloucester, who usurped the throne as Richard III. The two princes were never heard of again, and were probably murdered on their uncle's orders.

Edward VI (1537–53) King of England (1547–53), born in London, the son of Henry VIII by his third queen, Jane Seymour. During his reign, power was first in the hands of his uncle, the Duke of Somerset, then of John Dudley, Duke of Northumberland. He became a Protestant, and under the Protectors the English Reformation flourished.

Edward VII (1841–1910) King of the United Kingdom (1901–10), born in London, the eldest son of Queen Victoria. In 1863 he married Alexandra, daughter of Christian IX of Denmark. They had three sons and three daughters: **Albert Victor** (1864–92), **George** (1865–1936), **Louise** (1867–1931), **Victoria** (1868–1935), **Maud** (1869–1938), and **Alexander** (born and died 1871). As Prince of Wales, his behaviour led him into several social scandals.

Edward VIII (1894–1972) King of the United Kingdom (Jan–Dec 1936), born in Richmond, Greater London, the eldest son of George V. He succeeded his father in 1936, but abdicated in the face of opposition to his proposed marriage to Wallis Simpson, a commoner who had been twice divorced. He was given the title of **Duke of Windsor**, and the marriage took place in France in 1937.

Edward (Antony Richard Louis), Prince (1964–) Prince of the United Kingdom, the third son of Queen Elizabeth II. He joined the Royal Marines in 1986, but left the following year and began a career in the theatre, joining Andrew Lloyd Webber's Really Useful Theatre Company. In 1993 he formed his own company, Ardent Productions. He was made Earl of Wessex in honour of his marriage to **Sophie Rhys-Jones** (1965–) in 1999. They have a daughter, **Lady Louise Windsor** (2003–).

Edward the Black Prince (1330–76) Prince of England, born in Woodstock, Oxfordshire, the eldest son of Edward III. He was created Prince of Wales in 1343, and fought at Crécy (1346), where he won his popular title from his black armour. His later victories included Poitiers (1356). He had two sons: **Edward** (1356–70) and **Richard**, the future Richard II.

Edward the Confessor, St (c.1003–66) King of England (1042–66), the elder son of Ethelred the Unready and Emma of Normandy. Although in 1051 he probably recognized Duke William of Normandy (later William I) as his heir, on his deathbed he nominated Harold Godwinson (Harold II) to succeed, the Norman Conquest following soon after. He was canonized in 1161.

Edward the Elder (c.870–924) King of Wessex (from 899), the elder son of Alfred the Great. He established himself as the strongest ruler in Britain, annexing the S Danelaw (910–18), and taking control of Mercia (918).

Edward the Martyr, St (c.963–78) King of England (975–8). During his reign there was a reaction against the policies supporting monasticism espoused by his father, Edgar. He was murdered by supporters of his stepmother, Elfrida, and canonized in 1001.

Edwards, Blake, originally **William Blake McEdwards** (1922–) Director and writer born in Tulsa, OK. He is best known for *Breakfast at Tiffany's* (1961), and his series of *Pink Panther* films (1964–78) starring Peter Sellers. In 2004 he received a Lifetime Achievement Academy Award. He is married to the actress Julie Andrews.

Edwards, Huw (1961–) Television journalist and presenter, born in Llangennech, near Llanelli. He joined BBC Wales, becoming parliamentary correspondent (1986) and chief political correspondent for BBC News 24 (1988). He has presented the Six O'Clock News (1999–2002) and the Ten O'Clock News (2003–), and also several general-interest programmes, notably *The Story of Welsh* (2003).

Edwards, Jonathan (1966–) Triple jump athlete, born in London. His sporting achievements include Commonwealth Games gold (2002), Olympic gold (2000), European Championship title (1998), and two World Championship gold medals (1995, 2001). He holds the world record of 18·29 m, set at the 1995 Championships in Gothenburg, Sweden. He retired in 2003.

Edwin, St (584–633) King of Northumbria from 616, brought up in North Wales. Under him, Northumbria became united, and he obtained the overlordship of all England, save Kent. He was converted to Christianity (627), fell in battle at Hatfield Chase, and was afterwards canonized.

Egbert, in Anglo-Saxon **Ecgberht** or **Ecgbryht** (?–839) King of Wessex (802–39). His successes gave him mastery over S England from Kent to Land's End, and established Wessex as the strongest Anglo-Saxon kingdom.

Eichmann, (Karl) Adolf (1906–62) Nazi war criminal, born in Solingen, Germany. He became a member of the SS in 1932, and organizer of anti-Semitic activities. Captured by US forces in 1945, he escaped from prison, but was traced by Israeli agents, taken to Israel in 1960, and executed.

Eiffel, (Alexandre) Gustave (1832–1923) Civil engineer, born in Dijon, France. Apart from his most famous project, the *Eiffel Tower*, he also designed the framework of the Statue of Liberty, New York.

Einstein, Albert (1879–1955) Mathematical physicist, born in Ulm, Germany. He became world famous by his special (1905) and general (1916) theories of relativity, and was awarded the Nobel Prize for Physics in 1921. Director of the Kaiser Wilhelm Physical Institute in Berlin (1914–33), after Hitler's rise to power he left Germany, became a professor at the Institute of Advanced Study in Princeton, and spent the rest of his life attempting by means of his unified field theory (1950) to establish a merger between quantum theory and his general theory of relativity. He was also a champion of pacifism and liberalism.

Eisenhower, Dwight D(avid), nickname **Ike** (1890–1969) US general and 34th president (1953–61), born in Denison, TX. In 1942 he commanded Allied forces for the amphibious descent on French N Africa, and became Supreme Commander for the 1944 cross-Channel invasion of the continental mainland. His popularity swept him to victory in the presidential elections (1952) standing as a Republican, and he was re-elected in 1956.

El Cid *see* Cid, El

Eleanor of Aquitaine (c.1122–1204) Queen consort of Louis VII of France (1137–52) and of Henry II of England (1154–89). She was imprisoned (1174–89) for supporting the rebellion of her sons, two of whom became kings as Richard I (in 1189) and John (1199).

Eleanor of Castile (1246–90) Queen consort of Edward I of England (1254–90), the daughter of Ferdinand III. The *Eleanor Crosses* at Northampton, Geddington, and Waltham Cross are the survivors of the 12 erected by Edward at the halting places of her funeral cortège.

Elgar, Sir Edward (1857–1934) Composer, born in Broad Heath, Hereford and Worcester. The *Enigma Variations* (1899) and the oratorio *The*

Dream of Gerontius (1900) made him the leading figure of his day in English music. Other works included symphonies, concertos, and incidental music, and in 1924 he became Master of the King's Musick.

Elijah (9th-c BC) Hebrew prophet, whose activities are portrayed in four Bible stories (1 *Kings* 16–19; 2 *Kings* 1–2). He opposed the worship of Baal in Israel, and by virtue of his loyalty to God was depicted as ascending directly into heaven.

Eliot, George, pseudonym of **Mary Ann Evans** or **Marian Evans** (1819–80) Novelist, born at Arbury Farm, Astley, Warwickshire. She became the centre of a literary circle, one of whose members was G H Lewes, with whom she lived until his death (1878). Her major novels were *Adam Bede* (1859), *The Mill on the Floss* (1860), *Silas Marner* (1861), *Middlemarch* (1871–2), and *Daniel Deronda* (1876).

Eliot, T(homas) S(tearns) (1888–1965) Poet, critic, and playwright, born in St Louis, MO. The enthusiastic support of Ezra Pound led to his first book of poetry, *Prufrock and Other Observations* (1917), followed by *The Waste Land* (1922) and *The Hollow Men* (1925). Later works include his major poetic achievement, *Four Quartets* (1944), and a series of verse dramas, notably *Murder in the Cathedral* (1935) and *The Cocktail Party* (1950). He was awarded the Nobel Prize for Literature in 1948.

Elisha (second half of 9th-c BC) Hebrew prophet whose activities are portrayed in 1 *Kings* 19 and 2 *Kings* 2–9,13.

He was active in Israel under several kings from Ahab to Jehoash.

Elizabeth I, known as **the Virgin Queen** and later **Good Queen Bess** (1533–1603) Queen of England (1558–1603), the daughter of Henry VIII by his second wife, Anne Boleyn, born in Greenwich, London. She saw her role in Europe as a Protestant sovereign, and it is from this time that the Anglican Church was formally established. Mary, Queen of Scots, was thrown into her power (1568) and imprisoned, causing endless conspiracies among English Catholics. After the most sinister plot was discovered (1586), Elizabeth was reluctantly persuaded to execute Mary (1587), and subsequently persecuted Catholics. Philip of Spain then attacked England with his 'invincible armada' (1588), but was repelled. A strong, cruel, and capricious woman, the 'Virgin Queen' was nevertheless popular with her subjects, as indicated by her other byname, 'Good Queen Bess'; and her reign is seen as the period when England assumed the position of a world power.

Elizabeth II (1926–) Queen of the United Kingdom (1952–) and head of the Commonwealth, born in London, the daughter of George VI. She was proclaimed queen on 6 February 1952, and crowned on 2 June 1953. Her husband was created Duke of Edinburgh, later Prince Philip. They have three sons, Charles, Andrew, and Edward, and a daughter, Anne. In 2002, Queen Elizabeth celebrated her golden jubilee.

Elizabeth (Queen Mother), originally **Lady Elizabeth Bowes-Lyon**

(1900–2002) Queen Consort of Great Britain, born in St Paul's Walden, Bury, Hertfordshire. In 1923 she married the second son of George V. Princess Elizabeth (later Queen Elizabeth II) was born in 1926 and Princess Margaret in 1930. Her husband came to the throne as King George VI in 1936 and after his death (1952), she continued to undertake public duties around the world, becoming a widely loved figure. Her death generated a wave of popular emotion, and the nation marked her death with a level of ceremony not seen in the UK for half a century.

Ellington, Duke, popular name of **Edward Kennedy Ellington** (1899–1974) Composer, arranger, bandleader, and pianist, born in Washington, DC. Among his early successes were 'Black and Tan Fantasy' (1927) and 'Mood Indigo' (1930). His creative peak is generally said to be 1939–42, with such recordings as 'Take the A Train'. Later works included jazz suites, film scores, ballets, and a series of 'sacred concerts' (1968–74) performed in cathedrals around the world. His son, **Mercer Ellington** (1919–96), led the band after his death.

Emerson, Ralph Waldo (1803–82) Writer, born in Boston, MA. His works include many poems and essays, notably *The Conduct of Life* (1860), showing him to be a transcendentalist and a bold advocate of spiritual individualism.

Emin, Tracey (1963–) Multimedia artist, born in London. She gained attention with her controversial entry for the 1999 Turner Prize, 'My Bed'. Her first piece of public art, a sculpture entitled 'The Roman Standard', was unveiled in Liverpool in 2005.

Enfield, Harry (1961–) British comedian, actor, and writer, known for his character-based comedy shows. *Sir Norbert Smith – a Life?* (1989) won the Silver Rose at Montreux, as did *The End of an Era* (1994). He achieved national recognition after his own BBC television series in 1991–2, following this with *Harry Enfield and Chums* (1994, 1996).

Engels, Friedrich (1820–95) Socialist philosopher, and founder of 'scientific socialism', born in Barmen, Germany. He collaborated with Marx on the *Communist Manifesto* (1848), and spent his later years editing and translating Marx's writings.

Enoch Biblical character, the son of Jared, and the father of Methuselah. In the Graeco-Roman era his name became attached to Jewish apocalyptic writings allegedly describing his visions and journeys through the heavens (1, 2, and 3 *Enoch*).

Epicurus (c.341–270 BC) Greek philosopher, born in Samos. In 305 BC he established a school of philosophy at Athens, holding that pleasure, in the sense of freedom from pain and anxiety, is the chief good.

Epstein, Sir Jacob (1880–1959) Sculptor, born in New York City. Several of his symbolic sculptures, such as 'Ecce homo' (1934), led to accusations of indecency and blasphemy. In the 1950s, 'Christ in Majesty' (in aluminium; Llandaff Cathedral) and 'St Michael and the Devil' (in bronze;

Coventry Cathedral) won more immediate acclaim.

Erasmus, Desiderius, originally **Gerrit Gerritszoon** (1466–1536) Humanist, born in Rotterdam, The Netherlands. His masterpiece, *Colloquia* (1519), is an audacious handling of Church abuses. He also made the first translation of the Greek New Testament into English (1516).

Eriksson, Sven-Goran (1948–) Footballer and football manager, born in Torsby, Sweden. As manager, his clubs included Gothenburg (1980), Benfica (1982–84, 1989–91), AS Roma (1984–86), Fiorentina (1987–98), Sampdoria (1991–96), and Lazio (1997–2001). In 2001 he became manager of the England football team. It was announced early in 2006 that he would quit after the FIFA World Cup in June that year.

Ernst, Max(imillian) (1891–1976) Painter, born in Brühl, near Cologne, Germany. In 1919 he founded at Cologne the German Dada group, and later joined the Surrealist movement in Paris, his works including 'Oedipus Rex' (1921) and 'Polish Rider' (1954).

Esau Biblical character, the elder son of Isaac. He was depicted as his father's favourite son, but was deprived of Isaac's blessing and his birthright by his cunning brother Jacob (*Gen* 27).

Essex, Robert Devereux, 2nd Earl of (1566–1601) English soldier and courtier to Elizabeth I, born in Netherwood, Hereford and Worcester. He became a privy councillor (1593) and earl marshal (1597), but alienated the Queen's advisers, and there were constant quarrels with

Elizabeth. His six months' lord-lieutenancy of Ireland (1599) proved a failure, and he was imprisoned. He attempted to raise the City of London, was found guilty of high treason, and beheaded.

Ethelbert or **Æthelbert** (c.552–616) King of Kent (560–616). In his reign Kent achieved (c.590) control over England S of the Humber, and Christianity was introduced by St Augustine (597). To him we owe the first written English laws.

Ethelred I, also spelled **Æthelred** (c.830–71) King of Wessex (865–71), the elder brother of Alfred the Great. During his reign, the Danes launched their main invasion of England and established their kingdom (866), but were defeated at Ashdown, in the former county of Berkshire.

Ethelred II, known as **Ethelred the Unready**, also spelled **Æthelred** (c.968–1016) King of England (978–1016), the son of Edgar. He was forced into exile (1013) when Sweyn Forkbeard secured mastery over England. After Sweyn's death (1014), he returned to oppose Canute, but English resistance was broken when his son, Edmund Ironside, rebelled. 'Unready' is a mistranslation of *Unraed*, which means 'ill-advised'.

Ethelwulf, also spelled **Æthelwulf** (d.858) Anglo-Saxon king of England (839–56), the son of the West Saxon king, Egbert. In 851 he fought a victorious battle against the Danish army at Aclea in Surrey. In 856 he was deposed by rivals on his return from Rome, but continued to rule Kent until his death. Four of his sons became kings of Wessex, including Alfred the Great.

Euclid, Gr **Eucleides** (4th–3rd-c BC) Greek mathematician who taught in Alexandria c.300 BC, and who was probably the founder of its mathematical school. His chief extant work is the 13-volume *Elements*. The approach which obeys his axioms became known as *Euclidean geometry*.

Euler, Leonhard (1707–83) Mathematician, born in Basel, Switzerland. He was a giant figure in 18th-c mathematics, publishing on every aspect of pure and applied mathematics, physics and astronomy. His treatises on differential and integral calculus and algebra remained standard textbooks for a century, and his notations, such as e and π, have been used ever since.

Euripides (c.480–406 BC) Greek tragic playwright, born in Athens. He wrote about 80 dramas, of which 19 survive, including *Alcestis*, *Medea*, *Orestes*, *Electra*, *The Bacchae*, and *Iphigenia in Aulis*.

Evans, Sir Arthur (John) (1851–1941) Archaeologist, born in Nash Mills, Hertfordshire. He excavated the city of Knossos (1899–1935), discovering the remains of the civilization which in 1904 he named *Minoan*.

Evans, Chris (1966–) Disc-jockey and television presenter, born in Warrington. For Channel 4 he launched *The Big Breakfast* and hosted *Don't Forget Your Toothbrush* and *TFI Friday*. He presented breakfast shows for Radio 1 and later Virgin Radio, but was dismissed by Virgin in 2001 for breach of contract. In 2005 he joined BBC Radio 2, and also began hosting

OFI Sunday for ITV1. He married actress Billie Piper in 2001 (separated, 2005).

Eve, Trevor (1951–) Actor and producer, born in Birmingham, West Midlands. In 1980 he became well known for his lead in the television series *Shoestring*, and later TV appearances include *The Politician's Wife* (1995), *David Copperfield* (1999), *The Family Man* (2006), and the series *Waking the Dead* (2001–).

Everly Brothers, The American duo **Don Everly** (1937–) and **Phil Everly** (1939–), guitarists and vocalists. Their first major hit was 'Bye Bye Love' (1957), and the style – close harmonies over acoustic guitars and a rock-and-roll beat – became their trademark. They split up in 1973, but re-formed in 1983.

Evert (Lloyd), Chris(tine Marie) (1954–) Tennis player, born in Fort Lauderdale, FL. She won Wimbledon titles in 1974, 1976, and 1981, and the US singles title in 1975–80 and 1982.

Evita see Perón, Eva

Eyck, Jan van (c.1389–1441) Painter, born near Maastricht, The Netherlands. The greatest Flemish artist of the 15th-c, his most famous work is the altarpiece 'The Adoration of the Holy Lamb' (1432) in the Church of St Bavon, Ghent.

Eyre, Sir Richard (Charles Hastings) (1943–) Director, born in Barnstaple, Devon. He was artistic director of the Nottingham Playhouse (1973–8), producer of the BBC television's *Play for Today* series (1978–81), and artistic director of the National Theatre, London (1988–97). Among his feature films are *Iris* (2000) and *Stage Beauty* (2004).

Fabergé, Peter Carl, originally **Karl Gustavovich Fabergé** (1846–1920) Goldsmith and jeweller, born in St Petersburg, Russia. He is known for the creation of elaborate and fantastic objects, notably the imperial Easter eggs commissioned by Alexander III for his tsarina in 1884.

Fahrenheit, Gabriel (Daniel) (1686–1736) Physicist, born in Gdańsk, Poland (formerly Danzig, Germany). He invented the alcohol thermometer in 1709, and a mercury thermometer in 1714.

Fairbanks, Douglas (Elton), Snr, originally **Douglas Elton Ulman** (1883–1939) Film actor, born in Denver, CO. He made a speciality of swashbuckling hero parts, as in *The Three Musketeers* (1921), *Robin Hood* (1922), and *The Thief of Baghdad* (1924).

Fairbanks, Douglas (Elton), Jr (1909–2000) Film actor, writer, producer, and businessman, born in New York City, the son of Douglas Fairbanks, Snr. He made Hollywood movies in the style of his father, such as *Sinbad the Sailor* (1947), and later became a diplomat.

Fairfax (of Cameron), Thomas Fairfax, 3rd Baron (1612–71) English parliamentary general, born in Denton, North Yorkshire. In the Civil War, he distinguished himself at Marston Moor (1644), and in 1645 commanded the New Model Army, defeating Charles I at Naseby.

Faldo, Nick, popular name of **Nicholas Alexander Faldo** (1957–) Golfer, born in Welwyn Garden City, Hertfordshire. His successes include the Professional Golfing Association championships (1978, 1980, 1981), the Open Championship (1987, 1990, 1992), and the US Masters (1989, 1990, 1996). His 23 Ryder Cup wins (1977–97) are a record.

Falla, Manuel de (1876–1946) Composer, born in Cadiz, Spain. His works became famous for their colourful national Spanish idiom, and he is best known for his ballet, *The Three-Cornered Hat* (1919).

Fältskog, Agnetha *see* Abba

Faraday, Michael (1791–1867) Chemist, experimental physicist, and natural philosopher, born in Newington Butts, Surrey. His major work is the series of *Experimental Researches on Electricity* (1839–55), in which he reports a wide range of discoveries about the nature of electricity, notably electrolysis, and the relationship between electricity and magnetism.

Farouk (1920–65) Last reigning king of Egypt (1936–52), born in Cairo, the son of Fuad I. Egypt's defeat by Israel (1948) and continuing British occupation led to increasing unrest, and a coup forced his abdication and exile.

Farrow, Mia (1945–) Film actress, born in Los Angeles, CA. She starred in *Rosemary's Baby* (1968) and several Woody Allen films, notably *The Purple Rose of Cairo* (1985), *Hannah and Her Sisters* (1986), and *Husbands and Wives* (1992). Earlier married to Frank Sinatra (1966–8), her relationship with Woody Allen broke up in acrimony in 1992, following her discovery of Allen's affair with their adopted teenage daughter.

Fassett, Kaffe (1937–) Fashion designer, born in San Francisco, CA. In England from 1964, he formed a design company producing colourful knitting kits, needlepoint, and fabrics.

Fatima (c.605–33) The youngest daughter of the Prophet Mohammed, and wife of the fourth Muslim caliph, Ali; from them descended the *Fatimids*, the dynasty of Shiite caliphs, who ruled over Egypt and N Africa (909–1171), and later over Syria and Palestine.

Faulkner, William (Cuthbert), originally **Falkner** (1897–1962) Writer, born in New Albany, MS. His novels include *The Sound and the Fury* (1929), *As I Lay Dying* (1930), *Absalom, Absalom!* (1936), *Intruder in the Dust* (1948), and *The Reivers* (1962). He was awarded the Nobel Prize for Literature in 1949.

Fauré, Gabriel (Urbain) (1845–1924) Composer, born in Pamiers, France. Though chiefly remembered for his songs, including the evergreen *Après un rêve* (c.1865), he also wrote operas and orchestral pieces, and a much-performed *Requiem* (1887–90).

Fawkes, Guy (1570–1606) Catholic conspirator, born in York, North Yorkshire. He served in the Spanish army in The Netherlands (1593–1604), came to England at Catesby's invitation, and became a member of the Gunpowder Plot. Caught red-handed, he was tried and hanged.

Federer, Roger (1981–) Tennis player, born in Basel, Switzerland. In 2003 he became the first Swiss man to win a Grand Slam title when he became Wimbledon singles champion. During 2004 he won the Australian Open, the US Open, the ATP Masters, and retained the Wimbledon singles title. In 2005 he won the Wimbledon singles title for a third successive year, and won the US Open. He began 2006 ranked world number 1 and won the Australian Open title.

Fellini, Federico (1920–93) Film director, born in Rimini, Italy. His films, always from his own scripts, include (trans titles) *The Road* (1954, Oscar), *Nights of Cabiria* (1956, Oscar), *The Sweet Life* (1960, Cannes Festival prizewinner), *8½* (1963), *Fellini's Roma* (1972), and *I Remember* (1973, Oscar).

Ferdinand (of Castile), known as **the Catholic** (1452–1516) King of Castile as Ferdinand V (from 1474), of Aragon and Sicily as Ferdinand II (from 1479), and of Naples as Ferdinand III (from 1503), born in Sos, Aragon, Spain. In 1469 he married Isabella, sister of Henry IV of Castile, and ruled jointly with her until her death (1504). Under him, Spain gained supremacy following the discovery of America, and by 1512 he had become monarch of all Spain.

Ferdinand, Rio (Gavin) (1978–) Footballer, born in London. He made his debut for West Ham in 1996, joining Leeds in 2000 for a record fee of £18 million. He made his England debut in 1997 and was a member of the England squad for the FIFA World Cup (1998, 2002). In 2002 he became the world's most expensive defender when he was bought by Manchester United for £30 million.

Ferguson, Sir Alex(ander Chapman) (1941–) Football player and manager, born in Glasgow. As manager at Manchester United, his achievements include the FA Cup (1990), the European Cup Winners' Cup (1991), the League and Cup double (1994, 1996, 1999), and the European Cup (1999). In 2003 he received the FA Manager of the Decade award.

Ferguson, Sarah see Andrew, Duke of York

Fermat, Pierre de (1601–65) Mathematician, born in Beaumont-de-Lomagne, France. He became a lawyer, then turned to mathematics, making many discoveries in the properties of numbers, probabilities, and geometry. With Descartes, he was one of the two leading mathematicians in the early 17th-c.

Fermi, Enrico (1901–54) Nuclear physicist, born in Rome. In 1934 he and his colleagues split a number of nuclei by bombardment with neutrons, for which he was awarded the Nobel Prize for Physics in 1938. In the USA, he constructed the first US nuclear reactor in 1942.

Ferrari, Enzo (1898–1988) Racing-car designer, born in Modena, Italy. He became a racing driver in 1920, founded the company which bears his name in 1929, and in 1940 began designing his own cars.

Ferrier, Kathleen (1912–53) Contralto singer, born in Higher Walton, Lancashire. One of her greatest successes was Mahler's *Das Lied von der Erde* (The Song of the Earth) at the first Edinburgh Festival (1947).

Fielding, Helen (1958–) Novelist, born in Morley, West Yorkshire. She gained success with her comic novel *Bridget Jones's Diary* (1996; filmed 2001) – originally a weekly newspaper column about the fictional life of a single woman. A sequel, *Bridget Jones: The Edge of Reason*, appeared in 2000 (filmed 2004).

Fielding, Henry (1707–54) Writer, born at Sharpham Park, Glastonbury, Somerset. On Richardson's publication of *Pamela* (1740), he wrote his famous parody, *Joseph Andrews* (1742). *The History of Tom Jones, A Foundling* (1749) established his reputation as a founder of the English novel.

Fields, Dame Gracie, originally **Grace Stansfield** (1898–1979) Singer and variety star, born in Rochdale, Greater Manchester. With her sentimental songs and broad Lancashire humour, she won a unique place in the affections of British audiences, known for her theme tune, 'Sally' (1931).

Fields, W C, originally **William Claude Dukenfield** (1879–1946) Actor, born in Philadelphia, PA. He appeared in the Ziegfeld Follies, and established his comic persona in silent films, but his distinctive voice found its full scope with the coming of sound during the 1930s.

Fiennes, Joseph (Alberic) (1970–) Actor, born in Salisbury, Wiltshire, the brother of Ralph Fiennes. He became known after his role in the film *Elizabeth* (1998). Later films include *Shakespeare in Love* (1998), *Enemy at the Gates* (2000), and *Man to Man* (2005).

Fiennes, Ralph (Nathaniel) (1962–) Actor, born in Suffolk. His film debut was in *Emily Bronte's Wuthering Heights* (1991). Later films include *Schindler's List* (1993, Golden Globe, Oscar nomination), *The English Patient* (1996, Oscar nomination), *The End of the Affair* (1999), and *The Constant Gardener* (2005, Oscar nomination).

Fiennes, Sir Ranulph (Twisleton-Wykeham-) (1944–) Explorer, born in Windsor, England. He was the leader of several expeditions, including the Transglobe (1979–82), tracing the Greenwich Meridian across both Poles. With Michael Stroud he completed the first unsupported crossing on foot of the Antarctic in 1993, and in 2003 they successfully completed the challenge to run seven marathons in seven continents in seven days.

Fillmore, Millard (1800–74) US statesman and 13th president (1850–3), born in Summerhill, NY. Elected to Congress in 1833, he was vice-president to Zachary Taylor in 1848, becoming president on his death.

Finney, Albert (1936–) Actor, born in Salford, Greater Manchester. His performance in *Saturday Night and Sunday Morning* (1960) established him as a star, and he received Oscar nominations for *Tom Jones* (1963), *Murder on the Orient Express* (1974), *The Dresser* (1983), and *Under the Volcano* (1984). His work for television includes *The Gathering Storm* (2002, Emmy; Golden Globe).

Finney, Tom, popular name of **Sir Thomas Finney** (1922–) Footballer, born in Preston, Lancashire. He spent his playing career with Preston North End and is considered to have been one of the best wingers in the game. He was capped for England 76 times.

Firth, Colin (1960–) Actor, born in Grayshott, Hampshire. He received a BAFTA nomination for his role in the television production of *Pride and Prejudice* (1995), where his brooding performance as the handsome Mr Darcy attracted unprecedented public interest. His films include *Bridget Jones's Diary* (2001, sequel 2004) and *Where the Truth Lies* (2005).

Fischer, Bobby, popular name of **Robert (James) Fischer** (1943–) Chess player, born in Chicago, IL. He was world champion in 1972–5, taking the title from Spassky. Ranked as the greatest of all Grand Masters, he resigned his title in 1975, and did not then compete at a major international level until 1992, when he defeated Spassky in a much publicized match.

Fischer-Dieskau, Dietrich (1925–) Baritone, born in Berlin. One of the foremost interpreters of German *Lieder*, particularly the song-cycles of

Schubert, he has also appeared in a wide range of operatic roles.

Fishburne, Larry, popular name of **Laurence John Fishburne III** (1961–) Actor, born in Augusta, GA. He won a Tony Award for his performance in the Broadway play *Two Trains Running*. His films include *The Matrix* (1999) and its sequels (both 2003), and *Assault on Precinct 13* (2005).

Fisher, John, St (1469–1535) Clergyman and humanist, born in Beverley, East Riding. In 1527 he pronounced against the divorce of Henry VIII, and was sent with More to the Tower. In 1535 he was made a cardinal, and soon after was beheaded. He was canonized in 1935.

Fitzgerald, Ella (1918–96) Jazz singer, born in Newport News, VA. She joined Chick Webb's band and recorded several hits, notably 'A-tisket A-tasket' (1938). Her series of recordings for Verve (1955–9) in multi-volume 'songbooks' are among the treasures of American popular song.

Fitzgerald, F(rancis) Scott (Key) (1896–1940) Novelist, born in St Paul, MN. He captured the spirit of the 1920s jazz era in *The Great Gatsby* (1925). Other novels include *The Beautiful and the Damned* (1922) and *Tender is the Night* (1934).

Flanders, Michael (1922–75) Variety performer, born in London. He is best remembered for the revue *At The Drop of a Hat* (1956) and songs, such as the 'Hippopotamus Song', created and performed with Donald Swann.

Flatley, Michael (1958–) Dancer and choreographer, born in Chicago, IL.

In 1975 he became the first American to win the All World Championships in Irish dancing. He shot to fame after the success of his stage routine *Riverdance* (1994), and went on to create, choreograph, and star in the shows *The Lord of the Dance* (1996), *Feet of Flames* (1998), and *Celtic Tiger* (2005).

Flaubert, Gustave (1821–80) Writer, born in Rouen, France. His masterpiece, *Madame Bovary* (1857), was condemned as immoral and its author (unsuccessfully) prosecuted. *Three Tales* (trans, 1877) reveals his mastery of the short story.

Fleming, Sir Alexander (1881–1955) Bacteriologist, born near Darvel, East Ayrshire. He was the first to use antityphoid vaccines on human beings, pioneered the use of Salvarsan against syphilis, and in 1928 discovered penicillin, for which he shared the Nobel Prize for Physiology or Medicine in 1945.

Fleming, Ian (Lancaster) (1908–64) Writer and journalist, born in London. He achieved worldwide fame as the creator of a series of spy novels, starting with *Casino Royale* (1953), built round the exploits of his amoral hero James Bond.

Flintoff, Andrew, nickname **Freddie** (1977–) Cricketer, born in Preston, Lancashire. A fast bowler and batsman, he joined Lancashire County Cricket Club at age 17 and debuted for England against South Africa in 1998. In his first Ashes series, in England in 2005, he contributed to his country's victory with a tally of 24 wickets and 402 runs, winning England's Man of the Series Award. He captained England for the first time during the team's Test series against India in March 2006, taking over from an injured Michael Vaughan.

Flynn, Errol (Leslie Thomson) (1909–59) Actor, born in Hobart, Tasmania. *Captain Blood* (1935) established him as a hero of historical adventure stories, seen also in such films as *The Adventures of Robin Hood* (1938) and *The Sea Hawk* (1940). During the 1940s his off-screen reputation for drinking and womanizing became legendary.

Foale, Michael (1957–) Astronaut, born in Louth, Lincolnshire. In October 2003 he was chosen to command the International Space Station (ISS), spending 200 days performing routine maintenance and conducting scientific experiments, and thereby clocking up more hours in space than any other US astronaut.

Fokine, Michel, originally **Mikhail Mikhaylovich Fokine** (1880–1942) Dancer and choreographer, born in St Petersburg, Russia. He is credited with the creation of modern ballet from the artificial, stylized mode prevalent at the turn of the century.

Fonda, Henry (Jaynes) (1905–82) Actor, born in Grand Island, NE. His performances in *Young Mr Lincoln* (1939) and *The Grapes of Wrath* (1940) established him in the role of the American folk hero. His last major appearance was in *On Golden Pond* (1981, Oscar).

Fonda, Jane (Seymour) (1937–) Actress, born in New York City, the daughter of Henry Fonda. She married (1965–73) director Roger Vadim,

with whom she made *La Ronde* (1964) and *Barbarella* (1968). Later films include *Klute* (1971, Oscar), *Coming Home* (1978, Oscar), and *Monster-in-Law* (2005).

Fonteyn, Margot, in full **Dame Margot Fonteyn de Arias**, originally **Margaret Hookham** (1919–91) Ballerina, born in Reigate, Surrey. She joined the Sadler's Wells Ballet (later the Royal Ballet) in 1934, and became one of the leading ballerinas of the 20th-c, partnering Nureyev in the 1960s.

Foot, Michael (Mackintosh) (1913–) British statesman, born in Plymouth, Devon, the brother of Dingle and Hugh Foot. He served as secretary of state for employment (1974–6), and became deputy leader (1976–80) then leader (1980–3) of the Labour Party.

Ford, Anna (1943–) Broadcaster, born in Tewkesbury, Gloucestershire. She worked with Granada TV and the BBC before becoming an ITN newscaster (1978–80) and helping to present *TV am* (1980–2). She then worked as a freelance broadcaster and writer, and (1989–2006) with BBC news and current affairs.

Ford, Elbur *see* Hibbert, Eleanor

Ford, Gerald R(udolph) (1913–) US Republican statesman and 38th president (1974–7), born in Omaha, NE. Vice-president in 1973, he became president in 1974 when Nixon resigned over the Watergate scandal. The full pardon he granted to Nixon made him unpopular, and he was defeated in the 1976 presidential election by Carter.

Ford, Harrison (1942–) Actor, born in Chicago, IL. His films include *Star*

Wars (1977) and its two sequels, the series of 'Indiana Jones' films, beginning with *Raiders of the Lost Ark* (1981), *Witness* (1985, Oscar nomination), *The Fugitive* (1993), *What Lies Beneath* (2000), and *Firewall* (2005).

Ford, Henry (1863–1947) Automobile engineer and manufacturer, born in Dearborn, MI. He produced his first petrol-driven motor car in 1893, and in 1903 started the Ford Motor Co, pioneering the modern 'assembly line' mass-production techniques for his famous Model T (1908–9).

Ford, John, originally **Sean Aloysius O'Fearna** (1895–1973) Film director, born in Cape Elizabeth, ME. His portrayal of US pioneering history is seen in *Stagecoach* (1939), *The Informer* (1935, Oscar), and *The Grapes of Wrath* (1940, Oscar). Other films include *How Green Was My Valley* (1941, Oscar) and *The Quiet Man* (1952, Oscar).

Foreman, George (1948–) Boxer, born in Marshall, TX. He became the world heavyweight champion in 1973, knocking out Joe Frazier, but lost the title to Muhammad Ali in 1974. He returned to the ring in 1991, losing to Evander Holyfield, then regaining the title in 1994.

Forester, C(ecil) S(cott) (1899–1966) Writer, born in Cairo. Known especially for his creation of Horatio Hornblower, he also wrote biographical and travel books.

Formby, George (1904–61) Entertainer, born in Wigan, Greater Manchester. He appeared in a series of slapstick comedies as a shy young man with an irrepressible grin and ever-ready ukulele to accompany his risqué songs.

Forster, E(dward) M(organ) (1879–1970) Writer, born in London. His works include *Where Angels Fear to Tread* (1905), *The Longest Journey* (1907), *A Room with a View* (1908), *Howard's End* (1910), and his masterpiece, *A Passage to India* (1924).

Forsyth, Bruce, popular name of **Bruce Joseph Forsyth-Johnson** (1928–) Entertainer, born in Edmonton, Greater London. He is best known as the host of many UK television shows, such as *Sunday Night at the London Palladium* (1958–60), *The Generation Game* (1971–8, 1992–4), and *Strictly Come Dancing* (2003–).

Forsyth, Frederick (1938–) Writer of suspense thrillers, born in Ashford, Kent. His reputation rests on three taut thrillers, *The Day of the Jackal* (1971), *The Odessa File* (1972), and *The Dogs of War* (1974).

Foster, Jodie, originally **Alicia Christian Foster** (1962–) Film actress and director, born in Los Angeles, CA. After starring in such films as *Bugsy Malone* (1976) and *Taxi Driver* (1976), she later established herself as an adult actress in *The Accused* (1988, Oscar) and *The Silence of the Lambs* (1991, Oscar). Later films include *Contact* (1997) and *Flightplan* (2005).

Foster, Stephen (Collins) (1826–64) Songwriter, born in Pittsburgh, PA. He began writing 'minstrel songs', such as 'Oh! Susanna' (1848), 'Old Folks at Home' (1851), and 'Beautiful Dreamer' (1864), which became seminal works of the US tradition.

Foucault, (Jean Bernard) Léon

(1819–68) Physicist, born in Paris. He determined the velocity of light, and showed that light travels more slowly in water than in air (1850). By means of a freely suspended pendulum, he proved that the Earth rotates (1851).

Fowler, H(enry) W(atson) (1858–1933) Lexicographer, born in Tonbridge, Kent. In 1903 he began a literary partnership with his brother **F(rank) G(eorge) Fowler** (1871–1918) which led to *The King's English* (1906) and the *Concise Oxford Dictionary* (1911).

Fowler, Robbie (1975–) Footballer, born in Liverpool, Merseyside. He made his debut for Liverpool in 1993. He was twice voted the Professional Football Association's Young Player of the Year (1995, 1996), and made his full debut for England in 1996. After spells with Leeds United (from 2001) and Manchester City (from 2003), he rejoined Liverpool in 2006.

Fowles, John (Robert) (1926–) Writer, born in Leigh-on-Sea, Essex. His books include *The Magus* (1966), *The French Lieutenant's Woman* (1969; filmed 1981), *The Ebony Tower* (1974; televised 1984), and *Tessera* (1993).

Fox, George (1624–91) Founder of the Religious Society of Friends (Quakers), born in Fenny Drayton, Leicestershire. His life is a record of persecutions, imprisonments, and missionary travel to several parts of the world.

Foxx, Jamie, originally **Eric Morlon Bishop** (1967–) Actor and producer, born in Terrell, TX. He appeared in the TV comedy sketch show *In Living Color* (1990), and later had his own series *The Jamie Foxx Show* (1996). His feature films include *Ali* (2001), *Collateral* (2004, Golden Globe, Oscar nomination), *Ray* (2004, Golden Globe, Oscar), and *Jarhead* (2005).

Fra Angelico *see* Angelico, Fra

France, Anatole, pseudonym of **Jacques Anatole François Thibault** (1844–1924) Writer, born in Paris. He wrote several lively novels, which contrast with his later, satirical works, such as *Penguin Island* (trans, 1908) and *The Gods are Athirst* (trans, 1912). He was awarded the Nobel Prize for Literature in 1921.

Francis of Assisi, St, originally **Giovanni Bernardone** (?1181–1226) Founder of the Franciscan Order, born in Assisi, Italy. In 1205 he devoted himself to the care of the poor and the sick, and formed a brotherhood for which he drew up a rule repudiating all property. He was canonized in 1228.

Francis of Sales, St (1567–1622) Bishop and writer, born in Sales, France. A distinguished preacher, he became Bishop of Geneva (1602), where he helped to found a congregation of nuns of the Visitation. He was canonized in 1665.

Francis, Dick, popular name of **Richard Stanley Francis** (1920–) Jockey and novelist, born in Surrey. After retiring as a rider in 1957, he began writing popular thrillers with a racing background, such as *Forfeit* (1969), *Whip Hand* (1980), *Comeback* (1991), and *Win, Place, and Show* (2004).

Francis Xavier, St, Span **San Francisco Javier**, known as **the Apostle of the Indies** (1506–52) Roman Catholic missionary, born in

Navarre, Spain. One of the first seven members of the Jesuit order (1534), he began his missionary work in Goa, India (1542), travelling to the Malay Is (1545) and Japan (1549). He was canonized in 1622.

Franck, César (Auguste) (1822–90) Composer, born in Liège, Belgium. His reputation rests on a few masterpieces all written after the age of 50, the best known being a string quartet, a symphony, and the *Variations symphoniques* for piano and orchestra.

Franco (Bahamonde), Francisco, popular name **el Caudillo** ('the leader') (1892–1975) Spanish general and dictator (1936–75), born in El Ferrol, Galicia. In 1936 he joined the conspiracy against the Popular Front government, becoming *generalísimo* of the rebel forces. Between 1936 and 1939 he led the Nationalists to victory, and presided over the construction of an authoritarian regime that endured until his death.

Frank, Anne (1929–45) Jewish diarist, born in Frankfurt, Germany. Her family fled to The Netherlands in 1933, and after the Nazi occupation she hid with her family in Amsterdam from 1942 until they were betrayed in 1944. She died in Belsen. The diary she kept during her concealment was published in 1947.

Franklin, Benjamin (1706–90) US statesman, writer, and scientist, born in Boston, MA. His research into electricity proved that lightning and electricity are identical. He was actively involved in framing the Declaration of Independence (1776), and played a major part in the Fed-

eral Constitutional Convention (1787). In his retirement he wrote an acclaimed autobiography.

Franks, Tommy, popular name of **Thomas Ray Franks** (1945–) US general, born in Wynnewood, OK. He served in West Germany (1980s) and Korea, and was commander of the Third US Army, Fort McPherson, GA. Promoted to general (2000), he was appointed commander-in-chief of the US Central Command (2000–3). He had responsibility for the campaign in Afghanistan to destroy the Taliban regime (2001) and commanded the US-led invasion of Iraq (Mar–Apr 2003). He retired in 2003.

Fraser, Lady Antonia, *née* **Pakenham** (1932–) British writer. She is best known for her books about important historical figures, such as *Mary Queen of Scots* (1969, James Tait Black), *Kings and Queens of England* (1975, 1988), and *Marie Antoinette: The Journey* (2001). She married Harold Pinter in 1980.

Frazer, Sir James George (1854–1941) Social anthropologist, classicist, and folklorist, born in Glasgow. His major work was *The Golden Bough* (1890; rewritten in 12 vols, 1911–15).

Frazier, Joe, popular name of **Joseph Frazier** (1944–) Boxer, born in Beaufort, SC. He defeated Jimmy Ellis to become the world heavyweight champion (1970), but lost the title to George Foreman (1973). He retired in 1976, and staged an unsuccessful comeback fight in 1981.

Frears, Stephen Arthur (1941–) Director, born in Leicester, Leicestershire. He won international acclaim with his cult classic, *My Beautiful Launderette* (1985). Other films include *Dangerous Liaisons* (1988), *Dirty Pretty Things* (2002), and *Mrs Henderson Presents* (2005).

Freeman, Morgan (1937–) Actor, born in Memphis, TN. He made his Broadway debut in 1967 in an all-black production of *Hello, Dolly*. His film credits include *Street Smart* (1987, Oscar nomination), *Driving Miss Daisy* (1989), *Million Dollar Baby* (2004, Oscar), and *Paradise Now* (2006).

French, Dawn (1957–) Comedy writer and actress, born in Holyhead, Anglesey. She formed a comedy partnership with Jennifer Saunders, becoming widely known with the television series *French and Saunders* (from 1987). Her own series include *Murder Most Horrid* and *The Vicar of Dibley* (from 1994, Emmy, 1998). She is married to comedy performer Lenny Henry.

Freud, Sir Clement (Raphael) (1924–) British politician, writer, broadcaster, and caterer. Known for his books about food, and as a long-serving member of the BBC Radio 4 *Just a Minute* team (from 1968), he became a Liberal MP (1972–87).

Freud, Sigmund (1856–1939) Founder of psychoanalysis, born in Freiburg, Moravia (now Príbor, Czech Republic). His major work, *The Interpretation of Dreams* (trans, 1900), argued that dreams are disguised manifestations of repressed sexual wishes. In 1902 he was appointed to a professorship in Vienna, out of which grew the Vienna Psychoanalytical Society

(1908) and the International Psychoanalytic Association (1910).

Friends *see* Aniston, Jennifer; Cox, Courteney; Kudrow, Lisa; LeBlanc, Matt; Perry, Matthew; Schwimmer, David

Friml, (Charles) Rudolf (1879–1972) Composer, born in Prague. He settled in the USA in 1906, where he made his name as a composer of light operas, including *Rose Marie* (1924) and *The Vagabond King* (1925).

Frost, Sir David (Paradine) (1939–) Broadcaster and businessman, born in Tenterden, Kent. He presented the satirical revue, *That Was the Week That Was* (BBC, 1962–3), and hosted many programmes in Britain and the US. A co-founder of London Weekend Television, he was also co-founder and presenter of Britain's TV–am (1983). He presented the BBC's *Breakfast with Frost* from 1992–2005.

Frost, Robert (Lee) (1874–1963) Poet, born in San Francisco, CA. His works include *A Boy's Will* (1913), *New Hampshire* (1923, Pulitzer), *Collected Poems* (1930, Pulitzer), and *A Further Range* (1936, Pulitzer). He was regarded as the unofficial laureate of the USA.

Fry, Christopher, pseudonym of **Christopher Harris** (1907–2005) Playwright, born in Bristol. He wrote a series of major plays in free verse, often with undertones of religion and mysticism, including *A Phoenix Too Frequent* (1946) and *The Lady's Not For Burning* (1949).

Fry, Elizabeth (1780–1845) Quaker prison reformer, born in Norwich, Norfolk. After seeing the terrible conditions for women in Newgate prison, she devoted her life to prison reform at home and abroad.

Fry, Stephen (John) (1957–) Writer, actor, and comedian, born in London. At Cambridge University (1979–82) he joined the Footlights Revue where he met **Hugh Laurie** (1959–). They formed a comedy writing partnership, notably for the television series *A Bit of Fry and Laurie* (1987–95). He appeared in *Blackadder* (1986) and *Jeeves and Wooster* (1990–3), and his films include *Wilde* (1997) and *A Cock and Bull Story* (2005).

Fuchs, Sir Vivian Ernest (1908–99) Antarctic explorer and geologist, born in the Isle of Wight, UK. He is best known as the leader of the Commonwealth Trans-Antarctic Expedition (1955–8) which completed the first land crossing of Antarctica.

Fuller, R(ichard) Buckminster (1895–1983) Inventor, designer, poet, and philosopher, born in Milton, MA. He developed the Dymaxion ('dynamic and maximum efficiency') House in 1927, and the Dymaxion streamlined, omnidirectional car in 1932. In 1962 he became professor of poetry at Harvard.

Gable, (William) Clark (1901–60) Actor, born in Cadiz, OH. Growing popularity in tough but sympathetic parts soon labelled him 'the King of Hollywood', reaching its peak with his portrayal of Rhett Butler in *Gone With the Wind* (1939).

Gabriel, Peter (1950–) Singer and songwriter, born in Surrey. He co-founded the rock group Genesis, but left to pursue a solo career in 1975. A collection of his video hits, *CV* (1988), topped the UK music video chart. Later credits include the score for the controversial film *The Last Temptation of Christ* (1988). In 1982 he founded the 'World of Music, Arts and Dance' (WOMAD) festival.

Gaddafi or **Qaddafi, Colonel Muammar** (1942–) Libyan political and military leader, born into a nomadic family. He overthrew King Idris in 1969, and became Chairman of the Revolutionary Command Council, encouraging a return to the fundamental principles of Islam. An unpredictable figure, his support of violent revolutionaries in other countries has been a continuing source of international concern.

Gagarin, Yuri (Alekseyevich) (1934–68) Russian cosmonaut, born in Gagarin (formerly Gzhatsk), Russia. In 1961 he became the first man to travel in space, completing a circuit of the Earth in the *Vostok* spaceship satellite.

Gainsborough, Thomas (1727–88) Landscape and portrait painter, born in Sudbury, Suffolk. He moved to Bath in 1759, where he established himself with his portrait of Earl Nugent (1760). His best-known paintings include 'The Blue Boy' (c.1770), 'The Harvest Wagon' (1767), and 'The Watering Place' (1777).

Galileo, in full **Galileo Galilei** (1564–1642) Astronomer and mathematician, born in Pisa, Italy. He improved the refracting telescope (1610), and was the first to use it for astronomy. His bold advocacy of the Copernican theory brought ecclesiastical censure, and he was forced to retract before the Inquisition. The validity of his work was eventually given official recognition by the Roman Catholic Church in 1993.

Galliano, Sir John (Charles) (1960–) Fashion designer, born in Gibraltar. He received the British Fashion Council Designer of the Year Award in 1987, 1994, and 1995, and became designer-in-chief at Christian Dior in 1996.

Gallup, George (Horace) (1901–84) Public opinion expert, born in Jefferson, IA. In 1935 he founded the American Institute of Public Opinion, and evolved the *Gallup polls* for testing the state of public opinion.

Galsworthy, John (1867–1933) Novelist and playwright, born in Kingston Hill, Surrey. The six novels comprising *The Forsyte Saga* (1906–28) began a new vogue for 'serial' novels. His plays, such as *Strife* (1909) and *The Skin Game* (1920), illustrate his interest in social and ethical problems. He was awarded the Nobel Prize for Literature in 1932.

Galton, Sir Francis (1822–1911) Scientist and explorer, born in Birmingham, West Midlands. He is best known for his studies of heredity and intelligence, such as *Hereditary Genius* (1869), which led to the field he called *eugenics*.

Galway, Sir James (1939–) Flautist, born in Belfast. Since 1975 he has followed a successful solo career, playing on a solid gold flute of remarkable tonal range.

Gama, Vasco da (c.1469–1525) Navigator, born in Sines, Alentejo, Portugal. He led the expedition which discovered the route to India round the Cape of Good Hope (1497–9).

Gambon, Sir Michael (John) (1940–) Actor, born in Dublin. He joined the Royal Shakespeare Company (1982–3), and his notable television appearances include *The Singing Detective* (1986, BAFTA) and *Perfect Strangers* (2001, BAFTA). He played the role of Dumbledore in the films *Harry Potter and the Prisoner of Azkaban* (2004) and *Harry Potter and the Goblet of Fire* (2005).

Gandhi, (Mohandas Karamchand), known as **the Mahatma** (Hindi 'of great soul') (1869–1948) Indian nationalist leader, born in Poorbandar, Kathiawar. He studied law in London, and in 1893 went to South Africa, where he spent 20 years opposing discriminatory legislation against Indians. In 1914 he returned to India, where he became leader of the Indian National Congress, advocating a policy of non-violent non-co-operation to achieve independence. In 1930 he led a 320 km/200 mi march to the sea to collect salt in symbolic defiance of the government monopoly. After independence (1947), he tried to stop the Hindu–Muslim conflict in Bengal, a policy which led to his assassination by a Hindu fanatic.

Gandhi, Indira (Priyadarshini) (1917–84) Indian prime minister (1966–77, 1980–4), born in Allahabad, India, the daughter of Nehru. She became president of the Indian Congress Party (1959–60), minister of information (1964), and prime minister after the death of Shastri. She was unable to stem sectarian violence at home, and was assassinated by Sikh extremists.

Gandhi, Rajiv (1944–91) Indian prime minister (1984–9), born in Mumbai (Bombay), India, the eldest son of Indira Gandhi. After the death of his brother **Sanjay Gandhi** (1946–80) in an air crash, he was elected to his brother's parliamentary seat (1981). He became prime minister following the assassination of Indira Gandhi (1984), but was defeated in the 1989 election. He was assassinated while campaigning for the Congress Party.

Gandolfini, James (1961–) Actor, born in Westwood, NJ. He became well known for his role as Tony Soprano in the television series *The Sopranos*

(1999–), for which he received a Best Actor Golden Globe (1999) and three Emmy awards (2000, 2001, 2003).

Garbo, Greta, originally **Greta Lovisa Gustafsson** (1905–90) Film actress, born in Stockholm. In the USA from 1925, her successes included *Anna Christie* (1930), *Anna Karenina* (1935), *Camille* (1936), and *Ninotchka* (1939).

García Lorca, Federico *see* Lorca, Federico García

García Márquez, Gabriel *see* Márquez, Gabriel García

Gardner, Ava (Lavinnia), originally **Lucy Johnson** (1922–90) Film actress, born in Smithfield, NC. Once voted the world's most beautiful woman, she remained a leading lady for two decades, her films including *The Barefoot Contessa* (1954) and *Night of the Iguana* (1964).

Gardner, Erle Stanley (1889–1970) Crime novelist, born in Malden, MA. He is best known as the writer of the 'Perry Mason' books, beginning with *The Case of the Velvet Claws* (1933), which were made into a long-running television series.

Garfield, James A(bram) (1831–81) US Republican statesman and 20th president (Mar–Sep 1881), born in Orange, OH. He identified himself with the cause of civil service reform, irritating many in his own party, and was shot by a disappointed office-seeker.

Garfunkel, Art (1942–) Singer and actor, born in Forest Hills, NY. He teamed up with Paul Simon as a teenager, achieving major hits with 'The Sound of Silence' (1965) and the soundtrack for *The Graduate*. As a soloist, he achieved a UK number 1 with 'Bright Eyes' (1979). In 2004 the duo re-formed for a successful international tour.

Garibaldi, Giuseppe (1807–82) Italian patriot, born in Nice, France. At the outbreak of Italy's war of liberation, he sailed from Genoa (1860) with his 'thousand' volunteers and arrived in Sicily, overran much of S Italy, and drove King Francis of Naples from his capital.

Garland, Judy, originally **Frances Gumm** (1922–69) Actress and singer, born in Grand Rapids, MN. She became a juvenile film star in *Broadway Melody of 1938*, followed by *The Wizard of Oz* (1939) and *Meet Me in St Louis* (1944), directed by Vincente Minnelli, whom she later married.

Garrett, Lesley (1955–) Soprano, born in Doncaster, South Yorkshire. In 1984 she joined the English National Opera as principal soprano. Her television work includes two series of *Lesley Garrett Tonight* (BBC 1998, 2000), and among her albums are *Soprano in Red* (1995) and *So Deep is the Night* (2003).

Garrick, David (1717–79) Actor, theatre manager, and playwright, born in Hereford, Hereford and Worcester. In 1741 he won acting fame as Richard III, and for 30 years dominated the English stage. As joint manager of Drury Lane (1747–76) he encouraged innovations in scenery and lighting design.

Gascoigne, Paul, nickname **Gazza** (1967–) Footballer, born in Gateshead, Tyne and Wear. After Tottenham Hotspur signed him in 1988, he established himself as an outstanding player and a controversial personality, winning 57 caps for England. His career has been hindered by injury and he joined a succession of clubs, and in 2004 was briefly player-coach at Boston United.

Gaskell, Elizabeth (Cleghorn), *née* **Stevenson**, known as **Mrs Gaskell** (1810–65) Writer, born in London. She began to write in middle age, her works including *Mary Barton* (1848), *Wives and Daughters* (1865, televised 2000), and a biography of Charlotte Brontë.

Gates, Bill, popular name of **William Henry Gates** (1955–) Computer engineer and entrepreneur, born in Seattle, WA. In 1977 he co-founded Microsoft to develop and produce DOS, his basic operating system for computers, adopted in 1981 by IBM. One of the wealthiest men in the US by age 35, he founded the charitable Bill and Melinda Gates Foundation (2000).

Gauguin, (Eugène Henri) Paul (1848–1903) Post-Impressionist painter, born in Paris. From 1891 he lived mainly in Tahiti and the Marquesas Is, evolving his own style, *Synthétisme*, reflecting his hatred of civilization and the inspiration he found in primitive peoples.

Gaulle, Charles de *see* de Gaulle, Charles

Gaultier, Jean-Paul (1952–) Fashion designer, born in Paris. He joined the houses of Jacques Esterel and Jean Patou before producing his own independent collection in 1976. He reached a new audience as co-host of the magazine show *Eurotrash* on British television.

Gaunt, John of *see* John of Gaunt

Gavaskar, Sunil (Manohar) (1949–) Cricketer, born in Mumbai (Bombay), India. He played 125 Test matches for India, scoring a then record 10 122 runs, and 25 834 runs in first-class cricket at an average of 51·46 per innings.

Gazza *see* Gascoigne, Paul

Gebrselassie, Haile (1973–) Athlete, born in Arssi, Ethiopia. The dominant long-distance runner of the 1990s, he was four times world champion (1993, 1995, 1997, 1999) and twice Olympic champion (1996, 2000) at 10 000 m. He had set a total of 15 world records by 2000.

Gehry, Frank O (1929–) Architect, born in Toronto, Ontario, Canada. He opened his own Los Angeles firm in 1962. His work is characterized by sculptural design, 'brutalist' combinations of materials such as corrugated metal and chain-link fencing in residential applications, and undefined interiors. Among his best-known buildings is the Guggenheim Museum, Bilbao (1997). His awards include the Pritzker Architecture Prize (1989).

Geldof, Bob, popular name of **Robert Frederick Xenon Geldof** (1954–) Rock musician and philanthropist, born in Dublin. He led the successful rock group, the Boomtown Rats (1975–86). In 1984 he established the pop charity 'Band Aid' trust which raised £8 million for African famine relief through the release of the record 'Do they know it's Christmas?'. A later version was recorded (2004) to raise funds for famine-stricken Darfur in W Sudan, and in 2005 he organized the 'Live 8' charity pop concerts in support of the Make Poverty History campaign.

Genghis Khan, also spelled **Jingis** or **Chingis Khan** ('Very Mighty Ruler'), originally **Temujin** (1162/7–1227) Mongol conqueror, born in Temujin, Mongolia, on the R Onon. From 1211, in several campaigns, he overran the empire of N China, the Kara-Chitai, Kharezm, and other territories, and by his death the Mongol empire stretched from the Black Sea to the Pacific.

George I (of Great Britain) (1660–1727) King of Great Britain and Ireland (1714–27), born in Osnabrück, Germany, the great-grandson of James I of England. Elector of Hanover since 1698, he took relatively little part in the government of Britain, living in Hanover as much as possible.

George II (of Great Britain) (1683–1760) King of Great Britain and Ireland (1727–60), and Elector of Hanover, born at Herrenhausen, Hanover, the son of George I. In 1705 he married **Caroline of Ansbach** (1683–1737). His reign saw the crushing of Jacobite hopes at Culloden (1746), the foundation of British India after Plassey (1757), and the capture of Quebec (1759).

George III (1738–1820) King of Great Britain and Ireland (1760–1820), elector (1760–1815) and king (from 1815) of Hanover, born in London. Eager to govern as well as reign, he caused considerable friction, and with Lord North shared in the blame for the loss of the American colonies. In 1810 he suffered a recurrence of a mental derangement, and the Prince of Wales was made regent.

George IV (1762–1830) King of Great Britain and Hanover (1820–30), born in London, the eldest son of George III. In 1795 he married Princess Caroline of Brunswick, whom he tried to divorce when he was king. Her death in 1821 ended a scandal in which the people sympathized with the queen.

George V (1865–1936) King of the United Kingdom (1910–36), born in London, the second son of Edward VII. He married Princess Mary of Teck in 1893. His reign saw the Union of South Africa (1910), World War 1, the Irish Free State settlement (1922), and the General Strike (1926).

George VI (1895–1952) King of the United Kingdom (1936–52), born at Sandringham, Norfolk, the second son of George V. He married Lady Elizabeth Bowes-Lyon in 1923, and they had two children: Princess Elizabeth (later Queen Elizabeth II) and Princess Margaret. During World War 2 he set a personal example coping with wartime restrictions, continuing to reside in bomb-damaged Buckingham Palace, and visiting all theatres of war.

George, St (fl.3rd-c) Patron of chivalry, and guardian saint of England and Portugal. His name was early obscured by fable, such as the story of his fight with a dragon to rescue a maiden.

George, David Lloyd *see* Lloyd-George, David

George-Brown, Baron, originally **George (Alfred) Brown** (1914–85) British statesman, born in London. Deputy Leader of the Labour Party (1960–70), he unsuccessfully contested Wilson for party leadership in 1963. He was secretary of state for economic affairs (1964–6) and foreign secretary (1966–8).

Gere, Richard (1949–) Actor, born in Philadelphia, PA. He made his screen debut in 1975, and went on to star in such films as *Yanks* (1979), *American Gigolo* (1980), and *Pretty Woman* (1990). Later films include *Chicago* (2002) and *Shall We Dance?* (2004).

German, Sir Edward, originally **Edward German Jones** (1862–1936) Composer, born in Whitchurch, Shropshire. A composer of light opera, his works include *Merrie England* (1902), *Tom Jones* (1907), symphonies, suites, chamber music, and songs.

Geronimo, Indian name **Goyathlay** (1829–1909) Chiricahua Apache Indian, born along the Gila River in present-day Arizona. The best known of all Apache leaders, he forcibly resisted the internment of 4000 of his people on a reservation at San Carlos (1874), escaping from white control on several occasions.

Gershwin, George, originally **Jacob Gershvin** (1898–1937) Composer, born in New York City. In 1924 he began collaborating with his brother Ira as lyricist, producing numerous classic songs, such as 'Lady Be Good' (1924) and 'I Got Rhythm' (1930). He also composed extended concert works, such as *Rhapsody in Blue* (1924). His masterpiece was the jazz-opera *Porgy and Bess* (1935).

Gershwin, Ira, originally **Israel Gershvin**, pseudonym **Arthur Francis** (1896–1983) Songwriter, born in New York City. In 1924 he

began to work with his brother, producing such hits as 'I Got Plenty o' Nothin'' (1935) and 'They Can't Take That Away From Me' (1938).

Gervais, Ricky (Dene) (1962–) Actor, writer, and director, born in Reading, Berkshire. He shot to fame with his role as David Brent in the BBC television show *The Office* (2001–2), a series he co-wrote with Stephen Merchant. The show won double BAFTA awards for Gervais, as Best Sitcom and Best Comedy Performance (2002, 2003, 2004). He teamed up with Merchant again for the comedy series *Extras* (2005).

Getty, J(ean) Paul (1892–1976) Oil billionaire and art collector, born in Minneapolis, MN. He entered the oil business in his early twenties, and went on to acquire and control more than 100 companies, becoming one of the world's richest men.

Getz, Stan(ley) (1927–91) Jazz saxophonist, born in Philadelphia, PA. He formed his own groups, developing a distinctive 'cool' sound, and in the 1960s popularized a bossa-nova style.

Gibbon, Edward (1737–94) Historian, born in Putney, Surrey. After a visit to Rome in 1764 he began to plan for his major work, *The History of the Decline and Fall of the Roman Empire* (5 vols, 1776–88).

Gibson, Mel, originally **Columcille Gerard Gibson** (1956–) Film actor and director, born in Peekskill, NY. He became known following his lead role in *Mad Max* (1979) and its sequels (1981, 1985), later films including *Lethal Weapon* (1987) and its sequels (1989, 1991, 1998), and *Braveheart*, which he also directed (1995, Oscar Best Film). In 2004 he directed the controversial *The Passion of the Christ*.

Gide, André (Paul Guillaume) (1869–1951) Writer, born in Paris. His best-known works are *Fruits of the Earth* (trans, 1897) and *The Counterfeiters* (trans, 1926), his translations of *Oedipus* and *Hamlet*, and his *Journal*. He received the Nobel Prize for Literature in 1947.

Gielgud, Sir (Arthur) John (1904–2000) Actor and director, born in London. A leading Shakespearean actor, his many films include *The Prime Minister* (1940), *Arthur* (1970, Oscar), *Prospero's Books* (1991), and *Elizabeth* (1998). The London *Globe* theatre was renamed after him in 1994.

Giggs, Ryan (1973–) Footballer, born in Cardiff. He made his league debut for Manchester United in 1991, and later that year became the youngest-ever Welsh cap. He has twice been named the Professional Football Association's Young Player of the Year (1991–2). His honours with United include the FA Cup, Premier League Championship, and European Cup in the 1998–9 season. He gained his 50th cap for Wales in 2005.

Gilbert, Sir W(illiam) S(chwenck) (1836–1911) Parodist and librettist, born in London. He wrote much humorous verse under his boyhood nickname 'Bab', collected in 1869 as the *Bab Ballads*, and partnered Arthur Sullivan in writing 14 popular operas, from *Trial by Jury* (1875) to *The Gondoliers* (1889).

Gilbert and George Avant-garde artists: **Gilbert Proesch** (1943–), born in St Martin in Thurn, Italy, and **George Passmore** (1944–), born in Plymouth, Devon. They made their name in the late 1960s as performance artists (the 'singing sculptures'), with faces and hands painted gold, holding their poses for hours at a time.

Gilbert of Sempringham, St (c.1083–1189) Priest, born in Sempringham, Lincolnshire. He was the founder of the Gilbertine Order (1148), which was dissolved at the Reformation. He was canonized in 1202.

Giles, Bill, popular name of **William George Giles** (1939–) British weatherman, the head of the Weather Centre at the BBC (1983–2000). He joined the Meteorological Office in 1959, became a radio broadcaster in 1972, and moved to television in 1975. His books include *The Story of Weather* (1990).

Giles, Carl (1916–95) Cartoonist, born in London. From 1937 he produced his distinctive and popular humorous drawings, first for *Reynolds News*, then (from 1943) for the *Express* newspapers.

Gillespie, Dizzy, popular name of **John Birks Gillespie** (1917–93) Jazz trumpeter and composer, born in Cheraw, SC. As a band leader, often with Charlie Parker on saxophone, he developed the music known as *bebop*. His own big band (1946–50) was his masterpiece, affording him scope as both soloist and showman.

Gillette, King C(amp) (1855–1932) Inventor of the safety razor, born in Fond du Lac, WI. He was a travelling salesman for a hardware company, before founding his razor blade company in 1903.

Gilliam, Terry (1940–) Artist and film director, born in Minneapolis, MI. Originally known for his fantasy animations in TV's 'Monty Python's Flying Circus' (1969–74), he went on to direct such films as *Time Bandits* (1980), *Fear and Loathing in Las Vegas* (1998), and *The Brothers Grimm* (2005).

Ginsberg, Allen (1926–97) Poet of the 'beat' movement, born in Newark, NJ. *Howl* (1956), his epic poem, launched him as a public speaker against authoritarianism. Other collections include *Kaddish and Other Poems* (1961) and *Reality Sandwiches* (1963).

Giotto (di Bondone) (c.1266–1337) Painter and architect, the founder of the Florentine School of painting, born in Vespignano, Italy. His major work was the fresco cycle, 'The Lives of Christ and the Virgin', in the Arena Chapel, Padua (1305–8).

Gladstone, W(illiam) E(wart) (1809–98) British prime minister (1868–74, 1880–5, 1886, 1892–4), born in Liverpool. He was Chancellor of the Exchequer (1852–5, 1859–66), and in 1867 became leader of the Liberal Party. Frequently in office until 1894, he succeeded in carrying out a scheme of parliamentary reform, but his bills for Irish Home Rule were defeated.

Glass, Philip (1937–) Composer, born in Baltimore, MD. A proponent of minimalism in music, he attracted public notice with the first of his 12 operas, *Einstein on the Beach* (1976).

Later work includes *Monsters of Grace* (1998), and the film scores *Kundun* (1998) and *The Hours* (2002, BAFTA).

Glendower, Owen, Welsh **Owain Glyndwr** or **Owain ap Gruffudd** (c.1354–c.1416) Welsh chief, born in Powys. In 1400 he rebelled against Henry IV, proclaimed himself Prince of Wales, established an independent Welsh parliament, and joined the coalition with **Harry Percy** (1364–1403), who was defeated at the Battle of Shrewsbury.

Glenn, John H(erschel) (1921–) Astronaut, the first American to orbit the Earth, born in Cambridge, OH. In 1962 he made a three-orbit flight in the Friendship 7 space capsule. A senator since 1975, he sought the Democratic nomination for the presidency in 1984 and 1988.

Gloucester, Richard (Alexander Walter George), Duke of (1944–) British prince, the younger son of Henry, Duke of Gloucester (the third son of George V). In 1972 he married **Birgitte van Deurs** (1946–); they have one son, **Alexander, Earl of Ulster** (1974–), and two daughters, **Lady Davina Windsor** (1977–) and **Lady Rose Windsor** (1980–).

Godard, Jean-Luc (1930–) Film director, born in Paris. *Breathless* (trans, 1960) established him as one of the leaders of *Nouvelle Vague* cinema. His prolific output includes *Weekend* (1968), *Detective* (1984), *Hail, Mary* (trans, 1985), and *Nouvelle Vague* (1990).

Godiva, Lady (11th-c) An English lady and religious benefactress. According to tradition, she rode naked through Coventry in order to obtain the remission of a heavy tax imposed by her husband, Leofric, Earl of Chester, upon the townsfolk (1040).

Godwin, also spelled **Godwine** (?–1053) Anglo-Saxon nobleman and warrior, the father of Harold Godwinsson. In 1042 he helped to raise Edward the Confessor to the throne, and married him to his daughter Edith. Godwin's son Harold was for a few months Edward's successor.

Goebbels or **Göbbels, (Paul) Joseph** (1897–1945) Nazi politician, born in Rheydt, Germany. Head of the Ministry of Public Enlightenment and Propaganda (1933), and a bitter anti-Semite, his gift of mob oratory made him a powerful exponent of Nazism. In the Berlin bunker he and his wife committed suicide, after taking the lives of their six children.

Goering or **Göring, Hermann (Wilhelm)** (1893–1946) Nazi politico-military leader, born in Rosenheim, Germany. He joined the Nazi government in 1933, founded the Gestapo, set up the concentration camps, and in 1940 became economic dictator of Germany. Sentenced to death at the Nuremberg War Crimes Trial, he committed suicide.

Goethe, Johann Wolfgang von (1749–1832) Poet, dramatist, and scientist, born in Frankfurt, Germany. He captured the spirit of German nationalism with his drama, *Götz von Berlichingen* (1773), following this with his novel *The Sorrows of Young Werther* (trans, 1774). From 1776 he wrote much lyric poetry, inspired by his relationships with a series of women, notably Charlotte von Stein.

In his later years he wrote *Wilhelm Meister's Apprentice Years* (trans, 1796), continued as *Wilhelm Meister's Journeyman Years* (1821–9). His masterpiece is a version of *Faust*, published in two parts (1808, 1832).

Goldberg, Whoopi, originally **Caryn Elaine Johnson** (1955–) Film actress, born in New York City. She achieved instant fame with her role in *The Color Purple* (1985), winning a Golden Globe. Later films include *Ghost* (1990, Oscar for Best Supporting Actress), *Sister Act* and its sequel (1992, 1994), and *Get Bruce* (1999).

Goldblum, Jeff (1952–) Film actor, born in Pittsburgh, PA. He became well known for his roles in science-fiction films, such as *The Fly* (1986), *Jurassic Park* and its sequel (1993, 1997), and *Independence Day* (1996). Later films include *Mini's First Time* (2005).

Golding, Sir William (Gerald) (1911–93) Novelist, born near Newquay, Cornwall. His books include *Lord of the Flies* (1954), *Pincher Martin* (1956), *Rites of Passage* (1980, Booker), and *Close Quarters* (1987). He was awarded the Nobel Prize for Literature in 1983.

Gonzaga, Luigi, St, known as **St Aloysius** (1568–91) Jesuit priest, born near Brescia, Italy. In a plague at Rome he devoted himself to the care of the sick, but was himself infected and died. He was canonized in 1726, and is the Italian patron saint of youth.

Gooch, Graham (Alan) (1953–) Cricketer, born in Leytonstone, Greater London. As England captain (1988–93), he led a notable victory over the West Indies in Jamaica (1989). The leading England Test run-scorer, and most-capped player, he announced his retirement in 1995, with 8900 runs scored in 118 Tests.

Goodman, Benny, popular name of **Benjamin David Goodman**, nickname **the King of Swing** (1909–86) Clarinettist and bandleader, born in Chicago, IL. He formed his own orchestra in New York City (1934), and became one of the best-known leaders of the big-band era, making such recordings as 'Let's Dance' and 'One O'Clock Jump'.

Goodman, John (1952–) Film actor, born in St Louis, MO. He became well known for his role as the husband Dan in the television comedy series *Roseanne* (1988–97). His films include *Barton Fink* (1991), *The Flintstones* (1994), and *Beyond the Sea* (2004).

Goodyear, Charles (1800–60) Inventor, born in New Haven, CT. His research led to the invention of vulcanized rubber in 1844, and ultimately to the development of the rubber-manufacturing industry and the production of the tyres named after him.

Goons, The Four comedians who came together after World War 2 to create the Goon Show, which revolution-ized British radio comedy: **Spike Milligan**, **Peter Sellers**, **Harry Secombe**, and **Michael Bentine** (1922–96). They first performed on radio together in 1951: the show soon became *The Goon Show*, running for nine years and winning a worldwide band of devotees.

Gorbachev, Mikhail Sergeyevich (1931–) Soviet statesman, born in Privolnoye, Russia. General secretary of the Central Committee (1985–91), in 1988 he also became chairman of the Presidium of the Supreme Soviet (ie head of state) and in 1990 the first executive president of the USSR. He launched a radical programme of reform (*perestroika*) of the Soviet economic and political system, and a greater degree of civil liberty was allowed under the policy of *glasnost* ('openness' of information). In for-eign and defence affairs he pursued detente and nuclear disarmament with the West. He survived an attempted coup in August 1991, but resigned after the break-up of the USSR later that year.

Gordimer, Nadine (1923–) Novelist, born in Springs, South Africa. In novels such as *A Guest of Honour* (1971), *The Conservationist* (1974), and *A Sport of Nature* (1987), she adopts a liberal approach to problems of race and repression. A collection of short stories, *Loot*, appeared in 2003. She was awarded the Nobel Prize for Lit-erature in 1991.

Gordon, Charles George (1833–85) British general, born in Woolwich, Greater London. In 1860 he went to China, where he crushed the Taiping Rebellion, for which he became known as **Chinese Gordon**. Appointed Governor of the Sudan (1877), he was besieged at Khartoum for 10 months by the Mahdi's troops, and killed there two days before a relief force arrived.

Gore, Al(bert Arnold, Jr) (1948–) US vice-president (1993–2000), born in Washington, DC. A Democratic congressman (1977–85) and senator

(1985–92), he was elected vice-president to Clinton in 1992. He conceded defeat to George W Bush after five weeks of complex legal argument over the voting procedure in the presidential election in 2000.

Górecki, Henryk Mikolaj (1933–) Composer, born in Czernica, near Rybnik, Poland. His work was virtually unknown in the West until 1993, when his *Symphony No. 3: Symphony of Sorrowful Songs* (1973) reached number six in the British best-selling album charts, and sold over half a million copies worldwide.

Göring, Hermann *see* Goering, Hermann

Gorky, Maxim, pseudonym of **Alexey Maksimovich Peshkov** (1868–1936) Novelist, born in Nizhni Novgorod, Russia. He produced several Romantic short stories, then social novels and plays, notably the drama *The Lower Depths* (trans, 1902). An autobiographical trilogy (1915–23) contains his best writing. His birthplace was renamed Gorky in his honour (1929–91).

Gormley, Antony (Mark David) (1950–) Sculptor, born in London. He won the Turner Prize in 1994, and his later projects include the giant steel statue 'The Angel of the North' (1998) near Gateshead in Tyneside, and 'Another Place' (2005), 100 life-size iron figures rising out of the sand at Crosby Beach, Merseyside.

Gould, Shane (Elizabeth) (1956–) Swimmer, born in Brisbane, Queensland, Australia. She created Olympic history by being the first and only woman to win three individual gold swimming medals in

world record time. She retired in 1973, at the age of 17.

Gounod, Charles (François) (1818–93) Composer, born in Paris. His major works include the opera, *The Mock Doctor* (trans, 1858) and his masterpiece, *Faust* (1859). He also published Masses, hymns, and anthems, and was popular as a songwriter.

Gower, David (Ivon) (1957–) Cricketer, born in Tunbridge Wells, Kent. He was captain of England (1984–6, 1989), and for a time the leading Test run-scorer, with 8231 runs in Test cricket over 117 matches. He retired in 1993 and began a career in the media.

Goya (y Lucientes), Francisco (José) de (1746–1828) Artist, born in Fuendetodos, Spain. He became famous for his portraits, and in 1799 was made court painter to Charles IV, which led to 'The Family of Charles IV' (1800).

Grable, Betty, originally **Ruth Elizabeth Grable** (1916–73) Actress, born in St Louis, MO. She had her first major film role in *Hold 'em Jail* (1932), and became more established with *Pigskin Parade* (1936), and *Million Dollar Legs* (1939). She was adopted by American GI's during World War 2 as a pin-up girl.

Grace, W(illiam) G(ilbert) (1848–1915) Cricketer, born in Downend, South Gloucester. He twice captained the English team. His career in first-class cricket (1865–1908) as batsman and bowler brought 126 centuries, 54 896 runs, and 2876 wickets.

Grade (of Elstree), Lew Grade, Baron, originally **Louis Winogradsky** (1906–98) Theatrical impresario, born near Odessa, Ukraine, the eldest of three brothers who were to dominate British show-business for over 40 years. He arrived in Britain in 1912, along with his younger brother **Boris Grade**, who became **Baron Bernard Delfont of Stepney** (1909–94). Bernard entered theatrical management in 1941, and presented the annual Royal Variety Performance (1958–78). Lew headed several large film entertainment and communications companies.

Graf, Steffi (1969–) Tennis player, born in Brühl, nr Heidelberg, Germany. She won all four major titles in 1988, winning the Wimbledon singles title six more times (1989, 1991–3, 1995, 1996), and the French Open in 1999, retiring later that year. She married tennis player Andre Agassi in 2001.

Graham, Billy, popular name of **William Franklin Graham, Jr** (1918–) Evangelist, born in Charlotte, NC. A charismatic figure, since the 1950s he has conducted revivalist campaigns in the USA, UK, South America, the former USSR, and W Europe, invariably attracting large audiences. He received the Templeton Prize in 1982.

Graham, Martha (1894–1991) Dancer, teacher, and choreographer, born in Pittsburgh, PA. She started the Martha Graham School of Contemporary Dance in 1927, and became the most famous exponent of Expressionist modern dance in the USA.

Grahame, Kenneth (1859–1932) Writer, born in Edinburgh. He wrote several stories for children, the best known being *The Wind in the Willows*

(1908), dramatized in 1930 by A A Milne as *Toad of Toad Hall*.

Grainger, Percy (Aldridge), originally **George Percy Grainger** (1882–1961) Composer and pianist, born in Melbourne, Victoria, Australia. He lived in the USA for much of his life, championing the revival of folk music, but was one of the first to compose for electronic instruments.

Grammer, Kelsey (1955–) Actor, born on St Thomas, US Virgin Islands. He is best known for his role as Dr Frasier Crane, originally seen in *Cheers* (1982–93) and *Wings*, and then in *Frasier* (from 1993–2004, 32 Emmys).

Granger, Stewart, originally **James Lablanche Stewart** (1913–93) Film actor, born in London. He emerged as a leading romantic star in the 1940s, his films including *The Man in Grey* (1943), *King Solomon's Mines* (1950), *Beau Brummell* (1954), and *The Wild Geese* (1977).

Grant, Cary, originally **Archibald Leach** (1904–86) Film actor, born in Bristol. He went to Hollywood in 1928, and gave memorable performances for Hitchcock in *Suspicion* (1941), *Notorious* (1946), *To Catch a Thief* (1955), and *North by North-West* (1959).

Grant, Hugh (John Mungo) (1960–) Actor, born in London. He became internationally known following his role in *Four Weddings and a Funeral* (1994, Best Actor Golden Globe). Later films include *Notting Hill* (1999), *Bridget Jones's Diary* (2001), *Love Actually* (2003), and *Bridget Jones: The Edge of Reason* (2004).

Grant, Richard E(sterhuysen) (1957–) Actor, born in Mbabane, Swaziland.

He became known following his role as the down-and-out thespian in the film *Withnail and I* (1987). He made his directorial debut with *Wah-Wah* (2005), and television roles include *The Scarlet Pimpernel* (1998) and *A Christmas Carol* (1999).

Grant, (Hiram) Ulysses S(impson) (1822–85) US general and 18th president (1869–77), born in Point Pleasant, OH. In the Civil War (1861), he led Union forces to victory, first in the Mississippi Valley, then in the final campaigns in Virginia. Elected president in 1868 and 1872, he presided over the reconstruction of the South. His memoirs (1885–6) have been much acclaimed.

Granz, Norman (1918–2001) Concert impresario and record producer, born in Los Angeles, CA. He was chiefly known for his staging of the national and international tours called Jazz at the Philharmonic, and was widely recognized as a leading disseminator of jazz music around the world.

Grappelli, Stéphane (1908–97) Jazz violinist, born in Paris. He and Django Reinhardt were the principal soloists in the Quintet of the Hot Club of France (1934–9), the first European jazz band to exert an influence in the USA.

Graves, Robert (Ranke) (1895–1985) Writer, born in London. His best-known novels are *I, Claudius* and its sequel, *Claudius the God* (both 1934), which were adapted for television in 1976. His *Collected Poems* (1975) draws on more than 20 volumes.

Gray, Thomas (1716–71) Poet, born in London. His masterpiece is 'Elegy Written in a Country Churchyard' (1751), set at Stoke Poges, Buckinghamshire. He then settled in Cambridge, where he wrote his *Pindaric Odes* (1757).

Greco, El ('El' Span 'the', 'Greco' Ital 'Greek'), nickname of **Domenikos Theotokopoulos** (1541–1614) Painter, born in Candia, Crete, Greece. He settled in Toledo, Spain (c.1577), and became a portrait painter whose reputation fluctuated because of the suspicion which greeted his characteristic distortions, such as his elongated, flamelike figures. His most famous painting is probably the 'Burial of Count Orgaz' (1586).

Greenaway, Kate, popular name of **Catherine Greenaway** (1846–1901) Artist and book-illustrator, born in London. She became well known in the 1880s for her coloured portrayals of child life, in such works as *The Birthday Book* (1880). The *Greenaway Medal* is awarded annually for the best British children's book artist.

Greenaway, Peter (1942–) Film-maker and painter, born in Newport, Wales. *The Draughtsman's Contract* (1982) won him critical acclaim. His later works explore such preoccupations as sex, death, decay, and gamesmanship, and include *Drowning By Numbers* (1988), *Prospero's Books* (1991), and *8½ Women* (1999).

Greene, (Henry) Graham (1904–91) Writer, born in Berkhamsted, Hertfordshire. In his major novels, central religious issues emerge, especially concerning Catholicism, as in *Brighton Rock* (1938), *The Power and the Glory* (1940), *The End of the Affair* (1951), and *A Burnt-Out Case*

(1961). He also wrote plays, film scripts (notably, *The Third Man*, 1950), short stories, and essays.

Greer, Germaine (1939–) Feminist, writer, and lecturer, born in Melbourne, Victoria, Australia. Her controversial book *The Female Eunuch* (1970) portrayed marriage as a legalized form of slavery for women, and attacked the misrepresentation of female sexuality by male-dominated society. *The Whole Woman* (1999) takes stock of the situation of the feminist movement.

Gregory I, St, known as **the Great** (c.540–604) Pope (590–604), a Father of the Church, born in Rome. It was here that he saw some Anglo-Saxon youths in the slave market, and was seized with a longing to convert their country to Christianity. He reformed public ritual, and systematized the sacred chants, and was canonized on his death.

Gretzky, Wayne, nickname **the Great One** or **the Great Gretzky** (1961–) Ice-hockey player, born in Brantford, Ontario, Canada. He joined the Edmonton Oilers in 1979, and transferred to the Los Angeles Kings in 1988. He is the National Hockey League's all-time leading scorer. He retired in 1999.

Grey, Charles Grey, 2nd Earl (1764–1845) British prime minister (1830–4), born in Fallodon, Northumberland. He secured the passage of the 1832 Reform Bill, and carried the Act for the abolition of slavery in the colonies.

Grey, Lady Jane (1537–54) Queen of England for nine days in 1553, the great-granddaughter of Henry VII. In 1553 the Duke of Northumberland aimed to secure the succession by marrying Jane (against her wish) to his fourth son, Lord Guildford Dudley. Three days after Edward VI's death she was named as his successor, but was forced to abdicate in favour of Mary, and beheaded.

Grey, Zane, pseudonym of **Pearl Grey** (1872–1939) Novelist, born in Zanesville, OH. In 1904 he began to write Westerns, the best known of his many popular books being *Riders of the Purple Sage* (1912).

Grey-Thompson, Dame Tanni (1969–) Paralympian, born in Cardiff. Born with spina bifida and paralyzed from the waist down, she took up wheelchair racing and made her debut for Wales aged 15. Her first Olympic success was at Seoul in 1988 when she won the 400 m race, and went on to achieve a remarkable medal haul at successive games: Barcelona in 1992 (four golds, one silver), Atlanta in 1996 (one gold, three silver), Sydney in 2000 (four golds), Athens in 2004 (two golds). She was made a dame in 2005.

Gribbin, John Richard (1946–) Astronomer, writer, and broadcaster, born in Maidstone, Kent. His first book, *The Jupiter Effect* (1974) was followed by over 50 others, including *In Search of Schrödinger's Cat* (1984), and biographies of Stephen Hawking and Albert Einstein.

Grieg, Edvard (Hagerup) (1843–1907) Composer, born in Bergen, Norway. His works include the incidental music for Ibsen's *Peer Gynt* (1876), the A minor piano concerto, orchestral suites, violin sonatas, and numerous songs and piano pieces.

Griffith, Melanie (1957–) Actress, born in New York City. She appeared in a number of films as a teenager, and her adult career commenced with *Body Double* (1984). Later films include *Bonfire of the Vanities* (1990), *Lolita* (1997), and *Tempo* (2003). She married actor Antonio Banderas in 1996.

Grigson, Sophie, popular name of **Hester Sophia Frances Grigson** (1959–) British cookery writer and broadcaster. A newspaper cookery correspondent from 1986, she became widely known through her television programmes for Channel 4, such as *Sophie's Meat Course* (1995). Among her books are *Sophie Grigson's Feasts for a Fiver* (1999) and *Country Kitchen* (2004).

Grimm brothers Folklorists and philologists: **Jacob Ludwig Carl Grimm** (1785–1863) and **Wilhelm Carl Grimm** (1786–1859), both born in Hanau, Germany. They are best known for *Grimm's Fairy Tales* (trans, 3 vols, 1812–22). Jacob's *Germanic Grammar* (trans, 1819, revised 1822–40) is perhaps the greatest philological work of the age; he also formulated *Grimm's law* of sound changes.

Grisham, John (1955–) Novelist, born in Jonesboro, AR. A lawyer, his first novel, the crime thriller *A Time To Kill* (1989), was followed by a string of best sellers, many of which have been made into successful films. They include *The Firm* (1991), *The Rainmaker* (1995), and *The Broker* (2005).

Groening, Matt (1954–) Cartoonist, born in Portland, OR. He is known as creator of the popular cartoon family *The Simpsons* which debuted as a series in 1990, and won an Emmy for Best Animated Series. It celebrated its 350th episode in 2005.

Gromyko, Andrei Andreevich (1909–89) Soviet president (1985–8), born near Minsk, Belarus. As longest-serving foreign minister (1957–85), he was responsible for conducting Soviet relations with the West during the Cold War.

Gucci, Guccio (1881–1953) Fashion designer, born in Florence, Italy. He opened his first shop in Florence in 1920, becoming known for his leather craftsmanship and accessories. The first overseas shop opened in New York City in 1953.

Guevara, Che, popular name of **Ernesto Guevara (de la Serna)** (1928–67) Revolutionary leader, born in Rosario, Argentina. He was prominent in the Cuban revolution (1956–9), and left Cuba in 1965 to become a guerrilla leader in South America. He was captured and executed in Bolivia.

Guggenheim, Solomon R(obert) (1861–1949) Businessman and art collector, born in Philadelphia, PA, the son of Meyer Guggenheim. He collected Modernist paintings and established the Solomon R Guggenheim Foundation (1937), which later financed the Solomon R Guggenheim Museum, designed in 1959.

Guillem, Sylvie (1965–) Ballet dancer and choreographer, born in Paris. She trained at the Paris Opéra Ballet School (1977–80) and at age 16 joined the company's corps de ballet, gaining the status of *étoile* in 1984. From

1989 she became principal guest artist with the company.

Guillotin, Joseph Ignace (1738–1814) Physician and revolutionary, born in Saintes, France. He proposed to the Constituent Assembly, of which he was a deputy, the use of a decapitating instrument as a means of execution. This was adopted in 1791 and named after him (the *guillotine*).

Guin, Ursula Le *see* Le Guin, Ursula

Guinness, Sir Alec (1914–2000) Actor, born in London. Among his notable films are *Kind Hearts and Coronets* (1949), *The Lavender Hill Mob* (1951), and *The Bridge on the River Kwai* (1958, Oscar). Later roles included Ben Kenobi in the *Star Wars* series, and Smiley in the television version of Le Carré's novels (1979, 1982).

Gullit, Ruud (1962–) Football player and manager, born in Suriname. He played for Dutch clubs Feyenoord and PSV Eindhoven, and in 1987 was named European Footballer of the Year, later joining AC Milan for a then world record £7·5 million fee. He captained Holland to win the European Championship (1988), and with AC Milan won the European Cup (1989, 1990). After spells as manager at Chelsea and Newcastle United, he became coach at Feyenoord in 2004.

Gunnell, Sally (Janet) (1966–) Athlete, born in Chigwell, Essex. She achieved gold in the 100 m hurdles at the 1986 Commonwealth Games, and gold in the 400 m hurdles at the 1992 Olympics. In 1993–4 she was European Cup, Commonwealth, and World Cup champion hurdler.

Gutenberg, Johannes (Gensfleisch) (1400–68) Printer, regarded as the inventor of printing from movable type, born in Mainz, Germany. He entered into a partnership with Johann Fust who financed a printing press, but Fust later sued him for repayment of the loan and reclaimed the machinery. His best-known book is the *Gutenberg Bible* (c.1455).

Guthrie, Woody, popular name of **Woodrow Wilson Guthrie** (1912–67) Folk singer and songwriter, born in Okemah, OK. He took to the road during the Great Depression, and wrote hundreds of songs, lauding migrant workers, pacifists, and underdogs of all kinds, such as 'So Long, It's Been Good to Know You' and 'This Land is Your Land'.

Gwyn or **Gwynne, Nell**, popular name of **Eleanor Gwyn** (c.1650–87) Mistress of Charles II, possibly born in London. Originally an orange seller, she established herself as a comedienne at Drury Lane. She had at least one son by the king – Charles Beauclerk, Duke of St Albans.

Gyllenhaal, Jake, popular name of **Jacob Benjamin Gyllenhaal** (1980–) Actor, born in Los Angeles, CA. Born into a show business family, he made his film debut at age 10 in *City Slickers* (1991). He gained recognition for his role in *Donnie Darko* (2001), and later films include *The Day After Tomorrow* (2004), *Brokeback Mountain* (2005, Best Supporting Actor BAFTA and Oscar nomination), and *Jarhead* (2005).

Hackman, Gene (1931–) Film actor, born in San Bernardino, CA. His many films include *Bonnie and Clyde* (1967), *The French Connection* (1971, Oscar), *The Royal Tenenbaums* (2001, Golden Globe), and *Welcome to Mooseport* (2004).

Hadlee, Sir Richard (John) (1951–) Cricketer, born in Christchurch, New Zealand. New Zealand's best all-round cricketer, he made his Test debut in 1973, took 431 Test wickets, and scored 3124 Test runs, retiring in 1990.

Hadrian, in full **Publius Aelius Hadrianus** (76–138) Roman emperor (117–38), ward, protégé, and successor of the Emperor Trajan. He spent most of his reign touring the empire, consolidating frontiers, and promoting urban life. In Britain he initiated the building of the wall named after him.

Hadrian IV (Pope) *see* Adrian IV

Haggard, Sir H(enry) Rider (1856–1925) Novelist, born at Bradenham Hall, Norfolk. *King Solomon's Mines* (1885) made his work known, and was followed by *She* (1887) and several other stories.

Hague, William (Jefferson) (1961–) British politician, born in Rotherham, South Yorkshire. Elected an MP in 1989, he became minister of state for social security (1994–5) and minister for Wales (1995–7). He won the leadership of the Conservative Party following John Major's resignation in 1997. He resigned after the general election defeat of 2001, but returned in 2005 as shadow foreign secretary.

Haig (of Bemersyde), Douglas Haig, 1st Earl (1861–1928) British field marshal, born in Edinburgh. In 1915 he became commander of the British Expeditionary Force, waging a costly war of attrition, for which he was much criticized.

Haile Selassie I, originally **Prince Ras Tafari Makonnen** (1892–1975) Emperor of Ethiopia (1930–6, 1941–74), born near Harer, Ethiopia. He led the revolution in 1916 against Lij Yasu, and became regent and heir to the throne, westernizing the institutions of his country. The disastrous famine of 1973 led to his deposition, but he is still held in reverence by many, notably by Rastafarians.

Hailey, Arthur (1920–2004) Novelist, born in Luton, Bedfordshire. He became a naturalized Canadian in 1947. He has written many best-selling blockbusters about disasters, several of which became highly successful films, such as *Airport* (1968) and *Wheels* (1971).

Hailwood, Mike, popular name of **Stanley Michael Bailey Hailwood** (1940–81) Motor-cyclist, born in

Oxford, Oxfordshire. Between 1961 and 1967 he took nine world titles, and also won a record 14 Isle of Man Tourist Trophy races between 1961 and 1979.

Hain, Peter (Gerald) (1950–) British politician, born in Nairobi, Kenya. Labour MP for Neath (1991–), he joined the Foreign Office (1998) becoming minister for Europe after the 2001 general election. He was appointed secretary of state for Wales in 2002, combining this with the post of Northern Ireland secretary from 2005, and served as Leader of the Commons (2003–5).

Haitink, Bernard (1929–) Conductor, born in Amsterdam. He conducted the Amsterdam Concertgebouw Orchestra (from 1961) and the London Philharmonic (1967–79), and was appointed musical director at Glyndebourne (1978–88) and Covent Garden (1988–2002). He is also principal guest conductor of the Boston Symphony Orchestra (1995–).

Haley, Bill, popular name of **William John Haley** (1925–1981) Popular singer and musician, born in Highland Park, MI. With his group 'The Comets' he popularized rock-and-roll in the 1950s. His most famous song was 'Rock Around the Clock' (1955).

Halifax, Charles Montagu, 1st Earl of (1661–1715) English Whig statesman, born in Horton, Northamptonshire. He established the Bank of England (1694), and as Chancellor of the Exchequer (1694–5) introduced a new coinage. On George I's arrival (1714) he became prime minister.

Hall, Sir Peter (Reginald Frederick) (1930–) Theatre, opera, and film director, born in Bury St Edmunds, Suffolk. He became director of the Royal Shakespeare Company (1960–8), Covent Garden Opera (1969–71), and the National Theatre (1973–88). He formed his own production company in 1988, and became artistic director at the Old Vic in 1997.

Hallé, Sir Charles (1819–95) Pianist and conductor, born in Hagen, Germany. Driven to England by the Revolution of 1848, he settled in Manchester, where in 1858 he founded his famous orchestra.

Halley, Edmond (1656–1742) Astronomer and mathematician, born in London. He began a study of planetary orbits, and correctly predicted the return in 1758 of the comet now named after him.

Hals, Frans (c.1580–1666) Portrait and genre painter, probably born in Antwerp, Belgium. Among his best-known works are 'The Laughing Cavalier' (1624) and 'Gypsy Girl' (c.1628–30).

Hamilton, Emma, Lady, *née* **Emily Lyon** (c.1765–1815) Lord Nelson's mistress, probably born in Ness, Cheshire. In 1791 she married Sir William Hamilton, meeting Nelson in 1793. After their deaths she became bankrupt, and in 1814 fled to Calais, where she died.

Hammerstein, Oscar, II (1895–1960) Librettist, born in New York City. With composer Jerome Kern he wrote *Show Boat* (1927), and with Richard Rodgers he wrote *Oklahoma!* (1943, Pulitzer), *South Pacific* (1949,

Pulitzer), *The King and I* (1951), and *The Sound of Music* (1959).

Hammett, (Samuel) Dashiell (1894–1961) Crime writer, born in St Mary's Co, MD. He achieved international fame with his 'private eye' novels *The Maltese Falcon* (1930; filmed 1941) and *The Thin Man* (1932), which was also filmed and later made into a television series.

Hammond Innes, Ralph (1913–98) Writer and traveller, born in England. His popular adventure stories include *The Trojan Horse* (1940), *Atlantic Fury* (1962), and *Delta Connection* (1996).

Hampshire, Susan (1938–) British actress. She won Emmy awards for best actress in the television series *The Forsyte Saga* (1970), *The First Churchills* (1971), and *Vanity Fair* (1973). Later series include *Monarch of the Glen* (2000–5).

Hampton, Lionel (Leo), nicknames **Hamp** and **King of the Vibes** (1908–2002) Jazz musician and bandleader, born in Louisville, KY. He introduced the vibraphone into jazz, playing with Armstrong and with Goodman in the 1930s. He formed a permanent big band in 1940, continuing as a leader until the 1980s.

Hancock, Tony, popular name of **Anthony John Hancock** (1924–68) Comedian, born in Birmingham, West Midlands. He achieved national popularity with the radio and TV series *Hancock's Half Hour* (1954–61). A chronic alcoholic, he committed suicide while attempting a comeback on Australian television.

Handel, George Frideric (1685–1759) Composer, born in Halle, Germany.

His vast output included over 40 operas, about 20 oratorios, cantatas, sacred music, and orchestral, instrumental, and vocal works. While in London (from 1720), he developed a new form, the English oratorio, which proved to be highly popular. His most memorable work includes *Saul* (1739), *Israel in Egypt* (1739), and *Messiah* (1742).

Handy, W(illiam) C(hristopher) (1873–1958) Composer, born in Florence, AL. He formed his own publishing company, and was the first to introduce the 'blues' style to printed music, his most famous work being the 'St Louis Blues' (1914).

Hanks, Tom, popular name of **Thomas J Hanks** (1956–) Film actor, born in Oakland, CA. His many successful films include *Sleepless in Seattle* (1993), *Philadelphia Story* (1993, Oscar, Golden Globe), *Forrest Gump* (1994, Oscar), *Saving Private Ryan* (1998), *Cast Away* (2000, Golden Globe), and *The Terminal* (2004).

Hanna-Barbera Animated cartoonists. **William (Denby) Hanna** (1910–2001), born in Melrose, NM, was one of the first directors at the new MGM animation studio in 1937. He teamed up with **Joseph (Roland) Barbera** (1911–), born in New York City, who had joined MGM as an artist. They created the *Tom and Jerry* cartoons, winning seven Oscars between 1943 and 1952, and such television cartoon series as *The Flintstones*, *Yogi Bear*, and *Huckleberry Hound*.

Hannibal (247–182 BC) Carthaginian general and statesman, the son of Hamilcar Barca. In the Second Punic

War (218–202 BC), he completely surprised the Romans by his bold invasion of Italy from the N (with elephants), and inflicted a series of heavy defeats on them. Recalled to Africa (203 BC), he was defeated by Scipio and Zama.

Hansard, Luke (1752–1828) British printer. He and his descendants printed regular parliamentary reports from 1774 to 1889, and in 1943 *Hansard* became the official name for the reports.

Hardicanute, also spelled **Harthacnut** (c.1018–42) King of Denmark (1035–42), and the last Danish King of England (1040–2), the only son of Canute and Emma of Normandy. His death without children led to the restoration of the Old English royal line in the person of Edward the Confessor.

Harding, Warren G(amaliel) (1865–1923) US statesman and 29th president (1921–3), born in Corsica, OH. Emerging as a power in the Republican Party, he won the presidency in 1920, campaigning against US membership of the League of Nations.

Hardy, Oliver (Norvell) (1892–1957) *see* Laurel and Hardy

Hardy, Thomas (1840–1928) Novelist and poet, born in Upper Bockhampton, Dorset. His major novels include *The Return of the Native* (1878), *The Mayor of Casterbridge* (1886), *Tess of the D'Urbervilles* (1891), and *Jude the Obscure* (1896). He also wrote moving elegies to his first wife, Emma Gifford (d.1912), and the epic drama *The Dynasts* (1903–8).

Hare, Sir David (1947–) Playwright and director, born in St Leonard's-on-Sea, East Sussex. His politically engaged plays include *Slag* (1970) and *Plenty* (1978). *The Secret Rapture* (1988) won two awards for best play of the year, and later works include *Amy's View* (1997) and *A Breath of Life* (2002).

Hare, William *see* Burke, William

Hargreaves, James (c.1720–78) Inventor, probably born in Blackburn, Lancashire. He invented the spinning jenny in c.1764, but his fellow spinners broke into his house and destroyed his frame (1768).

Hargreaves, Roger (1935–88) Children's writer, born in Cleckheaton, West Yorkshire. He began writing after creating the storybook character 'Mr Tickle' for his son, Adam, in 1971. A hugely popular series of Mr Men books followed and in 1981 he began the series of Little Miss books.

Harman, Harriet (1950–) British stateswoman, born in London. She became a solicitor, and was legal officer for the National Council of Civil Liberties (1978–82). Elected a Labour MP in 1982, she held a number of shadow ministerial posts before becoming secretary of state for social security and minister for women (1997–8). She was appointed solicitor general after the 2001 election.

Harmsworth, Alfred (Charles William), 1st Viscount Northcliffe (1865–1922) Journalist and newspaper magnate, born near Dublin. In 1896 he revolutionized Fleet Street with his *Daily Mail*, introducing mass circulation journalism to the UK. In

1908, he became proprietor of *The Times*.

Harmsworth, Harold (Sydney), 1st Viscount Rothermere (1868–1940) Newspaper magnate, born in London. He founded the Glasgow *Daily Record* and in 1915 the *Sunday Pictorial*. After the death of his brother, Alfred, he acquired control of the *Daily Mail* and *Sunday Dispatch*.

Harold I, nickname **Harold Harefoot** (c.1016–40) King of England (1037–40), the younger son of Canute. Canute had intended that Hardicanute should succeed him in both Denmark and England; but in view of Hardicanute's absence in Denmark, Harold was accepted in England.

Harold II (c.1022–66) Last Anglo-Saxon king of England (1066), the second son of Earl Godwin. He defeated his brother Tostig and Harold Hardrada, King of Norway, at Stamford Bridge (Sep 1066), but William of Normandy then invaded England, and defeated him near Hastings (Oct 1066), where he died, shot through the eye with an arrow.

Harrelson, Woody (1961–) Actor, born in Midland, TX. He became well known for his role as the bartender in the popular TV series *Cheers* (1983–93). His feature films include *Indecent Proposal* (1993), *The People vs. Larry Flynt* (1996, Oscar nomination), and *North Country* (2005).

Harris, Jet *see* Shadows, The

Harris, Joanne (Michèle Sylvie) (1964–) Novelist, born in N England. Her first successful novel, *Chocolat* (1999; filmed 2000), was shortlisted for the Whitbread Book Award. Further books include *Blackberry Wine* (2000), *Holy Fools* (2003), and *Gentlemen and Players* (2005).

Harris, Joel Chandler (1848–1908) Humorist and dialect writer, born in Eatonton, GA. His *Uncle Remus* stories about 'Brer Rabbit' and 'Brer Fox', made him internationally famous, known especially for his distinctive use of Southern African-American folklore and dialect.

Harris, Rolf (1930–) Entertainer and artist, born in Bassendean, Western Australia. He joined the BBC children's department in 1954, and later had commercial success with his recordings. From 1994–2003 he fronted the TV series *Animal Hospital*. Known especially for his spontaneous paintings, he was commissioned to paint a portrait of Queen Elizabeth II to mark her 80th birthday in 2006.

Harrison, Benjamin (1833–1901) US statesman and 23rd president (1889–93), born in North Bend, OH, the grandson of William Henry Harrison. Elected a Republican senator in 1880, in 1888 he defeated Cleveland on the free trade issue, but failed to gain re-election in 1892.

Harrison, George (1943–2001) Singer, guitarist, and songwriter, born in Liverpool, Merseyside. He played lead guitar and sang with the Beatles, and developed an interest in Indian music and Eastern religion. His solo albums included *All Things Must Pass* (1970) and *Somewhere in England* (1981).

Harrison, Sir Rex, originally **Reginald Carey Harrison** (1908–90) Actor, born in Huyton-with-Roby, Lancashire. His charming, somewhat blasé style attracted many star comedy parts, such as in *Blithe Spirit* (1945), *The Constant Husband* (1958), and *My Fair Lady* (1964, Oscar).

Harrison, William Henry (1773–1841) US soldier, statesman, and ninth president (1841), born in Charles City Co, VA. He became a senator in 1824, and president in 1841, but died of pneumonia a month after his inauguration.

Hartnell, Sir Norman (1901–78) Fashion designer and court dressmaker, born in London. He began his own business in 1923, his work including costumes for leading actresses, wartime 'utility' dresses, and Princess Elizabeth's wedding and coronation gowns.

Harvey, Caroline *see* Trollope, Joanna

Harvey, William (1578–1657) Physician, born in Folkestone, Kent. His celebrated treatise, *On the Motion of the Heart and Blood in Animals* (trans, 1628), first described the circulation of the blood.

Hastings, Warren (1732–1818) British colonial administrator in India, born in Churchill, Oxfordshire. As Governor-General of Bengal (1774), he made the East India Company's power paramount in many parts of India. On his return to England (1784) he was charged with corruption, and after a 7-year trial was acquitted.

Hattersley, Roy (Sydney George), Baron (1932–) British statesman, born in Sheffield, South Yorkshire. He was secretary of state for prices and consumer protection (1976–9), and later held several Opposition posts, including shadow Chancellor, and deputy leader of the Labour Party (1983–92). He was created a life peer in 1997.

Havel, Václav (1936–) Playwright, president of Czechoslovakia (1989–92), and president of the Czech Republic (1993–2003), born in Prague. His writing was judged subversive, and he was imprisoned (1979–83), and again in 1989, but released and elected president by direct popular vote following the collapse of Communism.

Haw-Haw, Lord *see* Joyce, William

Hawking, Stephen (William) (1942–) Theoretical physicist, born in Oxford, Oxfordshire. His work has been concerned with cosmology, dealing with black holes, singularities, and the 'big bang' theory of the origin of the universe. His popular writing includes *A Brief History of Time* (1988). Since the 1960s he has suffered from a neuromotor disease, causing extreme physical disability.

Hawkins, Coleman (1904–69) Jazz tenor saxophonist, born in St Joseph, MO. He joined Fletcher Henderson's jazz orchestra (1923), popularizing the tenor saxophone, and recorded 'Body and Soul', a jazz landmark.

Hawkins, Sir John *see* Hawkyns, Sir John

Hawkyns or **Hawkins, Sir John** (1532–95) English sailor, born in Plymouth, Devon. He became navy treasurer (1573), served against the Armada (1588), and in 1595, with Drake, commanded an expedition to the Spanish Main.

Hawn, Goldie (Jeanne) (1945–) US actress, born in Washington, DC. She became known through her comedy roles in Rowan and Martin's TV review *Laugh In* (1968–70). Her films include *Private Benjamin* (1980), *Death Becomes Her* (1992), *The First Wives Club* (1996), and *The Banger Sisters* (2002).

Hawthorne, Nathaniel (1804–64) Writer, born in Salem, MA. His first major success was the novel *The Scarlet Letter* (1850), still the best known of his works.

Hawthorne, Sir Nigel (Barnard) (1929–2001) Actor, born in Coventry, West Midlands. A successful stage actor, he achieved television fame as Sir Humphrey Appleby in the series *Yes Minister* (1980) and its sequel (1986). His feature films included *The Madness of King George* (1994, Oscar nomination) and *The Fragile Heart* (1997, Best Actor BAFTA).

Haydn, Franz Joseph (1732–1809) Composer, born in Rohrau, Austria. Among his innovations were the four-movement string quartet and the 'classical' symphony. His prolific output includes 104 symphonies, some 50 concertos, 84 string quartets, 24 stage works, 12 Masses, orchestral divertimenti, keyboard sonatas, and diverse chamber, choral, instrumental, and vocal pieces.

Hayes, Rutherford B(irchard) (1822–93) US statesman and 19th president (1877–81), born in Delaware, OH. Under his presidency, the country recovered commercial prosperity after the Civil War. His policy included reform of the civil service and the conciliation of the Southern states.

Hayworth, Rita, originally **Margarita**

Carmen Cansino (1918–87) Film actress, born into a show business family in New York City. She partnered both Fred Astaire and Gene Kelly in musicals of the 1940s, and found her best-known lead in *Gilda* (1946).

Healey (of Riddlesden), Denis (Winston) Healey, Baron (1917–) British statesman, born in Eltham, Kent. He was secretary of state for defence (1964–70) and Chancellor of the Exchequer (1974–9). Unsuccessful in the Labour leadership contests of 1976 and 1980, he became deputy leader (1980–3), and in 1983 was appointed shadow foreign minister.

Heaney, Seamus (Justin) (1939–) Poet, born on a farm near Castledawson in Co Londonderry. Early works such as *Death of a Naturalist* (1966) and *Door into the Dark* (1969) established a deep bond between language and the land. Volumes of selected poems appeared in 1980, 1990, and 1998. Later work includes *The Spirit Level* (1996, Whitbread) and his reworking of the Anglo-Saxon epic poem *Beowulf* (1999, Whitbread). He received the Nobel Prize for Literature in 1995.

Hearst, William Randolph (1863–1951) Newspaper publisher, born in San Francisco, CA. His national chain of newspapers and periodicals included the *Chicago Examiner*, *Cosmopolitan*, and *Harper's Bazaar*, and his life inspired the Orson Welles film *Citizen Kane* (1941).

Heath, Sir Edward (Richard George), known as **Ted Heath** (1916–2005) British prime minister (1970–4), born in Broadstairs, Kent.

He was minister of labour (1959–60), Lord Privy Seal (1960–3), and Leader of the Opposition (1965–70). He was Father of the House from 1997 to his retirement in 2001.

Hedren, Tippi, originally **Nathalie Hedren** (1935–) Film actress, born in New Ulm, MI. She was discovered by Alfred Hitchcock, who cast her in *The Birds* (1963) and *Marnie* (1964). Later films include *Roar* (1981), *Deadly Spygames* (1989), and *Citizen Ruth* (1996). She is the mother of actress Melanie Griffith.

Heilbrun, Carolyn, *née* **Gold**, pseudonym **Amanda Cross** (1926–2003) Writer and teacher, born in East Orange, NJ. She published scholarly works, but was best known as a writer of popular mystery novels featuring Kate Fansler, also an urban college professor, as seen in *The Theban Mysteries* (1972), *A Trap for Fools* (1989), and *The Edge of Doom* (2002).

Heinz, H(enry) J(ohn) (1844–1919) Food manufacturer, born in Pittsburgh, PA. In 1876 he founded the business which was reorganized in 1888 as H J Heinz Co, and he became its president (1905–19).

Heisenberg, Werner (Karl) (1901–76) Theoretical physicist, born in Würzburg, Germany. He developed a method of expressing quantum mechanics in matrices (1925), and formulated his revolutionary principle of indeterminacy (the *uncertainty principle*) in 1927. He was awarded the Nobel Prize for Physics in 1932.

Helena, St (c.255–c.330) Mother of the Emperor Constantine (the Great), born in Bithynia, Asia Minor. The wife of Constantius Chlorus, she early became a Christian. In 326, according to tradition, she founded the basilicas on the Mt of Olives and at Bethlehem.

Heller, Joseph (1923–99) Novelist, born in New York City. His wartime experience formed the background for his first book, *Catch-22* (1961), which launched him as a successful novelist. A sequel, *Closing Time*, appeared in 1994.

Hemingway, Ernest (Miller) (1899–1961) Novelist and short-story writer, born in Oak Park, IL. Obsessed with war, big-game hunting, and bullfighting, his works include *A Farewell to Arms* (1929), *For Whom the Bell Tolls* (1940), and *The Old Man and the Sea* (1952, Pulitzer). He was awarded the Nobel Prize for Literature in 1954.

Hempleman-Adams, David (1956–) British explorer, born in Swindon, Wiltshire. In 1998 he completed the explorer's 'Grand Slam', having reached the North and South Poles and climbed the highest mountain on each continent, including Mt Everest. He is the first person to fly a balloon over the Andes (1998) and the North Pole (2000), and the first person to cross the Atlantic solo in an open wicker basket (2003).

Hendrix, Jimi, popular name of **James Marshall Hendrix** (1942–70) Rock guitarist, singer, and songwriter, born in Seattle, WA. In London he formed the Jimi Hendrix Experience, and the band's first single, 'Hey Joe', was an immediate success. His raucous blues style influenced heavy metal bands.

Hendry, Stephen (Gordon) (1969–) Snooker player, born in Edinburgh. He became a professional in 1985, and dominated the game in the 1990s, his wins including seven Embassy world championships (1990, 1992–6, 1999). In 2003 he added the British Open title to his achievements.

Hengist and Horsa (5th-c) Brothers, leaders of the first Anglo-Saxon settlers in Britain. Bede states that they were invited over by Vortigern, the British king, to fight the Picts in c.450.

Henin-Hardenne, Justine, *née* **Justine Henin** (1982–) Tennis player, born in Liège, Belgium. Her achievements include the French Open (2003, 2005), the US Open (2003), and the Australian Open (2004). She began 2006 ranked number 6 and reached the final of the Australian Open.

Henman, Tim(othy) (1974–) Tennis player, born in Oxford, Oxfordshire. He turned professional in 1993, and had become Britain's number 1 player by early 1997. He reached the semi-finals at Wimbledon in 1998, 1999, 2001, and 2002, and rose to fourth in the world rankings in 2002. He won the Paris Masters in 2003.

Henry I (of England) (1068–1135) King of England (1100–35) and Duke of Normandy (1106–35), the youngest son of William the Conqueror, and elder brother of Robert Curthose, Duke of Normandy. During his reign, the Norman Empire attained the height of its power. His only legitimate son, William Adelin, was drowned in 1120, and in 1127 he nominated his daughter, Empress Matilda, as his heir for both England and Normandy, but after Henry's death, the crown was seized by Stephen, son of his sister, Adela.

Henry II (of England) (1133–89) King of England (1154–89), born in Le Mans, France, the son of Empress Matilda and Geoffrey of Anjou. He invaded England in 1153, and was recognized as the lawful successor of the usurper, Stephen, founding the Angevin or Plantagenet dynasty of English kings. His reign is chiefly remembered for the conflict with Thomas Becket, his murder (1170), and the annexation of Ireland (1171).

Henry III (of England) (1207–72) King of England (1216–72), the elder son and successor, at the age of nine, of John. His arbitrary assertion of royal rights led to the rebellion of Simon de Montfort and the barons. He was captured at Lewes (1264), but defeated the rebels at Evesham (1265).

Henry IV (of England) originally **Henry Bolingbroke** (1366–1413) King of England (1399–1413), the first king of the House of Lancaster, the son of John of Gaunt, who was the fourth son of Edward III. In 1397 he supported Richard II against the Duke of Gloucester, but was banished in 1398. On returning to England, he induced Richard to abdicate in his favour, and defeated Henry Percy (Hotspur) and his followers at Shrewsbury (1403).

Henry V (of England) (1387–1422) King of England (1413–22), born in Monmouth, Monmouthshire, the eldest son of Henry IV. In 1415 he invaded France, and won the Battle of Agincourt against great odds. He was recognized as heir to the French throne, and married Charles VI's daughter, Catherine of Valois.

Henry VI (of England) (1421–71) King of England (1422–61, 1470–1), born in Windsor, S England, the only child of Henry V and Catherine of Valois. Although crowned King of France in Paris in 1431, he gradually lost England's French conquests. Richard, Duke of York, seized power as Lord Protector in 1454, and defeated the king's army at St Albans (1455), the first battle of the Wars of the Roses, deposing Henry in 1461. Richard Neville, Earl of Warwick, restored him to the throne (Oct 1470), his nominal rule ending when Edward IV returned to London (Apr 1471). After the Yorkist victory at Tewkesbury (May 1471), where his only son was killed, Henry was murdered in the Tower.

Henry VII (of England) (1457–1509) King of England (1485–1509), born at Pembroke Castle, Pembrokeshire, the grandson of Owen Tudor and Catherine of Valois, the widow of Henry V. He founded the Tudor dynasty by defeating Richard III at Bosworth (1485), married Elizabeth of York, and concluded peace with France.

Henry VIII (of England) (1491–1547) King (1509–47), born in Greenwich, Greater London, the second son of Henry VII. Soon after his accession he married Catherine of Aragon. From 1527 he determined to divorce Catherine, whose children, except for Mary, had died in infancy, and in defiance of the Roman Catholic Church was privately married to Anne Boleyn (1533). In 1534 it was enacted that his marriage to Catherine was invalid, and that the king was the sole head of the Church of England. In 1536 Catherine died, and Anne Boleyn was executed for infidelity. Henry then married Jane Seymour, who died leaving a son, afterwards Edward VI. In 1540 Anne of Cleves became his fourth wife, but dislike of her appearance caused him to divorce her speedily. He then married Catherine Howard (1540), who was executed on grounds of infidelity (1542). In 1543 his last marriage was to Catherine Parr, who survived him.

Henry, Lenny, popular name of **Lenworth George Henry** (1958–) Comedian and actor, born in Dudley, West Midlands. He joined the children's television show *Tiswas* in the 1970s, and went on to star in his own series *The Lenny Henry Show* (1984–95). He also hosts the annual BBC *Comic Relief* telethon. He is married to comedy actress Dawn French.

Henry, O, pseudonym of **William Sydney Porter**, also as **Oliver Henry**, **S H Peters** (1862–1910) Writer, master of the short story, born in Greensboro, NC. The first of his many volumes was *Cabbages and Kings* (1904), providing a romantic and humorous treatment of everyday life, and noted for their use of coincidence and trick endings.

Henry, Thierry (Daniel) (1977–) Footballer, born in Paris. He joined Arsenal Football Club in 1999. He was voted the Football Writers' Association Player of the Year (2003) and the Professional Football Association Player of the Year (2003, 2004), and has twice been runner-up for FIFA World Player of the Year (2003, 2004). In 2005 his 186th goal for Arsenal made him the club's leading goal scorer.

Henson, Jim, popular name of **James Maury Henson** (1936–90) Puppeteer, born in Greenville, MS. His 'Muppets' achieved nationwide popularity on the children's television workshop, *Sesame Street* (from 1969) and *The Muppet Show* (1976–81), appearing also in a string of films.

Hepburn, Audrey, originally **Eda van Heemstra** (1929–93) Actress and film star, born in Brussels, Belgium. She was given the lead in the Broadway production of *Gigi* (1951), and went on to win international acclaim for *Roman Holiday* (1953, Oscar). Other films included *The Nun's Story* (1959), *Breakfast at Tiffany's* (1961), and *My Fair Lady* (1964).

Hepburn, Katharine (Houghton) (1907–2003) Actress, born in Hartford, CT. From 1932 she attained international fame in films, notably in *Morning Glory* (1933), *Guess Who's Coming to Dinner* (1967), *The Lion in Winter* (1968), and *On Golden Pond* (1981), all of which gained her Oscars, and *The African Queen* (1952).

Hepworth, Dame (Jocelyn) Barbara (1903–75) Sculptor, born in Wakefield, West Yorkshire. She was one of the foremost non-figurative sculptors of her time, as seen in her *Contrapuntal Forms* (1951).

Hereward, known as **Hereward the Wake** (?–c.1080) Anglo-Saxon thegn who returned from exile to lead the last organized English resistance against the Norman invaders. He held the Isle of Ely against William the Conqueror (1070–1), and became legendary as an opponent of injustice.

Hergé, pseudonym of **Georges Rémi** (1907–83) Strip cartoonist, born in Etterbeek, Belgium. He created the *Tintin* strip, using the pseudonym Hergé, a phonetic version of his initials, RG.

Herman, Woody, popular name of **Woodrow Charles Herman** (1913–87) Bandleader, alto saxophonist, and clarinettist, born in Milwaukee, WI. He formed the white swing band called the Woodchoppers in 1936, following this with the Herman Orchestra (or 'Herd') in 1944.

Herod, known as **the Great** (c.73–4 BC) King of Judea (40 BC), the younger son of the Idumaean chieftain, Antipater. An able administrator, he did much to develop the economic potential of his kingdom. His cruelty is reflected in the Gospel account of the Massacre of the Innocents.

Herodotos or **Herodotus** (c.485–425 BC) Greek historian, born in Halicarnassus, Asia Minor. He travelled widely in the Middle East, collecting material for his great narrative history, which gave a record of the wars between the Greeks and the Persians.

Herriot, James, pseudonym of **James Alfred Wight** (1916–95) Veterinary surgeon and writer, born in Glasgow. Beginning in the 1970s, he brought the vet's world to the notice of the public with a number of best-selling books, such as *It Shouldn't Happen to a Vet.* Films and television series made his work widely known, especially the series *All Creatures Great and Small* (1977–80).

Hertz, Heinrich (Rudolf) (1857–1894) Physicist, born in Hamburg, Germany. His main work was on electromagnetic waves (1887), and he was the first to broadcast and receive radio waves. The unit of frequency is named after him.

Heseltine, Michael (Ray Dibdin), Lord (1933–) British Conservative statesman, born in Swansea, S Wales. He served as secretary of state for the environment (1979–83) and defence secretary (1983–6), later becoming environment secretary (1990–2), President of the Board of Trade (1992–5), and deputy prime minister (1995–7). He was made a Companion of Honour in 1997.

Hess, (Walter Richard) Rudolf (1894–1987) German politician, Hitler's deputy as Nazi Party leader, born in Alexandria, Egypt. In 1941, he flew alone to Scotland to plead the cause of a negotiated Anglo-German peace, and was held in Britain until the Nuremberg Trials (1946) when he was sentenced to life imprisonment. He remained in Spandau prison, Berlin, until his death.

Heston, Charlton, originally **John Charles Carter** (1923–) Actor and director, born in Evanston, IL. He is chiefly known for historic or heroic roles in such epics as *The Ten Commandments* (1956), *Ben Hur* (1959, Oscar), and *El Cid* (1961).

Hewitt, Lleyton (1981–) Tennis player, born in Adelaide, South Australia.

His wins include the Queen's Club Championship three years in succession (2000–2), the US Open singles title (2001), the ATP Tour World Championships (2001, 2002), and the 2002 Wimbledon singles title. At the beginning of 2006 he had a world ranking of 6.

Hewitt, Patricia (Hope) (1948–) British stateswoman, born in Canberra, Australia. Elected a Labour MP in 1997, she served as minister for trade and industry (1997–8), economic secretary to the Treasury (1998–9), information technology minister (1999–2001), trade and industry secretary and minister for women (2001–5), and minister for health from 2005.

Heyer, Georgette (1902–74) Writer, born in London. Her work includes historical novels, fictional studies of real figures in crisis, such as William I, and comedy detective novels. An authority on the Regency period, she had success with *Regency Buck* (1935).

Heyerdahl, Thor (1914–2002) Anthropologist, born in Larvik, Norway. In 1947 he proved, by sailing a balsa raft (the *Kon-Tiki*) from Peru to Tuamotu I in the S Pacific, that the Peruvian Indians could have settled in Polynesia. Later journeys included from Morocco to the West Indies in a papyrus boat, *Ra II* (1970).

Hiawatha, Indian name **Heowenta** (16th-c) Legendary Mohawk leader, born in present-day New York State. It is now generally accepted that he was a real person who was influential in founding the Five Nations League, an alliance of five Iroquois tribes.

Hibbert, Eleanor (Alice Burford)

(1906–93) Novelist, born in London. A prolific writer of romantic novels, she used several pseudonyms. As **Jean Plaidy** she wrote over 40 historical novels, beginning with *Together They Ride* (1945). Her other pseudonyms were **Eleanor Burford**, **Elbur Ford**, **Kathleen Kellow**, **Ellalice Tate**, **Victoria Holt**, and **Philippa Carr**.

Hickok, James Butler, popularly known as **Wild Bill Hickok** (1837–76) Frontier figure, born in Troy Grove, IL. He was marshal of Hays City (1869) and of Abilene (1871). He toured with Buffalo Bill's Wild West Show (1872–3) and was shot from behind by Jack McCall while holding the 'Dead Man's Hand' in poker.

Higgins, Alex(ander Gordon), nickname **Hurricane Higgins** (1949–) Snooker player, born in Belfast. He has had a tempestuous career after becoming the youngest world champion in 1972, at age 23. He won the title for a second time in 1982.

Higgins, John (1975–) Snooker player, born in Wishaw, Lanarkshire. His wins include the British Open (1995, 1998, 2004), the European Open (1997), the LG Cup (2005), the Embassy World Championship (1998, 1999), and the Masters (2006). During the 2003 British Open, he made history as the first player to compile maximum 147 breaks in successive matches.

Higgs, Peter (Ware) (1929–) Theoretical physicist, born in Newcastle-upon-Tyne, Tyne and Wear. He is best known for the *Higgs particle*, predicted via the *Higgs mechanism*

(1964), which is a generalization of ideas developed by Philip Anderson in the context of condensed matter physics, especially superconductivity, to relativistic quantum field theory.

Highsmith, Patricia (1921–95) Writer of detective fiction, born in Fort Worth, TX. Her first novel was *Strangers on a Train* (1949; filmed 1957), but her best novels describe the criminal adventures of her psychotic hero, Tom Ripley, beginning with *The Talented Mr Ripley* (1956).

Hill, Benny, popular name of **Alfred Hawthorne Hill** (1925–92) Comedian, born in Southampton, Hampshire. He gained national popularity with the saucy *Benny Hill Show* (1957–66), and spent over two decades writing and performing in top-rated television specials that were seen around the world.

Hill, Damon (Graham Devereux) (1960–) Motor-racing driver, born in London, the son of Graham Hill. His first Grand Prix was at Silverstone (1992), and he went on to win over 20 grands prix in the next four years, succeeding Nigel Mansell on the Williams team. He was world champion in 1996 and retired from Formula One in 1999.

Hill, (Norman) Graham (1929–75) Motor-racing driver, born in London. He was twice world champion (1962, 1968), and won the Monaco Grand Prix five times (1963–5, 1968–9).

Hill, Sir Rowland (1795–1879) Originator of penny postage, born in Kidderminster, Hereford and Worcester. In his *Post-office Reform: its Importance* *and Practicability* (1837), he advocated a simple rate of postage, to be prepaid by stamps, and in 1840 a uniform penny rate was introduced.

Hillary, Sir Edmund (Percival) (1919–) Mountaineer and explorer, born in Auckland, New Zealand. As a member of Hunt's Everest expedition he attained, with Tenzing Norgay, the summit of Mt Everest in 1953.

Hilton, Conrad (Nicholson) (1887–1979) Hotelier, born in San Antonio, NM. He formed the Hilton Hotels Corporation in 1946, which became Hilton International in 1948, one of the world's largest hotel organizations.

Himmler, Heinrich (1900–45) German Nazi leader and chief of police, born in Munich, Germany. In 1929 he became head of the SS, directed the Gestapo, and initiated the systematic killing of Jews. Captured by the Allies, he committed suicide.

Hindenburg, Paul (Ludwig Hans Anton von Beneckendorff und) von (1847–1934) German general and president (1925–34), born in Poznan, Poland (formerly Posen, Prussia). He won victories over the Russians (1914–15), but was forced to direct the German retreat on the Western Front (to the *Hindenburg line*).

Hindley, Myra *see* Brady, Ian

Hines, Earl (Kenneth), nickname **Fatha** ('Father') **Hines** (1903–83) Jazz pianist and bandleader, born in Duquesne, PA. He formed his own band in 1928, and his approach to solo improvisation, known as 'trumpet-style piano', was influential.

Hingis, Martina (1980–) Tennis player, born in Kosice, Slovak Republic. Raised in Switzerland, she played for that country, and in 1997 became the youngest ever world number 1. Her wins include the Wimbledon singles (1997), US Open (1997), and Australian Open (1997–9). Injury forced her retirement in 2003, but she returned to competitive tennis in 2006.

Hippocrates (c.460–c.377 BC) Physician, known as 'the father of medicine', and associated with the medical profession's *Hippocratic oath*, born on the island of Cos, Greece. The most celebrated physician of antiquity, he gathered together all that was sound in the previous history of medicine.

Hirohito *see* Showa Tenno

Hirst, Damien (1965–) Avant-garde artist, born in Bristol. He became known for works which made use of dead animals, preserved in formalin, such as 'Mother and Child Divided', and established his reputation after being awarded the Turner Prize in 1995.

Hislop, Ian (1960–) British writer, editor, and broadcaster. He became a television scriptwriter for *Spitting Image* (1984–9) and editor of the satirical magazine *Private Eye* (from 1986). He is also a team captain of BBC television's *Have I Got News For You* (1991–), and wrote the comedy sitcom *My Dad's The Prime Minister* (2003).

Hitchcock, Sir Alfred (Joseph) (1899–1980) Film director, born in London. He became a master of suspense, internationally recognized for his intricate plots and novel camera techniques. His films include *The Thirty-Nine Steps* (1935), *The Lady Vanishes* (1938), *Rebecca* (1940, Oscar), *Psycho* (1960), *The Birds* (1963), and *Frenzy* (1972).

Hitler, Adolf, popular name **der Führer** ('the Leader') (1889–1945) German dictator, born in Braunau, Upper Austria. In 1919 he joined a small political party which in 1920 he renamed as the National Socialist German Workers' Party. While in prison for attempting to overthrow the Bavarian government, he produced his political testament, *Mein Kampf* (1925, My Struggle). Made chancellor in 1933, he suspended the constitution, silenced all opposition, and brought the Nazi Party to power. His domestic policy was one of total Nazification, enforced by the Gestapo, and established concentration camps for political opponents and Jews. His aggressive actions in Czechoslovakia and Poland precipitated World War 2 (1939). With his early war successes, he increasingly ignored the advice of military experts, and the tide turned in 1942 after the defeats at El Alamein and Stalingrad. When Germany was invaded, he retired to an air-raid shelter under the Chancellery building in Berlin, where he went through a marriage ceremony with his mistress, Eva Braun. All available evidence suggests that Hitler and his wife committed suicide and had their bodies cremated.

Hobbs, Jack, popular name of **Sir John Berry Hobbs** (1882–1963) Cricketer, born in Cambridge, Cambridgeshire. He played in county cricket for Surrey (1905–34) and for England (1908–30). He made a record number of 197 centuries and 61 237 runs in first-class cricket.

Ho Chi-Minh, originally **Nguyen That Thanh** (1892–1969) Vietnamese prime minister (1954–5) and president (1954–69), born in Kim-Lien, North Vietnam. He led the Viet Minh independence movement in 1941, and directed the successful military operations against the French (1946–54), becoming President of North Vietnam.

Hockney, David (1937–) Artist, born in Bradford, West Yorkshire. Associated with the Pop Art movement from his earliest work, he has also worked in printmaking and photography, and designed sets and costumes. He is well known for his 'swimming pool' paintings.

Hoddle, Glenn (1957–) Football manager and player, born in Hayes, Greater London. He played for Tottenham Hotspur and AS Monaco, and was player/manager at Swindon Town and Chelsea. Appointed England manager (1996–9), he resigned after a controversial newspaper interview, and became manager of Southampton (2000), Tottenham (2001–3), and Wolverhampton Wanderers (from 2004).

Hodges, Johnny (1906–70) Jazz alto and soprano saxophonist, born in Cambridge, MA. He joined Duke Ellington's orchestra (1928–51), then led his own band with moderate success, rejoining in 1955 until his death.

Hoffman, Dustin (1937–) Actor, born in Los Angeles, CA. His first leading film role was *The Graduate* (1967), and this was followed by a number of similar 'anti-hero' roles, such as in *Midnight Cowboy* (1969). Later films include *All The President's Men* (1976), *Kramer v Kramer* (1979, Oscar), *Rain Man* (1988, Oscar), and *Finding Neverland* (2004).

Hogan, Paul (1941–) Comedian and actor, born in Lightning Ridge, New South Wales, Australia. He became internationally known for the films *Crocodile Dundee* (1986) and *Crocodile Dundee II* (1988), and has since become something of a national folk hero. *Crocodile Dundee in Los Angeles* appeared in 2001.

Hogarth, William (1697–1764) Painter and engraver, born in London. His highly detailed engravings of 'modern moral subjects' include 'A Rake's Progress' (1733–5), and his masterpiece, the 'Marriage à la Mode' (1743–5).

Holbein, Hans, known as **the Younger** (1497–1543) Painter, born in Augsburg, Germany, the son of **Hans Holbein the Elder** (c.1460–1524). His works include the celebrated 'Dead Christ' (1521) and the 'Dance of Death' woodcuts (1523–6). In 1526 he went to England where he painted portraits, notably of Henry VIII and his wives.

Holiday, Billie, originally **Eleanora Fagan**, nickname **Lady Day** (1915–59) Jazz singer, born in Baltimore, MD. In the late 1930s she worked with the big bands of Count Basie and Artie Shaw, singing such memorable ballads as 'Easy Living' (1937) and 'Yesterdays' (1939).

Holliday, Doc, popular name of **John**

Henry Holliday (1852–87) Gambler and dentist, baptized at Griffin, GA. After training as a dentist, he adopted a life of gambling, drinking, and gunfighting, and in Dodge City was involved in the gunfight at the OK Corral (1881).

Holloway, Stanley (1890–1982) Entertainer, born in London. He was a genial comedy actor in such Ealing film classics as *Passport to Pimlico* (1948) and *The Lavender Hill Mob* (1951), and was perhaps best known for his role of Alfred Doolittle in *My Fair Lady* on Broadway (1956–8; filmed 1964).

Holly, Buddy, popular name of **Charles Hardin Holley** (1936–59) Rock singer, songwriter, and guitarist, born in Lubbock, TX. With his band, The Crickets, he recorded such hits as 'That'll Be The Day', 'Peggy Sue', and 'Oh Boy'. After his death in a plane crash, he became an important cult figure.

Holm, Sir Ian (1931–) Actor, born in Ilford, Greater London. He achieved a major success at Stratford, when he played Prince Hal, Henry V, and Richard III in *The Wars of The Roses* (1963–4). After a period away from the stage, he played a widely acclaimed Lear in 1997.

Holmes, Dame Kelly (1970–) Athlete, born in Pembury, Kent. Her achievements include the 1500 m gold at the 1994 Commonwealth Games, 1500 m gold at the 2002 Commonwealth Games, and Olympic gold in the 800 m and 1500 m events at the 2004 Games in Athens. She was made a dame in 2005 and retired from athletics later that year.

Holroyd, Michael (de Courcy Fraser) (1935–) Biographer, born in London. His two-volume life of Lytton Strachey (1967–8) is recognized as a landmark in biographical writing. He married novelist Margaret Drabble in 1982.

Holst, Gustav (Theodore) (1874–1934) Composer, born of Swedish origin in Cheltenham, Gloucestershire. His major works include the seven-movement suite *The Planets* (1914–16), *The Hymn of Jesus* (1917), and his orchestral tone poem, *Egdon Heath* (1927).

Holt, Victoria *see* Hibbert, Eleanor

Holyfield, Evander (1962–) Boxer, born in Atlanta, GA. He became the World Boxing Association (WBA) heavyweight champion in 1996 and the International Boxing Federation heavyweight champion in 1998. He was undisputed heavyweight champion of the world in 1990–2. In 2001 he lost the WBA crown to John Ruiz.

Home of the Hirsel, Baron, formerly **Sir Alec Douglas-Home**, originally **Alexander Frederick Douglas-Home, 14th Earl of Home** (1903–95) British prime minister (1963–4), born in London. He was Commonwealth relations secretary (1955–60) and foreign secretary (1960–3, 1970–4). After Macmillan's resignation, he astonished everyone by emerging as premier, renouncing his peerage and fighting a by-election.

Homer, Greek **Homēros** (c.8th-c BC) Greek poet, to whom are attributed the great epics, the *Iliad*, the story of the siege of Troy, and the *Odyssey*, the tale of Odysseus's wanderings. Arguments have long raged over whether his works are in fact by the same hand, or have their origins in the lays of Homer and his followers (*Homeridae*).

Hoon, Geoffrey (1953–) British statesman, born in Derby, Derbyshire. He was an MEP (1984–94) and became Labour MP for Ashfield in 1992. He served in the Lord Chancellor's Department (1998) and the Foreign Office (1999), and as defence secretary (1999–2005), Leader of the Commons (2005–6), and minister for Europe in 2006.

Hoover, Herbert (Clark) (1874–1964) US statesman and 31st president (1929–33), born in West Branch, IA. His opposition to direct governmental assistance for the unemployed after the world slump of 1929 made him unpopular, and he was beaten by Roosevelt in 1932. The *Hoover Dam* is named after him.

Hoover, J(ohn) Edgar (1895–1972) US public servant, born in Washington, DC. He served as FBI director (1924–72), campaigning against city gangster rackets in the inter-war years, and against Communist sympathizers in the post-war period.

Hope, Bob, originally **Leslie Townes Hope** (1903–2003) Comedian, born in London. In partnership with Bing Crosby and Dorothy Lamour, he appeared in the highly successful *Road to ...* comedies (1940–52), and in many others until the early 1970s.

Hope, Christopher (1944–) Writer, born in Johannesburg, South Africa. His novels include *Kruger's Alp* (1984, Whitbread), *Serenity House* (1992, shortlisted for the Booker Prize), and *Heaven Forbid* (2002). Among his non-fiction works are *White Boy Running* (1988) and *Brothers Under the Skin: Travels in Tyranny* (2003).

Hopkins, Sir (Philip) Anthony (1937–) Actor, born in Port Talbot, S Wales. His films include *The Elephant Man* (1980), *The Silence of the Lambs* (1991, Oscar), *The Remains of the Day* (1994, BAFTA), *Amistad* (1997), and *Proof* (2005). He received a Golden Globe for lifetime achievement in 2006.

Hopkins, Gerard Manley (1844–89) Poet, born in London. He became a Catholic in 1866. An edition of his poems published in 1918 had a mixed reception, largely because of his experiments with 'sprung rhythm'; but a new edition in 1930 was widely acclaimed. His best-known poems include 'The Wreck of the *Deutschland*' and 'The Wind-hover'.

Horace, in full **Quintus Horatius Flaccus** (65–8 BC) Latin poet and satirist, born near Venusia, Italy. His earliest works were chiefly satires and lampoons, and through the influence of Virgil he came under the patronage of Maecenas. The unrivalled lyric poet of his time, his greatest work was the three books of *Odes* (19 BC).

Hordern, Sir Michael (Murray) (1911–95) Actor, born in Berkhamsted, Hertfordshire. A popular actor for 20 years, his major classical roles included King Lear (1960) and Prospero (1978), as well as several modern roles, such as in Tom Stoppard's *Jumpers* (1972) and Howard Barker's *Stripwell* (1975).

Horne, Lena (1917–) Singer and actress, born in Brooklyn, NY. A popular band singer, she went into films, becoming the first African-American to be signed to a long-term contract. She became known for her outspokenness about discrimination.

Horsa *see* Hengist and Horsa

Hoskins, Bob, popular name of **Robert William Hoskins** (1942–) Actor, born in Bury St Edmunds, Suffolk. He became well known with the television series *Pennies From Heaven* (1978), and his film credits include *The Long Good Friday* (1980), *Mona Lisa* (1986, BAFTA), *Who Framed Roger Rabbit* (1988), and *Mrs Henderson Presents* (2005).

Houdini, Harry, originally **Ehrich Weiss** (1874–1926) Magician and escape artist, born in Budapest. He gained an international reputation as an escape artist, freeing himself from handcuffs and other devices, often while imprisoned in a box under water or in mid-air.

Housman, A(lfred) E(dward) (1859–1936) Scholar and poet, born near Bromsgrove, Hereford and Worcester, the brother of Laurence Housman. He is best known for *A Shropshire Lad* (1896) and *Last Poems* (1922), but devoted much of his life (1903–30) to an annotated edition of Manilius.

Houston, Sam(uel) (1793–1863) US soldier and statesman, born in Lexington, VA. As commander-in-chief in the Texan War, he defeated the Mexicans on the San Jacinto in 1836, achieving Texan independence, and was then elected president of the republic. Houston, TX, is named after him.

Houston, Whitney (1963–) Singer and actress, born in Newark, NJ. The album *Whitney Houston* (1985, Grammy) included her first US number 1 hit single 'Saving All My Love For You'. In 1988 she broke a US chart record with seven consecutive number 1 hits. Her films include *The Bodyguard* (1992) and *The Preacher's Wife* (1996).

Howard, Catherine (?–1542) Fifth wife of Henry VIII, a grand-daughter of the 2nd Duke of Norfolk. She was married to the king in 1540, but after Henry learned of Catherine's alleged premarital affairs (1541), she was accused of treason and beheaded.

Howard, Elizabeth Jane (1923–) Novelist, born in London. The *Cazalet Chronicles* comprises *The Light Years* (1990), *Marking Time* (1991), *Confusion* (1993), and *Casting Off* (1995). Later novels include *Falling* (1999, televised 2005). Her third husband was Kingsley Amis.

Howard, John (Winston) (1939–) Australian prime minister (1996–), born in Sydney, New South Wales, Australia. He became an MP in 1974, and went on to serve as deputy-leader (1983–5) and leader of the Liberal Party in Opposition (1985–9, 1995–6). He became prime minister following his party's general election victory in 1996. He won a third term in 2001.

Howard, Michael (1941–) British statesman, born in Gorseinon, near Swansea. He was elected an MP in 1983, and after a series of ministerial posts became home secretary (1993–7). He served as shadow foreign secretary (1997–9) and shadow Chancellor (2001–3), and in 2003 was elected party leader. Defeated in the 2005 general election, he stepped down in December that year.

Howard, Ron(ald William) (1954–) Actor, director, and producer, born in Duncan, OK. He became known for his roles in the TV series *The Andy Griffith Show* (1960–8) and *Happy Days* (1973–80). He made his directorial debut with *Grand Theft Auto* (1977), and later films include *Apollo 13* (1995), *A Beautiful Mind* (2002, Oscar Best Director; Golden Globe Best Film), and *Cinderella Man* (2005).

Howard, Trevor (Wallace) (1916–88) Actor, born in Cliftonville, Kent. He sprang to stardom with *Brief Encounter* (1945), followed by *The Third Man* (1949) and *Outcast of the Islands* (1951). Work for television included *White Mischief* (1987).

Howe (of Aberavon), (Richard Edward) Geoffrey Howe, Baron (1926–) British statesman, born in Port Talbot, S Wales. He was Chancellor of the Exchequer (1979–1983), foreign secretary (1983–9), and deputy prime minister (1989–90), but resigned from the government over European monetary union.

Howe, Richard Howe, 1st Earl (1726–99) British admiral, born in London, the brother of William Howe. He commanded the British fleet (1776) during the American War of Independence. In the French Revolutionary Wars he defeated the French at 'the Glorious First of June' (1794).

Howerd, Frankie, originally **Francis Alex Howard** (1922–92) Comedian and actor, born in London. He appeared regularly on television and in films, his most famous role being that of a Roman slave in the television series *Up Pompeii* (1970–1; filmed 1971).

Hoyle, Sir Fred(erick) (1915–2001) Astronomer, mathematician, astrophysicist, and science-fiction writer, born in Bingley, West Yorkshire. He was known for his work on the origin of chemical elements, and was a leading proponent of steady-state cosmology, and a believer in an extraterrestrial origin for life on Earth.

Hu Jintao (1942–) Chinese president (2003–). A member of the Politburo standing committee in 1992, he was appointed vice-president in 1998, and succeeded Jiang Zemin as president in 2002 and as head of the Central Military Commission (2004–).

Hubbard, L(afayette) Ron(ald) (1911–86) Writer, and founder of the Scientology religion, born in Tilden, NE. His most famous work, *Dianetics: the Modern Science of Mental Health* (1950) became the basic text of the Scientology movement.

Hubble, Edwin (Powell) (1889–1953) Astronomer, born in Marshfield, MO. His work led to the discovery that the universe is expanding, establishing a ratio between the galaxies' speed of movement and their distance (*Hubble's constant*). The *Hubble Space Telescope* is named after him.

Hughes, Howard (Robard) (1905–76) Businessman, film producer, film director, and aviator, born in Houston, TX. He inherited his father's machine tool company (1923), ventured into films (1926), founded his own aircraft company, and broke several world air speed records (1935–8). He eventually became a recluse.

Hughes, Ted, popular name of **Edward (James) Hughes** (1930–98) Poet, born in Mytholmroyd, West Yorkshire. Best known for his distinctive animal poems, his first collections were *The Hawk in the Rain* (1957) and *Lupercal* (1960). He married US poet Sylvia Plath in 1956, and after her death edited her collected poems (1981). He became poet laureate in 1984. *Birthday Letters* (1998), a series of poems about his relationship with Plath, won several literary prizes.

Hugo, Victor (Marie) (1802–85) Writer, born in Besançon, France. The most prolific French writer of the 19th-c, his major works include the novel *The Hunchback of Notre Dame* (trans, 1831), the books of poems *Punishments* (trans, 1853) and *Les Contemplations* (1856), and his panoramic novel of social history, *Les Misérables* (1862).

Hume, (George) Basil, Cardinal (1923–99) Roman Catholic Benedictine monk. Abbot of Ampleforth (1963), he was created Archbishop of Westminster and a cardinal in 1976. He was the first Catholic bishop to be appointed to the Order of Merit, in 1999.

Hume, David (1711–76) Philosopher and historian, born in Edinburgh. His masterpiece, *A Treatise of Human Nature* (1739–40), extended the empiricist legacy of Locke and

Berkeley. Other works include the popular *Political Discourses* (1752) and his *History of England* (6 vols, 1754–62).

Hume, John (1937–) Northern Ireland politician, born in Londonderry, Co Londonderry. Leader of the Social Democratic Labour Party, in 1993 he and Sinn Féin leader Gerry Adams began a series of talks, the Hume–Adams peace initiative, intended to bring about an end to violence in Northern Ireland. He shared the 1998 Nobel Peace Prize with David Trimble for his efforts to find a peaceful solution to the conflict.

Humperdinck, Engelbert (1854–1921) Composer, born in Siegburg, Germany. He composed several operas, one of which, *Hänsel und Gretel* (1893), was highly successful.

Humperdinck, Engelbert, popular name of **Arnold George Dorsey** (1936–) Singer, born to British parents in Chennai (Madras), India, and brought up in Leicester, UK. In 1965 he changed his name and had his first hit single 'Release Me' (1967). After the 1970s his career as a cabaret artist blossomed in America.

Humphries, (John) Barry (1934–) Comic performer and satirical writer, born in Melbourne, Victoria, Australia. He is best known for his characters Sir Les Patterson and 'housewife megastar' Dame Edna Everage, who have frequently appeared on television and in film.

Humphrys, John (Desmond) (1943–) Television journalist and presenter, born in Cardiff. He began as a reporter with the BBC (1966) and was presenter on the *Nine O'Clock News*

(1981–6). He joined Radio 4's *Today* programme in 1987 and presents *On the Record* for BBC 1 (from 1993). In 2003 he became host of the revived classic TV quiz show *Mastermind*.

Hunniford, Gloria (1940–) British broadcaster, born in Portadown, Co Armagh. She became widely known with her daily radio programme for BBC's Radio 2 (1982–95), while participating in several shows, including BBC's *Gloria Live* (1990–3). She wrote *Next to You* (2005), a best-selling biography of her daughter, **Caron Keating** (1962–2004).

Hunt (of Llanfair Waterdine), (Henry Cecil) John Hunt, Baron (1910–98) Mountaineer, born in Marlborough, Wiltshire. In 1953 he led the first successful expedition to Mt Everest, and in 1958 led the British party in the British–Soviet Caucasian expedition.

Hurd (of Westwell), Douglas (Richard), Baron (1930–) British statesman, born in Marlborough, Wiltshire. He became Northern Ireland secretary (1984), home secretary (1985), and foreign secretary (1989–95).

Hurt, John (1940–) Actor, born in Chesterfield, Derbyshire. He won BAFTA awards for *Midnight Express* (1978) and *The Elephant Man* (1980). Among later films are *Rob Roy* (1995) and *Captain Corelli's Mandolin* (2001), and he starred in *The Alan Clark Diaries* (2004) for television.

Hurt, William (1950–) Actor, born in Washington, DC. He won a Best Actor Oscar for *Kiss of The Spiderwoman* (1985), and Oscar nominations for *Children Of A Lesser God*

(1986), *Broadcast News* (1987), and *A History of Violence* (2005).

Hussain, Nasser (1968–) Cricketer, born in Madras, India. A batsman, he joined Essex in 1987 and made his England debut in 1990. He achieved a career-best 207 runs against Australia at Edgbaston in 1997. Appointed England captain in 1999, he led his country to its first series victory over the West Indies on home soil since 1969. He retired in 2004.

Hussein, Saddam, also spelled **Sadam Husain** (1937–) President of Iraq (1979–2003), born in Takrit. Prominent in the 1968 revolution, he became vice-president of the Revolutionary Command Council in 1969. His attack on Iran (1980) led to a war of attrition which ended in 1988. He invaded Kuwait in 1990, but was forced to withdraw when he was defeated by a coalition of Arab and Western forces in Operation Desert Storm (1991). During the 1990s he continued to resist UN and US pressure for a programme of weapons inspection within Iraq. The country's apparent failure to comply with UN resolutions to eliminate its weapons of mass destruction led to a US-led military invasion in March 2003. He was deposed the next month, fled, and was captured by US forces and held as a prisoner-of-war. His trial for war crimes began in Baghdad in 2005, and was ongoing in 2006.

Huston, John (Marcellus) (1906–87) Film director, born in Nevada, MO.

His films include *The Treasure of the Sierra Madre* (1948, Oscar), *The African Queen* (1951), *Moby Dick* (1956), and the musical, *Annie* (1982).

Hutton, James (1726–97) Geologist, born in Edinburgh. The *Huttonian theory*, emphasizing the igneous origin of many rocks, was expounded in *A Theory of the Earth* (1795), which forms the basis of modern geology.

Hutton, Len, popular name of **Sir Leonard Hutton** (1916–90) Cricketer, born in Fulneck, West Yorkshire. Playing for England against Australia at the Oval in 1938, he scored a world record 364 runs. During his first-class career (1934–60) he scored 40 140 runs, including 129 centuries.

Hutton, Sir James Brian Edward, Lord (1931–) Judge, born in Belfast. He became Judge of the High Court of Justice (NI) (1979–88), Lord Chief Justice of Northern Ireland (1988–97), and Lord of Appeal in Ordinary (1997–2004). He was appointed to chair the enquiry (2003–4) into the circumstances surrounding the death of Dr David Kelly, the Ministry of Defence's chief scientific officer and weapons inspector.

Huxley, Aldous (Leonard) (1894–1963) Novelist and essayist, born in Godalming, Surrey, the grandson of T H Huxley. His reputation was made with his satirical novels *Crome Yellow* (1921) and *Antic Hay* (1923). Later novels include *Point Counter Point* (1928) and, his best-known work, *Brave New World* (1932).

Ibsen, Henrik (Johan) (1828–1906)
Playwright and poet, born in Skien,
Norway. His international reputation began with *Brand* and *Peer Gynt*
(1866–7). He regarded his historical
drama, *Emperor and Galilean* (trans,
1873) as his masterpiece, but his fame
rests more on his social plays, notably *A Doll's House* (trans, 1879) and
Ghosts (trans, 1881). In his last phase
he turned more to Symbolism, as in
The Wild Duck (trans, 1884), *Rosmers-
holm* (1886), and *The Master-Builder*
(trans, 1892). The realism of *Hedda
Gabler* (1890) was a solitary escape
from Symbolism.

Ignatius (of Antioch), St (c.35–c.107)
One of the apostolic Fathers of the
Church, reputedly a disciple of St
John, the second Bishop of Antioch.
He died a martyr in Rome.

Ignatius de Loyola, St *see* Loyola,
Ignatius of, St

Illingworth, Ray(mond) (1932–)
Cricketer and broadcaster, born in
Pudsey, West Yorkshire. A proficient
batsman and spin-bowler, he won 66
Test caps for England (36 as captain),
taking 122 wickets and scoring two
centuries. He was later appointed
chairman of selectors, Test and
County Cricket Board (1994–6), and
manager of the England team
(1995–6).

Imran Khan, in full **Ahmad Khan
Niazi Imran** (1952–) Cricketer, born
in Lahore, Pakistan. A fast bowler and
astute captain, he inspired Pakistan's
rise to prominence in world cricket.
After leading Pakistan to the 1992
World Cup, he retired with a Test
Match score of 3807 runs and 362
wickets. He married in 1995, and has
since been developing a career in
politics, forming his own party,
Pakistan Tehrik-i-Insaaf (Pakistan
Justice Movement).

Ingham, Sir Bernard (1932–) Journalist, born in Hebden Bridge, West
Yorkshire. A government press adviser (1976) and under-secretary in the
Department of Energy (1978–9), he
became nationally known after his
appointment as chief press secretary
to prime minister Margaret Thatcher
(1979–90).

Innes, Michael *see* Stewart, J I M

Ionesco, Eugène (1912–94) Playwright,
born in Slatina, Romania. After the
success of *The Bald Prima Donna*
(trans, 1950), he became a prolific
writer of one-act plays which came to
be seen as typical examples of the
Theatre of the Absurd, such as *The
Chairs* (trans, 1952) and *Rhinocéros*
(1960).

Irenaeus, St (c.130–c.200) One of the
Christian Fathers of the Greek
Church, probably born near Smyrna.
He is chiefly known for his opposi-
tion to Gnosticism, and for his
attempts to prevent a rupture

between Eastern and Western Churches over the computing of Easter.

Irons, Jeremy (John) (1948–) Actor, born in Cowes, Isle of Wight. A stage actor with the Royal Shakespeare Company, he became well known after his role in *The French Lieutenant's Woman* (1981) and the television series *Brideshead Revisited* (1981). Later films include *Reversal of Fortune* (1990, Oscar), *Stealing Beauty* (1996), and *Kingdom of Heaven* (2005).

Ironside, William Edmund Ironside, Baron (1880–1959) British field marshal, born in Ironside, Aberdeenshire. Chief of the Imperial General Staff at the outbreak of World War 2, he commanded the home defence forces (1940). The *Ironsides*, fast light-armoured vehicles, were named after him.

Irvine (of Lairg), Alexander Andrew Mackay Irvine, Baron (1940–) British judge. He was called to the bar in 1967, and became a QC (1978) and a deputy judge in the High Court (1987). Appointed shadow Lord Chancellor (1992–7), he then served as Lord Chancellor (1997–2003).

Irving, John (Winslow) (1942–) Novelist, born in Exeter, NH. His first three novels received little attention, but he made his name with *The World According To Garp* (1978; filmed 1982). Later books include *The Hotel New Hampshire* (1981; filmed 1984), *The Cider House Rules* (1985; filmed 1999, Oscar), and *Until I Find You* (2005).

Irving, Washington, pseudonym **Geoffrey Crayon** (1783–1859) Man of letters, born in New York City. Under his pseudonym he wrote *The Sketch Book* (1819–20), a miscellany containing such items as 'Rip Van Winkle' and 'The Legend of Sleepy Hollow'.

Isaac Biblical character, the son of Abraham by Sarah, through whose line of descent God's promises to Abraham were seen to continue. He was nearly sacrificed by Abraham at God's command (*Gen* 22).

Isabella I (of Castile), also known as **Isabella the Catholic** (1451–1504) Queen of Castile (1474–1504), born in Madrigal de las Altas Torres, Spain, the daughter of John II, King of Castile and León. In 1469 she married Ferdinand V of Aragon, with whom she ruled jointly from 1479.

Isaiah, Heb **Jeshaiah** (8th-c BC) The first in order of the major Old Testament prophets, the son of Amoz. A citizen of Jerusalem, he began to prophesy c.747 BC. According to tradition, he was martyred.

Isherwood, Christopher (William Bradshaw) (1904–86) Novelist, born in Disley, Cheshire. His best-known novels, such as *Goodbye to Berlin* (1939), were based on the decadence of post-slump, pre-Hitler Berlin, and later inspired *Cabaret* (musical 1966; filmed 1972). In collaboration with Auden, he wrote three prose-verse plays with political overtones.

Ishiguro, Kazuo (1954–) Novelist, born in Nagasaki, Japan. His third novel, *The Remains of the Day* (1989; filmed 1993), won the Booker Prize and established his reputation. Later books include *The Unconsoled* (1995) and *Never Let Me Go* (2005).

Ishmael Biblical character, the son of

Abraham by Hagar, his wife's maid. He was expelled into the desert with his mother after the birth of Isaac, and is considered the ancestor of the Bedouin tribes (the *Ishmaelites*).

Ivory, James (Francis) (1928–) Film director and writer, born in Berkeley, CA. With Ismail Merchant he formed Merchant-Ivory Productions in 1961. International success came with *Shakespeare Wallah* (1965), which he wrote with **Ruth Jhabvala** (1927–), and he went on to direct a series of films based on major works in English literature, such as *Howard's End* (1992, BAFTA Best Film).

Izzard, Eddie (1962–) British comedian, born in Aden, Yemen. He became nationally known in the UK through live videos of his major shows at the Ambassadors (1993) and the Albery (1995) in London, and won two Emmy awards for *Eddie Izzard: Dressed to Kill* (2000).

Jacklin, Tony, popular name of **Anthony Jacklin** (1944–) Golfer, born at Scunthorpe, North Lincolnshire. He won the 1969 Open at Royal Lytham, and in 1970 won the US Open at Hazeltine (the first British winner for 50 years). He was appointed non-playing captain of the European team in the Ryder Cup (1983–9).

Jackson, Andrew, nickname **Old Hickory** (1767–1845) US statesman and seventh president (1829–37), born in Waxhaw, SC. In his presidential campaign he gained the support of the mass of voters – a new development in US politics which came to be called 'Jacksonian democracy'.

Jackson, Betty (1949–) Fashion designer, born in Backup, Lancashire. She became chief designer with Quorum (1975–81), and is now design director of Betty Jackson Ltd. In 1985 she was British Designer of the Year and won the British Fashion Council award.

Jackson, Glenda (1936–) Actress and politician, born in Birkenhead, Merseyside. She became a leading member of the Royal Shakespeare Company before appearing in films, including *Women in Love* (1969, Oscar) and *A Touch of Class* (1973, Oscar). She became a Labour MP in 1992 and served as transport minister (1997–9).

Jackson, Jesse (Louis) (1941–) Clergyman and politician, born in Greenville, NC. A civil rights activist, in 1984 and 1988 he sought the Democratic nomination for the presidency, winning considerable support, and becoming the first African-American to mount a serious candidacy for the office.

Jackson, Mahalia (1911–72) Gospel singer, born in New Orleans, LA. Her strong religious background and the influence of contemporary blues music were evident in her singing style. Two notably successful records were 'Move On Up a Little Higher' and 'Silent Night'.

Jackson, Michael (1958–) Pop singer, born in Gary, IN. A child star with his brothers in the pop group The Jacksons, he sang on four consecutive number 1 hits. His first major solo album was *Off The Wall* (1979), and he consolidated his career with *Thriller* (1982) and *HIStory* (1995). He developed a reclusive lifestyle in adulthood, though continuing to tour widely. He was married to Lisa Marie Presley (1994–6) and Debbie Rowe (1996–9). In 2005 he faced trial on child molestation charges and was acquitted.

Jackson, Peter (1961–) Film director, writer, and producer, born in Pukerua, North Island, New Zealand.

Among his films is the multi-award-winning *The Lord of the Rings* trilogy: *The Fellowship of the Ring* (2001), *The Two Towers* (2002), and *The Return of the King* (2003). Awards included 11 Oscars, including Best Picture and Best Director. In 2005 he directed a remake of the 1933 film, *King Kong*.

Jack the Ripper Unidentified English murderer who, between August and November 1888, murdered and mutilated five prostitutes in the East End of London. The murderer was never discovered, but speculation about the murderer's identity was still continuing in the 1990s.

Jacob Biblical character, the son of Isaac, and patriarch of the nation Israel. He supplanted his elder brother Esau, obtaining his father Isaac's special blessing and thus being seen as the inheritor of God's promises. He fathered 12 sons, to whom Jewish tradition traced the 12 tribes of Israel.

Jacobi, Sir Derek (George) (1938–) Actor, born in London. He has made several film and television appearances, notably the title role in the television drama serial *I, Claudius* (1977). A member of the Royal Shakespeare Company since 1982, his main work continues to be in the theatre.

Jacobson, Dan (1929–) Novelist and short-story writer, born in Johannesburg, South Africa. He began writing in the 1950s, with *The Trap* (1955), later novels including *The Beginners* (1966), *Her Story* (1987), *The God-Fearer* (1993), and *All For Love* (2005).

Jagger, Mick, popular name of **Sir**

Michael Philip Jagger (1943–) Singer, born in Dartford, Kent. He formed his own rock group, The Rolling Stones, together with Keith Richard, Bill Wyman, Charlie Watts, and Brian Jones. He wrote and sang many of their hit singles including 'The Last Time' (1965) and 'I Can't Get No Satisfaction' (1965). Still popular after four decades, the group released the album *A Bigger Bang* in 2005.

James I (of England) (1566–1625) The first Stuart king of England (1603–25), also king of Scots (1567–1625) as James VI, born in Edinburgh, the son of Mary, Queen of Scots. On Elizabeth's death, he ascended the English throne as great-grandson of James IV's English wife, Margaret Tudor. At first well received, his favouritism brought him unpopularity. During his reign the Authorized (or King James) Version of the Bible was published (1611).

James II (of England) (1633–1701) King of England and Ireland (1685–8), also King of Scotland, as **James VII**, born in London, the second son of Charles I. After he became a convert to Catholicism, several attempts were made to exclude him from the succession. His actions in favour of Catholicism raised general indignation, and William, Prince of Orange, was formally asked to invade (1688). James escaped to France, and made an ineffectual attempt to regain his throne in Ireland, ending in the Battle of the Boyne (1690).

James, St ('Brother' of Jesus), also known as **St James the Just** (1st-c) One of the 'brothers' of Jesus of

Nazareth (*Matt* 13.55), and identified as the foremost leader of the Christian community in Jerusalem. According to Josephus, he was martyred by stoning (c.62).

James, St (Son of Alphaeus), also known as **St James the Less** (1st-c) One of the 12 apostles. He may be the James whose mother Mary is referred to at the crucifixion of Jesus.

James, St (Son of Zebedee), also known as **St James the Great** (1st-c) One of Jesus's 12 apostles, often listed with John (his brother) and Peter as part of an inner group closest to Jesus. According to *Acts* 12.2, he was martyred under Herod Agrippa I (c.44).

James, Clive (Vivian Leopold) (1939–) Writer, satirist, broadcaster, and critic, born in Sydney, New South Wales, Australia. Television critic for *The Observer*, his television programmes include *Saturday Night Clive*, as well as a series of 'documentaries' set in cities around the world.

James, Henry (1843–1916) Novelist, born in New York City. His work as a novelist falls into three periods. In the first he is mainly concerned with the impact of American life on older European civilization, as in *Roderick Hudson* (1875), *Portrait of a Lady* (1881), and *The Bostonians* (1886). His second period is devoted to purely English subjects, such as *The Tragic Muse* (1890), *What Maisie Knew* (1897), and *The Awkward Age* (1899). He reverts to Anglo-American attitudes in his last period, which includes his masterpiece, *The Ambassadors* (1903). The acknowledged master of the psychological novel, he was a major influence on 20th-c writing.

James, Jesse (Woodson) (1847–82) Wild West outlaw, born in Centerville, MO. He and his brother **Frank James** (1843–1915) led many robberies in and around Missouri, before Jesse was murdered by a gang member for a reward. Frank gave himself up, stood trial, and was released.

James, Dame Naomi (Christine) (1949–) Yachtswoman and writer, born in New Zealand. She became the first woman to sail solo around the world, and first woman solo around Cape Horn (Sep 1977–Jun 1978) on her yacht *Express Crusader*. In 1980 she entered the Observer Transatlantic Race, achieving the women's record for a single-handed Atlantic crossing.

James, P D, pseudonym of **Phyllis Dorothy White, Baroness James of Holland Park** (1920–) Detective-story writer, born in Oxford, Oxfordshire. Many of her novels feature Inspector Adam Dalgleish, such as *Shroud for a Nightingale* (1971), *A Taste for Death* (1986), *Original Sin* (1994), and *The Lighthouse* (2005).

Janáček, Leoš (1854–1928) Composer, born in Hukvaldy, Czech Republic. Devoted to the Czech folksong tradition, he wrote several operas, a Mass, instrumental chamber pieces, and song cycles.

Jansky, Karl (Guthe) (1905–50) Radio engineer, born in Norman, OK. His discovery (1932) of radio waves from outer space allowed the development of radio astronomy during the 1950s. The unit of radio emission strength, the *jansky*, is named after him.

Jardine, Al(an) *see* Beach Boys, The

Jason, Sir David (1940–) Actor, born in Edmonton, Greater London. Best known as a television actor, his many series include *Open All Hours* (1976, 1981–5), *Only Fools and Horses* (several series), and *A Touch of Frost* (1992–). In 2003 he was honoured with a BAFTA Fellowship.

Jefferson, Thomas (1743–1826) US vice-president (1797–1801) and third president (1801–9), born in Shadwell, VA. He took a prominent part in the first Continental Congress (1774), and drafted the Declaration of Independence (1776). His administration saw the war with Tripoli, the Louisiana Purchase (1803), and the prohibition of the slave trade.

Jenkins (of Hillhead), Roy (Harris) Jenkins, Baron (1920–2003) British statesman, born in Abersychan, Torfaen, S Wales. He served as Chancellor of the Exchequer (1967–70) and home secretary (1965–7, 1974–6), became president of the European Commission (1977–81), then co-founded the Social Democratic Party, becoming its first leader (1981–3).

Jenner, Edward (1749–1823) Physician, born in Berkeley, Gloucestershire. Having observed how an infection of the mild disease cowpox prevented later attacks of smallpox, in 1796 he inoculated a child with cowpox, then two months later with smallpox, and the child failed to develop the disease. This led to the widespread use of vaccination.

Jennings, Pat(rick) (1945–) Footballer, born in Newry, Co Down. A goalkeeper, he played for Watford, Tottenham Hotspur, and Arsenal, making 747 League appearances. He is Britain's most capped footballer, playing for Northern Ireland 119 times.

Jerome, St, originally **Eusebius Hieronymus** (c.342–420) Christian ascetic and scholar, born in Stridon, Croatia. He is chiefly known for making the first translation of the Bible from Hebrew into Latin (the Vulgate).

Jerome, Jerome K(lapka) (1859–1927) Humorous writer, novelist, and playwright, born in Walsall, Staffordshire. He is best known for his novel *Three Men in a Boat* (1889), which became a humorous classic.

Jesus Christ (c.6 /5 BC–AD c.30 /33) The central figure of the Christian faith, whose nature as 'Son of God' and whose redemptive work are fundamental beliefs for adherents of Christianity. 'Christ' became attached to the name 'Jesus' in Christian circles in view of the conviction that he was the Jewish Messiah ('Christ'). Jesus of Nazareth is described as the son of Mary and Joseph, and is credited with a miraculous conception by the Spirit of God. He was born in Bethlehem before the death of Herod the Great (4 BC), but began his ministry in Nazareth. After being baptized by John the Baptist in the Jordan, he gathered a group of 12 apostles, and began his public ministry. The main records of this ministry are the New Testament Gospels, which show him proclaiming the coming of the kingdom of God in the country of Galilee over a 3-year period. He was executed by crucifixion under the order of Pontius Pilate, perhaps because of the unrest Jesus's activities were causing. Accounts of his resurrection from the dead and later events are preserved in the Gospels, Pauline writings, and Acts of the Apostles.

Jewel, Jimmy *see* Jewel and Warriss

Jewel and Warriss Stage names of **Jimmy Jewel** (1909–95) and **Ben Warriss** (1909–93) Comedy partners, born in Sheffield, South Yorkshire. They achieved national fame as stars on BBC radio's *Up the Pole* (1947) and as cover stars of the weekly children's comic, *Radio Fun*.

Jiang Jieshi, or **Chiang Kai-shek** (1887–1975) Revolutionary leader of 20th-c China, the effective head of the Nationalist Republic (1928–49), born in Zhejiang. In 1918 he joined the separatist revolutionary government of Sun Yixian, and in 1925 launched an expedition against the Beijing government, entering Beijing in 1928. During the ensuing decade the Nationalist Party steadily lost support to the Communists, and was eventually defeated by Communist forces. He was forced to retreat to Taiwan (1949), where he headed an emigré regime.

Jingis Khan *see* Genghis Khan

Joan of Arc, St, Fr **Jeanne d'Arc**, known as **the Maid of Orléans** (c.1412–31) Traditionally recognized patriot and martyr, who halted the English ascendancy in France during the Hundred Years' War, born in Domrémy, France. At the age of 13 she heard saints' voices bidding her rescue France from English domination. She entered Orléans (1429), forced the English to retire, and took the Dauphin to be crowned Charles VII at Reims. Later captured, she stood trial (1431) for heresy and sorcery, and was burned. She was canonized in 1920.

Jobs, Steven (1955–) Computer inventor and entrepreneur, born in San Francisco, CA. He was co-founder with **Stephen Wozniak** (1950–) of the Apple Computer Co in 1976.

Joel, Billy (1949–) Singer, songwriter, and pianist, born in Long Island, NY. He earned a gold disc with the album *Piano Man* (1974); later albums include *Stormfront* (1989), *River of Dreams* (1993), and *Movin' Out* (2002).

Johansson, Scarlett (1984–) Actress, born in New York City. She gained recognition for her role in *The Horse Whisperer* (1998), and later films include *Girl with a Pearl Earring* (2003), *Lost in Translation* (2003, BAFTA Best Actress), and *Match Point* (2005).

John (of England), also known as **John Lackland** (1167–1216) King of England (1199–1216), born in Oxford, Oxfordshire, the youngest son of Henry II. He tried to seize the crown during Richard I's captivity (1193–4), but was forgiven and made successor by Richard, who thus set aside the rights of Arthur, the son of John's elder brother Geoffrey. After Arthur was murdered on John's orders (1203), Philip II of France marched against him and conquered all but a portion of Aquitaine (1204–5). In 1206 John refused to receive Stephen Langton as Archbishop of Canterbury; he was excommunicated (1209), and finally conceded (1213). Demands for constitutional reform by the barons led to the granting of the Magna Carta (1215), and his repudiation of the Charter brought the first Barons' War (1215–17).

John, St, also known as **John, son of Zebedee** and **John the Evangelist** (1st-c) One of the 12 apostles, the son of Zebedee, and the younger brother of James. He was said to have spent his closing years at Ephesus, after having written the Apocalypse, the Gospel, and the three Epistles which bear his name.

John XXIII, originally **Angelo Giuseppe Roncalli** (1881–1963) Pope (1958–63), born in Sotto il Monte, Italy. He convened the Second Vatican Council (1962–5) to renew the religious life of the Church, with the aim of eventual unity of all Christians.

John, Augustus (Edwin) (1878–1961) Painter, born in Tenby, Pembrokeshire. His favourite themes were gypsies, fishing folk, and naturally regal women, as in 'Lyric Fantasy' (1913); and he painted portraits of several political and artistic contemporary figures.

John, Sir Elton (Hercules), originally **Reginald Kenneth Dwight** (1947–) Rock singer and pianist, born in Pinner, Greater London. He was one of the top pop stars of the 1970s, known for such songs as 'Rocket Man' (1972) and 'Honky Cat' (1972), and for his clownish garb. His recording of 'Candle in the Wind '97', sung at the funeral of Princess Diana, became the largest-selling single in history. He also composed the music for the West End show *Billy Elliot* (2005). In 2005, he was joined

in an official civil partnership with his long-time companion, David Furnish.

John of Austria, Don, Span **Don Juan** (1547–78) Spanish soldier, the illegitimate son of the Emperor Charles V, born in Regensburg, Germany. He defeated the Moors in Granada (1570) and the Turks at Lepanto (1571).

John of Gaunt (1340–99) Duke of Lancaster, born in Ghent, Belgium, the fourth son of Edward III. He was highly influential as a peacemaker during the troubled reign of Richard II. On his second wife's death (1394) he married his mistress, Catherine Swynford, by whom he had three sons; from the eldest descended Henry VII.

John of the Cross, St, originally **Juan de Yepes y Álvarez** (1542–91) Christian mystic and poet, the founder with St Teresa of the Discalced Carmelites, born in Fontiveros, Spain. A Carmelite monk, his poems, such as *Spiritual Canticle* (trans), are highly regarded in Spanish mystical literature. He was canonized in 1726.

John the Baptist, St (1st-c) Prophetic figure in the New Testament Gospels, the son of a priest named Zechariah. He baptized Jesus and others at the R Jordan, and was executed by Herod Antipas.

John Paul I, originally **Albino Luciani** (1912–78) Pope (Aug–Sep 1978), born in Forno di Canale, Italy. He was the first pope to use a double name (from his two immediate predecessors, John XXIII and Paul VI). He died only 33 days later, the shortest pontificate of modern times.

John Paul II, originally **Karol Jozef**

Wojtyła (1920–2005) Pope (1978–2005), born in Wadowice, Poland, the first non-Italian pope in 450 years. A champion of economic justice and an outspoken defender of the Church in Communist countries, he was uncompromising on moral issues. He celebrated his silver jubilee in 2003. On his death, his body lay in state at St Peter's Basilica where over two million people queued to pay their last respects.

Johns, Jasper (1930–) Painter, sculptor, and printmaker, born in Augusta, GA. Attracted by the Dadaist ideas of Duchamp, he chose to paint flags, targets, maps, and other pre-existing images in a style deliberately clumsy and banal, and became one of the creators of Pop Art.

Johnson, Amy (1903–41) Pioneer aviator, born in Hull. She flew solo from England to Australia (1930), to Japan via Siberia (1931), and to Cape Town (1932), making new records in each case.

Johnson, Andrew (1808–75) US statesman and 17th president (1865–9), born in Raleigh, NC. He became vice-president (1865), and president on Lincoln's assassination (1865). A Democrat, his conciliatory policies were opposed by Congress, who wished to keep the Southern states under military government. He vetoed the congressional measures, was impeached, tried, and acquitted.

Johnson, Dame Celia (1908–82) Actress, born in Richmond, Surrey. Well-established on the stage, she had leading roles in the films *In Which We Serve* (1942) and *This Happy Breed* (1944), and is best remembered for her performance in *Brief Encounter* (1945).

Johnson, Lyndon Baines, also known as **LBJ** (1908–73) US statesman and 36th president (1963–9), born in Stonewall, TX. Vice-president in 1960, he became president after Kennedy's assassination, and was returned to the post in 1964. His administration passed the Civil Rights Act (1964) and the Voting Rights Act (1965), which helped African-Americans, but the escalation of the war in Vietnam led to unpopularity, and he retired in 1969.

Johnson, Magic, popular name of **Earvin Johnson** (1959–) Basketball player; born in Lansing, MI. He played 12 years as a guard for the Los Angeles Lakers (1980–91), was named to the All-NBA (National Basketball Association) team nine times (1983–91), and was voted the league's Most Valuable Player three times (1987, 1990, 1991). He retired from the NBA in 1992 when he tested positive for the HIV virus, but returned to play for the Lakers in 1996.

Johnson, Michael (1967–) Track athlete, born in Dallas, TX. Four-times world champion at 400 m (1993, 1995, 1997, 1999), he achieved the 200 m/400 m double at the 1995 championships, and an unprecedented male double of 200 m and 400 m gold medals at the 1996 (Atlanta) Olympics.

Johnson, Samuel, known as **Dr Johnson** (1709–84) Lexicographer, critic, and poet, born in Lichfield, Staffordshire. From 1747 he worked for eight years on his *Dictionary of the English Language*, started the moralistic periodical, *The Rambler* (1750), and wrote his philosophical romance *Rasselas* (1759). His reputation as man and conversationalist outweighs his literary reputation.

Johnston, Bruce *see* Beach Boys, The

Jolie, Angelina, in full **Angelina Jolie Voight** (1975–) Actress, born in Los Angeles, CA, daughter of actor Jon Voight. Her films include *Gia* (1998, Best Actress Golden Globe), *Girl, Interrrupted* (1999, Golden Globe; Best Supporting Actress Oscar), *Lara Croft: Tomb Raider* (2001, sequel 2003), and *Alexander* (2004).

Jolson, Al, originally **Asa Yoelson** (1886–1950) Actor and singer, born in Srednike (now Seredzius), Lithuania. Brought to the USA in 1893, he became known in the 1920s for such sentimental songs as 'Mammy', 'Sonny Boy', and 'Swanee'.

Jonathan (c.11th c BC) Biblical character, the son and heir of Saul (the first king of Israel) and loyal friend of David. David succeeded Saul as King of Israel, after Jonathan was killed fighting against the Philistines.

Jones, Inigo (1573–1652) The first of the great English architects, born in London. He introduced the Italian Palladian style into England, where his designs include the Queen's House at Greenwich (1616–35) and the Banqueting House in Whitehall (1619–22).

Jones, Marion (1975–) Track and field athlete, born in Los Angeles, CA. A sprinter and jumper, she won the 100 m World Championship in 1997. She became the first woman in history to win five athletics medals at a single Olympic Games (Sydney, 2000).

Jones, Sir Tom, originally **Thomas Jones Woodward** (1940–) Singer, born in Pontypridd, S Wales. He became known following his hit single, 'It's Not Unusual' (1965), and later hits include 'Green Green Grass of Home' (1966), 'What's New Pussycat?' (1965), and 'Delilah' (1968). He was knighted in 2006.

Jonson, Ben(jamin) (1572–1637) Playwright, born in London. His four chief plays are *Volpone* (1606), *The Silent Woman* (1609), *The Alchemist* (1610), and *Bartholomew Fair* (1614), and he also wrote several masques. A major influence on 17th-c poets (known as 'the tribe, or sons, of Ben'), he became poet laureate in 1617.

Joplin, Scott (1868–1917) Pianist and composer, born in Texarkana, AR. His 'Maple Leaf Rag' (1899) made ragtime music a national craze, and was the first of his several popular rags.

Jordan, Michael (Jeffrey), nickname **Air Jordan** (1963–) Basketball player, born in New York City. He played with the Chicago Bulls 1984–93 and from 1995, holds the record for most points in an NBA play-off game (63), and was a member of the USA Olympic gold medal-winning team in 1984 and 1992. In 1996 he took the NBA scoring title for the eighth time to break Wilt Chamberlain's record, and won it again in 1997. He won his sixth NBA title with the Chicago Bulls in 1998, finally retiring in 2003.

Joseph, St (1st-c BC) Husband of the

Virgin Mary, a carpenter in Nazareth, who last appears in the Gospel history when Jesus Christ was 12 years old (*Luke* 2.43).

Joseph Biblical character, the 11th son of Jacob. He is depicted as a favourite son (marked by the gift of a multi-coloured coat), sold into slavery by his jealous brothers, who rises to high office in Pharaoh's court. Eventually he is reconciled with his brothers.

Joseph of Arimathea, St (1st-c) In the New Testament a rich Israelite, a secret disciple of Jesus, and a councillor in Jerusalem. He went to Pontius Pilate and begged the body of Jesus, burying it in his own rock-hewn tomb (*Mark* 15.42–7).

Joséphine de Beauharnais, *née* **Marie Josèphe Rose Tascher de la Pagerie** (1763–1814) First wife of Napoleon Bonaparte, and French empress, born in Trois-Ilets, Martinique. She married Napoleon in 1796, and accompanied him on his Italian campaign. The marriage, being childless, was dissolved in 1809.

Joshua, Heb **Yehoshua** In the Old Testament, the son of Nun, of the tribe of Ephraim. Upon Moses' death he was appointed to lead the people into Canaan. The Book of Joshua is a narrative of the conquest and settlement of Canaan.

Josiah (7th-c BC) Biblical character, king of Judah (c.639–609 BC). He is credited with destroying pagan cults and attempting to centralize worship in Jerusalem and the Temple.

Joule, James (Prescott) (1818–89) Physicist, born in Salford, Greater Manchester. He showed that heat is a form of energy, and established the mechanical equivalent of heat. His name is preserved in the unit of work, the *joule*.

Jowell, Tessa (Jane Helen Douglas) (1947–) British stateswoman, born in London. A Labour MP from 1992, she held a number of shadow posts before becoming minister for public health (1997), employment minister, and secretary of state for culture, media and sport (2001–).

Joyce, James (Augustine Aloysius) (1882–1941) Writer, born in Dublin. His early work includes the short stories, *Dubliners* (1914), and *A Portrait of the Artist as a Young Man* (1916). *Ulysses* appeared in Paris in 1922, but was banned in the UK and USA until 1936. *Finnegans Wake* finally emerged in 1939. His work revolutionized the novel form through the abandonment of ordinary plot for 'stream of consciousness', and through his unprecedented exploration of language.

Joyce, William, nickname **Lord Haw-Haw** (1906–46) British traitor, born in New York City. Throughout World War 2 he broadcast from Radio Hamburg propaganda against Britain, gaining his nickname from his upper-class drawl. He was captured by the British, tried, and executed in London.

Judas Iscariot (1st-c) One of the 12 apostles of Jesus. He betrayed Jesus for 30 pieces of silver by helping to arrange for his arrest at Gethsemane by the Jewish authorities (*Mark* 14.43–6).

Jude, St or **Thaddeus** (1st-c) One of the

12 Apostles, called 'Judas (son) of James' (*Luke* 6.16). He is traditionally thought to have been martyred in Persia with St Simon.

Judith Old Testament Jewish heroine. In the Apocryphal Book of Judith, she is portrayed as a widow who entered the tent of Holofernes, general of Nebuchadnezzar, cut off his head, and so saved her native town of Bethulia.

Jung, Carl (Gustav) (1875–1961) sychiatrist, born in Kesswil, Switzerland. He met Freud in Vienna in 1907, became his leading collaborator, and was president of the International Psychoanalytic Association (1911–14). Increasingly critical of Freud's approach, his *The Psychology of the Unconscious* (trans, 1911–12) caused a break in 1913. He then developed his own theories, which he called 'analytical psychology'.

Kafka, Franz (1883–1924) Novelist, born in Prague, of German Jewish parents. His works include the short story *The Metamorphosis* (trans, 1916), and his posthumously published unfinished novels *The Trial* (trans, 1925), *The Castle* (trans, 1926), and *Amerika* (1927). He has influenced many authors with his vision of society (often called 'Kafkaesque') as a pointless, schizophrenically rational organization, with tortuous bureaucratic and totalitarian procedures.

Kahlo, Frida (1907–54) Artist, born in Coyoicoán, Mexico City. Pain and the suffering of women are recurring themes in her Surrealistic and often shocking pictures. She married Diego Rivera in 1928. A major exhibition of her work was held at London's Tate Modern in 2005.

Kalashnikov, Mikhail (1919–) Russian gun designer. He designed the *Avtomat Kalishnikova*, the AK-47 machine gun, of which over 50 million have been produced.

Kandinsky, Wasily or **Vasily Vasilyevich** (1866–1944) Painter, born in Moscow. In Russia (1914–21) he founded the Russian Academy and in 1922 took charge of the Weimar Bauhaus. He became a naturalized French citizen in 1939, and was a leader of the *Blaue Reiter* group.

Kant, Immanuel (1724–1804) Philosopher, born in Königsberg, Prussia (now Kaliningrad, Russia). His main work, now a philosophical classic, is the *Critique of Pure Reason* (trans, 1781) in which he provided a response to the empiricism of Hume. His views on ethics are set out in the *Foundations of the Metaphysics of Morals* (trans, 1785) and the *Critique of Practical Reason* (trans, 1788), and his views on aesthetics in the *Critique of Judgment* (trans, 1790).

Kapil Dev, Nihanj (1959–) Cricketer, born in Chandigarh, India. An allrounder, he led India to victory in the 1983 World Cup, and became the youngest player to perform a Test double of 2000 runs and 200 wickets. In 1994 he broke Hadlee's record by taking 432 wickets in his 130th Test match.

Kapoor, Anish (1954–) Artist and sculptor, born in Mumbai (Bombay), India, moving to London in 1973. He has exhibited at major venues around the world, and his awards include the Turner Prize (1991). In 2003 he won a competition to create the centrepiece for a planned memorial garden to British victims of the 11 September 2001 terrorist attacks in New York City.

Karadžić, Radovan (1945–) Militant leader of the Bosnian Serbs within Bosnia and Herzegovina, born in Petnijca, Montenegro (former Yugoslavia). In the 1990s he founded and became president of the Serbian Democratic Party. When Bosnia and Herzegovina declared independence, he declared himself president of the self-styled 'Serb Republic'. A period of purges followed. Following international efforts to bring him before the UN war crimes tribunal in The Hague, he resigned his presidency (1996) and has since been in hiding.

Karajan, Herbert von (1908–89) Conductor, born in Salzburg, Austria. In 1955 he was made principal conductor of the Berlin Philharmonic, with which he was mainly associated until his resignation in 1989.

Karloff, Boris, originally **William Henry Pratt** (1887–1969) Film star, born in London. He went to Hollywood, where he made his name as the monster in *Frankenstein* (1931), and appeared in many other popular horror films.

Karpov, Anatoly Yevgenyevich (1951–) Chess player and world champion (1975–85), born in Zlatoust, Russia. He became world champion by default after Fischer refused to defend his title (1975), and was unbeaten until losing to Kasparov in a controversial match (1985). He defeated Jan Timman in an official world championship match in 1993, and twice successfully defended the FIDE title (1996, 1998).

Kasdan, Lawrence (1949–) Film director, born in Miami Beach, FL. He gained a co-writer credit on *The Empire Strikes Back* (1980) before becoming a director with *Body Heat* (1981). Later films include *The Acci-*

dental Tourist (1989), *French Kiss* (1995), and *Dreamcatcher* (2003).

Kasparov, Gary (Kimovich) (1963–) Chess player, born in Baku, Azerbaijan. When he beat Karpov for the world title (1985) he became the youngest ever world champion, and is now the highest-ranked active player. He set up the Grandmasters' Association in 1987, and arranged a World Championship match in 1993 when he defeated Nigel Short. He lost his title to Vladimir Kramnik in 2000, and retired in 2005.

Kaufman, Philip (1936–) Film director and screenwriter, born in Chicago, IL. As an independent film-maker he wrote, produced, and directed his first film, *Goldstein* in 1964. He wrote the screenplays for *The Outlaw Josey Wales* (1975) and *Raiders of the Lost Ark* (1981). As director, his films include *The Unbearable Lightness of Being* (1988) and *Twisted* (2004).

Kay, John (1704 c.1764) Inventor, born near Bury, Greater Manchester. In 1733 he patented his flying shuttle, but his house was ransacked by a mob of textile workers, fearful for their livelihood, and he left for France (1753).

Kaye, Danny, originally **David Daniel Kominski** (1913–1987) Stage, film, and television entertainer, born in New York City. His films include *The Secret Life of Walter Mitty* (1946), *Hans Christian Andersen* (1952), and *The Court Jester* (1956), and he became known for his fundraising activities for UNICEF.

Keane, Roy (Maurice) (1971–) Footballer, born in Cork, Ireland. An all-round midfielder, he joined Manchester United in 1993 for £3·75 million, a record between British clubs at that time. He became captain in 1997. In 2000 he was voted The Football Writers' and the Professional Footballers' Association's Player of the Year. He left the club at the end of 2005 and signed for Scottish side Celtic.

Keaton, Buster, popular name of **Joseph Francis Keaton** (1895–1966) Film comedian, born in Piqua, KS. Renowned for his deadpan expression, he starred in and directed such silent classics as *Our Hospitality* (1923), *The Navigator* (1924), and *The General* (1926).

Keaton, Diane (1946–) Actress and director, born in Los Angeles, CA. She played opposite Woody Allen in the Broadway production of *Play It Again, Sam* (1969), then went on to star in several of his films, such as *Annie Hall* (1977, Oscar). She won Oscar nominations for *Marvin's Room* (1996) and *Something's Gotta Give* (2003).

Keaton, Michael (1951–) Film actor, born in Caraopolis, PA. His breakthrough came with *Mr Mom* (1983), and later films include *Beetlejuice* (1988), *Batman* (1989, sequel 1992), and *First Daughter* (2004).

Keats, John (1795–1821) Poet, born in London. His first book of poems was published in 1817. His poem *Endymion* (1818) was fiercely criticized, but he later produced *Lamia and Other Poems* (1820), a landmark in English poetry, which contains 'The Eve of St Agnes' and his major odes. His *Letters* (1848) are among the most celebrated in the language.

Keillor, Garrison, pseudonym of **Gary**

Edward Keillor (1942–) Writer and broadcaster, born in Anoka, MN. In 1974 he first hosted the live radio show, 'A Prairie Home Companion', delivering a weekly monologue set in the fictional mid-western town of Lake Wobegon. His books include the best-selling *Lake Wobegon Days* (1985) and *Love Me* (2003).

Keller, Helen (Adams) (1880–1968) Writer, born in Tuscumbia, AL. She lost her sight and hearing after an illness at 19 months, but was educated by Anne Sullivan, who taught her to speak, read, and write.

Kellogg, W(illie) K(eith) (1860–1951) Cereal manufacturer and philanthropist, born in Battle Creek, MI. He joined with his brother, **John H(arvey) Kellogg** (1852–1943), to develop a process of toasting wheat and corn into crisp flakes for a breakfast cereal. Their *corn flakes* revolutionized the breakfast-eating habits of the Western world.

Kellow, Kathleen *see* Hibbert, Eleanor

Kelly, David (Christopher) (1944–2003) British microbiologist, born in the Rhondda Valley, S Wales. He was appointed the Ministry of Defence's chief scientific officer and senior adviser to the proliferation and arms control secretariat, and was also senior adviser on biological warfare for the UN in Iraq (1994–9). In 2003 he became a key figure in the row between the government and the BBC over claims that Downing Street 'sexed up' a dossier on Iraq's weapons capability. Having been identified by the press, he became the centre of media attention, and committed suicide.

Kelly, Gene, popular name of **Eugene Curran Kelly** (1912–96) Dancer and actor, born in Pittsburgh, PA. His stage success in *Pal Joey* (1939) led to a Hollywood debut in *For Me and My Girl* (1942), followed by musicals such as *An American in Paris* (1951) and *Singin' in the Rain* (1952).

Kelly, Grace (Patricia), married name **Grimaldi, Princess Grace of Monaco** (1929–82) Film actress and princess, born in Philadelphia, PA. Her films included *High Noon* (1952), *Rear Window* (1954), and *The Country Girl* (1954, Oscar). In 1956 she married Prince Rainier III of Monaco, and retired from the screen. She was killed in a car accident.

Kelly, Ned, popular name of **Edward Kelly** (1855–80) Outlaw, born in Beveridge, Victoria, Australia. With his brother and two others he formed the Kelly gang. They carried out a series of daring robberies (1878–80) which, coupled with Ned's home-made armour, made them into legendary figures. He was hanged at Melbourne.

Kelman, James (1946–) Novelist and short-story writer, born in Glasgow. Regarded as one of the major talents in contemporary Scottish fiction, he won the Booker Prize in 1994 for *How Late It Was, How Late*. Later works include the novels *Translated Accounts* (2001) and *You Have to be Careful in the Land of the Free* (2004).

Kelvin (of Largs), William Thomson, 1st Baron (1824–1907) Mathematician and physicist, born in Belfast. He carried out fundamental research into thermodynamics, helping to develop the law of the conservation of energy and the absolute temperature scale (now given in kelvin). He also presented the dynamical theory of heat, and developed theorems for the mathematical analysis of electricity and magnetism.

Kempe, Rudolf (1910–76) Conductor, born near Dresden, Germany. He appeared frequently at Covent Garden, London, and was principal conductor of the Royal Philharmonic Orchestra (1961–75), then of the BBC Symphony Orchestra until his death.

Kendal, Felicity (Ann) (1947–) British actress, born in Olton, West Midlands. Well known for her part in the television series *The Good Life* (1974–8), later series include *Rosemary and Thyme* (from 2003). Much of her work is in the theatre.

Keneally, Thomas (Michael) (1935–) Writer, born in Kempsey, New South Wales, Australia. His novels are frequently historical, and include *Schindler's Ark* (1982, Booker; filmed as *Schindler's List*, 1993), *Towards Asmara* (1989), *The Great Shame* (1999), and *The Tyrant's Novel* (2003).

Kennedy, A(lison) L(ouise) (1965–) Novelist and short-story writer, born in Dundee, Scotland. Her first collection of short stories was the prize-winning *Night Geometry and the Garscadden Trains* (1990), and her first novel was *Looking for the Possible Dance* (1994, Somerset Maugham Award). Later novels include *Everything You Need* (1999) and *Paradise* (2004).

Kennedy, Charles (Peter) (1959–) British politician, born in Inverness, Highland. He was elected a Social Democratic MP (1983–), becoming

...ngest MP in the Commons. A ...pporter of merger with the Liberal Party, he was elected president of the new Liberal Democrat Party in 1990, and leader upon Paddy Ashdown's resignation in 1999. He quit as leader at the start of 2006.

Kennedy, Edward M(oore), known as **Ted Kennedy** (1932–) US politician, born in Brookline, MA, the youngest son of Joseph Kennedy. In 1969 he became the youngest ever majority whip in the US Senate, but his involvement that year in a car accident at Chappaquidick in which a woman companion (Mary Jo Kopechne) was drowned, dogged his political career, and caused his withdrawal as a presidential candidate in 1979.

Kennedy, Jackie see Onassis, Jacqueline Kennedy

Kennedy, John F(itzgerald), also known as **JFK** (1917–63) US statesman and 35th president (1961–3), born in Brookline, MA, the son of Joseph P Kennedy. He was the first Catholic, and the youngest person, to be elected president. His 'New Frontier' in social legislation involved a federal desegregation policy in education, and civil rights reform. He displayed firmness and moderation in foreign policy, in 1962 inducing Russia to withdraw its missiles from Cuba, and achieving a partial nuclear test-ban treaty with Russia in 1963. On 22 November, he was assassinated in Dallas, TX. The alleged assassin, Lee Harvey Oswald, was himself shot two days later during a jail transfer.

Kennedy, Nigel (Paul), professional name (from 1997) **Kennedy** (1956–)

British violinist. Noted for his unconventional style of dress, and for his remarkable playing ability, his recording of Vivaldi's *Four Seasons* held the number 1 spot in the UK Classical Chart for over a year (1989–90).

Kennedy, Robert F(rancis) (1925–68) US politician, born in Brookline, MA, the third son of Joseph Kennedy. An efficient manager of his brother John F Kennedy's presidential campaign, he was an energetic attorney general (1961–4), notable in his dealings with civil rights problems. After winning the Californian Democratic presidential primary election, he was killed in Los Angeles by Sirhan Sirhan.

Kent, Edward (George Nicholas Paul Patrick), Duke of (1935–) British prince, the eldest son of George, Duke of Kent. In 1961 he married Katharine Worsley, and they have three children: **George Philip Nicholas, the Earl of St Andrews** (1962–), **Helen Marina Lucy, Lady Helen Windsor** (1964–), and **Nicholas Charles Edward Jonathan, Lord Nicholas Windsor** (1970–). Lady Helen Windsor married Timothy Taylor to become Lady Helen Taylor.

Kent, George Edward Alexander Edmund, Duke of (1902–42) Son of King George V and Queen Mary. In 1934 he was created duke, and married **Princess Marina of Greece and Denmark** (1906–68). He was killed on active service.

Kent, Prince Michael of (1942–) British prince, the younger brother of Edward, Duke of Kent. He married in

1978 Baroness Marie-Christine Von Reibniz, and their children are **Frederick Michael George David Louis, Lord Frederick Windsor** (1979–) and **Gabriella Marina Alexandra Ophelia, Lady Gabriella (Ella) Windsor** (1981–).

Kenzo, in full **Kenzo Takada** (1940–) Fashion designer, born in Kyoto, Japan. Known for his innovative ideas and use of traditional designs, he creates clothes with both oriental and Western influences, and is a trendsetter in the field of knitwear.

Kepler, Johannes (1571–1630) Astronomer, born in Weil-der-Stadt, Germany. He announced his first and second laws of planetary motion in *New Astronomy* (trans, 1609), which formed the groundwork of Newton's discoveries. His third law was promulgated in *Harmony of the World* (trans, 1619).

Kermode, Sir (John) Frank (1919–) Literary critic, born in the Isle of Man. His works include *Romantic Image* (1957), *Forms of Attention* (1985), *Uses of Error* (1991), and *The Age of Shakespeare* (2004).

Kern, Jerome (David) (1885–1945) Songwriter and composer, born in New York City. He wrote a string of successful Broadway shows, notably *Show Boat* (1928). His songs include 'The Way You Look Tonight' and 'A Fine Romance'.

Kerouac, Jack, popular name of **Jean Louis Lebris de Kerouac**, pseudonyms **Jean-Louis, Jean Louis Incognito, John Kerouac** (1922–69) Writer, born in Lowell, MA. He is best known for *On the Road* (1957), a spontaneous work expressing the youthful discontent of the 'beat generation'.

Kerry, John (Forbes) (1943–) US politician, born in Denver, CO. He embarked on a career in law and worked as a prosecutor in Massachusetts before going into politics. In 1982 he was voted lieutenant governor for Massachusetts, and has been senator since 1984. In 2004 he secured the Democrat nomination for the US presidential election but was narrowly defeated by incumbent President George W Bush.

Keynes (of Tilton), John Maynard Keynes, Baron (1883–1946) Economist, born in Cambridge, Cambridgeshire. In both World Wars he was an adviser to the Treasury. The unemployment crises inspired his two great works, *A Treatise on Money* (1930) and *General Theory of Employment, Interest and Money* (1936).

Khan, Jahangir (1963–) Squash rackets player, born in Karachi, Pakistan. He won three world amateur titles (1979, 1983, 1985), a record six World Open titles (1981–5, 1988), and eight consecutive British Open titles (1982–9).

Khomeini, Ayatollah Ruhollah (1900–89) Iranian religious and political leader, born in Khomeyn, Iran. A Shiite Muslim opposed to the pro-Western regime of Shah Mohammed Reza Pahlavi, he was exiled in 1964. He returned to Iran amid great popular acclaim in 1979 after the collapse of the Shah's government, and became virtual head of state. Under his leadership, Iran underwent a turbulent 'Islamic Revolution' in which a return was made to the strict observance of Muslim principles and traditions.

Khrushchev, Nikita Sergeyevich (1894–1971) Soviet statesman, first secretary of the Soviet Communist Party (1953–64), and prime minister (1958–64), born in Kalinovka, Ukraine. He became first secretary soon after the death of Stalin, and three years later denounced Stalinism. Among the events of his administration were the 1956 Hungarian uprising, and the failed attempt to install missiles in Cuba (1962). He was replaced by Brezhnev and Kosygin, and went into retirement.

Khubilai Khan *see* Kublai Khan

Kidman, Nicole (Mary) (1967–) Film actress, born in Honolulu, HI. While living in Australia, she made her film debut in *Bush Christmas* (1983). Her US breakthrough came with *Dead Calm* (1989), and later films include *Moulin Rouge* (2000, Golden Globe), *The Hours* (2002, Oscar, Golden Globe, BAFTA), and *The Interpreter* (2005). She was married (1990–2001) to actor Tom Cruise.

Kierkegaard, Søren (Aabye) (1813–55) Philosopher and theologian, a major influence on 20th-c existentialism, born in Copenhagen. Regarded as one of the founders of existentialism, in *Concluding Unscientific Postscript* (trans, 1846), he attacked all philosophical system building.

King, Billie Jean, *née* **Moffat** (1943–) Tennis player, born in Long Beach, CA. Between 1961 and 1979 she won a record 20 Wimbledon titles, including the singles in 1966–8, 1972–3, and 1975. She also won 13 US titles (including four singles), four French titles (one singles), and two Australian titles (one singles).

King, Francis (Henry) (1923–) Writer, born in Adelboden, Switzerland. His novels include *The Dividing Stream* (1951), *The Needle* (1975), *The Ant Colony* (1991), and *Ash on an Old Man's Sleeve* (1996). He has also written short stories, poetry and travel books.

King, Larry, originally **Lawrence Harvey Zeiger** (1933–) Talk-show host, born in New York City. He joined CNN in 1985, taking *Larry King Live* to the top of the ratings by 1992, widely watched for its commentary and debate on contemporary events.

King, Martin Luther, Jr, originally **Michael L King** (1929–68) Clergyman and civil rights campaigner, born in Atlanta, GA. Known for his policy of passive resistance and his acclaimed oratorical skills, his greatest successes came in challenging the segregation laws of the South, and in 1964 he received the Kennedy Peace Prize and the Nobel Peace Prize. He was assassinated in Memphis, TN, by James Earl Ray.

King, Stephen (Edwin), pseudonyms **Steve King**, **Richard Bachman**, **John Swithen** (1947–) Novelist, born in Portland, ME. He achieved success with his first novel, *Carrie* (1974), and became known for his vivid treatment of horrific and supernatural themes. Later books (many of which have been filmed) include *The Shining* (1976), *Bag of Bones* (1998), and *Cell* (2006).

Kingsley, Sir Ben, originally **Krishna**

Bhanji (1943–) Actor, born in Snainton, North Yorkshire. A noted Shakespearean actor, he achieved fame for his title role in the film *Gandhi* (1980, Oscar). Other films include *Schindler's List* (1993), *House of Sand and Fog* (2003), and *Oliver Twist* (2005).

Kingsley, Charles (1819–75) Writer, born in Holne, Devon. A 'Christian Socialist', his social novels, such as *Alton Locke* (1850), had great influence at the time. His best-known works are *Westward Ho!* (1855), *Hereward the Wake* (1866), and his children's book, *The Water Babies* (1863).

Kinnock (of Bedwellty), Neil (Gordon) Kinnock, Baron (1942–) British Labour politician, born in Tredegar, Blaenau Gwent, Wales. He served as party leader (1983–92), and became a European Commissioner in 1994. In 1999 he held the post of vice president for administrative reform under the new president, Romano Prodi, stepping down at the end of 2004, when he became chair of the British Council.

Kinsey, Alfred (Charles) (1894–1956) Sexologist and zoologist, born in Hoboken, NJ. He is best known for his controversial studies, *Sexual Behavior in the Human Male* (1948, the so-called 'Kinsey Report') and *Sexual Behavior in the Human Female* (1953).

Kinski, Klaus, originally **Nikolaus Gunther Naksznski** (1926–91) Film actor, born in Sopot, Poland. He became known for his leading roles in the films of Werner Herzog, such as *Aguirre, Wrath of God* (1972) and *Fitzcarraldo* (1982), and for his role in *Nosferatu, the Vampyre* (1979).

Kipling, (Joseph) Rudyard (1865–1936) Writer, born of British parents in Mumbai (Bombay), India. His verse collections *Barrack Room Ballads* (1892) and *The Seven Seas* (1896) were highly successful, as were the two *Jungle Books* (1894–5). *Kim* appeared in 1901, and the classic *Just So Stories* in 1902. He was awarded the Nobel Prize for Literature in 1907.

Kissinger, Henry (Alfred) (1923–) US secretary of state (1973–6) and academic, born in Fürth, Germany. He became Nixon's adviser on national security affairs in 1969, was the main American figure in the negotiations to end the Vietnam War (for which he shared the 1973 Nobel Peace Prize), and became secretary of state under Nixon and Ford. His 'shuttle diplomacy' was aimed at bringing about peace between Israel and the Arab states.

Kitchener (of Khartoum and of Broome), (Horatio) Herbert Kitchener, 1st Earl (1850–1916) British field marshal, born near Ballylongford, Co Kerry, Ireland. Commander-in-chief in South Africa (1900–2), he brought the Boer War to an end. He then became commander-in-chief in India (1902–9), and secretary for war (1914), when he organized manpower on a vast scale ('Kitchener armies').

Kitt, Eartha (Mae) (1928–) Entertainer, singer, and actor, born in North, SC. Her vocal vibrancy, fiery personality, and cat-like singing voice made her a top international cabaret attraction and recording artiste.

Klee, Paul (1879–1940) Artist, born in

Münchenbuchsee, near Bern, Switzerland. He settled in Munich, became a member of the *Blaue Reiter* group (1911–12), and later taught at the Bauhaus (1920–32). After 1919 he worked in oils, producing small-scale, mainly abstract pictures, as in his 'Twittering Machine' (1922).

Klein, Calvin (Richard) (1942–) Fashion designer, born in New York City. He set up his own firm in 1968, and became known for the simple but sophisticated style of his clothes, including 'designer jeans'.

Klemperer, Otto (1885–1973) Conductor, born in Wrocław, Poland (formerly Breslau, Prussia). In his later years, he concentrated mainly on the German classical and Romantic composers, and was particularly known for his interpretation of Beethoven. He also composed six symphonies, a Mass, and *Lieder*.

Klerk, F W de *see* de Klerk, F W

Kline, Kevin (Delaney) (1947–) Film actor, born in St Louis, MO. Though known for his dramatic abilities, it was his comic role in *A Fish Called Wanda* (1988) that earned him an Oscar as Best Supporting Actor. Later films include *Chaplin* (1992), *Wild, Wild West* (1999), and *The Pink Panther* (2006).

Knievel, Evel, professional name of **Robert Craig Knievel** (1938–) Motorcycle stunt performer, born in Butte, MT. He carried out motorcycle stunts as a teenager, eventually forming Evel Knievel's Motorcycle Devils in 1965 and becoming known for his spectacular and dangerous performances. He later managed the stunt career of his son, Robbie Knievel.

Knightley, Keira (Christina) (1985–) Actress, born in London. Born into a show business family, she began acting at an early age and her first major part came in *Star Wars: Episode 1 – The Phantom Menace* (1999). Later films include *Bend It Like Beckham* (2002), *Pirates of the Caribbean: The Curse of the Black Pearl* (2003), and *Pride and Prejudice* (2005, Oscar nomination).

Knox, John (c.1513–72) Protestant reformer, born near Haddington, East Lothian. A Catholic priest, he was influenced by Wishart to work for the Lutheran reformation. He became a chaplain to Edward VI, but on Mary's accession (1553) fled to Geneva, where he was much influenced by Calvin. After returning to Scotland he founded the Church of Scotland (1560).

Knox-Johnston, Robin, popular name of **Sir William Robert Patrick Knox-Johnston** (1939–) British yachtsman, the first person to circumnavigate the world non-stop and single-handed, 14 June 1968–22 April 1969. He is also holder of the British Sailing Transatlantic Record (1986: 10 days, 14 h, 9 min), and he co-skippered *Enza*, achieving the world's fastest circumnavigation under sail (1994: 74 days, 22 h, 17 min, 22 s).

Kodály, Zoltán (1882–1967) Composer, born in Kecskemét, Hungary. Among his best-known works are the *Háry János* suite (1926) and several choral compositions, especially *Psalmus Hungaricus* (1923) and *Te Deum* (1936).

Koestler, Arthur (1905–83) Writer and journalist, born in Budapest. His masterpiece is the political novel, *Darkness at Noon* (1940). His nonfiction books and essays deal with politics, scientific creativity, and parapsychology, notably *The Act of Creation* (1964).

Kolbe, St Maximilian (Maria) (1894–1941) Franciscan priest, born near Łódź, Poland. He was arrested by the Gestapo in 1941, and imprisoned in Auschwitz, where he gave his life in exchange for one of the condemned prisoners. He was canonized in 1982.

Korda, Sir Alexander, originally **Sándor Laszlo Korda** (1893–1956) Film producer, born in Puszta, Hungary. His films include *The Private Life of Henry VIII* (1932), *The Third Man* (1949), and *Richard III* (1956).

Kosygin, Alexey Nikolayevich (1904–80) Russian premier (1964–80), born in St Petersburg, Russia. First deputy prime minister (with Mikoyan) from 1960, he succeeded Khrushchev as chairman of the Council of Ministers in 1964, but resigned in 1980 because of ill health.

Kray brothers Convicted British murderers, twin brothers who ran a criminal Mafia-style operation in the East End of London in the 1960s: **Ronald Kray** (1933–95) and **Reginald Kray** (1933–2000). They were tried in 1969, and sentenced to life imprisonment of not less than 30 years.

Kreisler, Fritz (1875–1962) Violinist, born in Vienna. From 1889 he became one of the most successful violin virtuosos of his day, and composed violin pieces, a string quartet, and an operetta, *Apple Blossoms* (1919), which was a Broadway success.

Kroc, Ray(mond A) (1902–84) Restaurateur, born in Chicago, IL, the founder of the McDonald's chain of fast-food restaurants. A milk-shake machine manufacturer in the 1950s, he was impressed by his customers, Mac and Dick McDonald, who sold hamburgers, French fries, and milkshakes from a stand. He bought the rights to operate similar stands, and by 1959 had opened his 100th store. In 2006, this number had reached 30 000 restaurants in more than 119 countries.

Kublai Khan, also spelled **Khubilai Khan** (1214–94) Mongol emperor of China (1279–94), the grandson of Genghis Khan. He established himself at Cambaluc (modern Beijing), and ruled an empire which extended as far as the R Danube. The splendour of his court was legendary.

Kubrick, Stanley (1928–99) Screen writer, film producer, and director, born in New York City. His films include *Spartacus* (1960), *Lolita* (1962), *2001: a Space Odyssey* (1965), *A Clockwork Orange* (1971), and *The Shining* (1980).

Kudrow, Lisa (1963–) Actress, born in Encino, CA. She became known for her role as Ursula in *Mad About You* (1992), then achieved major success as Phoebe Buffay (Ursula's 'twin sister') in the acclaimed television series *Friends* (1994–2004).

Kundera, Milan (1929–) Novelist, born in Brno, Czech Republic. In 1975 he settled in Paris. His works include

The Unbearable Lightness of Being (trans, 1984; filmed 1987) and *Immortality* (1991).

Küng, Hans (1928–) Roman Catholic theologian, born in Sursee, Switzerland. His questioning of Catholic doctrine, as in *Justification* (1965), *The Church* (1967), and *Infallible? An Inquiry* (1971), aroused controversy, and the Vatican withdrew his licence to teach as a Catholic theologian in 1979.

Kurosawa, Akira (1910–98) Film director, born in Tokyo. He was renowned for his adaptation of the techniques of the Noh theatre to film-making, in such films as *Rasho-mon* (1950) and *The Seven Samurai* (trans, 1954). Later films include *Kagemusha* (1980) and *Rhapsody in August* (1991).

Kurzweil, Raymond C (1948–) Computer scientist, a pioneer of reading technology, born in New York City, NY. Since the 1970s he has led the development of the first optical character recognition device, the first text-to-speech synthesizer, the first flat-bed scanner, the first orchestral music synthesizer, and a large vocabulary automatic speech recognizer. He received the major prize for inventors, the Lemelson-MIT Award, in 2001.

L

Laban, Rudolf von (1879–1958) Dancer, choreographer, dance theorist, and notator, born in Bratislava. In Manchester he established the Art of Movement Studio in 1948, now known as the Laban Centre, and also developed a system of dance notation, *Labanotation*.

Lacroix, Christian (1956–) Fashion designer, born in Arles, France. In 1987 he opened the House of Lacroix in Paris, making his name with ornate and frivolous clothes.

Lagerfeld, Karl (1939–) Fashion designer, born in Hamburg, Germany. He was design director at Chanel, and updated the Chanel look. Known for his high quality ready-to-wear clothing, he showed the first collection under his own label in 1984.

Laine, Cleo *see* Dankworth, Sir John

Laker, Sir Freddie, popular name of **Sir Frederick Alfred Laker** (1922–2006) Business entrepreneur, born in Kent. In 1966 he headed the successful Laker Airways Ltd, but was severely set back by the failure of the 'Skytrain' fares-buster project (1982).

From 1992 he was chairman and managing director of Laker Airways (Bahamas) Ltd.

Laker, Jim, popular name of **James Charles Laker** (1922–86) Cricketer and broadcaster, born in Bradford, West Yorkshire. He made test cricket history at Old Trafford in 1956 when he took 19 Australian wickets for 90 runs. During his career (1946–64) he took 1944 wickets.

Lalique, René (1860–1945) Jeweller and designer, born in Ay, France. His glass designs, decorated with relief figures, animals, and flowers, were an important contribution to the Art Nouveau and Art Deco movements.

Lamb, Charles, pseudonym **Elia** (1775–1834) Essayist, born in London. He achieved success through joint publication with his sister, **Mary** (1764–1847) of *Tales from Shakespear* (1807). His best-known works are the series of essays under his pseudonym, the *Essays of Elia* (1823–33).

Lamont (of Lerwick), Norman Lamont, Baron (1942–) British politician, born in Lerwick, Shetland Is. He became financial secretary to the Treasury in 1986 and Chancellor of the Exchequer in 1990. Following his replacement in the 1993 Cabinet reshuffle, he launched an attack on John Major's policies.

Lancaster, Burt(on Stephen) (1913–94) Film actor, born in New York City. Cast early on in a succession of tough-guy roles, later notable films include *From Here to Eternity* (1953), *Elmer Gantry* (1960, Oscar), *Birdman of Alcatraz* (1962), and *Local Hero* (1983).

Landseer, Sir Edwin (Henry)

(1802–73) Artist, born in London. Dogs and deer were his main subjects, often with the Highlands of Scotland as a backdrop, as in 'Monarch of the Glen' (1851). He modelled the four bronze lions at the foot of Nelson's Monument in Trafalgar Square (1867).

Lane, Sir Allen, originally **Allen Lane Williams** (1902–70) Publisher, born in Bristol. In 1935 he formed Penguin Books Ltd, where he began by reprinting novels in paper covers, a revolutionary step in the publishing trade.

Langdon, Harry (Philmore) (1884–1944) Comedian, born in Council Bluffs, IA. He appeared in several popular feature films, such as *The Strong Man* (1926) and *Long Pants* (1927), and is remembered for his character as a baby-faced innocent, bemused by the wider world.

Lanza, Mario, originally **Alfredo Arnold Cocozza** (1921–59) Tenor, born in Philadelphia, PA. Discovered while working in the family's grocery business, he went on to Hollywood to appear in several musicals, including his most famous role in *The Great Caruso* (1951).

Lara, Brian (Charles) (1969–) Cricketer, born in Cantaro, Trinidad, West Indies. In 1994 he broke several cricketing records, including a world record Test innings of 375 for the West Indies against England, and became the world's first batsman to score over 500 runs in one innings in first-class cricket. In 2005 he became the highest run-scorer in the history of Test cricket when he surpassed Allan Border's record of 11 174 runs.

Larkin, Philip (Arthur) (1922–85) Poet, librarian, and jazz critic, born in Coventry, West Midlands. *Collected Poems* was published posthumously (1988) and became a best seller, as did his *Letters* (1992). He also edited the *Oxford Book of Twentieth Century English Verse* (1973).

Lauda, Niki, popular name of **Nikolas Andreas Lauda** (1949–) Motor-racing driver, born in Vienna. He was three times world champion, in 1975, 1977 (both Ferrari), and 1984 (Marlboro McLaren), despite a horrific crash in 1976. He retired in 1985 after 25 career wins.

Lauder, Estée, originally **Josephine Esther Mentzer** (1908–2004) Businesswoman, born in New York City. She co-founded Estée Lauder Inc with her husband Joseph Lauder in 1946, and had great success with the fragrance 'Youth Dew' in the 1950s.

Laughton, Charles (1899–1962) Film and stage actor, born in Scarborough, North Yorkshire. Among his memorable films are *The Private Life of Henry VIII* (1932, Oscar), *The Barretts of Wimpole Street* (1934), *Mutiny on the Bounty* (1935), and *The Hunchback of Notre Dame* (1939).

Laurel and Hardy Comedians who formed the first Hollywood film comedy team. The 'thin one', **Stan Laurel** (1890–1965), originally **Arthur Stanley Jefferson**, was born in Ulverston, Lancashire, England, and went to the USA in 1910. The 'fat one', **Oliver Hardy** (1892–1957), was born near Atlanta, GA. They came together in 1926 and made many full-length feature films, but their best efforts are generally thought to be their early (1927–31) shorts.

Lauren, Ralph, originally **Ralph Lifshitz** (1939–) Fashion designer, born in New York City. In 1967 he joined Beau Brummel Neckwear and created the Polo range for men. He is famous for his American styles, such as the 'prairie look' and 'frontier fashions'.

Lavoisier, Antoine Laurent (1743–94) Chemist, born in Paris. In 1788 he showed that air is a mixture of gases which he called *oxygen* and *nitrogen*, and he devised the modern method of naming chemical compounds. His major work is the *Traité élémentaire de chimie* (1789). Although politically a liberal, he was guillotined on a contrived charge of counter-revolutionary activity.

Law, (Andrew) Bonar (1858–1923) British prime minister (1922–3), born in New Brunswick, Canada. In 1911 he became Unionist leader, and acted as colonial secretary (1915–16), Chancellor of the Exchequer (1916–18), and Lord Privy Seal (1919), before serving for a short time as premier.

Law, (David) Jude (1972–) Actor, born in London. His feature films include *Wilde* (1997), *The Talented Mr Ripley* (1999), *Cold Mountain* (2003, Oscar nomination), and *Alfie* (2004). He was married to actress Sadie Frost (1997–2003).

Lawrence, D(avid) H(erbert Richard) (1885–1930) Poet and novelist, born in Eastwood, Nottinghamshire. He achieved fame with *Sons and Lovers* (1913), but was prosecuted for obscenity after publishing *The Rainbow* (1915). Other major novels include *Women in Love* (1921),

The Plumed Serpent (1926), and *Lady Chatterley's Lover* (1928). He wrote many short stories, short novels, and travel books, and is also known for his letters.

Lawrence, T(homas) E(dward), known as **Lawrence of Arabia** (1888–1935) British soldier and writer, born in Tremadoc, Gwynedd. In 1916 he was appointed British liaison officer to the Arab Revolt, and was present at the taking of Aqaba (1917) and Damascus (1918). His account of the Arab Revolt, *Seven Pillars of Wisdom*, became one of the classics of war literature, and his exploits received so much publicity that he became a legendary figure.

Lawson (of Blaby), Nigel, Baron (1932–) British Conservative statesman, born in London. He served as financial secretary to the Treasury (1979–81), energy secretary (1981–3), and Chancellor of the Exchequer (1983–9).

Lawson, Nigella (1960–) Journalist and cookery writer, born in London. The daughter of politician Nigel Lawson, she became known with her Channel 4 television series, *Nigella Bites* (2001), with accompanying book. Other bestsellers include *How to be a Domestic Goddess* (2000) and *Feast* (2004).

Leach, Bernard (Howell) (1887–1979) Studio potter, born in Hong Kong. With Shoji Hamada, he established the Leach pottery at St Ives in Cornwall, where he made earthenware and stoneware, and played a crucial role in promoting handmade pottery which could be appreciated as art.

Leakey, L(ouis) S(eymour) B(azett)

(1903–72) Archaeologist and physical anthropologist, born in Kabete, Kenya. His great discoveries took place in East Africa, where he found remains of *Zinjanthropus* (1959), *Homo habilis* (1964), and *Kenyapithecus africanus* (1967).

Lean, Sir David (1908–91) Film director, born in Croydon, Greater London. His films include *Brief Encounter* (1945), *Bridge on the River Kwai* (1957, Oscar), *Lawrence of Arabia* (1962, Oscar), *Dr Zhivago* (1965), and *A Passage to India* (1984).

Lear, Edward (1812–88) Artist and writer, born in London. He is remembered for his illustrated books of travels, and for his books of nonsense verse, illustrated by his own sketches, beginning with *A Book of Nonsense* (1846).

Leavis, F(rank) R(aymond) (1895–1978) Literary critic, born in Cambridge, Cambridgeshire. He edited the journal *Scrutiny* (1932–53), and wrote several major critical works, notably *New Bearings in English Poetry* (1932), *The Great Tradition* (1948), and *The Common Pursuit* (1952). Throughout his work, much of it shared with his wife **Queenie Dorothy Leavis** (1906–91), he stresses the moral value of literary study.

LeBlanc, Matt (1967–) Actor, born in Newton, MA. He achieved success as Joey Tribbiani in the acclaimed television series *Friends* (1994–2004), and continued this role in a spin-off series, *Joey* (2004–).

Le Carré, John, pseudonym of **David John Moore Cornwell** (1931–) Novelist, born in Poole, Dorset. His first published novel, *Call for the Dead* (1961), introduced his 'anti-hero' George Smiley. Other works include *Tinker, Tailor, Soldier, Spy* (1974), *Smiley's People* (1980), *The Tailor of Panama* (1996), and *Absolute Friends* (2003). Many of his novels have been filmed or televised.

Le Corbusier, pseudonym of **Charles Edouard Jeanneret** (1887–1965) Architect and artist, born in La Chaux-de-Fonds, Switzerland. Settling in Paris in 1917, he met Ozenfant, who introduced him to Purism. His main interest was large urban projects and city-planning, and examples of his work are the *Unité d'habitation* ('Living unit'), Marseille (1945–50) and Chandigarh, the new capital of the Punjab.

Lee, Ang (1954–) Film director, producer, and screenwriter, born in Taipei, Taiwan. His award-winning films include *Sense and Sensibility* (1995, Oscar nomination), *Crouching Tiger, Hidden Dragon* (2000, four Oscars, four BAFTA awards, Golden Globe), and *Brokeback Mountain* (2005, Oscar, four Golden Globes).

Lee, Laurie (1914–97) Writer, born in Stroud, Gloucestershire. His autobiographical books *Cider With Rosie* (1959), *As I Walked Out One Midsummer Morning* (1969), and *I Can't Stay Long* (1975) are widely acclaimed for their evocation of a rural childhood and of life in the many countries he had visited.

Lee, Robert E(dward) (1807–70) Confederate general, born in Stratford, VA. He was in charge of the defences at Richmond, and defeated Federal forces in the Seven Days'

Battles (1862). His strategy in opposing General Pope, his invasion of Maryland and Pennsylvania, and other achievements are central to the history of the Civil War.

Lee, Spike, popular name of **Shelton Jackson Lee** (1957–) Film-maker, born in Atlanta, GA. *She's Gotta Have It* (1986) established him internationally. Later films, centred around African-American culture, include *Mo' Better Blues* (1990), *Get on the Bus* (1996), *She Hate Me* (2004), and *Inside Man* (2006).

Le Guin, Ursula K(roeber), *née* **Kroeber** (1929–) Science-fiction writer, born in Berkeley, CA. Her books include the 'Hain' novels, such as *The Left Hand of Darkness* (1969), and her 'Earthsea' trilogy: *A Wizard of Earthsea* (1968), *The Tombs of Atuan* (1971), and *The Farthest Shore* (1972). Later works include the short-story collection, *Changing Planes* (2003).

Lehár, Franz (1870–1948) Composer, born in Komárom, Hungary. He is best known for his operettas, including the internationally acclaimed *The Merry Widow* (1905).

Leibniz, Gottfried Wilhelm (1646–1716) Philosopher and mathematician, born in Leipzig, Germany. His great influence was primarily as a mathematician, and as a pioneer of modern symbolic logic, but he also wrote on history, law, and political theory, and his philosophy was the foundation of 18th-c Rationalism.

Leicester, Robert Dudley, Earl of, also known as **Baron Denbigh** and **Sir Robert Dudley** (c.1532–88) English nobleman, the favourite and possibly the lover of Elizabeth I. He continued to receive favour in spite of his unpopularity at court and two secret marriages. In 1588, he successfully commanded the forces against the Spanish Armada but died shortly afterwards.

Leicester (of Holkham), Thomas William Coke, Earl of (1752–1842) Agriculturist, born in London. One of the first agriculturists of England, people visited his estate from all over the world. Special meetings were held at sheep clipping time (*Coke's Clippings*), the last of which took place in 1821.

Leigh, Janet, originally **Jeanette Helen Morrison** (1927–2004) Actress, born in Merced, CA. Among her many films are *The Romance of Rosy Ridge* (1947), *Touch of Evil* (1958), *Psycho* (1962, Golden Globe, Oscar nomination), and *The Fog* (1980). Her third husband (1951–62) was actor Tony Curtis.

Leigh, Mike (1943–) Playwright and theatre director, born in Salford, Greater Manchester. He has scripted a distinctive genre based on actors' improvisations around given themes, his most successful work having a second life on film, as in *Bleak Moments* (1970), and on television, as in *Abigail's Party* (1977). Later films include the prizewinning *Secrets and Lies* (1996) and *Vera Drake* (2004).

Leigh, Vivien, originally **Vivian Hartley** (1913–67) Actress, born in Darjeeling, India. She married Laurence Olivier in 1940 (divorced 1961), and appeared opposite him in many classical plays. She is best remembered for her performances in the films *Gone With the Wind* (1939, Oscar) and *A Streetcar Named Desire* (1951, Oscar).

Lemmon, Jack, popular name of **John Uhler Lemmon** (1925–2001) Film and stage actor, born in Boston, MA. *Some Like It Hot* (1959) began a 7-film collaboration with director Billy Wilder. Other films include *Mister Roberts* (1955, Oscar), *Save the Tiger* (1973, Oscar), *Glengarry Glen Ross* (1992), and *The Odd Couple II* (1998).

Lenin, Vladimir Ilyich, originally **Vladimir Ilyich Ulyanov** (1870–1924) Marxist revolutionary, born in Simbirsk, Russia. At a congress in 1903 he caused the split between the Bolshevik and Menshevik factions, and in October 1917 led the Bolshevik revolution, becoming head of the first Soviet government. At the end of the Civil War (1918–21) he introduced the New Economic Policy, which his critics saw as a 'compromise with capitalism' and a retreat from strictly socialist planning. On his death, his body was embalmed and placed in a mausoleum near the Moscow Kremlin. His birthplace was renamed Ulyanovsk in his honour (1924–91).

Lennon, John (Winston) (1940–80) Pop star, composer, and songwriter, born in Liverpool, Merseyside. He was the Beatles rhythm guitarist, keyboard player, and vocalist, and a partner in the Lennon–McCartney song-writing team. He married Japanese artist **Yoko Ono** (1933–) in 1969, and the single recorded under the name of The Plastic Ono Band, 'Give Peace a Chance' (1969), became the

'national anthem' for pacifists. He was shot and killed by a deranged fan.

Leo I, St, known as **the Great** (c.390–461) Pope (440–61), probably born in Tuscany. One of the most eminent of the Latin Fathers, he summoned the Council of Chalcedon (451), where the intention of his 'Dogmatical Letter', defining the doctrine of the Incarnation, was accepted.

Leonard, 'Sugar' Ray (1956–) US boxer, born in Wilmington, DE. He became WBC world welterweight champion in 1979, and WBA light middleweight champion in 1981. He is the only boxer to have been world champion at five weights.

Leonardo da Vinci (1452–1519) Painter, sculptor, architect, and engineer, born in Vinci, Rome. In 1482 he settled in Milan, where he painted his 'Last Supper' (1498) on the refectory wall of Santa Maria delle Grazie. In 1500 he entered the service of Cesare Borgia in Florence as architect and engineer, and with Michelangelo decorated the Sala del Consiglio in the Palazzo della Signoria. About 1504 he completed his most celebrated easel picture, 'Mona Lisa' (Louvre). His notebooks contain original remarks on most of the sciences.

Lerner, Alan Jay (1918–86) Lyricist and librettist, born in New York City. He wrote radio scripts and contributed to satirical revues, and in 1942 he met composer Frederick Loewe. Their collaborations include such hit musicals as *Brigadoon* (1947), *My Fair Lady* (1956), *Gigi* (1958), *Camelot*

(1960), and *The Little Prince* (1974). Lerner wrote the words for two other musicals, *On A Clear Day You Can See Forever* (1965) and *Coco* (1969).

Lesseps, Ferdinand (Marie), vicomte de (Viscount of) (1805–94) French diplomat and entrepreneur, born in Versailles, France. In 1854 he began his campaign for the construction of a Suez Canal, finally completed in 1869. A later scheme for a sea-level Panama Canal had to be abandoned.

Lessing, Doris (May), *née* **Tayler** (1919–) Writer, born in Kermanshah, Iran. Brought up in Southern Rhodesia, her first published novel was *The Grass is Singing* (1950), a study of white civilization in Africa. Later works include the five-book sequence *Children of Violence*, and her best-known novel *The Golden Notebook* (1962).

Lester, Dick, popular name of **Richard Lester** (1932–) Film director, born in Philadelphia, PA. He came to Britain and gained success with two feature films starring The Beatles, *A Hard Day's Night* (1964) and *Help!* (1965). Later film credits include *Superman II* and its sequel (1980, 1983), *The Return of the Musketeers* (1989), and *Get Back* (1991).

Letterman, David (1947–) Television talk-show host, born in Indianapolis, IN. He became well known following guest-host appearances on the Johnny Carson Show (1979–80), hosted a late-night show for MBC from 1982, then in 1993 joined CBS as host of *Late Night with David Letterman*.

Leverhulme (of the Western Isles),

William Hesketh Lever, 1st Viscount, also known as **Baron Leverhulme of Bolton-Le-Moors** (1851–1925) Soap-maker and philanthropist, born in Bolton, Greater Manchester. In 1886, with his brother, James Darcy Lever, he began to develop a small soap works into a national business, founding the model industrial new town of Port Sunlight.

Levi Biblical character, the third son of Jacob by his wife Leah. It is debated whether his descendants ever formed one of the 12 tribes of Israel descended from Jacob's sons. They seem to have been a kind of priestly class.

Lévi-Strauss, Claude (1908–) Social anthropologist, born in Brussels. A major influence on contemporary anthropology, his four-volume study, *Mythologiques* (1964–72), studied the systematic ordering behind codes of expression in different cultures.

Levy, Andrea (1956–) Writer, born in London. Born to Jamaican parents, her early novels explore the problems faced by black British-born children of Jamaican emigrants. Later novels include *Small Island* (2004), which won the Orange Prize and the Whitbread Best Novel and Book of the Year.

Lewinsky, Monica (1973–) Former White House intern, born in San Francisco, CA. She joined the White House in 1995, moving to the Pentagon the next year. In 1999 she was called to give evidence in an impeachment trial involving claims of sexual harassment made by Paula Jones against President Clinton. It was alleged that Lewinsky had had a sexual relationship with him and that he had persuaded her to deny the affair. Clinton denied the affair while under oath, but later retracted the denial. Lewinsky continued to maintain a high profile after the trial and her memoir, *Monica's Story* (1999), became a best seller.

Lewis, (Frederick) Carl(ton) (1961–) Track and field athlete, born in Birmingham, AL. He won four gold medals at the 1984 Olympic Games, two more in 1988, and an unprecedented third consecutive gold medal in the long jump in 1992, he won another gold at the 1996 Games. He was awarded the gold medal for the 100 m in 1988 when Ben Johnson was disqualified.

Lewis, C Day *see* Day-Lewis, C

Lewis, C(live) S(taples) (1898–1963) Academic, writer, and Christian apologist, born in Belfast. His novel *The Screwtape Letters* (1942) is the best known of many works on Christian apologetics. *The Lion, the Witch and the Wardrobe* (1950) was the first in his *Chronicles of Narnia*, a classic children's series.

Lewis, Jerry Lee (1935–) Rock singer, country singer, and pianist, born in Ferriday, LA. His 1957 recordings 'Whole Lotta Shakin'' and 'Great Balls of Fire' became classics of rock, copied by successive generations of musicians.

Lewis, Lennox (1965–) Heavyweight boxer, born in London. Awarded the World Boxing Council (WBC) heavyweight title in 1993, he lost it in 1994 to Oliver McCall, but regained it from him in 1997. In 2001 he won the WBC and International Boxing Federation heavyweight titles and successfully defended them against Mike Tyson in 2002. He retained the WBC title in a controversial match with Vitali Klitschko in 2003, and retired from professional boxing in 2004.

Liberace, also known as **Walter Busterkeys**, originally **Wladziu Valentino Liberace** (1919–87) Entertainer, born in Milwaukee, WI. He developed an act of popular piano classics performed with a lavish sense of showmanship, and his television series, *The Liberace Show* (1952–7), won him an Emmy as Best Male Personality.

Lillee, Dennis (Keith) (1949–) Cricketer, born in Perth, Western Australia. A renowned fast bowler, during his career he took 355 wickets in 70 Tests.

Lincoln, Abraham (1809–65) US Republican statesman and 16th president (1861–5), born near Hodgenville, KY. He was elected president on a platform of hostility to the expansion of slavery. When the Civil War began (1861), he defined the issue in terms of national integrity, a theme he restated in the Gettysburg Address of 1863, and in the same year proclaimed freedom for all slaves in areas of rebellion. On 14 April 1865 he was shot at Ford's Theater, Washington by John Wilkes Booth, and died next morning.

Lindbergh, Charles (Augustus) (1902–74) Aviator, born in Detroit, MI. In 1927 he made the first non-stop solo transatlantic flight, from New York City to Paris, in the monoplane *Spirit of St Louis*. In 1932 his infant son was kidnapped and murdered, a sensational crime for which Bruno Richard Hauptmann was executed (1936).

Lindsay, Robert, popular name of **Robert Lindsay Stevenson** (1949–) Actor, born in Ilkeston, Derbyshire. He became well known as 'Wolfie' in the popular television sitcom *Citizen Smith* (1977). Later work for television includes *Hornblower* (1998–2003), *My Family* (2001–), and *Jericho* (2005). In musical theatre, his award-winning performances include *Me and My Girl* (1987) and *Oliver!* (1997).

Lindwall, Ray(mond Russell) (1921–96) Cricketer, born in Sydney, New South Wales, Australia. He took 228 wickets in 61 Tests, and also scored more than 1500 runs, including two Test centuries.

Lineker, Gary (Winston) (1960–) Footballer, journalist, and broadcaster, born in Leicester, Leicestershire. He played for Leicester City, Everton, Barcelona, Tottenham Hotspur, and in Japan. He made his England debut in 1984 (captain 1990–2), played in the 1986 and 1990 World Cups, and gained 80 caps. He was twice voted Player of the Year (1986, 1992). Since 1999 he has presented BBC's *Match of the Day*, and is a familiar figure on television commercials.

Linklater, Eric (Robert Russell) (1899–1974) Novelist, born in Dounby, Orkney Is, Scotland. While in the USA (1928–30) he wrote *Poet's Pub* (1929), the first of a series of satirical novels which include *Juan in America* (1931) and *Private Angelo* (1946).

Linnaeus, Carolus, Swed **Carl von Linné** (1707–78) Botanist, born in Råshult, Sweden. His *Systema naturae fundamenta botanica* (1735), *Genera plantarum* (1737), and *Species plantarum* (1753), expound his influential system of classification, in which names consist of generic and specific elements, with plants grouped hierarchically into genera, classes, and orders.

Lipman, Maureen (Diane) (1946–) Actress and writer, born in Hull. She has appeared in a number of West End productions and on television, and became widely known for her award-winning 'You got an Ology?' British Telecom TV commercial. She has written several humorous books, including *How Was It For You?* (1985). In 1973 she married the playwright Jack Rosenthal.

Lippershey, Hans or **Jan**, also spelled **Lippersheim** (c.1570–1619) Dutch optician, born in Wesel, Germany. He is one of several spectacle-makers credited with the discovery that the combination of a convex and a concave lens can make distant objects appear nearer. He is believed to be the inventor of the telescope (1608).

Lippi, Fra Filippo, known as **Lippo** (c.1406–69) Religious painter, born in Florence, Italy. His greatest work, on the choir walls of Prato Cathedral, was begun in 1452. His later works, deeply religious, include the series of 'Nativities'.

Lippmann, Walter (1889–1974) Journalist, born in New York City. Special writer for the New York *Herald Tri-*

bune, his daily columns became internationally famous, and he received the Pulitzer Prize for International Reporting in 1962.

Liszt, Franz (1811–86) Composer and pianist, born in Raiding, Hungary. From 1835 to 1839 he lived with the Comtesse d'Agoult, by whom he had three children, and in 1847 met Princess Carolyne zu Sayn-Wittgenstein with whom he lived until his death. A virtuoso pianist who gave concerts throughout Europe, his works include 12 symphonic poems, Masses, two symphonies, and a large number of piano pieces.

Little Richard, popular name of **Richard Wayne Penniman** (1935–) Rock-and-roll singer and pianist, born in Macon, GA. 'Tutti Frutti' (1955) brought him international popularity. Most of his recordings from 1958 to 1964 were of Gospel songs, but in the mid-1960s he made a comeback with his 'Whole Lot Of Shaking Goin' On', and other hits.

Lively, Penelope (Margaret), *née* **Low** (1933–) Novelist and children's writer, born in Cairo. Her children's books include *The Ghost of Thomas Kempe* (1973) and *The Revenge of Samuel Stokes* (1981). Among her adult novels are *Moon Tiger* (1987, Booker) and *Making It Up* (2005).

Liverpool, Robert Banks Jenkinson, 2nd Earl of (1770–1828) British prime minister (1812–27), born in London. He became foreign secretary (1801–4), home secretary (1804–6, 1807–9), and secretary for war and the colonies (1809–12). As premier, he oversaw the final years of the Napoleonic Wars and the War of 1812–14 with the USA.

Livingstone, David (1813–73) Missionary and traveller, born in Blantyre, South Lanarkshire. He discovered L Ngami and the Victoria Falls (1852–6), led an expedition to the Zambezi (1858–63), and discovered L Shirwa and L Nyasa. He disappeared while searching for the sources of the Nile, and was found in 1871 by Stanley, sent to look for him by the *New York Herald*.

Livingstone, Ken(neth Robert) (1945–) British politician, born in London. He was elected leader of the Greater London Council in 1981 and, following its demise, he became Labour MP for Brent East in 1987. He was an unsuccessful Labour candidate for the newly established position of Mayor of London in 2000, but stood as an independent and was elected (re-elected 2004). He was subsequently expelled from the Labour Party but readmitted in 2004.

Livy, in full **Titus Livius** (c.59 BC–AD 17) Roman historian, born in Patavium, Italy. His history of Rome, from its foundation to the death of Drusus (9 BC), comprised 142 books, of which 35 have survived.

Lloyd, Clive (Hubert) (1944–) Cricketer, born in Georgetown, Guyana. A batsman and fielder, he joined Lancashire (1968–86), and played in 110 Test matches for the West Indies (captain 1974–85), scoring 7515 runs and making 19 centuries.

Lloyd, Harold (Clayton) (1893–1971) Film comedian, born in Burchard, NE. He became one of America's most popular daredevil comedians in films such as *High and Dizzy* (1920) and *Safety Last* (1923), and he received an honorary Academy Award in 1952.

Lloyd, (John) Selwyn *see* Selwyn-Lloyd, Baron

Lloyd-George (of Dwyfor), David Lloyd George, 1st Earl (1863–1945) British Liberal prime minister (1916–22), born in Manchester, Greater Manchester. He was President of the Board of Trade (1905–8), Chancellor of the Exchequer (1908–15), minister of munitions (1915) and secretary for war (1916), and superseded Asquith as coalition prime minister, carrying on a forceful war policy. He negotiated with Sinn Féin, and conceded the Irish Free State (1921) – a measure which brought his downfall.

Lloyd-Webber, Andrew Lloyd Webber, Baron (1948–) Composer, born in London. With Tim Rice he wrote *Joseph and the Amazing Technicolour Dreamcoat* (1968) and the rock opera *Jesus Christ Superstar* (staged 1970). He has since composed the music for many West End hits, including *Evita* (1978), *Cats* (1981), *The Phantom of the Opera* (1986), *Sunset Boulevard* (1993), and *Woman in White* (2004). His brother **Julian** (1951–) is a cellist.

Lock, Tony, popular name of **Graham Anthony Richard Lock** (1929–95) Cricketer, born in Limpsfield, Surrey. A left-arm bowler for Surrey, he played 49 Tests for England and took 174 wickets, taking 10 or more wickets in a match on three occasions.

Locke, Bobby, popular name of **Arthur D'Arcy Locke** (1917–87) Golfer, born in Germiston, South Africa. He won four British Open championships (1949, 1950, 1952,

1957) and between 1947 and 1950 won 11 events on the US tour circuit.

Locke, John (1632–1704) Philosopher, born in Wrington, Somerset. His major work, the *Essay Concerning Human Understanding* (1690), accepted the possibility of rational demonstration of moral principles and the existence of God, but its reliance on the senses was the real starting point of British empiricism.

Lockwood, Margaret (1916–90) English actress, born in Karachi, Pakistan (formerly India). She made her film debut in *Lorna Doone* (1935), and starred in the Alfred Hitchcock film *The Lady Vanishes* (1938). In the late 1940s she was Britain's most popular leading lady, appearing regularly in theatre productions.

Lodge, David (John) (1935–) Novelist and critic, born in London. His novels include *Changing Places* (1975), *Small World* (1984; televised 1988), *Nice Work* (1988; televised 1989), and *Author, Author* (2004). Among critical works are *Language of Fiction* (1966) and *The Practice of Writing* (1996).

Lodge, Henry Cabot (1850–1924) US Republican politician, historian, and biographer, born in Boston, MA. He led the opposition to the Treaty of Versailles in 1919, and prevented the USA joining the League of Nations in 1920. His grandson, **Henry Cabot Lodge Jr** (1902–85) was US representative at the United Nations (1953–60).

Loewe, Frederick, known as **Fritz** (1904–88) Composer, born in Vienna. He went to the USA in 1924, and worked on a number of Broadway musicals in collaboration with

Alan Jay Lerner, including *Briga-doon* (1947) and *My Fair Lady* (1956).

Lomu, Jonah (1975–) Rugby union player, born in Mangere, New Zealand, of Tongan parents. Selected for the New Zealand All Blacks in 1994, he became internationally known as a member of the World Cup squad, his massive physique making him an awesome opponent. A kidney disorder forced his retirement in 2003 but he underwent a succesful kidney transplant operation in 2004, and returned to competitive rugby in 2005.

London, Jack, pseudonym of **John Griffith Chaney** (1876–1916) Novelist, born in San Francisco, CA. His books include *The Call of the Wild* (1903), the political novel *The Iron Heel* (1907), and several autobiographical tales, notably *John Barley-corn* (1913).

Longfellow, Henry Wadsworth (1807–82) Poet, born in Portland, ME. He published many works, notably *Ballads and Other Poems* (1841), including 'The Wreck of the Hesperus'. His most popular work was 'The Song of Hiawatha' (1855), and in 1863 appeared *Tales of a Wayside Inn*, which included the famous 'Paul Revere's Ride'.

Lope de Vega *see* Vega, Lope de

Lopez, Jennifer, popularly known as **J-Lo** (1970–) Actress and pop singer, born in the Bronx, New York City. She trained as a dancer, gained a part in the television series *In Living Color* (1990–3), and went on to star in the films *The Wedding Planner* (2001), *Maid in Manhattan* (2002), and *Mon-ster-in-Law* (2005). Her albums

include *J-Lo* (2001) and *Rebirth* (2005).

Lorca, Federico García (1898–1936) Poet, born in Fuente Vaqueros, Spain. His best-known works are *Songs* (trans, 1927) and *The Gypsy Ballads* (trans, 1928, 1935). Prose plays include the trilogy *Blood Wedding* (trans, 1933), *Yerma* (1934), and *The House of Bernarda Alba* (trans, 1936). He was assassinated in the Spanish Civil War.

Loren, Sophia, originally **Sofia Scicolone** (1934–) Film actress, born in Rome. Under contract to film producer **Carlo Ponti** (1912–), later her husband, she won an Oscar for *Two Women* (trans, 1961). Other films include *The Millionairess* (1961) and *Marriage Italian Style* (1964).

Lorenz, Konrad (Zacharias) (1903–89) Zoologist, born in Vienna. The founder of ethology, his studies led to a deeper understanding of behaviour patterns in animals, notably imprinting in young birds, and he shared the Nobel Prize for Physiology or Medicine in 1973. His books, such as *On Aggression* (1963) and *King Solomon's Ring* (1949) enjoyed wide popularity.

Lorrain, Claude *see* Claude Lorrain

Louis XIV, known as **le Roi soleil** ('the Sun King') (1638–1715) King of France (1643–1715), born in St Germain-en-Laye, the son of Louis XIII. In 1660 he married Maria Theresa, elder daughter of Philip IV of Spain, through whom he was later to claim the Spanish succession for his second grandson. His obsession with France's greatness led him into aggressive foreign policies, his major political rivals being the Austrian Habsburgs, particularly Leopold I. His attempt to create a Franco-Spanish Bourbon bloc led to the War of the Spanish Succession (1701–13), and there was also conflict with the Jansenists, the Huguenots, and the papacy. His long reign nonetheless marked the cultural ascendancy of France within Europe, symbolized by the Palace of Versailles.

Louis XVI (1754–93) King of France (1774–93), born in Versailles, France, the grandson of Louis XV. He was married in 1770 to the Archduchess Marie Antoinette, daughter of the Habsburg Empress Maria Theresa, to strengthen the Franco-Austrian alliance. He failed to give consistent support to ministers who tried to reform the outmoded financial and social structures of the country and was forced in 1789 to summon the States General. He resisted demands from the National Assembly for sweeping reforms, and was brought with his family from Versailles to Paris as hostages to the revolutionary movement. Their attempted flight to Varennes (1791) branded them as traitors. The monarchy was abolished, he was tried for conspiracy, and guillotined in Paris.

Louis, Joe, popular name of **Joseph Louis Barrow**, nickname **the Brown Bomber** (1914–81) Boxer, born in Lafayette, AL. He beat Braddock for the world heavyweight title in 1937, and held the title for a record 12 years, making a record 25 defences.

Louis Napoleon *see* Napoleon III

Louis-Philippe, known as **the Citizen King** (1773–1850) King of the French (1830–48), born in Paris, the eldest son of Philippe Egalité. At the Revolution he entered the National Guard, renounced his title to demonstrate his progressive sympathies, then lived in exile (1793–1814). After the July Revolution (1830) he was given the title of King of the French. Political corruption and economic depression caused discontent, and he abdicated at the onset of the 1848 revolution.

Love, Mike *see* Beach Boys, The

Lovell, Sir (Alfred Charles) Bernard (1913–) Astronomer, born in Oldland Common, Gloucestershire. Director of the Nuffield Radio Astronomy Laboratories at Jodrell Bank, he is distinguished for his pioneering work in radio telescope design, space research, and the physics of radio sources.

Lowe, Arthur (1914–82) Actor, born in Hayfield, Derbyshire. It was television that brought him his greatest popularity, first as Mr Swindley in *Coronation Street* (1960–5), then as the bumbling Captain Mainwaring in *Dad's Army* (1968–77).

Lowell, Robert (Traill Spence), Jr (1917–77) Poet, born in Boston, MA. His first collection was the autobiographical *Land of Unlikeness* (1944), followed by *Lord Weary's Castle* (1946, Pulitzer). Other confessional volumes include *Life Studies* (1959) and *The Dolphin* (1973).

Lowry, L(aurence) S(tephen) (1887–1976) Artist, born in Manchester, Greater Manchester. From 1939 he produced many pictures of the Lancashire industrial scene, mainly in brilliant whites and greys, peopled with scurrying stick-like men and women.

Loyola, Ignatius of, St, originally **Iñigo López de Recalde** (1491 or 1495–1556) Theologian and founder of the Jesuits, born in his ancestral castle of Loyola in the Basque province Guipúzcao. He founded with six associates the Society of Jesus in 1584, and wrote the influential *Spiritual Exercises*. He was canonized in 1622.

Lucan, Richard John Bingham, 7th Earl of, known as **Lord Lucan** (1934–?) British aristocrat, and alleged murderer. He disappeared in 1974, after police found the body of the Lucan family's nanny. Speculation about his whereabouts continues to this day.

Lucas, George (Walton) (1944–) Film director, screenwriter, and producer, born in Modesto, CA. He is best known as producer of the Indiana Jones series and as director/writer of the *Star Wars* series (1977, 1980, 1983, 1999, 2002, 2005). In 1975 he started Industrial Light and Magic, a company that creates special visual and audio effects for film and television.

Lucid, Shannon (1943–) US astronaut and biochemist, born in Shanghai, China. In 1996 she set a new record for the longest US space mission (188 days) in orbit aboard the *Mir* space station. She became the first woman to be awarded the Congressional Space Medal of Honor.

Lucy, St (?–303) Christian martyr, the patron saint of virgins and of the blind. According to legend, she was a virgin denounced as a Christian by a rejected suitor, and martyred under Diocletian at Syracuse.

Ludd, Ned (fl.1779) Farm labourer from Leicestershire. Legend has it that he destroyed some stocking frames c.1782, and it is from him that the *Luddite* rioters (1812–18) took their name.

Luke, St (1st-c) New Testament evangelist, a Gentile Christian, perhaps 'the beloved physician' and companion of St Paul (*Col* 4.14). He is first named as author of the third Gospel in the 2nd-c, and tradition has ascribed to him both that work and the Acts of the Apostles.

Lumet, Sidney (1924–) Film director, born in Philadelphia, PA. His films include *Twelve Angry Men* (1957), *The Pawnbroker* (1965), *Murder on the Orient Express* (1974), *Night Falls on Manhattan* (1996), and *Find Me Guilty* (2006).

Lumière brothers Chemists, born in Besançon, France: **Auguste (Marie Louis) Lumière** (1862–1954) and **Louis (Jean) Lumière** (1864–1948). In 1893 they developed a cine camera, the *cinématographe*, and showed the first motion pictures using film projection in 1895.

Luria, Alexander Romanovich (1902–77) Psychologist, born in Kazan, Russia. One of the founders of neuropsychology, his books include *The Man with a Shattered World* (trans, 1972) and *The Working Brain* (trans, 1973).

Luther, Martin (1483–1546) Religious reformer, born in Eisleben, Germany. During a visit to Rome (1510–11), he was angered by the sale of indulgences. In 1517 he drew up 95 theses on indulgences, which he nailed on the church door at Wittenberg, and publicly burned the papal bull issued against him. He was summoned to appear before the Diet at Worms, and was put under the ban of the Empire. The drawing up of his views in the Augsburg Confession marks the culmination of the German Reformation (1530). His translation of the Bible became a landmark of German literature.

Lutyens, Sir Edwin Landseer (1869–1944) Architect, born in London. His best-known projects are the Cenotaph, Whitehall (1919–20), and the laying out of New Delhi, India (1912–30).

Lyle, Sandy, popular name of **Alexander Walter Barr Lyle** (1958–) Golfer, born in Shrewsbury, Shropshire. His successes include the European Open (1979), the French Open (1981), the British Open (1985), and the US Masters Championship (1988).

Lynam, Desmond (Michael) (1942–) Sports broadcaster, born in Ennis, County Clare, Ireland. He joined the BBC in 1969 as a sports presenter, and became nationally known for such programmes as *Grandstand*, *Sportsnight*, and *Match of the Day*. In 2005 he became host of *Countdown*, the long-running Channel 4 quiz show.

Lyngstad, Anni-Frid *see* Abba

Lynn, Dame Vera, originally **Vera Welch** (1917–) British singer, born in London. A vocalist with Howard Baker's orchestra at the age of 15, she became highly popular during World War 2, hosting a BBC radio programme *Sincerely Yours*, and overseas servicemen voted her 'The Forces Sweetheart'. Her songs included 'White Cliffs of Dover' and 'We'll Meet Again'.

Lyttelton, Humphrey (1921–) Jazz trumpeter and bandleader, born in Windsor, S England. He formed a band in 1948, and became the leading figure in the British revival of traditional jazz. His group expanded to an octet, and presented a range of more modern jazz styles.

Ma, Yo-Yo (1955–) Cellist, born in Paris. He is noted for his warmth of playing, superlative technique, a repertoire stretching from Bach to the moderns, and an energetic stage presence.

McAdam, John Loudon (1756–1836) Inventor of macadamized roads, born in Ayr, South Ayrshire. Appointed surveyor to the Bristol Turnpike Trust (1816), he re-made the roads there with crushed stone bound with gravel. His *macadam surfaces* were adopted in many other countries.

McAleese, Mary (1951–) President of Ireland (1997–), born in Belfast. A professor of criminal law, in 1994 she became the first woman and Catholic pro-vice-chancellor at Queen's University, Belfast. Despite her northern background, she became the presidential successor to Mary Robinson in the 1997 election and was re-elected for a second 7-year term in 2004.

MacArthur, Dame Ellen (1976–) Yachtswoman, born in Whatstandwell, Derbyshire. In 2000 she entered the Vendée Globe yacht race in *Kingfisher* and made history by becoming the fastest woman ever to sail solo around the world (94 days, 4 hrs, 25 min, 40 s). In 2005 she sailed solo around the world in record time (71 days, 14 hrs, 18 min, 33 s) aboard trimaran *B&Q*, beating the previous record by almost 33 hours.

Macaulay, Dame (Emilie) Rose (1881–1958) Writer, born in Rugby, Warwickshire. She won a considerable reputation as a social satirist, with such novels as *Dangerous Ages* (1921). Her best-known novel is *The Towers of Trebizond* (1956).

Macaulay (of Rothley), Thomas Babington Macaulay, Baron (1800–59) Essayist and historian, born in Rothley Temple, Leicestershire. He established his powers as an orator in the Reform Bill debates, and became secretary of war (1839–41). He wrote the popular *Lays of Ancient Rome* (1842) and the *History of England from the Accession of James II* (1848–61), the fifth volume unfinished.

Macbeth (c.1005–57) King of Scots (1040–57), the legend of whose life was the basis of Shakespeare's play. The provincial ruler of Moray, he became king after slaying Duncan I in battle near Elgin. He was killed by Duncan's son, Malcolm Canmore.

McBride, Willie John, popular name of **William John McBride** (1940–) Rugby union player, born in Toomebridge, Co Antrim. He was with Ballymena from 1962, won a total of 63 caps, and played in 17 Tests on five British Lions tours.

McCartney, Sir (James) Paul (1942–)

Pop star and composer, born in Liverpool, Merseyside. The Beatles' bass guitarist, vocalist, and member of the Lennon–McCartney songwriting team, his debut solo album was *McCartney* (1970). In 1971 he formed the band Wings with his wife, **Linda** (1942–98, *née* **Eastman**). 'Mull of Kintyre' (1977) became the biggest selling UK single (2·5 million). With Carl Davis he wrote the *Liverpool Oratorio* (1991), and in 1997 composed the symphonic poem, *Standing Stones*. His 3000th concert was performed in St Petersburg, Russia, in 2004. He married **Heather Mills** (1968–) in 2002 (separated, 2006).

McCartney, Stella (1972–) British fashion designer, the daughter of Paul McCartney. She became chief designer at the French couture house Chloé in 1997, and received the Designer of the Year Award at the Vogue Fashion Awards in New York in 2000. She joined Gucci in 2001, showed the first collection under her own label later that year, and in 2003 opened retail outlets in London and Los Angeles.

McCourt, Frank (1930–) Writer and teacher, born in Brooklyn, New York City, NY. His family returned to their native Ireland when he was four, and settled in Limerick. His works include the best-selling memoir, *Angela's Ashes* (1996, Pulitzer), a sequel *Tis: A Memoir* (1999), and *Teacher Man* (2005).

McCoy, Tony, properly **Anthony Peter McCoy** (1974–) Jockey, born in Co Antrim, Northern Ireland. National Hunt Champion jockey since 1995, in 2002 he broke the record for the number of winners in a season (269 set on the flat by Sir Gordon Richards in 1947), finishing with a total of 289 winners. He rode his 1700th winner on Mighty Montefalco at Uttoxeter in 2002 to beat Richard Dunwoody's all-time British winners' record.

McCullers, (Lula) Carson, *née* **Smith** (1917–67) Writer, born in Columbus, GA. Her work reflects the sadness of lonely people, as in her first book, *The Heart Is a Lonely Hunter* (1940). Later works include *The Ballad of the Sad Café* (1951).

McCullough, Colleen (1937–) Novelist, born in Wellington, New South Wales, Australia. Her books include the best-selling *The Thorn Birds* (1977). Later novels include *A Creed for the Third Millennium* (1985) and *The Grass Crown* (1991).

McDonagh, Martin (1970–) Playwright, born in London. Brought up in London by Irish parents, much of his work is set in Ireland. In 1997 his first four plays were running simultaneously in London's West End: *The Leenane Trilogy* and *The Cripple of Inishmaan*. Later plays include *The Lieutenant of Inishmore* (2001) and *The Pillowman* (2003). He wrote and directed the Oscar-winning short film *Six Shooter* (2005).

Macdonald, Flora (1722–90) Scottish heroine, born in South Uist, Western Isles. After the rebellion of 1745, she conducted the Young Pretender, Charles Edward Stuart, disguised as 'Betty Burke', to safety in Skye. She was imprisoned in the Tower of London, but released in 1747.

MacDonald, (James) Ramsay (1866–1937) British prime minister (1924, 1929–31, 1931–5), born in Lossiemouth, Moray. In 1894 he joined the Independent Labour Party, becoming its leader (1911–14, 1922–31), and was prime minister and foreign secretary of the first British Labour government.

McDonald, Sir Trevor (1939–) Television journalist and newscaster, born in Trinidad. A reporter for ITN from 1973, he became nationally known for *News at Ten* (1990–9), and began presenting *Tonight With Trevor McDonald* in 1999. He presented ITN's late-night bulletin for many years until 2005.

McEnroe, John (Patrick) (1959–) Tennis player, born in Wiesbaden, Germany. He won four US Open singles titles (1979–81, 1984) and three Wimbledon singles titles (1981, 1983–4). His skill as a player was often overshadowed by his outbursts on court which led to professional censure on several occasions.

McGough, Roger (1937–) Poet and performer, born in Liverpool, Merseyside. He became known as one of the 'Liverpool Poets' together with **Adrian Henri** (1932–2000) and **Brian Patten** (1946–). A poet of bizarre irony and wit, he is well known for his public readings. Poetry collections include *Gig* (1973), *Waving at Trains* (1982), and *Everyday Eclipses* (2003).

McGregor, Ewan (1971–) Actor, born in Crieff, Perthshire. His feature films include *Shallow Grave* (1994), *Trainspotting* (1996), three *Star Wars* episodes (1999, 2002, 2005), *Moulin Rouge* (2000), and *Big Fish* (2004).

McGuigan, Barry, properly **Finbar Patrick McGuigan** (1961–) Boxer, born in Clones, Co Monaghan. In 1978 as an amateur he won the Irish bantamweight title and Commonwealth Games gold medal. Once professional, he won the British featherweight title (1983) and the world featherweight championship (1985). He was inducted into the International Boxing Hall of Fame in 2005.

McGuinness, Martin (1950–) Sinn Féin politician, born in Londonderry, Northern Ireland. A militant IRA supporter, he developed a major role as a political strategist during the Northern Ireland peace process in the 1990s. He became an MP, though not attending at Westminster, and Sinn Féin's senior minister in the Stormont Assembly. He became minister of education in the devolved Assembly in November 1999.

Mach, Ernst (1838–1916) Physicist and philosopher, born in Turas, Austria. He carried out experimental work in aeronautical design and projectiles, and his name has been given to a unit of velocity (*Mach number*) and to the angle of a shock wave to the direction of motion (*Mach angle*).

Machiavelli, Niccolò (di Bernardo dei) (1469–1527) Italian political theorist, born in Florence, Italy. His masterpiece is *The Prince* (trans, 1532), whose main theme is that all means may be used to maintain authority, and that the worst acts of the ruler are justified by the treachery of the governed. It was condemned by the pope.

Macintosh, Charles (1766–1843) Manufacturing chemist, born in Glasgow. He developed in 1823 a method of waterproofing cloth, which resulted in the manufacture of the raincoat, or *macintosh*.

Macke, August (1887–1914) Painter, born in Meschede, Germany. Profoundly influenced by Matisse, he founded the *Blaue Reiter* group together with Franz Marc. He was killed in action in France.

McKellen, Sir Ian (Murray) (1939–) Actor, born in Burnley, Lancashire. He co-founded the Actors' Company in 1972, and played many memorable parts for the Royal Shakespeare Company (1974–8). His feature films include *Richard III* (1995) and the *Lord of the Rings* trilogy (2001–3).

Mackenzie, Sir (Edward Montague) Compton (1883–1972) Writer, born in West Hartlepool, Co Durham. His many novels include *Sinister Street* (1913–14) and *Whisky Galore* (1947).

Mackerras, Sir (Alan) Charles (MacLaurin) (1925–) Conductor, born in Schenectady, NY. He was musical director of the Sadler's Wells (later English National) Opera, the Sydney Symphony Orchestra, and the Welsh National Opera, and later became principal guest conductor with the Scottish Chamber Orchestra (1992–5), and with the Czech Philharmonic from 1996.

McKinley, William (1843–1901) US statesman and 25th president (1897–1901), born in Niles, OH. His name was identified with the high protective tariff carried in the *McKinley Bill* of 1890. His first term as president saw the war with Spain (1898), with the conquest of Cuba and the Philippines. He was shot by an anarchist.

Mackintosh, Sir Cameron (Anthony) (1946–) British impresario. He financed Lloyd Webber's *Cats*, and later produced such musicals as *Little Shop of Horrors* (1983), *Les Misérables* (1985), *Phantom of the Opera* (1986), and *Miss Saigon* (1989). Later productions include *The Witches of Eastwick* (2000) and *Mary Poppins* (2004).

Mackintosh, Charles Rennie (1868–1928) Architect, designer, and painter, born in Glasgow. He became a leader of the 'Glasgow Style', a movement related to Art Nouveau, his designs including detailed interiors, textiles, furniture, and metalwork.

MacLaine, Shirley, stage name of **Shirley Maclean Beaty** (1934–) Actress, born in Richmond, VA, the sister of Warren Beatty. Her films include *Irma La Douce* (1963), *Sweet Charity* (1969), *Terms of Endearment* (1983, Oscar), *Postcards from the Edge* (1990), and *Bewitched* (2005).

Maclean, Alistair (1922–87) Writer, born in Glasgow. His first novel *HMS Ulysses* (1955) became an immediate best seller. Later books included *The Guns of Navarone* (1957) and *Where Eagles Dare* (1967). Many of his books were made into films.

Maclean, Donald (Duart) (1913–83) British traitor, born in London. He joined the diplomatic service in 1934, and from 1944 was recruited by Soviet intelligence as an agent. In 1951 he disappeared with Burgess, reappearing in Russia in 1956.

McLuhan, (Herbert) Marshall (1911–80) Writer, born in Edmonton, Alberta, Canada. His controversial views on the effect of the communication media are propounded in *The Gutenberg Galaxy* (1962), *Understanding Media* (1964), and *The Medium is the Message* (with Q Fiore, 1967).

Macmillan, (Maurice) Harold, 1st Earl of Stockton (1894–1986) British prime minister (1957–63), born in London, the grandson of Daniel Macmillan. He was minister of housing (1951–4), minister of defence (1954–5), foreign secretary (1955), and Chancellor of the Exchequer (1955–7). He gained unexpected popularity with his infectious enthusiasm, effective domestic policy ('most of our people have never had it so good'), and resolute foreign policy.

MacMillan, Sir Kenneth (1929–92) Ballet dancer, choreographer, and ballet company director, born in Dunfermline, Fife. He became artistic director of the Royal Ballet in 1970, and its principal choreographer in 1977.

McMillan, Terry (1951–) Novelist, born in Port Huron, MI. She began writing in her mid-thirties, publishing a string of best-selling novels including *Disappearing Acts* (1989), *Waiting to Exhale* (1992; filmed 1995), and *A Day Late and a Dollar Short* (2001).

McMurtry, Larry (Jeff) (1936–) Writer, bookseller, and academic, born in Wichita Falls, TX. His first novel *Horseman, Pass By* (1961), was filmed as the Academy Award-winning *Hud* (1963), and he wrote the screenplay for his novel *The Last Picture Show* (1966; Oscar Best Picture, 1972). His best-selling frontier epic *Lonesome Dove* (1985) won a Pulitzer Prize in 1986.

MacNeice, (Frederick) Louis (1907–63) Poet, born in Belfast. He became closely associated with the new British left-wing poets of the 1930s, especially Auden, with whom he wrote *Letters from Iceland* (1937). Other volumes include *Collected Poems* (1949), and several verse plays for radio.

McQueen, (Terence) Steve(n) (1930–80) Film actor, born in Slater, MO. He became the archetypal 1960s cinema hero/rebel with his performances in *The Great Escape* (1963), *The Cincinnati Kid* (1965), and *Bullitt* (1968). He was married (1973–8) to actress **Ali McGraw** (1938–).

McVeigh, Timothy (James) (1968–2001) Convicted bomber, born in Pendleton, NY. He became internationally known when he was charged with the bombing of the Alfred P Murrah US government building in Oklahoma City in 1995, in which 168 people died. At his trial in 1997, a Denver jury found him guilty of conspiracy and murder. After a series of failed appeals, he was executed by lethal injection.

Macy, William H (1950–) Actor, born in Miami, FL. He became a household name in 1994 when he appeared in the television series *ER*, and in 2003 he won an Emmy for his role in the TV mini-series *Door to Door*. His films include *Fargo* (1996), *Seabiscuit* (2003), and *Cellular* (2004).

Madison, James (1751–1836) US statesman and fourth president (1809–17), born in Port Conway, VA. He played a major role in the Constitutional Convention of 1787, becoming known as 'the father of the Constitution'. Secretary of state under Jefferson, and president for two terms, his administration saw the Napoleonic Wars and the War of 1812.

Madonna, in full **Madonna Louise Ciccone** (1958–) Pop singer, born in Rochester, MI. Her albums include *Madonna* (1983), *Like A Virgin* (1984), *Music* (2000), and *Confessions on a Dancefloor* (2005), and she has also acted in films, including *Desperately Seeking Susan* (1985) and *Evita* (1996). In a new departure, her first children's book, *The English Roses*, was published in 2003.

Magdalene, St Mary *see* Mary Magdalene, St

Magellan, Ferdinand (c.1480–1521) Navigator, born in Sabrosa or Porto, Portugal. He sailed in 1519 around the foot of South America to reach the ocean which he named the Pacific (1520). He was killed in the Philippines, but his ships completed the first circumnavigation of the world. The *Strait of Magellan* is named after him.

Magnani, Anna (1908–73) Actress, born in Alexandria, Egypt. She achieved recognition in *Rome, Open City* (trans, 1945) and *The Rose Tattoo* (1955, Oscar). Much of her later work was for the Italian stage and television.

Magnusson, Magnus (1929–) Writer

and broadcaster, born in Edinburgh of Icelandic parents. He is chiefly known as a radio and television presenter, most famously in the annual series of *Mastermind*. His books include *Vikings!* (1980) and *Treasures of Scotland* (1981).

Magritte, René (François Ghislain) (1898–1967) Surrealist painter, born in Lessines, Belgium. A leading member of the Belgian Surrealist group (1924), his major paintings include 'The Wind and the Song' (1928–9) and 'The Human Condition' (1934, 1935). He was an early innovator of the Pop Art of the 1960s.

Mahler, Gustav (1860–1911) Composer, born in Kalist, Czech Republic (formerly Bohemia). His mature works consist entirely of songs and nine large-scale symphonies (with a 10th left unfinished), the best known being the song-symphony *The Song of the Earth* (trans, 1908–9).

Mahomet *see* Mohammed

Maier, Hermann, nickname **The Herminator** or **Hermannator** (1972–) Skier, born in Flachau, Salzburg, Austria. His achievements include the European Cup (1996) and World Cup (1998, 2000, 2001, 2004), and in March 2001 he equalled the World Cup season record of 13 wins. Later that year, he nearly lost his right leg in a motorcycle accident but made a comeback in 2003.

Mailer, Norman (Kingsley), originally **Nachum Malech Mailer** (1923–) Writer, born in Long Branch, NJ. His best-known novels are *The Naked and the Dead* (1948), a panoramic World War 2 novel, and *American Dream* (1964). Identified with many of the US liberal protest movements, his political studies include *The Armies of the Night* (1968, Pulitzer).

Mainbocher, originally **Main Rousseau Bocher** (c.1890–1976) Fashion designer, born in Chicago, IL. He started a couture house in Paris in 1930, one of his creations being the wedding dress designed for the Duchess of Windsor (1937).

Maintenon, Françoise d'Aubigné, Marquise de (Marchioness of) (1635–1719) Second wife of Louis XIV of France, born in Niort, France. She married the poet Paul Scarron in 1652, but when left an impoverished widow she took charge of the king's two sons by her friend Mme de Montespan, and became the king's mistress. After the queen's death (1683), Louis married her secretly.

Major, Sir John (1943–) British prime minister (1990–7), born in London. He became an MP in 1976, and rose to become Treasury chief secretary in 1987. In 1989 he became foreign secretary, and soon after returned to the Treasury as Chancellor. He won the leadership contest following Mrs Thatcher's resignation, and became prime minister in 1990. He resigned as leader of the Conservative Party after they lost the 1997 general election.

Makarios III, originally **Mihail Khristodoulou Mouskos** (1913–77) Archbishop of the Orthodox Church of Cyprus, and president of Cyprus (1960–74, 1974–7), born in Ano Panayia, Cyprus. He reorganized the *enosis* (union) movement, was arrested in 1956, but returned in 1959 to become chief Greek-Cypriot minister in the new Greek–Turkish provisional government.

Malachy, St, originally **Máel Máedoc úa Morgair** (c.1094–1148) Monk and reformer, born in Armagh, Co Armagh. In 1139 he journeyed to Rome, visiting St Bernard at Clairvaux, and introduced the Cistercian Order into Ireland on his return in 1142. In 1190 he became the first Irishman to be canonized.

Malcolm X, originally **Malcolm Little** (1925–65) Political leader, born in Omaha, NE. He entered the Nation of Islam (Black Muslims) and became a leading spokesman for its separatist policies, but left the organization in 1964, and founded the Organization of Afro-American Unity. A factional feud ensued, culminating in his assassination by Black Muslim enemies during a rally in Harlem.

Mallon, Seamus (1936–) Northern Ireland politician, born in Markethill, Armagh, Northern Ireland. A member of the Social Democratic and Labour Party, he became a UK MP in 1986, and was elected to the new Northern Ireland Assembly in 1998, becoming deputy first minister (1999–2001).

Malory, Sir Thomas (?–1471) English writer, known for his work, *Le Morte D'Arthur* (The Death of Arthur). From Caxton's preface, we are told that Malory was a knight, and that he finished his work in the ninth year of the reign of Edward IV (1461–70).

Malouf, David (1934–) Novelist, born in Brisbane, Queensland, Australia. His books include *An Imaginary Life* (1978), *The Great World* (1991, Miles

Franklin Award), *Remembering Babylon* (1993), and *Dream Stuff* (2000).

Malthus, Thomas Robert (1766–1834) Economist, born near Dorking, Surrey. He is chiefly known for the *Essay on the Principle of Population* (1798) which argued that the population has a natural tendency to increase faster than the means of subsistence, and that efforts should be made to cut the birth rate, either by self-restraint or birth control.

Mamet, David (Alan), sometimes credited as **Richard Weisz** (1947–) Playwright and film director, born in Chicago, IL. His works include the play *American Buffalo* (1976), the screenplay *The Postman Always Rings Twice* (1981), and the novel *The Village* (1994). He received the Pulitzer Prize for Drama in 1984 for *Glengarry Glen Ross*. In 2004 he wrote and directed *Spartan*.

Mancini, Henry, popular name of **Enrico Mancini** (1924–94) Composer, born in Cleveland, OH. His Oscar-winning compositions include the songs 'Moon River' (1961) and 'Days of Wine and Roses' (1962). He composed the film score for *Breakfast at Tiffany's* (1961) and the theme for the *Pink Panther* films.

Mandela, Nelson (Rolihlahla) (1918–) South African president (1994–99), born in Transkei, South Africa. He joined the African National Congress in 1944, directed a campaign of defiance against the South African government, and in 1964 was sentenced to life imprisonment. Released in 1990, he was elected president of the African National Congress (1991–7), and was closely involved in the negotiations with President de Klerk which led to the first all-race elections in 1994. In 1993 he shared the Nobel Peace Prize with de Klerk for their work towards dismantling apartheid.

Mandela, Winnie, also **Madikizela-Mandela**, popular name of **Nomzano Zaniewe Winifred Mandela** (1934–) Former wife of Nelson Mandela, born in Bizana, South Africa. She married Mandela in 1958 (divorced 1996), and was frequently banned, detained, and jailed. She took an active role in the African National Congress until convicted on charges of kidnapping and assault. She made a political comeback in late 1993, and was given a ministerial role in the 1994 government, but was dismissed in 1995. A controversial and charismatic figure, she figured prominently in the proceedings of the Truth and Reconciliation Commission in 1997.

Mandelson, Peter (1953–) Politician, born in London. He became a Labour MP in 1992, and in 1998 was appointed president of the Board of Trade, and secretary of state for trade and industry. He resigned following his failure to declare a private mortgage loan from a cabinet colleague. Later appointed Northern Ireland Secretary, he was forced to resign again (2001) following a further controversy. He made a second political comeback in 2004 when he was appointed European Commissioner for trade.

Manet, Edouard (1832–83) Painter, born in Paris. His 'Déjeuner sur l'herbe' (1863, Luncheon on the

Grass) was rejected by the Salon, which remained hostile to him. He helped to form the group out of which the Impressionist movement arose.

Mann, Thomas (1875–1955) Novelist, born in Lübeck, Germany. His works include *Buddenbrooks* (1901), *Death in Venice* (trans, 1913; filmed 1971), *The Magic Mountain* (trans, 1924), and his greatest work, a modern version of the mediaeval legend, *Doktor Faustus* (1947). He was awarded the Nobel Prize for Literature in 1929.

Mansell, Nigel (1953–) Motor-racing driver, born in Birmingham, West Midlands. In 1992 he retired from Formula 1 racing after winning the driver's championship with eight wins, and joined the Haas-Newman Indy car racing team in the USA, becoming champion in 1993. He briefly returned to Formula 1 in 1995, driving for McLaren, then retired.

Mansfield, Katherine, pseudonym of **Kathleen Mansfield Murry**, *née* **Beauchamp** (1888–1923) Short-story writer, born in Wellington, New Zealand. In 1918 she married writer John Middleton Murry. Her chief works are *Prelude* (1917), *Bliss, and Other Stories* (1920), and *The Garden Party, and Other Stories* (1922), but she is also known for her revealing *Journal* (1927) and *Letters* (1928).

Manson, Charles (1934–) Cult leader, born in Cincinnati, OH. He set up a commune, and in 1969 members of his cult conducted a series of murders in California, including that of actress **Sharon Tate** (1943–69). He was spared the death penalty due to a Supreme Court ruling against capital punishment.

Mantel, Hilary (Mary) (1952–) Novelist, born in Hadfield, Derbyshire. Her books include *Fludd* (1989), *A Change of Climate* (1994), and *The Giant, O'Brien* (1999). In 1987 she won the first Shiva Naipaul Prize.

Mao Zedong, also spelled **Mao Tse-tung** (1893–1976) Leader of the Chinese communist revolution, born in Hunan province, the son of a farmer. He took a leading part in the May Fourth Movement (1919), then became a Marxist and a founding member of the Chinese Communist Party (1921). After the break with the Nationalists (1927), he evolved the guerrilla tactics of the 'people's war', and led the Communist forces on the Long March to Shanxi (1924). He ousted the regime of Jiang Jieshi from the Chinese mainland, and proclaimed the new People's Republic of China (1949). In 1958 he launched his Great Leap Forward in rural and agricultural development, and in 1965 the Cultural Revolution. After his death, a strong reaction set in against the excessive collectivism which had emerged, but his anti-Stalinist emphasis on rural industry and on local initiative was retained.

Maradona, Diego (1960–) Footballer, born in Lanus, Argentina. He captained Argentina to their second World Cup in 1986, only for his career to founder amid accusations of drug-taking. He returned to the World Cup side as captain in 1994, but was again suspended following a drug test. He retired in 1997.

Marat, Jean Paul (1743–93) French

revolutionary politician, born in Boudry, Switzerland. Elected to the National Convention, he became a leader of the Mountain, and advocated radical reforms. He was fatally stabbed in his bath by a Girondin supporter, Charlotte Corday; thereafter he was hailed as a martyr.

Marceau, Marcel (1923–) Mime artist, born in Strasbourg, France. In 1948 he founded the Compagnie de Mime Marcel Marceau, developing the art of mime, and becoming himself the leading exponent known especially for his white-faced character, Bip.

Marciano, Rocky, originally **Rocco Francis Marchegiano**, nickname **the Rock from Brockton** (1923–69) Heavyweight boxing champion, born in Brockton, MA. He made his name when he defeated the former world champion, Joe Louis, in 1951. When he retired in 1956 he was the only undefeated world heavyweight champion.

Marconi, Guglielmo (1874–1937) Physicist and inventor, born in Bologna, Italy. In 1899 he erected a wireless station at La Spezia, and formed the Marconi Telegraph Co in London. In 1899 he transmitted signals across the English Channel, and in 1901 across the Atlantic. He shared the Nobel Prize for Physics in 1909.

Marco Polo see Polo, Marco

Mare, Walter de la see de la Mare, Walter

Margaret (of Scotland), St (c.1046–93) Scottish queen, born in Hungary, sister of Edgar the Ætheling. She married Malcolm Canmore, and did much to assimilate the old Celtic Church to the rest of Christendom. She was canonized in 1250.

Margaret (Rose), Princess (1930–2002) British princess, born at Glamis Castle, Scotland, the second daughter of George VI. In 1960 she married Antony Armstrong-Jones (divorced, 1978), who was created Viscount Linley and Earl of Snowdon in 1961. The former title devolved upon their son, **David Albert Charles** (1961–), who married Serena Alleyne Stanhope in 1993. They also have a daughter, **Sarah Frances Elizabeth** (1964–), who married Daniel Chatto in 1994.

Margaret of Anjou (1430–82) Queen consort of Henry VI of England, probably born in Pont-à-Mousson, France. She married Henry in 1445, and owing to his mental weakness she was in effect sovereign. In the Wars of the Roses, she was defeated at Tewkesbury (1471), and imprisoned for four years in the Tower.

Margaret Tudor (1489–1541) Queen of Scotland, born in London, the eldest daughter of Henry VII. She became the wife of James IV of Scotland (1503), and the mother of James V, for whom she acted as regent.

Maria Theresa (1717–80) Archduchess of Austria, and Queen of Hungary and Bohemia (1740–80), born in Vienna, the daughter of Emperor Charles VI. In 1740 she succeeded to the Habsburg lands, her claim leading to the War of the Austrian Succession. In 1745 her husband was elected Holy Roman Emperor. Military conflict was renewed in the Seven Years' War, and in 1763 she was forced to recognize the status quo of 1756.

Marie Antoinette (Josèphe Jeanne) (1755–93) Queen of France, born in Vienna, the daughter of Maria Theresa and Francis I. She married Louis XVI (1770), and exerted a growing influence over him, arousing criticism for her extravagance and opposition to reform. In 1791 she and Louis tried to escape to Austria, but were caught and imprisoned in Paris. After the king's execution, she was later guillotined.

Marina, Princess *see* Kent, George, Duke of

Mark, St, also called **John Mark** (fl.1st-c) Christian disciple. He is described in the New Testament as 'John whose surname was Mark' (*Acts* 12.12, 25), and a helper of the apostles Barnabas and Paul during their first missionary journey. He is often considered the Mark who is accredited in 2nd-c traditions with the writing of the second Gospel.

Mark Antony *see* Antonius, Marcus

Markova, Dame Alicia, originally **Lilian Alicia Marks** (1910–2004) Prima ballerina, born in London. She danced with Ballets Russes in 1924, and in Britain formed a partnership with Anton Dolin which led to the establishment of the Markova-Dolin Company in 1935. She retired in 1963 and became a director of the Metropolitan Opera Ballet (1963–9).

Marks (of Broughton), Simon Marks, Baron (1888–1964) Businessman, born in Leeds, West Yorkshire. In 1907 he inherited the 60 penny bazaars which his father Michael Marks, with Thomas Spencer, had built up from 1884. In collaboration with Israel Sieff, he developed Marks and Spencer into a major retail chain.

Marlborough, John Churchill, 1st Duke of (1650–1722) English general, born in Ashe, Devon. In 1678 he married Sarah Jennings, a friend of Princess Anne, through whom he obtained advancement. He commanded the British forces in the War of the Spanish Succession (1701–13), winning several great victories, including Blenheim (1704) and Ramillies (1706), for which he was rewarded with Blenheim Palace and a dukedom. Forced by political interests to align himself with the Whig war party (1708), his influence waned with theirs after 1710.

Marley, Bob, popular name of **Robert Nesta Marley** (1945–81) Singer, guitarist, and composer of reggae music, born near Kingston, Jamaica. A Rastafarian, in 1965 he formed the vocal trio, The Wailers, who popularized reggae during the 1970s. His most famous songs include 'No Woman, No Cry' and 'I Shot the Sheriff'.

Marlowe, Christopher (1564–93) Playwright, born in Canterbury, Kent. His *Tamburlaine the Great* (c.1587) shows his discovery of the strength and variety of blank verse, and this was followed by *The Jew of Malta* (c.1590), *The Tragical History of Dr Faustus* (c.1592), and *Edward II* (c.1592). He was fatally stabbed in a tavern brawl.

Márquez, Gabriel (Gabo) García (1928–) Novelist, born in Aracataca, Colombia. A journalist in Europe (1950–65), he published his first novel in 1955. His best-known work is

One Hundred Years of Solitude (trans, 1967). *Love in a Time of Cholera* (trans title) appeared in 1985. He received the Nobel Prize for Literature in 1982.

Marr, Andrew (1959–) Journalist, broadcaster, and writer, born in Glasgow. He joined *The Scotsman* newspaper as a trainee business reporter in 1981, and later became political editor at *The Economist* (1988–92), editor for *The Independent* (1996), and BBC political editor (2000–5). He has presented *Start the Week* for Radio 4 since 2002, and became host of *Sunday AM* on BBC 1 in 2005.

Marryat, Frederick (1792–1848) Naval officer and novelist, born in London. He wrote novels based on his experiences of sea life, notably *Peter Simple* (1833) and *Mr Midshipman Easy* (1836). His best-known work is the children's story *The Children of the New Forest* (1847).

Marsalis, Wynton (1961–) Trumpeter and composer, born in New Orleans, LA. After many engagements as a classical virtuoso, he was recruited in 1980 to Blakey's Jazz Messengers, and left in 1982 to lead the first of a succession of small groups.

Marsh, Dame Ngaio (Edith) (1899–1982) Detective-story writer, born in Christchurch, New Zealand. Her series of novels and short stories, featuring Superintendent Roderick Alleyn of Scotland Yard, include *Vintage Murder* (1937), *Opening Night* (1951), and *Black as He's Painted* (1974).

Martin, St (c.316–c.400) Patron saint of France, born in Sabaria, Pannonia. He founded the first monastery near Poitiers (c.360), became famous for his sanctity, and was made Bishop of Tours (c.372).

Martin, Steve (1945–) Film actor, born in Waco, TX. He made his film debut in *The Absent Minded Waiter* (1977), which received an Oscar nomination for best short film. Later films include *Dirty Rotten Scoundrels* (1988), *Father of the Bride* and its sequel (1991, 1995), *Bringing Down the House* (2003), and *The Pink Panther* (2006).

Martín de Porres, St (1579–1639) South American saint, who spent his entire life in the Dominican Order in Lima, Peru, ministering to the sick and poor. Canonized in 1962, he is the patron saint of social justice.

Marvell, Andrew (1621–78) Poet, born in Winestead, Hull. He is remembered for his pastoral and garden poems, notably 'To His Coy Mistress' and 'Upon Appleton House' (c.1652–3), but he was also a pamphleteer and satirist.

Marvin, Hank *see* Shadows, The

Marx, Karl (Heinrich) (1818–83) Founder of modern international communism, born in Trier, Germany, the son of a Jewish lawyer. With Engels as his closest collaborator, he reorganized the Communist League, and in 1848 finalized the *Communist Manifesto*, which attacked the state as the instrument of oppression, and religion and culture as ideologies of the bourgeoisie. In 1849 he settled in London, where he wrote the first volume of his major work, *Das Kapital* (1867), and was a leading figure in the First International from 1864 until its demise in 1872.

Marx Brothers Family of film comedians, born in New York City, comprising **Julius** (1895–1977), or **Groucho**; **Leonard** (1891–1961), or **Chico**; **Arthur** (1893–1961), or **Harpo**; and **Herbert** (1901–79), or **Zeppo**. Another brother, **Milton** (?1897–1977), known as **Gummo**, left the act early on. Their main reputation was made in a series of films, such as *Animal Crackers* and *Monkey Business* (both 1932). Zeppo retired from films in 1935. Each had a well-defined stencil: Groucho with his wisecracks; Chico, the pianist with his own technique; and Harpo, the dumb clown and harp maestro. The team broke up in 1949.

Mary (Mother of Jesus), also known as **Our Lady** or **the Blessed Virgin Mary** (?–c.63) Mother of Jesus Christ. In the New Testament she is most prominent in the stories of Jesus's birth (Matthew and Luke), and only occasionally appears in Jesus's ministry. She remained in Jerusalem during the early years of the Church, and tradition places her tomb there. The belief that her body was taken up into heaven is celebrated in the festival of the Assumption, defined as Roman Catholic dogma in 1950. Her Immaculate Conception has been a dogma since 1854. Belief in the apparitions of the Virgin at Lourdes, Fatima, and in several other places attracts many thousands of pilgrims each year.

Mary I, Tudor (1516–58) Queen of England and Ireland (1553–8), born in Greenwich, the daughter of Henry VIII by his first wife, Catherine of Aragon. A Catholic, on her accession she repealed anti-Catholic legislation, and aimed to cement a union with Philip II of Spain. These aspirations provoked Wyatt's rebellion, followed by the execution of Jane Grey and the imprisonment of Mary's half-sister, Elizabeth.

Mary II (1662–94) Queen of Britain and Ireland from 1689, born in London, the daughter of the Duke of York (later James II) and his first wife, **Anne Hyde** (1638–71). She was married in 1677 to her cousin, William, Stadtholder of the United Netherlands. When James II fled to France, she was proclaimed queen, sharing the throne with her husband (later William III).

Mary, Queen of Scots (1542–87) Queen of Scotland (1542–67) and Queen Consort of France (1559–60), born at Linlithgow Palace, West Lothian, the daughter of James V of Scotland by his second wife, Mary of Guise. In 1565 she married her cousin, Lord Darnley, but was soon alienated from him. The murder of her secretary by Darnley and a group of Protestant nobles (1566) confirmed her insecurity, and the birth of a son (the future James VI) failed to bring a reconciliation. Darnley was mysteriously killed in 1567, the chief suspect being the Earl of Bothwell, who underwent a mock trial and was acquitted. Mary's involvement is unclear, but she consented to marry Bothwell. The Protestant nobles rose against her and she was compelled to abdicate. Placing herself under the protection of Queen Elizabeth, her presence in England gave rise to countless plots, and after the

Babington conspiracy (1586) she was executed.

Mary of Teck, in full **Victoria Mary Augusta Louise Olga Pauline Claudine Agnes** (1867–1953) Queen-consort of Great Britain, the wife of George V, born in London, the daughter of Francis, Duke of Teck. She married the king when Duke of York in 1893. After the abdication of her eldest son, Edward VIII, she strengthened the popular appeal of the monarchy throughout the reign of her second son, George VI.

Mary Magdalene, St (1st-c) Disciple of Jesus. *Magdalene* possibly means 'of Magdala', in Galilee. *Luke* 8.2 reports that Jesus exorcized seven evil spirits from her; thereafter she appears only in the narratives of Jesus's passion and resurrection.

Masefield, John (Edward) (1878–1967) Poet and novelist, born in Ledbury, Hereford and Worcester. His best-known poetical work is *Salt Water Ballads* (1902), and he also wrote novels, plays, and works for children, such as *The Box of Delights* (1935). He became poet laureate in 1930.

Mason, James (1909–84) Actor, born in Huddersfield, West Yorkshire. He was nominated for an Oscar for *A Star Is Born* (1954), *Georgy Girl* (1966), and *The Verdict* (1982), and was also acclaimed for *Lolita* (1962) and *The Shooting Party* (1984).

Massenet, Jules (Emile Frédéric) (1842–1912) Composer, born in Montaud, France. He made his name with the comic opera *Don César de Bazan* (1872) and his opera *Manon* (1884). Other works include oratorios, orchestral suites, music for piano, and songs.

Massine, Léonide, originally **Leonid Fyodorovich Miassin** (1896–1979) Ballet dancer and choreographer, born in Moscow. He was principal dancer in Diaghilev's Ballets Russes, and went on to choreograph such acclaimed works as *Parade* (1917) and *La Boutique fantasque* (1919).

Mastroianni, Marcello (1924–96) Actor, born in Fontana Liri, Italy. Fellini's *La dolce vita* (1959, The Sweet Life) established him as an international star. He received Oscar nominations for (trans titles) *Divorce, Italian Style* (1962), *A Special Day* (1977), and *Dark Eyes* (1987).

Mata Hari, (Malay 'sun'), pseudonym of **Margaretha Geertruide MacLeod**, *née* **Zelle** (1876–1917) Spy, born in Leeuwarden, The Netherlands. She became a dancer in France (1905), had many lovers – several in high military and governmental positions – and, found guilty of espionage for the Germans, was shot in Paris.

Matisse, Henri (Emile Benoît) (1869–1954) Painter, born in Le Cateau, France. From 1904 he was the leader of the Fauves, his most characteristic paintings displaying a bold use of brilliant areas of primary colour, organized within a rhythmic two-dimensional design.

Matthau, Walter, originally **Walter Matuschanskavasky** (1920–2000) US film actor, born in New York City. The son of Russian-Jewish immigrants, he began working in Yiddish theatre, then gained recognition on Broadway. His films include *The Odd*

Couple (1968), *Hello Dolly* (1969), *Cactus Flower* (1969), *Pirates* (1986), and *Hanging Up* (2000).

Matthew, St (1st-c) One of the 12 apostles in the New Testament, identified with Levi (in *Mark* 2.14 and *Luke* 5.27). According to tradition he was the author of the first Gospel, a missionary to the Hebrews, and a martyr.

Matthews, Sir Stanley (1915–2000) Footballer, born in Hanley, Staffordshire. He began his career with Stoke City (1931), before transferring to Blackpool (1947). He played for England 54 times, was twice Footballer of the Year (1948, 1963), and won the first European Footballer of the Year Award (1956).

Maugham, W(illiam) Somerset (1874–1965) Novelist, playwright, and short-story writer, born in Paris. His works include the novel *Of Human Bondage* (1915), and also *The Moon and Sixpence* (1919) and *Cakes and Ale* (1930). Best known for his short stories, *The Complete Short Stories* (3 vols) was published in 1951.

Maupassant, (Henri René Albert) Guy de (1850–93) Novelist and short-story writer, probably born at the Château de Miromesnil, Dieppe, France. He wrote some 300 short stories and several novels, including *A Woman's Life* (trans, 1883), and the autobiographical *Bel-Ami* (1885).

Maxwell, James C(lerk) (1831–79) Physicist, born in Edinburgh. In 1873 he published his great *Treatise on Electricity and Magnetism*, which gives a mathematical treatment to Faraday's theory of electrical and magnetic forces. His greatest work was his theory of electromagnetic radiation, which established him as the leading theoretical physicist of the century.

Maxwell, (Ian) Robert, originally **Ludvik Hoch** (1923–91) Publisher and politician, born in Slatinske Dòly, Czech Republic. He founded the Pergamon Press, became a Labour MP (1964–70), and chairman of the Mirror group of newspapers in 1984, but was forced to float the company on the London stock market in 1991. Following his death at sea, it transpired that he had secretly siphoned large sums of money from two of his companies and from employee pension funds.

Maxwell Davies, Sir Peter *see* Davies, Sir Peter Maxwell

Mazarin, Jules, known as **Cardinal Mazarin**, originally **Giulio Raimondo Mazzarino** (1602–61) Neapolitan clergyman, diplomat, and statesman, born in Pescine, Italy. He entered the service of Louis XIII (1639), and through Richelieu was elevated to cardinal, succeeding him as first minister (1642). Blamed by many for the Frondes, he twice fled the kingdom. He concluded the Peace of Westphalia (1648) and negotiated the Treaty of the Pyrenees (1659), ending the prolonged Franco-Spanish conflict.

Meacher, Michael (Hugh) (1939–) British statesman, born in Hemel Hempstead, Hertfordshire. He was a university lecturer before being elected Labour MP in 1970. He became a member of Labour's national executive committee (1983–8), and served as minister for the environment (1997–2003).

Mead, Margaret (1901–78) Anthropologist, born in Philadelphia, PA. She carried out field studies in the Pacific, writing academic and popular books such as *Coming of Age in Samoa* (1928) and *New Lives for Old* (1956). Increasingly she became a freelance media heavyweight, particularly well known for her views on educational and social issues.

Medawar, Sir Peter (Brian) (1915–87) Zoologist, born in Rio de Janeiro, Brazil. He pioneered experiments in the prevention of rejection in transplant operations, and in 1960 shared the Nobel Prize for Physiology or Medicine for research on immunological tolerance in relation to skin and organ grafting.

Mee, Arthur (Henry) (1875–1943) Journalist, editor, and writer, born in Stapleford, Nottinghamshire. He was most widely known for his *Children's Encyclopaedia* (1908) and *Children's Newspaper.*

Meehan, Tony *see* Shadows, The

Mehta, Zubin (1936–) Conductor, born in Mumbai (Bombay), India. His posts include conductor and musical director of the Los Angeles Philharmonic (1962–78) and the New York Philharmonic (1978–91). In 1977 he was appointed musical director of the Israel Philharmonic Orchestra, and made director for life in 1981.

Meir, Golda, originally **Goldie Myerson**, *née* **Mabovitch** (1898–1978) Israeli prime minister (1969–74), born in Kiev, Ukraine. She was minister of labour (1949–56) and foreign minister (1956–66). Her efforts for peace in the Middle East were halted by the fourth Arab–Israeli War (1973), and she was forced to resign.

Melba, Dame Nellie, professional name of **Helen Armstrong**, *née* **Mitchell** (1861–1931) Prima donna, born in Melbourne, Victoria, Australia. She appeared at Covent Garden in 1888, and the purity of her coloratura soprano voice won her worldwide fame. 'Peach Melba' and 'Melba toast' were named after her.

Melbourne, William Lamb, 2nd Viscount (1779–1848) British Whig prime minister (1834, 1835–41), born in London. He became home secretary (1830–4), and formed a close relationship with the young Queen Victoria. Defeated in the election of 1841, he resigned. His wife wrote novels as **Lady Caroline Lamb** (1785–1828).

Mellor, David (John) (1949–) British statesman. Elected a Conservative MP in 1979, he became minister for the arts (1990), chief secretary to the Treasury (1990–2), and secretary of state for national heritage (1992). He was forced to resign in 1992 following revelations about an extra-marital affair. He failed to retain his seat in the 1997 election, but was later appointed (1997–9) head of a football task force by the Labour minister for sport.

Melville, Herman (1819–91) Novelist, born in New York City. His journeys on a whaling ship were the subject matter of his first novels, *Typee* (1846) and *Omoo* (1847), and his masterpiece *Moby Dick* (1851). After 1857 he wrote only some poetry, leaving his long story, *Billy Budd, Foretopman*, in manuscript.

Mendel, Gregor (Johann) (1822–84) Biologist and botanist, born in Heinzendorf, Austria. Abbot of the Augustinian monastery in Brno (1868), he researched the inheritance characters in plants, and his experiments led to the formulation of his laws governing the nature of inheritance, which became the basis of modern genetics.

Mendelssohn(-Bartholdy), (Jakob Ludwig) Felix (1809–47) Composer, born in Hamburg, Germany, the grandson of Moses Mendelssohn. Among his early successes was the *Midsummer Night's Dream* overture (1826). A tour of Scotland inspired him with the *Hebrides* overture and the *Scottish Symphony*, and other major works include his oratorios *St Paul* (1836) and *Elijah* (1846).

Mendes, Sam(uel Alexander) (1965–) Theatre and film director, born in Reading, S England. He became artistic director of London's Donmar Warehouse (1992–2002), where he won Olivier Awards for *Company* (1996), *Uncle Vanya* (2002), and *Twelfth Night* (2002). His films include *American Beauty* (1999, two Oscars) and *Jarhead* (2005).

Menuhin, Yehudi Menuhin, Baron (1916–99) Violinist, born in New York City. A child prodigy, he went on to international renown, especially for his interpretation of Bartók and Elgar. In 1962 he founded a school for musically gifted children near London.

Mercator, Gerardus, originally **Gerhard Kremer** or **Cremer** (1512–94) Mathematician, geographer, and map-maker, born in Rupelmonde, Belgium. He is best known for introducing the map projection (1569) which bears his name, and in 1585 was the first to use the word *atlas* to describe a book of maps.

Merchant, Ismail, originally **Ismail Noormohamed Abdul Rehman** (1936–2005) Film producer, born in Mumbai (Bombay), India. In 1961 he collaborated with James Ivory in setting up a film production company, Merchant-Ivory Productions. Their films include *Shakespeare Wallah* (1965), *A Room With A View* (1985, Oscar nomination), and *The Remains of the Day* (1993).

Merckx, Eddy, nickname **the Cannibal** (1945–) Racing cyclist, born in Woluwe St Pierre, Belgium. He won the Tour de France five times (1969–72, 1974), the Tour of Italy five times, and all the major classics.

Mercouri, Melina, originally **Anna Amalia Mercouri** (1923–94) Film actress, born in Athens. She found international fame in 1960 in *Never on Sunday*. Always politically involved, she was exiled from Greece (1967–74), elected to parliament in 1977, and became minister of culture from 1981.

Merkel, Angela (Dorothea), *née* **Kasner** (1954–) German stateswoman and chancellor (2005–), born in Hamburg, Germany. In 1998 she was named Secretary-General of the Christian Democratic Union (CDU) Party, was chosen party leader in 2000, and ran unsuccessfully for the chancellorship in 2002. In the 2005 election she narrowly defeated Gerhard Schröder and became Germany's first female chancellor.

Messerschmitt, Willy, popular name of **Wilhelm Messerschmitt** (1898–1978) Aircraft engineer and designer, born in Frankfurt, Germany. During World War 2 he supplied the Luftwaffe with its foremost types of combat aircraft, and in 1944 produced the Me262 jet fighter.

Messiaen, Olivier (Eugène Prosper Charles) (1908–92) Composer and organist, born in Avignon, France. His music was motivated by religious mysticism, and he is best known for *Twenty Looks at the Infant Jesus* (trans, 1944) and the *Turangalila* symphony.

Methodius, St *see* Cyril, St

Metternich, Klemens (Wenzel Nepomuk Lothar), Fürst von (Prince of) (1773–1859) Austrian statesman, born in Koblenz, Germany. In 1809 he became foreign minister, and negotiated the marriage between Napoleon and Marie Louise. He took a prominent part in the Congress of Vienna, and between 1815 and 1848 was the most powerful influence for conservatism in Europe.

Michael, George, originally **Yorgos Kyriatou Panayiotou** (1963–) Singer and songwriter, born in Finchley, Greater London. A partner with **Andrew Ridgeley** (1963–) in the band Wham!, he released his debut solo single 'Careless Whisper' in 1985, which reached number 1 in the UK charts. His debut solo album, *Faith* (1988), stayed in the US charts for over a year. Later albums include *Ladies and Gentlemen* (1998) and *Patience* (2004).

Michelangelo, in full **Michelangelo di Lodovico Buonarroti Simoni** (1475–1564) Sculptor, painter, and poet, born in Caprese, Italy. In Florence he sculpted the marble 'David', and the 'Pietà' in the cathedral. In 1503 Julius II summoned him to Rome, where he was commissioned to design the pope's tomb, and decorated the ceiling of the Sistine Chapel with paintings (1508–12). In 1538 he was appointed architect of St Peter's, to which he devoted himself until his death.

Michelin, André (1853–1931) Tyre manufacturer, born in Paris. He and his younger brother **Edouard** (1859–1940) established the Michelin tyre company in 1888, and were the first to use demountable pneumatic tyres on motor cars.

Midler, Bette (1945–) Comedienne, actress, and singer, born in Honolulu, HI. She developed a popular nightclub act with outrageously bawdy comic routines. Her album *The Divine Miss M* (1974) won her a Best New Artist Grammy award, and among her films are *The Rose* (1979, Oscar nomination), *Scenes from a Mall* (1991), *The First Wives Club* (1996), and *The Stepford Wives* (2004).

Mies van der Rohe, Ludwig, also spelled **Miës**, originally **Ludwig Mies** (1886–1969) Architect and designer, born in Aachen, Germany. He was director of the Bauhaus at Dessau and Berlin (1930–3), and moved to Chicago in 1938. Among his major works are the Seagram Building in New York City (1956–8) and the Public Library in Washington, DC (1967). He also designed tubular-steel furniture, particularly the 'Barcelona chair'.

Mill, John Stuart (1806–73) Empiricist philosopher and social reformer, born in London, the son of James Mill. Leader of the Benthamite utilitarian movement, he helped form the Utilitarian Society. His major works include *A System of Logic* (1843), the essay *On Liberty* (1859), and *Utilitarianism* (1863).

Miller, Arthur (1915–2005) Playwright, born in New York City. His major works include *All My Sons* (1947), *Death of a Salesman* (1949, Pulitzer), and *The Crucible* (1953). His brief marriage to Marilyn Monroe (divorced 1961), and alleged early Communist sympathies, brought him considerable publicity.

Miller, (Alton) Glenn (1904–44) Trombonist and bandleader, born in Clarinda, IA. He achieved a distinctive sound with a saxophone–clarinet combination, his many successes including 'Moonlight Serenade' (his theme song), 'Little Brown Jug', and 'In the Mood' (1939). He joined the US Air Force in 1942, and took his orchestra to Europe, but he was killed while travelling in a small aircraft lost without trace over the English Channel.

Miller, Henry (Valentine) (1891–1980) Writer, born in New York City. His early books *Tropic of Cancer* (1934) and *Tropic of Capricorn* (1938), much of which is autobiographical and explicitly sexual, were not published in Britain and the USA until the early 1960s. Later work includes the series *Sexus* (1945), *Plexus* (1949), and *Nexus* (1960).

Miller, Sir Jonathan (Wolfe) (1934–) Actor, director, and writer, born in London. He qualified as a doctor, and his career has combined medical research with contributions to stage and television. He was part of the *Beyond the Fringe* team (1961–4), and has directed for several theatres, including the National Theatre, English National Opera, and the Old Vic.

Milligan, Spike, popular name of **Terence Alan Patrick Sean Milligan** (1918–2002) Humorist, born in Ahmadnagar, India. He became known as co-writer and performer in BBC radio's *The Goon Show* (1951–9). His irrepressible sense of the ridiculous was a major influence on British humour, and he published a variety of children's books, poetry, and comic novels.

Mills, Hayley (1946–) Film actress, born in London. She made her film debut in *Tiger Bay* (1959) with her father, John Mills. She won a special Oscar for her part in *Pollyanna* (1960), and went on to star in such films as *The Parent Trap* (1961), *Whistle Down The Wind* (1961), and *Appointment With Death* (1988).

Mills, Sir John (Lewis Ernest Watts) (1908–2005) Actor and director, born in Felixstowe, Suffolk. His early films include *Scott of the Antarctic* (1948) and *The Colditz Story* (1954), and for two generations he represented the figure of a fundamentally decent and reliable Englishman. He gained an Oscar for *Ryan's Daughter* in 1978. He married **Mary Hayley Bell** (1914–2005) in 1941; their daughters, Juliet and Hayley, are both actresses.

Mills, Juliet (Maryon) (1941–) Film actress, born in London, the daughter of Sir John Mills. Her films include *Carry on Jack* (1964), *Oh! What a Lovely War* (1969), and *Jonathan Livingston Seagull* (1973), as well as several television films, such as *A Stranger in the Mirror* (1993).

Milne, A(lan) A(lexander) (1882–1956) Writer, born in London. In 1924 he achieved world fame with his book of children's verse, *When We Were Very Young*, written for his son, Christopher Robin, who was immortalized with his toy bear Winnie-the-Pooh in such children's classics as *Winnie-the-Pooh* (1926).

Milosevic, Slobodan (1941–2006) President of Serbia (1990–2000) and Yugoslavia (1997–2000), born in Pozarevac, Serbia. The founder and president of the socialist party of Serbia, he became the focus of world attention during the Kosovo crisis and NATO confrontation in early 1999. In 2001 he was arrested and handed over to UN investigators to face a war crimes tribunal in The Hague. His trial began in 2002 and was ongoing in 2006, with repeated delays due to his health, but came to an unexpected end when he died in prison.

Milton, John (1608–74) Poet, born in London. His early works include *L'Allegro* and *Il Penseroso* (1632), *Comus* (1633), and *Lycidas* (1637). During the Civil War he chiefly wrote political pamphlets. Blind from 1652, after the Restoration he devoted himself wholly to poetry: his epic sacred masterpiece, *Paradise Lost* (completed in 1665), *Paradise Regained*, and *Samson Agonistes* (both 1671).

Minghella, Anthony (1954–) Director and screenwriter, born in Ryde, Isle of Wight. His credits as film director/writer include *Truly, Madly, Deeply* (1991), *The English Patient* (1996, Oscars for Best Film and Best Director), *The Talented Mr Ripley* (1999), and *Cold Mountain* (2003).

Mingus, Charles (1922–79) Jazz bassist, composer, and bandleader, born in Nogales, AZ. During the 1940s he worked with big bands, and from 1953 led groups called the 'Jazz Workshop', which experimented with atonality and other devices of European symphonic music.

Minnelli, Liza (May) (1946–) Singer and actress, born in Los Angeles, CA, the daughter of Vincente Minnelli and Judy Garland. A versatile performer, she is best known for her role in *Cabaret* (1972, Oscar), and later appeared with Dudley Moore in the *Arthur* films.

Minogue, Kylie (1968) Singer and actress, born in Melbourne, Victoria, Australia. She achieved fame for her role in the television soap opera *Neighbours*. In 1987 she began a successful recording career, and her UK number 1 hit singles include 'Can't Get You Out Of My Head' (from the album *Fever*, 2001).

Miró, Joán (1893–1983) Artist, born in Barcelona, Spain. In 1920 he settled in Paris and became a founder of Surrealism. His paintings are predominantly abstract, and his humorous fantasy makes play with a restricted range of pure colours and dancing shapes, as in 'Catalan Landscape' (1923–4).

Mirren, Dame Helen (1945–) Actress,

born in London. Her role as DCI Jane Tennison in the television series *Prime Suspect* (from 1991) made her a household name in the UK. Her feature films include *The Madness of King George* (1994), *Gosford Park* (2001), and *Calendar Girls* (2003).

Mitchell, George (John) (1933–) US lawyer and politician, born in Waterville, ME. Appointed senator for Maine in 1980, he achieved national prominence for his interrogation of Oliver North during the Iran-Contra investigation. He became internationally known as the mediator in charge of the talks in Northern Ireland leading to the Good Friday agreement in 1998, and again as the leader of the review of the peace process which led to the establishment of the devolved national Assembly in 1999.

Mitchell, Joni, *née* **Roberta Joan Anderson** (1943–) Singer and songwriter, born in McLeod, Alberta, Canada. She moved to the USA in the mid-1960s, and in 1968 recorded her first album. Many of her songs, notably 'Both Sides Now' (1971), have been recorded by other singers.

Mitchum, Robert (1917–97) Film actor, born in Bridgeport, CT. A leading man particularly associated with the post-war thriller, his films included *Night of the Hunter* (1955), *The Sundowners* (1960), *Farewell My Lovely* (1975), and *Mr North* (1988).

Mitford, Nancy (Freeman) (1904–73) Writer, born in London, the sister of Diana, Jessica, and Unity Mitford. She established a reputation with such witty novels as *The Pursuit of Love* (1945) and *Love in a Cold Climate*

(1949), and edited *Noblesse Oblige* (1956).

Mitterrand, François (Maurice Marie) (1916–96) French president (1981–95), born in Jarnac, France. He held several ministerial posts (1947–58), became a stubborn opponent of de Gaulle, and was appointed secretary of the Socialist Party in 1971. As president he embarked on a programme of nationalization and job creation in an attempt to combat stagnation and unemployment.

Mo, Timothy (Peter) (1950–) Novelist, born in Kowloon, Hong Kong. He attracted attention with his first novel, *The Monkey King* (1978), set in Hong Kong. Later books include *The Redundancy of Courage* (1991) and *Renegade or Halo Squared* (1999).

Mohammed or **Mahomet** (Western forms of Arabic **Muhammad**) (c.570– c.632) Prophet of Islam, born in Mecca, the son of Abdallah, a poor merchant. When he was 40, Gabriel appeared to him on Mt Hira, near Mecca, and commanded him in the name of God to preach the true religion. Four years later he was told to come forward publicly as a preacher, expounding the Qur'an, which had been revealed to him by God. When the Meccans rose against him, he sought refuge at Medina in 622 (the date of the Mohammedan Era, the *Hegira*), and engaged in war against the enemies of Islam. In 630 he took Mecca, where he was recognized as chief and prophet, and thus secured the new religion in Arabia. In 632 he undertook his last pilgrimage to Mecca, and there fixed the ceremonies of the pilgrimage (*Hajj*). He fell ill after his return, and died at the house of the favourite of his nine wives, Aïshah.

Molière, pseudonym of **Jean Baptiste Poquelin** (1622–73) Playwright, born in Paris. His major achievements include *The Affected Young Ladies* (trans, 1659), *The School for Wives* (trans, 1622), *Tartuffe* (1664), *The Misanthropist* (trans, 1666), and *Le Bourgeois Gentilhomme* (1670). One of the greatest French dramatists, many of his plays have been translated for performances in English theatres, giving him a considerable reputation abroad.

Molotov, Vyacheslav Mikhailovich (from Russ *molot*, 'hammer'), originally **Vyacheslav Mikhailovich Skriabin** (1890–1986) Russian prime minister (1930–41), born in Kukaida, Russia. He served as foreign minister (1939–49, 1953–6), emerging as the uncompromising champion of world Sovietism; his *nyet* ('no') at meetings of the UN became a byword, and fostered the Cold War.

Molyneux, Edward (Henry) (1891–1974) Fashion designer, born in London. He opened his own couture house in Paris in 1919, becoming famous for the elegant simplicity of his tailored suits with pleated skirts, and for his evening wear.

Mondrian, Piet, originally **Pieter Cornelis Mondriaan** (1872–1944) Artist, born in Amersfoort, The Netherlands. One of the founders of the *De Stijl* movement, he moved to Paris in 1909, his work becoming increasingly abstract. He is considered the leader of Neoplasticism.

Monet, Claude (1840–1926) Painter, born in Paris. He exhibited at the first Impressionist Exhibition in 1874, where his painting 'Impression: Sunrise' (1872) gave the name to the movement. Among his best-known works are several series of paintings of subjects under different aspects of light, such as 'Haystacks' (1890–1).

Monroe, James (1758–1831) US statesman and fifth president (1817–25), born in Westmoreland Co, VA. He recognized the Spanish American republics, and in 1823 promulgated the *Monroe Doctrine*, embodying the principle 'that the American continents ... are henceforth not to be considered as subjects for future colonization by any European power'.

Monroe, Marilyn, stage name of **Norma Jean Mortenson** or **Baker** (1926–62) Film star, born in Los Angeles, CA. After a childhood spent largely in foster homes, she became a photographer's model in 1946. She studied at Strasberg's Actors' Studio, and came to star as a sexy 'dumb blonde' in many successful films, such as *How to Marry a Millionaire* (1953), *Bus Stop* (1956) and *The Misfits* (1961), written for her by her third husband, Arthur Miller (divorced 1961). She died apparently from an overdose of sleeping pills, and has since become a symbol of Hollywood's exploitation of beauty and youth.

Monsarrat, Nicholas (John Turney) (1910–79) Novelist, born in Liverpool, Merseyside. During World War 2 he served in the navy, and out of his experiences emerged his best-selling novel, *The Cruel Sea* (1951; filmed 1953).

Montaigne, Michel (Eyquem) de (1533–92) Essayist and courtier, born at Château de Montaigne, Périgord, France. He is remembered for his *Essais* (1572–80, 1588) on the new ideas and personalities of the time, which introduced a new literary genre.

Montessori, Maria (1870–1952) Doctor and educationist, born in Rome. She opened her first 'children's house' in 1907, developing a system of education based on freedom of movement, the provision of considerable choice for pupils, and the use of specially designed activities and equipment.

Monteverdi, Claudio (1567–1643) Composer, born in Cremona, Italy. His works include eight books of madrigals (1587–1638), two operas, and the *Mass* and *Vespers of the Blessed Virgin* (1610), which contained tone colours and harmonies well in advance of their time.

Montezuma II (1466–1520) The last Aztec emperor (1502–20). A distinguished warrior and legislator, he died during the Spanish conquest of Cortés.

Montgomery (of Alamein), Bernard Law Montgomery, 1st Viscount (1887–1976) British field marshal, born in London. He commanded the 8th Army in N Africa, defeated Rommel at El Alamein (1942), played a key role in the invasion of Sicily and Italy (1943), and was appointed commander-in-chief, ground forces, for the Allied invasion of Normandy (1944). In 1945, the German forces surrendered to him on Lünenburg Heath.

Moore, Bobby, popular name of **Robert Frederick Chelsea Moore** (1941–93) Footballer, born in London. In a long career with West Ham United (1958–74) and Fulham (1974–7), he was capped a record 108 times, 90 of them as captain, a total later surpassed by Peter Shilton. He led the victorious England side in the 1966 World Cup.

Moore, Demi, originally **Demetria Guynes** (1962–) Film actress, born in Roswell, NM. She became well known following her role in *Ghost* (1990), later films including *The Butcher's Wife* (1991), *A Few Good Men* (1992), *Indecent Proposal* (1992), and *The Scarlet Letter* (1995). She was married to actor Bruce Willis (1987–98).

Moore, Dudley (Stuart John) (1935–2002) Actor, comedian, and musician, born in London. One of the *Beyond the Fringe* team (1960–64), he joined Peter Cook for the TV series *Not Only... But Also* (1964–70). His films include *10* (1979), *Arthur* (1981) and *Santa Claus – The Movie* (1985). An accomplished musician, he performed with his own jazz piano trio, and composed for several films and plays.

Moore, Henry (Spencer) (1898–1986) Sculptor, born in Castleford, West Yorkshire. His style is based on the organic forms and undulations found in landscape and natural rocks, and influenced by primitive African and Mexican art. Major collections can be seen at the Henry Moore Sculpture Center, Toronto,

The Tate Gallery, London, and at his home in Much Hadham, Hertfordshire.

Moore, Sir John (1761–1809) British soldier, born in Glasgow. He commanded the English army in Spain (1808–9), where he was forced to retreat to Coruña. There he defeated a French attack, but was mortally wounded (as recounted in the poem by Wolfe).

Moore, Julianne, originally **Julie Anne Smith** (1961–) Actress, born in Fayetteville, NC. She became known for her role in the TV soap *As The World Turns* (1985–8). Film credits include *The Hand That Rocks the Cradle* (1991) and *The Hours* (2002). She has twice been nominated for a Best Actress Oscar, for *Boogie Nights* (1997) and *Far From Heaven* (2002).

Moore, Michael (1954–) Film director, producer, and writer, born in Davison, Flint, MI. He began film-making with the groundbreaking documentary *Roger and Me* (1989). Later films, exploring topical issues in American society, include *Canadian Bacon* (1995), *Bowling for Columbine* (2002), and *Fahrenheit 911* (2004). Among his books is the best-selling *Stupid White Men* (2001).

Moore, Sir Patrick (Alfred Caldwell) (1923–) Amateur astronomer, writer, broadcaster, and musician, born in Pinner, Greater London. He is best known as the enthusiastic and knowledgeable presenter of the long-running BBC television programme *The Sky at Night* (1957–).

Moore, Sir Roger (George) (1927–) Film star, born in London. On television he won stardom as the hero of such series as *Ivanhoe* (1958), and *The Saint* (1962–9), and brought a lightweight insouciance to the role of James Bond in seven films between *Live and Let Die* (1973) and *A View to a Kill* (1985).

Moors Murderers *see* Brady, Ian

Mordecai (c.5th-c BC) Biblical hero. He is described in the Book of Esther as a Jew in exile in Persia, who gained the favour of King Xerxes, and used his influence to protect Jews from an edict issued against them. The event is commemorated by the annual Jewish feast of Purim.

More, Sir Thomas, also **St Thomas More** (1478–1535) English statesman and scholar, born in London. On the fall of Wolsey (1529), he became Lord Chancellor, but resigned in 1532 following his opposition to Henry's break with the Roman Catholic Church. On refusing to recognize Henry as head of the English Church, he was beheaded. A leading humanist scholar, as revealed in his Latin *Utopia* (1516), he was canonized in 1935.

Morecambe, Eric, originally **Eric Bartholomew** (1926–84) Comedian, born in Morecambe, Lancashire. He teamed up in 1943 with fellow entertainer, **Ernie Wise** (originally **Ernest Wiseman**) (1925–99), and as **Morecambe and Wise**, they became the leading British comedy double-act known especially for their shows on television.

Morgan, Edwin (George) (1920–) Poet, born in Glasgow. A versatile writer, he has produced powerful 'social' poems as well as much experimental writing. His work includes *Poems of Thirty Years* (1982), *You: Anti-War Poetry* (1991), and *Collected Poems* (1996). In 2004 he was appointed to the newly created post of national poet of Scotland.

Morgan, Sir Henry (c.1635–88) Buccaneer, born in Llanrumney, S Wales. Kidnapped as a child, he joined the buccaneers, leading many raids against the Spanish and Dutch in the West Indies and Central America. He later became Deputy Governor of Jamaica.

Morley, Robert (1908–92) Actor and writer, born in Semley, Wiltshire. In his film career, from 1938, he played many individual character parts, including the title role in *The Trials of Oscar Wilde* (1960). He was well known for his edited collections, such as *Robert Morley's Book of Bricks* (1979).

Morris, Desmond (John) (1928–) British zoologist and writer, born near Swindon, Wiltshire. His study of human behaviour in *The Naked Ape* (1967) became a best seller, and was followed by many television programmes on animal and social behaviour. Later books include *The Human Zoo* (1969), *Manwatching* (1977), *The Soccer Tribe* (1981), and *The Naked Woman* (2004).

Morris, Estelle (1952–) British stateswoman, born in Manchester, Greater Manchester. A teacher, she was elected a Labour MP in 1992, and became minister of state for the Department for Education and Employment (1997–8), minister for school standards (1997–2001), secretary of state for education and skills

(2001–2), and arts minister (2003–5). She resigned as an MP in 2005.

Morris, William (1834–96) Craftsman, poet, and political activist, born in Walthamstow, Greater London. Associated with the Pre-Raphaelite Brotherhood, in 1861 he founded the firm of Morris, Marshall, Faulkner & Co, which revolutionized the art of house decoration and furniture in England, and in 1890 he founded the Kelmscott Press. He also organized the Socialist League.

Morrison, Toni, née **Chloe Anthony Wofford** (1931–) Novelist, born in Lorain, OH. Her early titles include *The Bluest Eye* (1970) and *Song of Solomon* (1977). Two later novels, *Tar Baby* (1981) and *Beloved* (Pulitzer, 1988), confirmed her as a leading novelist of her generation, and she received the Nobel Prize for Literature in 1993.

Morrison, Van, popular name of **George Ivan Morrison** (1945–) Singer, musician, and songwriter, born in Belfast. His first solo hit was 'Brown-Eyed Girl' (1967) and a year later he released the highly acclaimed, surreal album *Astral Weeks*. Later albums include *The Healing Game* (1996), *Down the Road* (2002), and *Magic Time* (2005).

Mortensen, Viggo (1958–) Actor, born in Manhattan, NY. His film debut was in *Witness* (1985), but it was for his later role as the brave warrior Aragorn in *The Lord of the Rings* trilogy (2001–3) that he became well known. Later films include *Hidalgo* (2004) and *A History of Violence* (2005).

Mortimer, Sir John (Clifford) (1923–)

Playwright, novelist, and barrister, born in London. He came to public prominence as a dramatist with his one-act play *The Dock Brief* (1957), and his television screenplays include *I, Claudius* (1976) and *Brideshead Revisited* (1981). His novels featuring the disreputable barrister, Horace Rumpole, were adapted for television as *Rumpole of the Bailey*.

Morton, Jelly Roll, popular name of **Ferdinand Lemott** (1890–1941) Jazz pianist, composer, and bandleader, born in Gulfport, LA. His unaccompanied piano solos made best sellers of such tunes as 'King Porter Stomp' and 'Jelly Roll Blues', and he made powerful orchestral arrangements for his band, The Red Hot Peppers.

Moses (c.13th-c BC) Major character of Israelite history, portrayed in the Book of Exodus as the leader of the deliverance of Hebrew slaves from Egypt and the recipient of the divine revelation at Mt Sinai. Stories about his early life depict his escape from death as an infant, his upbringing in the Egyptian court, and his prediction of a series of miraculous plagues to persuade the Pharaoh to release the Hebrews. Traditions then describe Moses' leadership of the Israelites during their 40 years of wilderness wanderings.

Mosley, Nicholas, Baron Ravensdale (1923–) Writer, born in London. His novels include *Spaces of the Dark* (1951), *The Rainbearers* (1955), *Accident* (1964; filmed 1967), *Hopeful Monsters* (1990, Whitbread), and *Children of Darkness and Light* (1996).

Mosley, Sir Oswald (Ernald) (1896–1980) Politician, born in Lon-

don. He became leader of the British Union of Fascists, remembered for its anti-Semitic violence and its support for Hitler. Detained under the Defence Regulations during World War 2, in 1948 he founded another racialist party, the Union Movement.

Moss, Sir Stirling (1929–) Motorracing driver, born in London. He won many major races in the 1950s, but never a world title, though he was runner-up twice. A bad crash at Goodwood in 1962 ended his career.

Motion, Andrew (1952–) Poet, born in London. In 1995 he became professor of creative writing at the University of East Anglia. His works include *Selected Poems 1976–1997* (1998) and *Public Property* (2002), and he is also a biographer and novelist. He was made poet laureate in 1999.

Mountbatten (of Burma), Louis (Francis Albert Victor Nicholas) Mountbatten, 1st Earl (1900–79) British admiral and statesman, born in Windsor, S England, the younger son of Prince Louis of Battenberg and Princess Victoria of Hesse, the granddaughter of Queen Victoria. He became chief of Combined Operations Command (1942), and played a key role in preparations for D-Day. In 1943 he was appointed supreme commander in SE Asia, where he defeated the Japanese offensive into India (1944), and worked with Slim to reconquer Burma (1945). He received the Japanese surrender at Singapore, and in 1947 became last Viceroy of India prior to independence. He was assassinated by Irish terrorists.

Mountbatten, Prince Philip *see* Edinburgh, Duke of

Mouskouri, Nana (1934–) Singer, born in Chania, Crete, Greece. She made her first record in Greece in 1959, and went on to record 'The White Rose of Athens' (1962), which became a major European hit.

Moussorgsky, Modest (Petrovich), also spelled **Mussorgsky** or **Musorgsky** (1839–81) Composer, born in Karevo, Russia. His chief works are the opera *Boris Godunov* (1874) and the piano suite *Pictures from an Exhibition* (1874). Rimsky-Korsakov arranged or completed many of his unfinished works.

Mowlem, Mo, popular name of **Marjorie Mowlem** (1949–2005) British stateswoman, born in Watford, Hertfordshire. She became a Labour MP in 1987, and was appointed secretary of state for Northern Ireland (1997–9), and minister for the cabinet office and chancellor of the Duchy of Lancaster (1999–2001). She played a key part in achieving the Good Friday Agreement and in the establishment of the Northern Ireland Assembly.

Mozart, Wolfgang Amadeus (1756–91) Composer, born in Salzburg, Austria. A child prodigy, he toured Europe as a pianist when he was six. After some years in Salzburg he settled in Vienna. After his operas *The Marriage of Figaro* (1786) and *Don Giovanni* (1787), he was appointed court composer to Joseph II. Other major operas include *Così fan tutte* (1790) and *The Magic Flute* (1791). He wrote over 600 compositions (indexed by Köchel), including 41 symphonies, a Requiem Mass, and many concertos, string quartets, and sonatas.

Mugabe, Robert (Gabriel) (1924–) Zimbabwean prime minister (1980–) and president (1987–), born in Kutama, Zimbabwe. In 1963 he co-founded the Zimbabwe African National Union (ZANU), and joined with Nkomo in 1976 to form the Patriotic Front. Formerly a pragmatic Marxist, intending to turn Zimbabwe into a one-party state, multi-party elections were held in 1990, and references to 'Marxism–Leninism' were dropped from the 1991 constitution. He came to world attention in 2000 for initiating a land redistribution policy aimed at local white farmers, which was internationally condemned. He won a fifth term in office in 2002, but controversy surrounding the election process led to Zimbabwe's suspension from the Commonwealth, and later its withdrawal.

Muggeridge, (Thomas) Malcolm (1903–90) Journalist and sage, born in London. He was editor of *Punch* (1953–7), and appeared in several television series, such as *Let Me Speak* (1964–5). In 1982 he became a Roman Catholic, and wrote *Chronicle of Wasted Time*.

Muhammad *see* Mohammed

Muir, Frank (1920–98) Writer and broadcaster, born in London. He joined Denis Norden to become one of the best-known teams of comedy script-writers (1947–64), contributing to many shows on radio and television.

Muir, Jean (Elizabeth) (1933–95) Fashion designer, born in London. In

1966 she established her own company, Jean Muir, designing clothes noted for classic shapes, softness, and fluidity.

Mulligan, Gerry, popular name of **Gerald Joseph Mulligan** (1927–96) Jazz musician, born in New York City. A technically accomplished musician, he experimented to produce a distinctive sound which proved popular and commercially successful. His motion pictures include *Jazz on a Summer's Day* (1958).

Munch, Edvard (1863–1944) Painter, born in Löten, Norway. He was obsessed by subjects such as death and love, which he illustrated in an Expressionist Symbolic style, using bright colours and a tortuously curved design, as in 'The Scream' (1893).

Münchhausen, (Karl Friedrich Hieronymus), Freiherr von (Baron) (1720–97) Soldier, born in Bodenwerder, Germany. Proverbial as the narrator of ridiculously exaggerated exploits, he served in Russian campaigns against the Turks. A collection of stories attributed to him was produced in 1785 by **Rudolf Erich Raspe** (1737–94).

Munro, H(ector) H(ugh), pseudonym **Saki** (1870–1916) Writer, born in Akyab, Myanmar (formerly Burma). He is best known for his humorous and macabre short stories, as collected in *Reginald* (1904) and *Beasts and Superbeasts* (1914).

Murdoch, Dame (Jean) Iris (1919–99) Novelist and philosopher, born in Dublin. Her many novels include *Under the Net* (1954), *The Bell* (1958), and *The Sea, The Sea* (1978, Booker).

She also wrote plays, philosophical works, and critical studies.

Murdoch, (Keith) Rupert (1931–) Media proprietor, born in Melbourne, Victoria, Australia. He built a substantial newspaper and magazine publishing empire, including the *News of the World*, *The Sun*, *The Times*, and the *New York Post*. He also has major business interests in other media industries, and is owner of satellite broadcaster BSkyB in the UK.

Murphy, Eddie, popular name of **Edward Reagan Murphy** (1961–) Comic actor, born in New York City. His films include *Trading Places* (1983), *Beverly Hills Cop* and its sequel (1984, 1987), *Dr Dolittle* (1998), and *Daddy Day Care* (2003), and he made his directorial debut with *Harlem Nights* (1989).

Murphy-O'Connor, Cormac, Cardinal (1932–) Roman Catholic cardinal, born in Reading, England. He was appointed to the English College as rector (1971–7), became Bishop of Arundel and Brighton in 1997, and in 2000 Archbishop of Westminster. He was made a cardinal in 2001.

Murray, Andy (1987–) Tennis player, born in Dunblane, Perthshire. In 2004 he won the junior men's singles title at the US Open, turned professional in 2005, and that year became Britain's youngest Davis Cup player. In 2006 he won the San Jose Open, after which he became Britain's number 1 when his ranking rose to 42.

Murray, Bill, popular name of **William James Murray** (1950–) Actor, born in Wilmette, IL. He began his career on the 1970s US TV comedy show *Saturday Night Live*, and became known for his film role in *Ghostbusters* (1984). Later films include *Groundhog Day* (1993), *Lost in Translation* (2003, BAFTA, Golden Globe, Oscar nomination), and *Broken Flowers* (2005).

Mussolini, Benito (Amilcare Andrea), known as **il Duce** ('the Leader') (1883–1945) Dictator and prime minister of Italy (1922–43), born in Predappio, Romagna. In 1919 he helped found the *Fasci di Combattimento* as a revolutionary force, his success symbolized by the March on Rome (1922). His rule saw the introduction of a totalitarian system, and the formation of the Axis with Germany. His declaration of war on Britain and France was followed by defeat in Africa and the Balkans, and after the Allied invasion of Sicily (1943) he was overthrown and arrested (1943). Rescued by German paratroopers, he was placed in charge of the puppet Italian Social Republic, but in 1945 was captured by the Italian Resistance and shot.

Mussorgsky, Modest *see* Moussorgsky, Modest

Mustapha Kemal Atatürk *see* Atatürk, Mustafa Kemal

Myers, Mike (1963–) Actor, comedian, writer, and director, born in Scarborough, Ontario, Canada. A comedian on the television programme *Saturday Night Live* in 1988, he introduced the character 'Wayne Campbell'. He took the character to the big screen in the film *Wayne's World* (1992), and later films include three *Austin Powers* movies (1997, 1999, 2002), and the voice of Shrek (*Shrek*, 2001, 2004).

Nabokov, Vladimir (Vladimirovich) (1899–1977) Writer, born in St Petersburg, Russia. He emigrated to the USA where he published many short stories and novels, including the controversial *Lolita* (1958; filmed 1962), *Pale Fire* (1962), and a lyrical autobiography, *Speak Memory* (1967). Among 20th-c novelists he is highly regarded for his linguistic versatility and intellectual range.

Naipaul, Sir V(idiadhar) S(urajprasad) (1932–) Novelist, born in Chaguanas, Trinidad. He became known with *A House for Mr Biswas* (1961), a satire spanning three Trinidadian generations. Other works include *In a Free State* (1971, Booker), *A Bend in the River* (1979), and *Magic Seeds* (2004). He received the Nobel Prize for Literature in 2001.

Nanak, known as **Guru Nanak** (1469–1539) Religious leader, the founder of Sikhism, born near Lahore, India. A Hindu by birth and belief, he travelled to Hindu and Muslim centres in search of spiritual truth. His doctrine, set out later in the *Adi-Granth*, sought a fusion of Brahmanism and Islam.

Naomi (Heb 'my delight') Biblical character described in the stories of the Book of Ruth as the mother-in-law of Ruth and Orpah. After Naomi was widowed, she returned from Moab to Bethlehem with her daughters-in-law, and attempted to arrange the marriage of Ruth with Boaz, one of the secondary kinsmen of Naomi's deceased husband. The offspring of this union was said to be the grandfather of David.

Napier, John (1550–1617) Mathematician, born at Merchiston Castle, Edinburgh. He invented logarithms and also devised a calculating machine, using a set of rods called *Napier's bones*.

Napoleon I, Fr **Napoléon Bonaparte**, Ital **Napoleone Buonaparte** (1769–1821) French general and emperor (1804–15), born in Ajaccio, Corsica. He commanded the artillery at the siege of Toulon (1793), and in 1796 married Joséphine, widow of the Vicomte de Beauharnais. In the Revolutionary Wars he made gains in Italy, but his fleet was destroyed at the Battle of the Nile (1798). After the *coup d'état* of 18th Brumaire (1799) he assumed dictatorial power as First Consul, routing the Austrians at Marengo (1800), and consolidated French domination by the Peace of Amiens (1802). He assumed the title of emperor in 1804. War with England was renewed, and extended to Russia and Austria. Forced by England's naval supremacy at Trafalgar (1805) to abandon the notion of invasion, he defeated Austria, Russia, and Prussia (1805–7), becoming the arbiter of Europe. He sent armies into Portugal and Spain, which resulted in the unsuccessful Peninsular War (1808–14). In 1809 he divorced the childless Joséphine, and married Marie Louise of Austria, a son being born in 1811. He invaded Russia, but was forced to retreat (1812), and abdicated after defeat at Leipzig. He regained power for a time (the Hundred Days), but after defeat at Waterloo (1815), he again abdicated, and was banished to St Helena.

Napoleon III, until 1852 **Louis Napoleon**, originally **Charles Louis Napoleon Bonaparte** (1808–73) President of the Second French Republic (1848–52) and emperor of the French (1852–70), born in Paris, the third son of Louis Bonaparte and Hortense Beauharnais. He made abortive attempts on the French throne (1836, 1840) and was imprisoned, but after the 1848 Revolution was elected president, and assumed the title of emperor. He declared war on Prussia in 1870, but was defeated and went into exile.

Nash, John (1752–1835) Architect, born in London. He designed Regent's Park (1811–25) and Marble Arch, laid out Trafalgar Square and St James's Park, and recreated Buckingham Palace from old Buckingham House.

Nash, (Frederic) Ogden (1902–71) Humorous writer, born in Rye, NY. His subject-matter was the everyday life of middle-class America, which he described in a witty and acute manner taking outrageous rhyming liberties with the English language, frequently published in the *New Yorker*. His collections include *Hard Lines* (1931).

Nasser, Gamal Abdel (1918–70) Egyptian prime minister (1954–6) and president (1956–70), born in Alexandria. Dissatisfied with the corruption of the Farouk regime, he was involved in the military coup of 1952. He nationalized the Suez Canal, which prompted Britain and France to seek his forcible overthrow, and created a federation with Syria as the United Arab Republic (1958–61). He resigned after the six-day Arab–Israeli War (1967), but was persuaded to stay on, and died in office.

Nathanael, (Heb 'God has given') (fl.1st-c) New Testament character, who appears only in *John* (1:45–51). He is said to have been brought to Jesus by Philip, and is one of the first to confess Jesus as 'Son of God, King of Israel'.

Naughtie, (Alexander) James (1951–) Journalist and broadcaster, born in Milltown of Rothiemay, Aberdeenshire. He became presenter of the BBC's *The World At One* (1988–94), and joined Radio 4's *Today* team in 1994. He has also presented several documentary series, such as *The Thin Blue Line* (1993).

Navratilova, Martina (1956–) Tennis player, born in Prague. The winner of a record nine singles titles at Wimbledon (1978–9, 1982–7, 1990), she won 167 singles titles (including 18 Grand Slam events) and 165 doubles titles with her partner Pam Shriver (including 37 Grand Slam events), becoming the most prolific winner in women's tennis. In 2003 she secured a record-equalling 20th Wimbledon title when she won the mixed doubles final.

Nebuchadnezzar II, also spelled **Nebuchadrezzar** (c.630–562 BC) King of Babylon (605–562 BC). During his 43-year reign he rebuilt Babylon as a supreme nation, and in 597 captured Jerusalem, later deporting the Jews to Babylonia (586 BC).

Neeson, Liam (1952–) Film actor, born in Ballymena, Northern Ireland. He received an Oscar nomination for his role as Schindler in *Schindler's List* (1993), and later films include *Michael Collins* (1996), *Batman Begins* (2005), and *The Chronicles of Narnia* (2005).

Nefertiti (14th-c BC) Egyptian queen, the consort of Akhenaten, by whom she had six children. She is immortalized in the beautiful sculptured head found at Amarna in 1912.

Nehru, Jawaharlal, known as **Pandit** ('Teacher') **Nehru** (1889–1964) India's first prime minister (1947–64), born in Allahabad, India, the son of Motilal Nehru. He introduced a policy of industrialization, reorganized the states on a linguistic basis, and brought the dispute with Pakistan over Kashmir to a peaceful solution.

Nelson, Horatio (1758–1805) British admiral, born in Burnham Thorpe, Norfolk. In 1794 while commanding a naval brigade he lost the sight of his right eye, and later had his right arm amputated. In 1798 he followed the French fleet to Egypt, destroying it at Aboukir Bay. On his return to Naples, he fell in love with Emma, Lady Hamilton, and began a liaison with her which lasted until his death. In 1805 he gained his greatest victory, against the combined French and

Spanish fleet at Trafalgar, but was mortally wounded on his flagship, HMS *Victory*.

Nelson, Willie (Hugh) (1933–) Country singer, songwriter, and guitarist, born in Abbott, TX. After writing and recording many country-music hits in the 1960s, he later gained a wider audience with such albums as *Shotgun Willie* (1972) and *Stardust* (1978).

Neri, St Philip (1515–95) Mystic, born in Florence, Italy. In 1551 he became a priest, and gathered around him a following of disciples which became the Congregation of the Oratory (1564). He was canonized in 1622.

Nero, in full **Nero Claudius Caesar**, originally **Lucius Domitius Ahenobarbus** (37–68) Emperor of Rome (54–68), the son of Gnaeus Domitius Ahenobarbus and the younger Agrippina, daughter of Germanicus. His mother engineered his adoption by the Emperor Claudius, her fourth husband. After her murder (59), Nero neglected affairs of state, corruption set in, and he was blamed for the Great Fire of Rome (64). He was toppled from power by the army, and forced to commit suicide.

Nesbit, E(dith), maiden name and pseudonym of **Mrs Hubert Bland** (1858–1924) Writer, born in London. She is best remembered for her children's stories, notably *The Railway Children* (1906; filmed 1970), but she also wrote novels and ghost stories.

Netanyahu, Binyamin, nicknamed in Israel **Bibi** (1949–) Israeli prime minister (1996–9), born in Tel Aviv, Israel. He was elected to the Israeli parliament in 1988, becoming leader of the Likud Party in 1993. A hardliner on security issues, he campaigned on a platform of peace with security, and defeated Shimon Peres by a narrow margin in the 1996 elections.

Newcastle, Duke of see Pelham, Thomas

Newcomen, Thomas (1663–1729) Inventor, born in Dartmouth, Devon. By 1698 he had invented the atmospheric steam engine, and from 1712 this device was being used for pumping water out of mines.

Newman, John Henry, Cardinal (1801–90) Theologian, born in London into a Calvinist family. A vigorous member of the Oxford Movement, he composed a number of its tracts. A convert to Catholicism (1845), he joined the Oratorians, published a spiritual autobiography, *Apology for His Life* (trans, 1864), and was made a cardinal (1879).

Newman, Nanette (1934–) Actress and writer, born in Northampton, Northamptonshire. In 1959 she married Bryan Forbes, and appeared in a number of his films including *The L-Shaped Room* (1962) and *The Stepford Wives* (1974). Her popular books include *God Bless Love* (1972).

Newman, Paul (Leonard) (1925–) Film actor and director, born in Cleveland, OH. His many films include *Cool Hand Luke* (1967), *Butch Cassidy and the Sundance Kid* (1969), *The Sting* (1973), *The Color of Money* (1986, Oscar), and *Road to Perdition* (2002). He married the actress Joanne Woodward in 1958.

Newman, Randy, popular name of **Randall Stuart Newman** (1943–) Singer and songwriter, born in Los Angeles, CA. He established himself as a major songwriter, with something of a cult following, before his debut vocal album *Randy Newman* (1968). Later albums included *Sail Away* (1972), *Land of Dreams* (1988), and *Bad Love* (1999).

Newton, Sir Isaac (1642–1727) Physicist and mathematician, born in Woolsthorpe, Lincolnshire. In 1665–6 the fall of an apple is said to have suggested the train of thought that led to the law of gravitation. He studied the nature of light, and devised the first reflecting telescope. His *Mathematical Principles of Natural Philosophy* (trans, 1687) established him as the greatest of all physical scientists. He was involved in many controversies, notably with Leibniz over the question of priority in the discovery of calculus.

Nicholas, St (4th-c) Bishop of Myra, Lucia, and patron saint of Russia. His identification with Father Christmas began in Europe, and spread to America, where the name was altered to *Santa Claus*.

Nichols, Mike, originally **Michael Igor Peschkowsky** (1931–) Film and theatre director, born in Berlin. A US citizen from 1944, he has won seven Tony Awards for his theatre work, which includes *The Odd Couple* (1965). He also directed the hit musical, *Annie* (1977), and his films include *The Graduate* (1967, Oscar), *Catch-22* (1970), and *Closer* (2004). Television work includes *Angels in America* (2004, Emmy).

Nicholson, Jack (1937–) Film actor, born in Neptune, NJ. His major films include *One Flew Over the Cuckoo's*

Nest (1975, Oscar), *The Shining* (1980), *Terms of Endearment* (1983, Oscar), *The Witches of Eastwick* (1987), *About Schmidt* (2002, Golden Globe, Oscar nomination), and *Something's Gotta Give* (2003).

Nicklaus, Jack (William) (1940–) Golfer, born in Columbus, OH. His tournament wins include the (British) Open (1966, 1970, 1978), the US Open (1962, 1967, 1972, 1980), the US Professional Golfers Association a record-equalling five times (1963, 1971, 1973, 1975, 1980), and the US Masters a record six times (1963, 1965–6, 1972, 1975, 1986).

Nietzsche, Friedrich (Wilhelm) (1844–1900) Philosopher and critic, born in Röcken, Germany. His major work, *Thus Spake Zarathustra* (trans, 1883–5), develops the idea of the 'overman'. Much of his esoteric doctrine appealed to the Nazis, and he was a major influence on existentialism.

Nightingale, Florence, known as **the Lady of the Lamp** (1820–1910) Hospital reformer, born in Florence, Italy. She led a party of 38 nurses to organize a nursing department at Scutari, where she soon had 10 000 wounded under her care. She later formed an institution for the training of nurses, in London.

Nijinska, Bronislava (1891–1972) Ballet dancer and choreographer, born in Minsk, Belarus, the sister of Vaslav Nijinsky. She danced with the Diaghilev company in Paris and London (1909–14), and in 1921 joined Diaghilev as principal choreographer. After 1938 she worked mainly in the USA.

Nijinsky, Vaslav (1890–1950) Ballet dancer, born in Kiev, Ukraine, brother of Bronislava Nijinska. As the leading dancer in Diaghilev's Ballets Russes, he became phenomenally successful. His choreographic work included *The Rite of Spring* (trans, 1913), regarded as outrageous at the time.

Nimoy, Leonard (1931–) Actor, director, producer, and writer, born in Boston, MA. He came to be identified with the half-Vulcan/half-human character of Spock in the *Star Trek* series (1966–9). His work as a director includes *Three Men and a Baby* (1987) and *Holy Matrimony* (1994).

Nin, Anaïs (1903–77) Writer, born in Neuilly, France. Her early work includes novels and short stories, but her reputation as an artist and seminal figure in the new feminism of the 1970s rests on her sexually explicit *Journals* (1966–83).

Niro, Robert De *see* De Niro, Robert

Niven, David, popular name of **James David Graham Nevins** (1909–83) Actor, born in Kirriemuir, Angus. He became established in urbane romantic roles with an English style, his films including *Around the World in 80 Days* (1956), *Separate Tables* (1958, Oscar), *The Guns of Navarone* (1961), and *55 Days at Peking* (1963).

Nixon, Richard (Milhous) (1913–94) US Republican statesman and 37th president (1969–74), born in Yorba Linda, CA. He lost the 1960 election to Kennedy, but won in 1968, and was re-elected in 1972. He resigned in 1974 under the threat of impeachment, after several leading members of his government had been found guilty of involvement in the Watergate affair, but was given a full pardon by President Ford.

Noah Biblical character, depicted as the son of Lamech. He is described as a 'righteous man' who was given divine instruction to build an ark in which he, his immediate family, and a selection of animals were saved from a widespread flood over the Earth (*Gen* 6–9).

Nobel, Alfred Bernhard (1833–96) Chemist and industrialist, born in Stockholm. In 1866 he discovered how to make a safe and manageable form of nitroglycerin he called *dynamite*, and also invented smokeless gunpowder and (1875) gelignite. He left much of his fortune to endow annual prizes for physics, chemistry, physiology or medicine, literature, and peace.

Norden, Denis (1922–) British scriptwriter and broadcaster. With Frank Muir he formed a comedy scriptwriting duo (1947–64), contributing to many shows, such as *Take It From Here* (1947–58). He is well known as the television presenter of *It'll Be Alright on the Night* (1977–).

Norman, Barry (Leslie) (1933–) Writer and television film critic, born in London. In 1973 he joined BBC television as host of *Film '73*, then wrote and presented the show (1973–81, 1983–97) until joining Sky television in 1998. Other work includes the series *The Hollywood Greats* (1977–9, 1984–5).

Norman, Greg(ory John), nickname **the Great White Shark** (1955–) Golfer, born in Mount Isa, Queensland, Australia. He won the Aus-

tralian Open (1980, 1985, 1987), the (British) Open (1986, 1993), and the World Match Play Championship (1986).

North, Frederick, 8th Baron North (1732–92) British prime minister (1770–82), born in London. He was widely criticized both for failing to avert the Declaration of Independence by the North American colonies (1776) and for failing to defeat them in the subsequent war (1776–83).

Northcliffe, Lord *see* Harmsworth, Alfred

Nostradamus, Latin name of **Michel de Notredame** (1503–66) Physician and astrologer, born in St Rémy, France. His *Centuries* of enigmatic predictions in rhymed quatrains (two collections, 1555–8) brought him fame, and continue to be referred to today.

Novak, Kim, originally **Marilyn Pauline Novak** (1933–) Film actress, born in Chicago, IL. She became a leading box-office attraction of the 1950s – perhaps the last of the 'sex goddesses' produced by the Hollywood star system. Her films include *The Man With The Golden Arm* (1955), *Pal Joey* (1957), and *Vertigo* (1958).

Novello, Ivor, originally **David Ivor Davies** (1893–1951) Actor, composer, songwriter, and playwright, born in Cardiff. His most characteristic works were his 'Ruritanian' musical plays such as *Glamorous Night* (1935), *The Dancing Years* (1939), and *King's Rhapsody* (1949).

Nunn, Sir Trevor (Robert) (1940–) Stage director, born in Ipswich, Suffolk. His directorship of the Royal Shakespeare Company (1968–87) saw the opening of two new theatres in Stratford: The Other Place (1974) and The Swan (1986). He also directed the musicals *Cats* (1981), *Starlight Express* (1984), and *Aspects of Love* (1989). From 1997–2003 he was director of the Royal National Theatre.

Nureyev, Rudolf (Hametovich) (1938–93) Ballet dancer, born in Irkutsk, Russia. While touring with the Kirov Ballet in 1961, he obtained political asylum in Paris. He made his debut at Covent Garden with the Royal Ballet in 1962, and formed a famous partnership with Fonteyn. He was ballet director of the Paris Opéra (1983–9) and principal choreographer (1989–92).

Nyman, Michael (1944–) Pianist and composer, born in London. He formed the Michael Nyman Band in 1977, for which he composed several works in which his own piano playing is a driving force. His compositions include scores for the films of Peter Greenaway, and for the films *The Piano* (1993), *Carrington* (1995), and *The Libertine* (2004).

Oakley, Annie, popular name of **Phoebe Anne Oakley Moses** (1860–1926) Rodeo star and sharpshooter, born in Darke Co, OH. She formed a trick-shooting act with her husband, Frank E Butler, and from 1885 they toured with the Buffalo Bill Wild West Show. Her story was fictionalized in the Irving Berlin musical comedy *Annie Get Your Gun* (1946), starring Ethel Merman.

Oates, Lawrence (Edward Grace) (1880–1912) Explorer, born in London. In 1910 he joined Scott's Antarctic Expedition, and was one of the party of five to reach the South Pole in 1912. Lamed by severe frostbite, and convinced that his condition would fatally handicap his companions' prospect of survival, he walked out into the blizzard, sacrificing his life.

Oates, Titus (1649–1705) Conspirator, born in Oakham, Leicestershire. In 1678 he publicized a fictitious 'Popish Plot' to murder Charles II and restore Catholicism. Many innocent people were executed for complicity in it, but two years later he was found guilty of perjury, and imprisoned until the 1688 Revolution.

Obadiah, also called **Abdias** One of the 12 'minor' prophets of the Old Testament. He prophesies the fall of Edom in retribution for taking sides against Jerusalem, predicting judgment on the nations and the restoration of Israel.

O'Brien, (Josephine) Edna (1930–) Writer, born in Tuamgraney, Co Clare, Ireland. Her novels include *The Country Girls* (1960), *August Is a Wicked Month* (1965), *Wild Decembers* (1999), and *In the Forest* (2002). The best of several collections of short stories appear in *The Fanatic Heart* (1985).

O'Casey, Sean, originally **John Casey** (1880–1964) Playwright, born in Dublin. His early plays, such as *The Shadow of a Gunman* (1923) and *Juno and the Paycock* (1924), were written for the Abbey Theatre. Later works, more experimental and impressionistic, include *Cockadoodle Dandy* (1949) and *The Bishop's Bonfire* (1955). He was awarded the Hawthornden Prize in 1926.

Ockham, William of *see* William of Ockham

O'Connell, Daniel, known as **the Liberator** (1775–1847) Irish Catholic political leader, born near Cahirciveen, Co Kerry, Ireland. His election as MP for Co Clare precipitated a crisis in Wellington's government, which eventually granted Catholic Emancipation (1829), enabling him to take his seat in the Commons.

Odette, popular name of **Odette Hallowes**, formerly **Churchill** (to 1955) and **Sansom** (to 1946), née **Brailly**

(1912–95) French wartime resistance heroine, born in Amiens, France. Brought up in France, she married an Englishman in 1931 and moved to London. Sent to France as an agent, she was arrested by the Germans in 1943, and sent to Ravensbruck concentration camp. Her wartime exploits were retold in a successful film, *Odette* (1950), starring Anna Neagle.

Oe, Kenzaburo (1935–) Novelist and short-story writer, born in Shikoku, Japan. His books include *A Personal Matter* (1964; trans 1968), *The Silent Cry* (1967; trans 1974, Tanizaki Prize), *A Healing Family* (trans 1996), and *Grand Street 55* (trans 1999). He received the Nobel Prize for Literature in 1994.

Oersted *see* Ørsted, Hans Christian

Offa (?–796) King of Mercia (757–96). He was the greatest Anglo-Saxon ruler in the 8th-c, treated as an equal by Charlemagne. He was responsible for constructing Offa's Dyke, stretching for 113 km/70 mi along the Welsh border.

Offenbach, Jacques, originally **Jacob Eberst** (1819–80) Composer, born in Cologne, Germany. He composed many light, lively operettas, such as *Orpheus in the Underworld* (trans, 1858). He also produced one grand opera, *The Tales of Hoffmann*, which was not produced until 1881.

Ogilvy, Angus / James / Marina *see* Alexandra, Princess

O Henry *see* Henry, O

Ohm, Georg Simon (1787–1854) Physicist, born in Erlangen, Germany. *Ohm's law* was published in 1827 as a result of his research in

electricity, and the measure of resistance is now called the *ohm*.

Oldfield, Bruce (1950–) Fashion designer, born in London. He showed his first collection in London in 1975. He designs evening dresses for royalty and film stars, as well as ready-to-wear clothes.

Oldman, Gary (1959–) Film actor, producer, and director, born in London. He became known following his portrayal of punk rocker Sid Vicious in the film *Sid and Nancy* (1986). Later films include *Bram Stoker's Dracula* (1992), *Lost in Space* (1998), and *Batman Begins* (2005).

Oliver, Jamie (Trevor) (1975–) Chef, born in Clavering, Essex. In 1999 he made the popular cooking series *The Naked Chef* for BBC television, with an accompanying cookbook. Later books include *Jamie's Dinners* (2004) and *Jamie's Italy* (2005). In 2005 the Channel 4 series *Jamie's School Dinners* documented his 'crusade' to improve the standard of school dinners in England.

Oliver, King, popular name of **Joseph Oliver** (1885–1938) Cornettist, composer, and bandleader, born in Abend, LA. He moved to Chicago, where in 1922 he formed his Creole Jazz Band, several of his compositions, such as 'Dr Jazz', becoming part of the standard traditional repertoire.

Olivetti, Adriano (1901–60) Manufacturer, born in Ivrea, Italy. After a period in the USA, he successfully transformed the manufacturing methods of the typewriter firm founded by his father **Camillo Olivetti** (1868–1943).

Olivier (of Brighton), Laurence (Kerr) Olivier, Baron (1907–89) Actor, producer, and director, born in Dorking, Surrey. He played all the great male Shakespearean roles, while his versatility was underlined by his virtuoso display in *The Entertainer* (1957). His films include *Henry V*, *Hamlet*, and *Richard III*. In 1940 he married actress Vivien Leigh (divorced 1961), and then actress Joan Plowright. He became first director of the National Theatre (1963–73), and after 1974 appeared chiefly in films and on television, notably in *Brideshead Revisited* (1982) and *King Lear* (1983).

Omar Khayyám, also spelled **Umar Khayyám** (c.1050–c.1122) Poet, mathematician, and astronomer, born in Nishapur, Persia. He was known to the Western world as a mathematician, until in 1859 Edward FitzGerald published a translation of his *Rubáiyát* ('Quatrains') – though little or nothing of this may actually be by Omar.

Onassis, Aristotle (Socrates) (1906–75) Millionaire shipowner, born in Smyrna, Turkey. He built up one of the world's largest independent fleets, and was a pioneer in the construction of super-tankers. In 1968 he married Jacqueline Kennedy.

Onassis, Jacqueline Kennedy, *née* **Jacqueline Lee Bouvier**, popularly known as **Jackie Kennedy** (1929–94) US first lady (1961–3), born in Southampton, NY. She married John F Kennedy in 1953, and her stoic behaviour after Kennedy's death enhanced her standing with the public. In 1968 she married the Greek millionaire shipping magnate, Aristotle Onassis.

Ondaatje, Michael (1943–) Poet, novelist, and editor, born in Colombo, Sri Lanka. He moved to Canada in 1962, becoming a university lecturer. His novel *The English Patient* was co-winner of the Booker Prize in 1992 (filmed 1996, Oscar). *Handwriting: Poems* appeared in 1999, and the novel *Anil's Ghost* in 2000.

O'Neal, (Patrick) Ryan (1941–) Film actor, born in Los Angeles, CA. He became well known as Rodney Harrison in the television series *Peyton Place*, a character he played for nearly five years. His films include *Love Story* (1970), *Paper Moon* (1973), and *People I Know* (2002).

O'Neill, Eugene (Gladstone) (1888–1953) Playwright, born in New York City. His works *Beyond the Horizon* (1920), *Anna Christie* (1922), *Strange Interlude* (1928), and *Long Day's Journey Into Night* (1956) all gained Pulitzer Prizes. Other classics include *Desire Under The Elms* (1924), *Mourning Becomes Electra* (1931), and *The Iceman Cometh* (1946). He was awarded the Nobel Prize for Literature in 1936.

O'Neill, Jonjo, popular name of **John Joseph O'Neill** (1952–) National Hunt jockey, born in Castletownroche, Co Cork, Ireland. He twice became champion jockey (1977–8, 1979–80), riding 148 winners in one season. In 1990 he began a career as a trainer and has had many successes.

Ono, Yoko (1933–) Multimedia artist, born in Tokyo. At age 18 she moved with her family to Scarsdale, NY. In 1967 she met future husband John

Lennon. They collaborated on art, film, and musical projects, and became famous for their series of 'conceptual events' to promote world peace, including the 'bed-in' held in an Amsterdam hotel room during their honeymoon in 1969. She inaugurated the Lennon Ono Grant for Peace prize in 2002.

Oppenheimer, J(ulius) Robert (1904–67) Nuclear physicist, born in New York City. He became director of the atom bomb project at Los Alamos (1943–5). Opposing the hydrogen bomb project, in 1953 he was suspended from secret nuclear research as a security risk, but was awarded the Enrico Fermi prize in 1963.

Orbison, Roy (1936–88) Country-pop singer and songwriter, born in Vernon, TX. His hit records include 'Only The Lonely' (1960), 'Cryin'' (1961), and 'Oh, Pretty Woman' (1964), and tributes to his music have continued long after his death.

Orczy, Emma (Magdalena Rosalia Marie Josepha Barbara), Baroness (1865–1947) Writer, born in Tarna-Eörs, Hungary. *The Scarlet Pimpernel* (1905) was followed by many popular adventure romances.

Orff, Carl (1895–1982) Composer, born in Munich, Germany. He is best known for his operatic setting of a 13th-c poem, *Carmina Burana* (1937).

Ørsted, Hans Christian, also spelled **Oersted** (1777–1851) Physicist, born in Rudkøbing, Denmark. In 1820 he discovered the magnetic effect of an electric current. The unit of magnetic field strength is named after him.

Orton, Joe, popular name of **John Kingsley Orton** (1933–67) Playwright and actor, born in Leicester, Leicestershire. He pioneered a style of black farce in such plays as *What the Butler Saw* (1969), *Entertaining Mr Sloane* (1963), and *Loot* (1964–5). He was murdered by his male lover.

Orwell, George, pseudonym of **Eric Arthur Blair** (1903–50) Novelist and essayist, born in Motihari, Bengal, India. He developed his own brand of socialism in *The Road to Wigan Pier* (1937) and many essays. He is best known for his satire of totalitarian ideology in *Animal Farm* (1945), and for the prophetic study of political tyranny, *1984* (1949).

Osama bin Laden (1955–?) Saudi guerrilla leader, born in Riyadh of a Yemeni family. After succeeding in business he moved to Afghanistan, where he founded the al-Qaeda terrorist organization and called for a jihad against the 'Judao-Christian alliance occupying Islamic sacred land in Palestine and the Arabian Peninsula'. He was accused by the USA of being behind the bombing of the USS *Cole* warship in the port of Aden, Yemen in 2000. Subsequently he conducted his terrorist campaigns under the protection of the Taliban in Afghanistan. He was named as the chief suspect in the assaults on the World Trade Center, New York, and the Pentagon, Washington, in September 2001. His whereabouts are since unknown, but occasional tape-recordings purporting to come from him have been made public.

Osborne, John (James) (1929–94) Playwright, film producer, and actor, born in London. His play *Look Back in Anger* (1956; filmed 1958) established him as the first of the 'Angry Young Men'. Other works include *The Entertainer* (1957; filmed 1959) and *Inadmissible Evidence* (1964; filmed 1965).

Osbourne, Ozzie, popular name of **John Michael Osbourne** (1948–) Rock musician and television entertainer, born in Birmingham, West Midlands. He formed the rock group Rare Breed, later known as Black Sabbath. He achieved international recognition following the success of a weekly MTV reality show, *The Osbournes* (2002), co-produced by his wife and manager, **Sharon Osbourne** (1952–). His single 'Changes', performed with daughter Kelly, topped the UK charts in 2003.

O'Sullivan, Ronnie, popular name of **Ronald Antonio O'Sullivan** (1975–) Snooker player, born in Wordsley, Wolverhampton. He turned professional in 1992, and his achievements to date include the British Open (1994), two World Championship titles (2001, 2004), the European Open (2003), and the Masters (1995, 2005). Nicknamed 'the Rocket', he also compiled the fastest-ever 147 maximum break (5 min 20 sec), completed during the 1997 World Championships.

Oswald, St (c.605–642) Anglo-Saxon king of Northumbria (633–41), the son of Ethelfrith of Benicia. He established Christianity in Northumbria with St Aidan's help, and fell in battle with the pagan King Penda.

Oswald, Lee Harvey (1939–63) Alleged killer of President John F Kennedy, born in New Orleans, LA. The day after President Kennedy's assassination (22 November 1963) he was charged with his murder, but before he could come to trial, he was shot by nightclub owner Jack Ruby.

Otaka, Tadaaki (1947–) Japanese conductor. He made his professional debut in 1971, and went on to become conductor of the Tokyo Philharmonic Orchestra (1971–91, laureate 1991), and principal conductor of the BBC National Orchestra of Wales (1987–95, laureate 1996) and the Kioi Sinfonietta, Tokyo (1995–).

O'Toole, Peter (Seamus) (1932–) Actor, born in Connemara, Co Galway, Ireland. His performance in the film *Lawrence of Arabia* (1962) made him an international star. Later films include *The Lion in Winter* (1968), *The Last Emperor* (1987), *Troy* (2004), and *Lassie* (2005). Nominated seven times for an Academy Award, he received an honorary Oscar in 2003.

Our Lady *see* Mary (Mother of Jesus)

Ovett, Steve, popular name of **Steven Michael James Ovett** (1955–) Athlete, born in Brighton, East Sussex. Gold medallist in the 800 m at the 1980 Olympics, he also won a bronze in the 1500 m. He broke the world record at 1500 m (three times), one mile (twice), and two miles.

Ovid, in full **Publius Ovidius Naso** (43 BC–AD 17) Latin poet, born in Sulmo, Italy. His major works are the three-book *Ars amatoria* (Art of Love) and the 15-book *Metamorphoses* (Transformations), one of the most influential works from antiquity.

Owain Glyndwr *see* Glendower, Owen

Owen, Alun (Davies) (1926–94) Playwright, born in Liverpool, Merseyside. A prolific writer for television and radio, his works include *The Rough and Ready Lot* (1958), *Progress to the Park* (1959), and a musical collaboration with Lionel Bart, *Maggie May* (1964).

Owen (of the City of Plymouth), David (Anthony Llewellyn), Baron

(1938–) British statesman, born in Plymouth, Devon. He was secretary for health (1974–6) and foreign secretary (1977–9), and one of the 'Gang of Four' who formed the Social Democratic Party (SDP) in 1981, becoming leader in 1983. Retiring from parliament in 1992, he became, with Cyrus Vance, a UN peace envoy in former Yugoslavia (1992–3).

Owen, Michael (James) (1979–) Footballer, born in Chester, Cheshire. A centre-forward, he joined Liverpool FC in 1996, and became the youngest player in the 20th-c to win an England cap (1998). He was a team member in the 1998 World Cup, Euro 2000, and 2002 World Cup, and by early 2006 had won 75 caps. His many awards include European Footballer of the Year in 2001. He joined Real Madrid in August 2004, transferring to Newcastle United in 2005.

Owen, Wilfred (Edward Salter)

(1893–1918) Poet, born near Oswestry, Shropshire. His poems, expressing a horror of the cruelty and waste of war, were first collected in 1920 by Sassoon. He was killed in action a week before the armistice.

Owens, Jesse, popular name of **James** or **John Cleveland** (1913–80) Athlete, born in Danville, AL. Within 45 min on 25 May 1935 at Ann Arbor, MI, he set five world records (100 yd, long jump, 220 yd, 220 yd hurdles, 200 m hurdles). His long jump record stood for 25 years.

Oz, Amos, originally **Amos Klausner** (1939–) Novelist, born in Jerusalem, Israel. His novels describe the tensions of life in modern Israel, and include (trans titles) *Elsewhere, Perhaps* (1966), *In the Land of Israel* (1982), *Don't Call it Night* (1995), and *The Same Sea* (2001). He received the Israel Prize for Literature in 1998 and the 2005 Goethe cultural prize for his life's work.

Pachelbel, Johann (c.1653–1706) Composer and organist, born in Nuremberg, Germany. His works profoundly influenced J S Bach. His best-known composition is the Canon in D Major.

Pacino, Al(fredo) (1940–) Film actor, born in New York City. His films include *The Godfather* (1972, 1974, 1990), *Serpico* (1973), *Sea of Love* (1989), and *Scent of a Woman* (1992, Oscar). Work for television includes the drama mini-series *Angels in America* (2004, Best Actor Emmy).

Packer, Kerry (Francis Bullmore) (1937–2005) Media proprietor, born in Sydney, New South Wales, Australia, the son of Frank Packer. In the 1977–8 season his creation of 'World Series Cricket', contracting leading Test cricketers for a knock-out series of one-day matches and 'Super-Tests', led to disputes with national cricket bodies and many legal battles.

Paganini, Niccolo (1782–1840) Violin virtuoso, born in Genoa, Italy. He revolutionized violin technique, his innovations including the use of stopped harmonics. His composi-

tions include the celebrated 24 *Capricci* (1820).

Paige, Elaine (1951–) Actress and singer, born in London. Her performances in *Jesus Christ Superstar* (1972) and *Billy* (1974) established her as a musical actress. Later musicals include *Evita* (1978), *Cats* (1981), *Sunset Boulevard* (1994–5), and *The King and I* (2000).

Paisley, Bob, popular name of **Robert Paisley** (1919–96) Football manager, born in Hetton-le-Hole, Durham. It was during his spell as manager of Liverpool (1974–83) that the club became the most successful in England. He was Manager of the Year on six occasions.

Paisley, Rev Ian (Richard Kyle) (1926–) Militant Protestant clergyman and politician, born in Armagh, Co Armagh, Northern Ireland. He founded the Protestant Unionist Party, and became the Democratic Unionist Party (DUP) MP for North Antrim. A rousing orator, he is strongly pro-British, fiercely opposed to the IRA, Roman Catholicism, and the unification of Ireland. In the 2005 general election, the party won nine out of 18 Northern Irish seats in the House of Commons.

Palestrina, Giovanni Pierluigi da (c.1525–94) Composer, born in Palestrina, Italy. The most distinguished composer of the Renaissance, he composed over 100 Masses, motets, hymns, and other church pieces.

Palgrave, Francis Turner (1824–97) Poet and critic, born in Great Yarmouth, Norfolk. He edited the *Golden Treasury of Songs and Lyrical*

Poems (1861), better known as 'Palgrave's Golden Treasury'.

Palin, Michael (Edward) (1943–) Script-writer and actor, born in Sheffield, Yorkshire. He joined the BBC television team in *Monty Python's Flying Circus* (1969–74), co-wrote and acted in the Monty Python films, won a BAFTA award for his role in *A Fish Called Wanda* (1988), and has presented a popular series of travel documentaries for the BBC.

Palmer, Arnold (Daniel) (1929–) Golfer, born in Latrobe, PA. His wins include the (British) Open (1961–2), the US Open (1960), and the US Masters (1958, 1960, 1962, 1964).

Palmerston (of Palmerston), Henry John Temple, 3rd Viscount (1784–1865) British Liberal prime minister (1855–8, 1859–65), born in Broadlands, Hampshire. He became a Tory MP in 1807, served as secretary of war (1809–28), joined the Whigs (1830), and was three times foreign secretary (1830–4, 1835–41, 1846–51). His robust defences of what he considered to be British interests abroad secured him the name of 'Firebrand Palmerston'.

Paltrow, Gwyneth (1972–) Film actress, born in Los Angeles, CA. Her films include *Emma* (1996), *Shakespeare in Love* (1998, Oscar), *The Talented Mr Ripley* (1999), and *Proof* (2005). She married Chris Martin of UK pop band Coldplay in 2003.

Pancras, St (?–304) Christian martyr, the son of a heathen noble of Phrygia. He was baptized in Rome, but immediately afterwards was slain in the Diocletian persecutions while only a young boy.

Pankhurst, Emmeline, *née* **Goulden** (1857–1928) Suffragette, born in Manchester, Greater Manchester. She founded the Women's Franchise League (1889), and in 1903, with her daughter **Christabel Harriette** (1880–1958), the Women's Social and Political Union. From 1905 she actively fought for women's suffrage, on several occasions being arrested and going on hunger strike.

Paretsky, Sara (1947–) Writer of detective fiction, born in Ames, IA. Most of her books feature V I Warshawski, a female private detective. Her first novel, *Indemnity Only*, appeared in 1982; *Blood Shot* (1988) is often said to be her best work. She is a founder of Sisters in Crime, which promotes the work of women writers of detective fiction.

Park, Nick, popular name of **Nicholas Wulstan Park** (1958–) Film animator and director, born in Preston, Lancashire. In 1985 he joined Aardman Animations in Bristol where his work included *A Grand Day Out* (1989, BAFTA), introducing the plasticine characters of Wallace and his dog Gromit. His later Oscar-winning films (with Steve Box) featuring Wallace and Gromit are *The Wrong Trousers* (1993), *A Close Shave* (1995), and *Wallace and Gromit in the Curse of the Were-Rabbit* (2005).

Parker, Sir Alan (1944–) Film director and actor, born in London. He made his feature-length cinema debut with *Bugsy Malone* (1976). Later films include *Midnight Express* (1978), *Evita* (1996), *Angela's Ashes* (1998), and *The Life of David Gale* (2002).

Parker, Charlie, popular name of

Charles Parker Jr, nickname **Bird** or **Yardbird** (1920–55) Jazz alto saxophonist, born in Kansas City, KS. In New York, he joined Dizzy Gillespie and other musicians in expanding the harmonic basis for jazz. The new music, called *bebop*, developed an adventuresome young audience at the end of World War 2.

Parker Bowles, Camilla *see* Cornwall, Duchess of

Parkinson, C(yril) Northcote (1909–93) Political scientist, born in Barnard Castle, Durham. He wrote many works on historical, political, and economic subjects, but achieved wider renown by his serio-comic tilt at bureaucratic malpractices in *Parkinson's Law: the Pursuit of Progress* (1957).

Parkinson, Michael (1935–) Journalist and broadcaster, born in Cudworth, nr Barnsley, Yorkshire. He has produced and presented several television programmes, and is best known as the host of his own Saturday evening chat show *Parkinson* (BBC, 1971–82, 1998–2004). He joined ITV in 2004 where he continued to present the show.

Parks, Rosa (Lee McCauley) (1913–2005) Civil-rights activist, born in Tuskegee, AL. She settled in Montgomery, AL and worked for the National Association for the Advancement of Colored People and the Union of Sleeping Car Porters. On 1 December 1955, she refused to give up her bus seat to a white man. By forcing the police to remove, arrest, and imprison her, she became a test case of segregation ordinances.

In 1999 she received the Congressional Gold Medal of Honor.

Parnell, Charles Stewart (1846–91) Irish politician, born in Avondale, Co Wicklow, Ireland. In 1879 he became president of the Irish National Land League, and in 1886 allied with the Liberals in support of Gladstone's Home Rule Bill. He remained an influential figure until 1890, when a divorce scandal forced his retirement.

Parr, Catherine (1512–48) Sixth wife of Henry VIII, the daughter of Sir Thomas Parr of Kendal. She married Henry in 1543, and persuaded him to restore the succession to his daughters, Mary I and Elizabeth I.

Parsons, Tony (1953–) Journalist and novelist, born in Romford, Essex. During the 1990s he became a newspaper columnist and a regular panellist on BBC 2's *Late Review* programme. His novel, *Man and Boy* (1998), won Book of the Year at the British Book Awards, and later books include *One for My Baby* (2001) and *Stories We Could Tell* (2005).

Parton, Dolly (Rebecca) (1946–) Country singer, songwriter, and actress, born in Locust Ridge, TN. She took country-based music into the pop mainstream, her hits including 'Jolene' (1974) and 'Islands In The Stream' (1984). From 1982 she had success as a film actress, and also began to operate her own theme park, 'Dollywood'.

Pascal, Blaise (1623–62) Mathematician, physicist, theologian, and man-of-letters, born in Clermont-Ferrand, France. He invented a calculating machine (1647), the barometer, the hydraulic press, and the syringe. He defended Jansenism against the Jesuits (1656–7), and fragments jotted down for a case book of Christian truth were later published as the *Pensées* (1669, Thoughts).

Pasolini, Pier Paolo (1922–75) Film director and writer, born in Bologna, Italy. He became known for controversial, bawdy film adaptations, such as *The Gospel According to St Matthew* (trans, 1964), *The Decameron* (trans, 1971), and *The Canterbury Tales* (1973).

Passmore, George *see* Gilbert and George

Pasternak, Boris (Leonidovich) (1890–1960) Writer and translator, born in Moscow. His first novel, *Dr Zhivago*, was banned in the Soviet Union, but became an international success after its publication in Italy in 1957. Expelled by the Soviet Writers' Union, he was compelled to refuse the 1958 Nobel Prize for Literature.

Pasteur, Louis (1822–95) Chemist and microbiologist, born in Dôle, France. He established that putrefaction and fermentation were caused by microorganisms, and in 1881 showed that sheep and cows 'vaccinated' with the attenuated bacilli of anthrax received protection against the disease.

Patchett, Ann (1963–) Writer, born in Los Angeles, CA. Her novels include *The Patron Saint of Liars* (1992), *Taft* (1994), and *Bel Canto* (2001, PEN/Faulkner Award, Orange Prize). *Truth and Beauty* (2004), a non-fiction work, appeared in 2004.

Pathé, Charles (1863–1957) Film pioneer, born in Paris. In 1896 he founded Société Pathé Frères with his brothers Emile, Théophile, and Jacques, and by 1912 it had become one of the largest film production organizations in the world.

Patmore, Coventry (Kersey Dighton) (1823–96) Poet, born in Woodford, Essex. Associated with the Pre-Raphaelite Brotherhood, his major work, *The Angel in the House* (1854–62), was followed by his conversion to Catholicism, and he then wrote mainly on mystical or religious themes.

Paton, Alan (Stewart) (1903–88) Writer and educator, born in Pietermaritzburg, South Africa. From his concern with the racial problem in South Africa sprang several novels, notably *Cry, the Beloved Country* (1948), *Too Late the Phalarope* (1953), and *Ah, but Your Land is Beautiful* (1981).

Patou, Jean (1880–1936) Fashion designer, born in Normandy, France. He opened as a couturier in 1919, becoming noted for his designs for sports stars, actresses, and society ladies, and for his perfume, 'Joy'.

Patrick, St (c.385–461) Apostle of Ireland, born (perhaps) in South Wales. Ordained a bishop at 45, he became a missionary to Ireland (432), fixed his see at Armagh (432), and was probably buried there.

Patten, Chris(topher Francis) (1944–) British politician, born in London. He became secretary of state for the environment (1989) and Conservative party chairman (1991). Credited with masterminding the Tory victory in the 1992 election, he lost his own seat and was appointed Governor of Hong Kong (1992–7). He served as a European Commissioner (1999–2004), and was elected Chancellor of Oxford University in 2003.

Patterson, James (1949–) Novelist, born in New York City. His detective novels featuring FBI Agent Alex Cross include *Kiss The Girls* (1995; filmed 1997), *Violets are Blue* (2001), and *Mary, Mary* (2005).

Patton, George (Smith), Jr (1885–1945) US general, born in San Gabriel, CA. He played a key role in the Allied invasion of French N Africa (1942), led the US 7th Army in its assault on Sicily (1943), commanded the 3rd Army in the invasion of France, and contained the German counter-offensive in the Ardennes (1944).

Paul VI, originally **Giovanni Battista Montini** (1897–1978) Pope (1963–78), born in Concesio, Italy. He became known for his liberal views and support of social reform. He travelled more widely than any previous pope and initiated important advances in the move towards Christian unity.

Paul, St, originally **Saul of Tarsus** (?10–65/67 AD) Apostle to the Gentiles and theologian of the early Christian Church, born of Jewish parents at Tarsus, Cilicia. A persecutor of Christians, on his way to Damascus (c.34–35) he was converted by a vision of Christ. He carried out many missionary journeys in regions of the E Mediterranean, such as Galicia, Corinth, and Ephesus. He is said to have been executed by Nero in Rome (c.64). Thirteen New Testament letters are traditionally attributed to him.

Paul, Vincent de see Vincent de Paul

Pauli, Wolfgang (1900–58) Theoretical physicist, born in Vienna. In 1924 he formulated the 'exclusion principle' in atomic physics, and in 1931 postulated the existence of an electrically neutral particle (the neutrino). He was awarded the Nobel Prize for Physics in 1945.

Paulin, Tom (1949–) Poet, born in Leeds, West Yorkshire. His books include *A State of Justice* (1977), *Seize the Fire* (1990), and *The Invasion Handbook* (2002). He is also known in the UK as a contributor to television discussion programmes on the arts.

Pauling, Linus (Carl) (1901–94) Chemist, born in Portland, OR. He applied quantum theory to chemistry, and was awarded the Nobel Prize for Chemistry in 1954 for his contributions to the theory of valency. He became a controversial figure from 1955 as the leading scientific critic of US nuclear deterrent policy. Awarded the Nobel Peace Prize in 1962, he was the first person to receive two full Nobel Prizes.

Pavarotti, Luciano (1935–) Tenor, born in Modena, Italy. He won the international competition at the Teatro Reggio Emilia in 1961, and made his operatic debut the same year. He made his US debut in 1968, and is internationally known as a concert performer.

Pavlov, Ivan Petrovich (1849–1936) Physiologist, born in Ryazan, Russia. From 1902 he studied what later became known as *Pavlovian conditioning* in animals. A major influence on the development of behaviourism in psychology, he was awarded the

Nobel Prize for Physiology or Medicine in 1904.

Pavlova, Anna (1881–1931) Ballerina, born in St Petersburg. She became particularly known for her role in Fokine's *The Dying Swan* (1905), and after a period with Diaghilev's Ballets Russes, she began touring Europe with her own company (1909).

Paxman, Jeremy (Dickson) (1950–) British television presenter and journalist, born in Leeds, West Yorkshire. He joined the BBC 1 *Tonight* team in 1977, and later joined BBC 2's *Newsnight* (1989), on which he developed a reputation as a tough but fair interviewer. He became presenter of *University Challenge* in 1994.

Paz, Octavio (1914–98) Poet, born in Mexico City. A prolific writer, his best-known works include *Collected Poems* (1957–87), in Spanish and English, and the prose *One Earth, Four or Five Worlds* (trans, 1984). He received the Nobel Prize for Literature in 1990.

Peacock, Thomas Love (1785–1866) Writer, born in Weymouth, Dorset. His conversational satirical romances include *Headlong Hall* (1816), *Melincourt* (1817), and *Nightmare Abbey* (1818).

Peake, Mervyn (Laurence) (1911–68) Writer and artist, born in Kuling, China, where his father was a missionary. He is best known for his Gothic fantasy trilogy of novels, *Titus Groan* (1946), *Gormenghast* (1950, televised 2000), and *Titus Alone* (1959), and for the novel *Mr Pye* (1953), also televised.

Peary, Robert E(dwin) (1856–1920) Naval commander and explorer, born in Cresson, PA. He made eight Arctic voyages to the Greenland coast, in 1891–2 arriving on the E coast by crossing the ice. In 1909 he led the first expedition to the North Pole, reaching it on 6 April.

Peck, (Eldred) Gregory (1916–2003) Film star, born in La Jolla, CA. Among his best-known films are *Spellbound* (1945), *The Gunfighter* (1950), *Moby Dick* (1956), *To Kill a Mockingbird* (1962, Oscar), and *The Omen* (1976).

Peckinpah, Sam (1925–84) Film director, born in Fresno, CA. He portrayed a harshly realistic view of the lawless US West, accentuating the inherent violence, as in *Major Dundee* (1965) and *The Wild Bunch* (1969).

Peel, John, popular name of **John Robert Parker Ravenscroft** (1939–2004) Radio disc jockey and presenter, born in Heswall, Merseyside. In 1967 he began a long career with Radio 1 and from 1998 to 2004 presented Radio 4's popular *Home Truths*. At the time of his sudden death he was working on his autobiography. The book, *John Peel: Margrave of the Marshes*, was completed by his wife and family and published in 2005.

Peel, Sir Robert (1788–1850) British prime minister (1834–5, 1841–6), born near Bury, Greater Manchester. As home secretary (1822–7, 1828–30), he carried through the Catholic Emancipation Act and reorganized the London police force (who became known as *Peelers* or *Bobbies*). As prime minister, his decision to repeal the Corn Laws (1846) split his party and brought his resignation.

Pelé, popular name of **Edson Arantes do Nascimento** (1940–) Footballer, widely held to be the best player in the game's history, born in Três Corações, Brazil. His first-class career was spent at Santos (1955–74) and the New York Cosmos (1975–7), and he played in Brazil's winning World Cup team in 1958, 1962, and 1970. Regarded as a national hero in Brazil, he was appointed a sports minister in 1994 and received an honorary British knighthood in 1997.

Pelham, Henry (1696–1754) British statesman and prime minister (1743–54), born in London, the younger brother of Thomas Pelham. He was active in suppressing the Jacobite Rising of 1715 and became secretary for war in 1724.

Pelham (-Holles), Thomas, 1st Duke of Newcastle (1693–1768) British prime minister (1754–6, 1757–62), the brother of Henry Pelham. A Whig and a supporter of Walpole, he became secretary of state (1724–54), and was extremely influential during the reigns of George I and II.

Penderecki, Krzysztof (1933–) Composer, born in Debica, Poland. A leading composer of the Polish avant-garde, his works include *Threnody for the Victims of Hiroshima* (1960), operas, and a St Luke Passion.

Penn, Sean (Justin) (1960–) Actor, writer, producer, and director, born in Santa Monica, CA. Born into a show business family, his films include *Dead Man Walking* (1995, Best Actor Oscar nomination), *The Thin Red Line* (1998), *Mystic River* (2003, Best Actor Oscar), and *The Interpreter*

(2005). His first wife was Madonna (1985–9).

Penn, William (1644–1718) Quaker reformer and colonialist, born in London. In 1681 he obtained a grant of land in North America, which he called Pennsylvania in honour of his father, Admiral Sir William Penn (1621–70). He sailed in 1682, and governed the colony for two years.

Penrose, Sir Roger (1931–) Mathematical physicist, born in Colchester, Essex. In 1973 he became professor of mathematics at Oxford. His work with Stephen Hawking showed that general relativity predicates a 'big bang' creation of the universe (1970). He invented *twistors*, geometrical entities that can be used to describe space-time.

Pepys, Samuel (1633–1703) Diarist and naval administrator, born in London. His celebrated diary, from 1 January 1660 to 31 May 1669, is both a personal record and a vivid picture of contemporary life. Written in shorthand, it was not decoded until 1825.

Perceval, Spencer (1762–1812) British prime minister (1809–12), born in London. He was solicitor general (1801), attorney general (1802), and Chancellor of the Exchequer (1807). He was assassinated in the lobby of the House of Commons.

Peres, Shimon, originally **Shimon Perski** (1923–) Israeli Labour prime minister (1984–6, 1995–6), born in Valozhyn, Belarus (formerly Wolożyn, Poland). He entered into a unique power-sharing agreement with the Consolidation Party (Likud), becoming prime minister for two years, when Yitzhak Shamir took over. He served again as prime minister (1995–6), was minister of foreign affairs (2001–2), interim Labour leader in opposition (2003–4), and vice premier (2005–). He shared the Nobel Peace Prize with Yitzhak Rabin in 1994.

Pergolesi, Giovanni Battista (1710–36) Composer, born in Jesi, Italy. His comic intermezzo *La serva padrona* (1732) influenced the development of *opera buffa*. He wrote much church music, notably his great *Stabat Mater*.

Pericles (c.495–429 BC) General and statesman, a member of the aristocratic Alcmaeonid family, who presided over the 'Golden Age' of Athens, and virtually its uncrowned king (443–429 BC). His unremitting hostility to Sparta brought about the Peloponnesian War (431–404 BC).

Perkins, Anthony (1932–92) Actor, born in New York City. He is best known for his role as the maniacal Norman Bates in Hitchcock's *Psycho* (1960), with its three sequels (1983, 1986, 1990).

Perón, (Maria) Eva (Duarte de), known as **Evita** (1919–52) The second wife of Argentinian President Juan Perón, born in Los Toldos, Argentina. An actress before her marriage in 1945, she became a powerful political influence and the mainstay of the Perón government. The musical *Evita* (1979) was based on her life.

Perry, Fred(erick John) (1909–95) Lawn tennis and table tennis player, born in Stockport, Greater Manchester. He won the world table tennis title in 1929, the lawn tennis singles title at Wimbledon in 1934–6, and

was the first man to win all four major titles.

Perry, Matthew (1969–) Actor, born in Williamstown, MA. He became known for his role as Chandler Bing in the acclaimed television series *Friends* (1994–2004). Roles in feature films include *Fools Rush In* (1997) and *The Whole Nine Yards* (2000, sequel 2004).

Perugino (Ital 'the Perugian'), originally **Pietro di Cristoforo Vannucci** (c.1445–1523) Painter, born in Città della Pieve, Umbria. He established himself in Perugia, and painted several frescoes in the Sistine Chapel, Rome, notably 'The Giving of the Keys to St Peter' (1489).

Pestalozzi, Johann Heinrich (1746–1827) Educationist, born in Zürich, Switzerland. He wrote *How Gertrude Educates her Children* (trans, 1801), the recognized exposition of the Pestalozzian method, in which the process of education is seen as a gradual unfolding of the children's innate faculties. *Pestalozzi International Children's Villages* were established in Switzerland (1946) and Surrey, UK (1958).

Peter I (of Russia), known as **the Great** (1672–1725) Tsar of Russia (1682–1721) and emperor (1721–5), born in Moscow. He embarked on a series of sweeping military, domestic, and ecclesiastical reforms. His defeat of Sweden in the Great Northern War (1700–21) established Russia as a major European power and gained a maritime exit on the Baltic coast, where he founded his new capital, St Petersburg (1703).

Peter, St, originally **Simon** or **Simeon**

bar Jona ('son of Jona') (1st-c) One of the 12 apostles of Jesus, a fisherman living in Capernaum, who was renamed by Jesus as **Cephas** or Peter (meaning 'rock') in view of his leadership among the disciples. Immediately after Jesus's ascension, Peter appears as the leader of the Christian community in Jerusalem. Tradition says that he was executed in Rome (c.64), and he is regarded by the Roman Catholic Church as the first Bishop of Rome. Two New Testament letters bear his name.

Peterson, Oscar (Emmanuel) (1925–) Jazz pianist and composer, born in Montreal, Quebec, Canada. In 1949 he became an international star when he joined a concert tour called 'Jazz at the Philharmonic' in New York, known for his extraordinary keyboard facility.

Petipa, Marius (1818–1910) Ballet-master and choreographer, credited with the development of Russian classical ballet, born in Marseille, France. He went to St Petersburg in 1847 to join the Imperial Theatre, becoming ballet master in 1869.

Petit, Roland (1924–) Choreographer and dancer, born in Paris. In 1948 he founded Les Ballets de Paris de Roland Petit, which toured widely in Europe and the USA. He later founded the Ballet de Marseille (1972), and became its director.

Petrarch, in full **Francesco Petrarca** (1304–74) Poet and scholar, born in Arezzo, Italy. In 1327 at Avignon he first saw Laura (possibly Laure de Noves), who inspired him with a passion which has become proverbial for its constancy and purity, seen in the series of love poems the *Canzoniere*. Crowned poet laureate at Rome in 1341, he was the earliest of the great Renaissance humanists and wrote widely on the classics.

Pfeiffer, Michelle (1958–) Film actress, born in Santa Ana, CA. She gained recognition in *The Witches of Eastwick* (1987) and *Dangerous Liaisons* (1988). Later films include *Frankie and Johnny* (1991), *Up Close and Personal* (1996), *What Lies Beneath* (2000), and *White Oleander* (2002).

Phelps, Michael (1985–) Swimmer, born in Baltimore, MD. At the 2003 World Championships he won three gold medals and set new record times in the 200 m butterfly, 200 m individual medley, and the 400 m individual medley. At the 2004 Olympics he won gold in the butterfly (100 m and 200 m), and the individual medley (200 m and 400 m), setting a new record for the 400 m event. At the 2005 World Championships, his gold medals in the 200 m freestyle and 200 m individual medley brought his individual world titles to six.

Philby, Kim, popular name of **Harold Adrian Russell Philby** (1912–88) Double agent, born in Ambala, India. Already recruited as a Soviet agent, he was employed by the British Secret Intelligence Service (1944–6) as head of anti-Communist counter-espionage. In 1963 he disappeared to Russia, where he was granted citizenship.

Philip, St (1st-c) One of the disciples of Jesus, listed among the 12 (in *Acts* 1). He is prominent in John's Gospel, and tradition suggests he was martyred on a cross.

Philip, Prince *see* Edinburgh, Duke of

Philip Neri, St *see* Neri, St Philip

Phillips, Mark, Captain (1948–) Former husband of Princess Anne (1973–92), and a noted horseman. A regular member of the British equestrian team (1970–6), he won the team event gold medal at the Munich Olympic Games in 1972.

Phillips, Peter / Zara *see* Anne (Elizabeth Alice Louise), Princess

Phoenix, Joaquin (Rafael), also known as **Leaf Phoenix** (1974–) Film actor, born in San Juan, Puerto Rico. After work in television commercials and sitcoms, feature film success came with *To Die For* (1995). Later films include *Gladiator* (2000) and *Hotel Rwanda* (2004), and he received an Oscar nomination for his role as Johnny Cash in the biopic *Walk the Line* (2005). His brother was River Phoenix.

Phoenix, River (1970–93) Film actor, born in Madras, OR. He made his film debut in *Explorers* (1985), and received a Best Actor Oscar nomination for his role in *Running on Empty* (1988). Later films included *Indiana Jones and the Last Crusade* (1989) and *Love You To Death* (1990). His early death was due to a drugs overdose.

Piaf, Edith, popular name of **Edith Giovanna Gassion** (1915–63) Singer, born in Paris. Known as *Piaf*, from the Parisian slang for 'sparrow', she became legendary for her nostalgic songs, such as 'Non, je ne regrette rien'.

Piaget, Jean (1896–1980) Psychologist, born in Neuchâtel, Switzerland.

He is best known for his research on the development of cognitive functions in children, in such pioneering studies as *The Origins of Intelligence in Children* (trans, 1948).

Picasso, Pablo (1881–1973) Artist, born in Málaga, Spain. The dominant figure of early 20th-c art, his 'blue period' (1902–4), a series of striking studies of the poor, gave way to the life-affirming 'pink period' (1904–6), full of the incidents of circus life. He then turned to brown, and began to work in sculpture. His break with tradition came with 'Les Demoiselles D'Avignon' (1906–7), the first exemplar of analytical Cubism, a movement which he developed with Braque (1909–14). His major creation is 'Guernica' (1937).

Pierce, Franklin (1804–69) US statesman and 14th president (1853–7), born in Hillsborough, NH. As president he tried unsuccessfully to bridge the widening chasm between the South and the North.

Pierce, Mary (1975–) French tennis player, born in Montreal, Quebec, Canada. Her tournament victories include the Australian Open in 1995, the first Frenchwoman to win this title since 1967, and the French Open in 2000. She reached the Masters semi-final in 1993 and the Roland-Garros final in 1994. At the start of 2006 she had a world ranking of number 5.

Piero della Francesca (c.1420–92) Painter, born in Borgo San Sepolcro, Italy. His major work is a series of frescoes illustrating 'The Legend of the True Cross' (1452–66) in the choir of S Francesco at Arezzo.

Piggott, Lester (Keith) (1935–) Flat racing jockey, born in Wantage, Oxfordshire. He rode 4493 winners in Britain, and was champion jockey 11 times. After retiring he became a trainer but was imprisoned (1987–8) for tax offences. He then resumed his career as a jockey and retired in 1995.

Pilate, Pontius, Lat **Pontius Pilatus** (1st-c) Roman prefect of Judea, appointed by Tiberius in c.26. His fame rests entirely on his role in the story of Jesus of Nazareth, permitting his execution at the prompting of the Jewish authorities.

Pilger, John (Richard) (1939–) Journalist and documentary film-maker, born in Sydney, New South Wales, Australia. He has twice won the Year British Journalist of the Year award and is a winner of the UNESCO Peace Prize. His film *Year Zero* (1979) exposed the atrocities of Pol Pot to the world. Among his books are *Hidden Agendas* (1998) and *The New Rulers of the World* (2002).

Pilkington, Sir Alastair, originally **Lionel Alexander Bethune Pilkington** (1920–95) Glass manufacturer, born in Newbury, Berkshire. He joined the family firm of glassmakers, and in 1952 conceived a new technique for manufacturing plate glass.

Pinkerton, Allan (1819–84) Detective, born in Glasgow. He settled in Illinois, USA (1842) and founded the Pinkerton National Detective Agency (1850). During the Civil War he headed a Federal intelligence network.

Pinochet (Ugarte), Augusto (1915–) Chilean dictator (1973–90), born in Valparaíso, Chile. He led a military coup ousting the Allende government in 1973, and in 1980 enacted a constitution giving himself an eight-year presidential term (1981–9). In 1998 he became the centre of international attention when he was arrested in London for 'crimes of genocide and terrorism'. He was detained under house arrest but the UK government returned him to Chile in 2000 on the grounds of ill health. In 2004 the Court of Appeal stripped him of immunity from prosecution, thus paving the way for a trial on charges of human rights abuses during his rule. The case was ongoing in 2006.

Pinsent, Sir Matthew (Clive) (1970–) Rower, born in Dorset. In 1990 he teamed up with Steve Redgrave for the coxless pairs. His many honours include eight gold medals in the World Championship Coxless Pairs (1991, 1993–5, 1997–9, 2002) and Olympic gold Coxless Pairs (1992, 1996) and Coxless Fours (2000, 2004). He retired in 2004.

Pinter, Harold (1930–) Playwright and director, born in London. His plays include *The Birthday Party* (1958), *The Caretaker* (1960; filmed 1963), *The Homecoming* (1965), and *Moonlight* (1993). Among his screenplays are *The Servant* (1962) and *The Go-Between* (1969). His work is highly regarded for the way it uses the unspoken meaning behind inconsequential everyday talk to induce an atmosphere of menace. He received the Nobel Prize for Literature in 2005, and was made a Companion of Honour in 2002.

Piper, Billie (Paul) (1982–) Pop singer and actress, born in Swindon, Wiltshire. Her debut single, 'Because We Want To' (1998), made number 1 in the UK charts. She later focused on an acting career and in 2005 was cast as Rose Tyler, travelling companion to the Doctor in the revived cult BBC television series *Doctor Who*. She married Chris Evans in 2001 (separated, 2005).

Piquet, Nelson, originally **Nelson Souto Maior** (1952–) Motor-racing driver, born in Rio de Janeiro, Brazil. He was world champion in 1981, 1983 (both Brabham), and 1987 (Williams). He won 23 grand prix between 1978 and a serious accident in 1991.

Pissarro, Camille (1830–1903) Impressionist artist, born in St Thomas, West Indies. The leader of the original Impressionists, most of his works depicted the countryside around Paris, such as 'Boulevard Montmartre' (1897).

Pitman, Sir Isaac (1813–97) Educationist, and inventor of a shorthand system, born in Trowbridge, Wiltshire. In Bath he established a Phonetic Institute for teaching shorthand (1839–43), and brought out the *Phonetic Journal* (1842).

Pitney, Gene (1941–2006) Singer and songwriter, born in Hartford, CT. His hits as a writer include 'Rubber Ball' and 'Hello Mary Lou' (both 1961). Among his hit singles as a singer were '24 Hours From Tulsa' (1963) and 'Something's Gotten Hold Of My Heart' (1967).

Pitt, Brad (1963–) Film actor, born in Shawnee, OK. He became known after his appearance in *Thelma &*

Louise (1991), and later films include *Seven* (1995), *Troy* (2004), and *Mr & Mrs Smith* (2005). He was married to actress Jennifer Aniston (2000–5).

Pitt, William, 1st Earl of Chatham, also known as **Pitt the Elder** (1708–78) British statesman and virtual premier (1756–61, 1766–8), born in London. He led the young 'Patriot' Whigs, and in 1756 became secretary of state. The king's enmity led him to resign in 1757, but public demand caused his recall, though he was again compelled to resign when his Cabinet refused to declare war with Spain (1761).

Pitt, William, also known as **Pitt the Younger** (1759–1806) British prime minister (1783–1801, 1804–6), born in Hayes, Kent, the second son of the Earl of Chatham (William Pitt, the Elder). In his first ministry he carried through important reforms, negotiated coalitions against France (1793, 1798), and proposed a legislative union with Ireland (1800). He resigned rather than contest George III's hostility to Catholic emancipation.

Pius XII, originally **Eugenio Maria Giuseppe Giovanni Pacelli** (1876–1958) Pope (1939–58), born in Rome. Under his leadership during World War 2 he did much to help prisoners of war and refugees, but there has been continuing controversy over his attitude to the treatment of the Jews in Nazi Germany.

Pizarro, Francisco (c.1478–1541) Conquistador, born in Trujillo, Spain. In 1526 he and Almagro sailed for Peru, and in 1531 began the conquest of the Incas. In 1537, conflict with Almagro led to the latter's execution, and in revenge Almagro's followers assassinated Pizarro.

Plaidy, Jean *see* Hibbert, Eleanor

Planck, Max (Karl Ernst Ludwig) (1858–1947) Theoretical physicist, born in Kiel, Germany. His work on the law of thermodynamics and black body radiation led him to abandon classical Newtonian principles and introduce the quantum theory (1900), for which he was awarded the Nobel Prize for Physics in 1918.

Plater, Alan (Frederick) (1935–) Playwright, born in Jarrow-on-Tyne, Tyne and Wear. His work for television includes the series *Softly Softly* (1966–76) and the plays *Close the Coalhouse Door* (1968) and *The Last of the Blonde Bombshells* (2000). Notable novels are *The Beiderbecke Affair* (1985), *The Beiderbecke Tapes* (1986), and *The Beiderbecke Connection* (1992).

Plath, Sylvia (1932–63) Poet, born in Boston, MA. She married Ted Hughes in 1957, and he edited her collected poems in 1981. Her only novel, *The Bell Jar* (1963), was published under the pseudonym **Victoria Lucas** just before her suicide in London.

Plato (c.428–347 BC) Greek philosopher, probably born in Athens of an aristocratic family. He became a disciple of Socrates, and before 368 BC founded an Academy at Athens. His writings, which consist of 35 philosophical dialogues (eg *Laches*, *Republic*, *Sophist*) and a series of letters, have had a pervasive and incalculable influence on almost every period and tradition, rivalled only by that of his greatest pupil, Aristotle.

Player, Gary (Jim) (1935–) Golfer, born in Johannesburg, South Africa. His successes include the (British) Open (1959, 1968, 1974), the US Open (1965), the US PGA title (1962, 1972), and the US Masters (1961, 1974, 1978).

Pleasence, Sir Donald (1919–95) Actor, born in Worksop, Nottinghamshire. On the stage he scored a huge success as the malevolent tramp, Davies, in Harold Pinter's *The Caretaker* (1960), and went on to appear in many films, often as a villain, such as *Dr Crippen* (1962) and *Cul-de-Sac* (1966).

Plimsoll, Samuel (1824–98) Social reformer, known as 'the sailors' friend', born in Bristol. Concerned about the unseaworthiness of ships, he promoted the Merchant Shipping Act (1876), and the *Plimsoll line* on the side of a ship was named after him.

Plowright, Dame Joan (1929–) Actress, born in Brigg, Lincolnshire. Her stage performances include *The Entertainer* (1957) and *Roots* (1959), and among her films are *The Dressmaker* (1988), *Enchanted April* (1993, Golden Globe), and *Tea with Mussolini* (1998). She married Laurence Olivier in 1961.

Plutarch, Gr **Ploutarchos** (c.46–c.120) Historian, biographer, and philosopher, born in Chaeronea, Boeotia, Greece. His extant writings comprise essays and historical works, notably *Parallel Lives*. North's translation of his work into English (1579) was the source of Shakespeare's Roman plays.

Pocahontas, personal name **Matoaka** (1595–1617) American-Indian princess, born near Jamestown, VA, the daughter of Powhatan. She helped maintain peace between the colonists and Indians, and saved the life of English adventurer John Smith. In 1613 she married **John Rolfe** (1585–1622), and in 1616 went with him to England.

Poe, Edgar Allan (1809–49) Poet and story writer, born in Boston, MA. He became known with *Tales of the Grotesque and Arabesque* (1840), and several short stories, notably 'The Murders in the Rue Morgue' (1841), the first detective story. His weird and fantastic stories, dwelling by choice on the horrible, were both original and influential. His poem 'The Raven' (1845) won immediate fame.

Poitier, Sidney (1924–) Actor and director, born in Miami, FL. His films include *Lilies of the Field* (1963, Oscar), *In the Heat of the Night* (1967) and *Guess Who's Coming to Dinner* (1967). He has also directed a number of lowbrow comedies, such as *Stir Crazy* (1980) and *Ghost Dad* (1990).

Polanski, Roman (1933–) Polish filmmaker, born in Paris. His films include *Rosemary's Baby* (1968), *Tess* (1979), *Frantic* (1988), *The Ninth Gate* (1999), *The Pianist* (2002, BAFTA, Oscar), and *Oliver Twist* (2005). His second wife, American actress **Sharon Tate** (1943–69), was a victim in the Manson killings.

Poliakoff, Stephen (1952–) Playwright and film director, born in London. A run of plays including *Hitting Town* and *City Sugar* (both 1975) established his reputation. Later works include *Breaking the Sil-*

ence (1984) and *Sweet Panic* (2003). Among his plays for television are *Shooting the Past* (1999) and *Gideon's Daughter* (2006).

Polk, James K(nox) (1795–1849) US statesman and 11th president (1845–9), born in Mecklenburg Co, NC. During his presidency, Texas was admitted to the Union (1845), and after the Mexican War (1846–7) the USA acquired California and New Mexico.

Pollack, Sydney (1934–) Film director and producer, born in South Bend, IN. His films include *They Shoot Horses Don't They?* (1969), *Tootsie* (1982), *Out of Africa* (1985, 2 Oscars), *Up at the Villa* (2000), and *The Interpreter* (2005).

Pollock, (Paul) Jackson (1912–56) Artist, born in Cody, WY. The first exponent of Action Painting in America, his art developed from Surrealism to abstract art and the first drip paintings of 1947. This technique he continued with increasing violence and often on huge canvases, as in *One* (1950), which is 17 ft long.

Polo, Marco (1254–1324) Merchant and traveller, born in Venice, Italy. He accompanied his father and uncle on a visit to Kublai Khan in China (1271–5), where he became an envoy in his service. Returning home in 1295, he compiled *The Travels of Marco Polo* (trans), commonly believed to have given Europe the first eye-witness account of Chinese civilization.

Pol Pot, also called **Saloth Sar** (1926–98) Cambodian prime minister (1976–9), born in Kompong Thom Province, Cambodia. He became leader of the Khmer Rouge guerrillas, set up a totalitarian regime which caused the death, imprisonment, or exile of millions. Overthrown when the Vietnamese invaded Cambodia, he withdrew to the mountains to lead the Khmer Rouge forces. In 1997 he was captured by his former comrades, and after a show trial in the Cambodian jungle he was condemned to life imprisonment.

Pompadour, Jeanne Antoinette Poisson, marquise de (Marchioness of), known as **Madame de Pompadour** (1721–64) Mistress of Louis XV, born in Paris. A woman of remarkable grace, beauty, and wit, she assumed the entire control of public affairs, and for 20 years swayed state policy, appointing her own favourites. She was a lavish patroness of architecture, the arts, and literature.

Pompey, in full **Gnaeus Pompeius Magnus**, known as **Pompey the Great** (106–48 BC) Roman politician and general of the late Republic. His victories include those over the Marians (83–82 BC), Spartacus (71 BC), and Mithridates VI (66 BC). He was defeated by Caesar at Pharsalus (48 BC), and later assassinated.

Pontius Pilatus *see* Pilate, Pontius

Pope, Alexander (1688–1744) Poet, born in London. He became well known as a satirical poet and a master of the heroic couplet, notably in *The Rape of the Lock* (1712–14). Other major works include *The Dunciad* (1728, continued 1742), the *Epistle to Doctor Arbuthnot* (1735), the philosophical *Essay on Man* (1733–4), and a series of satires imitating the epistles of Horace (1733–8).

Popper, Sir Karl (Raimund) (1902–94) Philosopher, born in Vienna. Associated with the 'Vienna Circle' of philosophers, his major work on scientific methodology was *The Logic of Scientific Discovery* (trans, 1934). Later books include *The Open Society and its Enemies* (1945), a polemic directed against totalitarian systems.

Porres, St Martín de *see* Martín de Porres, St

Porsche, Ferdinand (1875–1951) Automobile designer, born in Hafersdorf, Germany. In 1934 he produced a revolutionary type of cheap car with the engine in the rear, to which the Nazis gave the name *Volkswagen* ('people's car'). The Porsche sports car was introduced in 1950.

Porter, Cole (Albert) (1892–1964) Composer, born in Peru, IN. He composed lyrics and music for many stage successes, such as *Kiss Me Kate* (1948) and *Can-Can* (1953). His songs include 'Night and Day' (1932) and 'Begin the Beguine' (1935). *High Society* (1956) was his most successful film musical.

Porter, Eric (Richard) (1928–95) Actor, born in London. He appeared with the Royal Shakespeare Company and the National Theatre, and made several film and television appearances, notably as Soames Forsyte in the BBC television series, *The Forsyte Saga*.

Porter, Peter (Neville Frederick) (1929–) Poet, born in Brisbane, Queensland, Australia. He settled in England in 1951, and his *Collected Poems* appeared in 1983. Later collections include *Dragons in their*

Pleasant Palaces (1997) and *Afterburner* (2004).

Portillo, Michael (Denzil Xavier)
(1953–) British Conservative statesman, born in London. He served as minister for transport (1988–90) and the environment (1990–2), chief secretary to the Treasury (1992–4), secretary of state for employment (1994–5), and secretary of state for defence (1995–7). He lost his seat in the 1997 general election but was returned in 1999, and became shadow Chancellor in 2000. He lost the Conservative leadership contest in 2001, and left politics after the 2005 general election.

Portland, Duke of *see* Bentinck, William Henry Cavendish

Potter, (Helen) Beatrix (1866–1943) Writer of children's books, born in London. She illustrated her books herself, creating such popular characters as *Peter Rabbit* (1900) and *Benjamin Bunny* (1904).

Potter, Dennis (Christopher George) (1935–94) Playwright, born in the Forest of Dean, Gloucestershire. His plays for television, often technically innovative and controversial, include *Vote, Vote, Vote for Nigel Barton* (1965), *Blue Remembered Hills* (1979, BAFTA), *The Singing Detective* (1986), and *Lipstick on Your Collar* (1993).

Poulenc, Francis (1899–1963) Composer, born in Paris. A member of *Les Six*, he was prominent in the reaction against Impressionism. His works include much chamber music and the ballet *Les Biches*, but he is best known for his many songs, such as *Fêtes galantes* (1943).

Pound, Ezra (Weston Loomis)
(1885–1972) Poet, born in Hailey, ID. He was an experimental poet, whom T S Eliot regarded as the motivating force behind modern poetry. His main work is *The Cantos*, a loosely knit series of poems, which he began during World War 1, and which were published in many instalments (1930–59).

Poussin, Nicolas (1594–1665) Painter, born near Les Andelys, France. The greatest master of French Classicism, his masterpieces include two sets of the 'Seven Sacraments'.

Powell, Anthony (Dymoke)
(1905–2000) Novelist, born in London. His series of novels called *A Dance to the Music of Time* (12 vols, 1951–75) covered 50 years of British upper middle-class life and attitudes. Later books include the memoirs *To Keep the Ball Rolling* (4 vols, 1976–82) and *The Fisher King* (1986).

Powell, Baden *see* Baden-Powell, Robert

Powell, Colin (Luther) (1937–) US army general, born in New York City. He was appointed head of the National Security Council (1987–9) and chairman of the joint chiefs-of-staff (1989–93), the first African-American officer to receive this distinction. He had overall responsibility for the US military operation against Iraq in 1990–1. George W Bush appointed him secretary of state (2001–4).

Powell, (John) Enoch (1912–98) British statesman, born in Birmingham, West Midlands. He became a Conservative minister of health (1960–3), and was dismissed from the shadow cabinet in 1968 for his outspoken attitude on racial integration. He was later elected an Ulster Unionist MP (1974–87).

Powell, Michael (1905–90) Film director, scriptwriter, and producer, born in Bekesbourne, Kent. With **Emeric Pressburger** (1902–88) he formed The Archers Company in 1942, and made a series of unusual and original features, such as *Black Narcissus* (1947) and *The Tales of Hoffman* (1951).

Powell, Robert (1944–) Actor, born in Salford, Lancashire. He became widely known through his role in *Jesus of Nazareth* (1977), later films including *Frankenstein* (1984), and *The Mystery of Edwin Drood* (1993). His television work includes *The Detectives* (1989, 1992–4), with co-star Jasper Carrott, and *The First Circle* (1991).

Pratchett, Terry (1948–) Writer, born in Beaconsfield, Buckinghamshire. He is best known for his series of fantasy novels, Discworld, which began in 1983 with *The Colour of Magic* and which had reached a 30th novel, *Thud!*, in 2005. *The Science of Discworld* appeared in 1999, with a second volume in 2002.

Pré, Jacqueline du *see* du Pré, Jacqueline

Preminger, Otto (1906–86) Film director and producer, born in Vienna. He emigrated to the USA in 1935, and after some years of directing on the Broadway stage, made *Laura* (1944), often considered his best film. Later films included *Porgy and Bess* (1959), *Exodus* (1960), and *The Human Factor* (1979).

Prescott, John (Leslie) (1938–) British politician, born in Prestatyn, Denbighshire. In 1997 he became deputy prime minister in Tony Blair's government, and has served as secretary of state for the Environment, Transport and the Regions (1997–2001), secretary of state at the Cabinet office and chancellor of the Duchy of Lancaster (2001–2), and after a Cabinet reshuffle in 2002 was given responsibility for local government and the regions until 2006.

Presley, Elvis (Aaron), originally **Aron** (1935–77) Rock singer, born in Tupelo, MS. In 1953 he recorded some sides for Sun Records in Memphis, TN, then in 1956 'Heartbreak Hotel' sold millions of copies. His performances, featuring much hip-wriggling and sexual innuendo, incited hysteria in teenagers. He made many records that sold in the millions, including 'Hound Dog', 'Love Me Tender', and 'Jailhouse Rock'. His Hollywood films such as *Loving You* (1957), *King Creole* (1958), and *GI Blues* (1960) became enormous moneymakers. He died at Graceland, his Memphis mansion, which is now a souvenir shrine for his many fans.

Pressburger, Emeric *see* Powell, Michael

Previn, André (George) (1929–) Conductor, composer, and pianist, born in Berlin. A notable jazz pianist, he became musical director of symphony orchestras at Houston, London, Pittsburgh, and Los Angeles, then composer laureate of the London Symphony Orchestra (1991), and conductor laureate (1992). He has written musicals, film scores, and orchestral works, and done much to bring classical music to a wider public.

Price, Vincent (Leonard) (1911–93) Actor and writer, born in St Louis, MO. Achieving his first major success with *The Fall of the House of Usher* (1960), he went on to star in a series of acclaimed Gothic horror movies, such as *The Pit and the Pendulum* (1961) and *The Abominable Dr Phibes* (1971).

Priestley, J(ohn) B(oynton) (1894–1984) Writer, born in Bradford, West Yorkshire. His humorous novels include *The Good Companions* (1929). He established his reputation as a playwright with *Dangerous Corner* (1932), *Time and the Conways* (1937), and other plays on space-time themes. He married the archaeologist Jacquetta Hawkes in 1953.

Prince, Hal, popular name of **Harold Smith Prince** (1928–) Stage director and producer, born in New York City. His Broadway musicals include *The Pajama Game* (1954), *West Side Story* (1957), and *Cabaret* (1968), and he also directed *Evita* (1978) and *The Phantom of the Opera* (1986). Later productions include *Whistle Down the Wind* (1997) and *Candide* (1997).

Prince, stage name by which **Prince Roger Nelson** is most widely known (1958–) Pop singer and composer, born in Minneapolis, MN. Named after the Prince Roger Trio, a jazz band in which his father was a pianist, international success followed the release of *1999* (1982), the film and album *Purple Rain* (1984), and *Batman* (1989). He changed his name to the unpronounceable glyph O(+> in 1993, and has since adopted the designation of **The Artist (formerly known as Prince)**.

Prodi, Romano (1939–) Italian prime minister (1996–8, 2006–), and president of the European Commission (1999–2004), born in Scandiano, Reggio Emilia, Italy. Minister for industry in 1978–9, he left to head a centre-left coalition *L'Ulivo*, which was successful in the 1996 elections and he became prime minister. As president of the European Commission, he introduced a new code of conduct.

Proesch, Gilbert *see* Gilbert and George

Profumo, John (Dennis) (1915–2006) British Conservative statesman. He became minister for foreign affairs (1959–60) and secretary of state for war (1960–3), but resigned after deceiving the House of Commons about the nature of his relationship with Christine Keeler, who at the time was also involved with a Russian diplomat. He then dedicated his life to charitable work.

Prokofiev, Sergey Sergeyevitch (1891–1953) Composer, born in Sontsovka, Ukraine. His vast range of works include seven symphonies, nine concertos, ballets, operas, suites, cantatas, sonatas, songs, and his most popular work, *Peter and the Wolf* (1936).

Prost, Alain, nickname **the Professor** (1955–) Motor-racing driver, born in St Chamond, France. He won the world title in 1985–6 (both for McLaren Porsche), was runner-up in 1983–4 and 1988, and won again in 1989 (for McLaren Honda) and 1993, when he announced his retirement.

Proulx, E(dna) Annie (1935–) Novelist, born in Norwich, CT. In 1988 her collected stories were published as *Heart Songs and Other Stories*. She turned to novel writing with *Postcards* (1992), and later works include *The Shipping News* (1994, Pulitzer) and *That Old Ace in the Hole* (2002). Her story *Brokeback Mountain* (1997) was adapted into a successful film in 2005.

Proust, Marcel (1871–1922) Novelist, born in Auteuil, France. In 1912 he produced the first part of his 13-volume masterpiece, *A la recherche du temps perdu* (trans Remembrance of Things Past). His massive novel, exploring the power of the memory and the unconscious, as well as the nature of writing itself, has been profoundly influential.

Ptolemy, in full **Claudius Ptolemaeus** (fl.127–145) Greek astronomer and geographer, who worked in the great library in Alexandria. His book known as *Almagest* ('the greatest') is the most important compendium of astronomy produced until the 16th-c, his Earth-centred universe becoming known as the *Ptolemaic system*.

Puccini, Giacomo (Antonio Domenico Michele Secondo Maria) (1858–1924) Operatic composer, born in Lucca, Italy. His first great success was *Manon Lescaut* (1893), but this was eclipsed by *La Bohème* (1896), *Tosca* (1900), *Madame Butterfly* (1904), and the unfinished *Turandot*.

Pugin, Augustus (Welby Northmore) (1812–52) Architect, born in London. He worked with Barry designing a large part of the decoration and sculpture for the new Houses of Parliament (begun 1840), and did much to revive Gothic architecture in England.

Pulitzer, Joseph (1847–1911) Newspaper proprietor, born in Makó, Hungary. In 1864 he emigrated to the USA, and made his fortune in newspapers. In his will he established annual **Pulitzer Prizes** in the fields of literature, drama, history, music, and journalism.

Pullman, George Mortimer (1831–97) Inventor and businessman, born in Brocton, NY. He designed the Pullman railroad sleeping-car (1865), and later introduced dining-cars (1868).

Pullman, Philip (1946–) Novelist, born in Norwich, Norfolk. Publishing works mostly for children, he gained success with his trilogy for young adults, *His Dark Materials*, comprising *Northern Lights* (1995, aka *The Golden Compass*), *The Subtle Knife* (1997), and *The Amber Spyglass* (2000; Whitbread Book of the Year, 2002).

Purcell, Henry (1659–95) Composer, born in London. Best known for his vocal and choral works, he also wrote much incidental state music and an opera, *Dido and Aeneas* (1689). Of his many songs, 'Nymphs and Shepherds' is well known.

Pushkin, Alexander Sergeyevich (1799–1837) Poet, born in Moscow. Hailed in Russia as its greatest poet, his first success was the romantic poem 'Ruslan and Lyudmila' (1820), followed by the verse novel *Eugene Onegin* (1828) and the historical tragedy *Boris Godunov* (1831).

Putin, Vladimir (Vladimirovich) (1952–) Russian president (1999–), born in Leningrad (now St Petersburg), Russia. He began his career in the KGB as an intelligence officer (1975–91). In 1998 he became head of the Federal Security and of President Yeltsin's Security Council, and was promoted prime minister in 1999. He became president in early 2000 and was re-elected in 2004.

Puttnam (of Queensgate), David (Terence) Puttnam, Lord (1941–) Film-maker, born in London. His films include *Bugsy Malone* (1976), *Chariots of Fire* (1981, four Oscars), *The Killing Fields* (1984), *Memphis Belle* (1990), and *My Life So Far* (1997).

Pym, Barbara (Mary Crampton) (1913–80) Novelist, born in Oswestry, Shropshire. She is best known for her series of satirical novels on English middle-class society, including *Excellent Women* (1952) and *Quartet in Autumn* (1977).

Pynchon, Thomas (Ruggles) (1937–) Novelist, born in Glen Cove, NY. An experimentalist, esoteric and elusive, his novels include *V* (1963), *The Crying of Lot 49* (1966), *Gravity's Rainbow* (1973), *Vineland* (1992), and *Mason and Dixon* (1997), all displaying a preoccupation with codes, quests, and coincidences.

Pythagoras (6th-c BC) Philosopher and mathematician, born in Samos, Greece. He settled at Crotona, Italy (c.530 BC) and founded a moral and religious school. The famous geometrical theorem attributed to him was probably developed later by members of the Pythagorean school.

Pythias (of Syracuse) *see* Damon and Pythias

Qaddafi, Muammar *see* Gaddafi, Colonel Muammar

Quaid, Dennis (1954–) Film actor, born in Houston, TX. His films include *Innerspace* (1987), *Postcards from The Edge* (1990), and *Cold Creek Manor* (2004). His television work includes the highly rated *Bill* and its sequel (1981, 1983).

Quant, Mary (1934–) Fashion designer, born in London. The geometric simplicity of her designs, especially the mini-skirt, and the originality of her colours, became an essential feature of the new young Chelsea look in the 1960s.

Quayle, Sir Anthony(1913–89) Actor and director, born in Ainsdale, Lancashire. He joined the Shakespeare Memorial Theatre Company as actor and theatre director (1948–56), and helped create the Royal Shakespeare Company (1960). His major films include *Lawrence of Arabia* (1962).

Quayle, (James) Dan(forth) (1947–) US politician, born in Indianapolis, IN. He worked as a lawyer, journalist, and public official, becoming a Republican member of the Congress (1977–81) and Senate (1981–8). He was elected vice-president under George Bush in 1988, and announced in 1999 that he would run for president in 2000, but later withdrew.

Queen, Ellery *see* Dannay, Frederic

Queensberry, Sir John Sholto Douglas, 8th Marquess of (1844–1900) British aristocrat, a patron of boxing, who supervised the formulation in 1867 of new rules to govern that sport, since known as the *Queensberry Rules*. In 1895 he was tried and acquitted for publishing a defamatory libel on Oscar Wilde.

Quine, Willard Van Orman (1908–2000) Philosopher and logician, born in Akron, OH. Much influenced by the Vienna Circle and the empiricist tradition, his books include *Mathematical Logic* (1940), *Word and Object* (1960), and *From Stimulus to Science* (1995).

Quinn, Anthony (1915–2001) Film actor, born in Chihuahua, Mexico. Of Irish-Mexican parentage, he grew up in the USA, and after a few stage roles he made his film debut in *Parole!* (1936). He went on to win Oscars for *Viva Zapata* (1952) and *Lust for Life* (1956), and gained critical acclaim in Fellini's *La Strada* (1954) and *Zorba the Greek* (1964).

Quisling, Vidkun (Abraham Lauritz Jonsson) (1887–1945) Diplomat and fascist leader, born in Fyresdal, Norway. In 1933 he founded the National Party in imitation of the German National Socialist Party, and became puppet prime minister in occupied Norway. He was executed in 1945. His name has since been used for anyone who aids an enemy.

Rabelais, François, pseudonym (an anagram of his name) **Alcofribas Nasier** (?1494–1553) Satirist, physician, and humanist, born in or near Chinon, France. He is remembered for a sequence of books beginning with the comic and satirical *Pantagruel* (1533) and *Gargantua* (1535), published under his pseudonym, condemned by the Church for their unorthodox ideas and mockery of religious practices.

Rabin, Yitzhak (1922–95) Israeli soldier and prime minister (1974–7, 1992–5), born in Jerusalem. He was made chief-of-staff in 1964, heading the armed forces during the Six-Day War (1967). He became Labour Party leader and also served as defence minister (1984–90). He shared the Nobel Peace Prize in 1994. He was assassinated by a right-wing Israeli law student.

Rachel Biblical character, the daughter of Laban and wife of Jacob, and the mother of Joseph and Benjamin. According to *Genesis* 29, Jacob worked 14 years to earn Rachel as his wife.

Rachmaninov, Sergey Vasilyevich, also spelled **Rachmaninoff** and **Rakhmaninov** (1873–1943) Composer and pianist, born in Nizhni Novgorod, Russia. He is best known for his piano music, which includes four concertos, the *Prelude in C Sharp Minor*, and his last major work, the *Rhapsody on a Theme of Paganini* (1934) for piano and orchestra.

Racine, Jean (Baptiste) (1639–99) Dramatic poet, born in La Ferté-Milon, France. Widely regarded as the master of tragic pathos, his major verse tragedies include *Andromaque* (1667), *Phèdre* (1677), and *Bérénice* (1679).

Radcliffe, Daniel (Jacob) (1989–) Actor, born in London. He gained his first TV role in *David Copperfield* (1999), and in 2001 was cast as Harry Potter in the feature film *Harry Potter and the Philosopher's Stone*. He continued the role in later Harry Potter films (2002, 2004, 2005).

Radcliffe, Paula (1973–) Athlete, born in Northwich, Cheshire. Her achievements include the 5000 m gold at the 2002 Commonwealth Games, 10 000 m gold at the 2002 European Championships, three times women's winner of the London Marathon (2002, 2003, 2005), and winner of the Chicago Marathon (2002) and New York Marathon (2004).

Rafsanjani, Ali Akbar Hashemi (1934–) Iranian president (1989–97), born in Rafsanjan, Iran. After the 1979 revolution, he helped to found the ruling Islamic Republican Party, and in 1980 was chosen as Speaker of the Majlis (Lower House).

Raglan (of Raglan), Lord Fitzroy James Henry Somerset, Baron (1788–1855) British general, born at Badminton, Gloucestershire, the son of the Duke of Beaufort. In 1854 he led an ill-prepared force against the Russians in the Crimea, where his ambiguous order led to the Charge of the Light Brigade (1854) at Balaclava.

Rahner, Karl (1904–84) Roman Catholic theologian, born in Freiburg, Germany. His multi-volume *Theological Investigations* combines the philosophy of existentialism with the tradition of Aquinas.

Raine, Craig (Anthony) (1944–) Poet, born in Shildon, Co Durham. Poetry editor at Faber and Faber (1981–91), his books include *The Onion, Memory* (1978), *Selected Poetry* (1992), *Clay: Whereabouts Unknown* (1996), and *A la recherche du temps perdu* (2000).

Rainier III, in full **Rainier Louis Henri Maxence Bertrand de Grimaldi** (1923–2005) Prince of Monaco (1949–2005), born in Monaco. In 1956 he married film actress Grace Kelly. They had two daughters, **Caroline Louise Marguerite** (1957–) and **Stephanie Marie Elisabeth** (1965–). He was succeeded by his son, **Prince Albert Alexandre Louis Pierre** (1958–).

Rakhmaninov, Sergei *see* Rachmaninov, Sergey

Raleigh, Sir Walter, also spelled **Ralegh** (1552–1618) Courtier, navigator, and writer, born in Hayes Barton, Devon. He became prime favourite of Elizabeth I, and in 1584 sent the first of three expeditions to America, but later lost influence at court. When his enemies turned James I against him, he was imprisoned (1603–16), and after a failed expedition to the Orinoco in search of a gold-mine, he was executed.

Rambert, Dame Marie, originally **Cyvia Rambam** (1888–1982) Ballet dancer and teacher, born in Warsaw. She settled in London in 1918, and in 1935 formed the Ballet Rambert, remaining closely associated with it through its change to a modern dance company in the 1960s.

Rameses or **Ramses II**, known as **the Great** (13th-c BC) King of Egypt (1304–1237 BC), whose long and prosperous reign marks the last great peak of Egyptian power. His many monuments include the great sandstone temples at Abu Simbel.

Rameses or **Ramses III** (12th-c BC) King of Egypt (1198–1166 BC), famous primarily for his great victory over the Sea Peoples. Tradition identifies him with the pharaoh who oppressed the Hebrews of the Exodus.

Ramses *see* Rameses

Ramsey, Sir Alf(red) (1920–99) Footballer and manager, born in Dagenham, Greater London. He played with Southampton and Tottenham Hotspur, managed Ipswich Town, and as manager of England (1963–74) saw his team win the World Cup in 1966.

Ramsey (of Canterbury), (Arthur) Michael Ramsey, Baron (1904–88) Archbishop of Canterbury (1961–74), born in Cambridge, Cambridgeshire. He worked for Church unity, making a historic visit to Pope Paul VI in the Vatican in 1966.

Rank (of Sutton Scotney), J(oseph) Arthur Rank, Baron (1888–1972)

Film magnate, born in Hull. He became chairman of many film companies, including Gaumont-British and Cinema-Television, and did much to promote the British film industry.

Ransome, Arthur (Michell) (1884–1967) Writer, born in Leeds, West Yorkshire. He wrote critical works and travel books before making his name with books for young readers, notably *Swallows and Amazons* (1930).

Rantzen, Esther (Louise) (1940–) Television presenter and producer, born in Berkhamsted, Hertfordshire. She is best known as the producer and presenter of BBC television's *That's Life* (1973–94), and for many documentary programmes. She also founded the charity 'Childline'.

Raphael, in full **Raffaello Sanzio** (1483–1520) Painter, born in Urbino, Italy. In 1508 he went to Rome, where he produced his greatest works, including the frescoes in the papal apartments of the Vatican, and the cartoons for the tapestries of the Sistine Chapel. In 1514 he succeeded Bramante as architect of St Peter's.

Raphael, Frederic (Michael) (1931–) Novelist, playwright, screenwriter, and biographer, born in Chicago, IL. He has adapted several of his novels for the screen, including *The Glittering Prizes* (1976), which became a popular television series. As a screenwriter, his work includes *Darling* (1965, Oscar) adapted from his own novel, and *Eyes Wide Shut* (1999).

Raspe, Rudolf Erich *see* Münchhausen, Freiherr von

Rasputin, Gri (?1871–1916) religious 'eld koye, Russia. dence of the and empress b through hypnos haemophiliac heir to the throne, Alexey. His political influence led to his murder by a group of aristocrats.

Rattigan, Sir Terence (Mervyn) (1911–77) Playwright, born in London. His plays include *French Without Tears* (1936), *The Winslow Boy* (1946), *The Browning Version* (1948), and *Ross* (1960).

Rattle, Sir Simon (Denis) (1955–) Conductor, born in Liverpool, Merseyside. He became widely acclaimed as the principal conductor of the City of Birmingham Symphony Orchestra (1990–98). Since 1981 he has been principal guest conductor of the Los Angeles Philharmonic, and joined the Berlin Philharmonic orchestra as chief conductor and artistic director in 2002.

Rau, Johannes (1931–2006) German politician and president (1999–2004), born in Wuppertal-Barmen, Germany. He became minister-president of the Social Democratic Party (1978–98), and chair of the party state organization (1977–99) before being elected federal president.

Rauschenberg, Robert (1925–) Avant-garde artist, born in Port Arthur, TX. One of the most aggressive US modernists, his collages and 'combines' incorporate a variety of rubbish (rusty metal, old tyres, frag-

, Maurice (1875–1937) Composer, born in Ciboure, France. His works include *Pavane for a Dead Princess* (trans, 1899), *Rapsodie espagnole* (1908), the 'choreographic poem' *La valse* (1920), and *Boléro* (1928), intended as a miniature ballet.

Rawsthorne, Alan (1905–71) Composer, born in Haslingden, Lancashire. His wide-ranging works include three symphonies, eight concertos, choral and chamber music, and several film scores.

Ray, Man, originally **Emanuel Rudnitsky** (1890–1976) Painter, photographer, and film-maker, born in Philadelphia, PA. He co-founded the New York Dadaist movement, experimented with new techniques in painting and photography, and during the 1930s produced *rayographs* (photographic images made without a camera).

Reagan, Ronald (Wilson) (1911–2004) US Republican statesman and 40th president, born in Tampico, IL. He went to Hollywood in 1937 and made over 50 films, beginning with *Love Is On the Air* (1937). He became Governor of California in 1966, stood unsuccessfully for the Republican presidential nomination in 1968 and 1976, but in 1980 defeated Jimmy Carter, and won a second term in 1984, defeating Walter Mondale. He introduced a major programme of economic change, took a strong anti-communist stand, especially in the Middle East and Central America, and introduced the Strategic Defense Initiative. In 1981 he was wounded in an assassination attempt. During his second term, he reached a major arms-reduction accord with Soviet leader Gorbachev.

Reardon, Ray(mond) (1932–) Snooker player, born in Tredegar, Blaenau Gwent, S Wales. The first of the great snooker players of the modern era, he was world professional champion six times (1970, 1973–6, 1978).

Redford, (Charles) Robert (1937–) Actor and director, born in Santa Barbara, CA. His films include *Butch Cassidy and the Sundance Kid* (1969), *The Sting* (1973), *All the President's Men* (1976), and *Out of Africa* (1985). He gained an Oscar for his direction of *Ordinary People* (1980), and directed and starred in *The Horse Whisperer* (1998).

Redgrave, Sir Michael (Scudamore) (1908–85) Actor, born in Bristol. His notable stage performances included Richard II (1951), Prospero (1952), and Uncle Vanya (1962), and his film career began with *The Lady Vanishes* (1938). He married the actress **Rachel Kempson** (1910–2003) in 1935, and their three children are all actors; **Vanessa** (1937–), **Corin** (1939–), and **Lynn** (1943–).

Redgrave, Sir Steve(n Geoffrey) (1962–) Rower, born in Marlow, Buckinghamshire. His main event is the heavyweight coxless pairs. He was the winner of five consecutive gold Olympic medals from 1984 to 2000, a feat accomplished by no other Olympic athlete. He also won seven World Championship gold medals and three Commonwealth Games gold medals, more than any other rower.

Redgrave, Vanessa (1937–) Actress, born in London, the daughter of Michael Redgrave. Her films include *Julia* (1977, Oscar), *The Bostonians* (1983), and *Howard's End* (1992). In 2003 she won a Tony Award for her performance in a revival of *Long Day's Journey into Night*. She is also well known for her active support of left-wing causes.

Redwood, John (1951–) British politician, born in Dover, Kent. Elected a Conservative MP in 1987, he was appointed secretary of state for Wales (1993–5). He was an unsuccessful contender for leader of his party, following John Major's resignation in 1997, and became shadow secretary of state for trade and industry (1997–2000) and deregulation spokesman (2004).

Reed, Sir Carol (1906–76) Film director, born in London. His major films include *Kipps* (1941), *The Fallen Idol* (1948), and *Oliver!* (1968, Oscar), but he is best known for *The Third Man* (1949).

Reeve, Christopher (1952–2004) Film actor, born in New York City. Universally known as the star of *Superman* and its sequels (1978, 1980, 1983, 1991), in 1994 he became wheelchair-bound following an accident. He founded the Christopher Reeve Paralysis Foundation in 1998 to promote research into spinal cord injuries.

Reeves, Keanu (1964–) Film actor, born in Beirut, Lebanon. *Bill and Ted's Excellent Adventure* (1989), and its sequel (1991), brought him international recognition. Later films include *Much Ado About Nothing* (1993), *The Matrix* (1999) and its sequels (both 2003), and *C* (2005).

Reiner, Rob (1945–) Film actor, ector, and producer, born in New York City. He became known for his role in *All in the Family* (1971–8, 2 Emmys). He has produced and directed several films, notably *When Harry Met Sally* (1989) and *Ghosts of Mississippi* (1996), and directed *The Story of Us* (1999) and *Alex and Emma* (2003).

Reinhardt, Django, popular name of **Jean Baptiste Reinhardt** (1910–53) Jazz guitarist, born in Liverchies, Belgium. He played in the Quintet of the Hot Club of France with Stéphane Grappelli (1934–9), and became the first European jazz musician to influence the music.

Reisz, Karel (1926–2002) Film and theatre actor, director, and producer, born in Ostrava, Czechoslovakia (now Czech Republic). He went to England as a child in 1938. His film credits include *Saturday Night and Sunday Morning* (1959), *Night Must Fall* (1963), and *The French Lieutenant's Woman* (1981). In later years he worked mainly as a theatre director.

Rembrandt (Harmenszoon van Rijn) (1606–69) Painter, born in Leyden, The Netherlands. He settled in Amsterdam (1631), where he ran a large studio and took numerous pupils. 'The Anatomy Lesson of Dr Nicolaes Tulp' (1632) assured his reputation as a portrait painter, and his masterpiece was 'The Night Watch' (1642). His preserved works number over 650 oil paintings, 2000 drawings and studies, and 300 etchings.

Remington, Eliphalet (1793–1861) US firearms manufacturer and inventor, born in Suffield, CT. He pioneered several improvements in small arms manufacture, including the first successful cast steel rifle barrel in the USA.

Rendell (of Babergh), Ruth Rendell, Baroness, originally **Ruth Barbara Grasemann**, occasional pseudonym **Barbara Vine** (1930–) Detective-story writer, born in London. Several of her detective stories feature Chief Inspector Wexford, such as *Shake Hands Forever* (1975), and she has also written mystery thrillers including *A Judgement in Stone* (1977). Many of her stories have been filmed or televised, notably in *The Ruth Rendell Mysteries*.

Renfrew (of Kaimsthorn), (Andrew) Colin Renfrew, Baron (1937–) Archaeologist, born in Stockton-on-Tees, Co Durham. Widely known for pioneering archaeological programmes on BBC television, notably in the *Chronicle* series, his books include *The Emergence of Civilization* (1972) and *The Cycladic Spirit* (1991).

Rennie, John (1761–1821) Civil engineer, born in Phantassie, East Lothian. He constructed several bridges, including the old Southwark and Waterloo Bridges over the R Thames, and designed London Bridge, London docks, and several other ports.

Renoir, Pierre Auguste (1841–1919) Impressionist artist, born in Limoges, France. His picture of sunlight filtering through leaves – *Le Moulin de la Galette* (1876, Louvre) – epitomizes his colourful, happy art.

Resnais, Alain (1922–) Film director,

born in Vannes, France. His major films are *Hiroshima mon amour* (1959) and the controversial *Last Year at Marienbad* (trans, 1961).

Respighi, Ottorino (1879–1936) Composer, born in Bologna, Italy. His works include nine operas, the symphonic poems *Fountains of Rome* (trans, 1916) and *Pines of Rome* (trans, 1924), and the ballet *La Boutique fantasque* (1919).

Reuter, Paul Julius, Freiherr (Baron) **von**, originally **Israel Beer Josaphat** (1816–99) Founder of the first news agency, born in Kassel, Germany. He developed the idea of a telegraphic news service, and in 1851 moved his headquarters to London.

Revere, Paul (1735–1818) US patriot, born in Boston, MA. On 18 April 1775, the night before Lexington and Concord, he started out for Concord, where arms were secreted. He was turned back by a British patrol, and his mission was completed by **Dr Samuel Prescott** (1751–?77), but it was Revere whom Longfellow immortalized for the 'midnight ride'.

Reynolds, Sir Joshua (1723–92) Portrait painter, born in Plympton, Devon. He left over 2000 works, including such notable paintings as 'Dr Samuel Johnson' (c.1756) and 'Sarah Siddons as the Tragic Muse' (1784). He became the first president of the Royal Academy (1768).

Rhodes, Cecil (John) (1853–1902) British colonial statesman, born in Bishop's Stortford, Hertfordshire. He secured the charter for the British South Africa Company (1889), whose territory was later named after him as Rhodesia. Prime minister of Cape

Colony (1890–6), he was a conspicuous figure during the Boer War (1899–1902), when he organized the defences of Kimberley.

Rhodes, Wilfred (1877–1973) Cricketer, born in Kirkheaton, West Yorkshire. He played for Yorkshire and England, and during his career (1898–1930) took a world record 4187 wickets and scored 39 722 runs. He performed the 'double' of 1000 runs and 100 wickets 16 times.

Rhodes, Zandra (1940–) Fashion designer, born in Chatham, Kent. She showed her first collection in 1969, and is noted for her distinctive, exotic designs in floating chiffons and silks.

Rhys, Jean, pseudonym of **Ella Gwendolen Rees Williams** (1894–1979) Writer, born in Roseau, Dominica. Her best-known novel is *Wide Sargasso Sea* (1966), a 'prequel' to Charlotte Brontë's *Jane Eyre*. She also wrote short stories and an autobiography.

Rhys-Jones, Sophie *see* Edward, Prince

Ribbentrop, Joachim von (1893–1946) German statesman, born in Wesel, Germany. He was responsible for the Anglo-German naval pact (1935), and became foreign minister (1938–45). Captured in 1945, he was executed at Nuremberg.

Ricci, Nina, originally **Maria Nielli** (1883–1970) Fashion designer, born in Turin, Italy. She joined Raffin in 1908, and stayed with him for 20 years, eventually becoming his business partner. She showed her first collection in 1932, and developed a wide range of further products in cosmetics, furs, and fashion accessories.

Rice, Condoleezza (1954–) US academic and Republican politician, born in Birmingham, AL. She joined Stanford University in 1981, became a professor of political science, and was the first woman and first African-American to become a Stanford provost (1993–9). In 2001 she was appointed national security adviser by George W Bush, and made secretary of state in 2004.

Rice, Tim, popular name of **Sir Timothy Miles Bindon Rice** (1944–) Lyricist, writer, and broadcaster, born in Buckinghamshire. He is best known for writing the lyrics for *Joseph and the Amazing Technicolour Dreamcoat* (1968), *Jesus Christ Superstar* (1971), and *Evita* (1978).

Richard I, known as **Richard Coeur de Lion** or **Richard the Lionheart** (1157–99) King of England (1189–99), born in Oxford, Oxfordshire, the third son of Henry II and Eleanor of Aquitaine. His reign was largely spent crusading and defending the Angevin lands in France. He was mortally wounded while besieging the castle of Châlus, Aquitaine.

Richard II (1367–1400) King of England (1377–99), born in Bordeaux, France, the younger son of Edward the Black Prince. His reign was dominated by a series of power struggles which led to the execution or banishment of several lords, including Henry Bolingbroke (later Henry IV). Bolingbroke invaded England unopposed, and Richard was deposed, dying in Pontefract Castle.

Richard III (1452–85) King of England

(1483–5), born in Fotheringhay Castle, Northamptonshire, the youngest son of Richard, Duke of York. He was created Duke of Gloucester (1461), and after the death of Edward IV, had himself crowned king. He was killed fighting Henry Tudor (later Henry VII) at Bosworth Field.

Richard, Cliff, popular name of **Sir Harry Roger Webb** (1940–) Pop-singer, born in Lucknow, India. He formed his own band in 1958, and with The Shadows was hailed as Britain's answer to American rock, his hits including 'Living Doll' (1959). He also made a series of family musical films, such as *The Young Ones* (1961) and *Summer Holiday* (1962). He became the UK's top selling singles artist in 2004 with 21 million records, overtaking The Beatles.

Richards, Emma (1975–) Yachtswoman, born in Helensburgh, Argylle and Bute. In her 18 m/60 ft yacht *Pindar*, she became the first woman and youngest person to complete the 29 000-mile Around Alone solo race. She departed from New York (Sep 2002) and after 135 days at sea crossed the finishing line at Newport, RI (May 2003) in fourth place.

Richards, Sir Gordon (1904–86) Jockey and trainer, born in Oakengates, Shropshire. Between 1921 and 1954 he rode a record 4870 winners in Britain, and was champion jockey a record 26 times (1925–53).

Richards, Viv, popular name of **Sir Isaac Vivian Alexander Richards** (1952–) Cricket player, born in Antigua. He captained the West Indies (1985–91), and scored 8540 runs in 121 Test matches, including 24 centuries. In England he played county cricket for Somerset (1974–86) and Glamorgan (1990–3).

Richardson, Miranda (1958–) Actress, born in Southport, Lancashire. Her films include *Empire of The Sun* (1987), *Damage* (1992, BAFTA for Best Supporting Actress), and *Wah-Wah* (2005). She also appeared as Queen Elizabeth in the BBC television comedy series *Blackadder* (1990).

Richardson, Sir Ralph (David) (1902–83) Actor, born in Cheltenham, Gloucestershire. His association with the Old Vic Company began in 1930, and he led its post-war revival. His films include *Anna Karenina* (1948), *A Doll's House* (1973), and *Invitation to the Wedding* (1983).

Richardson, Samuel (1689–1761) Novelist, born in Mackworth, Derbyshire. In using the epistolary method, as in *Pamela* (1740) and *Clarissa* (1748), he helped to develop the dramatic scope of the novel, then little regarded as a literary form.

Richelieu, Armand Jean du Plessis, Cardinal, duc de (Duke of) (1585–1642) French statesman, born in Richelieu, France. As chief minister (1624–42) he was the effective ruler of France. His principal achievement was to check Habsburg power, ultimately by sending armies into the Spanish Netherlands, Alsace, Lorraine, and Roussillon.

Rickman, Alan (1946–) Actor, born in London. He played a wide range of theatre roles, then became known for his film work, including *Truly, Madly, Deeply* (1991), *Robin Hood, Prince of Thieves* (1991, BAFTA Best Supporting

Actor), and *Rasputin* (1996, Emmy). He starred as Professor Snape in four 'Harry Potter' films (2001, 2002, 2004, 2005).

Ridgeley, Andrew *see* Michael, George

Ridley, Nicholas (c.1500–1555) Protestant martyr, born near Haltwhistle, Northumberland. An ardent reformer, he became Bishop of London (1550), and helped Cranmer prepare the Thirty-nine Articles. On the death of Edward VI he espoused the cause of Lady Jane Grey, and was executed.

Riefenstahl, Leni, popular name of **Berta Helene Amalie Riefenstahl** (1902–2003) Film-maker, born in Berlin. Her films include *Triumph of the Will* (trans, 1935), a compelling record of a Nazi rally at Nuremberg, and *Olympia* (1938), an epic documentary of the Berlin Olympic Games.

Rifkind, Sir Malcolm (Leslie) (1946–) British Conservative statesman, born in Edinburgh. He became secretary of state for Scotland (1986–90), transport (1990–2), defence (1992–5), and foreign secretary (1995–7). In 2005 he was appointed shadow secretary of state for work and pensions.

Rigg, Dame Diana (1938–) Actress, born in Doncaster, Yorkshire. She played Emma Peel in the popular 1960s *The Avengers* television series, then joined the National Theatre (1972). Among her films are *Evil Under the Sun* (1982), *A Good Man in Africa* (1994), and *Heidi* (2005). Television work includes *Mother Love* (1990, BAFTA).

Rimbaud, (Jean Nicolas) Arthur

(1854–91) Poet, born in Charleville, France. His works include *The Drunken Boat* (trans, 1871) and *Les Illuminations* (published 1876), a series of prose and verse poems, which show him to be a precursor of Symbolism.

Rimet, Jules (1873–1956) French football administrator. He promoted the Fédération Internationale de Football Association (FIFA), of which he was president (1921–56), and founded the World Cup competition (1930), his name being added to the title in 1946.

Rimsky-Korsakov, Nikolai (Andreyevich) (1844–1908) Composer, born in Tikhvin, Russia. He produced three great orchestral masterpieces, *Capriccio Espagnol*, *Easter Festival*, and *Sheherazade* (1887–8), after which he chiefly wrote operas, such as *The Golden Cockerel* (1907).

Rivaldo, popular name of **Rivaldo Vitor Borba Ferreira** (1972–) Footballer, born in Recife, Brazil. His clubs include FC Santa Cruz , Deportivo de La Coruña, Barcelona, AC Milan, Brazilian club Cruzeiro, and Greek side Olympiakos (2004–). His many awards include the Ballon d'Or and the FIFA World Footballer of the Year in 1999. He was a member of Brazil's World Cup squad in 2002.

Rivers, Joan, professional name of **Joan Alexandra Molinsky** (1933–) Comedienne and writer, born in Larchmont, NY. She became the regular guest host of *The Tonight Show* (1983–6), and hosted *The Late Show* (1986–7) and her own daytime talk show in 1989. She has also worked as a film director and recording artist, and her books include *Bouncing Back* (1997).

Rix, Brian, popular name of **Brian Norman Roger Rix, Lord Rix of Whitehall and of Hornsea** (1924–) Actor and manager, born in Cottingham, Yorkshire. He established a reputation for farce at the Whitehall Theatre with such productions as *Reluctant Heroes* (1950), *Dry Rot* (1954), and *Simple Spymen* (1958). He later left the stage for charity work and was chairman of Mencap (1988–98).

Roach, Hal, popular name of **Harald Eugene Roach** (1892–1992) Filmmaker, born in Elmira, NY. After producing many short silent comedies, he went on to make a wide range of sound feature films, such as *Way Out West* (1937) and *One Million BC* (1940).

Roach, Max(well) (1924–) Jazz drummer, bandleader, and composer, born in New Land, NC. He played with many of the pioneers of 'bop' and modern jazz, including Dizzy Gillespie, Charlie Parker, and Miles Davis.

Robards, Jason, Jr (1922–2000) Actor, born in Chicago, IL. Primarily known as a stage actor, in 1956 he won critical acclaim for his performances in Eugene O'Neill's *The Iceman Cometh* and *Long Day's Journey into Night*. He won Best Supporting Actor Oscars for *All the President's Men* (1976) and *Julia* (1977). He was married to the actress Lauren Bacall (1961–9).

Robbe-Grillet, Alain (1922–) Novelist, born in Brest, France. After his first novel, *The Erasers* (trans, 1953), he emerged as the leader of the *nouveau*

roman group. His film scenarios include *Last Year at Marienbad* (trans, 1961).

Robbia, Luca della (c.1400–82) Sculptor, born in Florence, Italy. He executed 10 panels for the cathedral there (1431–40), and a bronze door for the sacristy with 10 panels of figures in relief (1448–67). He established a business producing glazed terracottas which was carried on by his nephew **Andrea della Robbia** (1435–1525) and Andrea's son **Giovanni della Robbia** (1469–c.1529).

Robbins, Jerome (1918–98) Dancer and choreographer, born in New York City. He became director of New York City Ballet (1949–59), and joint ballet master (from 1983). He collaborated with Bernstein on *West Side Story* (1957), and won two Oscars for the 1961 Hollywood version.

Robbins, Tim (1958–) Film actor, director, and writer, born in West Govina, CA. His films include (as actor) *The Shawshank Redemption* (1994), *Mystic River* (2003), and *War of the Worlds* (2005), and (as producer, director, and writer) *Dead Man Walking* and *Cradle Will Rock* (1999).

Robert I *see* Bruce, Robert

Robert, Duke of Normandy *see* Henry I (of England)

Roberts, Julia, originally **Julie Fiona Roberts** (1967–) Film actress, born in Smyrna, Georgia. She became well known after *Steel Magnolias* (1989, Best Supporting Actress Oscar nomination) and *Pretty Woman* (1990). Her later films include *Notting Hill* (1999), *Erin Brockovich* (2000, Best Actress Oscar, BAFTA, Golden Globe), and *Closer* (2004).

Robertson (of Port Ellen), George (Islay MacNeill) Robertson, Baron (1946–) British statesman, born on the island of Islay, Scotland. He was elected an MP in 1978, rising to become spokesman on Scotland in the shadow cabinet (1993–7). He served as defence secretary (1997–9) in the Labour government, and was appointed secretary-general of NATO (1999–2003).

Robeson, Paul (Bustill) (1898–1976) Singer and actor, born in Princeton, NJ. He appeared in works ranging from *Show Boat* to *Othello*, gave song recitals, notably of Negro spirituals, and appeared in numerous films. In the 1950s, his left-wing views caused him to leave the USA for Europe (1958–63), and he retired after his return.

Robespierre, Maximilien François Marie Isidore de (1758–94) French revolutionary leader, born in Arras. A prominent member of the Jacobins, he emerged in the National Assembly as a popular radical, became a member of the Committee of Public Safety (1793), and for three months dominated the country, introducing the Reign of Terror and the cult of the Supreme Being. His ruthlessness led to his fall from power, and he was guillotined.

Robin Hood Legendary 13th-c outlaw who lived in Sherwood Forest in the N Midlands, England. Known for his archery, he protected the poor, and outwitted wealthy and unscrupulous officials, notably the Sheriff of Nottingham.

Robinson, Anne (1944–) Journalist and television presenter, born in Liverpool, Merseyside. A journalist for several newspapers, she also presented the BBC consumer programme *Watchdog* (1993–2001). In 2000 she became known as the formidable presenter of the quiz game *The Weakest Link*.

Robinson, Edward G, originally **Emanuel Goldenberg** (1893–1973) Film actor, born in Bucharest, Romania. He became famous with his portrayal of a vicious gangster in *Little Caesar* (1930), and went on to play hoodlums in such films as *Key Largo* (1948), and strong character parts as in *Double Indemnity* (1944).

Robinson, (William) Heath (1872–1944) Artist, cartoonist, and book illustrator, born in London. His fame rests mainly on his humorous drawings satirizing the machine age, displaying 'Heath Robinson' contraptions of absurd and complicated design but with highly practical and simple aims.

Robinson, Mary, *née* **Bourke** (1944–) Irish president (1990–7), born in Ballina, Co Mayo, Ireland. She left the Labour Party in protest against the Anglo-Irish Agreement (1985), and against all the odds defeated Brian Lenihan of the Fianna Fáil Party to take office as Ireland's first female president. She was the UN High Commisioner for Human Rights, 1997–2002.

Robinson, Sugar Ray, originally **Walker Smith, Jr** (1921–89) Professional boxer, born in Detroit, MI. He turned professional in 1940, and was never knocked out in 201 contests. He held the world welterweight title

(1946–51) and the world middleweight title (1950–1).

Rob Roy (Gaelic 'Red Robert'), nickname of **Robert MacGregor** or
Campbell (1671–1734) Highland outlaw, born in Buchanan, Stirling,
Scotland. He began a life of brigand-
age after his lands were seized (1712),
and was eventually captured and
imprisoned in London, but pardoned
in 1727. His life was romanticized in
the novel by Sir Walter Scott.

Robson, Dame Flora (McKenzie)
(1902–84) Actress, born in South
Shields, Durham. She gained fame in
historical roles in plays and films,
such as Queen Elizabeth I in *Fire over
England* (1931) and Thérèse Raquin in
Guilty (1944).

Rochas, Marcel (1902–55) Fashion
designer, born in Paris. He set up a
couture house in Paris in 1925,
launching his first fragrances in 1931,
and the sheepskin jacket in 1942. The
couture house closed upon his death
in 1955, but his wife Hélène took over
the perfume department until she
left the company in 1989.

Rockefeller, John D(avison)
(1839–1937) Industrialist and philanthropist, born in Richford, NY. In
1875 he founded with his brother
William Rockefeller (1841–1922) the
Standard Oil Company, securing
control of the US oil trade. He gave
over $500 million in aid of medical
research, universities, and churches,
and established in 1913 the **Rockefeller Foundation** 'to promote the
wellbeing of mankind'. His son, **John
D Rockefeller, Jr** (1874–1960) built
the Rockefeller Center in New York
City. His third son, **Nelson A(ldrich)**

Rockefeller (1908–79), became
Republican Governor of New York
State (1958–73), and was vice-
president (1974–7) under President
Ford.

**Rockingham, Charles Watson
Wentworth, 2nd Marquess of**
(1730–82) British prime minister
(1765–6, 1782). He repealed the Stamp
Act, affecting the American colonies,
and opposed Britain's war against the
colonists.

Roddenberry, Gene, popular name of
Eugene Wesley Roddenberry
(1921–91) Writer, and film and television producer, born in El Paso, TX.
He is best known as the creator and
producer of the science-fiction series
Star Trek.

Roddick, Andy, popular name of
Andrew Stephen Roddick (1982–)
Tennis player, born in Omaha, NE. A
junior number 1 world champion in
2000 (the youngest American to
achieve this position since rankings
began), he then turned professional,
winning the US Open (2000), the
French Open (2002–3), and reaching
the semi-finals at Wimbledon (2003).
At the beginning of 2006 he had a
world ranking of number 3.

Roddick, Dame Anita (Lucia) (1943–)
Retail entrepreneur, born in
Brighton, East Sussex. In 1976 she
opened her first shop selling beauty
products made from natural ingre-
dients, not tested on animals, and
supplied in refillable containers. In
2006 the Body Shop chain was
acquired by the French cosmetics
company L'Oréal.

Rodgers, (Charles) Richard
(1902–79) Composer, born in New

York City. With the lyricist **Lorenz Hart** (1895–1942) he had many successful songs, such as 'The Lady Is a Tramp' and 'My Funny Valentine'. He later collaborated in a series of hit musicals with Oscar Hammerstein II, notably *Oklahoma!* (1943, Pulitzer), *South Pacific* (1949, Pulitzer), *The King and I* (1951), and *The Sound of Music* (1959).

Rodin, (René François) Auguste (1840–1917) Sculptor, born in Paris. His greatest work was 'La Porte de l'enfer' (The Gate of Hell) for the Musée des Arts Décoratifs in 1880, on which he worked for some 30 years. Among his other works is 'The Thinker' (trans, 1904), in front of the Panthéon in Paris.

Roentgen, Wilhelm Konrad von *see* Röntgen

Rogers, Ginger, originally **Virginia Katherine McMath** (1911–95) Film actress, born in Independence, MO. She first danced with Fred Astaire in *Flying Down to Rio* (1933), going on to make nine other films with him. She won an Oscar for best actress in *Kitty Foyle* (1940).

Roget, Peter Mark (1779–1869) Physician and scholar, born in London. He is best known for his *Thesaurus of English Words and Phrases* (1852), which he wrote after his retirement from medical practice.

Rolling Stones, The Rock group, with members **Mick Jagger** (1943–), **Keith Richard** (1943–), **Bill Wyman** (1941–), **Charlie Watts** (1942–), **Ron Wood** (1947–), former member **Brian Jones** (1944–69), one of the most successful popular music groups to emerge in the 1960s.

Among their hits were 'Satisfaction' and 'Jumpin' Jack Flash'. Still recording after four decades, they released the album *A Bigger Bang* in 2005, and made a world tour in 2006.

Rollins, Sonny, popular name of **Theodore Walter Rollins** (1929–) Jazz saxophonist and composer, born in New York City. From the mid-1950s he emerged as an important voice in the 'hard bop' movement, and became a powerful improviser on tenor and soprano saxophones.

Rolls, C(harles) S(tewart) (1877–1910) Motorist and aeronaut, born in London. From 1895 he experimented with the earliest motor cars, forming a partnership with Henry Royce in 1906 for their production.

Romberg, Sigmund (1887–1951) Composer of operettas, born in Nagykanizsa, Hungary. He settled in the USA in 1909. His most famous works include *The Student Prince* (1924) and *The Desert Song* (1926).

Rommel, Erwin (Johannes Eugen) (1891–1944) German field marshal, born in Heidenheim, Germany. He led a Panzer division during the 1940 invasion of France, then commanded the Afrika Korps, where he achieved major successes, but was eventually driven into retreat. He condoned the plot against Hitler's life, and after its discovery committed suicide.

Ronaldinho, popular name of **Ronaldo de Assis Moreira** (1980–) Footballer, born in Porto Alegre, Brazil. His clubs include Paris Saint-Germain (2001) and Barcelona (from 2003). In his Brazilian national team debut (1999) he scored his first international goal to win the Copa America, and was a key player in his team's victory in the 2002 World Cup. His honours include FIFA World Player of the Year (2004, 2005), European Footballer of the Year (2005), and the Ballon d'Or (2005).

Ronaldo (Luiz Nazario de Lima), nickname **Ro-Ro** (1976–) Footballer, born in Itaguai, Brazil. A forward, he played for Cruzeiro, PSV Eindhoven, Barcelona, Inter Milan, and Real Madrid (from 2002). While at Barcelona he scored a Spanish league record of 34 goals in a season, his team also winning the European Cup Winners' Cup. He has been FIFA World Footballer of the Year three times (1996, 1997, 2002) and European Player of the Year twice (1997, 2002).

Ronay, Egon (1920–) Gastronome and writer, born in Hungary. He emigrated to England (1946), opened his own restaurant in London (1952–5), and founded the annual *Egon Ronay's Guide to Hotels and Restaurants* (1956).

Röntgen, Wilhelm Konrad von, also spelled **Roentgen** (1845–1923) Physicist, born in Lennep, Germany. In 1895 he discovered the electromagnetic rays which he called *X-rays*, and received the first Nobel Prize for Physics in 1901.

Rooney, Mickey, originally **Joe Yule, Jr** (1920–) Film actor, born in New York City. He became known for his child roles in the Mickey McGuire (1927–33) and Andy Hardy (1937–8) series, later films including *Boy's Town* (1938, Special Oscar) and *Breakfast at Tiffany's* (1961). He was married eight times, including once to film actress Ava Gardner. He returned to the stage in 1979 with the musical *Sugar Babes*, and won an Emmy for his television role in *Bill* (1982). In 2004, he starred in *Let's Put on a Show*, a musical memoir of his life in 300 films.

Rooney, Wayne (1985–) Footballer, born in Liverpool, Merseyside. In 2002 he made his premiership debut with Everton at age 16. In 2003 he became the youngest ever senior England international when he debuted as a substitute in a friendly match against Australia. He joined Manchester United in 2004. His awards include Best Young Player in Europe (2004) and FIFPro's World Young Player of the Year (2005).

Roosevelt, (Anna) Eleanor, *née* **Roosevelt** (1884–1962) Diplomat and humanitarian, born in New York City, the wife of Franklin D Roosevelt, whom she married in 1905, and the niece of Theodore Roosevelt. An independent activist, she had a strong part in shaping her husband's New Deal administration. During her widowhood she was a major figure in Democratic Party politics, and was much involved with the UN.

Roosevelt, Franklin D(elano), nickname **FDR** (1882–1945) US Democratic statesman and 32nd president (1933–45), born in Hyde Park, NY. He met the economic crisis with his *New Deal* for national recovery (1933), and became the only president to be re-elected three times. He strove in vain to ward off war, and was brought in by Japan's action at Pearl Harbor

(1941). He met with Churchill and Stalin at Teheran (1943) and Yalta (1945).

Roosevelt, Theodore, known as **Teddy Roosevelt** (1858–1919) US statesman and 26th president (1901–9), born in New York City. Elected Republican vice-president in 1900, he became president on the death (by assassination) of McKinley, and was elected in 1904 in his own right. An 'expansionist', he insisted on a strong navy, and introduced a *Square Deal* policy for social reform.

Roseanne, popular name of **Roseanne Barr** (1952–) Actor and producer, born in Salt Lake City, UT. After hosting a number of television specials and series, she became known for her realistic, unglamorized sitcom *Roseanne* (1988–97). Her film credits include *She-Devil* (1989) and *Blue in the Face* (1995).

Rosebery, Archibald Philip Primrose, 5th Earl of (1847–1929) British Liberal prime minister (1894–5), born in London. He became foreign secretary (1886, 1892–4) under Gladstone, whom he succeeded as premier.

Ross, Jonathan (1960–) Television and radio presenter, born in London. His prolific career as a presenter for BBC television includes the long-running *Film Night* (from 1999), and his award-winning talk show *Friday Night With Jonathan Ross* (2001–).

Ross, Nick, popular name of **Nicholas David Ross** (1947–) Broadcaster and journalist, born in London. He became a BBC reporter on several radio and television programmes, becoming nationally known for his investigative reporting in *Call Nick Ross* (from 1987). He has also presented a wide range of news and discussion television programmes, notably *Crimewatch UK* (from 1984).

Rossellini, Roberto (1906–77) Film director, born in Rome. His film *Rome, Open City* (trans, 1945) was made with hidden cameras in a style which came to be known as 'neo-Realism'. Later films include (trans titles) *Paisan* (1946) and *General della Rovere* (1959).

Rossetti, Dante Gabriel (1828–82) Poet and painter, born in London, the son of Gabriele Rossetti. A founder of the Pre-Raphaelite Brotherhood (c.1850), his early painting was on religious themes, such as 'The Annunciation' (1850). *Ballads and Sonnets* (1881) contains some of his best poetry.

Rossini, Gioacchino (Antonio) (1792–1868) Composer, born in Pesaro, Italy. Among his early successes were *Tancredi* (1813) and *The Italian Girl in Algiers* (trans, 1813), and in 1816 he produced his masterpiece, *The Barber of Seville*. Also known for his *Stabat Mater* (1841) and the *Petite messe solennelle* (1863), his overtures have continued to be highly popular items in concert programmes.

Roth, Philip (Milton) (1933–) Novelist, born in Newark, NJ. His books include *Portnoy's Complaint* (1969), the trilogy *Zuckerman Bound* (1989), *American Pastoral* (1998, Pulitzer), *The Human Stain* (2000; filmed 2003), and *The Plot Against America* (2004). He was married to Claire Bloom (dissolved, 1995).

Rothermere, Viscount *see* Harmsworth, Harold (Sydney)

Rothko, Mark, originally **Marcus Rothkovitch** (1903–70) Painter, born in Dvinsk, Russia (now Daugavpils, Latvia). His family emigrated to the USA in 1913. During the 1940s he was influenced by Surrealism, but by the early 1950s had evolved his own meditative form of Abstract Expressionism.

Rothschild, Meyer (Amschel) (1743–1812) Financier, the founder of a banking dynasty, born in Frankfurt, Germany. He began as a moneylender, and became the financial adviser of the Landgrave of Hesse. His five sons continued the firm, opening branches in other countries.

Rousseau, Jean-Jacques (1712–78) Political philosopher, educationist, and essayist, born in Geneva, Switzerland. His works include *Discourse on the Origin and Foundations of Inequality Amongst Men* (trans, 1755), his masterpiece, *The Social Contract* (trans, 1762), which was a great influence on French revolutionary thought, and his major work on education, *Emile*.

Rowland, Tiny, originally **Rowland W Furhop** (1917–98) Financier, born in India. He joined Lonrho (London and Rhodesian Mining and Land Company) in 1961, and became chief executive and managing director, stepping down in 1994.

Rowling, J(oanne) K(athleen) (1965–) Writer, born in Chipping Sodbury, Gloucestershire. A former teacher, her life changed following the publication of *Harry Potter and the Philosopher's Stone* (1997; filmed 2001). It was followed by *Harry Potter and the Chamber of Secrets* (1998; filmed 2002), *Harry Potter and the Prisoner of Azkaban* (1999; filmed 2004), *Harry Potter and the Goblet of Fire* (2000; filmed 2005), *Harry Potter and the Order of the Phoenix* (2003), and *Harry Potter and the Half-Blood Prince* (2005), with a further volume planned.

Royce, Sir (Frederick) Henry (1863–1933) Engineer, born in Alwalton, Cambridgeshire. In 1884 he founded the firm of Royce Ltd in Manchester, made his first car in 1904, and with C S Rolls founded Rolls-Royce, Ltd in 1906.

Rubens, (Peter Paul) (1577–1640) Painter, born in Siegen, Germany. His major works include a triptych 'The Descent from the Cross' (1611–14) in Antwerp Cathedral, 21 large subjects on the life and regency of Marie de Médicis of France, and many works painted while on diplomatic missions in Spain and England, such as 'Peace and War' (National Gallery, London).

Rubinstein, Helena (1870–1965) Beautician and business executive, born in Kraków, Poland. She moved in the 1890s to Australia, where she opened the country's first beauty salon, in Melbourne (1902), and in 1915 launched an international business empire from New York City.

Ruby, Jack L, originally **Jacob Rubenstein** (1911–67) Assassin, born in Chicago, IL. Two days after the assassination of President John F Kennedy, he shot and killed Lee Harvey Oswald, the alleged assassin of the president. He was sentenced to death in 1964, but died while await-ing a second trial.

Rumford, Count *see* Thompson, Sir Benjamin

Rumsfeld, Donald (Henry) (1932–) US Republican politician, born in Chicago, IL. He joined the Nixon administration as an assistant to the president (1969–72), and was chief-of-staff under Gerald Ford (1974–5), who also appointed him defence secretary (1975–7). Appointed defence secretary (2001–) by George W Bush, he was responsible for the US campaign during the Iraq War (2003).

Runcie (of Cuddesdon), Robert (Alexander Kennedy) Runcie, Baron (1921–2000) Archbishop of Canterbury (1980–91), born in Crosby, Lancashire. His period as archbishop was marked by a papal visit to Canterbury, ongoing contro-versies over homosexuality and women in the Church, and the Lambeth Conference of 1987.

Rundstedt, (Karl Rudolf) Gerd von (1875–1953) German field marshal, born in Aschersleben, Germany. In 1939 he directed the attacks on Poland and France, and directed the Ardennes offensive in 1944.

Rusedski, Greg (1973–) Tennis player, born in Montreal, Quebec, Canada. He became a British subject in 1995. A left-handed player, known for his very fast serves, he became British number 1 in 1997. By the end of the 1999 Wimbledon Championships he was ranked 10th in the world listings. A variety of injuries kept him off the circuit for much of 2002–3, and at the start of 2006 his world ranking was 40.

Rush, Geoffrey (1951–) Actor, born in Toowoomba, Queensland, Australia. Known as a theatre actor in Australia, he received international recogni-tion for his role as David Helfgott in the 1996 film *Shine* (Oscar, Golden Globe, BAFTA). Later films include *Shakespeare in Love* (1999) and *Candy* (2005).

Rush, Ian (1961–) Footballer, born in St Asaph, Denbighshire. He joined Liverpool in 1981, scoring 110 goals in 182 league matches. His later clubs include Juventus, Leeds United, and Newcastle United. He went to Wrexham as coach (1998–2000) and was later manager of Chester City (2004–5). He was a regular member of the Welsh international team from 1980, gaining 73 caps.

Rushdie, (Ahmed) Salman (1947–) Writer, born in Mumbai, India, of Muslim parents. He became widely known after his second novel, *Mid-night's Children* (1981, Booker). *The Satanic Verses* (1988) caused world-wide controversy for its secular treatment of Islam, and in 1989 he was forced to go into hiding because of a death sentence passed on him by Ayatollah Khomeini of Iran. Among later novels are *The Moor's Last Sigh* (1995, Whitbread) and *Shalimar the Clown* (2005).

Ruskin, John (1819–1900) Writer and art theorist, born in London. His major works include *Modern Painters* (1843–60), *The Seven Lamps of Archi-tecture* (1848), and *The Stones of Venice* (1851–3).

Russell, Bertrand (Arthur William)

Russell, 3rd Earl (1872–1970) Philosopher and mathematician, born in Trelleck, Monmouthshire. His major works were *Principles of Mathematics* (1903) and (with A N Whitehead) *Principia Mathematica* (1910–13). Later works included *An Enquiry into Meaning and Truth* (1940) and *Human Knowledge* (1948). After 1949 he became a champion of nuclear disarmament. The single most important influence on 20th-c analytic philosophy, he was awarded the Nobel Prize for Literature in 1950.

Russell, Jack, popular name of **John Russell** (1795–1883) Clergyman, born in Dartmouth, Devon. He developed the West Country smooth-haired, short-legged terrier, since named after him.

Russell, (Ernestine) Jane (Geraldine) (1921–) Film actress, born in Bemidji, MN. Known for her striking looks, she became one of the leading Hollywood sex symbols of the 1950s, her major films including *Paleface* (1948) and *Gentlemen Prefer Blondes* (1953).

Russell (of Kingston Russell), John Russell, 1st Earl, known as **Lord John Russell** (1792–1878) British Whig–Liberal prime minister (1846–52, 1865–6), born in London. He first became prime minister after the Conservative Party split over the repeal of the Corn Laws (1846), and also served as foreign secretary (1852–5, 1859), though forced to retire over alleged incompetence during the Crimean War.

Russell, Ken, popular name of **Henry Kenneth Alfred Russell** (1927–) Film director, born in Southampton, Hampshire. After several experimental studies for BBC television (eg Debussy, Isadora Duncan), he began to make feature films, including *Women in Love* (1969) and *The Devils* (1971), and for television *Lady Chatterley* (1993).

Ruth, Babe, popular name of **George Herman Ruth**, nicknames **the Bambino, the Sultan of Swat** (1895–1948) Baseball player, born in Baltimore, MD. He joined the New York Yankees in 1920, and when he retired in 1935 had scored 714 home runs, a figure not bettered until 1974. *The Babe Ruth Story* was filmed in 1984; *The Babe* in 1991.

Rutherford (of Nelson), Ernest Rutherford, 1st Baron (1871–1937) Physicist, born near Nelson, New Zealand. With Soddy he proposed that radioactivity results from the disintegration of atoms (1903), and later he developed the modern conception of the atom, receiving the Nobel Prize for Chemistry in 1908.

Rutherford, Dame Margaret (1892–1972) Theatre and film actress, born in London. She gained fame as a character actress and comedienne, and played Agatha Christie's 'Miss Marple' in a series of films from 1962. She won an Oscar for her role in *The VIPs* in 1964.

Ryan, Meg (1963–) Film actress, born in Fairfield, CT. She became well known after *When Harry Met Sally* (1989), later films including *Sleepless in Seattle* (1993), *French Kiss* (1995), *City of Angels* (1998), and *Against the Ropes* (2004).

Ryder (of Warsaw), Sue Ryder, Baroness (1923–2000) Philanthropist, born in Leeds, West Yorkshire. She established the Sue Ryder Foundation in 1953, now comprising some 80 centres worldwide, offering residential care for the sick and disabled. The Ryder-Cheshire Foundation linked her work with that of her husband, Leonard Cheshire.

Ryder, Winona (1971–) Film actress, born in Winona, MI. Her films include *Beetlejuice* (1988), *Edward Scissorhands* (1990), *Girl, Interrupted* (1999), and *The Darwin Awards* (2006). She won a Best Supporting Actress Oscar nomination for *The Age of Innocence* (1993), and a Best Actress nomination for her role as Jo in *Little Women* (1995).

Rylance, Mark (1960–) Actor and director, born in Kent. In 1994 he received an Olivier Award for Best Actor in Thelma Holt's production of *Much Ado About Nothing*. In 1995 he was appointed founding artistic director of Shakespeare's Globe Theatre in London, stepping down in 2005. His film work includes *Prospero's Books* (1991) and *Intimacy* (2000).

Ryle, Gilbert (1900–76) Philosopher, born in Brighton, East Sussex. He is best known for his book *The Concept of Mind* (1949), which argued against the mind/body dualism ('the ghost in the machine') proposed by Descartes.

Ryle, Sir Martin (1918–84) Radio astronomer, born in Brighton, East Sussex, the nephew of Gilbert Ryle. His development of interferometers enabled him to survey the most distant radio sources, and his work paved the way for renewed interest in the 'big bang' theory. He shared the Nobel Prize for Physics in 1974.

S

Saatchi & Saatchi Advertisers: **Charles Saatchi** (1943–) and **Maurice Saatchi** (1946–), both born in Iraq. They moved to England in 1947, set up an advertising agency in 1970, and became famous for their election campaign for the Conservative Party in 1978.

Sabin, Albert (Bruce) (1906–93) Microbiologist, born in Białystok, Poland. He is best known for his research into a live virus as a polio vaccine, which has replaced the Salk vaccine, as it gives longer-lasting immunity, and is capable of being given orally.

Sacks, Oliver (Wolf) (1933–) Neurologist, born in London. In New York City, he worked with patients who had contracted a form of sleeping sickness, and became known following his account of the brief cure they experienced after receiving treatment with L-dopa, *Awakenings* (1973; filmed, 1990). His insights into unusual syndromes, along with an appealing literary style, resulted in a series of best-selling books, such as *The Man who Mistook his Wife for a*

Hat (1986) and *The Island of the Colorblind* (1998).

Sackville-West, Vita, popular name of **Victoria Mary Sackville-West** (1892–1962) Poet and novelist, born at Knole, Kent. Her best-known novels are *The Edwardians* (1930) and *All Passion Spent* (1931). In 1913 she married Harold Nicolson, and her friendship with Virginia Woolf occasioned the latter's *Orlando* (1928).

Saddam Hussein *see* Hussein, Saddam

Sade, Marquis de, popular name of **Donatien Alphonse François, comte** (Count) **de Sade** (1740–1814) Writer, born in Paris. Condemned to death for his cruelty and sexual perversions (1772), he escaped, but was later imprisoned in the Bastille (1784–90), where he wrote *The 120 Days of Sodom* (trans, c.1784).

Safin, Marat (1980–) Tennis player, born in Moscow. He turned professional in 1997, and his achievements include the US Open and two Masters Series titles in 2000, and the Paris Masters in 2002. Twice runner-up in the Australian Open (2002, 2004), he won the title in 2005. At the beginning of 2006 he had a world ranking of number 11.

Sagan, Carl (Edward) (1934–96) Astronomer and writer, born in New York City. He worked on the physics and chemistry of planetary atmospheres and surfaces, and investigated the origin of life on Earth and the possibility of extraterrestrial intelligence. His popular books include *Cosmic Connection* (1973). In 1978 he received a Pulitzer prize for his nonfiction work *The Dragons of Eden*.

Sagan, Françoise, pseudonym of **Françoise Quoirez** (1935–2004) Novelist, born in Paris. At 18 she wrote the best-selling *Bonjour tristesse* (1954, Good Morning, Sadness). Later works include *Aimez-vous Brahms?* (1959, Do You Like Brahms?), and a volume of collected works, *Oeuvres*, appeared in 1993.

St Denis, Ruth, originally **Ruth Dennis** (1877–1968) Dancer, director, choreographer, and teacher, born in Somerville, NJ. With Ted Shawn, whom she married in 1914, she founded the Denishawn school and company (1915), and became known for her exotic, colourful, Eastern dances.

Saint-Exupéry, Antoine (Marle Roger) de (1900–44) Airman and writer, born in Lyon, France. His philosophy of 'heroic action' is found in such novels as *Night Flight* (trans, 1931), but he is best known for his popular children's fable for adults, *The Little Prince* (trans, 1943).

Saint-Laurent, Yves (Henri Donat Mathieu) (1936–) Fashion designer, born in Oran, Algeria. In 1962 he opened his own house, and launched the first of his 160 Rive Gauche boutiques in 1966, selling ready-to-wear clothes.

Saint Leger, Barry (1737–89) British army colonel. He is best known as the founder of the Classic horse race at Doncaster, South Yorkshire, first run in 1776 and named after him in 1778.

Saint-Saëns, (Charles) Camille (1835–1921) Composer and music critic, born in Paris. His many works include five symphonies, 13 operas, notably *Samson et Dalila* (1877), the popular *Carnival of the Animals* (trans, 1886), and concertos for piano, violin, and cello.

Saki *see* Munro, H H

Saladin, in full **Salah al-Din Yussuf ibn Ayub** (1137–93) Sultan of Egypt and Syria, born in Tekrit, Mesopotamia. He defeated the crusaders in 1187, recapturing almost all their fortified places in Syria, but a further crusade captured Acre in 1191, and he was defeated.

Sales, Francis of *see* Francis of Sales, St

Salinger, J(erome) D(avid) (1919–) Novelist and short-story writer, born in New York City. His fame rests on the novel *The Catcher in the Rye* (1951); other books include *Franny and Zooey* (1961) and, after a long period of silence, *Hapworth 16, 1924* (1997). He has become a recluse in his later years.

Salisbury, Marquess of *see* Cecil, Robert, 3rd Marquess; Cecil, Robert, 5th Marquess

Salk, Jonas (Edward) (1914–95) Virologist, discoverer in 1953 of the first vaccine against poliomyelitis, born in New York City. In 1953–4 he prepared inactivated poliomyelitis vaccine, given by injections, which (after some controversy) was successfully tested.

Salome (1st-c) The traditional name of the daughter of Herodias. She danced before Herod Antipas (*Mark* 6.17–28), and as a reward was given the head of John the Baptist.

Samaranch, Juan Antonio (1920–) Seventh president of the International Olympic Committee (IOC), born in Barcelona, Spain. He was elected president of the IOC in 1980, and on his retirement in 2001 he was made honorary life president.

Sampras, Pete (1971–) Tennis player, born in Washington, DC. He turned professional in 1988, and went on to become the youngest men's US Open singles champion (1990), winning again in 1993, 1995, 1996, and 2002. Other wins include Wimbledon a record seven times (1993–5, 1997–2000), setting a world record of 14 Grand Slam titles in the process. He retired in 2003.

Samson (c.11th-c BC?) Biblical character, a legendary hero of the tribe of Dan. When Delilah cut his hair, breaking his Nazirite vow, he lost his great strength, and was held by the Philistines until his hair grew back and he pulled down their temple upon them (*Jud* 13–16).

Samuel (Heb probably 'name of God') (11th-c BC) Biblical character, the last of the judges and first of the prophets. He presided over Saul's election as the first king of Israel, but anointed David as Saul's successor, rather than Saul's own son, Jonathan.

Sandburg, Carl (August) (1878–1967) Poet, born in Galesburg, IL. He won a Pulitzer Prize in 1950 for his *Complete Poems*, and also in 1940 for a popular two-part biography of Abraham Lincoln.

Sanger, Frederick (1918–) Biochemist, born in Rendcombe, Gloucestershire. He revealed the full sequence of the 51 amino acids in insulin, for which he was awarded the Nobel Prize for Chemistry in 1958. He then devised methods to elucidate the molecular structure of the nucleic acids, and received a second Nobel Prize for Chemistry in 1980 – the first to receive two such awards.

Sanger, Margaret (Louise), *née* **Higgins** (1879–1966) Social reformer and founder of the birth control movement, born in Corning, NY. She started the first US birth control clinic in New York City in 1916, but was charged with creating a 'public nuisance', and imprisoned for 30 days. After a world tour, she founded the American Birth Control League in 1921.

Sapper, pseudonym of **Herman Cyril McNeile** (1888–1937) Novelist, born in Bodmin, Cornwall. He achieved fame as the creator of 'Bulldog' Drummond, the aggressively patriotic hero of a series of thrillers, such as *The Final Count* (1926).

Sarah or **Sarai** (Heb 'princess') Biblical character, the wife and half-sister of Abraham, who is portrayed (*Gen* 12–23) as having accompanied him from Ur to Canaan. Long barren, she is said to have eventually given birth to Isaac in her old age.

Sarandon, Susan, originally **Susan Abigail Tomalin** (1946–) Film actress, born in New York City. She became well known after her role in *The Rocky Horror Picture Show* (1975). Later films include *The Witches of Eastwick* (1987), *Thelma and Louise* (1991), *Dead Man Walking* (1995, Oscar), and *Elizabethtown* (2005).

Sargent, Sir (Harold) Malcolm (Watts) (1895–1967) Conductor, born in Ashford, Kent. He conducted the Royal Choral Society from 1928, the Liverpool Philharmonic Orchestra (1942–8), and the BBC Symphony

Orchestra (1950–7), and from 1948 was the popular leader of the London Promenade Concerts.

Sartre, Jean-Paul (1905–80) Existentialist philosopher and writer, born in Paris. His novels include the trilogy, *The Roads to Freedom* (1945–9), and he also wrote many plays, such as *Huis clos* (1944, trans In Camera/No Exit). His philosophy is presented in *Being and Nothingness* (trans, 1943). In 1964 he was awarded (but declined) the Nobel Prize for Literature. In the later 1960s he became heavily involved in opposition to US policies in Vietnam.

Sassoon, Siegfried (Loraine) (1886–1967) Poet and novelist, born in Brenchley, Kent. His hatred of war was fiercely expressed in his *Counterattack* (1918) and *Satirical Poems* (1926).

Saul (11th-c BC) Biblical character, the first king to be elected by the Israelites. He became jealous of David, his son-in-law, feuded with the priestly class, and fell in battle with the Philistines.

Saul of Tarsus *see* Paul, St

Saunders, Jennifer (1958–) Comedy writer and actress, born in Sleaford, Lincolnshire. She teamed up with Dawn French in a comedy act, making several series of 'French and Saunders' for television. She became internationally known following the success, as writer and actress, of her comedy series *Absolutely Fabulous* (1993–5, 2001; Emmy, 1993).

Savile, Jimmy, popular name of **Sir James Wilson Vincent Savile** (1926–) Television and radio personality, born in Leeds, West York-

shire. He achieved fame with regular appearances on *Top of the Pops* (from 1963) and as host of *Jim'll Fix It* (from 1975).

Sayers, Dorothy L(eigh) (1893–1957) Writer, born in Oxford, Oxfordshire. She became a celebrated writer of detective stories, introducing her hero Lord Peter Wimsey in *Clouds of Witness* (1926), and later earned a reputation as a leading Christian apologist with her plays, radio broadcasts, and essays.

Scarfe, Gerald (1936–) Cartoonist, born in London. His cartoons, based on extreme distortion in the tradition of Gillray, have appeared in several periodicals and newspapers, notably *The Sunday Times*. He is married to actress Jane Asher.

Scargill, Arthur (1938–) Trade unionist, born in Leeds, West Yorkshire. He became president of the National Union of Mineworkers in 1981, and is primarily known for his strong, socialist defence of British miners, especially during the miners' strike of 1984–5.

Scarlatti, (Pietro) Alessandro (Gaspare) (1660–1725) Composer, born in Palermo, Sicily. He reputedly wrote over 100 operas (of which 40 survive complete), 10 Masses, c.700 cantatas, and oratorios, motets, and madrigals.

Scarlatti, (Giuseppe) Domenico (1685–1757) Composer, born in Naples, Italy, the son of Alessandro Scarlatti. He was a skilled harpsichordist, and is mainly remembered for the 555 sonatas written for this instrument.

Schiaparelli, Elsa (1890–1973) Fashion designer, born in Rome. Her designs were inventive and sensational, and she was noted for her use of colour, including 'shocking pink', and her original use of traditional fabrics.

Schlesinger, John (Richard) (1926–2003) Film director, born in London. His many films include *A Kind of Loving* (1962), *Billy Liar* (1963), *Midnight Cowboy* (1969, Oscar), *Marathon Man* (1976), and *Madame Sousatzka* (1989). Work for television included *An Englishman Abroad* (1983) and *Cold Comfort Farm* (1996).

Schoenberg, Arnold, also spelled **Schönberg** (1874–1951) Composer, born in Vienna. His *Chamber Symphony* caused a riot at its first performance in 1907 through its abandonment of the traditional concept of tonality, and he became known for his concept of '12-note' or 'serial' music, used in most of his later works.

Schönberg, Arnold *see* Schoenberg, Arnold

Schopenhauer, Arthur (1788–1860) Philosopher, born in Gdańsk, Poland (formerly Danzig, Germany). His chief work, *The World as Will and Idea* (trans, 1819), emphasizes the central role of human will as the creative factor in understanding. A collection of his writings, published as *Parerga und Paralipomena* (1851), influenced existentialism and other philosophical movements.

Schröder, Gerhard (1944–) German statesman and chancellor (1998–2005), born in Mossenberg, Germany. He qualified as a lawyer, and entered parliament as a social democrat in 1980. He became minister president of Lower Saxony in

1990, and defeated Helmut Kohl to become chancellor in 1998, winning a second term in 2002. He was defeated in the 2005 election by Angela Merkel.

Schubert, Franz (Peter) (1797–1828) Composer, born in Vienna. His major works include the Trout Piano Quintet (1819), the C major symphony (1825), and the B minor symphony (1822), known as the 'Unfinished'. He is particularly remembered as the greatest exponent of German songs (*Lieder*), which number c.600.

Schumacher, Michael (1969–) Motor-racing driver, born in Hürth-Hermuhlheim, Germany. He made his Formula One debut in 1990 and was world champion in 1994 and 1995. He joined Ferrari in 1996, and with them won the world championship three years in succession (2000–2), gained a record sixth title in 2003, and achieved a seventh title in 2004. His brother, **Ralf Schumacher** (1975–), is also a F1 motor-racing driver.

Schumann, Robert (Alexander) (1810–56) Composer, born in Zwickau, Germany. He produced a large number of compositions for piano, then married Clara Wieck, and under her influence began to write orchestral works, notably his A minor piano concerto (1845) and four symphonies. He also wrote chamber music and a large number of songs (*Lieder*).

Schwarzenegger, Arnold (1947–) US film actor, born near Graz, Austria. In the 1980s he became known for his roles in tough action films, including *Conan the Barbarian* (1982), *The Ter-*

minator (1984, sequels 1991, 2003), *Total Recall* (1990), and *Last Action Hero* (1992). He became an American citizen in 1983 and successfully ran for governor of California in 2003.

Schwarzkopf, (Olga Maria) Elisabeth (Friederike) (1915–) Soprano, born in Janotschin, Poland. She sang in the Vienna State Opera (1944–8) and at Covent Garden (1949–52). She first specialized in coloratura roles, and later appeared more as a lyric soprano, especially in recitals of *Lieder*.

Schweitzer, Albert (1875–1965) Medical missionary, theologian, musician, and philosopher, born in Kaysersberg, NE France (formerly Germany). In 1896 he made his famous decision that he would live for science and art until he was 30, then devote his life to serving humanity. True to his vow, despite his international reputation in music and theology, he began to study medicine in 1905, and after qualifying (1913) set up a hospital to fight leprosy and sleeping sickness at Lambaréné, French Equatorial Africa, where he remained for the rest of his life. He was awarded the Nobel Peace Prize in 1952.

Schwimmer, David (1966–) Actor and director, born in New York City. He became known for his role as Ross Geller in the acclaimed television series *Friends* (1994–2004). Feature films include *The Pallbearer* (1996), *Uprising* (2001), and *Duane Hopwood* (2005).

Scofield, (David) Paul (1922–) Actor, born in Hurstpierpoint, West Sussex. In the 1940s he began to distinguish himself in Shakespearean roles, and later starred in *King Lear* (1962), *Othello* (1980), and as Sir Thomas More in *A Man For All Seasons* (1960; filmed 1966). Later film credits include *The Crucible* (1996).

Scorsese, Martin (1942–) Film director, writer, and producer, born in Flushing, Long Island, NY. His many films include *Taxi Driver* (1976), *Raging Bull* (1980), the controversial *The Last Temptation of Christ* (1988), *GoodFellas* (1990), *Gangs of New York* (2002, Golden Globe Best Director; Oscar nomination), and *The Aviator* (2004, Golden Globe Best Film; 11 Oscar nominations).

Scott, George C(ampbell) (1927–99) Film actor, born in Wise, VA. His early roles included *The Hustler* (1961) and *Dr Strangelove* (1963). He won an Oscar for *Patton* (1969), but refused to accept it (the first actor to do so), and also refused the Emmy he won for *The Price* (1970). Later films included *Dick Tracy* (1989), *Malice* (1993), and *Country Justice* (1997).

Scott, Sir George Gilbert (1811–78) Architect, born in Gawcott, Buckinghamshire. He became the leading practical architect of the British Gothic revival, as seen in the Albert Memorial (1862–3), St Pancras Station and Hotel in London (1865), and Glasgow University (1865).

Scott, Sir Peter (Markham) (1909–89) Artist, ornithologist, and broadcaster, born in London, the son of Robert Falcon Scott. He began to exhibit his paintings of bird scenes in 1933, and led several ornithological expeditions in the 1950s. His writing and television programmes helped to popularize natural history. In 1946 he founded the UK's wetland conservation charity, the Wildfowl and Wetlands Trust.

Scott, R(obert) F(alcon) (1868–1912) Antarctic explorer, born in Devonport, Devon. In 1910 he led an expedition to the South Pole (17 Jan 1912), only to discover that the Norwegian expedition under Amundsen had beaten them by a month. All members of his party died.

Scott, Ronnie, originally **Ronald Schatt** (1927–96) Jazz saxophonist and night club owner, born in London. In 1959 he opened a club in the Soho district of London, and it quickly became an international jazz centre.

Scott, Sir Walter (1771–1832) Novelist and poet, born in Edinburgh. His ballads, such as *The Border Minstrelsy* (1802), made him the most popular author of the day. His historical novels fall into three groups: those set in the background of Scottish history, from *Waverley* (1814) to *A Legend of Montrose* (1819); a group which takes up themes from the Middle Ages and Reformation times, from *Ivanhoe* (1819) to *The Talisman* (1825); and his remaining books, from *Woodstock* (1826) until his death.

Scriabin, Alexander Nikolayevich (1872–1915) Composer and pianist, born in Moscow. His compositions include three symphonies, two tone poems, and 10 sonatas.

Searle, Ronald (William Fordham) (1920–) Artist, born in Cambridge, Cambridgeshire. He became widely known as the creator of the macabre schoolgirls of 'St Trinian's'.

Sebald, W(infried) G(eorg) (1944–2001) Novelist, born in Germany. He became professor of European Literature at the University of East Anglia. His books include *The Emigrants* (1996), *The Rings of Saturn* (1998), *Vertigo* (1999), and *Austerlitz* (2001).

Sebastian, St (?–288) Roman martyr, a native of Narbonne. He was a captain of the praetorian guard, and secretly a Christian. When his belief was discovered, Diocletian ordered his death.

Secombe, Sir Harry (Donald) (1921–2001) Comedian, singer, and media personality, born in Swansea, S Wales. A member of BBC radio's *The Goons* (1951–9), he starred on stage in *Pickwick* (1963) and on film in *Oliver!* (1968), recorded several albums as a professional singer, and hosted the religious television series *Highway* (1983–93).

Seeger, Pete(r) (1919–) Folk singer, songwriter, guitarist, and banjo player, born in New York City. In 1940 he started the 'protest' movement in contemporary folk music. With his group, the Weavers, his best-known songs include 'Where Have All the Flowers Gone?', 'If I Had a Hammer', and 'Little Boxes'.

Segovia, Andrés (1894–1987) Guitarist, born in Linares, Spain. He evolved a revolutionary guitar technique permitting the performance of a wide range of music, and many modern composers wrote works for him.

Seinfeld, Jerry (1954–) Comedian,

actor, and writer, born in Brooklyn, New York City. He began working in Manhattan comedy clubs, later becoming a household name with his successful long-running TV sit-com series *Seinfeld* (1990–9). His book of comic observations, *SeinLanguage* (1993), became a best seller.

Sellers, Peter (1925–80) Actor and comedian, born in Southsea, Hampshire. His meeting with Spike Milligan heralded *The Goon Show* (1951–9), which revolutionized British radio comedy. His films include *I'm All Right Jack* (1959), *Only Two Can Play* (1962), and *Being There* (1980), and his popularity was unrivalled as Inspector Clouseau in the series of films that began with *The Pink Panther* (1963).

Selwyn-Lloyd, (John) Selwyn (Brooke) Lloyd, Baron (1904–78) British Conservative statesman, born in Liverpool, Merseyside. He served as minister of state (1951), supply (1954–5), and defence (1955), as foreign secretary (1955–60), and as Chancellor of the Exchequer (1960–2).

Senna, Ayrton, in full **Ayrton Senna da Silva** (1960–94) Motor-racing driver, born in São Paulo, Brazil. He had 41 Grand Prix victories (second only to Alain Prost), and was World Formula One champion (1988, 1990, 1991). He was killed during the 1994 San Marino Grand Prix.

Sennett, Mack, originally **Michael** or **Mikall Sinnott** (1880–1960) Film director, producer, and actor, born in Richmond, Quebec, Canada. He made hundreds of shorts, establishing a tradition of knockabout slap-stick under the name of Keystone Komics (1912) and the Sennett Bathing Beauties (1920).

Seurat, Georges (Pierre) (1859–91) Artist, born in Paris. His works, such as 'Une Baignade, Asnières' (Bathers at Asnières, 1883–4), painted in a Divisionist style, show the marrying of an Impressionist palette to Classical composition.

Seuss, Dr, pseudonym of **Theodor Seuss Geisel**, other pseudonyms **Theo LeSieg** and **Rosetta Stone** (1904–91) Writer and illustrator of children's books, born in Springfield, MA. His famous series of 'Beginner Books' in reading started with *The Cat in the Hat* (1957).

Sewell, Anna (1820–78) Novelist, born in Great Yarmouth, Norfolk. She wrote *Black Beauty* (1877; filmed 1946, 1971, 1994), the story of a horse, written as a plea for the more humane treatment of animals.

Seymour, Jane (c.1509–37) Third queen of Henry VIII, the mother of Edward VI. Lady-in-waiting to Henry's first two wives, she married him 11 days after the execution of Anne Boleyn. She died soon after the birth of her son.

Shackleton, Sir Ernest Henry (1874–1922) Explorer, born in Kilkea, Co Kildare, Ireland. He nearly reached the South Pole in his own expedition of 1909, and in 1915 his ship *Endurance* was crushed in the ice, forcing him to make a perilous journey to bring relief for the crew.

Shadows, The British instrumental rock group, formed in 1958 with original members **Hank Marvin** (1941–), **Bruce Welch** (1941–), **Brian**

Bennett (1940–), **Jet Harris** (1939–), and **Tony Meehan** (1943–2005). Created to back singer Cliff Richard, they played on his numerous hit records and in concerts. In 1960 they became an independent group, and were an instant success with Marvin's resonant guitar sound and their trademark 'Shadow step', a three-step dance movement.

Shakespeare, William (1564–1616) Playwright, actor, and poet, born in Stratford-upon-Avon, Warwickshire, the son of John Shakespeare and Mary Arden. He married Anne Hathaway in 1582, who bore him a daughter, Susanna, in 1583, and twins Hamnet and Judith in 1585. He moved to London, possibly in 1591, and became an actor. His sonnets, known by 1598, fall into two groups: 1 to 126 are addressed to a fair young man, and 127 to 154 to a 'dark lady' who holds both the young man and the poet in thrall. The first evidence of his association with the stage is in 1594, when he was acting with the Lord Chamberlain's company of players. When the company built the Globe Theatre S of the Thames (1599), he became a partner. He later returned to Stratford (c.1610), living as a country gentleman at his house, New Place. The first collected works, the First Folio, appeared in 1623. It is conventional to group the plays into early, middle, and late periods, and to distinguish comedies (eg *A Midsummer Night's Dream*, 1595; *As You Like It*, 1599; *Twelfth Night*, 1600–2), tragedies (eg *Hamlet*, 1600–1; *Othello*, 1605–6; *King Lear*, 1605–6; *Macbeth*, 1605–6), and histories (eg *Richard II*, 1595; *Henry IV*, I and II, 1596–7; *Henry V*, 1599), recognizing other groups that do not fall neatly into these categories, such as the Greek and Roman plays (eg *Julius Caesar*, 1599) and the late comedies (eg *The Tempest*, 1613). The authorship of some plays (eg *Titus Andronicus*) is still a matter of controversy.

Shankar, Ravi, popular name of **Robindra Shankar** (1920–) Sitarist, born in Benares, India. Widely regarded as India's most important musician, he set up schools of Indian music, founded the National Orchestra of India, and in the mid-1950s became the first Indian instrumentalist to undertake an international tour. He is the father of US singer and musician **Norah Jones** (1979–). A second daughter, **Anoushka Shankar** (1982–), is a sitarist.

Sharapova, Maria (1987–) Tennis player, born in Nyagan, Siberia, Russia. At age nine she enrolled at a tennis academy in Florida, USA. She turned professional at 14, and in 2003 reached the fourth round at Wimbledon. Success came in 2004 when she won the singles title there, becoming Russia's first woman Wimbledon champion. At the start of 2006 she was ranked world number 4.

Sharif, Omar, originally **Michael Shalhouz** (1932–) Film actor, born in Alexandria, Egypt. He attracted international attention following his role in *Lawrence of Arabia* (1962), then starred in *Doctor Zhivago* (1965). Later films include *Funny Girl* (1968), *The Tamarind Seed* (1974), *The Mirror Has*

Two Faces (1996), and *One Night With the King* (2005).

Sharman, Helen (Patricia) (1963–) Britain's first astronaut, born in Sheffield, South Yorkshire. In 1989 she responded to an advertisement for trainee astronauts, and was eventually selected to be the British member of the Russian scientific space mission, Project Juno (1991), spending eight days in space.

Sharon, Ariel (1928–) Prime minister of Israel (2001–6) and soldier, born in Kfar Maalal, Palestine. He won a seat in the Knesset (1973), became minister of defence (1981–3) during the war in Lebanon, but was forced to resign. Re-elected to the Knesset (1999), he became chairman of the Likud after the resignation of Binyamin Netanyahu, and replaced Ehud Barak as prime minister in 2001. He won a second term in 2003. In late 2005, Sharon quit the Likud and formed his own party named Kadima. He suffered a stroke at the beginning of 2006 and remained in a coma in hospital.

Sharpe, Tom, popular name of **Thomas Ridley Sharpe** (1928–) Novelist, born in London. He was a lecturer in history (1963–71) before turning to full-time writing, beginning with *Riotous Assembly* (1971). Later novels include *Indecent Exposure* (1973), *Porterhouse Blue* (1974), a series introducing the character of Wilt (from 1976), and *The Midden* (1996).

Shatner, William (1931–) Actor and director, born in Montreal, Quebec, Canada. He became internationally known following the cult success of the *Star Trek* television series (1966–9), in which he played Captain James T(iberius) Kirk. He reprised the role in several feature film sequels, directing as well as acting in *Star Trek V: The Final Frontier* (1989). Later TV work includes the drama series *Boston Legal* (2005, Emmy).

Shaw, Artie, originally **Arthur Jacob Arshawsky** (1910–2004) Clarinet player and bandleader, born in New York City. He became internationally known after recording 'Begin the Beguine' (1938), and rivalled Goodman as a clarinet soloist. He married eight times, always to a well-known beauty, including actresses Lana Turner, Ava Gardner, and Evelyn Keyes.

Shaw, Fiona, professional name of **Fiona Mary Wilson** (1958–) Actress, born in Cork, Co Cork, Ireland. She has worked consistently with the Royal Shakespeare Company, often collaborating with the director Deborah Warner, most notably with *Richard II* (1995) in which she played the title role. Film work includes *My Left Foot* (1988), *Butcher Boy* (1996), and *Harry Potter and the Prisoner of Azkaban* (2004).

Shaw, George Bernard (1856–1950) Playwright, essayist, and pamphleteer, born in Dublin. In 1882 he turned to socialism, joined the committee of the Fabian Society, and became known as a journalist. Among his major plays are *Arms and the Man* (1894), *The Devil's Disciple* (1897), *Man and Superman* (1905), *Major Barbara* (1905), *The Doctor's Dilemma* (1906), *Pygmalion* (1913), and *Saint Joan* (1923). He was awarded the Nobel Prize for Literature in 1925.

Shearer, Alan (1970–) England footballer, born in Newcastle-upon-Tyne, Tyne & Wear. He played for Southampton and Blackburn Rovers, then transferred to Newcastle (1996) for a then world record fee of £15 million. He joined the England squad in 1992, becoming captain in 1996, and by mid-2000 (when he announced his international retirement) had won 62 caps. In 2006 he broke Jackie Milburn's record of 200 goals for Newcastle, and retired that year.

Sheba, Queen of (c.10th-c BC) Monarch mentioned in the Bible (1 *Kings* 10), perhaps from SW Arabia (modern Yemen). She is said to have journeyed to Jerusalem to test the wisdom of Solomon and to exchange gifts.

Sheene, Barry (Stephen Frank) (1950–2003) Motorcycle racer, born in London. He made his professional debut at age 18 and went on to win the British (1970) and European (1973) 750 cc titles. With Suzuki he won two successive 500 cc World Championships (1976, 1977). In 1982 he was seriously injured at Silverstone and surgeons rebuilt his legs using metal plates. He later retired to Australia (1987), where he became a popular TV commentator for motorsports.

Shelburne, William Petty Fitzmaurice, 2nd Earl of (1737–1805) British prime minister (1782–3), born in Dublin. He was President of the Board of Trade (1763) and secretary of state (1766), and became premier on the death of Rockingham.

Shelley, Mary (Wollstonecraft), *née* Godwin (1797–1851) Writer, born in London, the daughter of William Godwin and Mary Wollstonecraft. She eloped with Shelley in 1814, and married him two years later. She wrote several novels, notably *Frankenstein, or the Modern Prometheus* (1818).

Shelley, Percy Bysshe (1792–1822) Poet, born at Field Place, near Horsham, West Sussex. From 1818 he lived in Italy, where he wrote the bulk of his poetry, including odes, lyrics, and the verse drama *Prometheus Unbound* (1818–19).

Shem Biblical character, the eldest son of Noah, the brother of Ham and Japheth. His descendants are listed (in *Gen* 10), and he is depicted as the legendary father of 'Semitic' peoples, including the Hebrews.

Shepard, Alan (Bartlett), Jr (1923–98) The first US astronaut, born in East Derry, NH. His sub-orbital flight in a Mercury space capsule ('Freedom 7') took place on 5 May 1961, reached an altitude of 185 km/116 mi, and lasted 15 min. He was also commander of the Apollo 14 crew which landed on the Moon in 1971.

Shepard, Sam, popular name of **Samuel Shepard Rogers** (1943–) Playwright and actor, born in Fort Sheridan, IL. His works include *The Tooth of Crime* (1972), *Killer's Head* (1975), and *Buried Child* (1978, Pulitzer), and the screenplay *Paris, Texas* (1984). In 2005 he wrote the screenplay and starred in *Don't Come Knocking*.

Shepherd, Cybill (1950–) Film actress, born in Memphis, TN. She made an acclaimed film debut in *The Last*

Picture Show (1971), following this with *The Heartbreak Kid* (1973) and *Taxi Driver* (1976). Television work includes the series *Moonlighting* (1985–9), with Bruce Willis, and *Cybill* (1995–8).

Sher, Sir Antony (1949–) Actor and writer, born in Cape Town, South Africa. He joined the Royal Shakespeare Company in 1982, and became known for his innovative creations of Shakespearean characters. Among his films are *Mrs Brown* (1997) and *Shakespeare in Love* (1998). His books include *Woza Shakespeare!* (1996, with Gregory Doran).

Sheridan, Richard Brinsley (Butler) (1751–1816) Playwright, born in Dublin. His highly successful comedy of manners, *The Rivals* (1775), was followed by several other comedies and farces, notably *The School for Scandal* (1777).

Sheringham, Teddy, popular name of **Edward Paul Sheringham** (1966–) Footballer, born in Highams Park, London. A forward, he played for Millwall, Aldershot, Nottingham Forest, and Tottenham Hotspur, signing for Manchester United in 1997, and returning to Tottenham in 2001. He was an England team member in the 2002 World Cup campaign, winning 51 caps by the end of the 2003 season. He played for Portsmouth (2003–4) and then joined West Ham.

Sherrington, Sir Charles Scott (1857–1952) Physiologist, born in London. His research on the nervous system constituted a landmark in modern physiology, and he shared the Nobel Prize for Physiology or Medicine in 1932.

Shields, Carol (Ann Warner) (1935–2003) Novelist, born in Oak Park, IL. She became professor and chancellor of the University of Winnipeg. Her first novel, *Small Ceremonies* (1976), received the Canadian Authors Association Award for best novel. Later books include *The Stone Diaries* (1993, Pulitzer) and *Larry's Party* (1997, Orange Prize). Her final novel, *Unless* (2001), was shortlisted for the Booker and Orange prizes.

Shilton, Peter (1949–) Footballer, born in Leicester, Leicestershire. He played for Leicester City, Stoke City, Nottingham Forest, Southampton, and Derby County, and became the first England goalkeeper to gain over 100 caps. On his retirement he had gained a record 125 caps.

Shipman, Harold (Frederick) (1946–2004) Doctor and serial murderer, born in Nottingham, Nottinghamshire. A GP in Hyde, Greater Manchester, he was arrested in 1998 and later sentenced to life imprisonment for the murder of 15 of his elderly patients by injecting them with diamorphine. A public inquiry reported in 2002 that there had been 215 victims in all (from 1975), with another 45 likely, and a further 38 uncertain, making him Britain's worst ever serial killer. He committed suicide in prison.

Shoemaker, Willie, popular name of **William Lee Shoemaker**, nickname **the Shoe** (1931–2003) Jockey and trainer, born in Fabens, TX. He won more races than any other jockey –

8833 winners between 1949 and his retirement in 1989.

Short, Clare (1946–) British stateswoman, born in Birmingham, West Midlands. She became an MP in 1983, joined the shadow cabinet in 1995, and was spokesperson on transport (1995–6) and overseas development (1996–7). She served as secretary of state for international development in the Labour government (1997–2003).

Shostakovich, Dmitri Dmitriyevich (1906–75) Composer, born in St Petersburg, Russia. At first highly successful, his operas and ballets were for a time criticized for a failure to observe 'Soviet realism'. He wrote 15 symphonies, violin, piano, and cello concertos, chamber music, and choral works.

Showa Tenno ('Emperor') **Hirohito** (1901–89) Emperor of Japan (1926–89), the 124th in direct lineage, born in Tokyo. His reign was marked by wars against China (1931–2, 1937–45) and the USA and Britain (1941–5). In 1946 he renounced his legendary divinity to become a democratic constitutional monarch.

Shrapnel, Henry (1761–1842) British artillery officer. In c.1793 he invented the *shrapnel shell*, an anti-personnel device which exploded while in flight, scattering lethal lead shot.

Shute, Nevil, pseudonym of **Nevil Shute Norway** (1899–1960) Writer, born in London. After World War 2 he emigrated to Australia, which became the setting for most of his later books, notably *A Town Like Alice* (1949) and *On the Beach* (1957).

Sibelius, Jean (Julius Christian) (1865–1957) Composer, born in Tavastehus, Finland. A passionate nationalist, he wrote a series of symphonic poems, notably *Finlandia* (1899), as well as seven symphonies and a violin concerto.

Sickert, Walter (Richard) (1860–1942) Artist, born in Munich, Germany. The Camden Town Group (later the London Group) was formed under his leadership (c.1910), and he became a major influence on later English painters.

Sidmouth (of Sidmouth), Henry Addington, 1st Viscount (1757–1844) British prime minister (1801–4), born in London. His Tory administration negotiated the Peace of Amiens (1802), and he later became home secretary under Liverpool (1812–21).

Sidney, Sir Philip (1554–86) Poet, born in Penshurst, Kent. His literary work, written in 1578–82 but published posthumously, includes the unfinished pastoral romance, *Arcadia*, the *Defence of Poesie*, and a sonnet cycle, *Astrophel and Stella*.

Sikorsky, Igor (Ivan) (1889–1972) Aeronautical engineer, born in Kiev. He built and flew the first four-engined aeroplane in 1913, and in the USA developed the first successful helicopter, the VS-300 (1939).

Sillitoe, Alan (1928–) Writer, born in Nottingham, Nottinghamshire. His best-known novels include *Saturday Night and Sunday Morning* (1958) and *The Loneliness of the Long Distance Runner* (1959; filmed 1962), and he has also written poetry and children's books.

Simenon, Georges (Joseph Chris-

tian) (1903–89) Crime novelist, born in Liège, Belgium. He revolutionized detective fiction with his tough, morbidly psychological Inspector Maigret series, beginning in 1933.

Simeon Stylites, St (387–459) The earliest of the Christian ascetic 'pillar' saints. In c.420 he established himself on top of a pillar c.20 m/70 ft high at Telanessa, near Antioch, where he spent the rest of his life preaching. His imitators were known as *stylites*.

Simmons, Jean (1929–) Film actress, born in London. She made her film debut in 1942, and moved to Hollywood in 1950. Her films include *The Robe* (1953), *Spartacus* (1960), and *How to Make an American Quilt* (1995). Television work includes *The Thorn Birds* (1983).

Simnel, Lambert (c.1475–c.1535) Pretender to the throne, the son of a joiner. He bore a resemblance to Edward IV, and was set up in Ireland (1487) as his son, then as the Duke of Clarence's son, **Edward, Earl of Warwick** (1475–99). Crowned in Dublin as Edward VI, he landed in Lancashire, but was defeated.

Simon, (Marvin) Neil (1927–) Playwright, born in New York City. His first Broadway Show, *Catch a Star!*, opened in 1955, and a series of long-running successes followed in the 1960s, including *The Odd Couple* (1965). His later work includes *Biloxi Blues* (1985, Tony), *Lost in Yonkers* (1991, Pulitzer, Tony), and *Laughter on the 23rd Floor* (1996, Laurence Olivier Award).

Simon, Paul (1941–) Singer, songwriter, and guitarist, born in Forest Hills, NY. He teamed up with Art Garfunkel at the age of 15. Their first big hit, 'The Sound Of Silence' (1964), was followed in 1968 by the film *The Graduate*, with songs written by Simon, and they had a major success with the album *Bridge Over Troubled Water* (1970). His solo career, using Third-World choirs and percussionists, led to one of the most successful albums of the 1980s, *Graceland* (1986). *You're the One* appeared in 2000.

Simone, Nina, originally **Eunice Kathleen Waymon** (1933–2003) Jazz singer, pianist, and songwriter, born in Tryon, NC. Her early hits included 'I Loves You, Porgy' and 'My Baby Just Cares for Me' (1958), and she became known for her protest songs in the 1960s.

Simon Peter *see* Peter, St

Simpson, N(orman) F(rederick) (1919–) Playwright, born in London. The success of *A Resounding Tinkle* (1957), a zany disruption of middle-class normality, brought him to prominence. His absurdist approach is also seen in *One-Way Pendulum* (1959).

Simpson, O(renthal) J(ames) (1947–) Player of American football, born in San Francisco, CA. He joined the Buffalo Bills in 1968, leading the League as top rusher four times (1972–6). In 1994 he was arrested on a charge of murder, his court case achieving unprecedented media publicity in 1995. He was acquitted later that year. In 1997 a civil trial jury found him liable for the murders.

Sinatra, Frank, popular name of **Francis Albert Sinatra** (1915–98)

Singer and actor, born in Hoboken, NJ. One of the greatest singers of popular songs, he began in the 1940s, made several hit records, and starred on radio and in films. His appeal disappeared for some years, then was revived by his appearance in *From Here to Eternity* (1953, Oscar); later films include *High Society* (1956) and *The Manchurian Candidate* (1962). He produced his masterworks in a series of recordings (1956–65), notably the albums *Songs for Swinging Lovers* (1956) and *Come Fly With Me* (1959), and the songs 'That's Life' (1966) and 'My Way' (1969). His personal life always proved noteworthy, with turbulent marriages to Ava Gardner and Mia Farrow, among others, and alleged Mafia connections.

Singer, Isaac M(erritt) (1811–75) Inventor and manufacturer of sewing machines, born in Pittstown, NY. At Boston in 1852 he devised an improved single-thread, chain-stitch sewing machine. His company became the largest producer of sewing machines in the world.

Sirhan, (Bishara) Sirhan (c.1943–) Assassin of Senator Robert Kennedy, born in Palestine. He shot Kennedy for his pro-Israeli views, during the lead-up to the presidential nomination in 1968, and was sentenced to life imprisonment.

Sisley, Alfred (1839–99) Impressionist painter and etcher, born in Paris. He painted landscapes almost exclusively, particularly in the valleys of the Seine, Loire, and Thames.

Sitting Bull, originally **Tatanka Iyotake** (c.1831–90) Chief of the Dakota Sioux, born near Grand River, SD. He was a leader in the Sioux War of 1876–7, and led the defeat of Custer and his men at the Little Bighorn (1876). He escaped to Canada, but surrendered in 1881. He later toured with Buffalo Bill's Wild West Show. He returned to his people, and was killed when the army suppressed the 'ghost dance' religious movement.

Sitwell, Dame Edith (Louisa) (1887–1964) Poet, born in Scarborough, North Yorkshire, the sister of Osbert and Sacheverell Sitwell. Her experimental poetry was controversially received with *Façade* (1922); her later works, such as *The Outcasts* (1962), reflect a deeper religious symbolism.

Sitwell, Sir (Francis) Osbert (Sacheverell) (1892–1969) Writer, born in London, the brother of Edith and Sacheverell Sitwell. He gained notoriety with his satirical novel *Before the Bombardment* (1927), but is best known for his five-volume autobiographical series, beginning with *Left Hand: Right Hand* (1944).

Sitwell, Sir Sacheverell (1897–1988) Poet and art critic, born in Scarborough, North Yorkshire, the brother of Edith and Osbert Sitwell. His many volumes of poetry cover a period of over 30 years, from *The People's Palace* (1918) to *An Indian Summer* (1982).

Skinner, B(urrhus) F(rederic) (1904–90) Psychologist, born in Susquehanna, PA. A leading behaviourist, he was a proponent of operant conditioning, and the inventor of the *Skinner box* for facilitating experimental observations. His main scientific works include *The Behavior* *of Organisms* (1938) and *Verbal Behavior* (1957).

Slim (of Yarralumia and of Bishopston), William (Joseph) Slim, 1st Viscount (1891–1970) British field marshal, born in Bristol. In World War 2, his greatest achievement was to lead his reorganized forces, the famous 14th 'Forgotten Army', to victory over the Japanese in Burma.

Smetana, Bedřich (1824–84) Composer, born in Litomyšl, Czech Republic. His compositions, intensely national in character, include nine operas, notably *The Bartered Bride* (trans, 1866), and many chamber and orchestral works, including the series of symphonic poems *My Country* (trans, 1874–9).

Smiley, Jane (1952–) Novelist, born in Los Angeles, CA. An early short story, *Lily*, won the O Henry Award, and *A Thousand Acres* (1992), a modern retelling of the *King Lear* story, won a Pulitzer Prize and the National Book Critics Award. Later novels include *Horse Heaven* (2000) and *Good Faith* (2003).

Smith, Adam (1723–90) Economist and philosopher, born in Kirkcaldy, Fife. In 1776 he published *An Inquiry into the Nature and Causes of the Wealth of Nations*, the first major work of political economy.

Smith, Bessie, nickname **Empress of the Blues** (c.1895–1937) Blues singer, born in Chattanooga, TN. Considered one of the outstanding African-American artistes of her day, she made a series of classic blues recordings throughout the 1920s, and starred in the 1929 film, *St Louis Blues*.

Smith, Delia (1941–) Television chef and writer, born in Woking, Surrey. She published her first cookery book, *How to Cheat at Cooking*, in 1973, and her popularity increased with the many highly successful television series that followed. Later best-selling books include *Delia Smith's Christmas* (1990) and *How to Cook* (1999). A new series of books, *The Delia Collection*, began in 2003.

Smith, Dodie, in full **Dorothy Gladys Smith**, pseudonym **C L Anthony** (1896–1990) Playwright, novelist, and theatre producer, born in Whitefield, Greater Manchester. Among her best-known works are the play *Dear Octopus* (1938) and the children's book *The Hundred and One Dalmatians* (1956; filmed 1961 and 1996).

Smith, Joseph (1805–44) Religious leader, born in Sharon, VT. He received his first 'call' as a prophet in 1820, and in 1827 the *Book of Mormon* was delivered into his hands. He established the new Church of Jesus Christ of Latter-day Saints, and founded Nauvoo, IL (1840), becoming mayor, but was imprisoned for conspiracy, and killed by a mob.

Smith, Maggie, popular name of **Dame Margaret Natalie Smith** (1934–) Actress, born in Ilford, Essex. Her films include *The Prime of Miss Jean Brodie* (1969, Oscar) and *California Suite* (1978, Oscar), and she received BAFTA awards for her roles in *A Private Function* (1984), *A Room With a View* (1986), and *The Lonely Passion of Judith Hearne* (1987). Among later films are *Gosford Park* (2001) and *Ladies in Lavender* (2004).

Smith, Stevie, pseudonym of

Florence Margaret Smith (1902–71) Writer and novelist, born in Hull. She gained a reputation as an eccentrically humorous poet on serious themes, illustrated by 'Not Waving but Drowning' (1957).

Smith, Will, popular name of **Willard Christopher Smith Jr** (1968–) Film actor and rapper, born in Philadelphia, PA. His first major film role was in *Six Degrees of Separation* (1993), and later films include *Men in Black* (1997, sequel 2002), *I, Robot* (2004), and *Hitch* (2005). He continues to combine successful careers as an actor and recording artist.

Smollett, Tobias (George) (1721–71) Novelist, born in Cardross, Argyll and Bute. He achieved success with his picaresque novels *The Adventures of Roderick Random* (1748) and *The Adventures of Peregrine Pickle* (1751), and his masterpiece, *The Expedition of Humphry Clinker* (1771).

Smuts, Jan (Christiaan) (1870–1950) South African general and prime minister (1919–24, 1939–48), born in Malmesbury, Cape Colony, South Africa. He was a significant figure at Versailles, instrumental in the founding of the League of Nations in 1919. His coalition with the Nationalists in 1934 produced the United Party.

Smythe, Pat(ricia), married name **Koechlin** (1928–96) Show jumper, born in London. She won the European championship four times on *Flanagan* (1957, 1961–3), and in 1956 was the first woman to ride in the Olympic Games.

Snagge, John (Derrick Mordaunt) (1904–96) British broadcaster, whose voice came to represent the traditional values of the BBC. He provided the commentary on the Oxford and Cambridge Boat Race for many years (1931–80).

Snead, Sam(uel Jackson), nickname **Slammin' Sam** (1912–2002) Golfer, born in Hot Springs, VA. He won the (British) Open (1946), the US PGA Championship (1942, 1949, 1951), and the US Masters (1949, 1952, 1954).

Snicket, Lemony, pseudonym of **Daniel Handler** (1970–) Writer, born in San Francisco, CA. He became well known for his series of novels for children entitled *A Series of Unfortunate Events*, featuring the Baudelaire siblings, Violet, Klaus and Sunny. Books in the series include *The Bad Beginning* (1999), *The Vile Village* (2001), and *The Grim Grotto* (2004).

Snow, C(harles) P(ercy) Snow, Baron (1905–80) Novelist and physicist, born in Leicester, Leicestershire. He is known for a cycle of successful novels portraying English life from 1920 onwards, beginning with *Strangers and Brothers* (1940), and for his controversial lecture, *The Two Cultures and the Scientific Revolution* (1959). He married the novelist Pamela Hansford Johnson in 1950.

Snow, Peter (John) (1938–) Broadcaster and writer, born in Dublin. He became a newscaster and reporter for ITN (1962–6), and a diplomatic and defence correspondent (1966–79), joining the BBC as presenter of *Newsnight* in 1979. He also became known as the co-presenter of the general elections (1974–2005).

Snowdon, Antony Armstrong-

Jones, 1st Earl of (1930–) Photographer and designer, born in London. He designed the Aviary of the London Zoo in 1965, and later presented the conditions of the handicapped, both in photographic studies and in television documentaries. He married Princess Margaret in 1960 (divorced 1978).

Soane, Sir John (1753–1837) Architect, born in Goring, Oxfordshire. His designs include the Bank of England (1792–1833, now rebuilt), and Dulwich Picture Gallery (1811–14).

Sobers, Gary, popular name of **Sir Garfield St Aubrun Sobers** (1936–) Cricketer, born in Barbados. A great West Indian all-rounder, he is the only man to score 8000 Test runs and take 200 wickets. During his career (1953–74) he scored 28 315 runs in first-class cricket and took 1043 wickets.

Socrates (469–399 BC) Greek philosopher, born in Athens. His personality and his doctrines were immortalized in Plato's dialogues. He devoted his last 30 years to convincing the Athenians that their opinions about moral matters could not bear the weight of critical scrutiny. He was tried on charges of impiety and corruption of the youth by defenders of a restored democracy in Athens, found guilty, and put to death.

Soderbergh, Steven (1963–) Director, producer, and screenwriter, born in Atlanta, GA. He gained recognition with his directorial debut, *sex, lies, and videotape* (1989, Palme d'Or, Oscar nomination). Later films include *Kafka* (1991), *Erin Brockovich*

(2000), *Traffic* (2000, Oscar Best Director), and *Bubble* (2005).

Solomon (Hebrew Bible) (10th-c BC) King of Israel, the second son of David and Bathsheba. His outwardly splendid reign (1 *Kings* 1–11) saw the expansion of the kingdom and the building of the great Temple in Jerusalem. Credited with great wisdom, his name was attached to several biblical and extra-canonical writings.

Solzhenitsyn, Alexander (Isayevich) (1918–) Writer, born in Kislovodsk, Russia. *One Day in the Life of Ivan Denisovich* (trans, 1962) was acclaimed both in the USSR and the West, but his denunciation of Soviet censorship led to the banning of *Cancer Ward* (trans, 1968) and *The First Circle* (trans, 1968). He was awarded the Nobel Prize for Literature in 1970 (received in 1974). His later books include *The Gulag Archipelago* (trans, 1973–8), for which he was exiled (1974), returning to Russia in 1994.

Sondheim, Stephen (Joshua) (1930–) Composer and lyricist, born in New York City. He earned his first success with his lyrics for *West Side Story* (1957). His own highly successful musicals include *A Funny Thing Happened on the Way to the Forum* (1962), *Sweeney Todd* (1979), and *Sunday in the Park with George* (1984, Pulitzer). Later works include *Passion* (1994).

Sontag, Susan, originally **Susan Rosenblatt** (1933–2004) Critic and writer, born in New York City, NY. She first gained attention with her essay, 'Notes on Camp' (1964), and in 1966 published her ground-breaking collection *Against Interpretation*. She also wrote novels including *Death Kit* (1967) and *In America* (1999).

Soper, Donald (Oliver) Soper, Baron (1903–98) Methodist minister, born in London. Widely known for his open-air speaking on London's Tower Hill, he wrote many books on Christianity and social questions, particularly from the pacifist angle.

Sophocles (c.496–406 BC) Greek tragic playwright, born in Colonus Hippius. He wrote 123 plays, of which only seven survive: *Ajax*, *Electra*, *Women of Trachis*, *Philoctetes*, and his three major plays, *Oedipus Rex*, *Oedipus at Colonus*, and *Antigone*.

Soros, George (1930–) Financier and philanthropist, born in Budapest. In 1969 he set up the Quantum and Quota groups of hedge funds, which grew rapidly from his daring speculations, and in 1979 he began to establish a network of Soros Foundations, mainly in E and C Europe, to advance opportunities in education and business.

Sotheby, John (1740–1807) Auctioneer and antiquarian. In 1780 he became a director of the first sale room in Britain exclusively for books, manuscripts, and prints.

Sousa, John Philip (1854–1932) Composer and bandmaster, born in Washington, DC. He composed more than 100 popular marches, including 'The Stars and Stripes Forever' (1896), and also invented the *sousaphone*.

Southey, Robert (1774–1843) Writer, born in Bristol. Although made poet laureate in 1813, his prose became more widely known than his poetry,

and included a life of Nelson, a naval history, and his letters.

Soyinka, Wole, popular name of **Akinwande Oluwole Soyinka** (1934–) Writer, born near Abeokuta, Nigeria. His writing is deeply concerned with the tension between old and new in modern Africa, and his first novel, *The Interpreters* (1965), was called the first really modern African novel. He was awarded the Nobel Prize for Literature in 1986.

Spacey, Kevin, stage name of **Kevin Spacey Fowler** (1959–) Actor, born in South Orange, NJ. His film work includes *LA Confidential* (1997), *American Beauty* (1999, Oscar), *Beyond the Sea* (2004), and *Edison* (2005). Notable stage performances include *Lost in Yonkers* (1991) and *The Iceman Cometh* (1998). In 2003 he became artistic director of the Old Vic Theatre, London.

Spark, Dame Muriel (Sarah), *née* **Camberg** (1918–2006) Writer, born in Edinburgh. She is best known for her novels, notably *Memento Mori* (1959), *The Ballad of Peckham Rye* (1960), *The Prime of Miss Jean Brodie* (1961; filmed 1969), and *The Mandelbaum Gate* (1965, James Tait Black). Later works include *The Finishing School* (2004).

Spartacus (?–71 BC) Thracian-born slave and gladiator at Capua, who led the most serious slave uprising in the history of Rome (73–71 BC). He inflicted numerous defeats on the Roman armies sent against him, until defeated and killed by Crassus.

Spears, Britney (Jean) (1981–) Pop singer and actress, born in Kentwood, LA. The title track of her first album, *Baby One More Time* (1999), became a number 1 hit. Later albums include *Britney* (2001) and *Greatest Hits: My Prerogative* (2004). She made her film debut in *Crossroads* (2002).

Spector, Phil (1940–) Record producer, born in New York City. In the 1960s he developed a distinctive 'wall of sound' style using echo-effects and other innovative recording techniques, with hits by such groups as the Ronettes and the Crystals. His *Christmas Album* remains a festive classic. In 2004 he was arrested and charged with murdering actress Lana Clarkson, and his trial was set to begin in early 2007.

Speer, Albert (1905–81) Architect and Nazi government official, born in Mannheim, Germany. He was minister of armaments in 1942, but openly opposed Hitler in the final months of the war. Tried at Nuremberg, he was imprisoned for 20 years in Spandau, Berlin.

Spence, Sir Basil (Urwin) (1907–76) Architect, born in Mumbai (Bombay), India. He emerged as the leading post-war British architect, with his fresh approach to new university buildings, the pavilion for the Festival of Britain (1951), and the new Coventry Cathedral (1951).

Spencer-Churchill, Baroness *see* Churchill, Sir Winston

Spender, Sir Stephen (Harold) (1909–95) Poet and critic, born in London. One of the group of modern poets with Auden and Day-Lewis in the 1930s, his *Collected Poems, 1928–85* were published in 1985.

Spenser, Edmund (?1552–99) Poet, born in London. His first original work was a sequence of pastoral poems, *The Shepheardes Calender* (1579). His major work, *The Faerie Queene*, used a nine-line verse pattern which later came to be called the *Spenserian stanza*.

Spielberg, Steven (1947–) Film director, born in Cincinnati, OH. His many highly successful films include *Jaws* (1975), *Close Encounters of the Third Kind* (1977), *ET, The Extra-Terrestrial* (1982), *Indiana Jones and the Temple of Doom* (1984), *Who Framed Roger Rabbit?* (1988), *Jurassic Park* (1993), *Schindler's List* (1993, 7 Oscars, 2 BAFTAs), *Saving Private Ryan* (1998, Oscar), and *Munich* (2005, Oscar nomination).

Spillane, Mickey, pseudonym of **Frank Morrison Spillane** (1918–) Detective fiction writer, born in New York City. During the 1940s and 1950s, he wrote a series of novels featuring detective Mike Hammer. *Kiss Me Deadly* (1952) is a typical example of his work, in its representation of sadism, cheap sex, and casual violence.

Spinks, Leon (1953–) Boxer, born in St Louis, MO. He won a gold medal in the light heavyweight division at the 1976 Olympic Games, and went on to briefly hold the world heavyweight title in a split decision over Muhammad Ali in 1978. His brother **Michael Spinks** (1956–) also won the heavyweight title (1983), making them the only brothers to hold world boxing titles.

Spinoza, Baruch or **Benedictus de** (1632–77) Philosopher and theologian, born in Amsterdam. Regarded as one of the great Rationalist thinkers of the 18th-c, his major works include the *Tractatus Theologico-Politicus* (1670) and *Ethica* (published posthumously, 1677).

Spitz, Mark (Andrew) (1950–) Swimmer, born in Modesto, CA. His outstanding achievement came at the Munich Olympic Games (1972), when he became the first athlete to win seven gold medals at one Games.

Spock, Benjamin (McLane), popular name **Dr Spock** (1903–98) Paediatrician, born in New Haven, CT. In 1946 he published his best-selling *Common Sense Book of Baby and Child Care*. He was a People's Party candidate for the US presidency in 1972 and the vice-presidency in 1976.

Spode, Josiah (1755–1827) Potter, born in Stoke-on-Trent, Staffordshire. He inherited the pottery founded c.1770 by his father, **Josiah Spode** (1733–97), making it renowned for transfer-printed earthenware, stoneware, and superbly decorated bone china.

Springer, Jerry, popular name of **Gerald N Springer** (1944–) Television presenter, lawyer, and politician, born in London. He moved with his parents to Queens, NY in 1949. He began practising law in Cincinnati where he was elected mayor (1977–81). Also pursuing a career in broadcasting, he has hosted the *Jerry Springer Show* since 1991. A controversial show about his life, *Jerry Springer – The Opera*, opened in London's West End in 2003, winning several awards.

Springfield, Dusty, originally **Mary O'Brien** (1939–99) Pop singer, born in London. Originally part of The Springfields, her debut solo single 'I Only Want To Be With You' (1964) was a UK hit, as was her debut album, *A Girl Called Dusty* (1964). In the 1990s she acquired something of a cult following, as part of the renewed interest in music of the 1960s.

Springsteen, Bruce (Frederick Joseph) (1949–) Rock singer, guitarist, and songwriter, born in Freehold, NJ. In 1976, he released a hit in 'Born to Run', and by the mid-1980s had become the world's most popular white rock star. His albums include *Born in the USA* (1985), *Tunnel of Love* (1987), *The Ghost of Tom Joad* (1995), and *Devils and Dust* (2005).

Stalin, Joseph, originally **Joseph Vissarionovich Djugashvili** (1879–1953) Marxist revolutionary and virtual dictator of the Soviet Union (1928–53), born in Gori, Georgia. As a leading Bolshevik he played an active role in the October Revolution (1917), and in 1922 became general secretary of the Party Central Committee. In 1928 he launched the campaign for the collectivization of agriculture during which millions of peasants perished, and in 1934–8 inaugurated a massive purge of the party, government, armed forces, and intelligentsia. He took part in the conferences of Teheran, Yalta, and Potsdam which resulted in Soviet control over the liberated countries of post-war E and C Europe, his foreign policies contributing to the Cold War between the Soviet Union and the West. He was posthumously denounced by Khrushchev (1956), and under Gorbachev 'Stalinism' was officially condemned.

Stallone, Sylvester (1946–) Film actor, born in New York City. His career as an action-film hero began with *Rocky* (1976, 2 Oscars), which he also wrote. Later films include the *Rocky* sequels (1979, 1982, 1985, 1990), *Rambo* and its sequel (1985, 1988), *Assassins* (1995), *Get Carter* (2000), and *D-Tox* (2002).

Stanislavsky, originally **Konstantin Sergeyevich Alexeyev** (1863–1938) Actor, theatre director, and teacher, born in Moscow. In 1898 he helped to found the Moscow Arts Theatre, where his teaching on acting remains the basis of much Western actor-training and practice.

Stanley, Sir Henry Morton, originally **John Rowlands** (1841–1904) Explorer and journalist, born in Denbigh, Denbighshire. In 1867 he joined the *New York Herald*, and in 1869 was instructed to 'find Livingstone' in Africa, eventually doing so at Ujiji (1871). He later traced the Congo to the sea, and founded the Congo Free State.

Starr, Ringo, originally **Richard Starkey** (1940–) Drummer, singer, songwriter, and actor, born in Liverpool, Merseyside. He replaced Pete Best as The Beatles' drummer, and after the group's break-up in 1970 embarked on a solo career, and built up his 'All Starrs' band, which toured from 1989 onwards. He appeared in a number of films and in 1973 he produced the horror spoof, *Son of Dracula*.

Steadman, Alison (1946–) Actress, born in Liverpool, Merseyside. Major roles include *Abigail's Party* (1977, Best Actress, Evening Standard Awards), and *The Rise and Fall of Little Voice* (1992, Best Actress, Olivier Awards). Television work includes *Nuts in May* (1976), *Fat Friends* (2000–5), and *The Worst Week of My Life* (2004–5).

Steel (of Aikwood), David (Martin Scott), Lord (1938–) British Liberal politician, born in Kirkcaldy, Fife. He became Liberal leader (1976–88), and in 1981 led the party into an alliance with the Social Democratic Party, the parties successfully merging in 1987–8.

Steel, Danielle (Fernande Schuelein) (1947–) Writer, born in New York City. A best-selling writer of romantic fiction, she achieved success with her fourth novel, *The Promise* (1978). She has also published several works of non-fiction, and the Max and Martha series of children's books (1989).

Steiger, Rod(ney Stephen) (1925–2002) Film actor, born in Westhampton, NY. He became known following his role in *On the Waterfront* (1954). Later films include *The Pawnbroker* (1965), *In the Heat of the Night* (1967, Oscar), and *American Gothic* (1988).

Stein, Gertrude (1874–1946) Writer, born in Allegheny, PA. Her main works include *Three Lives* (1908), *Tender Buttons* (1914), and her most widely read book, *The Autobiography of Alice B Toklas* (1933). Her Paris home became a salon for artists and writers between the two World Wars.

Steinbeck, John (Ernst), pseudonym **Amnesia Glasscock** (1902–68) Novelist, born in Salinas, CA. His first novel of repute was *Tortilla Flat*

(1935), and soon after came his major work, *The Grapes of Wrath* (1939, Pulitzer; filmed 1940). Other books include *Of Mice and Men* (1937), *East of Eden* (1952), and the humorous *Cannery Row* (1945). He received the Nobel Prize for Literature in 1962.

Steiner, Rudolf (1861–1925) Social philosopher, the founder of anthroposophy, born in Kraljevec, Croatia. In 1912 he established his first 'school of spiritual science', or *Goetheanum*, in Dornach, Switzerland. The Rudolf Steiner Schools, and others, arose from his ideas, focusing on the development of the whole personality of the child.

Steinway, Henry (Engelhard), originally **Heinrich Engelhardt Steinweg** (1797–1871) Piano-maker, born in Wolfshagen, Germany. In 1850 he moved his piano factory from Brunswick to the USA, where he introduced many innovations into the instrument, such as a cast-iron frame.

Stendhal, pseudonym of **Marie-Henri Beyle** (1783–1842) Writer, born in Grenoble, France. He is best known for his novels, notably *Scarlet and Black* (trans, 1830) and *The Charterhouse of Parma* (trans, 1839), but also wrote biographies, critical works on music, art, and literature, and a famous *Journal* (1888).

Stephen (c.1090–1154) Last Norman king of England (1135–54), and son of Stephen-Henry, Count of Blois, and Adela, daughter of William the Conqueror. He had sworn to accept Henry I's daughter, Matilda, as queen, but seized the English crown on Henry's death. After 18 years of virtually continuous warfare, he was forced in 1153 to accept Matilda's son, the future Henry II, as his successor.

Stephen, St (1st-c) The first Christian martyr, (*Acts* 6–7). Charged by the Jewish authorities for speaking against the Temple and the Law, he was tried by the Sanhedrin, and stoned to death by the crowds in Jerusalem.

Stephenson, George (1781–1848) Railway engineer, born in Wylam, Northumberland. His most famous engine, the *Rocket*, running at 58 km/36 mi an hour, was built in 1829. He was an engineer for several railway companies.

Stephenson, Robert (1803–59) Civil engineer, born in Willington Quay, Northumberland, the son of George Stephenson. His designs include the Britannia Bridge over the Menai Strait in N Wales (1846–9), and bridges at Conwy, Montreal (Canada), and elsewhere.

Stephenson, Sir William, known as **Intrepid** (1896–1989) Secret intelligence chief, born in Point Douglas, near Winnipeg, Canada. In 1940 he was appointed British intelligence chief in North and South America. The novelist Ian Fleming, a member of his wartime staff, is said to have adopted him as a model for the character 'M' in the James Bond books.

Sterne, Laurence (1713–68) Novelist, born in Clonmel, Co Tipperary, Ireland. In 1759 he wrote the first two volumes of his comic novel *The Life and Opinions of Tristram Shandy*, other volumes appearing between 1761 and 1767.

Stevenson, Juliet (1956–) Actress, born in London. Her work for the theatre includes *Death and the Maiden* (1992, Olivier Award, Best Actress). Among her film credits are *Drowning by Numbers* (1988), *Truly, Madly, Deeply* (1991, Evening Standard Awards, Best Actress), and *Being Julia* (2004).

Stevenson, Robert Louis (Balfour) (1850–94) Writer, born in Edinburgh. His romantic fiction included *Treasure Island* (1883), *Kidnapped* (1886), *The Strange Case of Dr Jekyll and Mr Hyde* (1886), *The Master of Ballantrae* (1889), and the unfinished *Weir of Hermiston* (1896), considered his masterpiece.

Stewart, Alec (James) (1963–) Cricketer, born in Merton, Greater London. He began playing for Surrey in 1981, made his Test debut in 1990, and by the end of the 2003 season had played in a record 133 Tests, scoring 8463 runs and 15 centuries, and making 273 dismissals (a wicket-keeping record). He was England captain (1998–9), and retired from international and county cricket in 2003.

Stewart, Sir Jackie, popular name of **John (Young) Stewart** (1939–) Motor-racing driver, born in Milton, West Dunbartonshire. He won 27 world championship races between 1965 and 1973, and was world champion in 1969, 1971, and 1973.

Stewart, James (Maitland) (1908–97) Film star, born in Indiana, PA. His early films include *The Philadelphia Story* (1940, Oscar) and *It's a Wonderful Life* (1946). He made a series of outstanding Westerns (1950–5) and

two successes for Hitchcock, *Rear Window* (1954) and *Vertigo* (1958).

Stewart, J(ohn) I(nnes) M(ackintosh), pseudonym **Michael Innes** (1906–94) Critic, and writer of detective fiction, born in Edinburgh. His work as Michael Innes includes *The Secret Vanguard* (1940), *A Private View* (1952), and *A Family Affair* (1969).

Stewart, Patrick (1940–) Actor and playwright, born in Mirfield, West Yorkshire. He is best known for his role as Captain Jean-Luc Picard in the follow-up series of *Star Trek: The Next Generation* (1987). Later films include *Star Trek: First Contact* (1996), *Star Trek: Insurrection* (1998), and *X-Men* (2000, sequel 2003).

Stewart, Rod(erick David) (1945–) Singer and songwriter, born in London. He began a career as a soloist, and also joined The Faces (1969–75). His numerous hit songs include 'Maggie May' (1971) and 'Sailing' (1975). Albums include *Every Picture Tells A Story* (1971), *When We Were The New Boys* (1998), and *As Time Goes By* (2003).

Sting, originally **Gordon Matthew Sumner** (1951–) Singer, songwriter, and actor, born in Newcastle upon Tyne. Formerly with group The Police, his albums include *The Dream of the Blue Turtles* (1985), *Mercury Falling* (1996), and *Sacred Love* (2003). His films include *Quadrophenia* (1978), *Dune* (1984), and *Lock, Stock and Two Smoking Barrels* (1999). He has also been much associated with campaigns concerning the environment and Amnesty International.

Stockton, Earl of *see* Macmillan, Harold

Stoker, Bram, popular name of **Abraham Stoker** (1847–1912) Writer, born in Dublin. He is chiefly remembered for the classic horror tale *Dracula* (1897); other novels include *The Mystery of the Sea* (1902) and *The Lady of the Shroud* (1909).

Stokowski, Leopold, originally **Antoni Stanislaw Boleslawowicz** (1882–1977) Conductor, born in London. He conducted the orchestras of Philadelphia (1912–36), New York (1946–50), and Houston (1955–60), and in 1962 founded the American Symphony Orchestra in New York City.

Stooges, The Three Comedy trio, originally the **Horwitz** (later **Howard**) brothers, **Samuel** (1895–1955), **Moses** (1897–1975), and **Jerome (Jerry)** (1903–52), all born in New York. They were known by their respective nicknames of Shemp, Moe, and Curly. Shemp left for a solo career, and the trio of Moe, Curly, and friend **Larry Fine** (originally **Feinberg**, born in Philadelphia, PA (1902–75)) went on to feature film success. Their films were characterized by anarchic knockabout humour, with sound effects perfectly synchronized with their blows. Shemp returned, replacing Curly (d.1952), and in turn was replaced by **Joe Besser**, born in St Louis, MO (1907–88); he was then replaced by **Joe De Rita**, Curly Joe, born in Philadelphia, PA (1909–93).

Stopes, Marie (Charlotte Carmichael) (1880–1958) Pioneer advocate of birth control, suffragette, and palaeontologist, born in Edinburgh. Her book *Married Love* (1918) caused a storm of controversy, and she founded the first birth control clinic, in London (1921).

Stoppard, Miriam, *née* **Stern** (1937–) British physician, writer, and broadcaster. She is well known for her television series, especially *Miriam Stoppard's Health and Beauty Show* (from 1988). Among her books are *The Baby and Child Medical Handbook* (1984) and *Defying Age* (2003). She married Tom Stoppard in 1972 (divorced, 1992).

Stoppard, Sir Tom, originally **Tomas Straussler** (1937–) Playwright, born in Zlín, Czech Republic. Among his plays are *Rosencrantz and Guildenstern are Dead* (1967), *Jumpers* (1972), *Travesties* (1974), and *The Real Thing* (1982, Tony). His screenplays include *Empire of the Sun* (1987) and *Shakespeare in Love* (1998).

Storey, David (Malcolm) (1933–) Writer, born in Wakefield, West Yorkshire. His novels include *This Sporting Life* (1960), *Saville* (1976, Booker), and *Thin-Ice Skater* (2004). Among his plays are *The Changing Room* (1972) and *Life Class* (1974).

Stowe, Harriet (Elizabeth) Beecher, *née* **Beecher** (1811–96) Novelist, born in Litchfield, CT. She became famous through her *Uncle Tom's Cabin*, which immediately focused antislavery sentiment in the North. Her other novels include *Dred* (1856) and *The Minister's Wooing* (1859).

Strachey, (Giles) Lytton (1880–1932) Biographer, born in London. A member of the Bloomsbury group of writers and artists, he created a literary bombshell with his *Eminent Victorians* (1918), an impertinent challenge to the self-assured studies previously typical of this genre.

Stradivari or **Stradivarius, Antonio** (c.1644–1737) Violin maker, born in Cremona, Italy. He perfected the Cremona type of violin, and is thought to have made over a thousand violins, violas, and violoncellos between 1666 and his death; about 650 of these still exist.

Strasberg, Lee, originally **Israel Strassberg** (1901–82) Actor, director, and teacher, born in Budanov, Ukraine (formerly Budzanow, Austria). He emigrated to the USA in 1909, and in 1931 was involved in the formation of the Group Theater, evolving an influential teaching technique known as 'method acting'.

Stratton, Charles (Sherwood), nickname **General Tom Thumb** (1838–83) Midget showman, born in Bridgeport, CT. He measured only 63 cm/25 in until his teens, eventually reaching 101 cm/40 in. Barnum displayed him in his museum, from the age of five, and in 1863 his marriage to **Lavinia Warren** (1841–1919), also a midget, was widely publicized.

Strauss, Johann, known as **the Elder** (1804–49) Violinist, conductor, and composer, born in Vienna. He founded with **Josef Lanner** (1801–43) the Viennese Waltz tradition. He composed several marches, notably the *Radetzky March* (1848), and many waltzes.

Strauss, Johann, known as **the Younger** (1825–99) Violinist, conductor, and composer, born in Vienna, the eldest son of Johann Strauss (the Elder). He wrote over 400 waltzes, notably *The Blue Danube* (trans, 1867) and *Tales from the Vienna Woods* (trans, 1868). Other works include the operetta *Die Fledermaus* (1874, The Bat), and a favourite concert piece, *Perpetuum Mobile*.

Strauss, Richard (1864–1949) Composer, born in Munich, Germany. He is best known for his symphonic poems, such as *Till Eulenspiegel's Merry Pranks* (trans, 1894–5), and his operas, notably *Der Rosenkavalier* (1911). He also wrote concertos, songs, and several small-scale orchestral works.

Stravinsky, Igor (Fyodorovich) (1882–1971) Composer, born near St Petersburg, Russia. He became famous with his music for the Diaghilev ballets *The Firebird* (1910), *Petrushka* (1911), and *The Rite of Spring* (1913). Essentially an experimenter, after World War 1 he devoted himself to Neoclassicism, as in the opera-oratorio *Oedipus Rex* (1927) and the choral *Symphony of Psalms* (1930). Other major compositions include the *Symphony in C major* (1940), the opera *The Rake's Progress* (1951), and such later works as *Requiem Canticles* (1966), in which he adopted serialism.

Straw, Jack, popular name of **John Whitaker Straw** (1946–) British statesman, born in Buckhurst Hill, Essex. An MP from 1979, he joined the shadow cabinet as spokesman on education (1987–92), environment and local government (1992–3), local government (1993–4), and home affairs (1994–7). He became home secretary in the 1997 Labour government, secretary of state for foreign and Commonwealth affairs (2001–6), and Commons Leader (2006–).

Streep, Meryl (Louise) (1949–) Actress, born in Summit, NJ. Her many films include *Kramer vs. Kramer* (1979, Oscar), *The French Lieutenant's Woman* (1981), *Sophie's Choice* (1982, Oscar), and *Adaptation* (2002, Oscar nomination). Her television work includes the drama mini-series *Angels in America* (2004, Emmy).

Street-Porter, Janet (1946–) British television executive, presenter, and journalist. She entered independent television in 1975 as a presenter, later joining the BBC as head of Youth and Entertainment Features (1988–94). She was editor of the *Independent on Sunday* (1999–2001), becoming its editor-at-large in 2001.

Streisand, Barbra, originally **Barbara Joan Streisand** (1942–) Singer, actress, and director, born in New York City. She played the lead in the Broadway show *Funny Girl* (1964), which she repeated in the 1968 film version to win an Oscar. Later films include *Hello Dolly* (1969), *A Star Is Born* (1976), and *Yentl* (1983). Her 1965 television special, *My Name is Barbra*, won five Emmy Awards.

Strindberg, (Johan) August (1849–1912) Playwright, born in Stockholm. He first achieved fame with the novel *The Red Room* (trans, 1879). His plays *The Father* (trans, 1887) and *Miss Julie* (trans, 1888) brought him to the forefront as the exponent of naturalistic drama; later plays were more symbolic in form and religious in theme.

Strong, Sir Roy (Colin) (1935–) Art historian and museum director, born in London. He became director of London's National Portrait Gallery in 1967, and was later director of the Victoria and Albert Museum (1974–87). In 1992 he wrote and presented the BBC television series *Royal Gardens*.

Stuart or **Stewart, Prince Charles Edward (Louis Philip Casimir)**, known as **the Young Pretender** and **Bonnie Prince Charlie** (1720–88) Claimant to the British crown, born in Rome, Italy, the son of James Francis Edward Stuart. In 1745, he landed at Eriskay in the Hebrides and raised his father's standard. The clansmen flocked to him, Edinburgh surrendered, and he kept court at Holyrood. Victorious at Prestonpans, he invaded England, but was routed at Culloden (1746). With the help of Flora Macdonald he escaped to the Continent.

Stuart or **Stewart, Prince James (Francis Edward)**, also known as **the Old Pretender** (1688–1766) Claimant to the British throne, born in London, the only son of James II of England and his second wife, Mary of Modena. In 1715 he landed at Peterhead during the Jacobite rising, but left Scotland some weeks later, thereafter living mainly in Rome.

Stylites, Simeon *see* Simeon Stylites, St

Sullivan, Sir Arthur (Seymour) (1842–1900) Composer, born in London. From 1871 he became known for his collaboration with W S Gilbert in their series of comic operas, and also composed a grand opera, *Ivanhoe*

(1891), cantatas, ballads, a *Te Deum*, and hymn tunes.

Sullivan, Louis Henry (1856–1924) Architect, born in Boston, MA. His experimental, functional skeleton constructions of skyscrapers and office blocks, particularly the Gage building and stock exchange, Chicago, IL, earned him the title 'Father of Modernism'.

Sundance Kid, popular name of **Harry Longabaugh** or **Langbaugh** (1867–?1909) Outlaw, born in Phoenixville, PA. He teamed up with Butch Cassidy, and drifted throughout North and South America robbing banks, trains, and mines. It is generally held that he was fatally shot by a cavalry unit in Bolivia.

Surtees, John (1934–) Motor-racing driver and motor-cyclist, born in Westerham, Kent, the only man to win world titles on both two and four wheels. He won the 350 cc motor-cycling world title (1958–60) and the 500 cc title (1956, 1958–60), then won the motor-racing world title (1964).

Sutcliffe, Peter, known as **the Yorkshire Ripper** (1946–) Convicted murderer, born in Bingley, West Yorkshire. He murdered 13 women over five years in N England and the Midlands. Arrested in 1981, he was sentenced to life imprisonment.

Sutherland, Donald (1934–) Film actor, born in St John, New Brunswick, Canada. He became known for his role in *The Dirty Dozen* (1967), following this with *M*A*S*H* (1970) and *Klute* (1971). Among his later films are *Backdraft* (1991), *Cold*

Mountain (2003), and *Pride and Prejudice* (2005).

Sutherland, Graham (Vivian) (1903–80) Artist, born in London. He was an official war artist (1941–5), and later produced several memorable portraits, including 'Sir Winston Churchill' (1955). His large tapestry, 'Christ in Majesty', was hung in the new Coventry Cathedral in 1962.

Sutherland, Dame Joan (1926–) Operatic soprano, born in Sydney, New South Wales, Australia. She made her debut at Sydney in 1947, moved to London in 1951, and joined the Royal Opera, becoming resident soprano at Covent Garden. She retired in 1990. In 1954 she married the conductor **Richard Bonynge** (1930–).

Swank, Hilary (Ann) (1974–) Actress, born in Lincoln, NE. As a child she attended a local theatre group, and in 1990 moved to Los Angeles where she began acting professionally, gaining her breakthrough into films with *The Next Karate Kid* (1994). Later films include *Boys Don't Cry* (1999, Oscar) and *Million Dollar Baby* (2005, Oscar, Golden Globe).

Swedenborg, Emanuel, originally **Emanuel Swedberg** (1688–1772) Mystic and scientist, born in Stockholm. His monumental *Philosophical and Logical Works* (trans, 1734), was a mixture of metallurgy and metaphysical speculation on creation. He expounded his doctrines in such works as *The New Jerusalem* (1758), and in 1787 his followers (known as Swedenborgians) formed the Church of the New Jerusalem.

Swift, Jonathan (1667–1745) Clergyman and satirist, born in Dublin. He attacked religious dissension in *A Tale of a Tub* (1704), and produced a wide range of political and religious essays and pamphlets. His world-famous satire, *Gulliver's Travels*, appeared in 1726.

Swinburne, Algernon Charles (1837–1909) Poet and critic, born in London. He achieved success with his play *Atalanta in Calydon* (1865), and the first of his series of *Poems and Ballads* (1866). Later works include several critical studies of major authors.

Swithin or **Swithun, St** (?–862) Eng-lish saint and theologian. In 852 he was made Bishop of Winchester, where he died. When in 971 the monks exhumed his body to bury it in the rebuilt cathedral, the removal (on 15 July) is said to have been delayed by violent rains.

Synge, (Edmund) J(ohn) M(illing-ton) (1871–1909) Playwright, born near Dublin. He settled among the people of the Aran Is, who provided the material for his plays, notably *Riders to the Sea* (1904) and *The Playboy of the Western World* (1907), and became a major influence on Irish playwrights.

Taft, William Howard (1857–1930) US statesman and 27th president (1909–13), born in Cincinnati, OH. He secured an agreement with Canada that meant relatively free trade until 1910. His son **Robert Alphonso Taft** (1889–1953) became a Republican leader (1939–53), but was defeated as a candidate for presidential nomination on three occasions.

Tallis, Thomas (c.1505–85) English musician. One of the greatest contrapuntists of the English School, he wrote much church music, including a motet in 40 parts, *Spem in Alium*.

Tandy, Jessica (1909–94) Stage and film actress, born in London. She moved to the USA in 1930, and played in the original production of *A Streetcar Named Desire* (1947). She married **Hume Cronyn** (1911–2003), often appearing with him on stage. Her films include *Driving Miss Daisy* (1989, Oscar).

Tarantino, Quentin (Jerome) (1963–) Film director, producer, actor, and screenwriter, born in Knoxville, TN. The success of his first screenplays, *True Romance* (1987, released 1993)

and *Natural Born Killers* (released 1994), enabled him to finance *Reservoir Dogs* (1992), in which he was director, screenwriter, and actor. Later films include *Pulp Fiction* (1994, Oscar) and the two-part *Kill Bill* (2003).

Tarrant, Chris(topher John) (1946–) British television presenter, writer, and producer. He made programmes for Independent Television, such as *Tiswas* (1974), *OTT* (1981), and *Tarrant on Television* (from 1989), and in 1998 became a household name as presenter of the TV quiz show *Who Wants to be a Millionaire?*

Tasman, Abel Janszoon (1603–c.59) Navigator, born near Groningen, The Netherlands. In 1642 he discovered the area he named Van Diemen's Land (now Tasmania) and New Zealand, followed by Tonga and Fiji (1643).

Tate, Ellalice *see* Hibbert, Eleanor

Tate, Sir Henry (1819–99) Sugar magnate, art patron, and philanthropist, born in Chorley, Lancashire. He patented a method for cutting sugar cubes (1872) and attained great wealth as a Liverpool sugar refiner. He founded The Tate Gallery.

Tate, Sharon *see* Manson, Charles; Polanski, Roman

Tati, Jacques, popular name of **Jacques Tatischeff** (1908–82) Actor and film producer, born in Le Pecq, France. He made his reputation as the greatest film comedian of the postwar period, notably in *Mr Hulot's Holiday* (trans, 1953) and *My Uncle* (trans, 1958).

Tatum, Art(hur) (1910–56) Jazz pianist, born in Toledo, OH. He became the first supreme keyboard jazz virtuoso, known for his technique, drive, and improvisational powers.

Tavener, Sir John (Kenneth) (1944–) Composer, born in London. His music is predominantly religious, and includes the cantata *The Whale* (1966) and a sacred opera *Thérèse* (1979). His *Song for Athene* (1993), written to commemorate the death of a family friend, became nationally known when it was chosen as part of the funeral ceremony for Princess Diana in 1997. Among later works are *The Veil of the Temple* (2003).

Taylor, Dame Elizabeth (Rosemond) (1932–) Film star, born in London. Her early films include *Cat on a Hot Tin Roof* (1958) and *Butterfield 8* (1960, Oscar). *Cleopatra* (1962) provided the background to her well-publicized romance with Richard Burton, her co-star in several films, including *Who's Afraid of Virginia Woolf?* (1966, Oscar). She has been married eight times, twice to Burton. She received a BAFTA honorary fellowship in 1999.

Taylor, Lady Helen *see* Kent, Edward, Duke of

Taylor, Zachary (1784–1850) US general, statesman, and 12th president (1849–50), born in Montebello, VA. In the Mexican War (1846–8) he won a major victory at Buena Vista, though heavily outnumbered. The main issue of his presidency was the status of the new territories, and the extension of slavery there.

Tchaikovsky or **Tschaikovsky, Piotr Ilyich** (1840–93) Composer, born in Kamsko-Votkinsk, Russia. Among his greatest works are the ballets *Swan Lake* (1876–7), *The Sleeping Beauty*

(1890), and *The Nutcracker* (1892), the last three of his six symphonies, two piano concertos, and several tone poems, notably *Romeo and Juliet* and *Capriccio Italien*.

Teagarden, Jack, popular name of **Weldon Leo Teagarden** (1905–64) Jazz trombonist and singer, born in Vernon, TX. A featured soloist in Paul Whiteman's orchestra (1933–8), he led his own orchestra (1939–46), then joined Armstrong's All Stars (1947–51).

Tebbit (of Chingford), Norman (Beresford) Tebbit, Baron (1931–) British Conservative statesman, born in Enfield, Greater London. He served as employment secretary (1981–3) and secretary for trade and industry (1983–5), but his career was interrupted in 1984 when he was badly hurt during the IRA bombing of the Grand Hotel at Brighton. He was later party chairman (1985–7).

Teilhard de Chardin, Pierre (1881–1955) Geologist, palaeontologist, Jesuit priest, and philosopher, born in Sarcenat, France. His unorthodox ideas led to a Church ban on his teaching and publishing. His major work, *The Phenomenon of Man* (1938–40), was posthumously published.

Te Kanawa, Dame Kiri (1944–) Operatic soprano, born in Gisborne, New Zealand. She made her debut with the Royal Opera Company in 1970, and has since taken a wide range of leading roles, in 1981 singing at the wedding of the Prince and Princess of Wales.

Telemann, Georg Philipp (1681–1767) Composer, born in Magdeburg, Germany. His many works include church music, 46 passions, over 40 operas, oratorios, many songs, and a large body of instrumental music.

Telford, Thomas (1757–1834) Engineer, born near Langholm, Dumfries and Galloway. His many projects include the Ellesmere (1793–1805) and Caledonian (1803–23) canals, and the road from London to Holyhead, with the Menai Suspension Bridge (1826).

Tell, Wilhelm, Eng **William Tell** (13th–14th-c) Legendary Swiss patriot. According to tradition, he was compelled by a tyrannical Austrian governor to shoot an apple off his own son's head with a crossbow at a distance of 80 paces. Later, Tell slew the tyrant, initiating the movement which secured the independence of Switzerland.

Temple, Shirley, married name **Black** (1928–) Child film star, born in Santa Monica, CA. During 1934–8 she appeared in more than 20 feature films, such as *Stand Up and Cheer* (1934) and *Bright Eyes* (1934), and was consistently the top US movie star. She received an honorary Academy Award in 1934. Retiring from the screen, in her married status as **Mrs S T Black** she entered Republican politics, and was US Ambassador to Ghana (1974–6) and Czechoslovakia (1989–93).

Tennyson, Alfred Tennyson, 1st Baron, known as **Alfred, Lord Tennyson** (1809–92) Poet, born in Somersby, Lincolnshire. His major works include 'The Lady of Shallott' and 'The Lotus-eaters' (1842), 'In Memoriam' (1850), and a series of poems

on the Arthurian theme, *Idylls of the King* (1859–85). He became poet laureate in 1850.

Tenzing Norgay, known as **Sherpa Tenzing** (1914–86) Mountaineer, born in Tsa-chu, Nepal. In 1953 he succeeded in reaching the Everest summit with Edmund Hillary, for which he was awarded the George Medal.

Teresa of Ávila, St (1515–82) Saint and mystic, born in Ávila, Spain. Famous for her ascetic religious exercises and sanctity, in 1562 she re-established the ancient Carmelite rule, with additional observances. She was canonized in 1622.

Teresa (of Calcutta), Mother, originally **Agnes Gonxha Bojaxhiu** (1910–97) Christian missionary in India, born in Skopje, Yugoslavia (formerly Albania). Her sisterhood, the Missionaries of Charity, was founded in 1950, and in 1957 she began work with lepers, and in many disaster areas of the world. She was awarded the Nobel Peace Prize in 1979.

Teresa of Lisieux *see* Theresa of Lisieux, St

Tereshkova, Valentina (1937–) Cosmonaut, the first woman to fly in space, born in Maslennikovo, Russia. She was solo crew member of the three-day Vostok 6 flight launched on 16 June 1963.

Terfel, Bryn, originally **Bryn Terfel Jones** (1965–) Bass baritone, born in Pantglas, Caernarfonshire. He became known after winning the Lieder Prize in the Cardiff Singer of the World competition in 1989, and is twice winner of best male artist at the Classical Brit Awards (2004, 2005). In 2000 he established the annual Bryn Terfel's Faenol Festival held near Bangor, North Wales.

Terry-Thomas, originally **Thomas Terry Hoar Stevens** (1911–90) Film actor, born in Finchley, Greater London. He was the gap-toothed villain in dozens of post-World War 2 comedies, satirizing and eventually personifying the upper-class bounder in such films as *I'm All Right Jack* (1959), *School for Scoundrels* (1960), and *Those Magnificent Men In Their Flying Machines* (1965).

Tesla, Nikola (1856–1943) Physicist and electrical engineer, born in Smiljan, Croatia. His inventions included improved dynamos, transformers, electric bulbs, and the high-frequency coil which now bears his name. The unit of magnetic induction is named after him.

Thackeray, William Makepeace (1811–63) Novelist, born in Kolkata (Calcutta), India. His major novels are *Vanity Fair* (1847–8), *Pendennis* (1848), *Henry Esmond* (1852), and *The Newcomes* (1853–5). In 1860 he became the first editor of *The Cornhill Magazine*, where much of his later work appeared.

Thaddeus, St *see* Jude, St

Tharp, Twyla (1942–) Dancer, choreographer, and director, born in Portland, IN. She has choreographed and danced with her own group, and made new work for other ballet and modern dance companies. In 1996 she formed her own company, Tharp!

Thatcher (of Kesteven), Margaret (Hilda) Thatcher, Baroness, *née*

Roberts (1925–) British Conservative prime minister (1979–90), born in Grantham, Lincolnshire. She was minister of education (1970–4), and in 1975 became the first woman party leader in British politics. Her government instituted the privatization of nationalized industries and national utilities, tried to institute a market in state-provided health care and education, and reduced the role of local government as a provider of services. She resigned in 1990, following her opposition to full economic union with Europe, having become the longest-serving premier of the 20th-c.

Thaw, John (Edward) (1942–2002) Actor, born in Manchester, Greater Manchester. Best known for his television work, which included *The Sweeney* (1974–8), *Inspector Morse* (1987–2000), and *Kavanagh QC* (1995–2000), he won a number of BAFTA awards and was honoured with a fellowship in 2001. He married actress **Sheila Hancock** (1933–) in 1973.

Theresa, Mother *see* Teresa, Mother

Theresa, St *see* Teresa of Ávila, St

Theresa of Lisieux, St, originally **(Marie Françoise) Thérèse Martin**, also known as **the Little Flower** and **St Theresa of the Child Jesus** (1873–97) Saint, born in Alençon, France. She entered the Carmelite convent of Lisieux in Normandy at the age of 15, where she remained until her death from tuberculosis nine years later. Her account of her life was published posthumously as *Story of a Soul* (trans, 1898). She was canonized in 1925.

Theroux, Paul (Edward) (1941–)
Novelist and travel writer, born in
Medford, MA. His novels include
Saint Jack (1973; filmed 1979), *Picture
Palace* (1978, Whitbread Award), *The
Mosquito Coast* (1981, James Tait
Black; filmed 1987), and *Blinding Light*
(2005). His rail journeys are
recounted in such books as *The Great
Railway Bazaar* (1975).

Thomas, St (1st-c) A disciple of Jesus
Christ. He is most prominent in
John's Gospel, where he is also called
Didymus ('the Twin'), and portrayed
as doubting the resurrection until he
touches the wounds of the risen
Christ (*John* 20). He is the patron
saint of Portugal.

Thomas, D(onald) M(ichael) (1935–)
Novelist, poet, and translator, born
in Redruth, Cornwall. He became
known after his controversial novel
The White Hotel (1981). Other novels
include his first, *The Flute Player*
(1979), *Lying Together* (1990), and
Flying into Love (1992). He has also
translated major literary works from
Russian.

Thomas, Dylan (Marlais) (1914–53)
Poet, born in Swansea, S Wales. He
established himself with the publication of *Eighteen Poems* in 1934. His
Collected Poems appeared in 1953, and
he then produced his best-known
work, the radio 'play for voices',
Under Milk Wood (1954).

Thomas, (Philip) Edward, pseudonym **Edward Eastaway** (1878–1917)
Poet and critic, born in London. He
wrote most of his work during active
service between 1915 and his death in
action, just before the publication of
Poems (1917), under his pseudonym.

Thomas, Sir George (Alan)
(1881–1972) Badminton player, born
in Istanbul. He won a record 21 All-
England titles between 1903 and
1928, including the singles four times
(1920–3). In 1939 he presented the
Thomas Cup to be contested by
national teams.

Thomas, R(onald) S(tuart)
(1913–2000) Poet, born in Cardiff. A
rector in the Church of Wales
(1942–78), his collections include
Selected Poems, 1946–68 (1973), *Coun-
terpoint* (1990), and *No Truth with the
Furies* (1995).

Thomas, Terry *see* Terry-Thomas

Thomas (à) Becket *see* Becket, St
Thomas

Thomas Aquinas *see* Aquinas, St
Thomas

Thompson, Sir Benjamin, Graf
(Count) **von Rumford**, known as
Count Rumford (1753–1814) Administrator and scientist, born in
Woburn, MA. In 1784 he entered the
service of Bavaria, where he carried
out military, social, and economic
reforms, for which he was made a
count of the Holy Roman Empire. He
first showed the relation between
heat and work, a concept fundamental to modern physics. In 1799 he
returned to London, and founded
the Royal Institution.

Thompson, Daley, popular name of
Francis Morgan Thompson (1958–)
Athlete, born in London. An outstanding decathlete, he was world
champion (1983), European champion (1982, 1986), and Olympic
champion (1980, 1984).

Thompson, Emma (1959–) Actress,
born in London. In 1989 she

appeared in the film *Henry V*, directed by Kenneth Branagh, whom she married the same year (divorced 1996). Later films include *Howards End* (1992, Oscar), *Remains of the Day* (1993), *In the Name of the Father* (1994), *Sense and Sensibility* (1996, BAFTA), and *Nanny McPhee* (2005).

Thompson, John T(alafierro) (1860–1940) US soldier and inventor, born in Newport, KY. In 1918 he originated the Thompson submachine gun, which came to be known as the *Tommy gun*.

Thomson, Sir J(oseph) J(ohn) (1856–1940) Physicist, born in Cheetham Hill, Greater Manchester. He showed in 1897 that cathode rays were rapidly moving particles, and deduced that these 'corpuscles' (electrons) must be nearly 2000 times smaller in mass than the lightest known atomic particle, the hydrogen ion. He received the Nobel Prize for Physics in 1906.

Thomson, Sir William *see* Kelvin, 1st Baron

Thoreau, Henry (David), originally **David Henry Thoreau** (1817–62) Essayist and poet, born in Concord, MA. In c.1839 he began the walks and studies of nature which became his major occupation, recorded in a daily journal. His writings include the classic *Walden, or Life in the Woods* (1854).

Thorpe, Ian, known as **The Thorpedo** (1982–) Swimmer, born in Paddington, Sydney, Australia. In the 1998 World Championships he became the youngest male world champion in history by winning the 400 m freestyle. His remarkable medal haul includes: four gold (1998 Commonwealth Games), two gold (1998 World Championships), three gold (2000 Olympics), six gold (2001 World Championships), six gold (2002 Commonweath Games), two gold (2003 World Championships), two gold (2004 Olympics).

Thumb, General Tom *see* Stratton, Charles

Thurber, James (Grover) (1894–1961) Writer and cartoonist, born in Columbus, OH. His drawings first appeared in his book *Is Sex Necessary?* (1929), and there are several anthologies of his work, such as *Thurber's Dogs* (1955). He was also the creator of the fantasizing character Walter Mitty.

Thurman, Uma (Karuna) (1970–) Film actress, born in Boston, MA. The daughter of an American father and Swedish mother, she moved to New York to try her luck at acting, and gained recognition with her role in Quentin Tarantino's *Pulp Fiction* (1994). Later films include *Kill Bill: Vol.1* (2003; *Vol.2*, 2004), and *The Producers* (2005).

Tiberius, in full **Tiberius Julius Caesar Augustus** (42 BC–AD 37) Roman emperor (14–37), the son of Livia, and stepson and successor of the Emperor Augustus. The suspicious death of his heir Germanicus (19), followed by the excesses of his chief henchman, Sejanus, and the reign of terror that followed Sejanus's downfall (d.31), made him widely hated.

Tindale *see* Tyndale, William

Tintoretto, originally **Jacopo Robusti** (1518–94) Venetian painter, probably born in Venice, Italy, the son of a dyer (Ital *tintore*). His most spectacular works are sacred murals, notably the canvases decorating the Church and Scuola of S Rocco. Other major works include 'The Last Supper' (1547) and the 'Paradiso' (1588).

Tippett, Sir Michael (Kemp) (1905–98) Composer, born in London. His works include the oratorio, *A Child of our Time* (1941), the operas *The Midsummer Marriage* (1952) and *King Priam* (1961), four symphonies, a piano concerto, and string quartets.

Titchmarsh, Alan (Fred) (1949–) Gardener, broadcaster, and writer, born in Ilkley, West Yorkshire. He became a household name as presenter of the popular BBC radio series, *Gardener's World* (1996) and of TV's *Ground Force* (1997–2003). His books include *How To Be a Gardener* (2002, 2003), and he has also written a number of novels.

Titian, Ital **Tiziano Vecellio** (c.1490–1576) Venetian painter, born in Pieve di Cadore, Italy. For the Duke of Ferrara he painted three great mythological subjects, 'The Feast of Venus' (c.1515–18), 'Bacchanal' (c.1518), and 'Bacchus and Ariadne' (c.1523). Later works include 'Ecce Homo' (1543) and 'Christ Crowned with Thorns' (c.1570).

Tito, known as **Marshal Tito**, originally **Josip Broz** (1892–1980) Yugoslav statesman and president (1953–80), born in Kumrovec, Croatia. In 1941 he organized partisan forces against the Axis conquerors, and after the war became the country's first Communist prime minister (1945), then president (1953). He broke with Stalin and the Comin-

form in 1948, developing Yugoslavia's independent style of Communism (*Titoism*).

Titus, St (1st-c) In the New Testament, a Gentile companion of the apostle Paul. Ecclesiastical tradition makes him the first Bishop of Crete.

Tolkien, J(ohn) R(onald) R(euel) (1892–1973) Philologist and writer, born in Bloemfontein, South Africa. His interest in language and saga led to his books about a fantasy world in which the beings have their own language and mythology, notably *The Hobbit* (1937), *The Lord of the Rings* (3 vols, 1954–5; filmed 2001–3), and *The Silmarillion* (1977).

Tolstoy, Count Leo Nikolayevich (1828–1910) Russian writer, moralist, and mystic, born at Yasnaya Polyana, Russia. He became known for his short stories, then wrote his epic *War and Peace* (1865–9), followed by *Anna Karenina* (1875–7). After a spiritual crisis he made over his fortune to his wife and lived poorly as a peasant under her roof. His doctrines founded a sect, and Yasnaya Polyana became a place of pilgrimage.

Tomlinson, Ray (1941–) Computer engineer, the inventor of e-mail, born in Vale Mills, NY. In 1971 he devised a method of sending a message from a user on one computer to a user on a remote machine. He selected the @ symbol to separate the name of the user from the name of the machine to which the message was being sent.

Tom Thumb *see* Stratton, Charles

Torvill and Dean Figure skaters **Jayne Torvill** (1957–) and **Christopher Dean** (1958–), both from Nottingham, Nottinghamshire. World ice dance champions (1981–4), and Olympic champions (1984), they then turned professional, but returned to international competition in 1993–4, winning the gold medal in the 1994 European Championships and a bronze in the 1994 Winter Olympics.

Toscanini, Arturo (1867–1957) Conductor, born in Parma, Italy. He conducted at La Scala, Milan (1898–1908), the Metropolitan Opera House, New York (1908–15), and the New York Philharmonic (1926–36), and brought into being the Orchestra of the National Broadcasting Corporation of America (1937–53).

Toshack, John (1949–) Football player and manager, born in Cardiff. He began his career with Cardiff City (1966) and later signed for Liverpool (1970–8), where his honours include three league titles, two UEFA Cup wins, and one FA Cup. As manager, he was successful with a number of top European clubs during the 1980s and 1990s, including Real Madrid. Briefly in charge of Wales in 1994, he was appointed manager for a second time in 2004.

Toulouse-Lautrec (-Monfa), Henri (Marie Raymond) de (1864–1901) Painter and lithographer, born in Albi, France. Physically frail, at the age of 14 he broke both his legs, which then ceased to grow. He is best known for his paintings of Montmartre society, as in 'The Bar' (1898) and 'At the Moulin Rouge' (1892), but he also depicted fashionable society and produced several portraits.

Townsend, Sue (1946–) Novelist and playwright, born in Leicester, Leicestershire. She made her name through a series of novels introducing the character of Adrian Mole, beginning with *The Secret Diary of Adrian Mole Aged 13¾* (1982), later books including *The Cappuccino Years* (1999) and *Adrian Mole and the Weapons of Mass Destruction* (2004).

Townshend (of Rainham), Charles Townshend, 2nd Viscount, known as **Turnip Townshend** (1674–1738) British statesman, born in Raynham, Norfolk. Made secretary of state by George I (1714–16, 1721–30), he became a leading figure in the Whig ministry. He acquired his nickname for his proposal to use turnips in crop rotation.

Tracy, Spencer (Bonadventure) (1900–67) Actor, born in Milwaukee, WI. He received Oscars for *Captains Courageous* (1937) and *Boys' Town* (1938). In the 1940s and 1950s he played opposite Katharine Hepburn in eight outstanding comedies. Later films included *Judgment at Nuremberg* (1961) and *Guess Who's Coming to Dinner* (1967), again with Hepburn.

Trapido, Barbara (1942–) Novelist, born in Cape Town, South Africa. She emigrated to the UK in 1963. Her novels include *Brother of the More Famous Jack* (1982, Whitbread), *The Travelling Hornplayer* (1999), and *Frankie & Stankie* (2003).

Travolta, John (1954–) Film actor, born in Englewood, NJ. His major films include *Saturday Night Fever* (1977), *Grease* (1978), *Staying Alive* (1983), *Pulp Fiction* (1994), *Get Shorty* (1995, Golden Globe), and its sequel, *Be Cool* (2005).

Tremain, Rose (1943–) Novelist and short-story writer, born in London. Her novels include *Sadler's Birthday* (1976), *Sacred Country* (1992, James Tait Black), and *The Colour* (2003). Among her books of short stories are *Evangelista's Fan* (1994) and *The Darkness of Wallis Simpson* (2005).

Trevelyan, G(eorge) M(acaulay) (1876–1962) Historian, born in Welcombe, Warwickshire, the son of Sir George Trevelyan. Best known as a pioneer social historian, his *English Social History* (1944) was a companion volume to his *History of England* (1926).

Trevino, Lee (Buck), nickname **Supermex** (1939–) Golfer, born in Dallas, TX. He won his first US Open in 1968, and in 1971 established a golfing record by winning three Open championships (US, Canadian, British) in the same year.

Trevithick, Richard (1771–1833) Engineer and inventor, born in Illogan, Cornwall. He invented (1796–1801) a steam carriage, which ran between Camborne and Tuckingmill, and which in 1803 was run from Leather Lane to Paddington by Oxford St.

Trimble, David (1944–) Northern Ireland politician, born in Bangor, Northern Ireland. He became leader of the Ulster Unionist Party (UUP) in 1995, and came to prominence for his role in the peace negotiations of the mid-1990s, sharing the 1998 Nobel Peace Prize with John Hume for his efforts. Appointed first minister of the new Northern Ireland National Assembly in 1998, he resigned in 2001, but was re-elected later that year. In 2005 he resigned as leader of the UUP after losing his seat in the general election.

Trollope, Anthony (1815–82) Novelist, born in London. His novels in the 'Barsetshire' series include *The Warden* (1855), *Barchester Towers* (1857), and *Framley Parsonage* (1861). Later novels include *Phineas Finn* (1869) and *The Way We Live Now* (1875).

Trollope, Joanna (1943–) Writer and novelist, born in Gloucestershire. Her first novel was *Eliza Stanhope* (1978). Later books include *The Rector's Wife* (1991) and *Second Honeymoon* (2006). She has also written novels as **Caroline Harvey**, including *Legacy of Love* (1992) and *The Brass Dolphin* (1999).

Trotsky, Leon, pseudonym of **Lev Davidovich Bronstein** (1879–1940) Russian Jewish revolutionary, born in Yanovka, Ukraine. He joined the Bolsheviks and played a major role in the October Revolution. In the Civil War he was Commissar for War, and created the Red Army. After Lenin's death (1924) he was ousted from the Party by Stalin, expelled from the Soviet Union (1929), and assassinated in Mexico City.

Trueman, Freddy, popular name of **Frederick Sewards Trueman** (1931–) Cricketer and broadcaster, born in Stainton, South Yorkshire. A Yorkshire fast bowler (1949–68), he played in 67 Tests for England between 1952 and 1965, and took a record 307 wickets.

Truffaut, François (1932–84) Film critic and director, born in Paris. His first feature, *The 400 Blows* (trans, 1959) effectively launched the French *Nouvelle Vague* movement. Later films include *Shoot the Pianist* (1960), *Jules et Jim* (1962), *Fahrenheit 451* (1966), and *Day for Night* (trans, 1972, Oscar).

Truman, Harry S (1884–1972) US Democratic statesman and 33rd president (1945–53), born in Lamar, MO. His decisions included the dropping of two atom bombs on Japan, the post-war loan to Britain, and the sending of US troops to South Korea. He promoted the policy of giving military and economic aid to countries threatened by Communist interference (the *Truman Doctrine*). At home, he introduced a *Fair Deal* of economic reform.

Tschaikovsky, Piotr Ilyich *see* Tchaikovsky

Tull, Jethro (1674–1741) Agriculturist, born in Basildon, West Berkshire. He introduced several new farming methods, including the invention of a seed drill which planted seeds in rows (1701).

Turner, J(oseph) M(allord) W(illiam) (1775–1851) Landscape artist and watercolourist, born in London. His best-known works include 'The Fighting Téméraire' (1839) and 'Rain, Steam and Speed' (1844). His art foreshadowed Impressionism, and was championed by Ruskin.

Turner, Kathleen (1954–) Actress, born in Springfield, MO. She made her film debut in *Body Heat* (1981), and among later films are *Romancing the Stone* (1984) and *Peggy Sue Got Married* (1986). She provided the husky voice for Jessica Rabbit in the film *Who Framed Roger Rabbit?* (1988). Her stage performances include *The Graduate* in London (2000).

Turner, Tina, originally **Annie Mae Bullock** (1939–) Pop singer, born in Nutbush, TN. She achieved success in the rhythm-and-blues vocal duo, Ike and Tina Turner, before their marriage and professional partnership ended in 1976. Her solo hits include 'Let's Stay Together' (1983) and 'Private Dancer' (1985), and she recorded the title song for the James Bond film *Goldeneye* (1996).

Turpin, Dick, popular name of **Richard Turpin** (1706–39) Robber, born in Hempstead, Essex. He was hanged at York for murder. His legendary ride from London to York was probably actually carried out by '**Swift John Nevison**' (1639–84).

Tussaud, Marie, *née* **Grosholtz** (1761–1850) Modeller in wax, born in Strasbourg, France. She toured Britain with her life-size portrait waxworks, and in 1835 set up a permanent exhibition in London that still contains her own handiwork, notably images of Marie Antoinette, Napoleon, and Burke and Hare in the Chamber of Horrors.

Tutankhamen or **Tut'ankhamun** (14th-c BC) Egyptian pharaoh of the 18th dynasty (1361–1352 BC), the son-in-law of Akhenaten. He is famous only for his magnificent tomb at Thebes, discovered intact in 1922.

Tutin, Dame Dorothy (1931–2001) Actress, born in London. She played many leading roles in classical and modern plays, including Queen Victoria in *Portrait of a Queen* (1965), and her films included *Savage Messiah* (1972) and *The Shooting Party* (1984).

Tutu, Desmond (Mpilo) (1931–) Anglican clergyman, born in Klerksdorp, South Africa. He became Bishop of Lesotho (1977) and Johannesburg (1984), and Archbishop of Cape Town (1986), retiring in 1996. A fierce critic of the apartheid system, he was awarded the Nobel Peace Prize in 1984.

Twain, Mark, pseudonym of **Samuel Langhorne Clemens** (1835–1910) Writer, born in Florida, MO. *The Innocents Abroad* (1869) established his reputation as a humorist. His two masterpieces, *Tom Sawyer* (1876) and *Huckleberry Finn* (1884), drawn from his own boyhood experiences, are firmly established among the world's classics.

Twiggy, professional name of **Lesley Lawson**, *née* **Hornby** (1949–) Fashion model, actress, and singer, born in London. She became a modelling superstar at the 'age of 17, and was a symbol of the 'swinging sixties' in London's Carnaby Street. Her films include *The Boy Friend* (1971) and *The Blues Brothers* (1981).

Tyler, Anne, married name **Anne Modarressi** (1941–) Writer, born in Minneapolis, MN. Her novels include *If Morning Ever Comes* (1965), *The Accidental Tourist* (1985; filmed 1988), *Breathing Lessons* (1989, Pulitzer), *A Patchwork Planet* (1998), and *The Amateur Marriage* (2004).

Tyler, John (1790–1862) US statesman and 10th president (1841–5), born in Charles City Co, VA. He became president on the death of Harrison, only a month after his inauguration. His administration was marked by the annexation of Texas.

Tyler, Liv, originally **Liv Rundgren** (1977–) Actress, born in New York City. Her film debut was in *Silent Fall* (1994), and later work includes

Stealing Beauty (1996), *The Lord of the Rings* trilogy (2001–3), and *Lonesome Jim* (2004).

Tyler, Wat (?–1381) English leader of the Peasants' Revolt (1381). The rebels of Kent chose him as captain, and marched to London, where the Mayor, **William Walworth** (d.1385), had him beheaded.

Tynan, Kenneth (1927–80) Theatre critic, born in Birmingham, West Midlands. He was drama critic for *The Observer* (1954–63), became literary manager of the National Theatre (1963–9), and wrote the controversial revue *Oh! Calcutta* (1969).

Tyndale or **Tindale, William** (?–1536) Translator of the Bible, probably born in Slymbridge, Gloucestershire. In Cologne (1525) he completed his translation of the English New Testament, then moved to Antwerp (1531), where he worked on an Old Testament translation, but was accused of heresy, and executed. His work was a major influence on the Authorized Version of the Bible (1611).

Tyson, Mike, popular name of **Michael (Gerald) Tyson** (1966–) Boxer, born in New York City. He beat Trevor Berbick for the World Boxing Council (WBC) world heavyweight title in 1986, and added the World Boxing Association title in 1987, when he beat James Smith. Later that year he became the first undisputed champion since 1978, when he beat Tony Tucker. He lost the title in 1990, and in 1992 was jailed following a trial for rape (released, 1995). He regained the WBC heavyweight title in 1996, then vacated it soon afterwards.

Uccello, Paolo, originally **Paolo di Dono** (1397–1475) Painter, born in Pratovecchio, Italy. He applied the principles of perspective to his paintings, as seen in 'The Flood' (1447–8, Florence), his use of fore-shortening giving a sternly realistic effect.

Ullmann, Liv (Johanne) (1939–) Actress, born in Tokyo. Her films with Ingmar Bergman include *Cries and Whispers* (trans, 1972), *Face to Face* (trans, 1975), and *Autumn Sonata* (trans, 1978), and she also makes regular theatre appearances.

Ulvaeus, Björn *see* Abba

Ungaro, Emanuel (Maffeolti) (1933–) Fashion designer, born in Aix-en-Provence, France, of Italian parents. In 1965 he opened his own house, and in 1968 produced his first ready-to-wear lines.

Unser, Al (1939–) Motor-racing driver, born in Albuquerque, NM. He won the Indianapolis 500 four times (1970–1, 1978, 1987), beating his brother, **Bobby** (1934–), who won the race in 1968, 1975, and 1981. His son, **Al Unser, Jr** (1962–), also became a champion auto racer and was twice winner of the Indianapolis 500 (1992, 1994).

Unsworth, Barry (Forster) (1930–) Novelist, born in Wingate, Co Durham. His works include *The Greeks Have a Word for It* (1967), *Pascali's Island* (1980; filmed 1988), *Sacred Hunger* (1992, co-winner Booker), and *The Songs of the Kings* (2003).

Updike, John (Hoyer) (1932–) Writer, born in Shillington, PA. His novels, exploring human relationships in contemporary US society, include *Rabbit, Run* (1960), *Rabbit is Rich* (1981, Pulitzer), *Rabbit at Rest* (1990, Pulitzer), *The Witches of Eastwick* (1984; filmed 1987), and *Seek My Face* (2003). His several collections of short stories include *Licks of Love* (2001).

Uris, Leon (Marcus) (1924–2003) Novelist, born in Baltimore, MD. *Exodus* (1958) is his best-known book, depicting the early years of struggle to defend the state of Israel. Later novels included *Mitla Pass* (1989), *A God in Ruins* (1999), and *O'Hara's Choice* (2003).

Ursula, St (fl.4th-c) Legendary saint and martyr, said to have been killed by Huns in Cologne. She became the patron saint of many educational institutes, particularly the teaching order of the Ursulines.

Usama bin Laden *see* Osama bin Laden

Ustinov, Sir Peter (Alexander) (1921–2004) Actor and playwright, born in London. A prolific playwright, his works included *The Love of Four Colonels* (1951), *Romanoff and Juliet* (1956), and *Overheard* (1981). He acted in over 50 films, and in his later years established a reputation as a raconteur.

Utrillo, Maurice (1883–1955) Painter, born in Paris, the illegitimate son of Suzanne Valadon. A prolific artist, he produced picture-postcard views of the streets of Paris, particularly old Montmartre.

Uttley, Alison, *née* **Alice Jane Taylor** (1884–1976) Writer, born at Castle Top Farm, near Cromford, Derbyshire. She wrote a series of books for children, featuring much-loved characters such as 'Little Grey Rabbit' and 'Sam Pig'.

U2 Irish rock band, formed in Dublin in 1976, made up of **Bono** (real name Paul Hewson, 1960–), **the Edge** (real name David Evans, 1961–), **Adam Clayton** (1960–), and **Larry Mullen** (1961–). Their albums include *The Joshua Tree* (1987), *Achtung Baby* (1991), and *How To Dismantle An Atomic Bomb* (2004, five Grammys). Bono has campaigned actively on human-rights issues.

Vadim, Roger, originally **Roger Vadim Plemiannikov** (1928–2000) Film director, born in Paris. *And God Created Woman* (trans, 1956), starring his wife Brigitte Bardot, paved the way for further sex-symbol presentations of his later wives, Annette Stroyberg in *Dangerous Liaisons* (trans, 1959), Jane Fonda in *Barbarella* (1968), and his lover, Cathérine Deneuve, in *Vice and Virtue* (trans, 1962).

Valentine, St (?–c.269) Roman priest and Christian martyr, said to have been executed during the persecution under Claudius II, the Goth; but claims have been made for another St Valentine, supposedly Bishop of Turni, taken to Rome for martyrdom. The custom of sending lovers' greetings on 14 February has no connection with either saint.

Valentino, popular name of **Valentino Garavani** (1933–) Fashion designer, born in Rome. He opened his own house in Rome in 1959, achieving worldwide recognition with his 1962 show in Florence.

Valentino, Rudolph (1895–1926) Film actor, born in Castellaneta, Italy. His performances in *The Sheikh* (1921), *Blood and Sand* (1922), and other silent film dramas made him the leading 'screen lover' of the 1920s.

Valera, Eamon de see de Valera, Eamon

Valois, Dame Ninette de, originally **Edris Stannus** (1898–2001) Dancer, born in Blessington, Co Wicklow, Ireland. In 1931 she founded the Sadler's Wells Ballet (now the Royal Ballet), continuing as its artistic director until 1963, and is regarded as the pioneer of British ballet.

Van Allen, James (Alfred) (1914–) Physicist and pioneer in space physics, born in Mt Pleasant, IA. Using data from satellite observations, he showed the existence of two zones of radiation around the Earth (the *Van Allen radiation belts*).

Vanbrugh, Sir John (1664–1726) Playwright and baroque architect, born in London. He scored a success with his comedies *The Relapse* (1696) and *The Provok'd Wife* (1697). As architect, he designed Castle Howard, Yorkshire (1699–1726) and Blenheim Palace (1705–20).

Van Buren, Martin (1782–1862) US statesman and eighth president (1837–41), born in Kinderhook, NY. In 1824 he was a member of the group which founded the Democratic Party. Arriving in office during the financial panic of 1837, his measure introducing a treasury independent of private banks created opposition, and he was overwhelmingly defeated in 1840.

Vanderbilt, Cornelius, known as **Commodore** (1794–1877) Financier, born on Staten I, NY. By age 40 he had become the owner of steamers running to Boston and up the Hudson; and in 1849, during the gold rush, he established a route to California. At 70 he became a railroad financier. He endowed Vanderbilt University in Nashville, TN.

Vanderbilt, Harold S(tirling) (1884–1970) Industrialist, born in Oakdale, NY. He developed the current scoring system for contract bridge in 1925, invented the first unified bidding system, and presented the Vanderbilt Cup.

van der Post, Sir Laurens (Jan) (1906–96) Writer and philosopher, born in Philippolis, South Africa. He was best known for his books in the mixed genre of travel, anthropology, and metaphysical speculation, such as *Venture to the Interior* (1951) and *The Lost World of the Kalahari* (1958).

van Dyck, Sir Anthony (1599–1641) Painter, one of the great masters of portraiture, born in Antwerp, Belgium. In 1632 he went to London, where he was made painter-in-ordinary to Charles I, and produced thoroughly romantic pictures of the Stuart monarchy.

Van Dyke, Dick (1925–) Popular entertainer, born in West Plains, MO. His television series, *The Dick Van Dyke Show* (1961–6), was highly popular, and won him Emmies in 1962, 1964, and 1965. His film career includes *Mary Poppins* (1964), *Chitty Chitty Bang Bang* (1968), and *Dick Tracy* (1990).

van Gogh, Vincent (Willem) (1853–90) Painter, born in Groot-Zundert, The Netherlands. His first masterpiece was 'The Potato Eaters' (1885), a domestic scene of peasant poverty. At Arles, the Provençal landscape gave him many of his best subjects, such as 'Sunflowers' (1888) and 'The Bridge' (1888). One of the pioneers of Expressionism, he used colour primarily for its emotive appeal, and profoundly influenced 20th-c art.

van Nistelrooy, Ruud, properly **Rutgerus Johannes Martinius Ruud van Nistelrooy** (1976–) Footballer, born in Oss, The Netherlands. After playing for several Dutch clubs (from 1993) he moved to Manchester United for a British record transfer fee of £19 million in 2001. By the end of 2005 he had gained 36 international caps. He was voted the Professional Footballers' Association Player of the Year for 2002.

Vasarely, Viktor (1908–97) Painter, born in Pecs, Hungary. His particular kind of geometrical-abstract painting, which he began to practise c.1947, pioneered the visually disturbing effects that were later called Op Art.

Vasco da Gama *see* Gama, Vasco da

Vaughan, Michael (1974–) Cricketer, born in Eccles, Manchester. A batsman and bowler, he played county cricket for Yorkshire, made his Test debut for England in 1999, and was appointed Test captain in 2003. In the 2004 series against South Africa, England achieved a record-breaking eighth successive Test victory with a win in the opening match, and went on to win the series. In 2005 he captained England at home in their successful bid to regain the Ashes for the first time since 1987 in a closely fought series hailed as the best ever.

Vaughan, Sarah (Lois), nickname **Sassie** (1924–90) Jazz singer and pianist, born in Newark, NJ. Internationally acclaimed for her vibrato, range, and expression, her most notable hits include 'It's Magic' and 'I Cried for You'.

Vaughan Williams, Ralph (1872–1958) Composer, born in Down Ampney, Gloucestershire. He developed a national style of music deriving from English choral tradition. His works include nine symphonies, the ballet *Job* (1930), the opera *The Pilgrim's Progress* (1948–9), and numerous choral works, songs, and hymns. His scores for the stage and for films include *The Wasps* (1909).

Vega (Carpio), Lope (Félix) de (1562–1635) Playwright and poet, born in Madrid. He first made his mark as a ballad writer, and after 1588 produced a wide range of historical and contemporary dramas – about 2000 plays and dramatic pieces, of which over 400 still survive.

Velázquez, Diego (Rodriguez de Silva) (1599–1660) Painter, born in Seville, Spain. He is best known for his three late masterpieces, 'The Maids of Honour' (trans, 1655), 'The Tapestry Weavers' (c.1657), and 'Venus and Cupid', known as 'The Rokeby Venus' (c.1658).

Venables, Terry, popular name of **Terence Frederick Venables** (1943–) Football player and manager, born in London. From 1958 he played with Chelsea, Tottenham Hotspur, and Queens Park Rangers, then managed a number of clubs, including Barce-

lona (1984–7) and Tottenham Hotspur (1987–93). He was the English national team coach (1994–6), then coach to the Australian national team. He returned to English football as coach with Middlesbrough (2000) and as manager at Leeds United (2002–3).

Verdi, Giuseppe (Fortunino Francesco) (1813–1901) Composer, born in Le Roncole, Italy. The leading operatic composer of the day, his major successes include *Nabucco* (1842), *Rigoletto* (1851), *Il Trovatore* (1853), *La Traviata* (1853), and *Aïda* (1871). Later works include the Requiem (1874), *Otello* (1887), and *Falstaff* (1893).

Vergil *see* Virgil

Verlaine, Paul (Marie) (1844–96) Poet, born in Metz, France. He mixed with the leading Parnassian writers, and achieved success with his second book of poetry, *Fêtes galantes* (1869). Later works include *Songs Without Words* (trans, 1874), *Les Poètes maudits* (1884), short stories, and sacred and profane verse.

Vermeer, Jan (1632–75) Painter, born in Delft, The Netherlands. He painted small detailed domestic interiors, notable for their use of perspective and treatment of the various tones of daylight, such as 'Woman Reading a Letter' (c.1662).

Verne, Jules (1828–1905) Writer, born in Nantes, France. He developed a new vein in fiction, anticipating the possibilities of science, as seen in (trans titles) *Journey to the Centre of the Earth* (1864), *Twenty Thousand Leagues under the Sea* (1870), and *Around the World in Eighty Days* (1873).

Veronese, Paolo, originally **Paolo Caliari** (c.1528–88) Venetian decorative painter, born in Verona, Italy. His major paintings include 'The Marriage Feast at Cana' (1562–3), 'The Adoration of the Magi' (1573), and 'Feast in the House of Levi' (1573).

Veronica, St (1st-c) Woman of Jerusalem who, according to tradition, met Jesus Christ during his Passion, and offered him her veil to wipe sweat from his brow, with the result that the divine features were miraculously imprinted upon the cloth.

Versace, Gianni (1946–97) Fashion designer, born in Reggio di Calabria, Italy. He launched his own ready-to-wear collection in 1978, and became known for his glamorous styles, producing a range of siren dresses that became his trademark, and often using innovative materials and techniques. He was shot dead by an assassin outside his home in Miami Beach, Florida.

Verwoerd, Hendrik (Frensch) (1901–66) South African prime minister (1958–66), born in Amsterdam, The Netherlands. His administration was marked by the policy of apartheid, and the establishment of South Africa as a Republic (1962). He was assassinated in Cape Town.

Vespucci, Amerigo (1454–1512) Explorer, born in Florence, Italy. He promoted a voyage to the New World in the tracks of Columbus. His name was given to America through an inaccurate account of his travels, in which he is said to have discovered the mainland in 1497.

Victoria, in full **Alexandrina Victoria** (1819–1901) Queen of Great Britain (1837–1901) and (from 1876) Empress of India, born in London, the only child of George III's fourth son, Edward, and Victoria Maria Louisa of Saxe-Coburg. Taught by Lord Melbourne, her first prime minister, she had a clear grasp of constitutional principles. In 1840 she married Prince Albert, and had four sons and five daughters. Strongly influenced by her husband, after his death (1861) she went into lengthy seclusion, but with her recognition as Empress of India, and the celebratory golden (1887) and diamond (1897) jubilees, she increased the prestige of the monarchy.

Vidal, (Eugene Luther) Gore, pseudonym **Edgar Box** (1925–) Writer, born in West Point, NY. His many novels include several satirical comedies, such as *Myra Breckinridge* (1968) and *Duluth* (1983), the historical trilogy, *Burr* (1973), *1876* (1976), and *Lincoln* (1984), and a fictional history of America. Later works include a volume of memoirs, *Screening History* (1992), and the novel, *The Smithsonian Institution* (1999).

Vidor, King (Wallis) (1894–1982) Film director, born in Galveston, TX. He made the silent classics *The Big Parade* (1925) and *The Crowd* (1928); later films included *Northwest Passage* (1940) and the big screen epic *Solomon and Sheba* (1959). He received an honorary Oscar in 1979.

Villeneuve, Jacques (1971–) Motorracing driver, born in Quebec, Canada. In 1995 he became the youngest driver to win the PPG Indy Car World Series title. He joined

Formula One in 1996, driving for the Williams Renault team, finished second in the World Driver's Championship, and won the Championship in 1997.

Villeneuve, Pierre (Charles Jean Baptiste Sylvestre) de (1763–1806) French admiral, born in Valensole, France. In 1805 he was in charge of the French fleet at Trafalgar, where he was taken prisoner. Released in 1806, he committed suicide during his return to Paris to face Napoleon.

Vincent de Paul, St (c.1580–1660) Priest and philanthropist, born in Pouy, France. In 1625 he founded the Congregation of Priests of the Missions (or *Lazarists*, from their priory of St Lazare) and in 1634 the Sisterhood of Charity. He was canonized in 1737.

Vinci, Leonardo da *see* Leonardo da Vinci

Vine, Barbara *see* Rendell, Ruth

Virgil or **Vergil**, in full **Publius Vergilius Maro** (70–19 BC) Latin poet, born in Andes, Italy. His works include the *Eclogues* (37 BC) and the *Georgics*, or *Art of Husbandry* (36–29 BC), and for the rest of his life he worked on the *Aeneid*.

Virgin Mary *see* Mary (Mother of Jesus)

Visconti, Luchino (1906–76) Stage and film director, born in Milan, Italy. His first film, *Obsession* (trans, 1942) took Italy by storm, with its strict realism and concern with social problems. Later films included (trans titles) *The Leopard* (1963) and *Death in Venice* (1971).

Vivaldi, Antonio (Lucio) (1678–1741) Violinist and composer, born in Venice, Italy. The 12 concertos of *L'Estro Armonico* (1712) gave him a European reputation, and *The Four Seasons* (trans, 1725), an early example of programme music, proved highly popular. He also wrote many operas, sacred music, and over 450 concertos.

Vlaminck, Maurice de (1876–1958) Artist, born in Paris. By 1905 he was one of the leaders of the Fauves, using typically brilliant colour, then painted more Realist landscapes, and later developed a more sombre Expressionism.

Voight, Jon(athan) (1938–) Film actor, born in Yonkers, NY. He gained recognition for his role in *Midnight Cowboy* (1969, Oscar nomination). Among his many films are *Coming Home* (1978, Oscar), *Runaway Train* (1985, Oscar nomination), and *Holes* (2003). In 2001 he appeared with his daughter, actress Angelina Jolie, in *Lara Croft: Tomb Raider*.

Volta, Alessandro (Giuseppe Antonio Anastasio) (1745–1827) Physicist, born in Como, Italy. He experimented on current electricity, and developed the first electric battery (1800). His name is given to the unit of electric potential, the *volt*.

Voltaire, pseudonym of **François Marie Arouet** (1694–1778) Writer, the embodiment of the 18th-c Enlightenment, born in Paris. His works include the tragedy *Oedipe*, poetry, historical and scientific treatises, his *Lettres philosophiques* (1733), and the satirical short story, *Candide* (1759). From 1762 he produced a range of anti-religious writings and the *Dictionnaire philosophique* (1764).

von Braun, Wernher *see* Braun, Wernher von

Vonnegut, Kurt (Jr) (1922–) Novelist, born in Indianapolis, IN. His novels are satirical fantasies, usually cast in the form of science fiction, as in *Player Piano* (1952), *Breakfast of Champions* (1973; filmed 1999), *Galapagos* (1985), and *Timequake* (1997). He is best known for *Slaughterhouse-Five* (1969).

Vortigern (fl.425–50) Semi-legendary British king. According to Bede, he recruited Germanic mercenaries led by Hengist and Horsa to help fight off the Picts after the final withdrawal of the Roman administration from Britain (409).

Vygotsky, Lev Semenovich (1896–1934) Psychologist, born in Orsha, Belarus. His writings, such as *Thought and Language* (1934–62) and *Mind in Society* (1978), have had a major influence on Soviet and (since the 1960s) Western psychology, particularly on specialists in child development.

Wade, (Sarah) Virginia (1945–) Tennis player, born in Bournemouth, Dorset. Her successes include the Wimbeldon singles title (1977), the US Open title (1968), and the French championship (1972).

Wagner, (Wilhelm) Richard (1813–83) Composer, born in Leipzig, Germany. His *Rienzi* (1842) was a great success, but his next operas, including *Tannhäuser* (1845), were failures. He then began to write *The Rhinegold* (trans, 1853), *The Valkyries* (trans, 1856), *Siegfried* (1857), *The Mastersingers* (trans, 1867), and *Twilight of the Gods* (trans, 1874), opening the Bayreuth theatre in 1876 with a performance of the whole *Ring* cycle.

Wagner, Robert (John) (1930–) Film and television actor, born in Detroit, MI. His greatest popularity has been in television series, such as *It Takes A Thief* (1965–9), *Switch* (1975–7), and *Hart to Hart* (1979–84), in which he co-starred with **Stefanie Powers** (1942–).

Wain, John (Barrington) (1925–94) Writer and critic, born in Stoke-on-Trent, Staffordshire. His novels

include *Hurry on Down* (1953), *The Contenders* (1958), and *Young Shoulders* (1982, Whitbread), and he also wrote poetry (*Poems, 1949–79*), plays, and several books of literary criticism.

Waite, Terry, popular name of **Terence (Hardy) Waite** (1939–) Consultant, born in Bollington, Cheshire. As the Archbishop of Canterbury's special envoy, he was involved in negotiations to secure the release of hostages held in the Middle East, and was himself kidnapped in Beirut (1987–91).

Wakefield, Edward Gibbon (1796–1862) Originator of subsidized emigration from Britain, born in London. He proposed (1929) the sale of small units of crown land in the colonies to subsidize colonization by the poor from Britain (later called *Wakefield settlements*).

Walcott, Derek (Alton) (1930–) Poet and playwright, born in Castries, St Lucia, West Indies. He founded the Trinidad Theatre Workshop in 1959. His works include *Collected Poems 1948–84* (1986) and the epic *Omeros* (1990), and he was awarded the Nobel Prize for Literature in 1992.

Waldheim, Kurt (1918–) Austrian president (1986–92), born near Vienna. He was foreign minister (1968–70) and UN secretary-general (1972–81). His presidential candidature was controversial because of claims that he had been involved in wartime atrocities, but he denied the allegations.

Wales, Prince of *see* Charles, Prince of Wales

Wales, Princess of see Diana, Princess of Wales

Wałęsa, Lech (1943–) Polish president (1990–5), born in Popowo, Poland. A Gdańsk shipyard worker, he became leader of the independent trade union, Solidarity, which openly challenged the Polish government. He was detained (1981–2), and awarded the Nobel Peace Prize in 1983. He continued to be prominent in Polish politics, and gained a landslide victory in the 1990 election but was defeated by Alexander Kwasniewski in 1995.

Walker, Alice (Malsenior) (1944–) Writer, born in Eatonville, GA. She is best known for her novels, notably *The Color Purple* (1982, Pulitzer), later made into a successful film. Later novels include *By the Light of My Father's Smile* (1998), and she has also written volumes of short stories and essays.

Wall, Max (Wall George Lorimer) (1908–90) Actor and comedian, born in London. He built a reputation as one of the finest British comics of his time in music hall and radio performances with a laconic comedy routine.

Wallace, (Richard Horatio) Edgar (1875–1932) Writer, born in London. He wrote over 170 novels and plays, and is best remembered for his crime novels, such as *The Clue of the Twisted Candle*.

Wallace, Sir William (c.1270–1305) Scottish knight and champion of Scots independence, probably born in Elderslie, Renfrewshire. He routed the English army at Stirling (1297), and took control of the government of Scotland as 'Guardian', but was defeated at Falkirk (1298), and executed.

Waller, Fats, popular name of **Thomas Wright Waller** (1904–43) Jazz pianist, organist, singer, and songwriter, born in New York City. He played in the stride tradition, and wrote such hits as 'Ain't Misbehavin'' (1929) and 'Keeping Out of Mischief Now' (1932).

Wallis, Sir Barnes (Neville) (1887–1979) Aeronautical engineer and inventor, born in Ripley, Derbyshire. He designed the R100 airship, the Wellington Bomber, the 'bouncing bombs' which destroyed the Mohne and Eder dams, and in the 1950s the first swing-wing aircraft.

Walpole, Sir Robert, 1st Earl of Orford (1676–1745) Chief minister (1721–42) of George I and George II, born in Houghton, Norfolk. George I made him a privy councillor and (1715) Chancellor of the Exchequer. He was Chancellor again in 1721 and widely recognized as 'prime minister' – a title (unknown to the Constitution) which he hotly repudiated.

Walsingham, Sir Francis (c.1530–90) English secretary of state to Elizabeth I (1573–90), born in Chislehurst, Kent. A strong opponent of the Catholics, he developed a complex system of espionage at home and abroad, enabling him to reveal several plots against the Queen.

Walter, Harriet (Mary) (1959–) British actress. She has frequently worked with the Royal Shakespeare Company, her roles including Lady Macbeth (1999) and Beatrice (2002). Her films include *Sense and Sensibility*

(1996), *Onegin* (1999), and *Bright Young Things* (2003). She is an associate artist with Peter Hall's Cannon's Mouth theatre company.

Walters, Julie (1950–) Actress, born in Birmingham, West Midlands. Her films include *Educating Rita* (1983, BAFTA), *Billy Elliot* (2000, BAFTA Best Supporting Actress), *Calendar Girls* (2003), and *Wah-Wah* (2005). She partnered Victoria Wood in the television series *Wood and Walters* (from 1981). Stage work includes *All My Sons* (2001, Laurence Olivier Award).

Walton, Sir William (Turner) (1902–83) Composer, born in Oldham, Lancashire. He became known through his instrumental setting of poems by Edith Sitwell, *Façade* (1923). Other works include two symphonies, concertos for violin, viola, and cello, the biblical cantata *Belshazzar's Feast* (1931), and the opera *Troilus and Cressida* (1954).

Wanamaker, Sam (1919–93) Actor and director, born in Chicago, IL. He became known for his acting and directing on stage (notably in Shakespearean productions) and in films and television. In 1970 he founded the Globe Theatre Trust in London. His daughter, **Zoe Wanamaker** (1949–), is an actress, whose theatre work includes *Electra* (1988, Laurence Olivier Best Actress Award) and in television the popular sitcom *My Family* (2002–).

Warbeck, Perkin (c.1474–99) Pretender to the English throne, born in Tournai, Belgium. In 1492 he professed to be Richard, Duke of York, the younger of Edward's two sons who were murdered in the Tower. He made an ineffectual landing in Kent (1495), then landed in Cornwall (1497), but was executed.

Warhol, Andy, originally **Andrew Warhola** (1928–87) Artist and filmmaker, born in Pittsburgh, PA. He was a pioneer in 1961 of Pop Art, with his brightly coloured exact reproductions of familiar everyday objects such as the famous soup-can label. His films include the 3-hour silent observation of a sleeping man, *Sleep* (1963). In the 1960s he also turned to music, founding a rock revue called The Exploding Plastic Inevitable (1966–7). The Andy Warhol Museum opened in Pittsburgh in 1994.

Warne, Shane, popular name of **Shane Keith Warne** (1969–) Cricketer, born in Melbourne, Victoria, Australia. A hugely charismatic legspinner, in 2004 he became the first spin bowler to take 500 Test wickets. He was part of Australia's losing side in the 2005 Ashes series but gained praise for his all-round performance, receiving the Australia Man of the Series award, and becoming the first bowler to take 600 Test wickets. In 2000 he was named as one of Wisden's Five Cricketers of the Century.

Warner, Jack, originally **Jack Leonard Eichelbaum** (1892–1978) Film mogul, born in London, Ontario, Canada. In partnership with his older brothers **Harry** (1881–1958), **Albert** (1884–1967), and **Sam** (1887–1927), he set up studios in 1923. The Warners were the first to introduce sound into their films, and had great success with *The Jazz Singer* (1927). Jack's later productions included *My Fair Lady* (1964) and *Camelot* (1967).

Warren, Robert Penn (1905–89) Writer, born in Guthrie, KY. Recipient of two Pulitzer Prizes (for fiction in 1947, for poetry in 1958), he established an international reputation with his political novel, *All the King's Men* (1943, Pulitzer; filmed 1949).

Warriss, Ben *see* Jewel and Warriss

Warwick, Richard Neville, Earl, also known as **Warwick the Kingmaker** (1428–71) English soldier and politician, who exercised great power during the Wars of the Roses. He championed the Yorkist cause, captured Henry VI, and had his cousin, Edward of York, proclaimed king as Edward IV (1461). When Edward tried to assert his independence, Warwick joined the Lancastrians, and restored Henry VI to the throne (1470). He was killed by Edward IV at Barnet.

Washington, George (1732–99) Commander of American forces and first president of the USA, born in Bridges Creek, VA. He represented Virginia in the first (1774) and second (1775) Continental Congresses, and was given command of the American forces, where he displayed great powers as a strategist and leader. He inflicted notable defeats on the enemy at Trenton and Princeton (1777), then suffered defeats at the Brandywine and Germantown, but held his army together through the winter of 1777–8 at Valley Forge, and forced the surrender of Cornwallis at Yorktown in 1781. In 1787 he became president, remaining neutral while political parties were formed, but

eventually joining the Federalist Party.

Watson, James D(ewey) (1928–) Geneticist, born in Chicago, IL. With Francis Crick and Maurice Wilkins he helped to discover the molecular structure of DNA, sharing with them the Nobel Prize for Physiology or Medicine in 1962. He was awarded an honorary knighthood in 2001.

Watson, Russell (1974–) Tenor, born in Salford, Greater Manchester. His debut album, *The Voice* (2000), topped the UK classical chart for many months. Later albums include *Encore* (2001) and *Amore Musica* (2004).

Watson, Tom, popular name of **Thomas (Sturges) Watson** (1949–) Golfer, born in Kansas City, MO. He turned professional in 1971 and has won the (British) Open five times (1975, 1977, 1980, 1982–3), the US Open (1982), and the US Masters (1977, 1981).

Watt, James (1736–1819) Inventor, born in Greenock, Inverclyde. He studied steam as a motive force, went into partnership with Boulton, and manufactured a new engine at Birmingham (1774). Several other inventions followed, including the design of a steam locomotive (1784). The term *horse-power* was first used by him, and the SI unit of power is named after him.

Watteau, (Jean) Antoine (1684–1721) Rococo painter, born in Valenciennes, France. His best-known works include 'Embarkation for the island of Cythera' (trans, 1717) and 'Fêtes galantes' (Scenes of Gallantry) – quasi-pastoral idylls in court dress which became fashionable in high society.

Waugh, Evelyn (Arthur St John) (1903–66) Writer, born in London. His social satirical novels include *Decline and Fall* (1928), *Vile Bodies* (1930), and *Scoop* (1938). Later books include *Brideshead Revisited* (1945) and the 'sword of honour' trilogy: *Men at Arms* (1952), *Officers and Gentlemen* (1955), and *Unconditional Surrender* (1961).

Wayne, John, originally **Marion Michael Morrison**, nickname **the Duke** (1907–79) Film actor, born in Winterset, IA. He achieved stardom as the Ringo Kid in *Stagecoach* (1939), and went on to make over 80 films, many in the Western genre typically starring as a tough but warm-hearted gunfighter or lawman, such as *She Wore a Yellow Ribbon* (1949), *The Man who Shot Liberty Vallance* (1962), and *True Grit* (1969, Oscar).

Weaver, Sigourney, originally **Susan Alexandra Weaver** (1949–) Film actress, born in New York City. She became well known through her role as astronaut Ripley in the film *Aliens* (1979, sequels 1986, 1992, 1997). Later films include *Ghostbusters* (1984) and *Imaginary Heroes* (2005).

Webb Social reformers, historians, and economists: **Sidney James Webb** (1859–1947) and **(Martha) Beatrice Webb**, *née* **Potter** (1858–1943), born in London, and Standish, Gloucestershire, respectively. Married in 1892, he joined the Fabian Society, and she became involved with social problems, publishing their classic *History of Trade Unionism* (1894), *English Local Government* (9 vols,

1906–29), and other works. Sidney later served as President of the Board of Trade (1924) and dominions and colonial secretary (1929–30).

Webb, Beatrice *see* Webb

Webb, Karrie (1974–) Golfer, born in Ayr, Queensland, Australia. She won the Women's British Open title in 1995, the youngest ever winner, and won it again in 1997 and 2002. Further achievements include the Australian Ladies' Masters (1998, 1999, 2000), Du Maurier Classic (1999), US Women's Open (2000, 2001), and the LPGA title (2001).

Webb, Matthew (1848–83) Swimmer, the first man to swim the English Channel, born in Dawley, Shropshire. In 1875 he swam from Dover to Calais in 21 h 45 min.

Webb, Sidney James *see* Webb

Webber, Andrew Lloyd *see* Lloyd-Webber, Andrew

Weber, Carl (Maria Friedrich) von (1786–1826) Composer and pianist, born in Eutin, Germany. The founder of German Romantic opera, as seen in *Euryanthe* (1823) and *Oberon* (1826), he also wrote orchestral works, as well as piano, chamber, and church music, and many songs.

Webern, Anton (Friedrich Ernst von) (1883–1945) Composer, born in Vienna. One of Schoenberg's first musical disciples, he made wide use of 12-tone techniques. His works include a symphony, cantatas, several short orchestral pieces, chamber music, a concerto for nine instruments, and songs.

Webster, John (c.1580–c.1625) English playwright. He collaborated with several other writers, especially Thomas Dekker, but is best known for his two tragedies, *The White Devil* (1612) and *The Duchess of Malfi* (1623).

Webster, Noah (1758–1843) Lexicographer, born in Hartford, CT. He achieved fame with the first part (later known as 'Webster's Spelling Book') of *A Grammatical Institute of the English Language* (1783). He is best known for his *American Dictionary of the English Language* (2 vols, 1828), which was a major influence on US dictionary practice.

Wedgwood, Josiah (1730–95) Potter, born in Burslem, Staffordshire. In 1759 he opened a factory at Burslem, and a later one near Hanley, which he called 'Etruria'. Inspired by antique models, he invented unglazed black basalt ware and blue jasper ware with raised designs in white.

Weissmuller, Johnny, popular name of **(Peter) John** (originally **Jonas**) **Weissmuller** (1904–84) Swimmer and film star, born in Freidorf, Romania. He won the 100 m freestyle at the 1924 and 1928 Olympics, and the 400 m in 1928. His name is widely known for his starring role in 12 Tarzan films between 1932 and 1948.

Welch, Bruce *see* Shadows, The

Welch, Raquel, originally **Raquel Tejada** (1940–) Actress, born in Chicago, IL. She was launched as a sex symbol after her scantily clad appearance in *One Million Years BC* (1966). For her role in *The Three Musketeers* (1973) she received a Best Actress Golden Globe Award.

Weldon, Fay, originally **Franklin**, *née* **Birkinshaw** (1933–) Writer, born in Alvechurch, Worcestershire. Her work deals with contemporary feminist themes, as in *Female Friends* (1975), and caustic satires of male-dominated society, as in *Darcy's Utopia* (1989). Later books include *Big Girls Don't Cry* (1998) and *She May Not Leave* (2005).

Welles, (George) Orson (1915–85) Film director, producer, writer, and actor, born in Kenosha, WI. In 1938 his radio production of Wells's *War of the Worlds* was so realistic that it caused panic in the USA. In 1941, he wrote, produced, directed, and acted in the film *Citizen Kane*, a revolutionary landmark in cinema technique, and this was followed by *The Magnificent Ambersons* (1942). He played a variety of memorable stage and film roles, the most celebrated being that of Harry Lime in *The Third Man* (1949).

Wellesley, Arthur *see* Wellington, 1st Duke of

Wellington, Arthur Wellesley, 1st Duke of (1769–1852) British general and prime minister (1828–30), born in Dublin, the brother of Richard Wellesley. In the Peninsular War he drove the French out of Portugal and Spain, gaining victories at Talavera (1809), Salamanca (1812), and Toulouse (1814), then routed the French at Waterloo (1815). His period as prime minister weakened the Tory Party, which split over the question of Catholic emancipation.

Wells, H(erbert) G(eorge) (1866–1946) Writer, born in Bromley, Kent. He achieved fame with scientific fantasies such as *The Time Machine* (1895) and *War of the Worlds* (1898), and a range of comic social novels, notably *Kipps* (1905) and *The History of Mr Polly* (1910). A member of the Fabian Society, he also wrote several socio-political works.

Wells, John (Campbell) (1936–98) British actor, playwright, humorist, and director. He was known for his satirical contributions to *Private Eye* magazine, and on radio and television. His plays included *Mrs Wilson's Diary* (1968) and *Anyone for Denis?* (1981), in which he played the title role.

Welsh, Irvine (1957–) Writer, born in Edinburgh. He became known with his controversial first novel, *Trainspotting* (1993; filmed 1996), and later books include *Filth* (1998), and *Porno* (2002).

Wenceslaus or **Wenceslas, St**, known as **Good King Wenceslas** (c.903–935) Duke and patron of Bohemia, born in Stochov, Czech Republic. He encouraged Christianity in Bohemia, and was murdered by his brother, Boleslaw. He became the patron saint of Bohemia and Czechoslovakia.

Wenders, Wim, originally **Ernst Wilhelm Winders** (1945–) Film director, born in Düsseldorf, Germany. He has won several awards at Cannes, including best director for *Paris, Texas* (1984) and *Wings of Desire* (1987). Later films include *Buena Vista Social Club* (1999) and *Shoots Don't Come Knockin'* (2004).

Wesker, Sir Arnold (1932–) Playwright, born in London. His plays include the Kahn family trilogy, *Chicken Soup with Barley, Roots*, and *I'm Talking about Jerusalem* (1958–60). Later works include the play *Chips*

with Everything (1962), a collection of stories, *The King's Daughters* (1996), and a novel, *Honey* (2005).

Wesley, Charles (1707–88) Hymnwriter and evangelist, born in Epworth, Lincolnshire, the brother of John Wesley. After an evangelical conversion in 1738, he wrote over 5500 hymns, including the well-known 'Hark, the Herald Angels Sing' and 'Love Divine, All Loves Excelling'.

Wesley, John (1703–91) Evangelist and founder of Methodism, born in Epworth, Lincolnshire. In 1738, at a meeting in London, he experienced an assurance of salvation which led him to preach, but his zeal alarmed the parish clergy, who closed their pulpits against him. This drove him into the open air at Bristol (1739), where he founded the first Methodist chapel. His many writings included collections of hymns, sermons and journals, and a magazine.

West, Benjamin (1738–1820) Painter, born in Springfield, PA. He settled in London in 1763. The representation of modern instead of classical costume in his best-known picture, 'The Death of General Wolfe' (c.1771), was an innovation in English historical painting.

West, Frederick (1941–95) Serial murderer, born in Much Marcle, Herefordshire. He and his wife, **Rosemary** (1953–), born in Devon, were accused in 1994 of killing 10 women, among them the former wife and a daughter of Frederick West, following the discovery of numerous bodies buried in their garden and house in Gloucester. In 1995 Frederick was found hanged in his Birmingham prison cell while awaiting trial. Rosemary was convicted of 10 murders and sentenced to life imprisonment.

West, Mae (1893–1980) Actress, born in New York City. A child performer, she spent some years in vaudeville and on Broadway before her first film, *Night After Night* (1932). Throughout the 1930s a series of racy comedies exploited her voluptuousness, although under much pressure from censorship.

West, Morris (Langlo) (1916–99) Novelist, born in Melbourne, Victoria, Australia. His books, often of a religious or moral nature, include *Children of the Sun* (1955), *The Devil's Advocate* (1959; filmed 1977), and *Lazarus* (1990).

West, Dame Rebecca, pseudonym of **Cicily Isabel Andrews**, *née* **Fairfield** (1892–1983) Novelist and critic, born in London. She is best known for her studies arising out of the Nuremberg war trials: *The Meaning of Treason* (1949) and *A Train of Powder* (1955). Her novels include *The Thinking Reed* (1936) and *The Birds Fall Down* (1966). Her long association with H G Wells produced a son, the critic and author Anthony West (1914–87).

West, Timothy (Lancaster) (1934–) Actor and director, born in Bradford, West Yorkshire. A member of the Royal Shakespeare and other companies, his many television appearances include *Churchill and the Generals* (1979) and *Bleak House* (2005). Among his films is *Cry Freedom* (1986). He married Prunella Scales in 1963. Their son, actor **Sam**

West (1966–), is noted for his Shakespearean roles. He was appointed director of Sheffield's Crucible Theatre in 2000, and artistic director of Sheffield Theatres in 2005.

Westinghouse, George (1846–1914) Engineer, born in Central Bridge, NY. In 1863 he invented an air-brake for railways, and also the gas meter and a system of conducting natural gas through pipes safely into homes. A pioneer in the use of alternating current for distributing electric power, he founded the Westinghouse Electrical Co in 1886.

Wheatley, Dennis (Yates) (1897–1977) Novelist, born in London. He produced a popular mix of satanism and historical fiction, as in *The Devil Rides Out* (1935), *The Scarlet Impostor* (1942), and *The Sultan's Daughter* (1963).

Wheeler, Sir (Robert Eric) Mortimer (1890–1976) Archaeologist, born in Glasgow. He carried out notable excavations in Britain and in India, and was well known for spirited popular accounts of his subject, in books and on television.

Whicker, Alan (Donald) (1925–) British broadcaster and journalist, born in Cairo. He joined the BBC (1957–68), worked on the *Tonight* programme (1957–65), and began his *Whicker's World* documentary series in 1958.

Whipple, Fred (Lawrence) (1906–2004) Astronomer, born in Red Oak, IA. Known for his work on the Solar System, in 1950 he suggested that comets are composed of ice and dust, and later work has confirmed this 'dirty snowball' model. The Fred Lawrence Whipple Observatory in Amado, AZ, contains the largest mirror telescope in the USA.

Whistler, James (Abbott) McNeill (1834–1903) Artist, born in Lowell, MA. He is best known for his evening scenes ('nocturnes'), such as 'Old Battersea Bridge' (c.1872–5, Tate, London), and for the famous portrait of his mother (1871–2, Musée d'Orsay).

Whitefield, George (1714–70) Methodist evangelist, born in Gloucester, Gloucestershire. Associated with the Wesleys, he founded no distinct sect, but had many adherents in Wales and Scotland, who formed the Calvinistic Methodists. He played an important role in the Great Awakening in the USA.

Whitelaw, Billie (1932–) Actress, born in Coventry, West Midlands. A noted interpreter of Beckett, her performances include *Play* (1964), *Not I* (1973), and *Footfalls* (1976). Her films include *The Omen* (1976), *Jane Eyre* (1996), and *Quills* (2000).

Whitelaw, William (Stephen Ian) Whitelaw, 1st Viscount, popularly known as **Willie Whitelaw** (1918–99) British Conservative statesman, born in Nairn, Highland. He served as secretary of state for Northern Ireland (1972–3) and for employment (1973–4), home secretary (1979–83), and Leader of the House of Lords.

Whiteman, Paul (1890–1967) Jazz bandleader, composer, and arranger, born in Denver, CO. Known in his early days as 'the King of Jazz', he was the most popular bandleader of the 1920s and early 1930s, before the swing era.

Whiteread, Rachel (1963–) Artist and sculptor, born in London. She became known for her casts of ordinary domestic objects, such as wardrobes and baths. In 1993 she captured the public imagination with her life-sized cement cast of a three-storey terraced house in East London. The project gained her the Turner Prize and was demolished soon afterwards.

Whitman, Walt(er) (1819–92) Poet, born in West Hills, Long Island, NY. An outstanding proponent of free verse, his major poetic work was *Leaves of Grass* (1855), which grew in successive editions to over 400 pages. His later prose works include *Democratic Vistas* (1871) and *Specimen Days and Collect* (1882–3).

Whitney, Eli (1765–1825) Inventor, born in Westborough, MA. He invented a cotton-gin (patented 1793) for separating cotton fibre from the seeds, and in 1798 developed a new system for the mass-production of firearms.

Whittington, Dick, popular name of **Richard Whittington** (c.1358–1423) English merchant, supposed to have been the youngest son of Sir William Whittington of Pauntley in Gloucestershire. He set out at 13 to find work in London, where he became Lord Mayor (1397–9, 1406–7, 1419–20).

Whittle, Sir Frank (1907–96) Aviator and inventor of the British jet engine, born in Coventry, West Midlands. He developed a turbo-jet engine which successfully powered an aircraft flight in 1941.

Wicliffe, John see Wycliffe, John

Widdecombe, Ann (Noreen) (1947–) British stateswoman, born in Bath. She was elected as Conservative MP for Maidstone in 1987, became minister of state for employment (1994–5) and at the Home Office (1995–7), then shadow secretary for health (1998–9), and shadow home secretary (1999–2001). She is also a novelist.

Wilberforce, William (1759–1833) British politician, evangelist, and philanthropist, born in Hull. In 1788 he began the movement which resulted in the abolition of the slave trade in the British West Indies in 1807.

Wilde, Oscar (Fingal O'Flahertie Wills) (1854–1900) Writer, born in Dublin. Celebrated for his wit and flamboyant manner, he became a leading member of the 'art for art's sake' movement. His early work included his *Poems* (1881), the novel *The Picture of Dorian Gray* (1891), and several comic plays, notably *Lady Windermere's Fan* (1892) and *The Importance of Being Earnest* (1895). *The Ballad of Reading Gaol* (1898) and *De Profundis* (1905) reveal the effect of two years' hard labour for homosexual practices.

Wilder, Billy, originally **Samuel Wilder** (1906–2002) Film director, born in Sucha, Poland (formerly Austria). His films include *Double Indemnity* (1944), *The Lost Weekend* (1945, Oscar), *Stalag 17* (1953), *Sunset Boulevard* (1950), and *The Apartment* (1960, Oscar).

Wilder, Gene, originally **Jerome Silberman** (1935–) Film actor, writer, and director, born in Milwaukee, WI. He received a Best Supporting Actor Oscar nomination for *The Producers* (1968), later films including *Blazing Saddles* (1974) and *Young Frankenstein* (1974). In 1996 he starred in the London stage production of *Laughter on the 23rd Floor*.

Wilder, Thornton (Niven) (1897–1975) Writer, born in Madison, WI. His novels include *The Bridge of San Luis Rey* (1927, Pulitzer) and *The Ides of March* (1948). The plays *Our Town* (1938) and *The Skin of Our Teeth* (1942) both won Pulitzer Prizes.

Wilhelm I / II see William I (of Germany); William II (of Germany)

Wilkins, Maurice (Hugh Frederick) (1916–2004) Biophysicist, born in Pongaroa, New Zealand. His X-ray diffraction studies of DNA helped Crick and Watson determine its structure, and he shared with them the Nobel Prize for Physiology or Medicine in 1962.

Wilkinson, Jonny (1979–) Rugby Union player, born in Surrey. He signed as a fly-half for Newcastle Falcons, and made his debut for England in 1998. In the inaugural 2000 Six Nations campaign he established a new championship points tally. He scored all England's points in the 24–7 semi-final win over France in the 2003 World Cup, and in the final against Australia secured his country's victory with a drop-goal in the last minutes of extra time. He was appointed England captain in 2004 but has since been dogged by injury.

William I (of England), known as **the Conqueror** (c.1028–87) Duke of Normandy (1035–87) and the first Norman king of England (1066–87), the illegitimate son of Duke Robert of Normandy. When Harold Godwinson took the throne as Harold II, William invaded with the support of the papacy, defeated and killed Harold at the Battle of Hastings, and was crowned king in 1066. By the time of the Domesday Book (1086), the leaders of Anglo-Saxon society S of the Tees had been almost entirely replaced by a new ruling class closely tied to William by feudal bonds.

William I (of Germany), Ger **Wilhelm** (1797–1888) King of Prussia (1861–88) and first German emperor (1871–88), born in Berlin, the second son of Frederick William III. He placed Bismarck at the head of the ministry, and was victorious against Denmark (1864), Austria (1866), and France (1871).

William II (of England), known as **William Rufus** (c.1056–1100) King of England (1087–1100), the second surviving son of William the Conqueror. His main goal was the recovery of Normandy from his elder brother Robert Curthose. He also led expeditions to Wales (1095, 1097), and came to exercise a controlling influence over Scottish affairs. He was killed by an arrow while hunting in the New Forest.

William II (of Germany), Ger **Wilhelm**, known as **Kaiser Wilhelm** (1859–1941) German Emperor and King of Prussia (1888–1918), born in Potsdam, Germany, the eldest son of Frederick III and Victoria, daughter of Britain's Queen Victoria. He dismissed Bismarck (1890), and began a long period of personal rule, displaying a bellicose attitude in international affairs. During World War 1 he became a figurehead, and later abdicated.

William III (of Great Britain), known as **William of Orange** (1650–1702) Stadtholder of the United Provinces (1672–1702) and King of Great Britain (1689–1702), born in The Hague, the son of William II of Orange by Mary, the eldest daughter of Charles I of England. In 1677 he married his cousin, **Mary** (1662–94), the daughter of James II by Anne Hyde. Invited to redress the grievances of the country, he landed at Torbay in 1688 with an English and Dutch army, and forced James II to flee. He defeated James's supporters at Dunkeld (1689) and at the Boyne (1690), then concentrated on the War of the League of Augsburg against France (1689–97), in which he was finally successful.

William IV, known as **the Sailor King** (1765–1837) King of Great Britain and Ireland, and King of Hanover (1830–7), born in London, the third son of George III. He was the last monarch to use his powers to dismiss a ministry with a parliamentary majority when he sacked Melbourne in 1834.

William of Ockham or **Occam**, known as **the Venerable Inceptor** (c.1285–c.1349) Scholastic philosopher, born in Ockham, Surrey. He is especially known for his use of the principle of parsimony (*Ockham's razor*): 'Do not multiply entities beyond necessity.'

Williams, (George) Emlyn (1905–87) Playwright and actor, born in Pen-y-ffordd, Flintshire. He achieved success as a playwright with *A Murder Has Been Arranged* (1930) and *Night Must Fall* (1935), featured in several films, and gave widely acclaimed readings from Dickens and Dylan Thomas.

Williams, Hank, popular name of **Hiram King Williams** (1923–53) Country singer, composer, and guitarist, born in Mount Olive West, AL. His many hit records include 'Love-sick Blues' (1949) and 'Hey, Good Lookin''. His son, **Hank Williams Jr** (1949–), continues as a successful country singer and songwriter.

Williams, John (Christopher) (1942–) Guitarist, born in Melbourne, Victoria, Australia. Several modern composers have written works for him. In England from 1952, he founded a jazz and popular music group known as Sky (1979–84), and later formed the contemporary music group Attacca.

Williams, John (Towner) (1932–) Film composer and conductor, born in New York City. The leading screen composer of his generation, his early films included *Superman* (1978) and the *Star Wars* and *Indiana Jones* series. Later scores include *A.I. Artificial Intelligence* (2001) and *Memoirs of a Geisha* (2005, BAFTA).

Williams, J(ohn) P(eter) R(hys) (1949–) Rugby union player and physician, born in Bridgend, S Wales. He played rugby for London Welsh and Bridgend, as well as for Wales (captain, 1978) and the British Lions. He is the most capped Welshman, with 55 appearances.

Williams, Kenneth (1926–87) Actor and comedian, born in London. He starred in the radio series *Round the Horne* and was later a regular on *Just a Minute*. He also appeared in several of the *Carry On* series of comedy films, his affected style of speech making him instantly recognizable.

Williams, Mark (1975–) Snooker player, born in Cwm, S Wales. He turned professional in 1992. His first major tournament win was the Regal Welsh Open in 1996, and further titles include the Benson and Hedges Masters (1998, 2003), UK Championship (1999, 2002), World Professional Championship (2000, 2003), and the LG Cup (2003). He was ranked world number 1 in 2000–1 and 2003.

Williams, Robbie, popular name of **Robert Peter Williams** (1974–) Pop singer, born in Stoke-on-Trent, Staffordshire. At age 16 he joined British boy band *Take That* (1991), leaving four years later to pursue a solo career. Among his hit albums are *Life Thru a Lens* (1997), *Escapology* (2002), and *Intensive Care* (2005).

Williams, Robin (1952–) Film actor and entertainer, born in Chicago, IL. He starred in the television series *Mork and Mindy* (1978–82), and made his film debut in *Popeye* (1981). He earned Oscar nominations for *Good Morning Vietnam* (1987) and *Dead Poets Society* (1989), and a Best Supporting Actor Oscar for *Good Will Hunting* (1997). Later films include *Insomnia* (2002) and *The Final Cut* (2004).

Williams, Rowan (1950–) Anglican clergyman, born in Swansea, S Wales. Professor of divinity at Oxford (1986–92), he was consecrated Bishop of Monmouth in 1992, becoming Archbishop of Wales in 2000. In 2002 he succeeded George Carey as Archbishop of Canterbury.

Williams, Serena (1981–) Tennis player, born in Saginaw, MI, the sister of Venus Williams. Coached by her father, her singles titles include the US Open (1999, 2002), the French Open (2002), Wimbledon (2002, 2003), and the Australian Open (2003, 2005). At the beginning of 2006 she was ranked world number 15.

Williams (of Crosby), Shirley (Vivien Teresa Brittain) Williams, Baroness, *née* **Catlin** (1930–) British stateswoman, born in London. She was Labour secretary of state for prices and consumer protection (1974–6) and for education and science (1976–9). She became a cofounder of the Social Democratic Party in 1981, its first elected MP (1981–3), and its president (1982–7). From 2000–4 she was leader of the Liberal Democrats in the House of Lords.

Williams, Tennessee, pseudonym of **Thomas Lanier Williams** (1911–83) Playwright, born in Columbus, MS. He achieved success with *The Glass Menagerie* (1944). His later plays, almost all set in the Deep South against a background of decadence and degradation, include *A Streetcar Named Desire* (1947, Pulitzer), *Cat on a Hot Tin Roof* (1955, Pulitzer), *Suddenly Last Summer* (1958), and *Night of the Iguana* (1961). He also wrote short stories, essays, poetry, memoirs, and two novels.

Williams, Venus (1980–) Tennis player, born in Lynwood, CA. Coached by her father, she became the dominant female player of 2000, that year winning the Wimbledon singles title, the US Open, and Olympic gold. She retained the Wimbledon and the US Open singles titles in 2001, but in 2003 lost her Wimbledon crown to sister, Serena Williams, winning it again for a third time in 2005. She began 2006 ranked world number 10.

Williams, William Carlos (1883–1963) Writer and physician, born in Rutherford, NJ. He developed a distinctly American style for his shorter lyrics, which commanded attention from *Spring and All* (1923), and he adapted this for his 'personal epic', *Paterson* (5 vols, 1946–58). He also wrote plays, essays, a trilogy of novels, and criticism, including *In The American Grain* (1925).

Williamson, Malcolm (Benjamin Graham Christopher) (1931–2003) Composer, born in Sydney, New South Wales, Australia. His compositions include the operas *Our Man in Havana* (1963) and *The Red Sea* (1972), as well as a wide variety of orchestral, vocal, choral, and other works.

Willis, Bruce (1955–) Film actor, born in West Germany, but moved to the USA as a young child. He became known in the television series *Moonlighting* (1985–9), and achieved star status for his role in the *Die Hard* series (1988, 1990, 1995). Later films include *Pulp Fiction* (1994), *The Sixth Sense* (1999), and *Sin City* (2005).

Wilson, Sir Angus (Frank Johnstone) (1913–91) Writer, born in Bexhill, East Sussex. His works include the short stories *The Wrong Set* (1949), the novels *Anglo-Saxon Attitudes* (1956) and *The Old Men at the Zoo* (1961), and the play *The Mulberry Bush* (1955).

Wilson, Brian see Beach Boys, The

Wilson, Carl see Beach Boys, The

Wilson, Colin (Henry) (1931–) Novelist and writer on philosophy, sociology, and the occult, born in Leicester, Leicestershire. His books include *The Outsider* (1956), *The Mind Parasites* (1966), *Poltergeist!* (1981), and *Alien Dawn* (1999). His psychic interests brought him status as a cult figure in the 1980s.

Wilson, Colin St John (1922–) Architect, born in Cheltenham, Gloucestershire. His many design projects include the extension to the British Museum (1973–9) and the new British Library (1962–97) in Euston Road, London.

Wilson, Dennis see Beach Boys, The

Wilson, Edmund (1895–1972) Literary and social critic, born in Red Bank, NJ. He was a prolific and wide-ranging author, producing several studies on aesthetic, social, and political themes, as well as verse, plays, travel books, and historical works.

Wilson (of Rievaulx), (James) Harold Wilson, Baron (1916–95) British prime minister (1964–70, 1974–6), born in Huddersfield, West Yorkshire. He was President of the Board of Trade (1947–51), and in 1963 succeeded Gaitskell as Leader of the Labour Party. His economic plans were badly affected by a balance of payments crisis, leading to severe restrictive measures. Following his third general election victory, he resigned as Labour leader in 1976.

Wilson, Jacqueline (1945–) Writer, born in Bath. Her many books for children include *The Story of Tracy Beaker* (1992) and *Double Act* (1996), both successfully filmed for television. She was named the most borrowed author in the UK library lending chart for three successive years (2004–6), and in 2005 was made Children's Laureate.

Wilson, Richard (1936–) Actor and director, born in Greenock, Inverclyde. His film work includes roles in *A Passage to India* (1984) and *The Man Who Knew Too Little* (1997), but it was his characterization of Victor Meldrew in several series of *One Foot in the Grave* (1990–2000, BAFTAs in 1991 and 1993) that made him a national figure.

Wilson, (Thomas) Woodrow (1856–1924) US statesman and 28th president (1913–21), born in Staunton, VA. Elected Democratic president in 1912 and 1916, his administration saw the prohibition and women's suffrage amendments to the constitution, America's participation in World War 1, his peace plan proposals (the *Fourteen Points*), and his championship of the League of Nations. He received the Nobel Peace Prize in 1919.

Windsor, Duke of see Edward VIII

Windsor, George Philip Nicholas see Kent, Edward, Duke of

Windsor, Lady Davina *see* Gloucester, Richard, Duke of

Windsor, Lady Gabriella *see* Kent, Prince Michael of

Windsor, Lady Helen *see* Kent, Edward, Duke of

Windsor, Lady Louise *see* Edward, Prince

Windsor, Lady Rose *see* Gloucester, Richard, Duke of

Windsor, Lord Frederick *see* Kent, Prince Michael of

Windsor, Lord Nicholas *see* Kent, Edward, Duke of

Windsor, Prince Edward *see* Edward, Prince

Windsor, Princess Margaret *see* Margaret, Princess

Windsor, (Bessie) Wallis, Duchess of, *née* **Warfield**, previous married names **Spencer** and **Simpson** (1896–1986) Wife of Edward VIII, born in Blue Ridge Summit, PA. Well known in London society, she met Edward, the Prince of Wales, who made clear his intention to marry her, and was forced to abdicate. They married in 1937, subsequently living abroad.

Winfrey, Oprah (Gail) (1954–) Television talk-show host, actor, and producer, born in Kosciusko, MS. In 1986 she launched the highly successful *Oprah Winfrey Show* (38 Emmys). She established Harpo Productions in Chicago, her films including *The Color Purple* (1985, Oscar nomination) and *Beloved* (1998). She is also known as an activist in support of children's rights.

Wingate, Orde (Charles) (1903–44) British general, born in Naini Tal, India. In Burma (1942) he organized the Chindits – specially trained jungle-fighters drawn from British, Ghurka, and Burmese forces.

Winifred, St (7th-c) Legendary Welsh saint, a noble British maiden, beheaded by Prince Caradog for repelling his unholy proposals. The legend relates that her head rolled down a hill, and where it stopped a spring gushed forth – famous still as a place of pilgrimage, Holywell in Flintshire.

Winner, Michael (Robert) (1935–) Film producer and director, born in London. He has written the screenplay for many of his films, which include *The Big Sleep* (1977), *Death Wish* (and its sequels), and *Bullseye!* (1990). In 1998 he produced and directed *Parting Shots*.

Winslet, Kate (1975–) Actress, born in Reading, Berkshire. Her breakthrough into films came with *Heavenly Creatures* (1994), and later successes include *Sense and Sensibility* (1995), *Titanic* (1997), *Iris* (2001), and *Finding Neverland* (2004). She married director Sam Mendes in 2003.

Winston, Robert (Maurice Lipson), Baron (1940–) Obstetrician, gynaecologist, and broadcaster, born in London. In the 1970s he developed gynaecological microsurgery and undertook the first human tubal transplant, and in 1981 founded the National Health Service's in vitro fertilization (IVF) programme. He is well known as a television presenter of series such as *Child of Our Time* (BBC, 2001–5) and *Walking With Cavemen* (2003).

Wisdom, Sir Norman (1915–) Comedian, born in London. He made his stage debut in 1946, and appeared in variety and film (beginning with *Trouble in Store*, 1953) as an inadequate but well-meaning character in ill-fitting clothes. He announced his retirement in 2005 on his 90th birthday.

Wise, Ernie *see* Morecambe, Eric

Witherspoon, (Laura Jean) Reese (1976–) Film actress, born in Baton Rouge, LA. She made her film debut with *The Man in the Moon* (1991) and established her reputation with *Legally Blonde* (2001). In 2005, her performance as singer June Carter in the biopic of Johnny Cash, *Walk the Line*, won her a Best Actress Oscar and BAFTA.

Wittgenstein, Ludwig (Josef Johann) (1889–1951) Philosopher, born in Vienna. He produced major works on the philosophy of language, notably *Tractatus Logico-Philosophicus* (1921) and *Philosophical Investigations* (trans, 1953), in which he studies the 'language games' whereby language is given its meaning in actual use.

Wodehouse, Sir P(elham) G(renville) (1881–1975) Writer, born in Guildford, Surrey. A prolific writer, he produced a succession of over 100 novels, as well as many short stories, sketches, librettos, and lyrics. His best-known works fall within his 'country house' period, involving the creation of Bertie Wooster and Jeeves, as in *Quick Service* (1940) and *The Mating Season* (1949).

Wogan, Terry, popular name of **Michael Terence Wogan** (1938–) Broadcaster and writer, born in Lim-

erick, Ireland. His television shows include *Blankety Blank* (1977–81), the annual Eurovision Song Contests, and an early evening chat-show (1982–92), but he is also well known for his radio series, such as *Wake Up to Wogan* (1993–). He was awarded an honorary knighthood in 2005.

Wojtyła, Karol Jozef *see* John Paul II

Wolfe, James (1727–59) British soldier, born in Westerham, Kent. Sent to Canada during the Seven Years' War (1756–63), in 1758 he commanded in the famous capture of Quebec (1759), where he was killed.

Wolfe, Tom, popular name of **Thomas Kennerly Wolfe** (1931–) Journalist, pop-critic, and novelist, born in Richmond, VA. A proponent of New Journalism, his books include *The Electric Kool-Aid Acid Test* (1968). Among his novels are the best seller *The Bonfire of the Vanities* (1988) and *I Am Charlotte Simmons* (2004).

Wolfowitz, Paul (Dundes) (1943–) President of the World Bank (2005–), born in Brooklyn, NY. In 1981 he was appointed head of the US state department policy planning staff, and further posts include under-secretary for defence policy (1989–93), and deputy defence secretary (from 2001). In 2005 he took up the role of head of the World Bank.

Wolsey, Thomas, Cardinal (c.1475–1530) English cardinal and statesman, born in Ipswich, Suffolk. Under Henry VIII, he became Archbishop of York (1514) and a cardinal (1515). Made Lord Chancellor (1515–29), he was Henry VIII's leading adviser. When he failed to persuade the pope to grant Henry's divorce, he was arrested, and died while travelling to London.

Wonder, Stevie, originally **Steveland Judkins** or **Steveland Morris** (1950–) Soul singer, songwriter, and instrumentalist, born in Saginaw, MI. He was blind from birth, played the harmonica, drums, keyboards, and guitar from an early age, and was signed to Motown Records in 1961. His first album *Little Stevie Wonder: the 12-Year-Old Genius* (1963) was an immediate success. Later albums include *Natural Wonder* (1995) and *A Time to Love* (2005).

Wood, Elijah (Jordan) (1981–) Actor, born in Cedar Rapids, IA. After a number of small film parts he made his breakthrough with *Paradise* (1991). He became well known following his role as Frodo Baggins in *The Lord of the Rings* trilogy (2001–3), and later films include *Green Street* (2005).

Wood, Sir Henry (Joseph) (1869–1944) Conductor, born in London. In 1895 he helped to found the Promenade Concerts which he conducted annually until his death. He also composed operettas and an oratorio.

Wood, Victoria (1953–) Comedy performer and writer, born in Prestwich, Lancashire. The creator of all her own sketches, songs, and stand-up routines, her television career includes *Wood and Walters* (1981–2), *An Audience with Victoria Wood* (1988, BAFTA), and *Dinner Ladies* (1998–9). In 2005 she wrote and starred in the stage musical *Acorn Antiques*.

Woods, Tiger, popular name of **Eldrick Woods** (1976–) Golfer, born in Cypress, CA. He turned professional in 1996, and shot to fame after winning the US Masters at Augusta in 1997 at the age of 21. Later successes include the US PGA title (1999, 2000), the US Open (2000, 2002), the Open Championhip (2000, 2005), and the US Masters (2001, 2002, 2005). In 2005 he was voted the US PGA Tour Player of the Year for the seventh time in nine years.

Woolf, (Adeline) Virginia, *née* **Stephen** (1882–1941) Novelist, born in London. A leading member of the Bloomsbury Group, she made a major contribution to the development of the novel, in such works as *Mrs Dalloway* (1925), *To the Lighthouse* (1927), and *The Waves* (1931), noted for their impressionistic style. She is also known for her *Diary* (5 vols, 1977–84) and *Letters* (6 vols, 1975–80).

Woolworth, Frank W(infield) (1852–1919) Merchant, born in Rodman, NY. In 1879 he opened a store in Utica, NY, for 5-cent goods only; this failed, but a second store, in Lancaster, PA, selling also 10-cent goods, was successful. He then built a chain of similar stores, setting up the F W Woolworth Company in 1905.

Wordsworth, William (1770–1850) Poet, born in Cockermouth, Cumbria. *Lyrical Ballads* (1798), written with Coleridge, was the first manifesto of the new Romantic poetry. He settled at Dove Cottage, Grasmere, married Mary Hutchinson in 1802, and wrote much of his best work, including his poetic autobiography, *The Prelude* (1805, published in 1850). He became poet laureate in 1843.

Wren, Sir Christopher (1632–1723)

Architect, born in East Knoyle, Wiltshire. In 1669 he designed the new St Paul's (building begun 1675) and many other public buildings in London, such as the Greenwich Observatory and Kensington Palace.

Wren, P(ercival) C(hristopher) (1875–1941) Writer, born in Deptford, Devon. He joined the French Foreign Legion, and this provided him with the background of several novels of adventure, notably *Beau Geste* (1924).

Wright, Frank Lloyd (1867–1959) Architect, born in Richland Center, WI. He became known for his low-built, prairie-style residences, but soon launched out into more controversial designs, and is regarded as the leading designer of modern private dwellings, planned in conformity with the natural features of the land. Among his larger works is the Guggenheim Museum of Art in New York City.

Wright brothers Aviation pioneers: **Orville Wright** (1871–1948), born in Dayton, OH, and **Wilbur Wright** (1867–1912), born near Millville, IN. They were the first to fly in a powered heavier-than-air machine (17 Dec 1903), at Kitty Hawk, NC. They formed an aircraft production company in 1909.

Wrigley, William, Jr (1861–1932) Chewing-gum manufacturer, born in Philadelphia, PA. He successfully marketed the famous spearmint flavour (1899) and established the William Wrigley, Jr, Co.

Wycliffe or **Wicliffe, John**, also spelled **Wyclif, Wycliff** (c.1330–84) Religious reformer, born near Richmond, Yorkshire. He attacked the Church hierarchy, priestly power, and the doctrine of transubstantiation, and issued the first English translation of the Bible (1380). His opinions were condemned, and he was forced to retire. His followers were known as *Lollards*.

Wyler, William (1902–81) Film director, born in Mulhouse, France (formerly Germany). He received Oscars for *Mrs Miniver* (1942), *The Best Years of Our Lives* (1946), and *Ben Hur* (1959).

Wyndham, John, pseudonym of **John Wyndham Parkes Lucas Beynon Harris** (1903–69) Science-fiction writer, born in Knowle, West Midlands. His novels include *The Day of the Triffids* (1951), *The Kraken Wakes* (1953), and *The Midwich Cuckoos* (1957), as well as collections of short stories.

Xavier, Francis, St *see* Francis Xavier, St

Yamamoto, Yohji (1943–) Fashion designer, born in Tokyo. He started his own company in Tokyo in 1972, designing loose, functional clothes for men and women, featuring a great deal of black, which conceal rather than emphasize the body.

Yeats, W(illiam) B(utler) (1865–1939) Poet and playwright, born near Dublin. *The Wanderings of Oisin* (1888), a long narrative poem, established his reputation. His most popular plays were *The Countess Cathleen* (1892), *The Land of Heart's Desire* (1894), and *Cathleen ni Houlihan* (1903), and many of his best-known poems appeared in *The Tower* (1928), *The Winding Stair* (1929), and *A Full Moon in March* (1935). He received the Nobel Prize for Literature in 1923.

Yeltsin, Boris (Nikolayevich) (1931–) Russian president (1990–9), born in Butka, Russia. He was appointed Moscow party chief (1985), but after criticizing party conservatives for sabotaging *perestroika*, he was downgraded to a lowly administrative post (1987). He returned to public attention in 1989 as a member of the new Congress of USSR People's Deputies, and was elected president of the Russian Federation. His political standing increased when he led the protestors who defeated the Gorbachev coup (1991), and following the break-up of the Soviet Union he remained in power as president. Although successful in the 1996 elections, continuing ill health caused him major difficulties and he resigned in 1999.

Yentob, Alan (1947–) Television broadcaster, born in London. He joined the BBC (1968), edited *Arena* (1978–85), became controller of BBC 2 television (1988–93), then of BBC 1 (1993–6), and was appointed director of programmes (1996). In 2002 he became director of drama, entertainment and children's programmes, and in 2004 also took the role of BBC's creative director.

York, Alvin (Cullum) (1887–1964) US soldier and popular hero, born in Pall Mall, TN. While in France during World War 1, he led a small detachment against a German machine-gun emplacement, killing 25 of the enemy, and inducing 132 to surrender.

York, Prince Andrew, Duke of *see* Andrew, Duke of York

York, Princess Beatrice of *see* Andrew, Duke of York

York, Princess Eugenie of *see* Andrew, Duke of York

York, Michael, stage name of **Michael York-Johnson** (1942–) Actor, born in Fulmer, Buckinghamshire. His films include *Cabaret* (1971) and *Austin Powers: International Man of Mystery* (1997), and among his television appearances are *The Night of the Fox* (1990) and *A Knight in Camelot* (1998).

York, Richard, Duke of *see* Edward V

York, Richard, 3rd Duke of (1411–60) English nobleman, the father of Edward IV, Richard III, and George, Duke of Clarence. He loyally served the weak-minded Henry VI, and in 1460 was promised the succession, but was killed in a rising by Lancastrian forces.

Yorkshire Ripper, The *see* Sutcliffe, Peter

Young, Brigham (1801–77) Mormon leader, born in Whitingham, VT. Converted in 1832, he became president of the Church upon the death of Joseph Smith in 1844. He led the Mormons to Utah (1847), where they founded Salt Lake City. He established over 300 towns and settlements, had over 20 wives (estimates vary), and was the father of more than 40 children.

Young, Jimmy, professional name of **Sir Leslie Ronald Young** (1923–) British broadcaster and singer. He topped the charts with 'Unchained Melody' and 'The Man From Laramie' (1955), becoming the first British singer to have two consecutive number 1 hits. He presented the *Jimmy Young* BBC radio show during 1967–2002.

Young, Lester (Willis), nickname **Prez** (1909–59) Tenor saxophonist, born in Woodville, MS. He worked with a succession of bands in the mid-west, before joining the newly formed Count Basie Orchestra in 1934.

Young, Neil (Percival) (1945–) Singer, songwriter, and guitarist, born in Toronto, Ontario, Canada. Much influenced by Bob Dylan, he has released over 30 albums, including *Harvest* (1972), *Reactor* (1981), *Broken Arrow* (1996), and *Prairie Wind* (2005).

Z

Zamenhof, L(azarus) L(udwig), pseudonym **Doktoro Esperanto** (1859–1917) Oculist and philologist, born in Białystok, Poland. An advocate of an international language to promote world peace, he invented Esperanto ('one who hopes') in 1887.

Zanuck, Darryl F(rancis) (1902–79) Film producer, born in Wahoo, NE. He co-founded Twentieth-Century Pictures (later Twentieth-Century Fox) in 1933. Among his many successful films are *The Jazz Singer* (1927), *The Longest Day* (1962), and *The Sound of Music* (1965).

Zappa, Frank, popular name of **Francis Vincent Zappa** (1940–93) Avant-garde rock musician and composer, born in Baltimore, MD. He led the the satirical 'underground' band The Mothers of Invention, his albums including *Freak-Out!* (1966) and *We're Only in it for the Money* (1967).

Zarathustra *see* Zoroaster

Zeffirelli, Franco (1923–) Stage, opera, and film director, born in Florence, Italy. His films include *The Taming of the Shrew* (1966) and *Romeo and Juliet*

(1968), for television *Jesus of Nazareth* (1977), and film versions of the operas *La traviata* (1983) and *Otello* (1986). He received an honorary knighthood in 2004.

Zeiss, Carl (1816–88) Optician and industrialist, born in Weimar, Germany. In 1846 he established at Jena the factory which became noted for the production of lenses, microscopes, and other optical instruments.

Zellweger, Renée (Kathleen) (1969–) Actress, born in Katy, TX. She made her film debut in *My Boyfriend's Back* (1993). Later films include *Bridget Jones's Diary* (2001, sequel 2004), *Chicago* (2002), *Cold Mountain* (2003, Best Supporting Actress Oscar, BAFTA), and *Cinderella Man* (2005).

Zephaniah (7th-c BC) Old Testament prophet of the time of King Josiah of Judah. His account of a coming Day of Wrath inspired the mediaeval Latin hymn Dies Irae.

Zephaniah, Benjamin (Obadiah Iqbal) (1958–) Poet, born in Birmingham, West Midlands, who spent much of his childhood in Jamaica. His first book, *Pen Rhythms* (1981), was followed by *The Dread Affair* (1985), a passionate condemnation of aggression. Later collections include *Too Black, Too Strong* (2001) and *We Are Britain!* (2002).

Zeppelin, Ferdinand (Adolf August Heinrich), Graf von (Count of) (1838–1917) German army officer, born in Konstanz, Germany. In 1897–1900 he constructed his first airship, setting up a factory at Friedrichshafen.

Zeta-Jones, Catherine (1969–)

Actress and singer, born in Swansea, S Wales. She became known through her role in the BBC television series *The Darling Buds of May* (1991), and went on to feature film success with *The Mask of Zorro* (1998, sequel 2005). Later films include *Traffic* (2000), in which she co-starred with husband Michael Douglas (married 2000), *Chicago* (2002, BAFTA, Oscar Best Supporting Actress), and *The Terminal* (2004).

Zhang Yimou, sometimes credited as **Yi-Mou Zhang** (1951–) Film director and actor, born in Xian, China. In 1986 he started work at the Xian Film Studios, where he played the lead in Wu Tianming's *Lao jing* (1986, Old Well). His debut as a director came in 1987 with *Hong gao liang* (Red Sorghum), which won him critical acclaim. Later films include *Wo De Fu Qin Mu Qin* (2000, The Road Home) and *Shi mian mai fu* (2004, House of Flying Daggers).

Zhou Enlai, also spelled **Chou En-lai** (1898–1975) One of the leaders of the Communist Party of China, and prime minister of the Chinese People's Republic from its inception in 1949 until his death. He vastly increased China's international influence, and during the Cultural Revolution worked to preserve national unity against the forces of anarchy.

Zidane, Zinédine, nickname **Zizou** (1971–) Footballer, born in Castellane, near Marseille, France, the son of Algerian immigrant parents. He signed as a schoolboy for Cannes FC, and later joined Juventus. He was a key player for his country in the 1998 FIFA World Cup Final, scoring two goals in France's 3–0 victory over Brazil, and was hailed as a national hero. He was European Footballer of the Year (1998) and FIFA World Footballer of the Year (1998, 2000, 2003). In 2001 he signed for Real Madrid for a world record transfer fee of £47.2 million.

Zola, Emile (Edouard Charles Antoine) (1840–1902) Novelist, born in Paris. After his major novel, *Thérèse Raquin* (1867), he began the long series called *Les Rougon-Macquarts*, which contains such acclaimed studies as *Nana* (1880), *Germinal* (1885), and *The Beast in Man* (trans, 1890).

Zoroaster, Greek form of **Zarathustra** (6th-c BC) Iranian prophet and founder of the ancient Parsee religion which bears his name. He appears as a historical person only in the earliest portion of the Avesta.

Zwingli, Huldrych or **Ulrich**, Lat **Ulricus Zuinglius** (1484–1531) Protestant reformer, born in Wildhaus, Switzerland. He espoused the Reformed doctrines, obtaining the support of the civil authorities, but in 1524 split with Luther over the question of the Eucharist.

PENGUIN POCKET REFERENCE

THE PENGUIN POCKET DICTIONARY OF QUOTATIONS
EDITED BY DAVID CRYSTAL

The Penguin Pocket Dictionary of Quotations is essential reading for anyone searching for the perfect quotation – whether you need a snappy one-liner for a speech or a remark of brilliant insight for your written work. With this pithy and provocative selection of wit and wisdom, you will never be lost for words again.

- Includes quotations from a vast range of people, from film stars to politicians

- Arranged alphabetically by name of person quoted, with the original source for each quotation given

- Provides a full index of key words to help you find each quotation quickly and easily

PENGUIN POCKET REFERENCE

THE PENGUIN POCKET DICTIONARY OF BABIES' NAMES
DAVID PICKERING

The Penguin Pocket Dictionary of Babies' Names is essential reading
for all expectant parents wishing to choose the perfect name for their
child. It gives the meanings and stories behind thousands of names
from all parts of the world – ranging from the most well-known choices
to more unusual names.

– Gives variations and shortened forms for each name

– Highlights names popularized by books, films and celebrities

– Lists the most popular girls' and boys' names from 1700 to the
  present

– Shows how tastes for names have changed in the twenty-first century

PENGUIN POCKET REFERENCE

THE PENGUIN POCKET BOOK OF FACTS
EDITED BY DAVID CRYSTAL

The Penguin Pocket Book of Facts is a goldmine of information, figures and statistics on every conceivable subject – from the world's highest mountains and longest rivers to the gods of mythology, and from time zones to Nobel Prize winners. The ultimate one-stop factfinder, this is the essential book for browsers, crossword and trivia addicts, and for anyone who needs to check facts at home or at work.

– Up-to-date information about everything from astronomy to zoology

– Easy to use

– Illustrated throughout with maps and diagrams

PENGUIN POCKET REFERENCE

THE PENGUIN POCKET ENGLISH DICTIONARY

This pocket edition of the bestselling *Penguin English Dictionary* is the perfect reference book for everyday use. Compiled by Britain's foremost lexicographers, up to date and easy to use, it is the ideal portable companion for quick reference.

- Includes a wealth of words, phrases and clear definitions, with more information than other comparable dictionaries

- Covers standard and formal English, as well as specialist terms, slang and jargon

- Provides invaluable guidance on correct usage, commonly confused words and grammar and spelling

PENGUIN POCKET REFERENCE

POCKET ROGET'S® THESAURUS
GEORGE DAVIDSON

Roget's Thesaurus is the world's most trusted wordfinder and a writer's best friend, and this Pocket edition is ideal for helping you to find the exact words you need for all your written work. It will help improve your knowledge and use of the English language, build up your vocabulary and provide the key to stimulating and creative writing.

– Contains over 880 sections, covering objects, activities and abstract words and phrases

– Includes formal English, technical language, slang and jargon

– Provides full cross-referencing

'The indispensable guide to the English language' *Daily Express*

He just wanted a decent book to read ...

Not too much to ask, is it? It was in 1935 when Allen Lane, Managing Director of Bodley Head Publishers, stood on a platform at Exeter railway station looking for something good to read on his journey back to London. His choice was limited to popular magazines and poor-quality paperbacks – the same choice faced every day by the vast majority of readers, few of whom could afford hardbacks. Lane's disappointment and subsequent anger at the range of books generally available led him to found a company – and change the world.

'We believed in the existence in this country of a vast reading public for intelligent books at a low price, and staked everything on it'
Sir Allen Lane, 1902–1970, founder of Penguin Books

The quality paperback had arrived – and not just in bookshops. Lane was adamant that his Penguins should appear in chain stores and tobacconists, and should cost no more than a packet of cigarettes.

Reading habits (and cigarette prices) have changed since 1935, but Penguin still believes in publishing the best books for everybody to enjoy. We still believe that good design costs no more than bad design, and we still believe that quality books published passionately and responsibly make the world a better place.

So wherever you see the little bird – whether it's on a piece of prize-winning literary fiction or a celebrity autobiography, political tour de force or historical masterpiece, a serial-killer thriller, reference book, world classic or a piece of pure escapism – you can bet that it represents the very best that the genre has to offer.

Whatever you like to read – trust Penguin.